SPORTS MARKETING

A Strategic Perspective

SPORTS MARKETING

A Strategic Perspective

Matthew D. Shank
Associate Professor of Marketing
Northern Kentucky University

City of Westminster College
Maida Vale Learning Centre

PRENTICE HALL
Upper Saddle River, New Jersey 07458

Acquisition Editor: Gabrielle Dudnyk
Editorial Assistant: Michele Foresta
Editor in Chief: Natalie Anderson
Marketing Manager: Shannon Moore
Production Editor: Cindy Spreder
Permissions Coordinator: Monica Stipanov
Managing Editor: Dee Josephson
Manufacturing Buyer: Kenneth J. Clinton
Manufacturing Supervisor: Arnold Vila
Manufacturing Manager: Vincent Scelta
Design Manager: Patricia Smythe
Interior Design: Amanda Kavanaugh
Photo Research Supervisor: Melinda Lee Reo
Image Permission Supervisor: Kay Dellosa
Photo Researcher: Beth Boyd
Cover Design: Amanda Kavanaugh
Cover Illustration/Photo: Tom Raymond / Tony Stone Images; Jim Cummus / FPG International, LLC;
    Thomas Zimmerman / Tony Stone Images; Alan Thorton / Tony Stone Images.
Composition: Preparé

Library of Congress Cataloging-in-Publication Data

Shank, Matthew D.
    Sports marketing: a strategic perspective / Matthew D. Shank.
       p.   cm.
    Includes bibliographical references and index.
    ISBN 0-13-621871-7
    1. Sports—United States—Marketing. 2. Sports—Economic
aspects—United States. I. Title.
    GV716.S42   1999   98-46626
    796'—068'8—dc21   CIP

Prentice-Hall International (UK) Limited, London
Prentice-Hall of Australia Pty. Limited, Sydney
Prentice-Hall Canada Inc., Toronto
Prentice-Hall Hispanoamericana, S.A., Mexico
Prentice-Hall of India Private Limited, New Delhi
Prentice-Hall of Japan, Inc., Tokyo
Simon & Schuster Asia Pte. Ltd., Singapore
Editora Prentice-Hall do Brasil, Ltda., Rio de Janeiro

Printed in the United States of America

10 9 8 7 6 5 4 3 2 1

To My Parents

BRIEF CONTENTS

CONTENTS

Overview

In today's society, there is no escaping sports.

For most of us, sports touch our lives on a daily basis. We watch sports on television, read about sports in the newspaper, talk to friends about sports, purchase sports merchandise, participate in sports, and attend sporting events. Even if you have no interest in sports, you are exposed to sports in a variety of ways. Sports stars appear in advertising and the mass media, the Olympic coverage pre-empts your favorite television show, or your significant other incessantly follows the home team.

The sports industry has experienced tremendous growth in the last decade and is currently the 11th largest industry in the United States. Moreover, the sports industry is flourishing around the globe. The expansion of the sports industry has triggered a number of important outcomes: more sports-related jobs are being created, and more students are interested in careers in the sports industry. As student interest grows, demand for programs and classes in sports administration will also increase.

One of the functional areas of sports administration that is synonymous with the sports industry is sports marketing. Sports marketing is a multidimensional field of study encompassing a wide variety of activities. Typically, sports marketing is associated with professional sports team trying to increase attendance. However, the field of sports marketing can include everything from Nike's "I Can" advertising campaign to Joe's Garage's sponsorship of the local little league team.

In this book, we will discover the complex and diverse nature of sports marketing. Moreover, a framework will be presented to help explain and organize the strategic sports marketing process. Even if you are not a sports enthusiast, you will become excited about the unique application of marketing principles and processes to the sports industry.

Why This Book?

Programs and courses in sports marketing are emerging at universities across the country. Surprisingly, few sports marketing textbooks are written from a strategic marketing perspective. In writing this book, I sought to fill this void. In addition, my goals are to provide:

- *A framework or conceptual model of the strategic marketing process that can be applied to the sports industry.* The contingency framework is presented as a tool for organizing the many elements that influence the strategic sports marketing process. It recognizes the unpredictable nature of the sports industry and allows us to explore the complex relationship between the elements of sports marketing.

- *An appreciation for the growing popularity of women's sports and the globalization of sports.* Women's sports issues and international sports topics are integrated throughout the text, and are highlighted with a "Spotlight on Sports Marketing" feature.

- *An examination of current research in the area of sports marketing.* The study of sports marketing is still in its infancy, and academic research of interest to sports marketers—including sports sponsorships, using athletes as endorsers, and segmenting the sports market—has grown exponentially over the past five years. It is important that students learn how academic research is applied to the "real world" of sports marketing.

- *A balanced treatment of all aspects of sports marketing at all levels.* This book attempts to capture the diverse and rich nature of sports marketing by covering the marketing of athletes, teams, leagues, and special events. Although it is tempting to discuss only "major league" sports because of their intense media coverage, this book explores different sports (including cricket and beach volleyball) and different levels of competition (collegiate and recreational). Moreover, the book discusses the activities involved in marketing to participants of sports—another area of interest to sports marketers.

- *An introduction of the concepts and theories unique to sports marketing and a review of the basic principles of marketing in the context of sports.* Even though many of the terms and core concepts are repetitive, they often take on different meanings in the context of sports marketing. Consider the term *sports involvement.* Although you probably recognize the term *product involvement* from your principles of marketing or consumer behavior class, what is *sports involvement*— involvement with sports based on participation or watching sports? Is involvement with sports deeper and more enduring than it is for other products that we consume? How can sports marketers apply sports involvement to developing a strategic marketing plan? As you can see, the core marketing concept of involvement in the context of sports presents a whole new set of interesting questions and a more comprehensive understanding of sports marketing.

- *Comprehensive coverage of the functions of sports marketing.* Although some texts focus on specialized activities in sports marketing, such as sports sponsorship, this book seeks to cover all of the relevant issues in designing an integrated marketing strategy. Extensive treatment is given to understanding sports consumers as spectators and participants. In addition to planning the sports marketing mix (product, price, promotion, and place), we will examine the execution and evaluation of the planning process.

Ground Rules

This text is organized into four distinct but interrelated parts. Each part represents an important component in the strategic sports marketing process.

Part 1: Contingency Framework for Strategic Sports Marketing

In chapter 1, we introduce sports marketing and illustrate the breadth of the field. In addition, we will take a look at the unique nature of sports products and the sports marketing mix. Chapter 2 presents the contingency framework for strategic sports marketing. This chapter also highlights the planning, implementation, and control phases of the strategic sports marketing process. In chapter 3, the impact of the internal and external contingencies on the strategic sports marketing process is examined. Internal contingencies such as the sports organization's mission and organizational culture are considered, as are external contingencies such as competition, the economy, and technology.

Part 2: Planning for Market Selection Decisions

Chapter 4 presents an overview of the tools used to understand sports consumers—both participants and spectators. Each step in the marketing research process is discussed, illustrating how information can be gathered to aid in strategic decision making. Chapters 5 and 6 discuss participants and consumers of sports, respectively. Chapter 5 examines the psychological and sociological factors that influence our participation in sports, while chapter 6 looks at spectator issues such as fan motivation. In addition, we will discuss the relationship between the participant and spectator markets. Chapter 7 explores the market selection decisions of segmentation, targeting, and positioning in the context of sports.

Part 3: Planning the Sports Marketing Mix

Chapters 8–15 explain the sports marketing mix—the core of the strategic marketing process. Chapters 8 and 9 cover sports product issues such as brand loyalty, licensing, and the new product development process. Chapter 10 introduces the basic promotion concepts, and chapter 11 gives a detailed description of the promotion mix elements of advertising, public relations, personal selling, and sales promotions. Chapter 12, the final chapter on promotion, is devoted to designing a sports sponsorship program. In chapter 13, the sports distribution function is introduced. Then the discussion turns to sports retailing, the stadium as place, and sports media as a type of distribution channel. The final chapters of part 3 tackle the basic concepts of pricing (chapter 14) and pricing strategies (chapter 15).

Part 4: Implementation and Controlling the Strategic Sports Marketing Process

Although the previous sections focus on the planning efforts of the strategic marketing process, part 4 focuses on the implementation and control phases. Chapter 16 begins with a discussion of how sports organizations implement their marketing plans. In this chapter we see how factors such as communication, motivation, and budgeting all play a role in executing the strategic plan. We also examine how sports marketers monitor and evaluate the strategic plans after they have been implemented. Specifically, three forms of control—process, planning assumption, and contingency—are considered.

edagogical Advantages

To help students learn about sports marketing and make this book more enjoyable to read, the following features have been incorporated throughout the text.

- Text organized and written around the contingency framework for strategic sports marketing
- Each chapter incorporates global issues in sport and how they impact sports marketing
- *Sports Marketing Hall of Fame* featuring pioneers in the field integrated throughout the text
- Coverage of women's sports issues in each chapter
- Text incorporates up-to-date research in the field of sport marketing
- Internet exercises at the end of each chapter
- Experiential exercises at the end of each chapter that ask you to apply the basic sports marketing concepts and perform mini-research projects
- Case studies/vignettes throughout the text to illustrate core concepts and make the material come to life
- Detailed glossary of sports marketing terms
- Use of advertisements and photos to illustrate core concepts of sports marketing
- Appendix describing careers in sports marketing
- Appendix presenting Internet addresses of interest to sports marketers
- Video featuring interviews with Showtime Cable Network executives discussing the marketing of sports programming

cknowledgments

Although I am the sole author of this textbook, this project could never have been completed without the expertise and encouragement of many others. Although there are countless people to thank, I was greatly assisted by the thoughtful reviews that undoubtedly improved this text. These reviewers include:

Ketra Armstrong, *Ohio State University*
Chris Cakebread, *Boston University*
Joseph Cronin, *Florida State University*
Pat Gavin, *New Mexico State University*
Lynn Kahle, *University of Oregon*
Jerry Lee Goen, *Oklahoma Baptist University*
Deborah Lester, *Kennesaw State University*
Ann Mayo, *Seton Hall University*

David Moore, *University of Michigan*
Gregory Pickett, *Clemson University*
Joseph Terrian, *Marquette University*
Lou Turley, *Western Kentucky University*

In addition to these formal reviews, I am especially grateful to Tom Boyd, Miami University of Ohio, for testing portions of this manuscript in his sports marketing classes.

I am very grateful to many of my colleagues at Northern Kentucky University who have supported me throughout this process. However, several individuals certainly went above and beyond the call of friendship and duty. Thanks go to Fred Beasley for serving as a sounding board and constant supply of new ideas. Also, I wish to thank Dan Kent and Maria Falbo-Kenkel for their helpful editing of early drafts of the manuscript. Special thanks go to Kathie Verderber and Rebecca Ball for help in writing chapter 1 and chapter 16, respectively. Finally, thanks go to Rob Snyder for providing me with an endless supply of old *Sports Illustrated* issues.

In addition to my colleagues at NKU, thanks go to all of my students at NKU who have helped fuel my interest in sports marketing. In particular, thanks go to Steve Arey, Karen Lang, and Marc Oligee for assistance in finding relevant literature and Internet sites of interest. Deserving special mention and thanks is Lori Litzlemann for help in securing permissions for the many articles and advertisements appearing in this text.

A number of organizations have been very helpful in providing permission to use advertisements and articles throughout the text. Thanks go out to all the individuals within these organizations who have made this book more meaningful and readable for students.

One of the goals of this text was to provide real-world examples and applications that would make the material come to life. This effort was certainly enhanced through the assistance of Rod Taylor and Tom Wessling of the Optimum Group. Special thanks go to Rod Taylor, who spent countless hours editing the early stages of the manuscript and making it much more user-friendly and interesting.

Finally, I am indebted to the Prentice Hall team for making this idea for a text become a reality. Thanks go to Greg Duncan and Don Hull for initiating this process. In addition, thanks go to Audrey Regan whose extensive comments on several chapters set the tone for the entire book. Also, I wish to thank Cindy Spreder for taking this book through the production process. Lastly, thanks go to Gabrielle Dudnyk for her support, professionalism, and confidence throughout the project.

PART ONE

Contingency Framework
for Strategic Sports Marketing

CHAPTER 1

Emergence
of Sports Marketing

OBJECTIVES

**After completing this chapter,
you should be able to**

- Define sports marketing and discuss how the sports industry is related to the entertainment industry

- Describe a marketing orientation and how the sports industry can use a marketing orientation

- Examine the growth of the sports industry

- Discuss the simplified model of the consumer–supplier relationship in the sports industry

- Explain the different types of sports consumers

- Define sports products and discuss the various types of sports products

- Understand the different producers/intermediaries in the simplified model of the consumer–supplier relationship in the sports industry

- Discuss the elements in the sports marketing mix

- Explain the exchange process and why it is important to sports marketers

- Outline the elements of the strategic sports marketing process

Mary is a typical "soccer mom." At the moment she is trying to figure out how to persuade the local dry cleaner to provide uniforms for her daughter's Catholic Youth Organization soccer team.

George is the president of the local Chamber of Commerce. The ten-year plan for the metropolitan area calls for developing four new sporting events that will draw local support while providing national visibility for this growing metropolitan area.

Sam is an events coordinator for the local 10k road race which is an annual fund raiser for fighting lung disease. He is faced with the difficult task of trying to determine how much to charge for the event to maximize participation and proceeds for charity.

Ramiz is the Athletic Director for State U. In recent years the men's basketball team has done well in post-season play, therefore, ESPN has offered to broadcast several games this season. Unfortunately, three of the games will have to be played at 10 P.M. local time in order to accommodate the broadcaster's schedule. Ramiz is concerned about the effect this will have on season ticket holders because two of the games are on weeknights. He knows that the last Athletic Director was fired because the local fans and boosters felt that he was not sensitive to their concerns.

What Is Sports Marketing?

Many people mistakenly think of sports marketing as promotions or sports agents saying, "Show me the money." As the examples above show, sports marketing is more complex and dynamic. **Sports marketing** *is the specific application of marketing principles and processes to sport products and to the marketing of non-sports products through association with sport.*

Mary, the soccer mom, is trying to secure a sponsorship, that is, she needs to convince the local dry cleaner that they will enjoy a benefit by associating their service (dry cleaning) with a kid's soccer team.

As president of the Chamber of Commerce, George needs to determine which sports products will best satisfy his local customers' needs for sports entertainment while marketing the city to a larger and remote audience.

In marketing terms, Sam is trying to decide on the best pricing strategy for his sporting event.

Finally, Ramiz is faced with the challenge of balancing the needs of two market segments for his team's products. As you can see, each of these marketing challenges is complex and requires careful planning.

To succeed in sports marketing one needs to understand both the sports industry and the specific application of marketing principles and processes to sports contexts. In the next section we will introduce you to the sports industry. Throughout this book we will continue to elaborate on ways in which the unique characteristics of this industry complicate strategic marketing decisions. After discussing the sports industry, we will review basic marketing principles and processes with an emphasis on how these principles and processes must be adapted to the sports context.

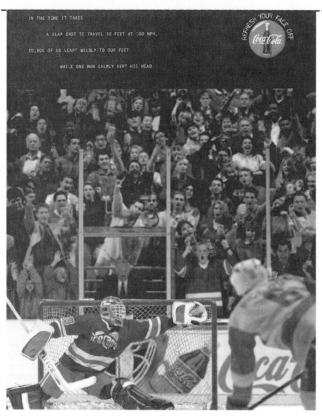

IN THE TIME IT TAKES
A SLAP SHOT TO TRAVEL 90 FEET AT 100 MPH,
20,000 OF US LEAPT WILDLY TO OUR FEET
WHILE ONE MAN CALMLY KEPT HIS HEAD.

REFRESH YOUR FACE OFF
Coca-Cola

■ Coca Cola's stadium signage is just one example of sports marketing.

Understanding the Sports Industry

Sport as Entertainment

Webster's defines **sport** as "a source of diversion or a physical activity engaged in for pleasure." Sport takes us away from our daily routine and gives us pleasure. Interestingly, "entertainment" is also defined as something diverting or engaging. Regardless of whether we are watching a new movie, listening to a concert, or attending an equally stirring performance by Michael Jordan, we are being entertained.

Most consumers view movies, plays, theatre, opera, or concerts as closely related forms of entertainment. Yet for many of us, sport is different. One important way in which sport differs from other common entertainment forms is that sport is spontaneous. A play has a script, and a concert has a program, but the action that entertains us in sport is spontaneous and uncontrolled by those who participate in the event. When we go to a comedic movie, we expect to laugh, and when we go to a horror movie we expect to be scared even before we pay our money. But the emotions we may feel when watching a sporting event are hard to determine. If it is a close contest and our team wins, we may feel excitement and joy. But if it is a boring event and our team loses, the entertainment *benefit* we receive is quite different. Because of its spontaneous nature, sport producers face a host of challenges that are different than those faced by most entertainment providers.

Nonetheless, successful sport organizations realize the threat of competition from other forms of entertainment. They have broadened the scope of their businesses seeing themselves as providing "entertainment." The emphasis on promotional events and stadium attractions that surround athletic events are evidence of this emerging entertainment orientation. Consider the NBA All-Star Game. What used to be a simple competition between the best players of the Western Conference and the best players of the Eastern Conference, has turned into an entertainment extravaganza. The event (not just a game anymore) lasts four days and includes slam-dunk contests, a rookie game, concerts, a three-on-three tournament for fans and plenty of other events designed to promote the NBA.[1]

Sporting goods organizations have also recognized their link to the entertainment industry. According to Jeffrey R. Bliss, who led Sara Lee's marketing efforts in the 1996 Olympics, "The industry is constantly watching for the next event, the next movie, the next star."[2] Similarly, Reebok Executive Vice President Robert Meers stated, "We've recognized for several years that sports is a part of entertainment. The market now is really sports, fashion, and music. We can't expect to ignore reality and survive."[3] Underscoring the notion of sport as entertainment is Richard Alder, president of the Atlanta Knights of the International Hockey League (IHL), who states that "This is a league for the masses and not the classes. [Minor league hockey] is entertainment with the ice as the stage. The NHL is the coat and tie league. We're not. They're the Mercedes, the best hockey league in the world. We're the Chevrolet. Of course, more people drive Chevys." Coincidentally, Alder worked for 16 years as a vice president of marketing for the Ringling Brother and Barnum & Bailey Circus.[4]

Organizations that have not recognized how sport and entertainment relate are said to suffer from marketing myopia. Coined by Theodore Levitt, **marketing myopia** is described as the practice of defining a business in terms of goods and services rather than in terms of the benefits customers seek. Sports organizations can eliminate marketing myopia by focusing on meeting the needs of consumers rather than on producing and selling sports products.

A Marketing Orientation

The emphasis on satisfying consumers' wants and needs is everywhere in today's marketplace. Most successful organizations concentrate on understanding the consumer and providing a sports product that meets consumers' needs while achieving the organization's objectives. This way of doing business is called a **marketing orientation**.

Marketing-oriented organizations practice the marketing concept that organizational goals and objectives will be reached if customer needs are satisfied. Organizations employing a marketing orientation focus on understanding customer preferences and meeting these preferences through the coordinated use of marketing. An organization is marketing oriented when it engages in the following activities.[5]

- **intelligence generation**—analyzing and anticipating consumer demand, monitoring the external environment, and coordinating the data collected
- **intelligence dissemination**—sharing the information gathered in the intelligence generation stage
- **responsiveness**—acting on the information gathered to make market decisions such as designing new products and services and/or developing promotions that appeal to consumers

Using the above criteria (intelligence gathering, intelligence dissemination, and responsiveness), a recent study examined the marketing orientation of minor league baseball franchises.[6] Results of the study indicate that minor league baseball franchises do not have a marketing orientation and that they need to become more consumer focused. Although the study suggests that minor league baseball franchises have not moved toward a marketing orientation, some sports organizations realize that profitability is based on adopting this business philosophy. One organization that has applied a marketing orientation and reaped the benefits is the Colorado Rockies.

Although he had no previous experience in the baseball industry, Rockies owner Jerry McMorris knew that the fans needed to be treated like customers. "I've always believed that to be successful in business, you have to give your customers fair value and treat them with courtesy and respect." His customer-orientation has paid off and although the team was not performing well on the field initially, the fans still supported the organization. This gave McMorris the ability to acquire better players and ultimately put a better product on the field.

In each of their first three seasons, the Rockies led the major leagues in attendance, drawing an incredible 10 million fans, in that time frame. Playing in Coors Field, the Rockies drew a total of 3.9 million fans in 1997. Tal Smith, the President of the Houston Astros, believes "the Rockies are one of the great success stories of professional sports. The fan interest and the revenue that has generated, pyramids the success. It allows them to go out and compete for the free agents, which makes the club better and, in turn, solidifies the team's popularity."[7]

Growth of the Sports Industry

Sport has become one of the most important and universal institutions in our society. The sports industry is the eleventh largest of all U.S. industry groups with a market value of the nation's output of sports goods and services at $152 billion in 1995.[8] For better or worse, sports are everywhere. The growth of sport and sports industry can be measured in different ways. Let us look at growth in terms of attendance, media coverage, employment, and the global market.

Growth in Attendance

Not only does sport spawn legions of "soccer moms and dads" who faithfully attend youth sport events, but for the past several years, fans have been flocking to major league sports in record numbers. The NFL experienced a record number of fans in the 1995 season (15,043,562), followed by its second highest regular season total in 1996 (14,612,417). The 1995–1996 season also produced record attendance at NBA games with a total of 20,513,218 fans enjoying the action. Similar to the NFL, last season the NBA experienced a slight dip in attendance (20,304,629), but still had its second highest figure in its history. After a poor showing in 1995 because of the players' strike, attendance has been growing for Major League Baseball (MLB). In 1995, the average attendance was 25,260 followed by increases in 1996 (26,889) and 1997 (28,445). The MLB's all-time average attendance record was 31,612, which took place in the strike shortened 1994 season. The NHL is poised to capitalize on the impending retirement of Michael Jordan and convert basketball fans to hockey fans. Tracing attendance over the past few years, regular season numbers have increased from 14,749 (1993–1994) to 16,548 (1996–1997) and the NHL shows no sign of slowing down.

Growth in Media Coverage

Although millions of Americans attend sporting events each year, even more of us watch sports on network and cable television or listen to sports on the radio. For example, while 70,000 fans were in attendance at Super Bowl XXXII in San Diego, NBC attracted an audience of 133.4 million viewers, making this game the third most-watched program in television history.[9] Likewise, some 170 million people watched CBS coverage of the Winter Olympic Games from Nagano, Japan,[10] however, this number is minimal compared to the estimated 3 billion people who watched worldwide. ESPN, the original sports-only network launched in 1979, reaches 70 million homes with its 8,760 hours of sports programming.[11]

Traditional networks are trying to keep pace with the demand for sports programming. NBC spent a record $2.3 billion to secure the broadcast and cable rights for the Olympic Games in 2004, 2006, and 2008. In addition, NBC paid $1.27 billion to televise the Olympics in 2000 and 2002. Add to this the recent four-year deal worth $2.64 billion paid by NBC and Turner Sports to televise NBA contests or the $18 billion paid by the networks to the NFL, and you can see the value of sports to the league and the networks.[12] These numbers show no signs of slowing down in the future.

The huge demand for sports broadcasting has led to the introduction of more sport-specific channels. New sports networks such as the Golf Channel, SpeedVision, and the Women's Sports Network are emerging because of consumer demand. This practice of "narrowcasting", reaching very specific audiences, seems to be the future of sports media.

In addition to traditional sports media, new media such as the Internet and pay-per-view cable television are growing in popularity. Satellite stations, such as Primestar and DIRECTV, allow spectators to subscribe to a series of sporting events and play a more active role in customizing the programming they wish to see. For example, DIRECTV offers the NHL Center Ice package where subscribers can choose from 30 out-of-market (i.e., not local) regular season NHL games a week for just $139.

Growth in Employment

Another way to explore the growth of the sports industry is to look at the number of people the industry employs. *The Sports Market Place Registry*, an industry directory, has more than 24,000 listings for sports people and organizations.[13] A *USA Today* report estimates that there are upwards of 4.5 million sports-related jobs in marketing, entrepreneurship, administration, representation, and media.[14] Consider all the jobs that are created because of sports-related activities such as building and staffing a new stadium.

The number of people working directly and indirectly in sports will continue to grow as sports marketing grows. Sports marketing creates a diverse workforce from the players who create the competition, to the photographers who shoot the competition (see Appendix A for a discussion of careers in sports marketing).

Growth in Global Markets

Not only is the sports industry growing in the United States, it is also growing globally. As the spotlight on international sports marketing discusses below, the European market is set to explode.

spotlight on international sports marketing

big league commercialization reaches european sports

Sports mania is hardly a new phenomenon in Europe, where in many countries soccer is almost a national religion. But sports as a business has long been decidedly minor league compared with the big-money madness across the Atlantic.

Driven by a revolution in European television, the commercialization of sports on a very American scale is spreading across Europe, with everything from merchandise for fans to theme restaurants to—no surprise—rising ticket prices.

Manchester United, the soccer team that is arguably the biggest commercial success in British sports. Last year the league that Manchester plays in pocketed $1.1 billion for four years of television rights, almost four times what it received in 1992, and Manchester will get a nice share of the take. The club rakes in an additional $29 million on merchandising. It owns its own stadium, and fans swarm through three sporting goods stores under the bleachers and line up for tables at the Red Cafe, the team restaurant.

What's propelling this wave of change? Mainly, European sports are being borne aloft by an explosion of cable and digital television as state broadcasting monopolies crumble. And while Manchester United is clearly in the front ranks of this revolution, the phenomenon shows no signs of stopping at the English Channel.

Not that the revolution is complete. In Milan, for instance, Adriano Galliani's eyes light up when he talks about Manchester United. Galliani is managing director of A.C. Milan, one of Italy's leading soccer franchises, but his club lost $25 million last year.

The money for television rights is divided among too many teams, he complains, and revenues from selling Milan jerseys and other paraphernalia are crimped by counterfeits. Besides all that, Mr. Galliani is struggling with the City of Milan over San Siro, the 85,000-seat stadium the city owns, where the team not only pays rent, but forfeits some of the revenues on food and parking.

Still, Italy's broadcasters paid $27 million to broadcast last year's soccer season, triple the

(continued)

sum five years ago. And in Germany the amount rose to $143 million from $81.5 million. With pay television fast arriving, revenues are expected to keep climbing. And the increased air time has led to a boom in sales of everything from jerseys to soccer balls to videocassettes of games.

Many changes are American-inspired, and companies like Disney and its ESPN network have acquired European partners. Sporting goods companies like Nike, Reebok, and the Footlocker unit of Woolworth, as well as the merchandising arms of the National Football League and the National Basketball Association, are profiting by elbowing in, like good rebounders.

But if all this sounds like an echo of what happened in the United States, European sports executives are taking change a step further. Plans are afoot to transform franchises into leisure businesses, with restaurants and pubs, vacation clubs, and television stations. And in contrast to sports in America, where most teams are the playthings of rich individuals, the European teams are turning to the stock market for capital.

In Britain, 18 soccer teams have listed stocks. Last year, Italy's government transformed the nation's soccer teams from nonprofit organizations into for-profit corporations, paving the way for stock market listings. Germany is expected to take a similar step next year.

Much of the change still affects only soccer, which rules the roost in Europe, in contrast to America, where football, basketball, baseball, tennis, and hockey vie for public attention. But lesser sports are caught up in the change as well. In Britain, several rugby franchises, like the Sheffield Eagles, have sold shares, and cricket, baseball's venerable cousin, has shortened game times to primp itself for television.

In Italy, where Formula One auto racing is the No. 2 spectator sport, the Ferrari unit of Fiat has parlayed its success into $10 million in licensing income for things like Ferrari shirts, caps, and jackets.

"Only in the last few years have sports come out of the wildness," said Richard Baldwin, a partner at Deloitte and Touche in London who specializes in the business of sports.

The changes have their downsides for fans. In Britain, soccer ticket prices rose an average of 11 percent in five years. And fan anger over the shifting of sports to pay-for-view TV is growing. In the Netherlands, protests were so loud over a new pay-per-view venture that it had to close down.

The flood of money also has inflated players' salaries. This summer, the Italian soccer club Inter set a European record when it offered a package of $42 million for the dazzling young Brazilian forward, Ronaldo. Share prices of soccer franchises are extremely volatile. In August, the index that tracks Britain's publicly traded soccer teams crashed to 650 from almost 900 in February, as the market became inundated with new issues and a 1995 European Union decision allowing free movement of players began to inflate salaries further.

Moreover, the rampant commercialization is provoking a backlash among some fans and owners. "Is it good for the fans?" asked Cristian Ratti, a 23-year-old law student and Inter fan who browsed recently among Inter jerseys at a Footlocker in Milan. "Sure. Morally, I'm not so sure."

The pace of change varies. British Sky Broadcasting, controlled by Rupert Murdoch's News Corporation, created the national market for satellite television. Britain now has more than six million satellite dishes, compared with virtually none in Italy and Spain.

The struggle for overall control of television revolves increasingly around sports. Last year, when an Italian media entrepreneur, Vittorio Cecchi Gori, outbid the national network, RAI, for soccer rights, the Government annulled the result and made both sides share the rights. In Spain, a private digital broadcaster, Canal Satelite Digital, is battling for soccer rights with a Government sponsored company, Via Digital.

The changes in British soccer were accelerated by a wave of soccer violence in the 1980s and the deaths of 96 fans in 1989 at the Hillsborough Stadium in Sheffield. Under Government pressure, the league reorganized itself, stadiums were refurbished, and a drive began to attract more women and families.

All this cost money, of course, which is why the teams turned to the stock market. Though only two American teams are quoted on a stock exchange—the Boston Celtics, in basketball, and the Florida Panthers, in hockey—in Britain a trickle soon became a flood.

In Spain, last year's national soccer champions, Atlético de Madrid, plans to go public, and in Italy, Bologna hired Nomura Securities to plan an offering.

Some sports executives are apprehensive about the heavy spending for players, which produces losses at many of Britain's soccer clubs. "The single biggest challenge will be to control what players earn," Mr. Baldwin of Deloitte said.

Yet other experts dismiss such concerns, saying the big franchises like Manchester must exploit their popularity. "The real challenge for these teams is not how to expand their fan base, but how to reach them as customers," said Max Alexander, an associate at Oliver & Ohlbaum, a London firm that advises sports teams.

Already, franchises like Manchester and Newcastle United run merchandising megastores and theme restaurants at the stadium and in nearby malls, and are examining the possibility of starting their own cable channels to broadcast great games of the past, interviews with players and features about soccer. Some experts see room for vacation theme clubs and marketing abroad. "These aren't sports clubs," Mr. Alexander said, "they're leisure businesses."

American sportswear companies have reacted by sponsoring European teams and athletes and plastering the new television channels with ads, giving European rivals like Adidas a run for their money. Nike uses Ronal-

do in its ads, and has a $200 million, 10-year deal to sponsor Brazil's national soccer team, the defending World Cup champion. Last year, Nike's sales in Europe totaled $1.83 billion, twice the level five years earlier.

In 1987, Footlocker opened its first European store in Germany, and now operates 234 stores in seven countries. "Anything associated with Michael Jordan is hot throughout the world," said Juris Pagrabs, a Footlocker spokesman.

That is the kind of talk that perks up ears at the National Basketball Association, which has cashed in on the popularity of basketball in Europe. Merchandise like licensed jerseys, basketballs, and backboards took off so fast after the triumphal march of the NBA Dream Team through the 1992 Barcelona Olympics that the league opened marketing offices in Paris, London, and Barcelona, and expects to open others soon in Germany and Italy.

Paul Zilk, senior vice president of NBA International in Paris, said about $500 million of the NBA's retail revenue of $3.5 billion is generated outside North America, half of it in Europe. With royalty rates of 10 to 15 percent, the NBA is thought to pocket about $25 million to $35 million from sales of licensed merchandise in Europe, and an equal amount from television rights. Mr. Zilk said he expected sales in Europe to grow annually "in excess of 15 percent, and we're pushing for 20 percent."

The NBA sponsors basketball programs in schools in Britain, France, and Germany; a recent NBA survey of 28,000 teenagers in 44 countries found that in Western Europe, 88 percent recognized the league's logo, and 93 percent that of the Chicago Bulls.

It is no coincidence that watching the Milan soccer team develop its business is a little like watching Mr. Murdoch in the United States, where his empire includes interests in the Knicks and Rangers in New York, and the Los Angeles Dodgers. Milan is owned by Silvio Berlusconi, the Italian entrepreneur-turned-politician, who in the 1980s cracked Italy's state television monopoly

(continued)

by founding his own private commercial channels.

Milan's Mr. Galliani, who admires the American approach to sports and traveled to Salt Lake City in the spring to see the third and fourth games of the NBA playoffs between the Utah Jazz and the Chicago Bulls, sees the future of franchises like Milan essentially as providers of programming for Europe's growing number of television channels.

"We are a content provider," he said, "and we see ourselves as a major."

Source: John Tagliabue, "Europe Enters the Big Leagues," *The New York Times,* September 10, 1997, C1, C4. Copyright © 1997 by *The New York Times,* Reprinted by permission.

The Structure of the Sports Industry

There are many ways to discuss the structure of the sports industry. We can look at the industry from an organizational perspective. In other words, we can understand some things about the sports industry by studying the different types of organizations that populate the sports industry such as local recreation commissions, national youth sports leagues, intercollegiate athletic programs, professional teams, and sanctioning bodies. These organizations use sports marketing to help them achieve their various organizational goals. For example, agencies such as the United States Olympic Committee (USOC) use marketing to secure the funding necessary to train and enter American athletes into the Olympic Games and Pan American games.

The traditional organizational perspective, however, is not as helpful to potential sports marketers as a consumer perspective. When we examine the structure of the sports industry from a consumer perspective, the complexity of this industry and challenge to sports marketers becomes obvious. Figure 1.1 shows a **simplified model of the consumer–supplier relationship**. The sports industry consists of three major elements: consumers of sport, the sports products that they consume, and the suppliers of the sport product. In the next sections, we will explore each of these elements in greater detail.

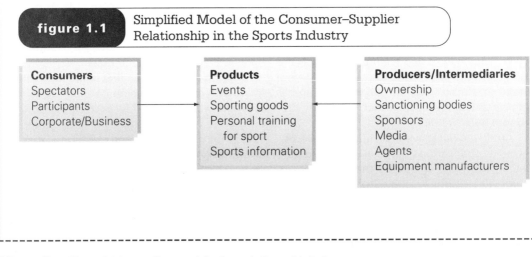

figure 1.1 Simplified Model of the Consumer–Supplier Relationship in the Sports Industry

Consumers
Spectators
Participants
Corporate/Business

Products
Events
Sporting goods
Personal training
    for sport
Sports information

Producers/Intermediaries
Ownership
Sanctioning bodies
Sponsors
Media
Agents
Equipment manufacturers

■ Sports marketing fills the stands.

The Consumers of Sport

The sports industry exists to satisfy the needs of three distinct types of consumers: spectators, participants, and sponsors.

The Spectator as Consumer

If the sporting event is the heart of the sports industry, then the spectator is the blood that keeps it pumping. **Spectators** are consumers who derive their benefit from the observation of the event. The sports industry, as we know it, would not exist without spectators. Spectators observe the sporting event in two broad ways. They attend the event or they experience the event via one of several sports broadcast media.

Spectator consumers are also of two types. Some are individuals, while others are corporations. As shown in Figure 1.2, there are two broad types of consumers: individual consumers and corporate consumers. Similarly, there are two broad ways in which consumers can spectate: in-person or via the media. This creates four distinct consumer groups. Individuals can attend events in person by either purchasing single event tickets or series (season) tickets. Not only do individuals attend sporting events, so too do corporations. Today stadium luxury boxes and conference rooms are designed specifically with the corporate consumer in mind. Many corporate consumers can purchase special blocks of tickets to sporting events. At times, there may be a tension between corporate consumers' and individual consumers' needs. Many feel that corporate consumers, able to pay large sums of money for their tickets, are pushing out the individual consumer and raising ticket prices.

Both individual spectators and corporations can also watch the event via a media source. The corporate consumer in this case is not purchasing the event for its own viewing, but, rather, acting as an intermediary to bring the spectacle to the end user

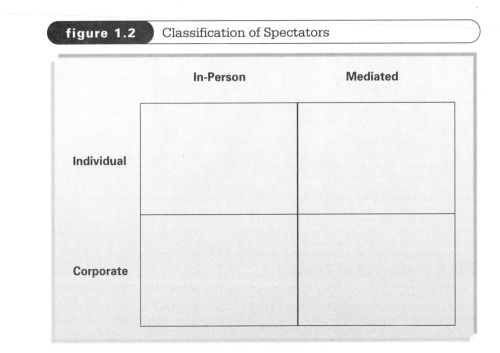

figure 1.2 Classification of Spectators

	In-Person	Mediated
Individual		
Corporate		

groups or audience. For example, CBS (the corporate consumer) purchases the right to televise the Masters Golf Tournament. CBS then controls how and when the event is experienced by millions of individual spectators who comprise the television audience.

Historically the focus of the sports industry and sports marketers was on the spectator attending the event. The needs of the consumer at the event were catered to first, with little emphasis on the viewing or listening audience. Due to the power of the corporate consumer, the focus has changed to pleasing the media broadcasting the sporting event to spectators in remote locations. Many season ticket holders are dismayed each year when they discover that the starting time for events has been altered to fit the ESPN schedule. Because high ratings for broadcasted sporting events translates into breathtaking deals for the rights to collegiate and professional sports, those who present sporting events are increasingly willing to accommodate the needs of the media at the expense of the on-site fan. The money associated with satisfying the needs of the media is breathtaking. For example, in 1997 the NFL signed a contract with a major television network for nearly $18 billion dollars.[15] Less than a month later, the players also reaped the benefits of this contract by having the salary cap raised to slightly over $52 million. Identifying and understanding the different types of spectator consumption is a key consideration for sports marketers when designing a marketing strategy.

table 1.1

US Sports Participation Trends (millions of people who do sports/fitness/outdoor activities on a "frequent basis")							
Participation In	1987	1990	1992	1994	1995	1996	%1996 v. 1987
Any Sports/Fitness/ Outdoor Activity	68.5	77.5	70.4	85.8	89.5	81.6	+19.1
Sports	34.4	36.3	32.2	43.8	43.3	41.5	+20.6
Fitness	39.6	47.4	43.5	50.7	54.4	47.3	+19.4
Outdoor	11.3	11.6	9.8	12.1	13.2	12.2	+8.0

Source: Courtesy of Sporting Goods Manufacturers Association.

The Participant as Consumer

In addition to watching sports, more people are becoming active **participants** in a variety of sports at a variety of competitive levels.[16] Table 1.1 shows the growth in participation. As the number of participants grows, the need for sports marketing expertise in these areas also increases. There are various types of participant consumers.

As you can see there are two broad classifications of sports participants: those that participate in unorganized sports and those that participate in organized sports.

Unorganized Sport Participants

Organized Sport Participants

    Amateur
            Youth Recreational Instructional
            Youth Recreational Elite
            Schools
            Intercollegiate

    Professional
            Minor/Secondary
            Major

Unorganized sports are the sporting activities that people engage in that are not sanctioned or controlled by some external authority. Kids playing a pick-up game of basketball, teenagers skateboarding, or people playing street roller hockey, as well as fitness runners, joggers, and walkers are only a few of the types of sporting activities that millions of people participate in each day. The number of people who participate

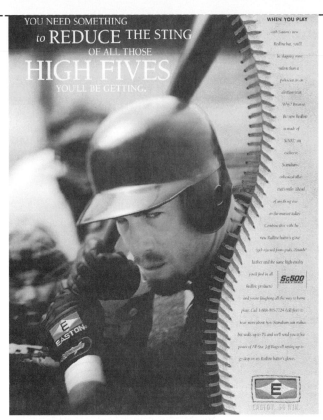

■ Easton markets to the highly involved sports participant.

in unorganized sports is difficult to estimate. We can see how large this market is by looking at the unorganized sport of home fitness. In 1996, 43 million Americans worked out with free weights.[17] We can see that the size of the market for unorganized sports is huge, and there are many opportunities for sports marketers to serve the needs of these consumers.

■ Unorganized sports participation also interests sports marketers.

Organized sporting events refer to sporting competitions that are sanctioned and controlled by an authority such as a league, association, or sanctioning body. There are two types of participants in organized events: amateur and professional.

Amateur sporting events refer to sporting competitions for athletes who do not receive compensation for playing the sport. Amateur competitions include recreational youth sports at the instructional and elite (also known as "select") levels, high school sports controlled at the state level through leagues, intercollegiate sports (NCAA Division 1-3, NAIA, NJCAA) and adult community-based recreational sports. Professional sports are also commonly classified by minor league or major league status.

Sponsors as Consumer

Other equally important consumers in sports marketing are the many business organizations that choose to sponsor sports. In **sports sponsorship**, the consumer (in most cases a business) is exchanging money or product for the right to associate its name or product with a sporting event. The decision to sponsor a sport is complex. The sponsor must not only decide on what sport(s) to sponsor but must also consider what level of competition (recreational through professional) to sponsor. They must choose whether to sponsor events, teams, league, or individual athletes.

WHEN TEAMWORK
IS THE DESTINATION
VICTORY HAPPENS
ALONG THE WAY

Ricoh proudly sponsors the USA Volleyball Team
This artwork was created in part with Ricoh copiers © 1994 Ricoh Corporation

RICOH

■ Ricoh leverages their sponsorship of the USA volleyball team.

table 1.2

Sponsorship Dollars Spent by Sport (in millions)			
	1996	1997	1998 (estimated)
Motorsports	$920	$998	$1055
Golf	555	614	650
Pro Sports Leagues/Teams	365	384	457
Olympic Teams	290	307	396
Tennis	260	269	287

Source: Courtesy of IEG Sponsorship Report, Chicago.

Although sponsorship decisions are difficult, sponsorship is growing in popularity for a variety of reasons. As Pope discusses in his excellent review of current sponsorship thought and practices,[18] sponsorship can help achieve corporate objectives (e.g., public awareness, corporate image building, community involvement), marketing objectives (reaching target markets, brand positioning, increasing sales), media objectives (generate awareness, enhance ad campaign, generate publicity), and personal objectives (management interest). Although $3 billion were spent by corporations on sports sponsorships in 1995, that number reached approximately $5 billion in 1996. In 1996, 40 corporations spent approximately $500 million alone on sponsorships for the Summer Olympic Games.[19] Table 1.2 presents a breakdown of three years of sponsorship spending for some of the top sport areas. In each sport sponsorship revenues increased, though the rate varied by sport.[20]

The Sports Product

Perhaps the most difficult conceptual issue for sports marketers is trying to understand the nature of the sports product. Just what is the sports product that participants, spectators, and sponsors consume? A **sports product** is a good, a service, or any combination of the two that is designed to provide benefits to a sports spectator, participant, or sponsor.

Goods/Services

Goods are defined as tangible, physical products that offer benefits to consumers. Sporting goods include equipment, apparel, and shoes. We expect sporting good retailers to sell tangible products such as tennis balls, racquets, hockey equipment, exercise equipment, and so on. By contrast, **services** are defined as intangible, non-physical products. A competitive sporting event (i.e., the game itself) and an ice-skating lesson are examples of sport services.

Sports marketers sell their products based on the **benefits** the products offer to consumers. In fact, products can be described as "bundles of benefits." Whether as participants, spectators, or sponsors, sports products are purchased based on the benefits consumers derive. Ski Industry America, a trade association interested in marketing the sport of snowshoeing, understands the benefit idea and suggests that the benefits offered to sports participants by this sports product include: great exercise, little athletic skill, and low cost (compared to skiing). It is no wonder snowshoeing has recently emerged as one of the nation's fastest growing winter sport.[21]

Spectators are also purchasing benefits when they attend or watch sporting events. For example, some 2 million spectators and 3.5 billion viewers watched some portion of the 1996 Olympic Games in Atlanta.[22] The Olympic Games provide consumers with benefits such as entertainment, ability to socialize, and feelings of identification with their countries' teams and athletes. Moreover, organizations such as Staples, which paid $100 million over 20 years for the naming rights to Los Angeles's downtown sports complex to open in 1999, believe the association with sports will be worth far more than the investment.[23] The benefits that organizations receive from associating with the sports product include enhanced image, increased awareness, and increased sales of their products.

Different Types of Sports Products

Sports products can be classified into four categories. These include: sporting events, sporting goods, sports training, and sports information. Let us take a more in-depth look at each of these sports products.

Sporting Events

The primary product of the sports industry is the **sporting event**. By primary product we are referring to the competition, which is needed to produce all of the related products in the sports industry. Without the game there would be no licensed merchandise, collectibles, stadium concessions, and so on. You may have thought of sports marketing as being important for only professional sporting events, but the marketing of collegiate sporting events and even high school sporting events is becoming more common.

Historically, a large distinction was made between amateur and professional sporting events. Today, that line is becoming more blurred. For example, the Olympic Games, once considered the bastion of amateur sports, is now allowing professional athletes to participate for their countries. Most notably, the rosters of the Dream Teams of USA Basketball fame and the USA Hockey team are almost exclusively professional athletes. This has been met with some criticism. Critics say that they would rather give the true amateur athletes their chance to "go for the gold."

Athletes Athletes are participants who engage in organized training in order to develop skills in particular sports. Athletes who perform in competition or exhibitions can also be thought of as sports products. Michael Jordan, Rebecca Lobo, and Ken Griffey Jr. are thought of as "bundles of benefits" that can satisfy consumers of sport both on and off the court. The latest athlete to achieve this "superproduct" status is the 21-year-old, multimillion dollar phenomenon named Eldrick "Tiger" Woods. Tiger seems to have it all. He is handsome, charming, young, multiethnic, and most important—talented. Tiger's sponsors certainly think he is worth the money. Nike,

Titleist, and the All-Star Cafe have all purchased a piece of Tiger for a total of $67 million in sponsorship fees.[24] But, the "bundle of benefits" that accompany an athlete vary from person to person. The benefits associated with Dennis Rodman are different from those associated with Grant Hill or gold medal winner Tara Lipinski. Regardless of the nature of the benefits, today's athletes are not thinking of themselves as athletes, but entertainers. "Being like Mike [Jordan] means being a polished celebrity who can slam, spike and strut for the highlight reel; give good sound bite without embarrasing himself, his sport and his sponsors; and be able to find that Disneyland film crew amid the pandemonium of winning a world championship."[25]

Arena   A final sports product that is associated with the sporting event is the site of the event—typically an arena or stadium. Today, the stadium is much more than a place to go watch the game. It is an entertainment complex that may include restaurants, bars, picnic areas, and luxury boxes. Most stadium seating is designed for entertainment purposes. For example, ChoiceSeat was introduced at SuperBowl XXXII and promises to be the stadium seat of the future. The ChoiceSeat is a Pentium-powered touch screen that allows individuals to access real-time camera views from a variety of camera angles, replays, player and game statistics, and merchandising information. With this new technology, the seat within the stadium becomes an attractive product to market.[26] As Roger Goodell of the NFL states, "Our teams have to be in high quality stadiums because that's half of the sports experience."

Sporting Goods

Sporting goods represent tangible products that are manufactured, distributed, and marketed within the sports industry. The sporting goods and recreation industry, consisting of four segments, was a $62 billion dollar industry in 1997.[27] The four segments and their relative contribution to the industry sales figure include: sports equipment ($17.1 billion), sports transportation products such as recreational vehicles and water scooters ($17.0 billion), sports apparel ($18.6 billion), and athletic footwear ($9.5 billion). Although sporting goods are usually thought of as sports equipment, apparel, and shoes, there are a number of other goods that exist for consumers of sport. Sporting goods include equipment, licensed merchandise, collectibles, and memorabilia.

Equipment   Sports equipment experienced a 4.1 percent increase in sales growth from 1996 to 1997. The largest product category, in terms of sales, was exercise equipment ($3.2 billion) followed by golf equipment ($2.75 billion), firearms and hunting ($1.9 billion), fishing ($1.6 billion), camping ($1.6 billion), and in-line skating equipment ($513 million).[28] Interestingly, a comprehensive survey of 1,607 adults was conducted in the fall of 1997 to determine households' ownership and usage of exercise equipment. The research found one-half of all U.S. households (50.1 percent) own at least one piece of exercise equipment. In addition, over two-thirds of the Americans say that they use their equipment regularly. In his discussion of the study's findings, Gregg Hartley, of the Fitness Products Council, stated "The stereotype is that most home exercise equipment just ends up gathering dust, but now there is solid evidence that millions of people (54.5 adults) are using the equipment to good results."[29]

Licensed Merchandise   Another type of sporting good that is growing in sales is licensed merchandise. **Licensing** is a practice whereby a sports marketer contracts with other companies to use a brand name, logo, symbol, or characters. In this case, the brand name may be a professional sports franchise, college sports franchise, or a sporting event. Licensed sports products usually are some form of apparel such as team hats, jackets, or jerseys. Licensed sports apparel accounts for 60 percent of all sales. Other licensed sports products such as novelties, sports memorabilia, trading cards, and even home goods are also popular.

The Licensing Letter reported that sales of *all* licensed sports products reached $13.8 billion in 1996, a three percent increase over the $13.4 billion in 1995 retail sales. Based on research from the National Sporting Goods Manufacturers Association, U.S. retail sales of licensed products for the four major professional sports leagues (NBA, NFL, MLB, and NHL) and colleges/universities have more than doubled in the 1990s from $5.35 billion in 1990 to $10.9 billion in 1996.[30]

Through this period, the various major professional sports leagues developed a sprawling network of licensing arrangements with more than 600 companies. Another 2,000 companies have arrangements with the various college/university licensing groups. As far as the retail distribution of product, a network of "fan shops" grew to over 450 in number and licensed products found their way into sporting goods stores, department stores, and, eventually, the mass merchants. In order to compete most of the major sporting good chains and many department stores developed separate areas devoted exclusively to licensed goods.[31] Sales of licensed sports products will continue to grow as other "big league" sports gain popularity. For example the PGA had sales of over $20 million in 1994 and NASCAR has seen the sale of licensed goods increase from around $60 million in 1990 to nearly $500 million in 1994.

Collectibles and Memorabilia   One of the earliest examples of sports marketing can be traced to the 1880s when baseball cards were introduced. Consider life before the automobile and the television. For most baseball fans, the player's picture on the card may have been the only chance to see that player. Interestingly, the cards were featured as a promotion in cigarette packages rather than bubble gum. Can you imagine the ethical backlash that this practice would have produced today?

Although the sports-trading card industry reached $1.2 billion in 1991, industry-wide yearly sales plummeted to $700 million in 1995.[32] What caused this collapse? The answer is too much competition. From the beginning of the 1995 baseball season through the end of the 1995 basketball season, there were 23 sports card lines (a line typically contains different sports cards for each brand) distributed by the Topps company, 22 by Fleer, 22 by Pinnacle, 15 by Upper Deck, 7 by Dondruss, 7 by Pacific, 4 by Collectors Edge, 3 by Classic, and 2 by Playoff.

David Leibowitz, an industry analyst, commented that "With the channel of distribution backed up and with too much inventory, it was hard to sustain prices, let alone have them continue to rise." There is, however, some evidence that the industry will rebound. Card shop owners reported that all baseball card sales increased from the Topps Mickey Mantle Commemorative set and from Cal Ripken Jr.'s consecutive

■ The sports collector's dream—the Baseball Hall of Fame.

game record and hype. In addition, the 1998 McGwire–Sosa home run race was a boost to the market. Says Leibowitz, "The worst is over. Barring some negative event, the (trading card) companies could start putting some impressive numbers on the board."[33]

Personal Training for Sports

Another growing category of sports is referred to as **personal training**. These products are produced to benefit participants in sports at all levels and include: fitness centers, health services, sports camps, and instruction.

Fitness Centers and Health Services   When the New York Athletic Club was opened in 1886, it became the first facility opened specifically for athletic training. From its humble beginning in New York, the fitness industry has seen an incredible boom. "Pumping iron" was a common phrase in the 1970s and early 1980s. Moreover, the 1970s aerobics craze started by Dr. Ken Cooper added to the growth of health clubs around the country.

It is no secret that a physically fit body is becoming more important to society. The growth of the fitness industry follows a national trend for people to care more about their health. In 1993, there were 11,655 clubs in the United States billed as "health and fitness" centers. In 1997, this number had grown 14.6 percent to more than 13,354 clubs. Moreover, health club membership climbed to a record high 20.8 million people and is expected to double by 2010. Why are people joining health clubs in record numbers? According to a 1997 study conducted by the International Health, Racquet, and Sportsclub Association, people purchased memberships at health clubs to improve health (80 percent), to look better (75 percent), for physical therapy (39 percent), and to deal with stress (30 percent).[34]

Sports Camps and Instruction   Sports camps are organized training sessions designed to provide instruction in a specific sport (e.g., basketball, soccer, etc.). Camps are usually associated with instructing children, however, the "fantasy sports camp" for aging athletes has received considerable attention in the past few years. Fantasy sports camps typically feature current or ex-professional athletes, and the focus is more on having fun than actual instruction. Nearly every major league baseball team now offers some type of fantasy camp for adults. For example, the Boston Red Sox Fantasy Camp (for ages 30 and over) allows you to be a major leaguer for a week. The experience consists of social activities, games, and instruction with former Red Sox players, but this does not come cheap. The price for participating is $3,500 per person.[35]

Along with camps, another lucrative sports service is providing personal or group instruction in sports. The difference between instruction and camps is the ongoing nature of the instruction versus the finite period and intense experience of the camp. For example, taking golf or tennis lessons from a professional typically involves a series of half-hour lessons over the course of months or sometimes years. Contrast this with the camp that provides intense instruction over a week-long period.

Sports Information

The final type of sports product that we will discuss is sports information. **Sports information** products provide consumers with news, statistics, schedules, and stories about sports. In addition, sports information can provide participants with instructional materials. Sports specific newspapers (e.g., *The Sporting News*), magazines (e.g., *Sports Illustrated*), Internet sites (e.g., cnnsi.com), television (e.g., FoxSports), and radio (e.g., WFAN) can all be considered sports information products. All of these forms of media are experiencing growth both in terms of products and audience. Consider the following examples of new sports information media. ESPN launched its new magazine in March 1998 to compete with *Sports Illustrated*, which leads all sports magazines with a circulation of over 3 million.[36] In addition, the ESPN2 audience has increased 215 percent since 1995 to more than 55 million homes.[37]

The fastest growing source of sports information is on the World Wide Web. The ESPN Chilton Sports Poll estimates that 17 percent of all computer owners and people with access to computers get sports information on-line. This percentage jumps to 27 percent when people with a high level of sports interest are asked about using

■ The USTA Official Web site provides sports information for the tennis enthusiast.

on-line, sports information.[38] Due to the tremendous amount of information that sports fans desire (e.g., team stats, player stats, league stats) and the ability of Web sites to supply such information, Web sites and sports marketing make a perfect fit. One example of the success of providing sports information via the World Wibe Web is ESPNet (ESPN's Web site).

ESPN is not only introducing a new magazine, it has become a leader in providing over 140,000 daily users with sports information on its Web site. ESPN's site has been so successful because it targets the right customers, has a great product, leverages the ESPN name, and has one of the highest advertising rates on the Web.[39]

The Multidimensional Nature of the Sports Product

As you can see from our previous discussion, there are a wide variety of sports products. Our earlier definition of the sports product incorporated the distinction between goods and services. Although this is a traditional approach to categorizing consumer products, the complexity of the sports product makes the goods-services classification inadequate. Consider the rich diversity of the sports products that we have just considered. Everything from a hockey puck to the NCAA championship game of the Final Four in basketball is included in our definition. Because of this diversity and complexity, we have added an additional dimension to the sports product known as the body–mind continuum. The body–mind continuum is based on the notion that some sports products benefit consumers' minds, while other products act on consumers' bodies. Figure 1.3 illustrates the multidimensional nature of sports products using two dimensions: goods/services and body/mind. These dimensions make up the **sports product map**.

As you can see, we have positioned some sports products on this map. Exercise equipment is shown as a good that works on the body of the consumer. At the other end of the map, attending or watching a sporting event is considered a service that acts on the mind of consumers. Perhaps we can best describe the differences based on the mind/body and goods/services dimension by exploring sports camps. Sports camps for children are primarily instructional in nature. The primary product being sold is the opportunity for kids to practice their physical skills. On the other hand, the fantasy camp targeting adults is a product that acts more on the mind than body. The adults are purchasing the "fantasy" to interact with professional athletes rather than the physical training.

figure 1.3   The Sports Product Map

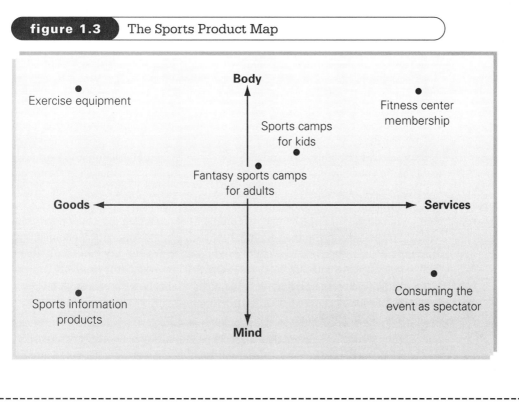

Understanding where sports products fall on this map is critical for sports marketers. Marketers must understand how they want their sports product to be perceived by consumers so they can understand what benefits to stress. For example, the marketers of a sporting event may want to sell the intangible excitement or the tangible features of the arena. This strategic decision is based on a number of factors that will be considered in detail throughout this text.

Producers/Intermediaries

Producers and intermediaries represent the manufacturers of sports products or the organizations that perform some function in the marketing of sports products. Organizations or individuals that perform the function of producer or intermediary include team owners, sanctioning bodies, agents, corporate sponsors, media, and sporting goods manufacturers. In the following paragraphs we will take a look at each of these producers and intermediaries as they relate to the various sports products.

Sports Labor   Owners of professional sports franchises, partnerships that own sporting events, and universities that "own" their athletic teams all represent producers of sporting events. One of the unique aspects of the sports industry is that often times businesspeople purchase a team because they always dreamed of becoming involved in sports. Typically, sports owners are entreprenuers who have made their riches in other businesses before deciding to get involved in the business of sports. All too often these owners may be realizing a dream, but fail to realize a profit. Just think of the risks in owning your own team. Pro sports teams have seasonal revenue streams, few chances to expand, and frequent labor problems and are dependent on the health of just a select few employees.

Many sports related financial ownership deals—be it racehorses, minor league baseball teams, indoor soccer franchises—score high on appeal and low on profits. J.W. Stealey, sole owner of the Baltimore Spirit, professional indoor soccer team, exemplifies the typical sports owner. He says, "Sports has always been my life. Owning a team is, to be honest, an ego kind of a deal, with all the attention from the media and involvement with the players." However, there is just one catch. "Although I keep expecting us to turn a profit, we never have."[40] Although ownership of professional franchises is still a dream for many individuals, corporations are quickly becoming the dominant force in ownership. In particular, media giants are purchasing teams to own their sports programming. Irwin Stelzer, a Washington economist, says "Buying a team is just a surer way of buying the rights [to programming]. Teams with media parents include the Dodgers (Fox), Angels (Walt Disney and ABC), Bears (Time Warner), and Cubs (Tribune)."[41] Interestingly, the NFL forbids corporate ownership of franchises.

Sanctioning Bodies   Sanctioning bodies are organizations that not only market sports products, but, more importantly, delineate and enforce rules and regulations, determine the time and place of sporting events, and provide athletes with the structure necessary to compete. Examples of sanctioning bodies include the NCAA, NFL, NHL, IOC (International Olympic Committee), and NASCAR. Sanctioning bodies can be powerful forces in the sports industry by regulating the rules and organizing the structure of the leagues and sporting events.

The PGA (Professional Golf Association) of America is one of the largest sanctioning bodies in the world. It is comprised of more than 22,000 members that promote the game of golf to "everyone, everywhere." In addition to marketing the game of golf, the PGA organizes tournaments for amateurs and professional golfers, holds instructional clinics, and hosts trade shows.[42] Although the PGA has a long history of advancing golf, this sanctioning body recently suffered from the controversial Casey Martin case. Casey Martin is a professional golfer with a disease known as Klippel-Trenaunay-Webber Syndrome. This chronic and progressive disease attacks the calf muscle and tibea, making walking extremely difficult. To date, the PGA rules forbid players from using golf carts during competition. However, Casey Martin sued the PGA for the right to ride in a cart and compete professionally. Martin argued that the PGA must abide by the regulation of the ADA (Americans with Disabilities Act). In February 1998 Casey Martin won his case and the court ordered that he be allowed to ride during competition. This victory for Martin was the first decision to invoke the ADA as it applies to a professional athlete. Another interesting twist to this case is that Martin is sponsored by Nike, which is also the title sponsor of the Nike Tour. Nike CEO Phil Knight publicly supported Martin and will feature him in the Nike "I Can" advertising campaign.

Sponsors   Sponsors represent a sport intermediary. As we discussed, corporations can serve as a consumer of sport. However, corporations also supply sporting events with products or money in exchange for association with the event. The relationship between the event, the audience, and the sponsor is referred to as the event triangle.[43] The basis of the event triangle is that the event, the audience, and the sponsor are all interdependent or depend upon each other to be successful. All three groups work in concert to maximize the sport's exposure. The events showcase talented athletes and attract the audience who watch the event in-person or through some medium. The audience, in turn, attracts the sponsor who pays the event to provide them with access to the audience. In addition, the sponsor promotes the event to the audience which helps the event reach its attendance goals. It is safe to say that sponsors represent an important intermediary or link between the event and the final consumers of sports—the audience.

Media   Earlier in this chapter, we commented on the growth of media in bringing sporting events to consumers. In fact, the media, which is considered an intermediary, may be the most powerful force in sports today and is getting stronger. Televised sports pulled in roughly $3.5 billion in sales in 1995 with the major networks (ABC, NBC, CBS, and FOX) accounting for over 70 percent of the market.[44] The primary revenue generator for these networks is selling prime advertising time. As the price of advertising time rises, so does the cost of securing broadcast rights, however, the networks are willing to pay.

Sports organizations cannot survive with the mass exposure of the media, and the media needs sports to satisfy the growing consumer demand for this type of entertainment. As the demand for sports programming increases, innovations in media will emerge. For example, in the next millennium interactive media will allow fans to control what game they are watching and what appears on the screen. The television audiences would be able to view player and game statistics at their convenience.

Agents   Another important intermediary in bringing the athlete to the consumer is the sports **agent**. From a sports marketing perspective, sports agents are intermediaries whose primary responsibility is leveraging athletes' worth or determining their bargaining power. The first "super-agent" in sports was Mark McCormack (see Sports Marketing Hall of Fame). Prior to his emergence, agents had never received the exposure and recognition that they enjoy today. Interestingly, it is not the agents themselves that have provoked their current rise to prominence, but rather the increased bargaining power of their clients.

The bargaining power of the athletes can be traced to two factors. First, the formation of new leagues in the 1970s, such as the American Basketball Association (ABA) and the World Hockey Association (WHA) resulted in increased competition to sign the best athletes. This competition drove the salaries to higher levels than ever before and made agents more critical. Second, free agency and arbitration has given players a chance to shop their talents on the open market and question the final offer

Sports Marketing hall of fame

MARK McCORMACK

Many people trace the beginnings of modern sports marketing to one man—Mark McCormack. In 1960, Mark McCormack, a Cleveland lawyer, signed an agreement to represent Arnold Palmer. With this star client in hand, McCormack began the International Management Group, better known as IMG. Today, IMG is a multinational sports marketing organization that employs over 2,000 people, has sales of over $1 billion, and represents some of the finest professional athletes in the world.

In addition to his contribution to sports marketing in the United States, McCormack has globalized sports marketing. He opened an Asian office of IMG in Tokyo in 1969, led in the sponsorship of events in Europe, and continues to expand into the Middle Eastern markets. One example of McCormack's enormous reach into international markets is IMG's Trans World International. TWI is the largest independent producer of sports programming in the world. One of its shows, Trans World Sports, is viewed in more than 325 million homes in over 76 countries.

Adapted from Zachary Schiller, Julia Flynn, and Jonathan B. Lerine, "Advantage, Mark McCormack?" *Business Week*, September 27, 1993, 64.

of owners. In addition, owners are now able to pay players the higher salaries because of the multimillion dollar national television contracts and cable television revenues.

Although most people associate agents with contract negotiations, agents do much more. Here are some of the other responsibilities of the agent:[45]

- determines the value of the player's services
- convinces a club to pay the player the aforementioned value
- develops the package of compensation to suit the players needs
- protects the player's rights under contract (and within the guidelines set by the collective bargaining agreement)
- counsels the player about post-career security, both financial and occupational
- finds a new club upon player free agency
- assists the player in earning extra income from endorsements, speeches, appearances, and commercials
- advises an athlete on the effect their personal conduct has on their career

Sports Equipment Manufacturers   **Sports equipment manufacturers** are responsible for producing and sometimes marketing sports equipment used by consumers who are participating in sports at all different levels of competition. Some sporting equipment manufacturers are still associated with a single product line whereas others carry a multitude of sports products. For example, Platypus Sporting Goods only manufacturers cricket balls. On the other hand, Wilson manufactures football, volleyball, basketball, golf, tennis, baseball, softball, racquetball/squash, and youth sports equipment.

Although it is obvious that equipment manufacturers are necessary to supply the equipment needed to produce the competition, they also play an important role in sports sponsorship. Sports equipment manufacturers become sponsors because of the natural relationship that they have with sports. For instance, Rawlings, one of the best known baseball glove manufacturers, sponsors the American and National League Golden Glove Award which is given to the best defensive players in their position. Spalding sponsors the NCAA Volleyball Championship by supplying the official game balls. In addition, Spalding is the official game ball of the WNBA.

asic Marketing Principles and Processes Applied to Sport

The Sports Marketing Mix

Sports marketing is commonly associated with promotional activities such as advertising, sponsorships, public relations, and personal selling. Although this is true, sports marketers are also involved in product and service strategies, pricing decisions, and distribution issues. These activities are referred to as the **sports marketing mix** which is defined as the coordinated set of elements that sports organizations use to meet their marketing objectives and satisfy consumers' needs.

The basic marketing mix elements are the sports product, price, promotion, and distribution. When coordinated and integrated the combination of the basic marketing mix elements are known as the marketing program. The marketing mix or program elements are controllable factors because sports marketing managers have control over each of the elements. In the following sections we take a closer look at the four marketing mix elements as they apply to the sports industry.

Product Strategies

One of the basic sports marketing activities is developing product and service strategies. In designing product strategies, decisions regarding licensing, merchandising, branding, and packaging are addressed. In addition, sports marketing managers are responsible for new product development, maintaining existing products, and eliminating weak products. MLB's decision to develop a new logo, the Washington Bullets changing their team name to the Wizards, and Nike introducing a new line of golf shoes are product issues of interest to sports marketers.

Because so much of sports marketing is based on services rather than goods, understanding the nature of services marketing is critical for the sports marketing manager. Services planning entails pricing of services, managing demand for services, and evaluating service quality. For instance, sports marketing managers want to know fans' perceptions of ticket ushers, concessions, parking, and stadium comfort. These service issues are especially important in today's sports marketing environment because fans equate value with high levels of customer service.

Distribution Strategies

Traditionally, the role of distribution is finding the most efficient and effective way to get the products into the hands of the consumers. Issues such as inventory management, transportation, warehousing, wholesaling, and retailing are all under the control of distribution managers. The advent of sporting good superstores such as Dick's Sporting Goods or the Sports Authority, offering sports memorabilia on the Home Shopping Network, and marketing sports products on the Internet are examples of the traditional distribution function at work. Sports marketing managers are also concerned with how to deliver sports to spectators in the most effective and efficient way. Questions such as where to build a new stadium, where to locate a recreational softball complex, or how to distribute tickets most effectively are potential distribution issues facing sports marketers.

Pricing Strategies

One of the most critical and sensitive issues facing sports marketing managers today is pricing. Pricing strategies include setting pricing objectives, choosing a pricing technique, and making adjustments to prices over time.

The price of tickets for sporting events; fees for personal seat licenses, pay-per-view, television sports programming; and the rising costs of participating in recreational sports such as golf, are all examples of how the pricing function impacts sports marketing.

Promotion Strategies

Just ask someone what comes to mind when they think of sports marketing, and the likely response is advertising. They may think of athletes such as Michael Jordan or Cal Ripken endorsing a product or service. Although advertising is an element of promotion, it is by no means the only one. In addition to advertising, promotional elements include communicating with the various sports publics through sponsorships, public relations, personal selling, or sales promotions. Together these promotional elements are called the promotion mix. When designing promotional strategies, sports marketers must consider integrating their promotions and using all aspects of the promotion mix.

The Exchange Process

Understanding the exchange process is central to any successful marketing strategy. As generally defined, an **exchange** is a marketing transaction in which the buyer gives something of value to the seller in return for goods and services. For an exchange to occur, several conditions must be satisfied:

- there must be at least two parties
- each party must have something of value to offer the other
- there must be a means for communication between the two or more parties
- each party must be free to accept or decline the offer
- each party must feel that it is desirable to deal with the other(s)

Traditionally, a marketing exchange consists of a consumer giving money to receive a product or service that meets their needs. Other exchanges, not involving money, are also possible. For example, trading a Reggie Jackson rookie baseball card for Dave Winfield and Don Mattingly cards represents a marketing exchange between two collectors.

Examples of elements that make up other exchanges appear in Figure 1.4. The two parties in the exchange process are called exchange players. These two participants are consumers of sport (spectators, participants, or sponsors) or producers/intermediaries of sport. Sports spectators exchange their time, money, and/or personal energy with sports teams in exchange for the entertainment and enjoyment of watching the contest. Sports participants exchange their time, energy, and money for the joy of sport and the better quality of life that participating in sports brings. In sponsorships, organizations exchange money or products for the right to associate with a sporting event, player, team, or other sports entity.

Although these are rather elementary examples of the exchange process, one of the things that makes sports marketing so unique is the complex nature of the exchange process. Within one sporting event multiple exchanges will occur. Consider a Winston Cup NASCAR event. There are exchanges between spectators and the track ownership (money for entertainment); spectators and product vendors who are licensed by NASCAR (money for goods associated with racing); track owner and NASCAR sanctioning body (money for organizing the event and providing other event services); media and NASCAR (event broadcast coverage for money); product

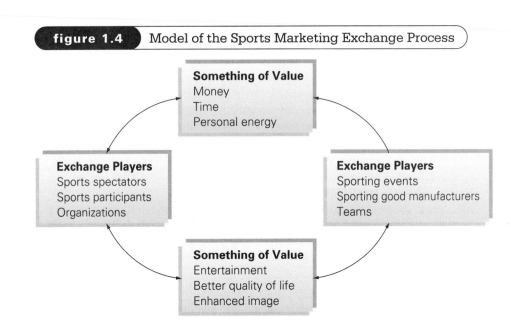

figure 1.4 Model of the Sports Marketing Exchange Process

Something of Value
Money
Time
Personal energy

Exchange Players
Sports spectators
Sports participants
Organizations

Exchange Players
Sporting events
Sporting good manufacturers
Teams

Something of Value
Entertainment
Better quality of life
Enhanced image

sponsors and driving team owner (promotional benefits for money); track owner and driving team owner (producer of the competition for money). As you may imagine, trying to sort out all of these exchanges, much less determine the various marketing strategy involved in each exchange, is a complicated puzzle that can only be solved by having a full understanding of the industry within each sport. Although the nature of each sporting event and industry is slightly different, designing a marketing strategy incorporates some fundamental processes that span the sports industry.

The Strategic Sports Marketing Process

Sports marketers manage the complex and unique exchanges process in the sports industry by using the strategic sports marketing process. The **strategic sports marketing process** is the process of planning, implementing, and controlling marketing efforts to meet organizational goals and satisfy consumers' needs.

In order to meet these organizational goals and marketing objectives, sports marketers must first anticipate consumer demand. Sports marketers want to know what motivates consumers to purchase, how they perceive sports products or services, how they learn about sports product, and how they choose certain products over others.

One way sports marketers anticipate demand is by conducting marketing research to gather information about the sports consumer. Another way that sports marketers anticipate demand is by monitoring the external environment. For instance, marketing research was used to determine the feasibility of locating a new NASCAR speedway in Northern Kentucky. According to developer, Jerry Carroll, "The report was two volumes and it not only said a major racetrack would work in this area, but it would be a grand slam." In addition, Carroll anticipated demand by examining the external environment. He found out that there are about 51 million people within a 300 mile radius of the proposed track and that "NASCAR fans, and other racing fans, don't think anything of driving 300 miles for a race."[46]

Next, sports marketers examine different groups of consumers, choose the group of consumers in which to direct the organization's marketing efforts, and then determine how to position the product or service to that group of consumers. These market selection decisions are referred to as segmentation, targeting, and position. The final aspect of the planning phase is to offer products that are promoted, priced, and distributed in ways that appeal to the targeted consumers.

Following the planning phase of the strategic sports marketing process, the next step is implementation. Implementation refers to executing or carrying out the plans. In order for implementation to be successful, the sports organization must consider a number of organizational design elements including: communication, staffing, skills, coordination, rewards, information, creativity, and budgeting.

Once the plans have been implemented, the final step of the strategic sports marketing process is referred to as the control phase. During the control phase plans are evaluated to determine whether organizational objectives have been met. If objectives are not being reached, adjustments are made to planning and the process continues.

To gain a better understanding of the strategic marketing process, we will look at the following spotlight on women in sports marketing. Notice that the WNBA clearly emphasizes the strategic marketing process. The WNBA, using the marketing might of the NBA, designed its strategic marketing process to generate immediate awareness and interest in the league. On the other hand, the ABL appears to be emphasizing its superior product rather than developing a comprehensive marketing strategy.

spotlight on women in sports marketing:

women's hoop league out-glitzes rival
WNBA gets the attention despite less talent than the ABL

Glory. That is the name of the Atlanta team in the women's professional American Basketball League, a fact you may not know given that there was little glory to be found on a recent media day here.

Only one local television camera appeared. The interview room had no tables and no chairs; players sat on the floor. No one was being fussed over for network promos or cereal-box shoots or for ads for McDonald's Chicken McNuggets. Such fussing is a hallmark of the rival league, the Women's National Basketball Association, launched to much hoopla by the powerful National Basketball Association. The ABL, started last year by an independent group of entrepreneurs, is still a marketing neophyte and mainly sticks to its hoops.

Teresa Edwards, who has played on a record four U.S. Olympic teams and is now the player-coach of the Glory, greets the press unadorned of even a shoe-endorsement deal. Where, she is asked, is her piece of the chicken-nuggets action? Where is the Glory's glory? She bristles.

(continued)

"We're not about greed," she says. "I'm not thinking, how much can I get out of television commercials and endorsements. We want to play good basketball. That's the important thing."

Her words have a pointed edge and a point: Women's basketball, swaddled in a warm, fuzzy blanket during its recent ascent in popularity, sits precariously atop the same fault line of outsized riches and celebrity that rumbles beneath all sports. When two separate professional women's basketball leagues were established within a year of each other—each hoping to capitalize on the goodwill generated by the U.S. women's victory at the Atlanta Olympics—the stage was set for conflict.

The ABL acknowledges that it can't match the WNBA's marketing power and instead touts itself as the league with better talent. Its teams bought ads in their local markets during the telecasts of WNBA games this summer. The blunt message: "We're no summer league. We're the big league."

Ouch. "The ABL approach to the game is to give women the opportunity to play in the U.S. as a career, like the men," says Robert Fiondella, the chairman of Phoenix Home Life Mutual Insurance Co., which owns 20 percent of the league. "Then you play in the winter, when the men play, and you pay enough money so they don't have to do anything else." A number of WNBA players, he notes, are heading overseas to supplement their summer salaries.

Last year, ABL players averaged $70,000, with a minimum of $40,000 and a maximum of $125,000. This year the average will rise to $80,000, with the maximum moving to $150,000 for a 44-game schedule. The WNBA, which played 28 games, has a sliding scale, from $10,000 to $50,000. It plans at least a 10 percent boost next summer (and possibly a few more games). It lured Ms. McCray with a six-figure salary, which includes promotional responsibilities. Three other young marquee players, Rebecca Lobo, Lisa Leslie, and Sheryl Swoopes, have similar contracts. In both cases, it is the leagues, not individual teams, that pay the players.

Indeed, the ABL fancies itself as the David to the WNBA Goliath and is accumulating ammunition—mainly money—to bring in top players. It created a licensing department, headed by a former executive at Elvis Presley Enterprises, to boost revenue. Reebok, the ABL's shoe and apparel partner, is tripling the volume of league gear in the market. Mr. Lacob and Phoenix Mutual each invested $3 million and stand by to add more. "We're committed that it doesn't fail," says Phoenix's Mr. Fiondella, and officials are considering becoming the first pro league to go public to raise capital.

Raising awareness is just as critical. "It's pretty tough competing with the WNBA marketing machine," says Glory general manager D. J. Mackovets, who is working overtime to fill the 6,000 seats in the team's arena. "We need to get our product in front of people. When we win, people will come back. It will be like a snowball."

Adapted from Roger Thurow, "Women's Hoops League Out-Glitzes Rival," *The Wall Street Journal*, September 27, 1997, B12.

SUMMARY

The sports industry is experiencing tremendous growth and sports marketing is playing an important role in this emerging industry. Chapter 1 provided a basic understanding of sports marketing and the sports industry. Sports marketing *is the specific application of marketing principles and processes to sport products and to the marketing of non-sports products* *through association with sport.* The study and practice of sports marketing is complex and interesting because of the unique nature of the sports industry.

Today, sports organizations define their businesses as entertainment providers. In addition, sports organizations know that in order to be successful in the competitive environment of sports, they must practice a marketing orientation. An organization with a marketing orientation concentrates on understanding consumers and providing sports products that satisfy consumers' needs.

Sports marketing will continue to grow in importance as sports become more pervasive in the U.S. culture and around the globe. This phenomenal growth of the sports industry can be seen and measured in a number of ways. We can identify growth by looking at the increasing numbers of sport spectators, the growth of media coverage, the increase in sports participation, rising employment opportunities, and the growth in sports internationally. To better understand this growing and complex industry, a simplified model of the consumer-supplier relationship was presented.

The simplified model of the consumer-supplier relationship in the sports industry consists of three major elements: consumers of sport, sports products, and producers/intermediaries. Three distinct types of sports consumers are identified in the model. These consumers of sport include spectators who observe sporting events, participants who take part in sporting events, and sponsors who exchange money or product for the right to be associated with a sporting event. The spectators, participants, and sponsors use sports products.

A sports product is a good, service, or any combination of the two that is designed to provide benefits to a sports consumer. The primary sports product consumed by sponsors and spectators is the sporting event. Products related to the event are athletes like Michael Jordan and arenas like the United Center which both provide their own

unique benefits. Other categories of sports products common to the sports industry include sporting goods (equipment, apparel and shoes, licensed merchandise, collectibles, and memorabilia), personal training services for sports (fitness centers and sports camps), and sports information (news and magazines). Because there is a variety of sports products it is useful to categorize these products using the sports product map.

Producers and intermediaries represent the third element of the simplified model of the consumer-supplier relationship in the sports industry. Producers include those organizations or individuals that help "manufacture" the sporting event such as owners, sanctioning bodies, and sports equipment manufacturers. Intermediaries are also critical to the sports industry because they bring the sport to the end-user of the sports product. Sponsors, the media, and agents are the three intermediaries presented in this chapter.

Although sports marketers must have a thorough understanding of the sports industry to be successful, the tool of their trade is the sports marketing mix. The sports marketing mix is defined as the coordinated set of elements that sports organizations use to meet their marketing mix objectives and satisfy consumers' needs. The elements of the marketing mix are sports products, distribution or place, pricing, and promotion.

In addition to the marketing mix, another central element of marketing is the exchange process. The exchange process is defined as a marketing transaction in which the buyer gives something of value to the seller in return for goods and services. One of the things that makes the sports industry so unique is the complex nature of the exchange process and the many exchanges that take place within a single sporting event.

To manage the complexities of the sports industry and achieve organizational objectives, sports marketers use the strategic sports marketing process. The strategic sports marketing process consists of three major parts: planning, implementation, and control. The planning process begins by understanding consumers' needs, selecting a group of consumers with similar needs, and positioning the sports product within this group of consumers. The final step of the planning phase is to develop a marketing mix that will appeal to the targeted group of consumers and carry out the desired positioning. The second major part of the strategic sports marketing process is putting the plans into action or implementation. Finally, the plans are evaluated to determine whether organizational objectives and marketing goals are being met. This third, and final, part of the strategic sports marketing process is called control.

KEY TERMS & CONCEPTS

agents

amateur sporting event

benefits

exchange process

goods

licensing

marketing myopia

marketing orientation

organized sporting event

participant

personal training

producers/intermediary

services

simplified model of the consumer–supplier relationship

spectator

sport

sporting events

sporting goods

sports equipment manufacturer

sports information

sports marketing

sports marketing mix

sports product

sports product map

sports sponsorship

strategic sports marketing process

REVIEW QUESTIONS

1. Define sports marketing and discuss how sports are related to entertainment?

2. What is a marketing-orientation and how do sports organizations practice a market orientation?

3. Discuss some of the ways that the sports marketing industry is growing?

4. Outline the simplified model of the consumer–supplier relationship in the sports industry.

5. What are the three distinct types of sports consumers? What are the different types of spectators? How are sports participants categorized?

6. Define sports products. What are the different types of sports products discussed in the simplified model of the consumer–supplier relationship in the sports industry?

7. Describe the different producers/intermediaries in the simplified model of the consumer–supplier relationship in the sports industry.

8. What are the basic elements of the sports marketing mix?

9. What is the marketing exchange process and why is the exchange process critical for sports marketers?

10. Define the strategic sports marketing process and discuss the various elements in the strategic sports marketing process.

EXERCISES

1. Provide five recent examples of sports marketing that have been in the news and describe how each relates to our definition of sports marketing.

2. How does sport differ from other forms of entertainment?

3. Provide an example of a sports organization that suffers from marketing myopia and another sports organization that defines its business as entertainment. Justify your choices.

4. Attend a high school, college, and professional sporting event and comment on the marketing orientation of the event at each level of competition.

5. Provide three examples of how you would *measure growth* in the sports marketing industry. What evidence do you have that the number of people participating in sports is growing?

6. Discuss the disadvantages/advantages of attending sporting events versus consuming a sporting event through the media (e.g., television or radio).

7. Develop a list of all of the sports products produced by your college/university. Which are goods and which are services? Identify ways in which the marketing of the goods differs from the services.

8. Choose any professional sports team and describe how it puts the basic sports marketing functions into practice.

INTERNET EXERCISES

1. Using Internet sites, support the growth of the sporting goods industry.

2. Compare and contrast the Internet sites of three professional sports teams. Which site has the strongest marketing orientation? Why?

NOTES

1. Leigh Montville, "February Frenzy," *Sports Illustrated,* February 20, 1995, 49–54.

2. Jerry Schwartz, "Long-Time Makers of Sporting Goods Consider the Possibility that Their Game Has Passed Them By," *The New York Times,* February 25, 1997, C9.

3. Ibid.

4. Michael Farber, "Putting on a Show," *Sports Illustrated,* October 17, 1994, 30–33.

5. A.K. Kohli and B.J. Jaworski, "Marketing Orientation: The Construct, Research Propositions, and Managerial Implications," *Journal of Marketing,* 54 (2): 1–18.

6. Jeffery D. Derrick, "Marketing Orientation In Minor League Baseball." <http://www.cad.gu.edu.au/market/cv...al_of_sport_marketing/derrick.html>

7. Roger Thurow, "The Rockies' Money Mountain High," *The Wall Street Journal,* October 6, 1995, B11.

8. "Archives." *The Business of Sports.* <http://bizsports.com/newsarchive/214.html>

9. "Close Game Helps Super Bowl Rating." *Super Bowl XXXII.* <http://www.sportserver.com/newsroo.../feat/archive/012698/nfl45018.html>.

10. "Sportsline USA Traffic Reaches All-Time High." *About SportsLine—CBS SportsLine.* <http://about.sportsline.com/releases/olytraf.htm>

11. Tim Jones, "The Boom in Sports on TV," *Chicago Tribune,* May 12, 1996, B1.

12. "NBA To Double Its Money in New Deal." *CNNSI.* <http://cnnsi.com/basketball/nba/news/1997/11/10/nba—contract>

13. Stedman Graham, Joe Jeff Goldblatt, and Lisa Delphy, *The Ultimate Guide to Sport Event Management and Marketing,* (Chicago, IL: Irwin, 1995) 6.

14. "TV Sports: The $3.5 Billion Ticket." *Broadcasting & Cable,* May 13, 1996, 34–35.

15. "ABC, ESPN Ready for Some Football: NBC, TNT Left out By NFL." *ESPN Sports Zone.* <http://espnet.sportszone.com/nfl/news/980113/00533127.html>

16. "1998 State of the Industry Report." *Sporting Goods Manufactures Association.* <http://www.sportlink.com/research/1998_research/industry/98soti.html>

17. Ibid.

18. Nigel Pope. "Overview of Current Sponsorship Thought." <http://www.cad.gu.edu.au/cjsm/pope21.htm>

19. "IEG Sponsorship Report." *IEG Network.* <http://www.sponsorship.com/forum/assertionsindex>.

20. Ibid.

21. Geoffrey Smith. "Sports: Walk, Don't Schuss." *Business Week.* <http://www.businessweek.com/1997/49/b3556153.htm>.

22. "Atlanta—The Numbers Game." <http://www.olympic.nbc.com/general/numbers.html>.

23. "Archives." *The Business of Sports.* <http://www.bizsports.com/newsarchive/123/new.html>.

24. "Tiger, Inc." *Business Week,* April 28, 1997, 32–36.

25. Jeff Jensen, "All the Sports World's a Stage," *Advertising Age,* vol. 65, October 24, 1994, 1, 3–4.

26. "Venue Media Teams with Williams to Provide ChoiceSeat Interactive Network at Super Bowl XXXII," *Yahoo!—The Williams Companies Inc Company News.* <http://biz.yahoo.com/bw/980123/venue_medi_1.html>.

27. "The Sports and Recreation Industry Reaches $62 Billion," *Sporting Goods Manufacturers Association* . <http://www.sportlink.com/press_room/1998_releases/m98-07.html>.

28. Ibid.

29. Ibid.

30. *Sports Licensed Products Report Sporting Goods Manufactures Association.* <http://www.sportlink.com/research/...h/industry/98_licensed_report.html>.

31. *1998 State of the Industry Report, Sporting Goods Manufactures Association.* <http://www.sportlink.com/research/1998_research/industry/98soti.html>.

32. John Garrity, "House of Cards," *Sports Illustrated,* July 29, 1996, 104–106.

33. Ibid.

34. Martin G. Letscher, "Sports, Fads and Trends," *American Demographics,* vol. 19, Number 6 (June, 1997): 53–56.

35. Jane Bennett Clark, "Take a Swing at a Sports Camp," *Kiplinger's Personal Finance Magazine,* April, 1997, 130.

36. "Top Magazines by Paid Circulation." *Ad Age Dataplace.* <http://www.adage.com>.

37. "ESPN2 Audience up 215% since 1995." *ESPN Sports Zone.* <http://espn.sportszone.com/editors/studios/980202ratings.html>.

38. "1998 State of the Industry Report." *Sporting Goods Manufacturers Association.* <http://www.sportlink.com/research/1998_research/industry/98soti.html>.

39. M. Gunter, "Web + Sports = Profit: Right?" *Fortune,* March 4, 1996, 197–198.

40. Jill Andresky Frasier, "Root, Root, Root for Your Own Team," *Inc.*, July 1997, 111.

41. Michael Santoli, "How to Own Your Own Sports Team," *The Wall Street Journal*, September 27, 1996, B17.

42. "The Role of the PGA of America." <http://www.pga.com/FAQ/pga_role.html>.

43. Phil Schaaf, *Sports Marketing: Its Not Just A Game Anymore,* (Amhearst, MA: Prometheus Books, 1995) 46–75.

44. "TV Sports: The $3.5 Billion Ticket," *Broadcasting & Cable,* May 13, 1996, 34–35, 38, 46.

45. "Frequently Asked Questions." *Sim-Gratton, Inc.* <http://home.istar.ca/~simagent/fag.html>

46. Andrea Tortora. "NASCAR Track City's Future?" *The Enquirer.* <http://www.enquirer.com/editions/1997/11/16/loc_kynascar.html> (November 16, 1997).

CHAPTER 2

Overview
of the Contingency Framework
for Strategic Sports Marketing

OBJECTIVES

After completing this chapter, you should be able to

- Understand the contingency framework for strategic sports marketing

- Describe and apply the strategic sports marketing process

- Define the internal and external contingencies and relate them to the strategic sports marketing process

- Explain the planning decisions fundamental to the strategic sports marketing process

- Describe how and why sports marketers understand consumers' needs

- Understand the concepts of segmentation, targeting, and positioning

- Identify the elements of the sports marketing mix

- Describe the implementation phase of the strategic sports marketing process

- Discuss the control phase of the strategic marketing process

- Identify different ways to assess the success of your planning

Trying to put a new spin on a 70-year-old brand is no easy task. For decades, the Globetrotters thrilled fans of all ages across the world. While the NBA is basking in popularity, the Globetrotters nearly dropped the ball. The problem was that the Globetrotters organization didn't change with the times. Its act grew stale while the NBA grew hip. The solution—unveil a new strategic marketing direction, keeping in mind the changing environment and internal strengths and weaknesses of the Globetrotters.

Mannie Jackson, team owner and former Globetrotter player, attempted to capitalize on the strengths of the Globetrotters. The team boasted a Q-score (measure of recognition and appeal) second only to Michael Jordan among athletes. In addition, the team is recognized not only in the United States, but around the world. As Jackson points out, "There's a lot of equity in the brand, and so now we are trying to build it, protect it, and embellish it."

Jackson has already realized the long-standing appeal his team has with families and small children. According to Jon Jameson, vice president of marketing at Denny's restaurants, the team "stands for quality, family entertainment, and outstanding role models for children." Although the Globetrotters' clean-cut image may be a curse for the older end of the youth market, they are one of the few entertainment properties that appeal to the six to ten age group.

What has Jackson done to rejuvenate the Globetrotters marketing mix? During the first year of Jackson's tenure (1993), the team boasted updated music and comedy bits, added a team mascot, and recruited an additional touring team. Jackson also cut all but four of the team's players and beefed up scouting to make the team more competitive.

■ Owner Manny Jackson and the Harlem Globetrotters.

The team also unveiled some big-name sponsorships, naming Reebok its official outfitter and signing a deal with Walt Disney World to use its new fieldhouse as a training camp. The partnerships are part of the team's effort to develop its licensing program, both by increasing the number of products beyond the dozen or so current offerings and by expanding the distribution. The team started selling the merchandise on its Web site and is scheduled to open its first retail store in Arizona.

The Globetrotters surpassed the 2.5 million mark in attendance for the 1998 "What Sports Should Be" tour, a 20 percent increase over the 1997 tour. Additionally, Globetrotters merchandise sales increased by 17 percent from 1997. All of this shows—strategic marketing pays off.

Source: Cyndee Miller, "Globetrotters Dribble Out A New Marketing Plan," *Sports Marketing*, September 23, 1996, 34. Courtesy of the Marketing News.

As the preceding article illustrates, the foundation of any effective sports organization is a sound, yet flexible, strategic framework. The process should be systematic and well-organized, but must be readily adaptable to changes in the environment. Each strategic marketing process may have unique characteristics, but the fundamentals are all the same. To help us make sense of the complex and rapidly changing sports industry, we will use a contingency framework to guide the strategic sports marketing process. For the remainder of this chapter, let us look at an overview of this process.

Contingency Framework for Strategic Sports Marketing

Sports marketing managers must be prepared to face a continually changing environment. Think about what can happen over the course of an event or a season. The team that was supposed to win the championship cannot seem to win a game. The star player gets injured halfway through the season. Attendance at the sporting event is affected by poor weather conditions. Team owners threaten to move the franchise, build new stadiums, and change personnel. All this impacts the sports marketing process.

At the collegiate level, a different set of situations may alter the strategic marketing process. For example, players may be declared ineligible because of grades, star players may leave school early to join the professional ranks, programs may be suspended for violation of NCAA regulations, or conferences may be realigned.

One example of a crisis situation at the collegiate level occurred when an announcement was made that one of the NCAA football program's most competitive and visible universities would be leaving the conference. This school's decision to leave the conference would have a tremendous impact on all of the schools in the conference. It was also speculated that the school's leaving the conference would have a direct impact on its local economy and the revenues from the football program.

A study was conducted to determine the perception of the local business community with respect to the economic impact of the football program.[1] Findings revealed that the university and conference had a high social impact on the community, but less of an economic one on the individual business owners. Businesses that held season tickets felt even stronger than non-season ticket holders about the positive impact the football program had on the community. Based on these findings, recommendations were made to promote the fact that the athletic program had a positive economic impact on the community. Unfortunately, recommendations such as the one just described were suggested after the crisis occurred.

The authors of this study advised taking a more proactive approach in the future, which would either avoid or prepare for crisis situations. More specifically, the authors suggested two remedies for identifying or resolving crises. First, sports organizations should conduct frequent marketing audits to review performance and identify market opportunities and threats. Second, formal marketing plans should be constructed and continually monitored to avoid or adapt to crisis situations. Most importantly, the authors stated that "a marketing plan could have been developed that would have blueprinted the team's approach to avoiding the impending crisis (perhaps lobbying efforts, new team recruitment, etc.) and defined a **contingency strategy** for adoption if the crisis were to prove inevitable."

It is also possible for positive opportunities to occur within the marketing environment. For example, the football program at Northwestern University, a perennial cellar-dweller in the Big Ten Conference, suddenly emerged as a national power in the mid-1990s. The Miracle Mets of 1969 made an unexpected late season run and eventually captured the World Series. The 1980 U.S. Olympic hockey team is yet another example of a team that defied the odds. These are all positive "crises" that presented opportunities for sports marketers.

Sports marketers need to be prepared for either positive or negative changes in the environment. These factors are out of the control of the sports marketer, but they must be acknowledged and managed. Sports marketers must be prepared to cope with these rapid changes. One model that provides a system for understanding and managing the complexities of the sports marketing environment is called the **contingency framework for strategic sports marketing**.

Contingency Approaches

Contingency models were originally developed for managers who wished to be responsive to the complexities of their organization and the changing environments in which they operate.[2] Several elements of the contingency framework make it especially useful for sport marketers. First, sports marketers operate in unpredictable and rapidly changing environments. They can neither predict team or player success nor control scheduling or trades. A quote by New York Mets Marketing Vice President, Michael Aronin, who spent 13 years with Clairol, captures the essence of this idea: "Before, I had control of the product, I could design it the way I wanted it to be. Here the product changes every day and you've got to adapt quickly to these changes."[3]

Second, the contingency approach suggests that no one marketing strategy is more effective than another. However, one particular strategy may be more appropriate than another for a specific sports organization in a particular environment. For example, sports marketers for the Boston Red Sox have years of tradition on their side that influence their strategic planning. This marketing strategy, however, will not necessarily meet the needs of the expansion Arizona Diamondbacks. Likewise, strategies for a NCAA Division I program are not always appropriate for a Division II program. The contingency framework can provide the means for developing an effective marketing strategy in all of these situations.

Third, a contingency model uses a systems perspective, one that assumes an organization does not operate in isolation but interacts with other systems. In other words, while an organization is dependent on its environment to exist and be successful, it can also play a role in shaping events outside the firm. Think about the Chicago Black Hawks and all the resources required from the environment to produce the core product—entertainment. These resources include professional athletes, owners, management and support personnel, minor league franchises to supply talent, facilities, other competitors, and fans. The different environments that the Chicago Black Hawks actively interact with and influence include the community, the NHL, sponsors, employees and their families, and the sport itself. Understanding the relationship between the organization and its many environments is fundamental to grasping the nature of the contingency approach. In fact, the complex relationship that sports organizations have with their many publics (e.g., fans, government, businesses, other teams) is one of the things that makes sports marketing so unique.

One way of thinking about the environments that impact sports organizations is to separate them on the basis of internal versus external contingencies. The external contingencies are factors outside of the organization's control; the internal are considered controllable from the organization's perspective. It is important to realize that both the internal and external factors are perceived to be beyond the control (though not the influence) of the sports marketer.

The essence of contingency approaches is trying to predict and strategically align the strategic marketing process with the internal and external contingencies. This alignment is typically referred to as strategic fit or just "fit." Let us look at the contingency approach shown in Figure 2.1 in greater detail.

figure 2.1 Contingency Framework for Strategic Sports Marketing

STRATEGIC SPORTS MARKETING PROCESS

EXTERNAL CONTINGENCIES (CHAPTER 2)

Competition
Legal/Political
Demographics
Technology
Culture
Physical environment
Economy

fit

PLANNING

1. Understanding consumers' needs
   A. Market research (chapter 4)
   B. Consumers as participants (chapter 5)
   C. Consumers as spectators (chapter 6)

2. Market selection decisions (chapter 7)
   A. Market segmentation
   B. Target markets
   C. Positioning

3. Marketing mix decisions (chapters 8–15)
   A. Sports products
   B. Pricing
   C. Promotion
   D. Place

IMPLEMENTATION (chapter 16)

CONTROL (chapter 16)

fit

INTERNAL CONTINGENCIES (CHAPTER 2)

Organization's vision
Organization's mission
Organization's objectives
 & marketing goals
Organization's strategy
Organization's culture

The focus of the contingency framework for sports marketing, and the emphasis of this text, is the strategic sports marketing process. The three primary components of this process are planning, implementation, and control. The planning phase begins with understanding the consumers of sports. As previously discussed, these consumers may be participants, spectators, or perhaps both. Once information regarding the potential consumers is gathered and analyzed, market selection decisions can be made. These decisions are used to segment markets, choose the targeted consumers, and position the sports product against the competition. The final step of the planning phase is to develop the sports marketing mix that will most efficiently and effectively reach the target market.

Effective planning is merely the first step in a successful strategic sports marketing program. The best laid plans are useless without a method for carrying them out and monitoring them. The process of executing the marketing program, or mix, is referred to as implementation. The evaluation of these plans is known as the control phase of the strategic marketing plan. These two phases, implementation and control, are the second and third steps of the strategic sports marketing process.

As you can see from the model, a contingency framework calls for alignment, or fit, between the strategic marketing process (planning, implementation, and control) and external and internal contingencies. Fit is based on determining the internal strengths and weaknesses of the sports organizations, as well as examining the external opportuntities and threats that exist. **External contingencies** are defined as all influences outside of the organization that can impact the organization's strategic marketing process. These external contingencies include factors such as competition, regulatory and political issues, demographic trends, technology, culture and values, and the physical environment. **Internal contingencies** are all the influences within the organization that can impact the strategic marketing process. These internal contingencies usually include the vision and mission of the organization, organizational goals and strategies for reaching those goals, and the organizational structure and systems.

Overview of the Strategic Sports Marketing Process: The Heart of the Contingency Framework

The **strategic sports marketing process** was defined in chapter 1 as the process of planning, implementing, and controlling marketing efforts to meet organizational goals and satisfy consumers' needs (see also Figure 2.2). The **planning phase**, which is the most critical, begins with understanding the consumers of sport through marketing research and identifying consumer wants and needs. Next, market selection decisions are made, keeping the external and internal contingencies in mind. Finally, the marketing mix, also known as the four P's, is developed to meet the identified consumer needs.

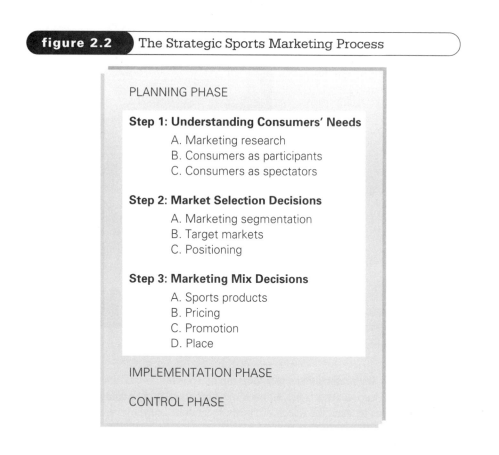

figure 2.2 The Strategic Sports Marketing Process

PLANNING PHASE

Step 1: Understanding Consumers' Needs
      A. Marketing research
      B. Consumers as participants
      C. Consumers as spectators

Step 2: Market Selection Decisions
      A. Marketing segmentation
      B. Target markets
      C. Positioning

Step 3: Marketing Mix Decisions
      A. Sports products
      B. Pricing
      C. Promotion
      D. Place

IMPLEMENTATION PHASE

CONTROL PHASE

Once the planning phase is completed, plans are executed in the **implementation phase**. In this second phase of the strategic sports marketing process, decisions such as who will carry out the plans, when will the plans will be executed, and how will the plans be executed are addressed. After implementing the plans, the third phase is to evaluate the response to the plans to determine their effectiveness. This is called the **control phase**. Let us examine the three phases of the strategic sports marketing process in greater detail.

The Planning Phase

Understanding Consumers' Needs

The first step in the planning phase is conducting marketing research to identify and examine sports consumers' needs. Marketing research is conducted using a variety of techniques. Surveys, the most widely used marketing research tool, are conducted at sporting events, over the telephone, or by mail to understand the attitudes and purchase behaviors (e.g., attendance) of sport consumers. Questions concerning who attends

■ Different consumers receive different benefits from fitness classes.

sporting events, the reasons that consumers attend sporting events, and consumers' attitudes towards various sports are all used by sports marketing managers to help formulate strategies to meet the needs of sports spectators and those who participate in sports.

An example of an area where sports marketers use marketing research to identify the needs of consumers can be found in the fitness industry. A survey was conducted by American Sports Data asking individuals why they most recently joined a health club. Young adults under the age of 35 thought it was important to join a health club in order to look better, increase strength, develop muscles, and meet new friends. On the other hand, the over-35 crowd joined to improve their health, deal with stress, or as medical or physical therapy.[4] Understanding the unique needs of these different groups of consumers is essential in designing appropriate marketing strategies that will meet these specific needs.

Market Selection Decisions

The process of selecting appropriate markets and positioning your sports entity effectively is the next stage in the planning phase of the strategic sports marketing process. **Market selection decisions** are sometimes referred to as STP, or segmentation, targeting, and positioning. These decisions should only be made after careful evaluation of the consumers' needs. It is important to bear in mind that the all of the steps in the strategic marketing process follow a sequential order and are systematically organized. Only after choosing a target can the sports entity be positioned to that distinct market segment. Let us examine each of these steps.

major league baseball international: segmenting the market based on where people live

In an effort to expand its fan base, Major League Baseball is looking to international markets. Though most people realize that baseball is extremely popular in Latin America and Asia, baseball is also the fourth most popular sport among kids in Germany. Baseball may be losing popularity in America, but it is growing internationally. To support and foster this growth, a division of Major League Baseball called Major League Baseball International (MLBI) was formed.

MLBI has a number of programs designed to encourage both the spectator and the participant consumer markets abroad. Programs for participants include the Envoy Program; Pitch, Hit and Run; and baseball festivals. The Envoy Program sends amateur coaches overseas to teach players the fundamentals of the game. In 1997, some 200,000 players were coached in 30 countries. The Pitch, Hit, and Run program operated in Australia, Japan, Taiwan, Germany, Puerto Rico, Korea, and the United Kingdom in 1997. Designed to teach kids ages 9 to 12 the fundamentals of the game, the program will introduce baseball to over 700,000 youths by 1998. Baseball festivals have also been de-signed by MLBI to introduce baseball to new audiences. Similar to MLB's All-Star Fan Fest, participants are given a chance to take their turn at bat in the cage, get their fastball clocked on radar, and even have their own baseball cards made. This event has expanded to 12 cities and, according to Tim Brosman of MLBI, "The baseball festival offers entertainment for the entire family and is a great way to get international fans more actively involved."

MLBI is also developing ways to attract spectators to the game of baseball. Most notably, two MLBI games will be aired live each week in the United Kingdom. MLBI also provides live broadcasting of the All-Star game to some 205 million fans in 205 countries.

In addition to these "products," Major League Baseball has opened a stand-alone (i.e., no adjacent retailers selling competing products to share traffic) MLB Club Shop in downtown Tokyo, and the Padres have opened a retail shop in Tijuana, Mexico. MLB will continue to expand in international market segments as long as U.S. retailers such as Foot Locker, J.C. Penney, and The Sports Authority experience international growth.

Source: The Official Site of Major League Baseball. <http://www.majorleaguebaseball.com/mlbi>.

Segmentation

Grouping consumers based on common needs is referred to as **market segmentation**. Sports marketers frequently segment markets based on one or a combination of the following characteristics:

- demographics (age, sex, marital status, occupation, education, ethnic background)
- geographic (where people live)
- geodemographic (the demography that defines a region where people live)
- benefits (what consumers desire in products and services)
- behavioral (consumption and usage patterns)
- psychographic (personality and lifestyle)

■ Dutch Boy segmenting the consumer market.

Demographics are perhaps the most popular way to segment sports consumers because of the ease of capturing demographic data. Table 2.1 provides a demographic comparison of motor sports fans. With this information, organizations could choose to sponsor the motor sport whose fans' demographic profile most closely matches its desired target market. Other considerations when choosing a target market(s) are discussed next.

Target Markets

After choosing the appropriate method or basis for categorizing groups of consumers, target market(s) must be chosen. **Target marketing** is described as choosing the segment(s) that will allow an organization most efficiently and effectively to attain its marketing objectives. As discussed, these marketing objectives are formulated prior to the market selection decisions. Therefore, target markets represent the group of consumers around which the entire strategic sports marketing process is built.

In order to choose successful market segments, sports marketers must keep the following requirements in mind. Target markets must be[5]

table 2.1

Demographic Comparison of Motor Sports Fans

Demographic Variables	Motor Sports				
	Drag Racing	Go-Kart Racing	Motorcycle Racing	Road Racing	Stock Car Racing
Average Age	36	25	45	36	40
Median Income	$40,000	$36,000	$35,000	$53,000	$41,000
Sex					
Male	70%	78%	76%	69%	62%
Female	30	22	24	31	38
Marital Status					
Married	52	N/A	58	53	64
Single	38	N/A	15	40	22
Widowed/Divorced	10	N/A	27	7	14
Occupation					
Blue collar	48	48	58	20	44
White collar	36	32	26	76	27
Self-Employed/Other/ Unemployed	8	10	15	8	19
Student/retired	8	10	1	8	10
Education (highest grade completed)					
Some High School	8	8	6	4	12
High School Graduate	42	66	43	28	48
Some College	31	20	24	32	24
College Graduate	16	6	15	30	16
Post-graduate	3	N/A	2	6	N/A

Source: Speedsouth Demographics Comparison. <http://www.speedsouth.com/democompare.html>.

- sizable (large enough in terms of the number of consumers)
- measurable (characteristics of the market are easily identifiable, such as gender or geographic region)
- reachable (must have a means of accessing the consumers)
- demonstrate behavioral variation (consumers within a market must share common needs, while consumers outside of the target market behave differently)

Positioning

The final market selection decision is positioning. **Positioning** is fixing the sports product in the minds of the target market. In other words, how does the target market perceive your product or service? For example, many minor league hockey franchises position their sport as fun-filled, family entertainment at a low price. For example, the International Hockey League (IHL), considered one of the most marketing-oriented sports leagues, has adopted a philosophy of providing major league sports at minor league prices. To implement this positioning, the IHL ran a print advertisement stating

> *Major League Entertainment. Minor League Price. Most professional sports leagues seem to have forgotten one key component when structuring their ticket prices. The fan. In fact, unless you're independently wealthy or you've just won the lottery, you probably can't afford to attend many games, much less bring your family. Not so in the IHL. We've combined major league entertainment with an average ticket price of about $10 to become the number one fan value in professional sports today. So check out an IHL game in a major league market near you and see what you might be missing. We guarantee it won't be all your spending money.*[6]

Arena football positions itself as a hard-hitting, action-packed game that can be watched in the comfort of an air-conditioned arena.[7] Turner Sports Broadcasting positions its televised NBA games as live, unscripted, and completely unpredictable drama (some of the unique characteristics of sport).

■ Cleveland Golf positioning its wedges.

The key to proper positioning is understanding what the target market wants or needs from the product/service. Marketing research is necessary to understand consumers' perceptions of positioning. The NHL recently put the market selection decisions of segmentation, targeting, and positioning into practice as discussed in the article, "NHL Looks to Fuel Image With New Marketing Push."

NHL looks to fuel image with new marketing push

Seeking to capitalize on the league's renewed momentum, the NHL has designed a diverse marketing attack. At the heart of the marketing plan is developing a mix that will appeal to the league's most fervent fans, the 18 to 34 demographic. In order to further develop this target market, the NHL will unveil its first agency-created image ad campaign. The campaign will position hockey and the NHL as the "coolest game on the earth." The NHL will break the $10 million ad campaign on Fox, ESPN, and each NHL team's local television carrier.

Also key to these new market selection decisions is partnering with more than a dozen companies. The NHL hopes this will appeal to sponsors, as commercial clutter will be kept to a minimum. One major sponsor, Quaker State, will launch a promotion called "Cool Collectibles" offering free and reduced price NHL merchandise through catalogues distributed in cases of its product. Also, this season (1996) Dodge will support NHL All-Star Game fan balloting, sponsored by Russell Athletic and conducted through Sears stores, with ads appearing in *Sports Illustrated* and *USA Today*. Another sponsor, Anheuser-Busch, is developing new marketing plans behind its hockey spokesmen, "The Hanson Brothers" (from the movie *Slap Shot*).

The NHL will also test a new program called "NHL Freeze Play." The educational program, sponsored by the Campbell Soup Co., is a six-week tutorial on ice hockey. If all goes well, Campbell will facilitate registration for the program in 20 markets.

Finally, the NHL is close to building its own NHL-brand ice rink/entertainment centers. While this marketing program may seem diverse, all of these efforts are designed to build loyalty among the chosen target market and position the NHL and hockey as the "Coolest Game on Earth."

Source: Jeff Jensen, "NHL Looks to Fuel Image with New Marketing Push," *Advertising Age*, September 30, 1996, 8.

Marketing Mix Decisions

After the market selection decisions are made, the **marketing mix decisions** are fully developed. The objective of the marketing mix is to implement the positioning established by the chosen target market. This is done by coordinating the marketing mix variables, or the four P's—product, price, place, and promotion.

Sports Products

As discussed in the first chapter, a sports product is a good, service, or any combination of the two that is designed to provide benefits to a sports spectator, participant, or sponsor. These benefits may be intangible or tangible. For example, the competition and entertainment generated by the San Diego State University Aztecs versus the University of Wyoming Cowboys football game is an intangible service that is consumed by thousands of fans at the game, watching on television, or listening to the radio. The football used in the game and manufactured by Wilson Sporting Goods, however, is a pure good with tangible attributes, including the size of the ball, the type of leather used, and the price.

spotlight on women in sports marketing

NHL, NFL design products for women fans

Imagine the hit-'em-hard Colorado Avalanche's trademark letter "A" nestled on a knit shirt with a hint of femininity. Or an Emmitt Smith T-shirt pared to petite size.

The NHL and NFL plan to test-market feminine versions of team logo apparel next season in hopes of capitalizing on the growing number of women fans. "We are developing an apparel direction which will not be gender-specific, but from a size, from a fabric…from a coloration point of view will reach out to the women's market," said Bernadette Mansur, vice president of NHL corporate communications.

The NFL also is looking at jumpers, workout gear, and even nightgowns, said Susan Rothman of NFL Properties Inc., the league's marketing division. The NBA and Major League Baseball already have some women's products in stores.

The market growth is coming from female baby boomers and Generation Xers who tend to watch and participate more in sports. Many are mothers who became hooked on sports after ferrying children to youth league games. In a recent study, the Sports Marketing Group/Dallas found the NBA's popularity increased 70 percent among women between 1989 and 1993; the NFL, 45 percent; and MLB, 40 percent. Alternatively, men increased 10 percent, 1 percent, and 7 percent, respectively.

Where there are fans, there are women. And there are dollars to be spent on team merchandise, from towels to bedding to dog leashes to kitchen oven mitts to men's cologne. Because of the importance of this segment, the leagues are trying to gauge the impact of women buyers on the market.

The Women's Sports Federation estimates women make 89 percent of the purchases of sporting apparel and logo merchandise. The NHL shows women who buy merchandise for themselves represent about 35 percent of total sales. The NBA estimates 44 percent of adults who purchase and wear licensed product are women. NFL Properties estimates that 43 percent of the fan base is women, and 70 percent of those fans purchase merchandise. In the future, licensed sports products designed for women will certainly become the rule rather than the exception.

Source: Reprinted with permission from *Marketing News*, published by the American Marketing Association, Sandy Shore, August 26, 1996, vol. 30, no. 18, p. 8.

Pricing

Price is simply something of value that is given in exchange for something else of value. For example, money paid in exchange for admission to a sporting event; salary paid to basketball star Juwan Howard ($110 million over seven years) in exchange for his talents; the time volunteers donate to the ATP Tennis Tournament in exchange for the thrill of getting to meet the players and watch the event for free are all forms of pricing. It is the job of sports marketers to set and control pricing. More importantly, the price must reflect the quality of the product as well as how the product is promoted and distributed to consumers.

Place

As discussed in chapter 1, place or distribution takes on several meanings in the context of sports marketing. Traditionally, place is associated with getting goods to the customer in an efficient manner. A channel of distribution is the chain of marketing organizations that interact to bring the product from producer to end user. For example, Mizuno manufactures baseball gloves, which are then sold and shipped to The Sports Authority retail outlets, which are then purchased by the consumer.

The other, equally important, distribution issue for sports marketers is bringing the competition to the fans. New technologies, such as the Internet and satellite television, are making this easier than ever before. MLB and its media partners, such as ESPN, have also recognized the need to provide sports programming when viewers desire entertainment. For example, witness the advent of Sunday-night baseball. Historically, baseball games were played only on Sunday afternoons, but now, the growth of larger prime-time audiences hungry for sports have caused teams to change their traditional scheduling. Issues involving whether to build new sports faciles and where to locate them are equally critical sport distribution issues.

Promotion

All forms of promotion are based on communicating with consumers. Sports marketers communicate with target groups through advertisements, public relations efforts, sales promotions, personal selling, and sponsorships. Each one of these elements, or a combination of these elements, comprise a firm's promotional efforts. This is known as the promotional mix.

Implementation Phase

The best plan is only a plan, that is, good intentions, unless it degenerates into work. The distinction that makes a plan capable of producing results is the commitment of key people to work on specific tasks.[7]

At this stage of the strategic sports marketing process, we gathered information about potential consumers, made market selection decisions, and developed our marketing mix. Now that we completed our planning phase, the next step is to put our plan into action. This step of the strategic sports marketing process is called implementation. During this phase, promotional efforts, distribution plans, product issues, and pricing strategies are all carried out. The best plans are meaningless unless properly implemented.

One example of the ramifications of implementation gone bad is the Philadelphia KiXX, indoor professional soccer team. Fans interested in purchasing tickets were instructed to call the team via its toll-free number which ends in KiXX. Mistakenly, many fans misdialed KICKS instead. Much to the fans suprise, the KICKS extension connects them to a fantasy sex line rather than the team's ticket office.[8]

What steps need to be taken during implementation and by whom? The successful implementation of a marketing plan requires that specific activities take place. The major activities that are necessary for implementing a plan, shown in Table 2.2, include: organizing, leadership and interaction, resource acquisition and allocation, coordinating and timing of activities, and information management.[9]

Organizing

Organizing is the first of the functional activities associated with implementation. In the marketing sense, organizing is the assigning of tasks, the grouping of tasks into organizational units, and allocating resources to organizational units. One of the key issues to consider in this aspect of implementation is how the sports organization should be structured to best carry out the strategic marketing process.

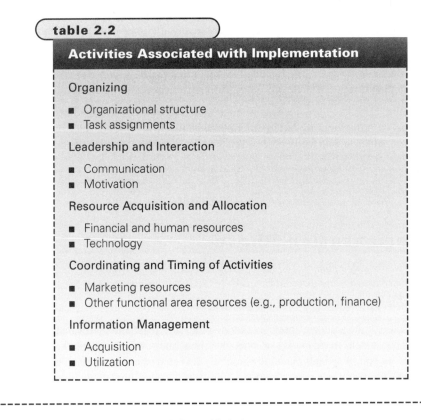

table 2.2

Activities Associated with Implementation

Organizing

- Organizational structure
- Task assignments

Leadership and Interaction

- Communication
- Motivation

Resource Acquisition and Allocation

- Financial and human resources
- Technology

Coordinating and Timing of Activities

- Marketing resources
- Other functional area resources (e.g., production, finance)

Information Management

- Acquisition
- Utilization

One example of a traditional organizational structure is the functional organization, where marketing activities are carried out by specialized departments such as advertising, marketing research, new product development, and so on. Other sports organizations find it more effective to organize by product type, customer type, geographic region, or perhaps use a hybrid organization, which combines all these features.

As previously discussed, sports organizations operate in extremely turbulent environments, where frequent and unpredictable changes are characteristic. For example, it is common for professional sports organizations to experience high turnover in the front office as well as on the field. Organization structures that provide flexibility enhance organizational effectiveness.

Leadership and Interaction

Two additional activities that are required to implement marketing plans successfully are having strong leaders and interacting well with others within the sports organization. Marketing leaders must emerge who can communicate the strategic sports marketing process within and outside the organization. For instance, the marketing department must communicate the importance of fan relation efforts to the players. These leaders must also have the ability to motivate their workforce so that the plans are implemented effectively and efficiently.

Sports marketing managers must excel at communicating the importance of their plans to employees within the organization, also known as internal customers. For sports marketing plans to succeed, management must sometimes focus on internal marketing—marketing efforts aimed at a company's own employees who have contact with the ultimate consumer of the sport or sports product.

Resource Acquisition and Allocation

Another of the activities necessary for implementation is the ability to acquire and allocate human, financial, and technological resources. Sports organizations are downsizing just like the rest of corporate America, and managers are continually being

■ Leadership off the court.

asked to do more with less. This includes carrying out plans developed in the strategic sports marketing process.

One example of financial trouble resulting from inefficient human resource allocation is Pro Beach Volleyball where the players serve as management and labor at the same time. By doing so they are forced to choose between their own short-term gain and the leagues' long-term best interest.

Coordinating and Timing of Activities

The coordination and timing of marketing activities is essential to a successful marketing effort. An advertisement designed to run during the holiday season could be destroyed if it is plagued by mistakes in timing and coordination.

Similarly, marketers must be quick to respond to sudden changes in team or player popularity. For example, when the Cincinnati Bengals signed Boomer Esiaison to a contract in 1997, demand for seats increased immediately, quickly changing the promotional strategy.

■ Slazenger coordinating its marketing efforts around the holidays.

Information Management

In order to make sound decisions regarding the implementation of the strategic marketing plan, information is critical. Having access to the necessary information and being able to interpret that information is the foundation of information management. Some of these types of information and how they are used to reformulate planning are discussed in the next section.

ⓒontrol Phase

The process of measuring results, comparing the results to the marketing objectives, communicating the results to the entire organization, and modifying the plan to achieve the desired results is known as the control phase. Upon implementing the sports marketing plan, the organization must attempt to understand whether or not the plan is achieving the desired results. If the plan is meeting or exceeding the proposed marketing objectives, no modifications are necessary. This, however, rarely occurs. More likely than not, changes will be necessary. For example, the Wilson Sporting Goods company decided to downsize its golf division in 1996, eliminating 85 positions because it failed to reach company profit goals for the past few years.[10]

Measuring Results

The results measured by the sports organization depend on the nature of the objectives set in the previous phase of the sports marketing plan. Assessment can be thought of in broad terms—to determine the overall success of the marketing plan. A marketing audit may then be conducted to explore the organization's marketing efforts. Alternately, assessment can be conducted to determine the success of very specific objectives. Let us briefly examine sales analysis, profitability analysis, customer satisfaction measurement, and marketing audits.

Sales Analysis

One common marketing objective that must be continuously monitored is sales data. The formal process of examining sales figures is called sales analysis. Sales analysis is a comparison of current sales with past sales, industry sales, sales by competitors, and forecasting sales as a method of evaluating a firm's performance.[11]

In the control phase of the strategic sports marketing process, sales analysis usually is based on examining sales relative to objectives set by forecasting sales. Through the use of simple analytical techniques, sales figures can be evaluated in a number of ways. For example, sales can be measured in unit volume, which is based on the number of units sold. Sales can also be assessed based on dollar volume, or the monies received from sales. In addition, sales can be measured relative to competitors in the industry or by market share. Market share is the proportion of an organization's total sales in a particular market.

Although each of these units of measurement (i.e., unit volume, dollar volume, market share) is useful, the most comprehensive and effective approach is to explore all these measures when conducting a sales analysis. Each method provides the organization with a slightly different perspective on their overall marketing efforts.

In addition to looking at the big picture, or total aggregate sales figure, sports marketers routinely examine more specific components of their overall sales. Often, the big picture is not the best picture. Smaller units of analysis—such as sales figures by geographic region, product categories, customer type, or even individual salespeople are generally more useful in guiding the strategic sports marketing process.

Profitability Analysis

One of the primary methods for evaluating the success of any sports organization is profitability. Profitability refers to the amount of money an organization earns after expenses or the difference between revenues generated by products and the cost incurred.

The most basic unit of measuring profitability is the profit margin. Expressed as the ratio of profits to revenues, profit margins are another "hard" measure of an organization's health. As with sales analysis, the organization's overall profit margin is important, but perhaps not as useful as examining the profitability of various product lines or services offered. Therefore, profitability analysis may best be conducted on smaller units to help guide the strategic sports marketing process.

Customer Satisfaction

Although sales and profits represent traditional hard measures of success, customer satisfaction has become one of the most critical objectives as more sports organizations strive for a customer or marketing orientation. Customer satisfaction is difficult to quantify, so multiple measurement methods can be useful.

Informally, organizations can assess customer satisfaction levels by communicating and listening to their customers' wants and needs. More formally, customer hotlines, observation of customers, and comment/complaint cards are used to gauge customer satisfaction. In addition to these measures, the most common form of evaluating customer satisfaction is conducting marketing surveys.

Marketing Audit

Very specific objectives can be measured by examining things such as sales, profits, and customer satisfaction. For a more holistic view of the sports marketing organization, a marketing audit is recommended. A marketing audit is a systematic and exhaustive appraisal of an organization's marketing activities.

What makes a marketing audit effective? First, an effective audit is systematic. That means the audit is organized and follows a logical process—its goal is a series of action items to guide strategic marketing planning. In addition, a systematic audit is unbiased. A marketing audit should be performed by an independent, outside source that can remain objective during the process. An effective audit should also be exhaustive. That is, the audit should seek to cover all of the firm's marketing activities in as much detail as possible. Finally, marketing audits should be conducted on a regularly scheduled timetable.

In order to conduct an audit, sports marketing managers should meet with an independent outside source to agree upon the timing, format, and objectives of the audit. Most importantly, the scope of the audit, or the number of activities to examine, would be agreed upon. Sports marketing audits usually include a review of the following areas: marketing orientation, marketing objectives, strategic planning process, target markets, products and services, promotion, planning, pricing, and distribution issues. Some sample marketing audit questions are shown in Table 2.3.

table 2.3

Sampling of Marketing Audit Questions

I. Market Orientation

1. Has the firm established a marketing orientation? That is, has the firm identified the benefits that particular customers seek and developed programs based on this input?
2. Is the firm's main goal to maximize customer satisfaction or to get as many customers as possible?

II. Marketing Planning

A. *The External Environment*

1. Social: What major social and lifestyle trends will have an impact on the firm? What action has the firm been taking in response to these trends?
2. Competition: Which organizations are competing with us directly by offering a similar product? Which organizations are competing with us indirectly by securing our prime prospects' time, money, energy, or commitment?
3. Technological: What major technological changes are occurring that affect the firm?

B. *Needs Assessments*

1. Are needs assessments undertaken?
2. Have secondary data been used in the needs assessments? If so, is the information current? Classified in a useful manner? Impartial? Reliable? Valid?
3. What does the firm want to learn from the needs assessments?

C. *Objectives and Mission*

1. What is the mission of the firm? What business is it in? How well is its mission understood throughout the organization? Five years from now, what business does it wish to be in?
2. What are the stated objectives of the organization? Are they formally written down? Do they lead logically to clearly stated marketing goals?

III. Target Market Strategies

1. Are the members of each product's target markets homogeneous or heterogeneous with respect to geographic, sociodemographic, and behavioral characteristics?
2. Is the size of each market segment sufficiently large or important to develop a unique marketing mix for it?
3. Are the market segments measurable and accessible? That is, are the market segments accessible to distribution and communication efforts?

(continued)

table 2.3 *(continued)*

Sampling of Marketing Audit Questions

4. What publics other than target markets (financial, media, government, citizen, local, general, and internal) represent opportunities or problems for the firm?
5. What steps has the firm taken to deal effectively with key publics?

IV. Distribution Decisions

1. Should the firm try to deliver its offerings directly to customers, or can we better deliver selected offerings by involving other organizations?
2. Are members of the target market willing and able to travel some distance to buy the product?
3. How good is access to facilities? Can it be improved? Which facilities need priority attention in these areas?

V. Product Strategies

1. What are the major products offered by the firm? Do they complement each other, or is there unnecessary duplication?
2. Where is the firm and each major product in its life cycle (calculated by using market share or sales)?

VI. Pricing Strategies

1. What are the firm's objectives in pricing each product?
2. What discounts are offered and with what rationale?
3. Has the firm considered psychological dimensions of price in its initial price decisions as well as in its price revision decisions?

VII. Promotion Strategies

1. Are there clear objectives for each element of the promotion mix? How are promotion activities related to these objectives?
2. How does a typical customer find out about the firm's products? Word of mouth? Personal selling? Advertising? Publicity?
3. How is public relations normally handled by the firm? By whom?
4. What is the specific purpose of each sales promotion activity? Why is it offered? What does it try to achieve?
5. What level of sponsorship opportunity do you have (i.e., local versus global)?
6. Are you actively selling your sponsors all of the services that they may need (e.g., luxury boxes, program advertisements, signage, ticket mention, employee nights, promotional services, etc.)?

Source: Principles of Marketing, 2/e, by Lamb/Hair/McDaniel, Copyright © 1994. Reprinted by permission of South-Western College Publishing, a division of International Thomson Publishing, Inc., Cincinnati, Ohio 45227.

Chapter 2 provides an overview of the contingency framework for the strategic sports marketing process. Although there are many ways to think about constructing a sports marketing plan, it is best to lay a foundation that is prepared for the unexpected. The contingency framework is especially useful for sports marketers because of the complex and uncertain conditions in which the sports organization operates. The unexpected changes that occur over the course of a season or event may be positive or negative. The changes that occur may be either controllable or uncontrollable events that impact the sports organization. Uncontrollable occurrences are typically in the marketing environment and are referred to as external contingencies, while internal contingencies are within the control of the organization (sometimes beyond the scope of the marketing function).

The contingency framework includes three major components: the internal contingencies, the external contingencies, and the strategic sports marketing process. The external contingencies, or uncontrollable factors, that influence the strategic marketing process, include competition, regulatory and political issues, demographic trends, technology, sociocultural issues, and the physical environment. The internal contingencies, which also impact strategic marketing decisions, include vision and mission of the organization, marketing goals and organizational objectives, organizational culture, and organizational design issues. The external and internal contingencies will be the focus of chapter 3.

The heart of the contingency framework is the strategic sports marketing process, which is defined as the process of planning, implementing, and controlling marketing efforts to meet organizational goals and satisfy consumers' needs. The planning phase has three steps. It begins with marketing research to examine the needs of current and potential markets. These consumer markets may be differentiated on the basis of participants or spectators. Next, market selection decisions are formulated. These include market segmentation, or dividing consumers into homogeneous groups based on common characteristics. The similarities among consumers are based on demographics (e.g., age, sex, income), psychographics (lifestyle), geographics (where the consumer lives), geodemographics (what consumers look like who live in a particular region), benefits (what the consumer wants in the sports product), and behavioral (consumption and usage patterns). Once the market is segmented, sports marketers must select the target market. The target market is defined as the segment that will allow an organization to reach its marketing objectives most efficiently and effectively. The final market selection decision is positioning. Positioning refers to fixing the sports product in the minds of the target market. In other words, how do we want our target market to perceive our sports product? What benefits do we want to sell?

The final step in the planning stage is to develop the appropriate marketing mix to reach the selected target market and achieve the desired positioning. The sports marketing mix consists of product, pricing, promotion, and place decisions. It is critical that the elements of the marketing mix, or the four P's, be coordinated. We want to assure that the pricing is aligned with the perceived quality of the product and that the place the sports product is delivered is consistent with the promotional message received by consumers. In sports marketing, the coordination of the marketing mix can be especially challenging because marketers have so little control over the core product or the competition itself. For example, it is not easy to lower ticket prices if the team is performing poorly.

The implementation phase of the strategic sports marketing process refers to carrying out or executing the plans just discussed. Obviously, the best plans are worthless unless they are properly acted upon or implemented. The success of implementation is based on how the sports organization is set up, how leaders communicate and motivate the employees, the marketing and financial resources available, and information management.

The third and final phase of the strategic sports marketing process is the control phase. The control phase is the process of measuring results, comparing the results to the marketing objectives, and revising objectives based on the evaluation of the objectives. The results of the marketing efforts are based on analyzing sales figures, profits, and customer satisfaction. A more global assessment of the sports organizations' marketing efforts is gained by conducting a marketing audit. The audit explores all of the critical marketing areas, such as the marketing orientation of the organization, market selection decisions, and the marketing mix variables.

KEY TERMS & CONCEPTS

contingency framework for
   strategic sports marketing
control phase
external contingencies
implementation phase

internal contingencies
marketing audit
marketing mix decisions
market segmentation
market selection decisions

planning phase
positioning
strategic sports marketing
   process
target marketing

REVIEW QUESTIONS

1. Describe the contingency framework for strategic sports marketing. Why is the contingency approach especially useful to sports marketers?

2. Outline the strategic marketing process and comment on how it is related to the external and internal contingencies.

3. How do sports marketers attempt to understand consumers' needs? Why is this such an important first step in the planning process?

4. What are the three broad market selection decisions? Why is the market selection decision portion of the strategic marketing process sometimes considered to be the most important?

5. Define and discuss segmentation, target markets, and positioning.

6. What is the marketing mix? Why is it important to have an integrated marketing mix?

7. What is meant by the implementation phase of the strategic marketing process? Describe the activities commonly associated with implementing the marketing plan.

8. What is meant by the control phase of the strategic marketing process? How are the results of the planning phase evaluated?

9. Describe a marketing audit. When should a marketing audit be conducted and by whom? What are some of the broad categories of a marketing audit?

EXERCISES

1. Interview the marketing manager of a sporting goods retailer or sports organization about their strategic sports marketing process. Ask how the external and internal contingencies affect planning.

2. Find two sports organizations that, in your opinion, have undergone or are about to undergo a crisis situation. How should these organizations handle the crisis from a marketing perspective?

3. Choose three teams in the same sport (Braves, Indians, Yankees) or three sports products in the same product category (e.g., Titleist, Cobra, and Ping golf clubs) and discuss how each makes market selection decisions. Comment specifically on similarities and differences in segmentation, targeting, and positioning.

4. Companies choose different sponsorship opportunities to reach different segments and target markets. Give examples of three different sponsorship opportunities and their perspective market segments and target markets.

5. Describe the marketing mix for the following sports products and services:
   - Wilson Sporting Goods tennis equipment
   - University of Notre Dame football program
   - Golf lessons at a local country club
   - Local high-school basketball program
   - Air Jordans from Nike

6. Develop a hypothetical professional sports franchise in the sport of your choice and discuss the marketing mix you would implement. How are your marketing mix decisions related to your market selection decisions?

7. Construct and then conduct a brief marketing audit of your university's athletic program.

INTERNET EXERCISES

1. Find the Web site of any minor league hockey franchise and based on their site, describe how they are segmenting their consumer/fan market.

2. Find three sponsorship opportunities via the Internet and describe the target market(s) the sponsorship is trying to reach.

3. Discuss the marketing mix for an on-line sporting goods store.

NOTES

1. E. Stephen Grant and R. Edward Bashaw, "A Collegiate Football Program Confronts a Sports Marketing Crisis: Results and Implications of a Descriptive Study," *Sports Marketing Quarterly*, vol. IV, no. 1 (1995): 35–40.

2. W. Richard Scott, *Organizations: Rational, Natural, and Open Systems* (Englewood Cliffs, NJ: Prentice Hall 1987), 87–89.

3. Bernard J. Mullin, Stephan Hardy, and William Sutton, *Sport Marketing* (Champaign, IL: Human Kinetics Publishers 1993), 16.

4. Martin G. Letscher, "Sports, Fads and Trends," *American Demographics*, vol. 19, no. 6, (June 1997): 53–56.

5. Joel Evans and Barry Berman, *Marketing*, 5th ed., (New York, NY: Macmillan, 1992), 255–226.

6. Michael Farber, "Putting on a Show," *Sports Illustrated*, October 17, 1994, 30–33.

7. Peter Drucker, *Management: Tasks, Responsibility, Practices* (New York, NY: Harper Row, 1974).

8. William Power, "Soccer Team Discovers There Are Lots of Ways to Get Your Kicks," *The Wall Street Journal*, December 5 1997, B1.

9. Adapted from William Zikmund and Michael D'Amico, *Marketing*, 4th ed., (St. Paul, MN: West Publishing, 1993).

10. Chuck Stogel, "Struggling Wilson Downsizes, Looks for More Innovation in Golf," *Brandweek*, September 9, 1996, 16.

11. Courtland Bovee and John Thill, *Marketing* (New York, NY: McGraw-Hill, 1992), 190–192.

CHAPTER 3

External and Internal Contingencies

After completing this chapter, you should be able to

- Describe external contingencies and explain how they impact the strategic sports marketing process

- Discuss the importance of monitoring external contingencies and environmental scanning

- Describe the major internal contingencies and explain how they impact the strategic sports marketing process

- Explain and conduct a SWOT analysis

As discussed in chapter 2, the strategic marketing process must carefully consider the "fit" between external and internal contingencies. To review, external contingencies are those factors outside the control of the organization that can impact marketing decisions. For instance, the growing emphasis on technology or women as participants of sports must be considered when developing new sports products. Internal contingencies are those factors controlled by the organization, such as its vision and mission, organizational objectives, and organizational culture.

A complex relationship exists between internal contingencies and the strategic marketing process. Sports marketers must make sure that the marketing strategies are aligned with the broader organizational purpose. This purpose is often based on changes that occur in the environment. It is at this point that external and internal contingencies must complement one another. Let us look further at the various factors that make up the external and internal contingencies.

(E)xternal Contingencies

As defined in chapter 2, environmental contingencies are all influences outside of the organization that might impact the strategic sports marketing process. External contingencies include competition, technology, cultural/social trends, physical environment, political/legal/regulatory environment, demographics, and the economy. Let us take a brief look at each of these factors and how they might impact marketing strategy.

Competition

Assessing the competitive forces in the marketing environment is one of the most critical components in the strategic sports marketing process. **Competition** is the attempt all organizations make to serve similar customers.[1]

Sellers realize that, in order to successfully reach their objectives, they must know who the competition is—both today and tomorrow. In addition, sellers must understand the strengths and weaknesses of their competitors and how competitor strategies will impact their own planning. An example of many "sellers" attempting to fill the same customer need can be found in Indy Car racing.

Competition between "the old" and "the new" ensued when the 80th Indianapolis 500 took on the first U.S. 500. As Tony George, president of the Indianapolis Motor Speedway, suggested, "It's a crucial day for us." The world was watching to see whether Indy could withstand a boycott by Championship Auto Racing Teams, Inc. (CART), which had most of the world's most popular drivers on its side. Seventeen rookie drivers were in the field of 33 at Indy, but it was the U.S. 500 drivers that provided the day's embarrassing moment when 12 cars piled up approaching the starting line.[2]

The Nature of Competition

Sports marketers most often categorize their competition as product related. There are three types of product-related competition. The first of these is termed **direct competition**, the competition between sellers producing similar products/services. High school football games on a Friday night in a large metropolitan area pose direct competition in that the "product" being offered is very similar. One interesting example of direct competition is found with the game schedule of the NBA Indiana Pacers. High school basketball is so popular in Indiana that the Pacers rarely play a home game on Friday or Saturday night because of the competition posed by high school games.

Another type of product competition is between marketers of substitute products and service, the competition between a product and a similar substitute product. For example, when several professional sports teams have scheduled an overlap, a consumer may have to choose among attending the Philadelphia 76ers (NBA), the Philadelphia Phillies (MLB), or the Philadelphia Eagles (NFL). Another example of substitute products is when spectators choose to watch a sporting event on television or listen to a radio broadcast rather than attend the event.

The third type of product-related competition, called **indirect competition**, is more general in nature and may be the most critical of all for sports marketers. Marketers of sporting events at any level realized that their true competition is other forms of entertainment. Professional, collegiate, and high school sporting events compete with restaurants, concerts, plays, movies, and all other forms of entertainment for the consumer dollar.

Indirect competition is present when even the popular USC and UCLA football games fail to sell out their respective home stadiums (the Rose Bowl and the L.A. Coliseum). There is simply too much entertainment competition in Southern California compared to Ann Arbor, Michigan (University of Michigan) or South Bend, Indiana (Notre Dame).

Technology

Technology represents the most rapidly changing environmental influence. New technologies impact the field of sports marketing daily. Advances in technology have a direct impact on how sports marketers perform their basic marketing functions, while others aid in the development of new sports products. For example, new technologies are emerging in advertising, stadium signage, and distributing the sports product. Internet sites are one of the fastest growing new technologies to impact sports marketing (see appendix B for examples of Internet sites of interest to sports marketers). In 1998, IBM planned for more than 40 million hits at superbowl.com, the official site of the Super Bowl.[3] ESPN's SportsZone, which premiered in March 1995, is in the top ten most frequently visited sites. Geoff Reiss, the page's publisher, stated that the site currently gets a phenomenal 4 million to 5 million hits daily. Interestingly, Reiss points out, "the number of hits dips significantly during college vacation periods." Among his service's users, 48 percent are aged 18 to 24. Another 34 percent are aged 25 to 34, and 95 percent of SportsZone's users are men whose average household income is $55,000.[4]

Another on-line sports organization receiving considerable attention is SportsLine USA. This service, which had its commercial release in 1995, claimed a half million hits per day in 1996.[5] In 1997, SportsLine was renamed CBS Sportsline as a result of an exclusive agreement with CBS Sports. Along with its popular CBS SportsLine (www.sportsline.com), SportsLine USA also publishes the *Vegas Insider*, owns the Golf Channel, owns the official Orange Bowl Site, and is the official Web site for several famous athletes. Most notably, it publishes the official Web sites of Michael Jordan, Tiger Woods, and Shaquille O'Neal. Even with this impressive lineup, ESPN's SportsZone is still number one in sports on-line services, largely because of the promotion it receives from its cable television network.

Internet sites have been developed to provide information on sports (e.g., www.NASCAR.com), sites of sporting events (www.talladega.com), teams (www.penske.com), and individuals (www.wallace.com). In addition, even live broadcasts of sporting events are now being transmitted via the Internet. AudioNet, Inc. (www.audionet.com) was one of the pioneers of live game broadcasts via the Internet beginning in 1995. The Web site now features play-by-play of 130 college and professional teams. Its Internet broadcast of the 1997 Super Bowl drew a half million listeners, an Internet record for the largest audience ever.[6]

Although the NBA and the NHL have been leaders in the Internet broadcast movement, MLB and the NFL have lagged behind. Some teams, however, have taken it

Some will be there

for every point.

Every triumph.

Every tear.

But hey, you've got a job.

www.usopen.org

www.usopen.org. Powered by IBM. Instant scores, player bios, everything.

IBM

Solutions for a small planet™

■ Providing sports information via the Internet.

upon themselves to offer high-tech, play-by-play. The Baltimore Orioles' flagship station, WBAL, went on-line with all of the Orioles' games in 1997 with great success. Station manager Jeff Beauchamp says "We have gotten e-mail from servicemen listening to games overseas. We've heard from transplants to other parts of the country who write how wonderful it is to follow the team you grew up with."[7]

Out-of-Market Technology

One of the latest technologies that will impact both consumers' ability to watch sports and marketers' ability to define their target audience more narrowly is "out-of-market sports packages." Out-of-market packages utilize direct-to-home (DTH) technology to give subscribers a selection of sports telecasts not available on regular cable. Currently, there are three major companies offering these packages—DIRECTV, Primestar Partners, and Liberty Satellite. Dennis P. Wilkinson, Primestar senior vice-president of marketing, says that the packages appeal both to displaced sports fans who want to watch their former favorite team and to die-hard sports fans hungry for any games.

Major League Baseball, the NHL, the NFL, and the NBA have all negotiated deals to transmit games to viewers outside the home and visiting team markets. Fans pay from as much as $159 a season to subscribe to "NFL Sunday Ticket," an out-of-market package of 200 NFL regular season games, to as low as $99 to receive the NBA's Team Pass, featuring the games of one out-of-market team. The total "out-of-market" market consists of roughly four million subscribers. However, industry experts say the packages will provide a steady revenue stream once the DTH companies build a sizable subscriber base.[8]

In addition to the Internet and DTH satellite, other new technologies are surfacing on a daily basis and changing the way sports are marketed. For instance, stadium signage has become dynamic rather than stationary. A Budweiser sign behind home plate may change into a promotion for McDonalds during the course of an inning or a pitch. The Fox network has designed a unique technology to allow televised hockey to be easier to follow for viewers. The puck is trailed by a flashing light to make it possible to keep up with a 100 mph slapshot. Another technological advancement making it easier for fans to follow the action will be the MaskCam. ESPN will introduce the MaskCam, a camera built into the umpire's mask, during its coverage of the College World Series.[9] Additionally, more traditional technologies, such as an ever-expanding cable network and in-home shopping, are giving more choices to consumers of sport.

So far, our discussion of technology is based more on how technology influences the spectators and distribution of sport. How do technologically advanced products impact sports participants and their performance? While most sporting goods have experienced major technological improvements over the past decade, two sports that live and die by technology are golf and tennis.

The tennis racquet revolution is not being dictated by larger sweet spots or new space-age, materials, but simply longer raquets. This new racquets range from 1 to 2 inches longer than the standard 27-inch racquet and are well within the 32 inch legal limit set by the International Tennis Federation. *Tennis* Technical Advisor, Tracy

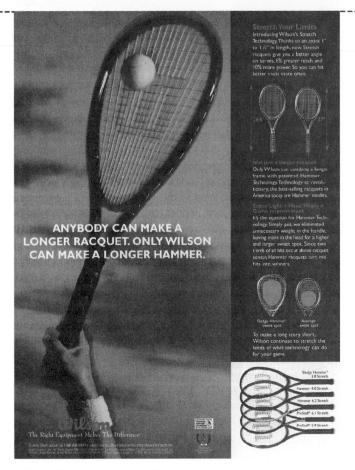

The latest in tennis technology: The longer racquet.

Leonard says, "the extra long is definitely the most significant racquet innovation since the wide-body. It is the third element of power, and equally significant to crushing the ball as were the large head and wide-beam breakthroughs."[10]

Howard Brody, a University of Pennsylvania physicist who specializes in racquet science adds:

From my calculations, it gives the player definite advantages—it increases serving accuracy by 5 percent per extra inch, and you don't have to be a physicist to figure out the benefit of more reach, especially on shots that normally hit the top of the frame. If my opponent has one, I'd better get one too, especially if I'm a shorter player. A guy like (5-foot-8) Michael Chang will gain even a bigger advantage than taller tour pros. Two years from now, it's possible that the extra long racquets will be the only racquets you can buy.[11]

In addition to changing the way sports are played, technology is altering the ways sports are consumed by fans at the event. Over time, technologies will allow fans to

Technology can take you only so far.

Though our business at Canon is to push technology to the limit, we are also aware of its limitations. To us, technology's applications are only as great as the capabilities of those it serves. Which is why Canon is as interested in the expansion of human potential as we are in the acceleration of technological innovation. To this end, Canon is deeply involved in projects that benefit people, especially the young. Canon's support of sports programs, such as Junior Golf, is a prime example. It is our belief that the lessons learned on the playing field—discipline, perseverance, determination and fair play, among them—are essential to the full development of human potential beyond athletics, maybe even beyond the bounds of technology as we know it. Now imagine how far that can take us all.

Canon

■ The finest technology still has not replaced hard work.

become more and more interactive. For example, Diamond Sports has equipped stadium seats with a handset that allows fans to vote on a figure skating champion. This same technology could be extended for other "made or marketing" events, such as the NBA's Slam-Dunk Contest.

While some marketers have a hard time grasping the special language of technology, they still agree that a whole new culture of technology has emerged. Phoenix Suns owner Jerry Colanglo describes the new wave of emerging technology and what this will mean for his new stadium built for the Arizona Diamondbacks:

We're going to load the park up with interactive technologies and virtual reality game stations from which you can see the field. I want to build an interactive virtual Cooperstown West into the stadium. I also want to have a computerized dossier on every fan who comes into my park, so I can know what technological services and experiences each customer desires. This new technology means we can wire into every pocketbook.[12]

Other new stadiums are following this technological revolution. The Portland Trail Blazers' new home, the Rose Garden, will eventually be equipped with a tiny video screen at each seat so fans can check out replays, player statistics, promotions, and a variety of information previously restricted to large stadium scoreboards.

Computer-driven video sports is another area of technological impact. Video sports games are called simulations due to their lifelike approximation of real sporting events. In fact, the danger for franchises lies in fans caring more about these games and simulations than they do for the "real" sports.

Nearly one out of every four video games sold is sports related. The magnitude of this number is seen in both the 35 million video game devices sold annually and the $6 billion video game industry. Paul Allen, co-founder of Microsoft and owner of the NBA's Portland Trail Blazers, believes that "the only thing holding back sports simulation products is the level of reality that can be achieved." Microsoft is planning to release a new baseball game that is a "true to life experience," according to programmer Rich Choi. Teams can be drawn from any of the 12,500 professional players from 1901 to the present.[13]

Cultural and Social Trends

Culture is described as the shared values, beliefs, language, symbols, and tradition that are passed on from generation to generation by members of a society. Perhaps the most important aspect of any culture is the shared and learned values. **Cultural values** are widely held beliefs that affirm what is desirable by members of a society. Several of the core American values of interest to sports marketers include individualism, youthfulness, achievement and success, and family.

Sports are symbolic of many core American values. In fact, what could be more American than baseball, our national pastime? ESPN used this rich tradition in a series of television advertisements promoting its Major League Baseball coverage. These advertisements, featuring Abraham Lincoln and Nicholas Turturro (of television's *NYPD Blue*), claimed "It's baseball—you're American—watch it."

All of these core values are directly or indirectly relevant to sports marketing. For instance, certain sports and/or sporting events stress individualism. Individualism is based on nonconformance or the need to be unique. Nothing could be more directly linked to individualism than the X-treme Games, featuring sports such as skateboarding and street luge.

The central or underlying value inherent in all sports is achievement and success. Virtually every sports marketing theme is either directly or indirectly linked to the achievement and success of an individual athlete or a team.

Youthfulness is another core American value that is continually stressed by sports marketers. People participate in sports and watch sports to feel young and have fun. Those in the mature market are making strides at staying in shape; they are also watching their own age cohorts still participating in sports at a professional level via any number of senior tours (men's and women's golf, tennis, bowling). In addition, products like Ginsana (the "All-Natural Energizer") endorsed by Scottie Pippen of the Chicago Bulls, helps the young and old feel "young and energized."

Another core American value is family and the need to feel a sense of belonging. According to a recent study, one sports activity that seems to be growing in popularity

■ The mature market: Staying young and having fun in record numbers.

as a result of the renewed emphasis on family values is home basketball. In 1996, over 10 million Americans said that they played hoops most often at home, instead of at the gym or on the playground. This growing number of home basketball participants (23 percent of the total basketball participation market) is based on dads, and increasingly moms, playing hoops with the kids.[14]

Physical Environment

Natural resources and other characteristics of the natural world have a tremendous impact on sports marketing. For instance, the climate of a region dictates the types of sports that are watched and played in that area. In fact, various sports were developed *because* of the physical characteristics of a region. Skiing and hockey in the North and surfing on the Coasts are obvious examples.

Sports marketers attempt to control the physical environment for both spectators and sports participants. For example, the 1997 Australian Open (tennis) was hit by a heat wave that affected both players and spectators. Tournament officials closed the roof on center court and artificially controlled the physical environment. Many players, however, wanted their matches rescheduled, and others argued that they had trained for the heat. This attempt to artificially control mother nature seems to have backfired, or at least come under scrutiny.[15]

Artificial turf replaced natural grass surfaces in stadiums in the late 1960s. In the 1990s, all new stadiums being built have switched back to natural grass. Grass not only seems to be easier on the athletes in terms of potential injuries, but fans seem to appreciate the "natural" look of grass. Likewise, domed stadiums seem to have run their (un)natural course. The newer stadiums are all open air venues, which have greater appeal for spectators. The retro-look, built-of-brick, newer stadiums have created a nostalgic atmosphere of "baseball as it was meant to be played."

The Japanese have seen the future of snow skiing . . . and it's indoors. The Laport Ski Dome in suburban Tokyo is trying to redefine the sport of snow skiing. The dome is essentially a $400 million, 17-story refrigerator on stilts, which is billed as the world's first and largest indoor skiing area with "real" snow.

For the modest price of $70, skiers can enjoy three hours of runs on a slope that is 536 yards long, 93 yards wide, 88 yards high, and has a vertical drop, at some points, of 264 feet. Like many things in Japan, the dome is mechanized to the point of intimidation.

The dome provides rental of all the necessary equipment, including video cameras to capture the experience. Once properly suited, a gentle moving sideway (people mover) de-livers skiers to the slope. Video screens show live pictures of the slope while people wait to arrive at the summit. At 23°F, the dome claims that its "patented crystals provide a deluxe snow texture that would never fall in a natural environment." As one skier claims, "the snow is substantial but not heavy, easy to shove around, and feels like velvet under my skis."

In addition to the controlled temperature and the snow, the dome plays pop music and has pastel patterns of light beamed on the snow to manipulate the atmosphere even more. Whether or not the dome is "the equivalent of a northern European mountain resort", as it claims to be, is debatable. However, the dome is the ultimate example of marketing influencing a sport by controlling the physical environment.

Adapted from Sheila Young, "Sking the Dome," *Snow Country*, November 1995, 63–65.

In addition to the climate, the physical environment of sports marketing is concerned with conservation and preserving natural resources. This trend towards conservation is most often referred to as "green marketing." Marketing ecologically-responsible products and being conscious about the effects of sports on the physical environment is one of the concerns of green marketing. For instance, many golf course management groups have come under attack from environmentalists concerned about the effect of phosphate-based chemicals used in keeping golf courses green.[16] Other groups have criticized the sport of fishing as cruel and unusual punishment for the fish.

Political, Legal, and Regulatory Environment

Sports marketers are continually faced with political, legal, and regulatory issues that impact their strategic decisions. Politics have always played a major role in sports and are becoming an increasingly important part of the sports landscape. In professional sports, politicians are involved in promoting or discouraging passage of stadium tax issues. Since 1953 most stadiums have been owned by city governments.[17] The question is "How far does one go in sacrificing taxpayers' wealth to promote civic pride?" Additional evidence of the relationship between government and sports marketing is the growing number of sports commissions. Since 1980, the number of sports commissions, designed to attract sporting events to cities, states, or regions, has increased from 10 to roughly 135.[18]

An example of a legal issue that impacts sports marketers is the law of trademark licensing, which protects trademark rights such as league names, team names, and logos. As the sale of licensed merchandise continues to grow, more and more trademark infringement lawsuits are being pursued. For instance, the California Angels (recently renamed the Anaheim Angels) had to defend their trademark rights when a large department store ran an advertisement featuring three children dressed up in California Angels uniforms. The department store failed to create a licensing arrangement with the Angels and later had to pay for their oversight. With the sale of millions of dollars of licensed merchandise on the line, professional and collegiate sports organizations are on the lookout for counterfeit merchandise or other violations of licensing law.[19]

A regulatory body or agency is responsible for enacting laws or setting guidelines for sports and sports marketers. Regulatory agencies can either be controlled by government or nongovernment agencies. One example of a nongovernment regulatory body that has tremendous control over sports and sports marketing practices is The Federation Internationale de Football Association (FIFA). FIFA is the international federation for the world's most popular sport, soccer. Formed in 1904, FIFA's mandate is to promote soccer through development programs for youth and to supervise international competition to ensure that the rules and regulations of the game are being followed. In addition, FIFA is responsible for maintaining the unified set of rules for soccer called the *Laws of the Game*.

Although FIFA is concerned with regulating the game itself, it also controls many facets outside the game that have an impact on sports marketing. For example, FIFA is committed to improving stadiums for the fans and protecting them against the rising costs of attendance. Another example of FIFA's control over sports marketing is that virtual advertising—superimposing marketing messages on the field during televised broadcasts—is forbidden.

In addition, FIFA works with ISL Marketing to secure sponsors for major soccer events, such as the World Cup. As a regulatory agency, FIFA attempts to make sure that the sponsors do not intrude in any way on the integrity of the game. FIFA General Secretary Joseph Blatter describes the delicate but beneficial relationship between FIFA and its sponsors as follows: "It's important for the sponsors not to influence—or even try to influence—the game itself, any more than it is FIFA's role or intention to influence how these companies do their own business."[20]

Demographic

Assessing the **demographic environment** entails observing and monitoring population trends. These trends are observable aspects of the population, such as the total number of consumers and their composition (i.e., age or ethnic background) or the geographic dispersion of consumers. Let us look at several aspects of the demographic profile of the Unites States, including size of the population, age of the population, shifts in ethnic groups, and population shifts among geographic regions.

Size of the Population
Currently, the U.S. population stands at 270 million consumers and is growing at a rapid pace. It is estimated that by the year 2000, the U.S. population will have increased

by as much as 8 million.[21] As with the U.S. population, the world population is also expanding at an alarming rate. The present world population is over 6 billion and is growing at a rate of 160 million per year. This is of special interest to sports marketers of U.S. leagues who are considering expansion into international markets.

Age

Age is one of the most common variables used in segmenting and targeting groups of consumers. As such, sports marketers must continually monitor demographic shifts in the age of U.S. consumers. The "graying of America" has and will continue to exert a huge influence. The older adult population is expected to grow at a rate of 62 percent by the year 2010, while the U.S. population as a whole is projected to increase at a rate of 19 percent.[22] This trend is a function of the baby boom generation growing older.

Studies show that by the year 2015, mature adults will make up almost 25 percent of the entire population; this number will grow even larger to comprise one-third of the population by the year 2050.[23] This means that in about 50 years, one out of every three Americans will be 55 years of age or older.[24] Apparently, with new technological advances bringing about breakthroughs in medicine, a lower mortality rate, and preventive approaches to health, Americans are living longer.

Moreover, the 76-million-strong baby boom generation is already entering midlife and will soon age. Four out of every ten adults in the United States are baby boomers; by the year 2000, they will be at least 35 years old. Also of significance is the baby bust generation (children of baby boomers), that follows in the wake of its parental tidal wave. In 1995, there were 19.6 million children under five years old, compared to the 16 million in 1980.[25]

Shifts in Ethnic Groups

The United States has been called a melting pot because of its diversity and multiethnic population. The number of white Americans is diminishing, while roughly 17 percent of the U.S. population is represented by some minority group. While all minority groups are growing, the fastest growing segment between 1980 and 1990 was Asian-Americans. This group nearly doubled in size, although Asian-Americans still represent only 3.8 percent of the U.S. population. The next fastest growing minority was Hispanic-Americans, who represent 11.2 percent of the U.S. population. African-Americans still remain the largest minority group, with 12.7 percent of the population.[26]

Each of these ethnic groups are important subcultures that share a portion of the larger (white) American culture, but also have unique consumption characteristics. There are a number of benefits in developing a marketing mix that appeals to specific ethnic groups. For example, the Dodgers' attendance boomed in the early 1980s, when they featured pitcher Fernando Valenzuela, who appealed to the Hispanic market in Los Angeles.

Population Shifts

Over the next three decades, the greatest population shift will be evident in the South and West.[27] The states with the highest growth in absolute number of people are

California, Texas, and Florida. There is no definitive explanation for this shift, although some believe it is due to the previously discussed aging of America or the growth of employment opportunities in these areas. Keep in mind that, until 1957 when the Brooklyn Dodgers moved to Los Angeles, there were no Major League Baseball teams west of St. Louis.

Along with exploring population shifts by state, sports marketers must assess the dispersion of people within an area. Are people moving back to urban areas, or is the "flight to the suburbs" still occurring? The 1990 census showed the greatest growth to be in suburban areas. There are still fewer people living in or moving back to the central city. These measures of population dispersion are having an impact on where new professional teams are locating and where new stadia are being built.

The Economy

The economic environment is another important but uncontrollable factor for sports marketers to consider. Economic factors that impact sports organizations can be described as either macroeconomic elements or microeconomic elements. A brief explanation of each follows.

Macroeconomic Elements

Economic activity is the flow of goods and services between producers and consumers. The size of this flow and the principle measure of all economic activity is called the gross national product, or GNP. The business cycle, which closely follows the GNP, is one of the broadest macroeconomic elements. The four stages of the business cycle are

Prosperity—the phase in which the economy is operating at or near full employment, and both consumer spending and business output are high.

Recession—the downward phase, in which consumer spending, business output, and employment are decreasing.

Depression—the low phase of the business cycle, in which unemployment is highest. Consumer spending is low, and business output has declined drastically.

Recovery—the upward phase when employment, consumer spending, and business output are rising.

Each of these cyclical phases influences economic variables, such as unemployment, inflation, and consumers' willingness to spend. Decisions about the strategic sports marketing process are affected by these fluctuations in the economy. If the country is in either a recession or a depression, consumers may be reluctant to purchase nonessential goods and services, such as sporting goods or tickets to sporting events. On the other hand, ticket sales may boom during times of economic growth. Additionally, the growth period may have an even greater impact on corporate demand for luxury boxes and season tickets.

Although the relationship between the purchase of sporting goods and tickets to sporting events is likely to be associated with good economic times, this may not always be the case. During a recession or depression, sports may serve as a rallying point for people. Consumers can still feel good about their teams even in times of economic hardship. This is one of the important, but sometimes neglected, societal roles of sport.

Microeconomic Elements

While **macroeconomic elements** examine the big picture, or the national income, **microeconomic elements** are those smaller elements that make up the big picture. One of the micro elements of concern to sports marketers is consumer income levels. As economist Paul Samuelson points out, "Mere billions of dollars would be meaningless if they did not correspond to the thousand and one useful goods and services that people really need and want."[28] Likewise, having sports products would be meaningless if consumers could not afford to purchase them. A primary determinant of a consumer's ability to purchase is his or her income level.

Consumer income levels are specified in terms of gross income, disposable income, or discretionary income. Of these types of income, discretionary is of greatest interest to sports marketers. This is the portion of income that the consumer retains after paying taxes and purchasing necessities. Sports purchases are considered a nonnecessity and therefore are related to a consumer's or family's discretionary income. According to a new analysis by TGE Demographics, Inc., two-thirds of American households have some discretionary income they can spend on nonecessities. In addition, the number of families with discretionary income is expected to rise.[29]

Monitoring the External Contingencies

As discussed, external contingencies are dynamic, and sports marketers must keep abreast of these continually changing influences. A systematic analysis of these external factors is the first step approached by sports marketers using the contingency framework. In addition, as the sports industry becomes more competitive, one of the keys to success will be identifying new market opportunities and direction through assessing the external contingencies. The method that is used to monitor the external contingencies is known as environmental scanning.

Environmental Scanning

An outward-looking, environmental focus has long been viewed as a central component of strategic planning. In fact, it has been argued that the primary focus of strategic planning is "to look continuously outward" and to keep the organization in step with the anticipated changes in the external environment. This process of monitoring external contingencies is called environmental scanning. More formally, **environmental scanning** is a firm's attempt to continually acquire information on events occurring outside their organization in order to identify and interpret potential trends.[30]

A sports organization can do several things to enhance its environmental scanning efforts. First, the organization can identify who will be responsible for environmental scanning. The only way to move beyond the pressures of daily business activities is to include environmental scanning responsibilities in the job description of key members of the organization.

Second, the organization can provide individuals conducting the environmental scan with plenty of information on the three C's: customers, competition, and company. Your scanners cannot correctly monitor the environment without having a solid base of information about the following: customer expectations and needs; the strengths, weaknesses, distinctive competencies, and relative market positioning of the competition; and the strengths, weaknesses, distinctive competencies, and relative market positioning of your own company—as well as the major developmental opportunities that await exploitation.

Third, the organization can assure integration of scanned information through structured interactions and communication. All too often information needed to recognize new market opportunities is identified but never gets disseminated among the various functional areas. That is, marketing, finance, and operations may all have some information, or pieces to the puzzle, but unless these individuals share the information, it becomes meaningless. Organizations with the most effective environmental scanning systems schedule frequent interactions among their designated scanners.

Fourth, the organization can conduct a thorough analysis of ongoing efforts in order to improve the effectiveness of environmental scanning activities. This systematic study consists of evaluating the types of scanning data that are relevant and available to managers. This focus on previous environmental scanning efforts can often lead to the identification of new market opportunities.

Fifth, the organization can create a culture that values a "spirit of inquiry." When an organization develops such a spirit, it is understood that the environmental scanning process is necessary for success. In addition, it is understood that environmental scanning is an ongoing activity that is valued by the organization.

Environmental scanning is an essential task for recognizing the external contingencies and understanding how they might impact marketing efforts. However, there are two reasons why environmental scanning practices fail to identify market opportunities or threats. First, the primary difficulty in effectively scanning the environment lies in the nature of the task itself. As scanning implies, sports marketers must look into the future and predict what will likely take place. To make matters even more difficult, these predictions are based on the interaction of the complex variables previously mentioned, such as the economy, demographics, technology, and so on. Second, predictions about the environment are based on data. Sports marketers are exposed to enormous amounts of data and only with experience can individuals selectively choose and correctly interpret the "right data" from the overwhelming mass of information that is available to them.

(I)nternal Contingencies

Organizational leaders develop a strategic direction based on the external contingencies that were just discussed. These strategic choices for the organization are also shaped by the core values of the decision makers. In turn, these strategic decisions provide the direction of the strategic sports marketing process. Although the sports marketer should have an understanding of internal contingencies and how they influence the strategic marketing process, they are thought of as more managerial in nature. In other words, these organizational decisions are usually made by top management rather than sports marketing managers.

Internal contingencies are all influences within the orgainzation that can impact the strategic sports marketing process. Let us describe some of the internal contingencies that sports marketers must consider within the contingency framework.

Vision and Mission

One of the first steps in developing a strategic direction for an organization is shaping a vision. The **vision** has been described as a long-term road map of where the organization is headed. It creates organizational purpose and identity. A well-written vision should be a prerequisite for effective strategic leadership in an organization. The vision should address the following:

- Where does the organization plan to go from here?

- What business do we want to be in?

- What customer needs do we want to satisfy?

- What capabilities are required for the future?

As you can see, the organizational questions addressed in the vision are all oriented towards the future. The mission, on the other hand, is a written statement about the organization's present situation. The purpose of a written mission statement is to inform various stakeholders (for example, consumers, employees, general public, suppliers) about the direction of the organization. It is particularly useful for motivating employees internally and for communicating with consumers outside of the organization. Here are examples of mission statements constructed by New Balance athletic footwear company and the Green Bay Packers.

Mission of New Balance
To be recognized as the world's leading manufacturer of high-performance footwear. We support this mission by conducting our internal and external relationships according to these core values: Teamwork; Total Customer Satisfaction; Integrity.[31]

Mission of the Green Bay Packers

The Green Bay Packers' mission is to be a dominating force in professional football's competitive arena.

On the field, the Packers will continually strive to present their fans with the highest level of performance quality available.

In their operating activities and relations with the NFL, the Packers will also continually strive for excellence in the quality of work performed.

On-field and operating personnel will, at all times, maintain the highest ethical and moral standards in their actions, recognizing that they are all representatives of the Packers franchise and traditions.

Overall, the Packers will commit themselves to doing their part in representing the State of Wisconsin with competitiveness, respect, and dignity.[32]

These mission statements address several key questions.

- What business are we currently in?

- Who are our current customers?

- What is the scope of our market?

- How do we currently meet the needs of our customers?

In addition to addressing these four key questions, the mission statements for New Balance and the Green Bay Packers also contain statements about the core values of the organization. In fact, these core values are fundamental to carrying out the vision and mission of the organization.

How do mission and vision influence the strategic sports marketing process? Both vision and mission define the consumers of sport in broad terms. For example, New Balance sees its customers from a global perspective, while the Packers use the term "fans" to represent its consumers. Also, vision and mission define the products and services that are being marketed to consumers. New Balance, in stating its core product is high-performance footwear, takes a somewhat limited view in defining its products and services. In addition, the vision and mission help identify the needs of consumers and ultimately guide the marketing process in meeting these needs.

Nike provides an excellent illustration of the dependent relationship among vision, mission, and the strategic marketing process.[33] Originally, the product was aimed towards the serious track athlete who wanted a low-priced, high-quality performance shoe for competition. By 1969, Nike had begun to build a strong brand reputation as the shoe for competitive athletes. Over time, however, Nike redefined and broadened its vision and mission. In 1978, footwear represented 97 percent of Nike's total sales. Today, this percentage has decreased to roughly 67 percent as Nike produces footwear and apparel to meet the needs of almost every consumer in global markets. Nike's strategic decision to sell more than just high-performance footwear aimed to only the serious athlete has changed the entire marketing mix. Now, more Nike products are being sold at more places than ever before. In fact, Nike's mission is "to maximize profits to the shareholders through products and services that enrich people's lives."[34]

Organizational Objectives and Marketing Goals

Organizational Objectives

The objectives of the organization stem from the vision and mission. They convert the vision and mission into performance targets to be achieved within a specified timeframe. **Objectives** can be thought of as signposts along the road that help an organization focus on its purpose as stated in the mission statement. More specifically, an objective is a long-range purpose that is not quantified or limited to a time period.[35]

Organizational objectives are needed to define both financial and strategic direction. Two types of objectives are typically developed by organizational leaders: financial objectives and strategic objectives. Financial objectives specify the performance that an organization would like to achieve in terms of revenues and profits. Achieving these financial performance objectives is critical to the long-term survival of the organization. Some examples of financial objectives include the following:

- growth in revenues
- increase in profit margins
- improved return on investment (ROI)

Strategic objectives are related to the performance and direction of the organization. Achieving strategic objectives is critical to the long-term market position and competitiveness of an organization. While strategic objectives may not have a direct link to the bottom line of an organization, they ultimately have an impact on its financial performance. Here are a few examples of general strategic objectives:

- increased market share
- enhanced community relations efforts
- superior customer service

Marketing Goals

Marketing goals guide the strategic marketing process and are based on organizational objectives. A **goal** is a short-term purpose that is measurable and challenging yet attainable and time specific.[36]

Here is a sampling of common marketing goals:

- Increase ticket sales by 5 percent over the next year

- Introduce a new product or service each year

- Generate 500 new season ticketholders prior to the next season

- Over the next six months, increase awareness levels from 10 perccent to 25 percent for women between the ages of 18 to 34 regarding a new sports product

Although multiple goals are acceptable, goals in some areas (e.g., marketing and finance) may conflict, and care must be taken to reduce any potential conflict. After developing marketing goals, the organization may wish to examine them based on the following criteria:[37]

- *Suitability*—the marketing goals must follow the direction of the organization and support the organization's business vision and mission.

- *Measurability*—the marketing goals must be evaluated over a specific timeframe (such as the examples just discussed).

- *Feasibility*—the marketing goals should be within the scope of what the organization can accomplish, given its resources.

- *Acceptability*—the marketing goals must be agreed upon by all levels within the organization. Top management must feel that the goals are moving the organization in the desired direction; middle managers and first line supervisors must feel the goals are achievable within the specified timeframe.

- *Flexibility*—the marketing goals must not be too rigid, given uncontrollable or temporary situational factors. This is especially true when adopting the contingency framework.

- *Motivating*—the marketing goals must be reachable but challenging. If the goals are too easy or too hard, then they will not direct behavior towards their fulfillment.

- *Understandability*—the marketing goals should be stated in terms that are clear and simple. If any ambiguities arise, people may inadvertedly work against the goals.

- *Commitment*—employees within the sports marketing organization should feel that it is their responsibility to ensure that goals are achieved. As such, managers must empower employees so that everyone in the organization is committed and will act to achieve goals.

- *People participation*—as with commitment, all employees in the organization should be allowed to participate in the development of marketing goals. Greater employee involvement in setting goals will foster greater commitment to goal attainment.

- *Linkage*—as discussed earlier, marketing goals must be developed with an eye toward achieving the broader organizational objectives. Marketing goals incongruent with organizational direction are ineffective.

Organizational Strategies

Organizational strategies are the means by which the organization achieves its organizational objectives and marketing goals. While the organizational vision, mission, objectives, and goals are the "what," the organizational strategy is the "how." It is, in essence, the game plan for the sports organization. Just as football teams adopt different game plans for different competitors, sports organizations must be able to readily adapt to changing environmental conditions. Remember, flexibility and responsiveness are the cornerstones of the contingency framework.

In general, there are four levels of strategy development within organizations: corporate strategy, business strategy, functional strategy, and operational strategy.[38] The relationship among these strategy levels is pictured in Figure 3.1. Notice that there must be a good fit among the levels, vertically and horizontally for the firm to succeed.

Corporate-level strategies represent the overall game plan for organizations that compete in more than one industry. Business-level strategies define how a business unit gains advantage over competitors within the relevant industry. Functional-level strategies are those developed by each functional area within a business unit. For example, the strategic sports marketing process is the functional-level strategy developed by sports marketing managers, just as finance strategy is the perview of their finance manager counterparts. The operational-level strategies are more narrow in scope. Their primary goal is to support the functional level strategies. Let us take a look at the relationship among the four levels of strategy at the Walt Disney Company to see how a good fit among strategies can lead to overall organizational effectiveness.[39]

---

figure 3.1 Relationship between Levels of Strategy

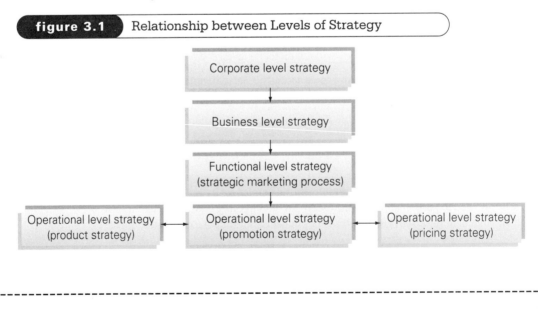

The Walt Disney Company is a diversified company with interests in three related entertainment industries. The entertainment industries of interest to Disney are broadcasting (ABC Television Networks, ABC Radio Networks, ESPN, ESPN2, ESPN News, and the Disney Channel); creative content (films, publishing, consumer products, ABC productions, music, and interactive products); and theme parks (theme parks, resorts, NHL Mighty Ducks, and the Anaheim Angels). Interestingly, the professional sports franchises are described as part of the theme park segment. Also of interest is that the ownership of the sports teams support the entertainment mission of Disney.

The corporate strategy for Disney is based on competing globally in all three entertainment industries. The corporate strategy should allow Disney to obtain the broader organizational goals and pursue its vision and mission.

At the business level, Disney management specifies strategies for each business unit within each of the three groups. For example, the Mighty Ducks and the Angels would each have a unique business-level strategy, even though they are in the same group—theme parks. These strategies are aimed at gaining competitive advantage within each relevant industry. However, each business-level strategy must support the corporate-level strategy, goals, vision, and mission.

At Disney, there are numerous functional areas within the organization. For example, the Angels functional areas may include finance/administration; general management/operations; business affairs; civic affairs; sales, and marketing. Leadership within each of these functional areas would be responsible for designing their own strategies to meet their respective business-level strategies.

Finally, within the functional areas such as sales and marketing, operational-level strategies are developed. Promotion, ticket sales, product, and pricing strategies must all be designed and coordinated to attain the sales and marketing objectives set forth in the functional-level strategy. As you can see, sports marketing managers responsible for each operational unit must be concerned with satisfying not only their own goals, but the objectives of the broader organization as well.

Corporate Level

Most professional sports franchises are owned by individuals or corporations that have many business interests. Sometimes these businesses are related, and sometimes the professional sports franchise is nothing more than a hobby of a wealthy owner. Today, the latter is becoming far less common as corporations include sports franchises in their portfolio. Even more rare is the sports franchise owned and operated as the primary, if not sole, source of owner income (e.g., Mike Brown family and the Cincinnati Bengals).

There are typically two types of diversified companies—those that pursue related diversification and those that pursue unrelated diversification. In related diversification, the corporation will choose to pursue markets in which they can achieve synergy in marketing, operations, and/or management. In other words, the corporation looks for markets that are similar to their existing products and markets. The underlying principle in related diversification is that a company that is successful in existing markets is more likely to achieve success in similar markets. Unrelated diversification, on the other hand, refers to competing in markets that are dissimilar to existing markets. The primary criteria for choosing markets is based on spreading financial risk over different markets.

Professional sports franchises can be owned privately by one or more individuals, publicly owned corporations, or some combination of both. Today, roughly 52 public companies own at least some of the 130 or so major league franchises.[40] At least one-third of these 52 companies are media franchises that view sport as a very related and natural diversification. Time Warner Media owns baseball, basketball, and hockey teams. The Tribune Company, which owns superstation WGN, also owns the Chicago Cubs. GE, which owns NBC, also owns the NY Knicks and NY Rangers. The list goes on and on. Along with the media giants, the leagues are recognizing the advantages of team ownership by corporations that are involved in related markets.

Developing Corporate-Level Strategy   Corporate-level strategies must make three types of decisions. First, top managers must determine in which markets they want to compete. Sports organizations have a core product/service, plus they also compete in ancillary markets. The core product has been defined as the game itself and the entertainment that is provided to consumers, while secondary markets include sale of licensed merchandise, fantasy sports camps, sports magazines, sports art, and so on. The leaders of a sports organization must also attempt to identify ways of capitalizing on the similarities in markets. For instance, fans for the core product often represent a natural target market for additional products and services. Examples such as Disney and the media moguls owning sports franchises illustrate the synergy in markets.

The second type of decision deals with enhancing the performance within each of the chosen markets. Top managers constantly need to monitor the mix of markets in which the organization competes. This evaluation might lead to decisions that involve pursing growth in some markets or leaving others. These decisions are based on the performance of the market and the ability of the organization to compete successfully within each market.

The third type of decision involves establishing investment priorities and placing organizational resources into the most attractive markets. For a sports organization, this could involve decisions regarding stadium renovation, player contracts, or investing more heavily in merchandising. Corporate decisions within a sports organization must constantly recognize that the core product, the competition itself, is necessary to compete in related markets.

Business-Level Strategy

The next level of strategic decision making is referred to as business-level, or competitive, strategies. Business-level strategies are based on managing one business interest within the larger corporation. The ultimate goal of business-level strategy decisions is to gain advantage over competitors. In the sports industry, these competitors may be other sports organizations in the area or simply entertainment, in general.

One strategic model for competing at the business level contains four approaches to gaining the competitive advantage. These approaches include low-cost leadership; differentiation; market niche based on lower cost; and market niche based on differentiation. Choices of which of the four strategies to pursue are based on two issues: strategic market target and strategic advantage.

Strategic market targets can include a broader market segment or a narrow, more specialized market niche. Strategic advantage can be gained through becoming a low-cost provider or creating a real or perceived differential advantage.

The focus of low-cost leadership is to serve a broad customer base at the lowest cost to any provider in the industry. While there may be a number of competitors pursuing this strategy, there will be only one low-cost leader. Many minor league teams compete as low-cost leaders due to the lower operating costs relative to their major league counterparts. Differentiation strategies attempt to compete on the basis of their ability to offer a unique position to a wide variety of consumers. Typically, companies differentiate themselves through products, services, or promotions. With differentiation strategies, companies can charge a premium for the perceived value of the sports product. Professional sports franchises attempt to differentiate themselves from competitors by providing a high-quality product on and off the field. This is done through a unique blend of sports promotion, community relations, stadium atmosphere, and a winning team.

Although low-cost leadership and differentiation strategies have mass market appeal, the market niche strategies are concerned with capturing a smaller market segment. These market segments may be based on consumer demographics, geographic location, lifestyle, or a number of other consumer characteristics. Within the market niche chosen, sports organizations can gain strategic advantage through a focus on low cost or differentiation. Two examples of low-cost market niche strategy include Pro Beach Volleyball where tournament ticket prices range from $6 to $10 typically and the Pro Rodeo Cowboys Association (PRCA) whose events are priced between $10 and $12.

Functional-Level Strategy

Each of the functional areas of the organization (for example, marketing, personnel, operations) must also develop a game plan that supports the business-level and corporate-level initiatives. Again, the contingency framework calls for "fit" between each of the levels of strategy within the organization. It is also important to coordinate among each of the functional areas. For example, the marketing strategies should dovetail with personnel strategies and operations strategies. The strategic marketing process discussed in chapter 2 provides the functional-level strategy for the organization's marketing efforts.

Operational-Level Strategy

Within the strategic sports marketing process, several narrower strategies must be considered. For example, plans must be designed, implemented, and evaluated in areas such as promotion, new product and service development, pricing, sponsorship, and ticket distribution. Each of these strategies at the operational level must also fit the broader strategic marketing process, as well as be integrated across the marketing function.

Organizational Culture

As we discussed earlier in the chapter, culture is described as the shared values, beliefs, language, symbols, and tradition that is passed on from generation to generation by members of a society. Culture can impact the importance placed on sports by a region or nation, whether or not we participate in sports, and even the types of sports we enjoy playing or watching. A similar concept applied to organizations is called organizational culture. **Organizational culture** is the shared values and assumptions of organizational members that shape an identity and establish preferred behaviors in an organization.[41]

As one of the internal contingencies, organizational culture influences the sports marketer in a number of ways. First, the organizational culture of a sports organization dictates the value placed on marketing. For instance, the Cincinnati Reds have only one person guiding their marketing efforts. Contrast this with the Toronto Blue Jays, who have 12 employees in marketing, and you begin to see the relative value an organization can place on the sports marketing function.

Second, organizational culture is important because it is linked with organizational effectiveness. In a study of campus recreation programs, organizational culture was found to be positively associated with organizational effectiveness.[42] That is, a positive culture is associated with an effective organization. A positive culture rewards employees for their performance, has open communication, has strong leadership, encourages risk-taking, and is adaptive. The ability to adapt to change is one of the most important dimensions' from the contingency framework perspective.

Third, the organizational culture of professional sports organizations and college athletic programs not only have an impact on the effectiveness of the organization, but can influence consumers' perceptions of the organization. For example, the Oakland Raiders, under owner Al Davis, have an organizational culture that values risk-taking and doing anything necessary to get the job done. This organizational culture translated to the team's successful and ruthless performance on the field. Subsequently, the fans began to adopt this outlaw image. Ultimately, the black and silver bad boys of football have attracted a fan following that has come to expect this rebel image.

University athletic departments and their programs are also defined by the organizational culture. Athletic programs are known to either value education or attempt to win at all costs. In Cincinnati, two Division I basketball programs have organizational cultures that, on the surface, couldn't be more different. Xavier University is known for its emphasis on academics (high student-athlete graduation rates) and athletics, whereas the University of Cincinnati program is sometimes jokingly referred to as "Hugs Thugs" (named after head coach Bob Huggins). In this case, the athletic programs have influenced consumers' perceptions and may also influence the broader university culture.

Assessing the Internal and External Contingencies: SWOT Analysis

To this point, we have looked at both the external and internal contingencies. In order to guide the strategic sports marketing process, an organization conducts a SWOT analysis. SWOT is an acronym for strengths, weaknesses, opportunities, and threats. The strengths and weaknesses are controllable factors within the organization. In other words, a firm must evaluate its own strengths and weaknesses based on the internal contingencies. The opportunities and threats are assessed as a result of the external contingencies found in the marketing environment. These elements may be beyond the control of the sports organization.

The strategic sports marketing process must first examine its own internal contingencies. These internal strengths and weaknesses include human resources, financial resources, and whether or not organizational objectives and marketing goals are being met with the current marketing mix. Products and services, promotional efforts, pricing structure, and methods of distribution are also characterized as either strengths or weaknesses.

After assessing the organizational strengths and weaknesses, the firm identifies external opportunities and threats found in the marketing environment. As discussed earlier in the chapter, sports marketing managers must monitor the competition; demographic shifts; the economy; political, legal, and regulatory issues; and technological advances. Each of these external factors may impact the direction of the strategic marketing process.

The intent of conducting a SWOT analysis is to help sports marketers recognize or develop areas of strength capable of exploiting environmental opportunities. When sports marketers observe opportunities that match a particular strength, a strategic window is opened. More formally, **strategic windows** are limited periods of time during which the characteristics of a market and the distinctive competencies of a firm fit together well and reduce the risks of seizing a particular market opportunity.[43] For example, the founders of the Roller Hockey League hope to capitalize on the growing trend in in-line skating. In addition to capitalizing on strengths, sports marketers develop strategies that eliminate or minimize organizational weaknesses.

At this stage, you should have a broad understanding of how each of the external contingencies may impact your marketing plan. Table 3.1 provides a common list of questions to consider when developing the opportunities and threats (OT) portion of your SWOT analysis.

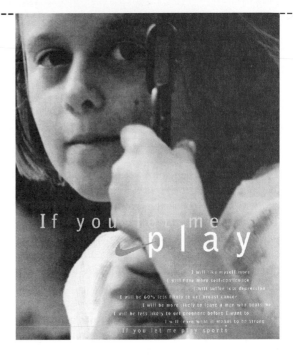

■ Many sports marketers realize new opportunities based on the growth in women's sports.

table 3.1

Assessing External Contingencies

1. **Social:** What major social and lifestyle trends will have an impact on the sports participants and/or spectators? What action has the firm been taking in response to these trends?
2. **Demographics:** What impact will forecasted trends in the size, age, profile, and distribution of population have on the firm? How will the changing nature of the family, the increase in the proportion of women in the work force, and changes in ethnic composition of the population affect the firm? What action has the firm taken in response to these developments and trends? Has the firm reevaluated its traditional sports products and expanded the range of specialized offerings to respond to these changes?
3. **Economic:** What major trends in taxation and in income sources will have an impact on the firm? What action has the firm taken in response to these trends?
4. **Political, Legal, and Regulatory:** What laws are now being proposed at federal, state, and local levels that could affect the strategic marketing process? What recent changes in regulations and court decisions have affected the sports industry? What action has the firm taken in response to these legal and political changes?
5. **Competition:** Which organizations are competing with us directly by offering a similar product? Which organizations are competing with us indirectly by securing our customers' time, money, energy, or commitment? What new competitive trends seem likely to emerge? How effective is the competition? What benefits do our competitors offer that we do not?
6. **Technological:** What major technological changes are occurring that affect the sports organization and sports industry?

T he contingency for strategic sports marketing consists of three components: the strategic sports marketing process, external contingencies, and internal contingencies. The purpose of chapter 3 was to gain a better understanding of the external and internal contingencies that impact the strategic sports marketing process. External contingencies are those elements outside the control of the sports organization. Alternatively, internal contingencies are managed by the sports organization.

Because the marketing environment is so complex and dynamic, sports marketers use a method for monitoring external contingencies called environmental scanning. Environmental scanning is the sports organization's attempt to acquire information continually on events occurring outside of the organization and to identify and interpret potential trends. Sports marketers must continually monitor the environment to look for opportunities and threats that may impact the organization.

The external contingencies that impact the strategic sports marketing process include competition; technology; cultural and social trends; physical environment; political, legal, and regulatory environment; demographic trends; and the economy. As with any industry, understanding competitive threats that exist is critical to the success of all sports organizations. Competition for sporting events and sports organizations comes in many forms. Typically, we think of competition as being any other sporting event. However, other forms of entertainment are also considered competitive threats for sports organizations. Technological forces represent another external contingency. Advances in technology are changing the way that consumers watch sports, play sports, and receive their sports information. Cultural/social trends must also be carefully monitored. Core values, such as individualism, youthfulness, and the need for belonging, can have an impact on the target markets chosen and how sports products are positioned to spectators and participants. The physical environment, such as the climate and weather conditions, is another external con-

tingency that can have a tremendous influence on the success or failure of sporting events. Another of the uncontrollable factors is the political, legal, and regulatory environment. Proposed legislation, such as the banning of all tobacco advertising and sponsorship at sporting events, could have a tremendous impact on the motosports industry. Demographic trends are another critical external contingency that must be monitored by sports marketers. For instance, the graying of America will bring about changes in the levels of participation in sports and the types of sports in which the "mature market" will participate. Finally, the economic conditions should be considered by sports marketers. Sports marketers must monitor the macroeconomic elements, such as the national economy, as well as microeconomic issues, such as the discretionary income of consumers in the target market.

In addition to external contingencies, internal contingencies also play a significant role in shaping the strategic sports marketing process. Internal contingencies, thought of as managerial, controllable issues, include vision and mission of the sports organization; organizational objectives and marketing goals; organizational strategies; and organizational culture. The vision and mission of the sports organization guide the strategic sports marketing process by addressing questions such as: What business are we in? Who are our current customers? What is the scope of our market? How do we currently meet the needs of our customers? The organizational objectives and marketing goals stem from the vision and mission of the sports organization. The objectives of the organization are long term and sometimes unquantifable. Alternatively, marketing goals are short term, measurable, and time specific. It is extremely important to remember that the marketing goals are directly linked to decisions made in the strategic sports marketing process. Another internal contingency that influences the strategic sports marketing process is organizational strategy. The organizational strategy is how the sports organization plans on carrying out its vision, mission, objectives, and goals. There are four different levels of strategy development within the organization. These include corporate-level strategies, business-level strategies, functional-level strategies, and operational-level strategies. Marketing is described as a functional-level strategy. The operational-level strategies such as pricing and promotion must fit the broader strategic sports marketing process. A final internal contingency is the organizational culture or the shared values and assumptions of organizational members that shape an identity and establish preferred behaviors in an organization.

External and internal contingencies are systematically considered prior to the development of the strategic marketing process. The process that many organizations use to analyze internal and external contingencies is called a SWOT analysis. SWOT is an acronym for strengths, weaknesses, opportunities, and threats. The strengths and weakness are internal, controllable factors within the organization that may influence the direction of the strategic sports marketing process. For example, human resources within the organization may represent a strength or a weakness within any organization. On the other hand, the opportunities and threats are uncontrollable aspects of the marketing environment (e.g., competition and economy). The purpose of conducting a SWOT analysis is to help sports marketers recognize how the strengths of their organization can be paired with opportunities that exist in the marketing environment. Conversely, the organization may conduct a SWOT analysis to identify weaknesses in relation to competitors.

KEY TERMS & CONCEPTS

competition

cultural values

culture

demography

direct competition

economic activity

environmental scanning

indirect competition

internal contingencies

macroeconomics

marketing environment

microeconomics

objectives

organizational culture

organizational strategies

out-of-market technology

physical environment

political and regulatory environment

strategic windows

technology

REVIEW QUESTIONS

1. Define the marketing environment. Are all elements of the marketing environment considered uncontrollable? Why or why not?

2. What is environmental scanning? Why is environmental scanning so important? Who conducts the environmental scan, and how is one conducted?

3. Define competition. What are the different types of competition?

4. How has technology influenced the sports marketing industry? Discuss how "out-of-market" technology benefits sports spectators.

5. Identify several cultural/social trends in our society and describe their impact on sport and sports marketing.

6. What are the core American values, and why are they important to sports marketers?

7. How does the physical environment play a role in sports marketing? How can sports marketers manipulate or change the physical environment?

8. Define the political and regulatory environment. Cite several examples of how this can influence or dictate sports marketing practices.

9. Describe the different demographic trends of interest to sports marketers. How will these demographic trends influence the strategic marketing process?

10. Differentiate between macro- and microeconomic elements. Which (macro or micro elements) do you feel plays a important role in sports marketing? Why?

11. How can sports marketers assess the external environment? What are some sources of secondary data that may assist in understanding the current and future external environment?

EXERCISES

1. Describe all of the ways that the changing marketing environment will have an impact on NASCAR racing. How should NASCAR prepare for the future?

2. Your university's athletic program has a number of competitors. List all potential competitors and categorize what type of competition each represents.

3. Find examples of how technology has influenced the sporting goods industry, a professional sports franchise, and the way spectators watch a sporting event. For each example indicate the technology that was used prior to the new technology.

4. Develop advertisements for athletic shoes that reflect each of the core American values discussed in the chapter.

5. Interview five international students and discuss the core values used by sports marketers in their culture. Do these values differ from the core American values? For example, do the British value individualism more or less than Americans? What evidence do they have to support their claims?

6. How does the physical environment of your geographic area/location play a role in sports marketing?

7. Describe how changing demographic trends have led to the development of new sports leagues, the shifting of professional sports franchises, and new sports products. Provide three specific examples of each.

INTERNET EXERCISES

1. Experience a portion of any sporting event via Internet broadcast. What did you enjoy the most about this experience, and what could be done to improve this technology?

2. Find three sports products on the Internet that stress technological developments. Do the companies communicate their technological advantages differently?

3. Search the Internet for articles/sites that discuss the pros and cons of the banning of tobacco advertisements at sporting events.

1. Bill Bearden, Thomas Ingram, and Buddy LaForge, *Marketing*, 2nd ed., (New York, NY: Irwin/McGraw Hill, 1998).

2. Ed Hinton, "Sunday Drivers," *Sports Illustrated*, June 3, 1996, 20–24.

3. Sharon Machlis, "Super Bowl on the Web" *Computerworld*, January 19, 1998, 1, 14.

4. Marc Spiegler, "Betting on Web Sports," *American Demographics*. <http://www.marketingtools.com>. (May 1996).

5. Sportsline USA. "Traffic Reaches All-Time High." <http://about.sportsline.com/releases/olytraf.htm>.

6. Marc Spiegler. "Betting on Web Sports."

7. Mark Hyman, "Do You Love The Orioles and Live in L.A.?" *Business Week*, May 12, 1997, 108.

8. Rich Brown, "Latest in Sports Marketing: Out-of-Market," *Broadcasting & Cable*, May 13, 1996, 41.

9. "The Business of Sport." News Archives. <http://www.bizsports.com/newsarchive/69new.htm> (June 2–June 6, 1997).

10. Bill Gray, "Long Time Coming," *Tennis*, September 1995, 32–35.

11. Ibid.

12. Donald Katz, "Welcome to the Electronic Arena—The Digital Age Is Upon Us, and the Sporting World Will Never be the Same," *Sports Illustrated*, July 3, 1995, 60–77.

13. Ibid.

14. "Family Values: Basketball At Home Growing More Popular." <http://biz.yahoo.com/bw/971201/american_basketball_1.html>.

15. "New Balls, Cool Rules for Australian Open." <http://www.pointcast.com> (October 8, 1997).

16. Ron Chepesiuk, "The Greening of America," *Wildlife Conservation*, vol. 96, no. 4, July 1993, 54–59. Rob Shapard, "Environment at the Fore Front: Keys for Greener Municipal Golf Courses." *American City and Country*, vol. 112, no. 4, April 1997, 52–59.

17. D.V. Baim, *The Sports Stadium As a Municipal Investment*, (Westport, CT: Greenwood, 1994).

18. "States and Sports: Hawaii Eyes Tourism Dollars." <http://www.sportserver.com>.

19. Maxine S. Lans, "Sports Team Logos are Big Business," *Marketing News*, vol. 29, no. 12, June 5, 1995, 6.

20. "For the Good of the Game." <http://www.fifa.com/fifa/handbook/fgg/fgg.intro.html> (1996).

21. U.S. Census Bureau. *National Population Projections*. <http://www.census.gov/population/www/projections/natproj.htm/>.

22. W. Lazer and E. Shaw, "How Older Americans Spend Their Money," *American Demographics*, (September 1987): 36–41.

23. H. Spotts and C. Schewe, "Communicating with the Elderly Consumer: The Growing Health Care Challenge," *Journal of Health Care Marketing*, (September 1989): 36–44.

24. Judith Waltrip, "Secrets of the Age Pyramids," *American Demographics*, August 1992, 46.

25. U.S. Census Bureau. *Current Population Reports: Population Projections of the United States by Age, Sex, Race and Hispanic Origin: 1995 to 2050.* <http://www.census.gov/prod/1/pop/p25-1130/>.

26. U.S. Census Bureau, *Population Estimates for the U.S. by Sex, Race, and Hispanic Origin, Selected Years from 1990 to 1998.* <http://www.census.gov/population/www/estimates/nation3.html>.

27. U.S. Census Bureau. *Current Population Reports, Population Projections: States, 1995-2025.* <http://www.census.gov/prod/www/Abs/p25-1131.html>.

28. Paul A. Samuelson, *Economics*, 10th ed. (New York, NY: McGraw Hill, 1976).

29. Berna Mider, "Fun Money" *American Demographics*, vol. 19, no. 3, March 1977, 33.

30. Matthew D. Shank and Robert A. Snyder, "Temporary Solutions: Uncovering New Market Opportunities in the Temporary Employment Industry," *Journal of Professional Services Marketing*, vol. 12, no.1, (1995), 5–17.

31. Fact Sheet (NB). <http://.www.newbalance.com/bean/misson.html>.

32. "Green Bay Packers: Community—Mission Statement." <http://www.packers.com/community/mission.html> (1997–98).

33. Kenneth Labich, "Vice vs. Reebok: A Battle for Hearts, Minds & Feet," *Fortune*, September 18, 1995, 90–106. Bik Saporito, "Can Nike Get Unstuck?" *Time*, March 30, 1998, 48–53.

34. Nike Inc., 1994 Annual Report. Reprinted with permission of Nike, Inc.

35. Subhash C. Jain, *Marketing Planning and Strategy*, 3rd ed. (Cincinnati, OH: South-Western Publishing, 1990).

36. Ibid.

37. George Steiner, *Strategic Planniing* (New York, NY: Free Press, 1979).

38. Aurthur Thompson and A.J. Strickland, *Strategic Management: Concepts and Cases*, 10th ed. (New York, NY: Irwin/McGraw Hill, 1998).

39. Team Marketing Report, "Inside the Ownership of Professional Team Sports," 1997, 29–30.

40. Ronald Grover, Amy Barrett, Richard Melcher, "Playing for Keeps," *Business Week,* September 22, 1997, 32–33.

41. E.H. Schein, *Organizational Culture and Leadership*, (San Francisco, CA: Josey-Bass, 1988).

42. W. James Weese, "Do Leadership and Organizational Culture Really Matter?" *Journal of Sport Management*, (1996), 197–205.

43. George S. Day, *Strategic Market Planning*, (St. Paul, MN: West, 1984).

C H A P T E R

4

Research Tools
for Understanding Sports
Consumers

O B J E C T I V E S

After completing this chapter, you should be able to

- Discuss the importance of marketing research to sports marketers

- Explain the fundamental process for conducting sports marketing research

- Identify the various research design types

- Describe the process for questionnaire development

- Understand how to prepare an effective research report

The Albany River Rats of the American Hockey League recently conducted a detailed study to gather information that would guide the planning phase of their strategic marketing process. The research objectives were to examine media usage, consumption behavior, and intentions (e.g., number of games attended, likelihood of attending again) and to explore the demographic characteristics of River Rat fans (e.g., age and gender). In addition, the study was designed to look at how survey responses differed according to fan demographics. For instance, are males more or less likely than females to attend a River Rat's game in the future?

To meet these research objectives, fans were asked to complete a survey at River Rat home games. A total of 1,421 surveys were returned and used for data analysis. Survey questions included:

- How many River Rat games have you attended?
- Would you come to a game again?
- What are the best two nights of the week to attend a River Rats game?
- What radio stations do you listen to?
- On what radio stations have you heard River Rat commercials?
- What newspapers do you read?
- What are your favorite television stations?
- Do you find the intermissions fun?
- Demographic information (age, gender, occupation, hometown)

Analysis of the overall fan base helped guide the strategic marketing process for the River Rats. More specifically, the survey helped to target their advertising efforts more efficiently.

Adapted from Mark Hinkle, "River Rats Fan Survey Results and Analysis," March 2, 1995, Unpublished technical report.

As the River Rat example illustrates, marketing research is a fundamental tool for understanding and ultimately satisfying customers' needs. As described in chapter 1, one way of demonstrating a marketing orientation is to gather information that is used for decision making. Another way of establishing a marketing orientation is to disseminate information and share the marketing information with those responsible for making decisions. Marketing research is viewed as an essential element in marketing-orientated organizations.

The information gathered through marketing research can be as basic as where consumers live, how much money they make, and how old they are. Research also provides information for decision makers in identifying marketing opportunities and threats; segmenting markets; choosing and understanding the characteristics of target markets; evaluating the current market positioning; and making marketing mix decisions.

More specifically, marketing research may provide answers to questions such as

- What new products or services would be of interest to consumers of sport?
- What do present and potential consumers think about our new ad campaign?
- How does the advertising and promotion mix impact purchase decisions?
- What are the latest changes or trends in the marketplace?

- How are consumers receiving sports information and programming?
- What are sports fans spending, and what are they buying?
- Who are the biggest sponsors of professional sports leagues or college sports?
- How interested are fans in my team, my players, and in the sport itself?
- How do consumers perceive my team, league, or event relative to competitors?
- What's the best way to promote my sports product or service?
- Who participates in sports, and what sports are they are participating in? Also, where are they participating, and how often?
- Are current consumers satisfied with my sports products and services? What are the major determinants of customer satisfaction?
- What price are consumers willing to pay for my sports product or service?
- What image does the team, player, or event hold with current consumers and potential consumers?

These are just a few of the questions that may be addressed through marketing research. **Marketing research** is the systematic process of collecting, analyzing, and reporting information to enhance decision making throughout the strategic sports marketing process.

Three key issues emerge from this definition. First, marketing research must be systematic in its approach. Systematic research is both well-organized and unbiased. The well-organized nature of good research is dependent on adherence to the marketing research process, which will be discussed later in this chapter. A researcher must also be careful not to have his or her mind made up about the results of a study prior to conducting it, therefore, the researcher must conduct the study in an unbiased manner.

Second, the marketing research process involves much more than collecting data and then reporting it back to decision makers. The challenge of research lies in taking the data collected, analyzing it, and then making sense of the data. Marketing researchers who can collect data, dump it in the computer, and spit out reports are a dime a dozen. The most valuable marketing researcher is the person who has the ability to examine the data and then make recommendations about how the information should be used (or not used) in the strategic marketing process.

Third, the importance of marketing research is found in its ability to allow managers to make informed decisions. Without the information gathered in research, management decision making would be based on guesses and luck. As Woody Hayes, Ohio State's great football coach, once said about the forward pass, "Three things can happen and two of them are bad!"

Finally, the definition states that marketing research is useful throughout the entire strategic sports marketing process. Traditionally, the focus of marketing research has been on how the information can be used in better understanding consumers during the planning phase of the strategic sports marketing process. It is also important to realize that marketing research is relevant at the implementation and control phases of the strategic marketing process. For example, research is used in the control phase to determine whether marketing goals are being met. The following case illustrates how research was used to evaluate the performance of sponsorship.

The Twin Cities Region of Norwest Bank Minnesota, N.A. completed a three-year contract for sole sponsorship of the Norwest Cup, a professional bike race featuring 75 world-class bikers from around the world. Though successful in terms of crowd and media exposure, the substantial financial commitment—more than half the annual budget for community relations and sponsorships—had company executives asking the question, "Is this event worth our investment?"

To help Norwest executives answer this question and make an informed decision, the company turned to marketing research. The primary objective of the research was to decide whether to renew or drop sponsorship of the Norwest Cup. Secondary research objectives were

■ To assess the value of the Norwest Cup and other sponsorships to Norwest
■ To define how community relations activities affect consumer choices
■ To compare Norwest and the Norwest Cup to other companies and community events
■ To identify the components of an effective and appropriate community relations program for Norwest

These objectives were addressed by designing a questionnaire and administering it to a representative sample of 500 consumers in the Twin Cities region. Research findings included the following:

■ Companies get more "points" for addressing education, the environment, and human services needs than they do sponsoring sports events
■ Special events make people feel good, but add little value; only one market segment would miss the Norwest Cup if it was discontinued
■ Norwest lags behind its corporate colleagues in being recognized for "making a difference" in the community
■ Norwest Cup is the right idea as an advertising opportunity aimed at building awareness but not as a way to demonstrate community support

Norwest decided to cancel its sponsorship of the Cup based on this study. The recommendation was to focus on community relations programs and spend dollars on education, perhaps a scholarship program, and to emphasize charitable giving through the Norwest Foundation. In withdrawing its support of the bike race, Norwest announced plans to shift those dollars to new programs aimed at addressing the critical and urgent needs of the community.

Source: "Researching the Value of a Sponsorship." <http://www.precentral.com/c9norwest.htm>. Courtesy of EMMI, Inc.

(T)he Marketing Research Process

As previously mentioned, marketing research is conducted using a systematic process, or the series of interrelated steps shown in Figure 4.1. Before discussing each of the steps in the research process in greater detail, two points should be kept in mind. First, the basic framework or process for conducting marketing research does not change, although every marketing research problem will. For example, the Detroit Red Wings

| figure 4.1 | Marketing Research Process |

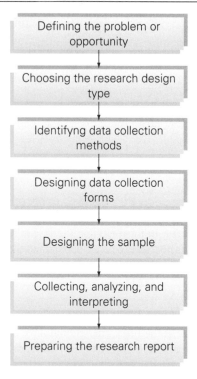

Defining the problem or opportunity

Choosing the research design type

Identifyng data collection methods

Designing data collection forms

Designing the sample

Collecting, analyzing, and interpreting

Preparing the research report

may engage in research to understand fan satisfaction or the effectiveness of a be-tween-period promotion. Each of these research questions are different. However, the basic marketing research process used to address each question is the same.

Second, you should understand that the steps of the research process are inter-dependent. In other words, defining the problem in a certain way will impact the choice of research design. Likewise, selecting a certain type of research design will influence the selection of data collection tools. Let us now examine each of the steps in the research process.

Defining the Problem or Opportunity

The first and most important step of the marketing research process for sports mar-keters is to define the problem or opportunity. **Problem definition** requires the re-searcher to specify what information is needed to either assist in solving problems or identifying opportunities. If the research addresses the correct problem or opportuni-ty and seeks to properly define the problem or opportunity, then the project could be successful. However, the data collected may be useless if it is not the information needed by the sports marketing manager.

table 4.1

Issues Addressed at Initial Research Meeting

- A brief background or history of the organization or individual(s) requesting the research
- A brief background of the types of research the organization has done in the past, if any
- What information the organization wants and why (i.e., what they plan to do with the information once it is obtained)?
- Who is the targeted population of interest for this research?
- What are the expectations in terms of the timeframe for the research and costs of conducting the study?

How does the researcher identify problems or opportunities that confront the sports organization? Initially, information is gathered at a meeting between the researcher and his or her client. In this meeting, the researcher should attempt to collect as much information as possible to better understand the need for research. Table 4.1 shows a list of the typical questions or issues addressed at the first information-gathering meeting.

Research Objectives

Based on this initial meeting, the researcher should have collected the proper information to develop a set of research objectives. Research objectives describe the various types of information needed in order to address the problem or opportunity. Each specific objective will provide direction or focus for the rest of the study.

Here's an example of the research objectives developed for the 1997 Sport Sponsorship Survey conducted by Sports & Media Challenge.[1] The broad purpose of the study was to provide information that would assist corporate sports sponsors in better aligning themselves with sports personalities and organizations. More specifically, the research objectives were as follows:

- Rank the most desired characteristics and attributes preferred by sponsors
- Determine the best process to select personalities and teams for sponsorship purposes
- Determine the current level of satisfaction and any problems associated with sponsorship purposes
- Determine the level of sponsorship activity and future trends
- Determine the types of sports and endorsers needed for sponsorship purposes
- Profile the types of companies using sports sponsorship as a marketing tool

Writing a Marketing Research Proposal

In order to ensure agreement on the direction of the research between the researcher and the client, a research proposal is developed. A **research proposal** is a written blueprint that describes all the information necessary to conduct and control the study.

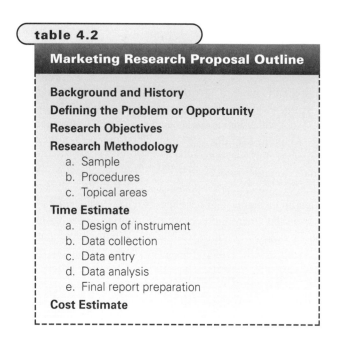

table 4.2

Marketing Research Proposal Outline

Background and History
Defining the Problem or Opportunity
Research Objectives
Research Methodology
    a. Sample
    b. Procedures
    c. Topical areas
Time Estimate
    a. Design of instrument
    b. Data collection
    c. Data entry
    d. Data analysis
    e. Final report preparation
Cost Estimate

The elements of the research proposal include background for the study, research objectives based on the need for the research, research methodology, timeframe, and cost estimates. An outline for developing a research proposal is shown in Table 4.2.

Choosing the Research Design Type

Once the researcher is certain that the problem is correctly defined, the research design type is considered. The **research design** is the framework for a study that collects and analyzes data. Although every study is unique and requires a slightly different plan to reach the desired goals and objectives, three research design types have emerged. These design types are called exploratory, descriptive, and causal designs. Whatever research design or designs are ultimately chosen, it is important to remember *the crucial principle in research is that the design of the research should stem from the problem.*[2]

Exploratory Designs

Exploratory designs are useful when research problems are not well defined. For instance, the general manager for the River Rats may say that ticket sales are down, but he is unsure why. In this case, an exploratory research design would be appropriate because there is no clear-cut direction for the research. The research is conducted to generate insight into the problem or to gain a better understanding of the problem at hand. For example, the researcher may recommend examining AHL attendance trends or conducting one-on-one interviews with team management to determine their ideas about the lack of attendance. Because exploratory research design types address vague problems, a number of data collection techniques are possible. These data collection techniques will be addressed during the next phase of the research process.

Descriptive Designs

If the research problem is more clearly defined, then a descriptive design is used. A descriptive design type describes the characteristics of a targeted group by answering questions such as who, what, where, when, and how often. The targeted group or population of interest to the decision maker might be current season ticketholders, people in the geographic region who have not attended any games, or a random group of people in the United States.

The River Rats study used a descriptive research design. The targeted group in this case was fans attending River Rat home games. Characteristics of the group of interest in the study included where the fans were coming from (geographic area), how often they attended games, when they were most likely to attend games (weekends, weekdays, day, evening), and demographics, such as age and gender.

In addition to describing the characteristics of a targeted group, descriptive designs show the extent to which two variables differ or correlate. For example, a researcher may wish to examine the relationship between game attendance and merchandising sales. Or, using the River Rat's example, researchers wished to understand the relationship between age of the fans and likelihood of attending games in the future. A descriptive research design type would allow us to examine the relationship or correlation between these two variables (age and future attendance).

If a positive relationship was found between age and likelihood of attending games in the future, then the older you get, the more likely you would be to attend future River Rat games. That is, as the age of the fan increases, the likelihood of going to future games also increases (see Figure 4.2a). On the other hand, a negative relationship means that as age increases, the likelihood of going to games decreases (see Figure 4.2b). Knowing the shape of this relationship will help the River Rat's marketers make decisions on who to target and how to develop the appropriate marketing mix for this group. What do you think the relationship between age and attendance would look like?

figure 4.2   Descriptive Research Designs

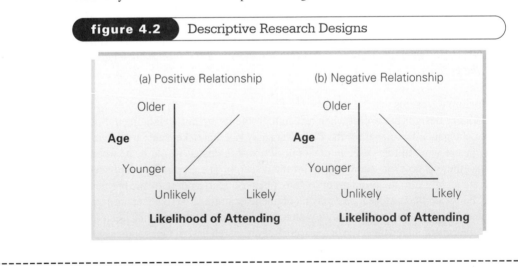

Causal Designs

Using a descriptive design, we can explore the relationship between two variables, such as age and likelihood of attending games in the future. However, what this does not tell us is that age *causes* the likelihood of attending to either increase or decrease. This can only be determined through a causal design.

Causal designs are useful when problems are very clearly defined. More specifically, causal designs examine whether changing the level of one variable causes the level of another variable to change. This is more commonly called a cause-and-effect relationship.

In an example of a causal design, the River Rats could conduct a study to determine whether varying the level of advertising on a local radio station has any effect on attendance. In this case, level of advertising is the independent variable and attendance is the dependent variable. The **dependent variable** is the variable to be explained, predicted, or measured (i.e., attendance). The **independent variable** is the variable that can be manipulated or altered in some way (i.e., level of advertising or perhaps whether to advertise at all).

In order to show cause-and-effect relationships, three criteria must be satisfied. The first criterion for causality is that the occurrence of the causal event must precede or be simultaneous to the effect it is producing. Using our example, advertising must precede or occur at the same time as the increase in attendance to demonstrate a cause-and-effect relationship.

The second criterion for causality involves the extent to which the cause and the effect vary together. This is called **concomitant variation**. If advertising expenditures are increased, then season ticket sales should also increase at the same rate of change. Likewise, when advertising spending is decreased, season ticket sales should also decline. Keep in mind, however, that concomitant variation does not prove a cause-and-effect relationship, but is a necessary condition for it.

A third criterion used to show causal relationships requires the elimination of other causal factors. This means that another variable or variables may produce changes in the independent variable. This possibility is called a spurious association or spurious correlation. In the dynamic sports marketing environment, it could be very difficult to isolate and eliminate all possible causal factors. For instance, an increase in attendance may be due to the success of the team, ticket prices, and/or addition of other promotions (e.g., puck night) rather than increased advertising. A researcher must attempt to either eliminate these other potential factors, hold them constant, or adjust the results to remove the effects of any other factors.

Identifying Data Collection Techniques

As with the previous steps in the research process, decisions regarding data collection techniques are very much a function of problem definition and research design type. If the research problem is loosely defined and requires an exploratory research design, then there are more alternatives for collecting that information. On the other hand, for well-specified problems using a causal design, the choice of data collection techniques decreases dramatically.

Data collection techniques can be broadly categorized as secondary or primary. **Secondary data** refer to data that have already been collected but are still related to the research question. This data may come from within the sports organization or from outside of the organization. For example, useful internal secondary data might include a history of team merchandise sales figures, event attendance figures, or fan satisfaction studies that had been conducted previously. External secondary data, or data from outside of the organization, may come from any number of sources that will be presented later in this chapter.

Although a researcher should always try to use existing data before conducting his or her own inquiries, it is sometimes impossible to find data relevant to the problem at hand. In that case, research must turn to the other data collection alternative, primary data. **Primary data** is information gathered for the specific research question at hand.

Before turning our discussion to the various types of primary and secondary data, it is important to note that both types of data are useful in understanding consumers. For example, sports marketers from the Phoenix Cardinals may want to look at trends in merchandising sales for each NFL team before undertaking a study to determine why their sales have decreased. In this case, secondary data is a useful supplement to the primary data they would also need to collect.

Secondary Data

As just mentioned, secondary data may be found within the sports marketing organization (internal secondary data) or from outside sources (external secondary data). External secondary data can be further divided into the following categories:[3]

- government reports and documents
- standardized sports marketing information studies
- trade and industry associations
- books, journals, and periodicals

Government Reports and Documents

As we discussed in chapter 3, environmental scanning is an essential task for monitoring the external contingencies. Government reports and documents are excellent sources of data for sports marketers exploring the marketing environment. Government sources of data can provide demographic, economic, social, and political information at the national, state, and local levels. This information is generally abundant and obtained at no cost. There are thousands of government sources that are useful for environmental scanning. In fact, many are now published on the Internet. Let us look at a few of the most useful sources of government data.

Bureau of the Census of the U.S. Department of Commerce (www.census.gov)
One of the most comprehensive sources of secondary data that is readily available via the Internet is census information. Here are some of the census documents that may be of interest: Census of Population; Census of Retail Trade; Census of Service Industries; and Census of Manufacturing Industries.

The Statistical Abstract of the United States (www.census.gov/stat_abstract)
Published each year by the Bureau of the Census, the *Statistical Abstract of the United States* is an excellent place to begin your search for secondary data. In addition to more general statistical information on the population and economy, the *Statistical Abstract* has a section entitled "Parks, Recreation and Travel." Within this section, statistics can be found on both participants and spectators.

Chambers of Commerce   Usually, Chambers of Commerce have multiple sources of demographic information about a specific geographic area, including education, income, and businesses (size and sale volume). This type of information can be helpful to sports marketers conducting research on teams or events within a metropolitan area.

Small Business Administration (SBA)   Studies sponsored by the SBA can be a valuable source for the environmental scan. The sources include statistics, maps, national market analysis, national directories, library references, and site selection.

spotlight on international sports marketing:

measuring the mood of international sports consumers

Trusting the opinions of the average sports fan is a dangerous game. Most of us suffer from a selective blindness that enables us to justify abysmal failings in our favorite teams and stars. However, a survey that gathered information the lifestyle choices of all sports fans—and thus established reliable patterns of behavior—would clearly be a valuable data source.

As it happens, such a survey exists in the United States, and it will soon be available in Europe. It is called the ESPN Chilton Sports Poll, and it canvasses the opinions of 50,000 Americans each year. Such is the demand for the data that clients include Reebok, Nike, Ford, General Motors, Toyota, and Coca-Cola. In addition, the ESPN Chilton Poll is the only research tool used by all the major sports leagues in the United States. The NBA, NFL, and Major League Baseball head a list of clients that also includes Major League Soccer, the ATP Tennis Tour, and PGA Golf.

The ESPN Chilton Poll is the brain child of Richard Luker, Ph.D., a former professor at Temple University who is now executive director of the poll. He conceived of the idea in the late 1980s. "When CBS lost half a billion dollars on a baseball deal, I began to ask what people in sport used as intelligence for pricing—and found very little research. I recognized an opportunity and began early development in 1990s."

Dr. Luker knew he would need a recognized sports partner if his poll was to have commercial credibility and singled out ESPN and *Sports Illustrated* as the best alternatives. Subsequently, it became clear that ESPN and its sister company, Chilton Research Services, would provide Luker with the support he needed, "So I approached them and the Sports Poll was set up in 1994 as a 50–50 joint venture between the two—though it is run fairly autonomously. ESPN has access to the data in the same way as other clients."

(continued)

Each month 150 interviewers conduct 1,000 telephone conversations in all areas of the United States. "We take a holistic view of how sports work from the perspective of the average citizen," says Luker. "Before the poll, the impact of sport was measured by television ratings. But we were determined to provide a full profile of what a person likes, watches, and buys."

The average interview is 32 minutes long and covers subjects from sports fans' attitudes, the Internet, and their views on which stars are best for commercial endorsements. Season ticket ownership, media consumption, and magazine subscription are also covered. In addition to the baseline questions, a customized survey can also be created for clients who want to know who drives what car or buys what merchandise. Every call is indexed by region, gender, income, and racial group. Attitudes toward particular sports are tracked in and out of season.

The findings in the United States suggest a voracious appetite for sport, with 89 percent of people fitting the description of fan. Although in line with other consumer spending activities, 70 percent of spending is done by 30 percent of the fans. Luker describes the U.S. interest in sport "as a near-religious experience. Sport is everywhere in the United States. You can't go 10 minutes without confronting sport in some guise. It is a completely integrated activity with the typical sports fan following six sports. Sixty-seven percent of the United States check results every day."

Luker's next ambition is to bring the same rigorous analysis to Europe, although he is fully aware of the difficulties. "You can't just transplant the poll, which makes it a lot of fun for me. I like a project when it is impossible— and this is close to that.

"Originally, we thought we'd do a snapshot of sports in Europe, but we came to the conclusion that it would not be appropriate. Now we believe a major baseline data collection is called for. I want 5,000 completed surveys for each of 10 to 15 European countries in order to provide the first fully articulated picture of sports in Europe." He is also planning a thorough analysis of the impact of the Olympics on a European audience. Luker estimates it will cost $1 million for the baseline study and insists that the commitment is there from his major U.S. clients. "They are willing to spend more on my European data than on the United States."

Luker has spent time in Europe preparing the groundwork for the new operation. "The big challenge is whether it is fair to talk about pan-European communications." In a judgment typical of an academic, he answers; "Yes and no. Each country has its own, quite parochial, sociology of sport, and we can't be assured that it will carry over to neighboring countries."

That said, his feeling is that "Europe is two to five years away from a crossover in some national sports championships. The availability of cross-national channels will contribute to that development." Luker is not convinced that Europeans have the same fervor for sports as their U.S. counterparts. "The closest you get is soccer. And beyond that there are real rumblings in rugby. But these are isolated sports, unlike in the United States where fans support lots of sports." He remains open-minded about what he will uncover in Europe. "There are bound to be some surprises. I expect our initial assumptions about which country is into sports and which isn't may prove to be wrong."

The plan is to launch the baseline survey before the end of 1997 and begin ongoing tracking in 1998. This timescale depends on the U.S. operation, however. "Our client base has doubled since the start of this year," says Luker, "so I'm spending a lot of my time staffing up on the U.S. poll at the moment." In addition, ESPN Chilton is getting an increasing number of requests for consultancy rather than just data delivery.

Source: Sport Business, Int. "Measuring the Mood of Our Market." <http://www.sportbusiness.com/>. Courtesy of Sport Business, Ltd.

Standardized Sports Marketing Information Studies

Although government sources of secondary data are plentiful, they are generally more useful for looking at national or global trends in the marketing environment. Standardized sports marketing information studies, such as the ESPN Chilton Poll, focus more specifically on sports consumers and markets. In fact, these sources of secondary data can provide extremely specialized information on consumers of a specific sport (e.g., golf) at a specific level of competition or interest (avid golfers). Table 4.3 shows some of the standardized studies available for better understanding golfers.

These types of studies are called standardized because the procedures used to collect the information and the type of data collected are uniform. Once the information is collected, it is then sold to organizations who may find the data useful. Although the data collected are more specific than other sources of secondary data, the data may still not directly address the research question. Table 4.4 shows a sampling of the standardized sources of secondary data that may be useful to sports marketers.

table 4.3

Standardized Golf Market Research Studies from the Research Resource Center

Golf Digest Equipment Subscriber Study (1996/$55): A research study that provides a detailed portrait of the avid golfer in today's marketplace. It provides insight into an avid golfer's lifestyle, playing habits, and equipment purchasing trends.

Golf Digest Subscriber Study (1996/$90): This study gives extended research information on the avid golfer's lifestyle. The data include information on golfer's investments and finances, purchasing, and travel tips.

Golf Operations Survey of the Golf Market (1997/$125): This report offers a unique view into the golf industry as perceived by golf retailers who read Golf Shop Operations each month. It identifies the latest market trends in golf equipment and apparel by facility type and geographic region.

Golf World Subscriber Study (1997/$90): These data provide an insightful portrait of some of the most frequent and better-skilled golfers in the marketplace. It provides insights into these low handicapped players' lifestyles, playing habits, and equipment purchasing trends.

Source: "Golf Market Studies." <http://www.golf.com/business/rrc/marketresearc.htm>. Courtesy of *Golf Digest,* the Golf Company Research Residence Center.

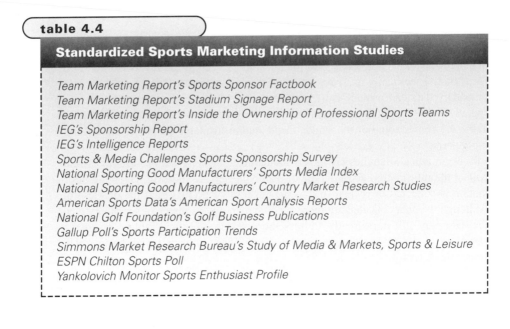

table 4.4

Standardized Sports Marketing Information Studies

Team Marketing Report's Sports Sponsor Factbook
Team Marketing Report's Stadium Signage Report
Team Marketing Report's Inside the Ownership of Professional Sports Teams
IEG's Sponsorship Report
IEG's Intelligence Reports
Sports & Media Challenges Sports Sponsorship Survey
National Sporting Good Manufacturers' Sports Media Index
National Sporting Good Manufacturers' Country Market Research Studies
American Sports Data's American Sport Analysis Reports
National Golf Foundation's Golf Business Publications
Gallup Poll's Sports Participation Trends
Simmons Market Research Bureau's Study of Media & Markets, Sports & Leisure
ESPN Chilton Sports Poll
Yankolovich Monitor Sports Enthusiast Profile

spotlight on women in sports marketing:

the women's sports foundation as a source of information

The Women's Sports Foundation is a national, member-based, nonprofit educational organization that promotes lifelong participation of all girls and women in sports and fitness. Established in 1974 by Billie Jean King, its founder; Donna de Varona, its first president; and many other champion female athletes, the foundation seeks to educate the public, encourage females' participation in sport, and support gender equity in sport.

One of the foundation's programs is educating the public. More specifically, the foundation works to improve public understanding of the benefits of sports and fitness for females of all ages. To support this educational objective, the foundation has a number of publications and research reports that serve as excellent sources of secondary data.

■ The growing number of women's sports participants are being monitored through secondary marketing research.

Publications

A Parent's Guide to Girls' Sports

Women's Athletic Scholarship Guide

Paying Fair: A Guide to Title IX in College and High-School Sports

Sports Talk: The Women's Sport Foundation Newsletter

Women's Sports Experience

Balancing Act

Research

The Wilson Report: Moms, Dads, Daughters, and Sports

The Women's Sports Foundation Report: Minorities in High School Sports

Miller Lite Report on Sports and Fitness in the Lives of Working Women

Source:"Women's Sports Foundation." <http://www.lifetimetv.com/WoSport/stage/INTERACT/html/about.html>. Courtesy of Women's Sports Foundation.

Trade and Industry Associations

The preceding discussion of the Women's Sports Foundation is just one example of an association that provides information of interest to sports marketers. There are hundreds of associations that can be helpful in the quest for information. Sports associations range from the very broad in focus (e.g., NCAA) to the more specific (e.g., The Association of Black Sporting Goods Professionals). Here is just a small sampling of trade and sport associations:

North American Society for Sport Management

European Association for Sport Management

International Sports Marketing Association

Australian Sports Marketing Association

Sporting Goods Manufacturers Association

National Collegiate Athletic Association

Books, Journals, and Periodicals

In addition to the books and journals listed below, a comprehensive list of referenced articles published in sports marketing is available, at no cost, from the University of Connecticut's Laboratory for Leisure, Tourism, and Sport. The reference list can also be found on the Internet (playlab.uconn.edu/frl.htm). In addition, a comprehensive list of periodicals related to sport can be found on the Sport Information Resource Center's Web site (www.sirc.ca/perlist.html).

Books

IEG's Complete Guide to Sponsorship

Sport Marketing (Mullins, Hardy & Sutton)

Sports Marketing: Competitive Business Strategies for Sport (Brooks)

Sport Marketing (Pitts and Stotlar)

Team Marketing Report's Newsletter

Successful Sports Marketing and Sponsorship Plans (Potlar)

Sports Marketing: Global Marketing Perspectives (Schlossberg)

Sports Marketing: It's Not Just a Game Anymore (Schaaf)

Sports Marketing: Famous People Sell Famous Products (Pemberton)

Sports Marketing: The Money Side of Sports (Pemberton)

Sports Marketing/Team Concept (Leonardi)

The Sports Marketing Guide (Wascovich)

Keeping Score: An Inside Look at Sports Marketing (Carter)

Ultimate Guide to Sport and Event Marketing (Graham, Goldblatt, Delpy)

Academic Journals of Interest to Sports Marketers

Cyber-Journal of Sports Marketing

Sports Marketing Quarterly

Journal of Sport Behavior

Journal of Sport and Social Issues

Journal of Sport Management

Journal of Services Marketing

Primary Data

Data collected specifically to answer your research questions are called primary data. There are a wide variety of primary data collection techniques. Again, remember that your method of collecting primary data is dependent on the earlier choice of research design. Let us look briefly at some of the primary data collection methods and their pros and cons.

Depth Interviews

Depth interviews are a popular data collection technique for exploratory research. Sometimes called "one-on-ones," depth interviews are usually conducted as highly unstructured conversations that last about an hour. *Unstructured* means that the researcher has a list of topics that need to be addressed during the interview, but the conversation can take its natural course. As the respondent begins his or her response, new questions may then emerge and require further discussion.

The primary advantage of depth interviews is that detailed information is gathered on the research question. Researchers may also prefer depth interviews to other primary methods when it is difficult to coordinate any interface with the target population. Just think of the difficulty in trying to organize research using professional athletes as the target population. For instance, a sports marketing researcher may want to determine what would be the characteristics of a successful athlete endorser. To address this research question, depth interviews may be conducted with professional athletes who have been successful endorsers, athletes who have never endorsed a product, brand managers of products being endorsed, or any other individuals who may provide insight into the research question. The responses given in these interviews would then be used to determine the characteristics of a successful endorser.

Depth interviews may also be appropriate when studying complex decision making. For example, researchers may wish to find out how others influence your decision to attend a sporting event. The information gathered in the depth interviews at the initial phase of this research may then be used in the development of a survey or some other type of primary research. In yet another example, depth interviews were used in a recent study to understand the decision-making process used by corporate sponsors.[4]

Focus Groups

Another popular exploratory research tool is focus groups. A **focus group** is a moderately structured discussion session held with eight to ten people. The discussion focuses on a series of predetermined topics and is led by an objective, unbiased moderator. Much like depth interviews, focus groups are a qualitative research tool used to gain a better understanding of the research problem at hand. For instance, focus groups may be useful in establishing a team name or logo design, what food to offer for sale in the concession areas, how best to reposition an existing sporting goods retailer, or what kinds of things would attract children to a collegiate sporting event. Let us look at two examples of sports organizations that have benefited from focus groups.

The San Jose Sharks conducted 32 focus groups in the Bay Area to address key marketing variables, such as positioning, logo design, ticket distribution, broadcasting and the media, and community issues. The results and discussion from these groups provided the direction for the strategic sports marketing process.[5] In another example, the Huffy Sports Company used focus group information to help

■ Focus group and observers.

design new labeling for its basketball units and accessory packaging. Through these focus groups, Huffy assessed consumer response to the visual copy elements of the proposed labeling. One finding that directed the labeling decision was that all the focus group participants preferred labeling that incorporated the NBA logo and NBA players.[6]

Conducting focus groups, like the Huffy Sports and San Jose Shark examples, requires careful planning. Table 4.5 provides questions and answers that must be considered when planning and implementing focus groups.

Projective Techniques

Another source of data collection is through the use of projective techniques. **Projective techniques** refer to any of a variety of methods that allow respondents to project their feelings, beliefs, or motivations onto a relatively neutral stimulus. Projective techniques were developed by psychologists to uncover motivations or to understand personality. The most famous projective technique is the Rorschach Test, which asks respondents to assign meaning to a neutral inkblot. While the Rorschach may have no value for sports marketing researchers, other projective techniques are useful. For instance, sentence completion, word association, picture association, and cartoon tests could be employed as data collection techniques. Figure 4.3 demonstrates the use of sentence completion to gain insight into consumer attitudes toward Fila. The responses to these sentences could be analyzed to determine consumer perceptions of the target market for Fila (question 1), the brand image of Fila (question 2), and product usage (question 3).

Surveys

Data collection techniques are more narrowly defined for descriptive research design types. As stated earlier, a descriptive study describes who, where, how much, how often, and why people are engaging in certain consumption behaviors. In order to capture this information, the researcher would choose to conduct a survey. Surveys allow sports marketing researchers to collect primary data such as awareness, attitudes, behaviors, demographics, lifestyle, and other variables of interest.

Surveys that are considered "snapshots" and describe the characteristics of a sample at one point in time are called **cross-sectional studies**. For example, if a high

---

figure 4.3   Sentence Completion Test

1. People who wear Fila footwear are _____ .

2. When I think of Fila, I _____ .

3. I would be most likely to buy Fila shoes for _____ .

table 4.5

Planning and Implementing Focus Groups

Q. How many people should be in a focus group?

A. Traditionally, focus groups are composed of eight to ten people. However, there is a current trend toward mini-groups of five to six people. Mini-groups are easier to recruit and allow for better and more interaction among focus group participants.

Q. How many people should I recruit, if I want eight people in my group?

A. The general rule of thumb is to recruit 25 percent more people than the number needed. For example, if you are planning on holding mini-groups with six people, you should recruit eight. Unfortunately, some respondents will not show up for the group, even if there is an incentive for participation.

Q. What is a good incentive for participants?

A. Naturally, a good incentive depends largely on the type of individual you wish to attract for your group. For example, if your group wishes to target runners who might be participating in a local 10K race, $35 to $50 may be the norm, including dinner or light snacks. However, if your group requires lawyers to discuss the impact of Title IX on the NCAA, an incentive of $75 to $100 may be more appropriate. In addition to or instead of cash, noncash incentives could also serve as an incentive for participation. For example, free tickets or merchandise may work better than cash for some groups.

Q. Where should the focus groups be conducted?

A. The best place to conduct focus groups is at a marketing research company that has up-to-date focus group facilities. The facility is usually equipped with a one-way mirror, videotape, microphones connected to an audio system, and an observation room for clients. In addition, more modern facilities have viewing rooms that allow the client to interact with the moderator via transmitter while the group is being conducted.

Q. How should I choose a moderator?

A. There is no rule of thumb, but research has identified a set of characteristics that seem to be consistent among good moderators. These characteristics include the following: quick learner, friendly leader, knowledgeable but not all-knowing, excellent memory, good listener, a facilitator—not a performer, flexible, empathic, a "big-picture" thinker, and a good writer. In addition, a good moderator should have a high degree of sports industry knowledge or product knowledge.[7]

Q. How many groups should be conducted?

A. The number of groups interviewed is dependent upon the number of different characteristics that are being examined in the research. For example, Notre Dame may want to determine whether regional preferences exist for different types of merchandise. If so, two groups may be conducted in the North, two groups in the South, and so on. Using the previous example, if lawyers were the participants in a focus group, two or three total groups may suffice. Any more than this and the information would become redundant and the groups would become inefficient.

Q. What about the composition of the groups?

A. A general rule of thumb is that focus group participants should be homogenous. In other words, people within the group should be as similar as possible. We wouldn't want satisfied, loyal fans in the same group as dissatisfied fans. Similarly, we wouldn't want a group to be composed of both upper-level managers and the employees that report to them. In the latter case, lower-level employees may be reluctant to voice their true feelings.

school athletic program wanted to measure fan satisfaction with its half-time promotions at a basketball game, cross-sectional design would be utilized. However, if a researcher wished to investigate an issue and examine responses over a longer period of time, a **longitudinal study** would be utilized. In this case, fan satisfaction would be measured, improvements would be made to the half-time promotions based on survey responses, and then fan satisfaction would be measured again at a later time. Although longitudinal studies are generally considered more effective, they are not widely used due to time and cost constraints.

Experiments

For well-defined problems, causal research is appropriate. As stated earlier, cause-and-effect relationships are difficult to confirm. **Experimentation** is research in which one or more variables are manipulated while others are held constant; the results are then measured. The variables being manipulated are called independent variables, while those being measured are called dependent variables.

An experiment is designed to assess causality and can be conducted in either a laboratory or a field setting. A laboratory, or artificial setting, offers the researcher greater degrees of control in the study. For example, Major League Baseball may wish to test the design of a new logo for licensing purposes. Targeted groups could be asked to evaluate the overall appeal of the logo while viewing it on a computer. The researchers could then easily manipulate the color and size of the logo (independent variables) while measuring the appeal to fans (dependent variable). All other variation in the design would be eliminated, offering a high degree of control.

Unfortunately, a tradeoff must be made between experimental control and the researchers' ability to apply the results to the "real purchase situation." In other words, what we find in the lab might not be what we find in the store. Field studies, therefore, are conducted to maximize the generalizablity of the findings to real shopping experiences. For example, MLB could test the different colors and sizes of logos by offering them in three different cities of similar demographic composition. Then, MLB could evaluate the consumer response to variations in the product by measuring sales. This common approach to experimentation used by sports marketers is called test marketing.

Test marketing is traditionally defined as introducing a new product or service in one or more limited geographic areas. Through test marketing, sports marketers can collect many valuable pieces of information related to sales, competitive reaction, and market share. Information regarding the characteristics of those purchasing the new products or services could also be obtained. First Union Bank recently ran a two-week test market to determine consumer preference for two debit cards. One of the debit cards featured NASCAR driver Wally Dallenbach and the other was an Atlanta Braves card. The test showed that consumers preferred the NASCAR card— 1,800 people chose the Dallenbach version compared to only 300 that chose the Braves card.[8]

Although test marketing information is invaluable to a sports marketer wishing to roll out a new product, it is not without its disadvantages. One of the primary disadvantages of test marketing is cost and time. Products must be produced, promotions or ads developed, and distribution channels secured—all of which cost money. In addition, the results of the test market must be monitored and evaluated at an additional cost. Another problem related to test marketing is associated with competitive activity. Often, competitors will offer consumers unusually high discounts on their products or services in order to skew the results of a test market. In addition, competitors may be able to quickly produce a "me-too," imitation product or service by the time the test market is ready for a national rollout.

The problems of cost, time, and competitive reaction may be alleviated by means of a more nontraditional test market approach called a **simulated test market**. Typically, respondents in a simulated test market participate in a series of activities, such as (1) receiving exposure to a new product or service concept (2) having the opportunity to purchase the product or service in a laboratory environment (3) assessing attitudes towards the new product or service after trial and (4) assessing repeat purchase behavior.

Designing Data Collection Instruments

Once the data collection method has been chosen, the next step in the marketing research process is designing the data collection instrument. Data collection instruments are required for nearly all types of data collection methods. Guides are necessary for depth interviews and focus groups. Data collection forms are needed for projective techniques. Even experiments require data collection instruments.

One of the most widely used data collection instruments in sports marketing is the questionnaire or survey. All forms of survey research require the construction of a questionnaire. The process of designing a questionnaire is shown in Figure 4.4.

Specify Information Requirements

In the first step of **questionnaire design**, the information requirements must be specified. In other words, the researcher asks what information needs to be gathered via the questionnaire. This should have been addressed if the problem was carefully defined in the initial step of the research process. Remember, in the first step of the marketing research process, research objectives were developed based on the information requirements that were specified. The research objectives are a useful starting point in questionnaire design, as they indicate what broad topic will be addressed in the study.

Decide Method of Administration

The method of administration is the next consideration in questionnaire design. The most common methods of administration are via mail, phone, or personal interview. Each method has its own unique advantages and disadvantages that must be considered (see Table 4.6). For example, if a short questionnaire is designed to measure fan

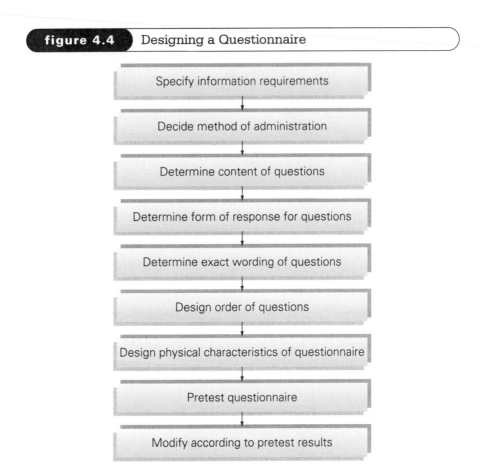

figure 4.4 Designing a Questionnaire

Specify information requirements

↓

Decide method of administration

↓

Determine content of questions

↓

Determine form of response for questions

↓

Determine exact wording of questions

↓

Design order of questions

↓

Design physical characteristics of questionnaire

↓

Pretest questionnaire

↓

Modify according to pretest results

Source: Gilbert A. Churchill, Jr., *Basic Marketing Research*, 3d ed., copyright © 1996 by The Dryden Press, reproduced by permission of the publisher.

attitudes toward the new promotion, then a phone survey may be appropriate. However, if the research is being conducted to determine preference for a new logo, then mail or personal interviews would be necessary.

Determine Content of Questions

The content of individual questions is largely governed by the method of administration. However, several other factors must be kept in mind. First, does the question address at least one of the research objectives? Second, are several questions necessary to answer an objective? Contrary to popular belief, more is not always better. Third, does the respondent have the information necessary to answer the question? For example, a respondent may not be able to answer questions regarding personal seat licenses if they do not have a full understanding or description of what is meant by a PSL. Finally, will the respondent answer the question?

table 4.6

Comparison of Methods of Administration

| Issues | Method of Administration | | | |
	Mail	Telephone	Stadium/Event Interviews	Internet
Costs	inexpensive	moderately expensive	most expensive because of time	inexpensive
Ability to use complex survey	little, since self-administered	same	greatest since interviewer is present	little, since self-administered
Opportunity for interviewer bias	none	same	greatest since interviewer is present	none
Response rate	lowest	moderate	greatest	low
Speed of data collection	slowest	high	medium to high	high

Sometimes respondents possess the necessary information, but they elect not to respond. For instance, questionnaires may sometimes ask sensitive questions (e.g., income levels) that respondents will not answer.

Determine Form of Response

After deciding upon the content of the questions, the form of response should be considered. The form of the response is dependent on the degree of structure in the question. Unstructured questionnaires use a high number of open-ended questions. These types of questions allow respondents to provide their own responses rather than having to choose from a set of response categories provided by the researcher. The following are examples of open-ended questions:

- How do you feel about personal seat licenses?
- How many years have you been a season ticketholder?
- How will the personal seat license impact your attitude towards the team?

Determine Exact Wording of Questions

One of the most rigorous aspects of questionnaire design is deciding on the exact wording of questions. When constructing questions, the following pitfalls should be avoided:

- **Questions should not be too lengthy.** Lengthy, run-on questions are difficult to interpret and have a higher likelihood of being skipped by the respondent.
- **Questions should not be ambiguous.** Clarity is the key to good survey design. For instance, "Do you like sports?" may be interpreted in two very different ways. One respondent may answer based on participation, while another may answer from a spectator's viewpoint. In addition, there may be ambiguity in how the respondent defines sport. Some respondents would call billiards a sport, while others may define it as a game.
- **Questions should not be double-barreled or contain two questions in one.** For example, "Do you enjoy collecting and selling baseball cards?" represents a double-barreled questions. This should be divided into two separate questions. "Do you enjoy collecting baseball cards?" and "Do you enjoy selling baseball cards?"
- **Questions should not lack specificity.** In other words, clearly define the questions. "Do you watch sports on a regular basis?" is a poorly written question in that the respondent does not know the researcher's definition of regular. Does the researcher mean once a week or once a day?
- **Questions should not be technical in nature.** Avoid asking respondents questions that will be difficult for them to answer. For instance "What type of swing weight do you prefer in your driver?" may be too technical for the average golfer to answer in a meaningful fashion.

Determine Question Sequence

Now that the question wording has been determined, the researcher must determine the proper sequence of the questions. First, a good questionnaire starts with broad, interesting questions that hook the respondent and capture his or her attention. Similarly, questions more narrow in focus, such as demographic information, should appear at the end of the questionnaire. Second, questions that focus on similar topical areas should be grouped together. For example, a fan satisfaction questionnaire may include sections on satisfaction with concessions, satisfaction with stadium personnel, or satisfaction with game promotions.

Finally, proper question sequencing must consider branching questions and skip patterns. Branching questions direct respondents to questions based on answers to previous questions. For example, the first question on a questionnaire may be, "Have you ever been to a River Rats game?" If the respondent answers "yes," he or she might continue with a series of questions concerning customer satisfaction. If the respondent answers "no," then he or she might be asked to skip forward to a series of questions regarding media preferences. Because branching questions and skip patterns are sometimes confusing to respondents, they should be avoided if at all possible.

Design Physical Characteristics of Questionnaire

One of the final steps in the questionnaire development process is to consider carefully the physical appearance of the questionnaire. If the questionnaire is cluttered and looks unprofessional, respondents will be less likely to cooperate and complete the instrument. Other questionnaire design issues include

- Questionnaire should look simple and easy to fill out

- Questionnaire should have subheadings for the various sections

- Questionnaire should provide simple and easy-to-understand instructions

- Questionnaire should leave sufficient room to answer open-ended questions

Pretest

After the questionnaire has been finalized and approved by the client, the next step in the questionnaire design process is to pretest the instrument. A **pretest** can be thought of as a "trial run" for the questionnaire to determine if there are any problems in interpreting the questions. In addition to detecting problems in interpreting questions, the pretest may uncover problems with the way the questions are sequenced.

An initial pretest should be conducted with both the researcher and respondent present. By conducting the pretest through personal interview, the researcher can discuss any design flaws or points of confusion with the respondent. Next, the pretest should be conducted using the planned method of administration. In other words, if the survey is being conducted over the phone, the pretest should be conducted over the phone.

The number and nature of the respondents should also be considered when conducting a pretest. The sample for the pretest should mirror the target population for the study, although it may be useful to have other experienced researchers examine the questionnaire before full-scale data collection takes place. The number of people to pretest depends on time and cost considerations. Although pretests slow down the research process, they are invaluable in discovering problems that would otherwise make the data collected meaningless.

Designing the Sample

After the data collection instrument has been designed, the research process turns to selecting an appropriate sample. A **sample** is a subset of the population of interest from which data is gathered that will estimate some characteristic of the population. Securing a quality sample for sports marketing research is critical. Researchers rarely have the time or money to communicate with everyone in the population of interest. As such, developing a sample that is representative of this larger group of consumers is required.

In order to design an effective and efficient sample, a variety of sampling techniques are available. Sampling techniques are commonly divided into two categories: **nonprobability sampling** and **probability sampling**. The primary characteristic of nonprobability sampling techniques is that the sample units are chosen subjectively by the researcher. As such, there is no way of ensuring whether the sample is representative of the population of interest. Probability sampling techniques are objective procedures in which sample units have a known and nonzero chance of being selected for the study. Generally, probability sampling techniques are considered stronger because the accuracy of the sample results can be estimated with respect to the population.

Nonprobability Sampling

The three nonprobability sampling techniques commonly used are convenience, judgment, and quota sampling. **Convenience sampling techniques** are also called accidental sampling because the sample units are chosen based on the "convenience" of the researcher. For example, a research project could be conducted to assess fans' attitudes toward high-school soccer in a large metropolitan area. Questionnaires could be handed out to fans attending Friday night games at three different high schools. These individuals are easy to reach, but may not be representative of the population of interest (in this case, high school fans in the area).

Other researchers may approach the same problem with a different data collection method. For example, three focus groups might be conducted to gain a better understanding of the fans' attitudes towards high-school soccer. Using this scenario, long-time, loyal soccer fans might be chosen as participants in the three focus groups. These participants represent a **judgment sample** because they are chosen subjectively and based on the judgment of the researcher they best serve the purpose of the study.

A quota sampling technique may also be used to address the research problem. In **quota sampling**, units are chosen on the basis of some control characteristic or characteristics of interest to the researcher. For instance, control characteristics such as gender and year in school may be appropriate for the soccer study. In this case, the researcher may feel that there may be important distinctions between male and female fans and between freshmen and seniors. The sample would then be chosen to capture the desired number of consumers based on these characteristics. Often, the numbers are chosen so that the percentage of each sample subgroup (e.g., females and juniors) reflect the population percentages.

Probability Sampling

As stated earlier, the stronger sampling techniques are known as probability sampling. In probability sampling, the sample is chosen from a list of elements called a sampling frame. For example, if students at a high school define the population of interest, the sampling frame might be the student directory. The sample would then be chosen objectively from this list of elements.

Although there are many types, a simple random sample is the most widely used probability sampling technique. Using this technique, every unit in the sampling frame has a known and equal chance of being chosen for the sample. A probability sampling technique, such as simple random sampling, allows the researcher to calculate the degree of sampling error, so the researcher knows how precisely the sample reflects the true population.

Sample Size

Another question that must be addressed when choosing a sample is the number of units to include in my sample, or the sample size. Practically speaking, sample sizes are determined largely on the basis of time and money. The more precise and confident the researcher wants to be in his or her findings, the greater the necessary sample size.

Another important determinant in sample size is the homogeneity of the population of interest. In other words, how different or similar are the respondents. To illustrate the effect of homogeneity on sample size, suppose the River Rats are interested in determining the average income of their season ticketholders. If the population of interest includes all the season ticketholders and each person has an income of $50,000, then how many people would we need to have a representative sample? The answer, because of this totally homogenous population, is one. Any one person that would be in our sample would give us the true income of River Rat season ticketholders.

As you can see from this brief discussion, sample size determination is a complex process based on confidence, precision, the nature of the population of interest, time, and money. Larger samples tend to be more accurate than smaller ones, but researchers must treat every research project as a unique case that has an optimal sample size based on the purpose of the study.

Data Analysis

After the data have been collected from the population of interest, data analysis takes place. Before any analytical work occurs, the data must be carefully scrutinized to ensure its quality. Researchers call this the editing process. During this process, the data is examined for impossible responses, missing responses, or any other abnormalities that would render the data useless.

Once the quality of the data is ensured, coding begins. Coding refers to assigning numerical values or codes to represent a specific response to a specific question. Consider the following question:

How likely are you to attend River Rats' games in the future?

1. extremely unlikely
2. unlikely
3. neither unlikely nor likely
4. likely
5. extremely likely

The response of *extremely likely* is assigned a code of 1, *unlikely* a code of 2, and so on. Each question in the survey must be coded to facilitate data analysis.

After editing and coding are completed, you are ready to begin analyzing the data. Although there are many sophisticated statistical techniques (and software programs) to choose from to analyze the data, researchers usually like to start by "looking at the big picture." In other words, researchers want to describe and summarize the data before they begin to look for more complex relationships between questions.

Often, the first step in data analysis is to examine two of the most basic informational components of the data—central tendency and dispersion. Measures of central tendency (also known as the mean, median, and mode) tell us about the typical response, while measures of dispersion (range, variance, standard deviation) refer to the similarity of responses to any given question.

table 4.7

Frequency Distribution or One-Way Table

How likely are you to attend River Rats' games in the future?

		Respondents	
		Number	Percentage
1	extremely unlikely	20	13.3
2	unlikely	30	20.0
3	neither unlikely or likely	25	16.7
4	likely	45	30.0
5	extremely likely	30	20.0
	Total	150	100%

To give us a good feel for the typical responses and variation in responses, frequency distributions are often constructed. A frequency distribution, such as the one shown in Table 4.7, provides the distribution of data pertaining to categories of a single variable. In other words, frequency distributions or one-way tables show us the number (or frequency) of cases from the entire sample that fall into each response category. Normally, these frequencies or counts are also converted into percentages.

After one-way tables or frequency distributions are constructed, the next step in data analysis involves examining relationships between two variables. A crosstabulation allows us to look at the responses to one question in relation to the responses to another question. Two-way tables provide a preliminary look at the association between two questions. For example, the two-way table shown in Table 4.8 explores

table 4.8

Two-Way Table or Crosstabulation

Likelihood of attending River Rats' games in the future?	Gender	
	Male	Female
1 extremely unlikely	5	15
2 unlikely	5	25
3 neither unlikely or likely	10	15
4 likely	30	15
5 extremely likely	25	5
Total	75	75

the relationship between the likelihood of going to River Rats' games and gender. Upon examination, the two-way table clearly shows that females are less likely to attend River Rats' games in the future than males. Implications of this finding may include the need to conduct future research to better understand why women are less likely to attend River Rats' games than males and designing a marketing mix that appeals to women.

Preparing a Final Report

The last step in the marketing research process is preparing a final report. Typically, the report is intended for top management of the sports organization, who can either put the research findings into action or shelve the project. Unfortunately, the greatest research project in the world will be viewed as a failure if the results are not clearly communicated to the target audience.

How can you prepare a final report that will assist in making decisions throughout the strategic marketing process? Here are some simple guidelines for preparing actionable reports.

- **Know your audience.** Before preparing the oral and/or written report, determine your audience. Typically, the users of research will be upper-management who do not possess a great deal of statistical knowledge or marketing research expertise. Therefore, it is important to construct the report so that it is easily understood by the audience who will use the report, not by other researchers. One of the greatest challenges in preparing a research report is presenting technical information in a way that is easily understood by all users.

- **Be thorough, not overwhelming.** By the time they are completed, some written research reports resemble volumes of the *Encyclopedia Britannica*. Likewise, oral presentations can drag on for so long that any meaningful information is lost. Researchers should be sensitive to the amount of information that they convey in an oral research report. Oral presentations should show only the most critical findings, rather than every small detail. Generally, written reports should include a brief description of the background and objectives of the study, how the study was conducted (methodology), key findings, and marketing recommendations. Voluminous tables should be located in an appendix.

- **Carefully interpret the findings.** The results of the study and how it was conducted are important, but nothing is as critical as drawing conclusions from the data. Managers who use the research findings often have limited time and no inclination to carefully analyze and interpret the findings. In addition, managers aren't interested in the findings alone, but what marketing actions can be taken based on the findings. Be sure not to neglect the implications of your research when preparing both oral and written reports.

(C) hapter 4 focuses on the tools used to gather information to make intelligent decisions throughout the strategic sports marketing process. More specifically, the chapter describes the marketing research process in detail. Marketing research is defined as the systematic process of collecting, analyzing, and reporting information to enhance decision making throughout the strategic sports marketing process.

The marketing research process consists of seven interrelated steps. These steps include defining the problem; choosing the research design type; identifying data collection methods; designing data collection forms; designing the sample; collecting, analyzing and interpreting data; and preparing the research report. The first step is defining the problem and determining what information will be needed to make strategic marketing decisions. The tangible outcome of problem definition is to develop a set of research objectives that will serve as a guide for the rest of the research process.

The next step in the marketing research process is to determine the appropriate research design type(s). The research design is the plan that directs data collection and analysis. The three common research design types are exploratory, descriptive, and causal. The choice of one (or more) of these design types for any study is based on the clarity of the problem. Exploratory designs are more appropriate for ill-defined problems, while causal designs are employed for well-defined research problems.

After the research design type is chosen, the data collection method(s) is selected. Once again, decisions regarding data collection are contingent upon the choice of research design. Data collection consists of two types—secondary and primary. Secondary data refers to data that has already been collected, either within or outside the sports organization, but still provides useful information to the researcher. Typically, sources of secondary data include government reports and documents; trade and industry associations; standardized sports marketing information studies;

and books, journals, and periodicals. Primary data is information that is collected specifically for the research question at hand. Common types of primary data collection techniques include, but are not limited to; depth interviews, focus groups, surveys, and experiments.

The fourth step in the research process is to design the data collection instrument. Regardless of whether you are collecting data by depth interviews, focus groups, or surveys, data collection instruments are necessary. The most widely used data collection technique in sports marketing research is the questionnaire. As such, it is important that sports marketing researchers understand how to construct a questionnaire properly. The steps for questionnaire design include specifying information requirements, deciding the method of administration (i.e., mail, phone, intercept), determining the content of questions, determining the form of response for questions, deciding on the exact wording of the questions, designing the order of the questions, designing the physical characteristics of the questionnaire, pretesting the questionnaire, and modifying it according to pretest results.

Once the data collection forms are constructed, the next step in the research process is choosing a sampling strategy. Rarely, if ever, can we take a census where we communicate with or observe everyone of interest to us in a research study. As such, a subset of those individuals is chosen to represent the larger group of interest. Sampling strategy identifies how we will choose these individuals and how many people we will choose to participate in our study.

Data analysis is the next step in the marketing research process. Before the data can be analyzed, however, it must be edited and coded. The editing process ensures that the data being used for analysis is of high quality. In other words, it makes sure that there are no problems, such as large amounts of missing data or errors in data entry. Next, coding takes place. Coding refers to assigning numerical values to represent specific responses to specific questions. Once the data have been edited and coded, data analysis is conducted. The method of data analysis depends on a variety of factors, such as how to address the research objectives. The last step in the marketing research process is to prepare a final report.

Oral and written reports typically discuss the objectives of the study, how the study has been conducted, and the findings and recommendations for decision makers.

KEY TERMS & CONCEPTS

concomitant variation

cross sectional studies

data collection techniques

experiment

focus groups

longitudinal studies

management problem statement

marketing research

methodology

nonprobability sampling

pretest

primary data

probability sampling

problem definition

projective techniques

questionnaire design

research design

research objectives

research problem statement

research proposal

secondary data

simulated test market

sports marketing research

test marketing

REVIEW QUESTIONS

1. Define sports marketing research. Describe the relationship between sports marketing research and the strategic marketing process.

2. What are the various steps in the marketing research process?

3. Define problem/opportunity definition and explain why this step of the research process is considered to be the most critical.

4. What are some of the basic issues that should be addressed at a research request meeting?

5. Outline the steps in developing a research proposal.

6. Define a research design. What are the three types of research designs that can be used in research? How does the choice of research design stem from the problem definition? Can a researcher choose multiple designs within a single study?

7. Describe some of the common data collection techniques used in sports marketing research. How does the choice of data collection technique stem from the research design type?

8. What are some of the central issues that must be considered when conducting focus groups?

9. What are the pros and cons of laboratory studies versus field studies?

10. Outline the nine steps in questionnaire design. What are some of the most common errors in the wording of questions?

11. Define nonprobability sampling and probability sampling techniques. What are three types of nonprobability sampling?

12. What is a sampling frame? How do researchers decide on the appropriate sample size for a study?

13. What are some of the guidelines for preparing oral and written research reports?

EXERCISES

You are interested in purchasing a new minor league baseball franchise. The franchise will be located in your area. In order to reduce the risk in your decision making, you have requested that a sports marketing firm submit a detailed research proposal. The following questions pertain to this issue:

1. What is the broad problem/opportunity facing you in this decision? Write the research objectives based on the problem formulation.

2. What type of research design type do you recommend?

3. The sports marketing firm has submitted the following preliminary questionnaire. Please provide a detailed critique of their work.

   Age: _____   Gender: _____

   Are you likely to go to a baseball game at the new stadium?
   Yes ____   No ____

   How many minor league games did you go to last year?
   0–3 ____   4–6 ____   6–9 ____   10 + ____

   What types of promos would you like to see?
   Beer Night ____   Straight-A Night ____   Polka Night ____

4. Now that you have looked at their survey, create a questionnaire of your own. Would any other data collection techniques be appropriate, given the research problem?

5. What sampling technique(s) do you recommend? How is the correct sample size determined, given your choice of sampling technique?

INTERNET EXERCISES

1. Using secondary data sources on the Internet, find the following and indicate the appropriate URL (Internet address):

   a. Number of women who participated in high-school basketball last year
   b. Attendance at NFL games last year
   c. Sponsors for the New York City Marathon
   d. Universities that offer graduate programs in sports marketing

2. Using the Internet, find at least five articles that relate to the marketing of NASCAR.

3. Using the Internet, locate three companies that conduct sports marketing research. What types of products and services do the companies offer?

1. "1997 Sports Sponsorship Survey." <http://www.mediachallenge.com/survey/CSsurvey.html>.

2. Gilbert Churchill, *Basic Marketing Research*, 3rd ed., (Ft. Worth, TX: Dryden Press, 1996).

3. Ibid.

4. Kristie McCook, Douglas Turco, and Roger Riley. "A Look At The Corporate Sponsorship Decision Making Process." *Cyber Journal of Sport Marketing*, vol. 1, no. 2 (1997). <http://www.cad.gu.edu.au/market/cy…rnal_of_sport_marketing/mcook.html>.

5. Jon Roe, "Team Nickname Can Be Vital to Financial Success," *Star Tribune*, January 22, 1998, 70.

6. "Focus Group Research Prompts New Labeling on Huffy Sports Packaging." <http://www.sportlink.com/new_products/huffy2.html>.

7. Gilbert Churchill, *Basic Marketing Research*, 3rd ed., (Fort Worth, TX: Dryden Press, 1996).

8. "IEG Network: Assertions." <http://www.sponsorship.com/forum/assertions.html>.

Understanding Participants as Consumers

After completing this chapter, you should be able to

- Define participant consumption behavior

- Explain the simplified model of participant consumption behavior

- Describe the psychological factors that impact participant decision making

- Identify the various external factors influencing participant decision making

- Describe the participant decision-making process

- Understand the different types of consumer decision making

- Discuss the situational factors that influence participant decision making

Under a full moon, 21 kayaks embark on a trip down the Potomac River outside Washington, D.C. The paddlers are a group of otherwise sedate executives and federal workers. "I used to be a couch potato," says kayaker Judith King, a 56-year-old editor. As cicadas serenade and lightning splinters the dark sky, King says, "I can't believe people sit home and watch television when they could be doing this."

The sports are all the same, but the conditions are new. Nighttime joggers, cyclists, backpackers, skaters, swimmers, and canoeists are growing in number. There are no statistics, but tour operators report increasing demand for nighttime hiking and boating excursions. Additionally, the Consumer Products Safety Commission recently began a study to explore the safety of bike reflectors.

Although everyone agrees that nighttime sports are becoming more popular, why this is so still remains unanswered. Some speculate that the growing number of shift workers in the United States has contributed to the demand for nighttime sports. Others who work normal, but long, hours say that it is their only time for recreation.

Whatever the reason, "No one is satisfied with the common outdoor experience anymore," says Richard MacNeil, a professor at the University of Iowa's Department of Sport, Health, Leisure, and Physical Studies. "Night makes things more adventurous."

Unfortunately, night also makes things more dangerous for the typical participant. The need to reduce the hazards of nighttime sport has spawned a number of new, high-visibility products from sporting goods manufacturers. For example, two seasons ago Nike made reflectors standard equipment on all of its running shoes. Luminator footballs and soccer balls are being sold for nighttime play. NightRanger and Night Quest night-vision binoculars are being used to illuminate shadowy wildlife. For nighttime skaters, there are "Comet Wheels," whose mini-batteries power the wheels of in-line skates.

Understanding the emergence of night sports participation, sports marketers will have the opportunity to respond to a new group of consumers with new product lines. The potential also exists for new sports to be developed specifically for nighttime play. After all, grown-ups everywhere are coming out to play after dark.

Adapted from Michael J. McCarthy, "More People Take Up Starlight Skating, Twilight Tennis," *The Wall Street Journal*, September 5, 1996, B1.

As the article illustrates, people will go to great lengths to participate in sports. Think about the sports and recreational activities in which you have participated during the past month. Maybe you have played golf or tennis, lifted weights, or even gone hiking. According to data from the National Sporting Goods Association provided in Table 5.1, millions of Americans participate in a variety of physical activities every year.

At this point you may be asking yourself, "Why are sports marketers concerned with consumers who participate in sports?" Recall from our discussion of sports marketing in chapter 1 that one of the basic sports marketing activities was encouraging consumers to participate in sports. Sports marketers are responsible for organizing events such as the Boston Marathon, the Iron Man Triathlon, or the Gus Macker 3-on-3 Basketball Tournament where thousands of consumers participate in sports. Moreover, sports marketers are involved in marketing the equipment and apparel necessary for the participation in sports. As you might imagine, sports participants constitute a large and growing market both in the United States and internationally.

table 5.1

Top Twenty Participant Sports in the United States

Activity/Sports	Number of Participants (in millions)
1. Bowling	53.3
2. Basketball	45.1
3. Free weights	43.2
4. Billiards	42.2
5. Freshwater fishing	42.1
6. Tent camping	41.2
7. Treadmill exercise	36.1
8. Stationary cycling	34.8
9. Fitness walking	33.2
10. Running/Jogging	32.3
11. In-Line skating	29.1
12. Golf	26.3
13. Fitness bicycling	26.2
14. Exercise to music	24.1
15. Volleyball	23.6
16. Resistance machines	22.5
17. Swimming (fitness)	21.8
18. Softball (slow pitch)	20.5
19. Hiking/Backpacking	20.0
20. Football (touch)	18.2

Source: National Sportings Goods Manufacturers Association. "America's Top 25 Participation Sports."
Courtesy of Sporting Goods Manufacturers Association.

spotlight on international sports marketing:

the german sports participation market

One of the most sports-minded countries in the world is Germany. In fact, Germany represents Europe's largest sporting goods equipment market with sales of some $6 billion dollars. Additionally, there are roughly 62,000 sports clubs with some 25 million members (in a country of 80 million people). Finally, German consumers spent an average of $750 dollars on sports equipment compared to $695 dollars for the U.S. participant.

When most people think about German sports, the first thing that comes to mind is soccer, and it remains a popular participation activity. The other fast growing sports in Germany include: basketball; hiking/treking; in-line skating; golf; walking; mountain biking, baseball; camping; and exercising with machines. Interestingly, these sports mirror the hottest activities in the United States and represent an opportunity for U.S. manufacturers. German

(continued)

retailers say that consumers are continually asking for sports equipment that is "Made in the U.S A."

What is the most popular sports activity in Germany? A recent study conducted by the German Federation of Sporting Goods Retailers found that outdoor sports, along with swimming, was ranked first in popularity among 34 percent of the population. Billions of dollars are spent each year by Germans to support this outdoor sports way of life. For example, some 2 billion dollars are spent on outdoor clothing. Even more is spent on other outdoor supplies such as tents, bikes (some 60 million bikes in a country of 80 million people), sunglasses, and backpacks. Interestingly, German consumers are very quality and image conscious. This is fine with the retailers who can demand higher prices for their products. This is also good news for U.S. manufacturers, whose highest quality sporting goods are very well received by the German market.

Source: "Sporting & Recreation Equipment Market in Germany." World Federation of the Sporting Goods Industry, <http://sporting.com/international/countrymarket/cm_5.html>

To successfully compete in the expanding sports participant market, sports organizations must develop a thorough understanding of participant consumption behavior and what affects it. **Participant consumption behavior** is defined as actions performed when searching for, participating in, and evaluating the sports activities that consumers feel will satisfy their needs. You may have noticed that this definition relates to the previous discussion of the marketing concept and consumer satisfaction. Sports marketers must understand why consumers choose to participate in certain sports and what the benefits of participation are for consumers. For instance, do we play indoor soccer for exercise, for social contact, to feel like part of a team, or to enhance our image? Also, the study of participant consumer behavior attempts to understand when, where, and how often consumers participate in sports. By understanding consumers of sport, marketers will be in a better position to satisfy their needs.

■ Three lifelong sports participants in training.

The definition of participant consumption behavior also incorporates the elements of the participant decision-making process. The decision-making process is the foundation of our model of participant consumption. It is a five-step process that consumers use when deciding which sports or activities to participate. Before turning to our model of participant consumption behavior, it must be stressed that the primary reason for understanding the participant decision-making process is to guide the rest of the strategic sports marketing process. Without a better understanding of sports participants, marketers would simply be guessing about how to satisfy their needs.

Model of Participant Consumption Behavior

To help organize all this complex information about sports participants, we have developed a model of participant consumption behavior that will serve as a framework for the rest of our discussion (see Figure 5.1). At the center of our model is the participant decision-making process, which is influenced by three components: (1) internal or psychological processes such as motivation, perception, learning and memory, and attitudes; (2) external or sociocultural factors, such as culture, reference groups, and family; and (3) situational factors that act on the participant decision-making process.

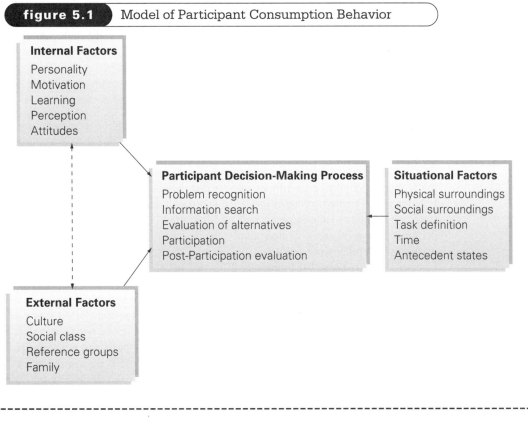

figure 5.1 Model of Participant Consumption Behavior

Internal Factors
Personality
Motivation
Learning
Perception
Attitudes

Participant Decision-Making Process
Problem recognition
Information search
Evaluation of alternatives
Participation
Post-Participation evaluation

Situational Factors
Physical surroundings
Social surroundings
Task definition
Time
Antecedent states

External Factors
Culture
Social class
Reference groups
Family

Participant Decision-Making Process

Every time you lace up your running shoes, grab your tennis racquet, or dive into a pool, you have made a decision about participating in sports. Sometimes these decisions are nearly automatic because, for example, we might jog nearly every day. Other decisions, such as playing in a golf league, require more careful consideration because of the time and cost involved. The foundation of our model of participant consumption behavior is trying to understand how consumers arrive at their decisions.

Participant decision-making is a complex, cognitive process that brings together memory, thinking, information processing, and making evaluative judgments. The five steps that make up the process used to explain participant decision-making are shown in Figure 5.1. It is important to remember that every individual consumer arrives at decisions in a slightly different manner because of his or her own psychological make-up and his or her environment. However, the five-step participant decision-making process moving from problem recognition through post-participation evaluation, is relatively consistent among consumers and must be understood by sports marketers in order to develop strategies that fit with consumer's needs.

As we progress through the participant decision-making process, let's consider the case of Jack, a 33-year-old male who just moved from Los Angeles to Cincinnati. Jack has always being active in sports and would like to participate in an organized sports league. Because of work and family commitments, Jack only has the time to participate in one league. He is unsure about what sport to participate in, although he does have a few requirements. Because he is a newcomer to the city, Jack would like to participate in a team sport in order to meet new people. Also, he wants the league to be moderately competitive so as to keep his competitive juices flowing. Finally, he would like to remain injury free, so the sport needs to be non- or limited-contact. Let us see how Jack arrives at this important decision by using the participant decision-making process.

Problem Recognition

The first step in the participant decision-making process is problem recognition. During problem recognition, consumers realize that they have a need that is not presently being met. **Problem recognition** is the result of a discrepancy between a desired state and an actual state large enough and important enough to activate the entire decision-making process.[1] Stated simply, the desired state reflects the "ideal" of the participant. In other words, What is the absolute best sport for Jack to participate in, given his unique needs? If there is a difference between ideal and actual levels of participation, then the decision-making process begins.

The desire to resolve a problem and to reach goals, once recognized by consumers, are dependent on two factors: (1) the magnitude or size of the discrepancy and (2) the relative importance of the problem. Let us look at how these two factors would impact problem recognition. Jack currently jogs on a daily basis and wishes to participate in a competitive, organized, and aggressive team sport. Is the discrepancy between actual state (individual, recreational, nonaggressive) and desired state (team

■ Many consumers see a discrepancy between the "ideal" and "actual" body.

play, competitive, aggressive) large enough to activate the decision-making process? Let's assume that it is and consider the second condition of problem recognition, the importance of the problem.

The second condition that must be met for problem recognition to occur is that the goal must be important enough to Jack. Some consumers may recognize the difference between participating in recreational sports versus an organized league. Would the benefits of participating in the new organized league (hopefully making some friends and being more competitive) outweigh the time, expense, and energy required to play? If the problem is important enough to Jack, then he moves on to the next stage of the decision-making process—information search.

What strategic implication does problem recognition hold for sports marketers? Generally, we would first identify the actual and desired states of sports participants or potential participants. Once these states have been determined, sports marketers can offer activities and events that will fill these needs and eliminate "problems." In addition, sports marketers can attempt to alter the perceived ideal state of consumers. For example, it is common for health clubs to show the "ideal" body that can be achieved by purchasing a membership and working out.

Information Search

After problem recognition occurs, the next step in the participant decision-making process is information search. **Information search** occurs when a participant seeks relevant information that will help him or her resolve the problem. The sources of information sought by consumers can be broken down into two types: internal and external sources. **Internal sources** of information are recalled from our own memories and are based on previous exposure to sports and activities. The internal information activated from memory can provide us with a wealth of data that may impact the decision-making process. Jack has spent most of his life participating in sports and recreational activities, so information based on past experience is readily available. For instance, since Jack has played in an organized league in the past, he would use internal information to recall his experiences. Did he enjoy the competition of organized sport? Why did he stop participating in the sport?

External sources of information are environmentally based and can occur in three different ways. First, Jack might ask **personal sources**, such as friends or family, to provide him with information about the possible organized team sports in which to participate. Friends and family are important information sources that can have a great deal of influence on our participation choices. Second, **marketing sources**, such as advertisements, sales personnel, brochures, and Web sites on the Internet are all important information sources. In fact, sports marketers have direct control over this source of information, so it is perhaps the most critical from the perspective of the sports organization. The third type of external information source is called an **experiential source**. Jack may watch games in several different sports leagues to gather information. His decision is influenced by watching the level of competition.

Some participants may require a great deal of information before making a decision, while others require little to no information. The amount of information and the number of sources used is a function of several factors, such as the amount of time available, the importance of the decision, the amount of past experience, and the demographics and psychographics of the participants.

The extent of the information search also depends on the **perceived risk** of the decision. Perceived risk stems from the uncertainty associated with decision making and is concerned with the potential threats inherent in making the wrong decision. For individual sports participants, perceived risk surfaces in many different forms. Perceived risk may be the embarrassment of not having the skill necessary to participate in a competitive league (social risks) or being concerned about the money needed to participate (economic risks). Also, an important perceived risk for many other adult participants is health and safety (safety risks).

At this stage of the participant decision-making process, sports marketers must understand as much as they can about the information sources used by consumers. For instance, marketers for the Cincinnati Recreational Commission want to know the information sources for teams, what is the most effective way to provide teams with information, how much information is desired, and to whom they should provide this information. Moreover, sports marketers want to understand the perceived risks for potential participants such as Jack. This information is essential for developing an effective promotional strategy that targets both teams and individual participants.

Evaluation of Alternatives

Now that the information search has yielded all the available participation alternatives that have some of the basic characteristics that appeal to Jack, he must begin to evaluate the alternatives. Jack thinks about all of the organized, team sports in which he might participate and chooses a subset to which he will give further consideration. The few sports given the greatest consideration are called the **evoked set** of alternatives. Jack's evoked set might consist of four sports: softball, basketball, bowling, and indoor soccer.

After consumers develop their evoked set, comprised of acceptable alternatives, they must evaluate each sport based on the important features and characteristics. These features and characteristics that potential consumers are looking for in a sport are called **evaluative criteria**. The evaluative criteria used by Jack includes team sport, organized or league play, moderate level of competition, and moderately aggressive sport. It is important to realize that each of the four evaluative criteria carries a different weight in Jack's overall decision-making process. To continue with our example, let's say that Jack attaches the greatest importance to participating in a team sport. Next, Jack is concerned with participating in a league or organized sport. The level of aggression is the next most important criterion to Jack. Finally, the least important factor in choosing from among the four sports is the level of competition.

In complex decision making, Jack would evaluate each of the sports against each of the evaluative criteria. The final decision regarding participation is based on which sport measures best against the various factors that he deems to be important. The two most important criteria—team sport and league play—are satisfied for each of the four sports in the evoked set. In other words, all of the sports that Jack is evaluating are team sports, and all have league play. Therefore, Jack moves on to his next criteria, level of aggression. Ideally, Jack wants to remain injury free so he eliminates indoor soccer and basketball from further consideration. Bowling seems to be a clear winner in satisfying this criteria, and Jack is aware of several competitive bowling leagues in the area. As such, Jack decides to participate in a bowling league.

The evaluation of alternatives has two important implications for sports marketers. First, sports marketers must ensure that their sports are included in the evoked set of potential consumers. To accomplish this objective, consumers must first become aware of the alternative. Second, sports marketers must understand what evaluative criteria are used by potential consumers and then must develop strategies to meet consumers' needs based on these criteria. For example, marketers of bowling have determined that there are two different participant bowling markets: league or organized bowlers and recreational bowlers.

Recreational bowlers are growing in numbers and care most about the facilities at which they bowl and the related services provided. The evaluative criteria used by recreational bowlers might include the type of food served, other entertainment offered (e.g., arcade games and billiards), and the atmosphere of the bowling alley. League bowlers, on the other hand, constitute a diminishing market. This segment of bowlers cares most about the location of the bowling center and the condition of the lanes.[2]

Participation

The evaluation of alternatives has led us to what marketers consider the most important outcome of the decision-making process—the participation decision. The participation stage of the decision-making process might seem to be the most straightforward, but many things need to be considered other than actually deciding what sport to play. For instance, the consumer's needs may shift to the equipment and apparel needed in order to participate. Jack may decide that he needs a new bowling ball, shoes, and equipment bag to look the part of bowler for his new team. Thus, marketers working for equipment manufacturers are interested in Jack's participant consumption behavior. In addition, Jack may have to decide which bowling alley offers the best alternative for his needs. He may choose a location close to home, one that offers the best price, or the alley that has the best atmosphere. Again, these criteria must be carefully considered by sports marketers, because participants make choices regarding not only what sports they wish to participate in, but where they wish to participate.

Other things might occur that alter the intended decision to participate in a given sport. At the last minute, Jack's co-workers may talk him out of playing in a competitive men's league, in lieu of a co-rec, work league. There might be a problem finding an opening on a roster, which would also change Jack's decision-making process at the last moment. Perhaps the bowling team that Jack wanted to join is scheduled to play during a trip that he had planned. All these "unexpected pleasures" may occur at the participation stage of the decision-making process.

Post-Participation Evaluation

You might think that the decision-making process comes to an abrupt halt after the participation decision, but there is one more very important step—**post-participation evaluation**. The first activity that may occur after consumers have made an important participation decision is **cognitive dissonance**. This dissonance occurs because consumers experience doubts or anxiety about the wisdom of their decision. In other words, people question their own judgment. Let us suppose Jack begins participating in a competitive bowling league, and the first time he bowls, he is embarrassed. His poor level of play is far worse than everyone else on the team. Immediately, he begins to question his decision to participate.

Whether or not dissonance occurs is a function of the importance of the decision, the difficulty of the choice, the degree of commitment to the decision, and the individual's tendency to experience anxiety.[3] Jack does not know his teammates well and only paid $50 to join the league, so he may decide to quit the team. On the other hand, he does not want to let his team down and ruin his chance of making new friends, so high levels of dissonance may cause him to continue with the team. In either case, the level of dissonance that Jack feels is largely based on his own personality and tendency to experience anxiety.

Another important activity that occurs after participation begins is evaluation. First, the participant develops expectations about what it will be like to play in this competitive bowling league. Jack's expectations may range from thinking about how much physical pain the sport will cause to thinking about how many new friends he will make as a result of participating. Next, Jack evaluates his actual experience after several games. If expectations are met or exceeded, then satisfaction occurs. However, if the experience or performance is poorer than expected, then dissatisfaction results. The level of satisfaction Jack experiences will obviously have a tremendous impact on future participation and word-of-mouth communication about the sport.

Types of Consumer Decisions

We have just completed our discussion of Jack's decision-making process and have failed to mention one very important thing. Not all decisions are alike. Some are extremely important and therefore take a great deal of time and thought. Because we are creatures of habit, some decisions require little or no effort. We simply do what we have always done in the past. The variety of decisions that we make about participation in sport can be categorized into three different types of participation decision processes. The decision processes, also known as levels of problem solving, are habitual problem solving, limited problem solving, and extensive problem solving.

Habitual Problem Solving

One type of decision process that is used is called **habitual problem solving (or routinized problem solving)**. In habitual problem solving, problem recognition occurs, followed by limited internal information search. As we just learned, internal search comes from experiences with sports stored in memory. Therefore, when Jack is looking for information on sports next year, he simply remembers his previous experience and satisfaction with bowling. The evaluation of alternatives is eliminated for habitual decisions since no alternatives are considered. Jack participates in bowling again, but this time there is no dissonance and limited evaluation occurs. In a sense, Jack's decision to participate in bowling becomes a habit or routine each year.

Limited Problem Solving

The next type of consumer decision process is called **limited problem solving**. Limited problem solving begins with problem recognition and includes internal search and sometimes limited external search. A small number of alternatives are evaluated using a few evaluative criteria. In fact, in limited problem solving, the alternatives being evaluated are often other forms of entertainment (e.g., movies, concerts). After purchase, dissonance is rare and a limited evaluation of the product occurs. Participation in special sporting events, such as a neighborhood 10K run or charity golf outing, are examples of sporting events that lend themselves to limited problem solving.

Extensive Problem Solving

The last type of decision process is called **extensive problem solving (or extended problem solving)** because of the exhaustive nature of the decision. As with any type of decision, problem recognition must occur for the decision-making process to become initiated. Heavy information search (both internal and external) is followed by the evaluation of many alternatives on many attributes. Post-purchase dissonance and post-purchase evaluation are at their highest levels with extensive decisions. Jack's initial decision to participate in the bowling league was an extensive decision due to his high levels of information search, the many sports alternatives he considered, and the comprehensive nature of his evaluation of bowling.

For many people who are highly involved in sports, participation decisions are more extensive in nature, especially in the initial stages of participating in and evaluating various sports. Over time, what was once an extensive decision becomes routine. Participants choose sports that meet their needs, and the decision to participate becomes automatic. It is important for marketers to understand the type of problem solving used by participants so that the most effective marketing strategy can be formulated and implemented.

Ⓟsychological/Internal Factors

Now that we have looked at the participant decision-making process, let's turn our focus to the internal, or psychological, factors. Personality, motivation, learning, and perception are some of the basic **psychological/internal factors** that will be unique to each individual and guide sports participation decisions.

Personality

One of the psychological factors that may have a tremendous impact on whether we participate in sports, the sports in which we participate, and the amount of participation, is personality. Psychologists have defined **personality** as a set of consistent responses an individual makes to the environment.

Although there are different ways to describe personality, one common method used by marketers is based on specific, identifiable personality traits. For example, individuals can be thought of as aggressive, orderly, dominant, or nurturing.[4] Consider the potential association between an individual's personality profile and the likelihood of participating in a particular sport. The self-assured, outgoing, assertive individual may be more likely than the apprehensive, reserved, and humble person to participate in any sport. Moreover, the self-sufficient individual may participate in more individual sports (e.g., figure skating, golf, tennis) than the group-dependent individual.

In a recent study, Generation X-ers were found to be more interested in fast-paced, high-risk activities, such as rock climbing and mountain biking.[5] As such, action sports may be a good choice for the happy-go-lucky, venturesome personality type of the Generation X-ers. Action or Extreme sports are defined as the pantheon of aggressive, non-team sports including snowboarding, in-line skating, super modified shovel racing, wakeboarding, ice and rock climbing, mountain biking and snow mountain biking.[6] Another example of the relationship between sports participation and personality traits can be seen in Table 5.2. As illustrated, golfers most often de-

■ A growing number of consumers participate in high risk sports.

scribed themselves as responsible, family-oriented, self-confident, and intelligent. The poorest descriptors for golfers were *bitter*, *sick a lot*, *extravagant*, and *risk-averse*. Interestingly, golfers described themselves as team players, although they participate in this highly individual sport.

table 5.2

Golfer's Self Reported Traits and Personality Characteristics

Best Descriptors	%	Poorest Descriptors	%
Responsible	80%	Bitter	3%
Family-Oriented	75	Sick a Lot	3
Self-Confident	70	Extravagant	6
Intelligent	66	Risk-Averse	6
Fun-Loving	64	Virgin	6
Team Player	63	Fun-Loving	8
Sensitive	62	Lonely	8
Ambitious	61	Outside the Mainstream	14
Competent	61	Sexy	15
Practical	60	Born Again	16

Source: Yankolovich Partners, "How Golfers are Likely to Describe Themselves," *Yankolovich Monitor Sports Enthusiast Profile.*

Although personality and participation may be linked, care must be taken not to assume a causal relationship between personality and sports participation. Some believe that sports participation might shape various personality traits (i.e., sports is a character builder). Other researchers feel that we participate in sports because of our particular personality type. To date, little research supports the causal direction of the relationship between personality and participation in sport.

Not only does personality dictate whether or not someone participates in sport, it may also be linked with participation in particular types of sports. The violent, aggressive personality type may be drawn to sports such as football, boxing, or hockey. On the other hand, the shy, introverted personality type may be more likely to participate in individual sports, such as tennis and running. Knowing the relationship between participation and personality profiles can help sports marketers set up the strategic sports marketing process so that it will appeal to the appropriate personality segment. In addition, sports marketers of large participant sporting events use personality profiles to attract potential corporate sponsors who may want to appeal to the same personality segment.

Motivation

Why do people participate in sports? What benefits are people looking for from participating in sport, and what needs do participating in sport satisfy? Results from a recent study suggest that there are three basic reasons for participation (see Table 5.3).

The study of human motivation helps to better understand the underlying need to participate in sports. **Motivation** is an internal force that directs behavior towards the fulfillment of needs. In our earlier discussion of the participant decision-making process, problem recognition resulted from having needs that are not currently being met. As the definition indicates, motivation is discussed in terms of fulfilling unmet needs. While there is no argument that all humans have needs, there is disagreement about the number of needs and the nature of them.

table 5.3

Why People Participate in Sport

Personal Improvement
Release of tension/relaxation, sense of accomplishment, skill mastery, improved health and fitness, other people's respect for one's athletic skill, release of aggression, enjoyment of risk taking, personal growth, development of positive values, sense of personal pride

Sport Appreciation
Enjoyment of the game, sport competition, thrill of victory

Social Facilitation
Time spent with close friends or family, sense of being part of a group

Source: George Milne, William Sutton, and Mark McDonald, "Niche Analysis: A Strategic Measurement Tool for Managers," *Sport Marketing Quarterly*, vol. 5, no. 3, (1996): 17–21.

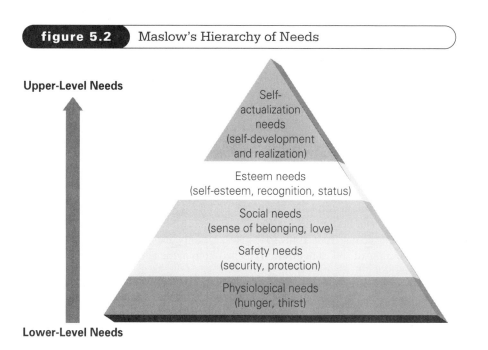

figure 5.2 Maslow's Hierarchy of Needs

Upper-Level Needs

Self-actualization needs (self-development and realization)

Esteem needs (self-esteem, recognition, status)

Social needs (sense of belonging, love)

Safety needs (security, protection)

Physiological needs (hunger, thirst)

Lower-Level Needs

Source: A.H. Maslow, *Motivation and Personality*, 2nd ed., (New York, NY: Harper and Row, 1970).

One popular theory of human motivation based on classification of needs is called **Maslow's Hierarchy of Needs** (see Figure 5.2). Maslow's Hierarchy of Needs consists of five levels. According to Maslow, the most basic, primitive needs must be fulfilled before the individual can progress to the next level of need. Once this higher level of need is satisfied, the individual is then motivated to fulfill the next higher level of need. Let us look at the hierarchy of needs as it relates to participation in sports.

The first and most basic level of needs in Maslow's hierarchy are called **physiological needs**. These are the biological needs that people have—to eat, drink, and meet other physiological needs. For some individuals, there may be a physiological need to exercise and have some level of activity. Once this lower order need is met, safety needs are addressed.

Safety needs are concerned with physical safety, as well as the need to remain healthy. Sports equipment manufacturers address the need participants have for physical safety. With respect to the need for health, many participants cite that the primary reason for joining health clubs is to maintain or improve their health.

The next need level is based on **love and belonging**. Many people choose to participate in sport because of the social aspects involved. One of the early need theories of motivation includes "play" as a primary social need.[7] For some individuals, sports participation is their only outlet for being part of a group and interacting with others. The need to be part of a team and be respected by teammates has been demonstrated in a number of studies.

As these social needs are satisfied, **esteem** needs of recognition and status must be addressed. Certainly, sport plays a major role in enhancing self-esteem. For example, bungee jumping provides an excellent illustration of how sport influences esteem. The president of the U.S. Bungee Association (USBA), Casey Dale, describes the motives of people who use risky activities as a self-image booster. "People are less satisfied than they used to be with being pigeonholed by what they do, so they want to change their self-image. A quick fix is to become this extreme, risk-taking individual. All of a sudden, Bill the accountant goes bungee jumping off a 20-story bridge, and all of his co-workers see him in a new light."[8]

Finally, the highest order need, **self-actualization**, should be met. This refers to the individual's need to "be all that you can be" and is usually fulfilled through participation in mountain climbing, triathlons, or any sport that pushes an individual to the utmost of his or her physical and mental capacities. For example, ultramarathons in which runners compete in 100K road races certainly test the will of all participants. Another example of self-actualization can be found in the amateur athlete who trains his or her whole life for the Olympic Games.

As a sports marketer, strategies for increasing participation may be enhanced if you identify and understand the needs of consumers. In some instances, participation might be fulfilling more than one need level. Consumers may be satisfying physiological needs, safety needs, social needs, esteem needs, or possibly self-actualization needs. For instance, marketing a health-club membership might appeal to consumers wishing to fulfill any of the need levels in the hierarchy. The members' physiological needs are being met through exercise. Safety needs might be met by explaining that the club has state-of-the-art exercise equipment that is designed to be safe for all ages

■ Sports participants fulfilling the need for self-actualization.

and fitness levels. Social needs are addressed by describing the club as a "home away from home" for many members. The need for esteem for health-club members might be easily satisfied by depicting how good they will look and feel after working out. Finally, self-actualization needs may be fulfilled by working out to achieve the ideal body.

The needs that have just been presented can be described in two ways: motive direction and motive strength. Motive direction is the way that a consumer attempts to reduce tension by either moving towards a positive goal or moving away from a negative outcome. In the case of sports participation, an individual wishes to get in good physical condition and may move toward this goal by running, biking, lifting weights, and so on. Likewise, this same individual may wish to move away from eating fatty foods and drinking alcohol.

Of particular interest to sports marketers is the strength of the sports participation motive. Motivational strength is the degree to which an individual chooses to actively pursue one goal over another. In sports marketing, the strength of a motive is characterized in terms of **sports involvement**. Sports involvement is the perceived interest in and personal importance of sports to an individual participating in a sport.[9]

Triathletes are an excellent example of an extreme level of sports involvement because of the importance placed on training for events. In their study, Hill and Robinson demonstrated that extreme involvement in a sport affects many aspects of the athletes' lives.[10] Participation could have positive effects, such as increased self-esteem, improved moods, and a better sense of overall wellness. Conversely, high involvement in a sport (e.g., triathlon) may produce neglected responsibilities of work, home, or family and/or feelings of guilt, stress, and anxiety. Said simply, extremely involved individuals frequently have a difficult time balancing their lives.

Sports marketers are interested in involvement because it has been shown to be a relatively good predictor of sports-related behaviors. For example, a recent study found that level of involvement was positively related to the number of hours people participate in sports, the likelihood of planning their day around a sporting event, and the use of sports-related media (e.g., television, newspaper, magazines).[11] Knowledge of sports involvement can help sports marketers develop strategies for both low-involvement and high-involvement groups of potential participants.

Perception

Think for a moment about the image you have of the following sports: soccer, hockey, and tennis. You might think of soccer as a sport that requires a great deal of stamina and skill, hockey as a violent and aggressive sport, and tennis as a sport for people who belong to country clubs. Ask two friends about their images of these same sports, and you are likely to get two different responses. That is because each of us has our own views of the world based on past experience, needs, wants, and expectations.

Your image of sport results from being exposed to a lifetime of information. You talk to friends and family about sports, you watch sports on television, and listen to sports on the radio. In addition, you may have participated in a variety of sports over the course of your life. We selectively filter sports information based on our own view of the world. Consumers process this information and use it in making decisions about participation.

The process in which consumers gather information and then interpret that information based on their own past experience is described as perception. **Perception** is defined as the complex process of selecting, organizing, and interpreting stimuli such as sports.[12] Ultimately, our perception of the world around us influences participant consumer behavior. The images that we hold of various sports and of ourselves dictate, to some extent, what sports we participate in. One of the primary goals of sports marketing is to shape your image of sports and sports products.

Before sports marketers can influence your perceptions, they must get your attention. **Selective attention** describes a consumer's focus on a specific marketing stimulus based on their needs and attitudes. For example, you are much more likely to pay attention to advertisements for new golf clubs if you are thinking about purchasing a set.

Sports marketers fight with other sports and nonsports marketing stimuli for the limited capacity that consumers have for processing information. One job of the sports marketer is to capture the attention of the potential participant. But how is this done? Typically, sports marketers capture our attention through the use of novel promotions, using large and colorful promotional materials, and by developing unique ways of communicating with consumers.

While sports marketers attempt to influence our perceptions, each participant brings a unique set of experiences, attitudes, and needs that impact the perceptual process. Generally speaking, consumers perceive things in ways that are consistent with their existing attitudes and values. This process is known as **selective interpretation**. For example, someone who has played hockey all his or her life may not see it as a dangerous and violent sport, while others hold a different interpretation.

Finally, **selective retention**, or the tendency to remember only certain information, is another of the influences on the perceptual process. Selective retention is remembering just the things we want to remember. The hockey player does not remember the injuries, the training, or the fights—only the victories.

Although sports marketers cannot control consumers' perceptions, they can and do influence our perceptions of sports through their marketing efforts. For example, a sports marketer trying to increase volleyball participation in boys ages 8 to 12 must first attempt to understand their perception of volleyball. Then the sports marketer tries to find ways of capturing the attention of this group of consumers, who have many competing sports and entertainment alternatives. Once they have the attention of this group of potential participants, a marketing mix is designed to either reinforce their perception of volleyball or change the existing image.

In addition to understanding consumers' image of volleyball, sports marketers are also interested in other aspects of perception. For instance, how do potential participants perceive advertisements and promotional materials about the sport? What are the parents' perception of volleyball? Do the parents perceive volleyball to be costly? The answer to all of these questions depends on our own unique view of the world, which sports marketers attempt to undestand and shape.

Learning

Another psychological factor that impacts our participation decisions is learning. **Learning** is a relatively permanent change in response tendency due to the effects of experience. These response tendencies can be either changes in behavior (participation) or in how we perceive a particular sport. Consumers learn about and gather information regarding participation in various sports in any number of ways. **Behavioral learning** is concerned with how various stimuli (information about sports) elicit certain responses (feelings or behaviors) within an individual. **Cognitive learning**, on the other hand, is based on our ability to solve problems and use observation as a form of learning. Finally, **social learning** is based on watching others and learning from their actions. Let us look briefly at these three theories of learning as they apply to sports participation.

Behavioral Learning

One behavioral learning theory of importance to sports marketers is operant conditioning. Conditioning teaches people to associate certain behaviors with certain consequences of those behaviors. A simplified model of operant conditioning is illustrated in Figure 5.3.

Let us illustrate the model of operant conditioning using snow-skiing participation. We may decide to try snow-skiing (specific behavior) as a new sport. Next and unfortunately, our behavior is punished as we continually fall down, suffering social embarrassment, and are uncomfortably cold. Finally, the likelihood of engaging in this behavior in the future is decreased because of the negative consequences of the earlier attempts at skiing. On the other hand, if the skiing participant is rewarded through the enjoyment of the sport and being with others, then he or she will continue to ski more and more.

The theory of operant conditioning lies at the heart of loyalty to a sport. In other words, if the sports we participate in meet our needs and are reinforcing them, then we will continue to participate in those sports. The objective of the sports marketer is to try to heighten the rewards associated with participating in any given sport and diminish any negative consequences.

Cognitive Learning

Although much of learning is based on our past experience, learning also takes place through reasoning and thought processes. This type of approach to learning is known

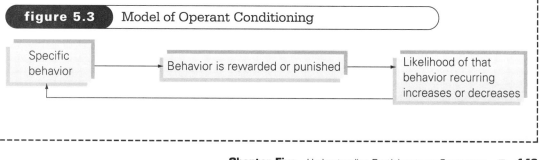

| figure 5.3 | Model of Operant Conditioning |

Specific behavior → Behavior is rewarded or punished → Likelihood of that behavior recurring increases or decreases

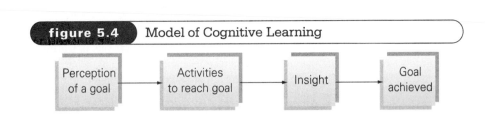

figure 5.4 Model of Cognitive Learning

| Perception of a goal | → | Activities to reach goal | → | Insight | → | Goal achieved |

as cognitive learning. **Cognitive learning** is best known as learning through problem solving or insight, as shown in Figure 5.4.

Consider a goal that concerns some of us, weight loss. Once this goal is established, consumers search for activities that allow them to achieve the goal. The activities necessary to achieve weight loss might include dieting, participating in aerobics, weight training, playing basketball, or jogging. When the consumer finally realizes what specific activities he or she feels are necessary to achieve the desired goal, insight occurs. Finally, and hopefully, the goal of weight loss is achieved.

With cognitive learning, the focus of sports marketers is to first understand the goals of potential consumers or participants. In addition, marketers must make potential participants aware of how the sport or sports product will help participants achieve their goals.

Social Learning

Much of our learning takes place by watching how others are rewarded or punished for their actions. This way of learning is called **social learning**. As children we watched our friends, family members, and our heroes participate in various sports. To a large extent, this early observation and learning dictates the sports in which we choose to participate later in life. In social learning, we not only see someone benefiting from sport, but we learn how to participate in the sport ourselves.

■ An Olympic hopeful learning through observation.

Those individuals that we choose to observe and the process of observation are called models and modeling, respectively. The job of the sports marketer is to present positive models and present sports in a positive light, so that others will perceive the benefits of sports participation. For example, MaliVia Washington may be seen as a role model for young African-American athletes thinking about participating in tennis, or Kerri Strug may be a model for young women interested in gymnastics.

Attitudes

Because of the learning and perceptual processes, consumers develop attitudes towards participating in sports. **Attitudes** are learned thoughts, feelings, and behaviors towards some given object. What is your attitude towards participation in bowling? One positive aspect of bowling is the chance to interact socially with other participants. On the other hand, bowling does not burn a lot of calories and may be seen as expensive. Your overall attitude towards bowling is made up of these positive and negative aspects of the sport.

Attitudes represent one of the most important components of the overall model of sports participation because they ultimately guide the decision-making process. Our attitudes are formed on the basis of an interaction between past experience and the environment in which we live. A simple model of attitude formation or how attitudes are developed is shown in Figure 5.5.

figure 5.5 Model of Attitude Formation

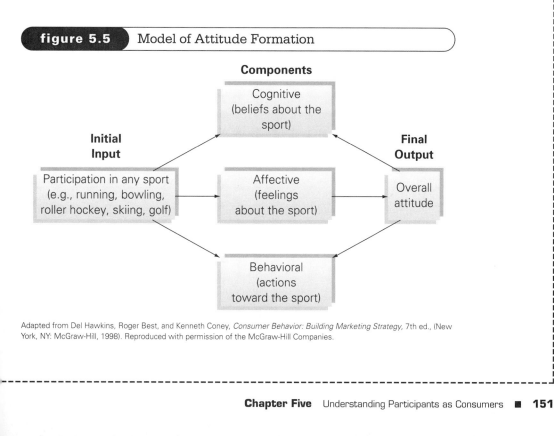

Adapted from Del Hawkins, Roger Best, and Kenneth Coney, *Consumer Behavior: Building Marketing Strategy,* 7th ed., (New York, NY: McGraw-Hill, 1998). Reproduced with permission of the McGraw-Hill Companies.

As the model of attitude formation suggests, an attitude is based on our thinking, feeling, and actions towards a sport. These three components interact to form an overall attitude. Let us look briefly at the three components: cognitive, affective, and behavior.

The **cognitive component** of attitude holds the beliefs that people have towards the object. Beliefs can be either a statement of knowledge regarding bowling or thoughts someone has towards bowling. They are neither right nor wrong and vary from individual to individual. For example, here are some beliefs about participation in bowling that consumers might hold:

- Bowling is expensive
- Bowling is time consuming
- Very few women bowl
- Bowling is for old people (Note: the largest participant group for bowling is 18- to 34-year-olds)

The **affective component** of attitude is based on feelings or emotional reactions to the initial stimulus. Most beliefs, such as the ones shown for cognitive attitude, have a related affective evaluation. More recently, affect, or feelings, have taken a more central role in explaining attitudes than beliefs or behaviors. In other words, some people equate attitudes with feelings that are held towards an object.[13]

Here are some potential affective statements:

- I hate bowling
- Bowling is a boring sport

The final component is called the **behavioral component** and is based on participants' actions. In other words, does the individual participate in bowling? How often does the individual bowl? What are the individual's behavioral intentions, or how likely will they be to bowl in the future?

Generally, sports marketers must understand consumer attitudes in order to maintain or increase participation in any given sport. Only after attitudes have been assessed can sports marketing strategies be formulated to improve upon or change existing attitudes. In our previous example, bowling equipment manufacturers and bowling alley management companies would need to change the beliefs that potential participants have about bowling. Additional strategies may attempt to change potential participants' feelings about bowling by repositioning the sport's current image. Finally, marketers may get potential participants to try bowling, which could lead to possible changes in the beliefs and feelings about the sport.

ociological/External Factors

Now that we have looked at the major internal or psychological factors that influence participation decisions, let us turn our attention to the sociological fators. The **external, or sociological, factors** are those influences outside of the individual participant that influence the decision-making process. The external factors are also referred to as sociological because they include all aspects of society and interacting with others.

The external factors discussed in this chapter include culture, social class, reference groups, and family.

Culture

Participating in sports and games has been one of the most long-standing traditions of civilization. Since the time of the ancient Greeks, participation in sports has been expected and highly valued.[14] In the United States, sports have been criticized for playing too important a role in our society. Many detractors have frowned at public monies being spent to finance private stadiums for professional athletics or institutions of higher education spending more on hiring a new coach than on a new president for the university (for example, the University of Minnesota football coach's salary is $500,000, or $275,000 more than the University president hired on the same day).

Culture is the learned values, beliefs, language, traditions, and symbols shared by a people and passed down from generation to generation. One of the most important aspects of this definition of culture includes the learning component. **Socialization** occurs when we learn about the skills, knowledge, and attitudes necessary for participating in sports. Sports marketers are interested in better understanding how the socialization process takes place and how they might influence this process.

A model of sports socialization is presented in Figure 5.6, which provides a framework for understanding how children learn about sports. Although the sports socialization process begins at younger and younger ages, it extends throughout the life of the individual. Sports marketers are interested in learning how the socialization process differs on the basis of gender, income, lifestyle of the family, and the number of children in the family.

Also having a tremendous impact on the process are the socializing agents. These factors represent the direct and indirect influences on the children. Sports marketers are also interested in understanding the relative impact of each of the socializing agents on a child's interest in participating in sports. For instance, is watching parents or professional athletes a better predictor of sports participation among children? One study has shown that children look to parents first, but if they are unacceptable or unwilling role models, children turn to other people.[15]

The learning mechanisms of observation and reinforcement are just two ways that the socialization process is facilitated. As discussed earlier, observation refers

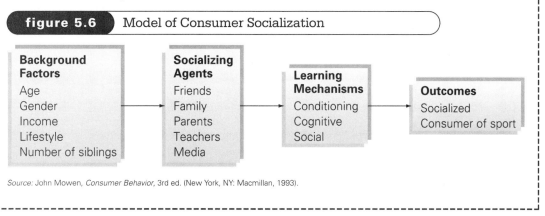

figure 5.6   Model of Consumer Socialization

Background Factors	Socializing Agents	Learning Mechanisms	Outcomes
Age	Friends	Conditioning	Socialized
Gender	Family	Cognitive	Consumer of sport
Income	Parents	Social	
Lifestyle	Teachers		
Number of siblings	Media		

Source: John Mowen, *Consumer Behavior*, 3rd ed. (New York, NY: Macmillan, 1993).

to looking to others as models for sports participation. For example, older siblings may serve as models for sports participation at earlier ages, while friends may become a more important learning mechanism as children age. Reinforcement may occur as children receive praise for participation in sport from parents, coaches, and friends.

The final element in the socialization model is the emergence of a socialized sports participant. Here, the child becomes actively engaged in sports participation. From the sports marketer's perspective, when children participate in sports at an early age, they may have better potential to become lifelong participants. Certainly, sporting goods manufacturers are interested in having children associate their brands with the enjoyment of sport at the earliest possible age. Aside from the learning that takes place during the socialization process, values represent another important aspect of any culture. **Values** are widely held beliefs that affirm what is desirable in a culture. Several of the core values that reflect U.S. culture are shown in Table 5.4.

Some of the core American values listed in Table 5.4 have intimate ties to sports participation in the United States. Obviously, the last value mentioned, fitness and health, relates directly to our preoccupation with participating in sports. The activity value has a direct impact on the way Americans spend their leisure time, including sports participation. Likewise, achievement and success is a theme that is continually underscored as consumers participate in sports.

Although not directly related, other core U.S. values may tangentially impact sports participation. For example, the value of individualism and being oneself may manifest itself in the types of sports or activities in which we choose to participate. Many sports, such as surfing, hang-gliding, climbing, and hiking, allow a consumer

table 5.4

Core American Values

Core American Value	Descriptor
Achievement and success	Sense of accomplishment
Activity	Being active or involved
Efficiency and practicality	Saves time and effort; solves problems
Progress	Continuous improvement
Material comfort	Money; status
Individualism	Being themselves
Freedom	Democratic beliefs
External conformity	Adaptation to society
Humanitarianism	Overcoming adversity; supporting
Charity	Giving to others
Youthfulness	Looking and acting young
Fitness and health	Exercise and diet

Source: Leon Shiffman and Leslie Kanuk, *Consumer Behavior*, 5th ed. (Englewood Cliffs, NJ: Prentice Hall, 1994).

to express his or her own personality. Youthfulness is also expressed through participation in sport as consumers keep "young at heart" by staying active. Consumers may also participate in sporting events to help raise money for charities.

Social Class

Throughout history people within various cultural systems have been grouped together based on social class. Whether it is the "haves" versus the "have nots" or the "upper class" versus the "lower class," social class distinctions have always been present. **Social class** is defined as the homogeneous division of people in a society sharing similar values, lifestyles, and behaviors that can be hierarchically categorized.

Important to this definition is the idea that individuals are divided into homogeneous classes, or strata. Typically, social strata are described in terms of a hierarchy ranging from lower class to upper class. Consumers are grouped into the various social classes based on the interaction of a number of factors. Occupation, income, and education are usually considered the three primary determinants of social class. In addition, possessions (e.g., home and car) and affiliations (e.g., club membership, professional organizations, community organizations) are also thought to be important factors.

Although researchers agree that there are distinct social strata, there is little agreement on how many categories there are in the hierarchy. For instance, some researchers believe that a seven-tiered structure (as illustrated in Figure 5.7) explains social class in the United States. Others, however, believe in a simple two-tiered system (i.e., upper and lower).

Regardless of the class structure, sports marketers are interested in social class as a predictor of whether or not a consumer will participate in sports and, if they do participate, the types of sports in which a consumer might participate. For instance, a recent study has shown that the number of people participating in soccer varies by household income.[16] Other research has shown that more than 1 in 4 Americans would like to have more time for leisure activities such as bowling and softball. A disproportionate number of these people who want more leisure time are lower income, blue-collar workers.[17] In addition, the Fish and Wildlife Service found that anglers are above-average in income and are moderately well-educated.[18]

Reference Groups

"Be Like Mike" and "I am Tiger Woods" illustrate the power of reference group influence. More formally, **reference groups** are individuals who influence the information, attitudes, and behaviors of other group members. Sports participation is heavily influenced through the various reference groups to which an individual may belong.

Witness the Tiger Woods phenomenon and the hordes of children who have now begun to participate in golf as a result of his influence. This type of reference group, which has an impact on our participation in sports as well as on our purchase of sports products, is called an aspirational group. Although many famous athletes recognize the influence they can have on children, others refuse to accept the responsibility that reference group influence demands (e.g., Charles Barkley of the NBA stating "I'm not a role model").

Sports Marketing — hall of fame

THE BABE: BABE DIDRIKSON ZAHARIAS

Mildred "Babe" Didrikson Zaharias was known by sports fans all over as the "best at everything." Her early success as an all-around athlete began as she played on basketball, softball, and track and field teams, named the Golden Cyclones, sponsored by the Employers Casualty Insurance Company. Babe represented the Golden Cyclones by herself in the 1932 Olympic track and field qualifying trials and entered eight of the ten events. She ended up winning six of the events, and her legend was born.

As an amateur, Babe won two gold medals and one silver in track and field events at the 1932 Olympics. She began a professional career that included stints in basketball, baseball, boxing, football, and hockey. Didrikson's most impressive sport of all, however, was golf. Returning to amateur status in golf, Babe ran up an unprecedented 17 straight wins, including a victory in the 1947 British Women's Amateur—never before won by an American. In 1949, she was one of the founding members of the LPGA.

In addition to her impressive athletic achievements, Babe was the consummate sports promoter and marketer. For example, she participated in publicity stunts such as harness racing and pitching against New York Yankee Joe Dimaggio. She published a book of golfing tips, had her own line of golf clubs through Spalding Sporting Goods, and appeared in movies such as the classic *Pat and Mike*.

Through her example and performance, Babe Didrikson Zaharias legitimized women's sports. Her excellence in so many sports made her a marketer's dream. Just imagine her today.

Source: Elizabeth Lynn, *Babe Didrikson Zaharias: Champion Athlete*, (New York, NY: Chelsea House, 1989).

Celebrity athletes are not the only individuals who have an impact on sports participation. Friends and co-workers are also considered a **primary reference group** because of the frequent contact that we have with these individuals and the power they have to influence our decisions. Many of us participate in sports because friends and co-workers have urged us to join their team, play a set of tennis, or hit the links. Primary reference groups may exert a powerful influence among high-school athletes as participation continues to grow at this level.

six million-plus played prep sports

The number of athletes participating in U.S. high school sports last season topped the 6 million mark for only the second time since figures were first compiled in 1971.

According to figures released by the National Interscholastic Athletic Administrators Association, over 3.6 million boys and 2.3 million girls participated in high school sports in the 1995–1996 season. These figures are based on the information from each of the state high school associations. Participation by boys increased for the fourth consecutive year, and the number of female athletes rose for the seventh straight year.

For girls, basketball remains the most popular sport, with 445, 869 participants, followed by track and field (379,060), volleyball (357,576), and fast-pitch softball (305,217). The sport with the largest increase in participation for girls was fast-pitch softball. Interestingly, 791 girls played high school football.

Football continues to dominate male sports participation (957,573), followed by basketball (545,596), track and field (454,645), and baseball (444,476). Track and field had the largest percentage increase in participation for boys.

Adapted from Dave Schutte, "6 Million-Plus Played Preps Sports Last Year," *Cincinnati Enquirer*, December 26, 1996, D4.

Family

Another primary reference group that has one of the greatest influences on sports participation is the family. As you might guess, family plays a considerable role because sports marketers target families as spectators. But how does family influence participation in sport? Consider families of friends or your own family. It is common for family members to exert a great deal of influence on each other with respect to decisions about sports participation and activities. For example, children may either directly or indirectly get parents involved in a sport (e.g., in-line skating, soccer, or biking) so that the entire family can participate together. Conversely, parents may urge their kids to get off the couch and get involved in sports.

Traditionally, fathers have had the greatest impact on their children's (mostly their sons) sports participation. Dad might have encouraged junior to play organized football because he did or go fishing because his father took him fishing. Of course, these scenarios are vanishing, as is the traditional family structure.

Long gone are the days of the mom, dad, two kids, and a dog. Long gone is the *Leave It to Beaver* mentality where fathers are breadwinners and mothers are homemakers. Today's modern family structure typically includes things like dual income

■ Girls' sports participation is eroding traditional gender roles.

Imagine a coloring book depicting young girls participating in a variety of sports. Within the drawings to be colored are names of sponsors such as Reebok and Spalding. This vision, called the *Girl's Sports Book*, has now become a reality and is being sold at Oshman's Sporting Goods stores.

Although the concept of a sports coloring book for girls may seem unique, it is just an illustration of the emergence of women in sports. In the sporting goods market, women buy more than half of the merchandise at some chains for their own use.

It is estimated that nearly one in three women today play sports of some sort, compared to 1 in 27 in the 1970s. Women now have the opportunity to play sports, and younger generations have the support of both mothers and fathers. But just what sports are being played? Data from the National Sporting Goods Association indicates that exercise walking, swimming, exercising with equipment, and camping are the most popular sports for women. Step aerobics and aerobic walking are the fastest growing sports for women.

This tremendous growth in women's sports participation is thought by most people to be tied to Title IX, the government mandate that high schools and colleges offer equal sports opportunities for girls. Not only has this caused a surge in participation at the high school and college ranks, but women are continuing to take the field after graduation, both as recreational and professional athletes.

Sporting goods manufacturers and retailers could not be more pleased with the new opportunity to market to women. Manufacturers have responded by designing equipment specifically to meet the female body. They are taking the lower center of gravity and lesser upper body strength into account. Re-

tailers are starting to target women with their merchandising and promotional efforts.

Oshman's Sporting Goods seems to have taken the lead in marketing to women sports participants. The store has developed clinics for women in sports and developed grants to support women's sports programs. Marilyn Oshman, daughter of founder Jake Oshman, said that the goal of the Women & Sports Program is "to provide leadership and vision in acknowledging the importance of women and sports and to support the development of sports opportunities for girls and women of all ages."

Some other efforts to produce sporting goods designed specifically for women include the following:

- Spalding's 28.5-inch basket for women (versus a 30-inch basket for men)
- Spalding softball gloves that feature more narrow hand openings and fingers
- Louisville Slugger softball bats that are 25 oz.
- Browning's 12-gauge shotgun that weighs less than the traditional version
- Terry Precision Bikes producing a special smaller framed model for women

Other examples of the growing women's sports market include the formation of professional sports leagues, such as the American Basketball League, the Women's NBA, the National Grass Volleyball League, the National Indoor Volleyball Association, and the Women's Fast Pitch League. Additional signs of the times include the introduction of the *Women's Sports Wire*, a newsletter for women's sports news, and the formation of the Women's Sports Marketing Group. The Women's Sports Marketing Group grew out of the need to understand how to properly market to women.

Adapted from Richard Halverson, "Women Take to the Field," *Discount Store News*, October 7, 1996, 59, 61, 63.

families with no kids (DINKS), divorced parents, single parents, or parents who are dually employed with kids (DEWKS).

Each of these modern family structures may influence participation in sports for both adults and children. For instance, dual-income families with no kids may have the time and the money to participate in a variety of "country club" sports. On the other hand, single or divorced parents may face time and financial constraints. Sports products such as the "10-minute workout" and 30-minute aerobic classes are targeted to working moms on the move. Additionally, the tremendous increase in sales of home exercise equipment may be traced back to the constraints of the modern family structure.

Childrens' ability to participate in organized sport may also be hampered by the single parent family, although women are increasingly taking on the traditional male sex role of coach, sports participant, and sports enthusiast. Also, fathers are increasingly encouraging daughters to participate in sport, another sign of changing sex roles.

Situational Factors

Now that we have looked at how the psychological and sociological factors influence the participant decision-making process, let us turn to the situational factors. Unlike the psychological and sociological factors that are relatively permanent in nature, the situational factors are temporary aspects that impact participation. For instance, the culture in which we make our participation decision is considered a long-term environmental factor. Likewise, personality is a set of consistent responses that we make to our environment. However, **situational factors** are those temporary factors within a particular time or place that influence the participation decision-making process.[19]

Consider the following examples of situational influences on participant behavior. Your best friend is in town and, although you do not normally enjoy golfing, you do so anyway to spend time with your friend. You typically run five miles per day, but an unexpected ice storm put a halt to your daily exercise routine. You have to study for final exams, so you settle for a 30-minute workout versus your normal 75 minutes. Each of these examples represents a different type of situational influence on participant decision making.

Consumer researchers have identified five situational influences that impact decision making. The five primary types of situational influences include physical surroundings; social surroundings; time; reason for participation, or task definition; and antecedent states. Let us briefly look at each in the context of participant decision making.

Physical Surroundings

The location, weather, and physical aspects of the participation environment comprise the **physical surroundings**. In sports participation, the physical surroundings play an extremely important role in decision making. When the weather outside is good, people who might not normally participate in sports do so. Likewise, the weather can have a situational influence on where we choose to participate. The runner described in the earlier example may decide to jog indoors rather than skip the workout. In addition to the weather, location might influence our decision to participate. For example, nonskiers may be tempted to try skiing if they are attending a sales conference in Vail or Aspen. Other aspects of the physical environment, such as a perfectly groomed championship golf course or scenic biking trail can also influence our participation decisions in a positive manner. From the perspective of the sports marketer, any attempt to increase participation must carefully consider the physical surroundings. Even the worst athletes in the world enjoy playing in nice facilities.

Social Surroundings

The effect of other people on a participant during participation in a sport is another situational influence, called **social surroundings**. In other words, who we are with may have a positive or negative impact on participation decisions. The earlier golf example presented a case where the presence of a friend caused the person to participate. Likewise, golfing in the presence of unfamiliar co-workers in a corporate outing can be an unpleasant and intimidating experience. In this case, participation might be avoided altogether.

Crowds represent another social situation that is usually avoided. For example, if the tennis courts or golf courses are full, you might decide to participate in another sport that day. Biking and hiking represent two other activities where crowds are usually perceived to have a negative impact on participation. In other words, people generally do not like to bike or hike in large crowds. However, some people may take pleasure when participating among large crowds. Consider, for example, runners who feel motivated when participating in events with thousands of other runners.

Time

The effect of the presence or absence of **time** is the third type of situational influence. In today's society, there are increasing time pressures on all of us. Changes in family structure, giving rise to dual income families and single parents, have made time for participation in sports even more scarce. Slightly more than half of all U.S. residents under the age of 50 complain of a lack of leisure time and this percentage is even higher for dual-income families. How many times have you heard someone say "I don't have the time to work out today?"

Because of time constraints, sports marketers are concentrating on ways to make our participation activities more enjoyable and more time-effective. For example, few of us can afford to take five hours out of our day to enjoy 18 holes of golf. As such, golfing associations are always communicating ways to speed up play. Similarly, few of us feel like we have the time to drive to the gym each day. The marketers' response to this was the development of the 30-minute workout and the enormous home health equipment industry.

Reason for Participation or Task Definition

Another situational influence, **task definition**, refers to the reasons that occasion the need for consumers to participate in a sport. In other words, the reason the consumer is participating impacts their decision-making process. Some participants may use jet

■ Social surroundings may have a negative or positive influence on participation.

skis or scuba dive once a year while they are on vacation. Other consumers may participate in a fantasy baseball camp, once in a lifetime.

These examples represent special occasions or situational reasons for participating. Moreover, the participation occasion may dictate the sports apparel and equipment we choose. For example, a consumer participating in a competitive softball league might wear cleats, long softball pants, and batting gloves. On the other hand, the recreational participant playing softball at the company picnic would only bring a glove.

Antecedent States

Temporary physiological and mood states that a consumer brings to the participant situation are **antecedent states**. In certain situations, people may feel worn out and lack energy. This physiological state may motivate some people to workout and become reenergized at the end of a long day of work. On the other hand, feeling tired can elicit another response in others, such as "I'm too tired to do anything today."

Certainly, other situational mood states, such as being "stressed out," can activate the need to participate in sports or exercise. On the other hand, feeling tired or hungry can cause us to decide against participation. At the very least, our mood can influence our decision to ride or walk 18 holes of golf.

It is important to remember that antecedent means "prior to" or "before." Therefore, the mood or physiological condition influences our decision making. For example, people who are experiencing bad moods may turn to sports to lift their spirits. Contrast this with someone who feels great because they have just participated in a sporting event.

SUMMARY

(T)he focus of chapter 5 is understanding the sports participant as a consumer of sports. Sports marketers are not only concerned with consumers who watch sporting events, but the millions of consumers who participate in a variety of sports. To successfully market to sports participants, sports marketers must understand everything they can about these consumers and their consumption behaviors. Participant consumption behavior is defined as the actions performed when searching for, participating in, and evaluating the sports activities that consumers feel will satisfy their needs.

To simplify the complex nature of participant consumption behavior, a model was developed. The model of participant consumption behavior consists of four major components: the participant decision-making process; internal or psychological factors; external or sociological factors; and situational variables. The participant decision-making process is the central focus of the model of participant consumption behavior. It explains how consumers make decisions about whether to participate in sports and in which sports to participate. The decision-making process is slightly different for each of us and is influenced by a host of factors. However, the basis of the decision-making process is a five-step procedure that consumers progress through as they make decisions. These five steps include problem recognition, information search, evaluation of alternatives, participation, and post-participation evaluation. The complexity of this process is highly dependent on how important the decision is to participants and how much experience consumers have had making similar decisions.

The internal or psychological factors are those things that influence our decision-making process. These psychological factors include personality, motivation, perception, learning, and attitudes. Personality is a set of consistent responses we make to our environment. Our personality can play a role in which sports we choose to participate in or whether or not we participate in any sports. For example, an aggressive personality type may be most likely to participate in boxing or hockey. Motivation is the reason that we participate in sports. Some of the more common reasons that we participate in sports are for personal improvement, appreciation of sport, and/or social facilitation. The strength of our motives to participate in sports is referred to as sport involvement. Another important psychological factor that influences our participation decisions is perception. Perception influences our image of the various sports and their participants, as well as shapes our attitudes towards sports participation. Learning also impacts our participant behavior. We learn whether or not to participate in sports because we are rewarded or punished by our participation (behavioral theories), because we perceive sports as a way to achieve our goals (cognitive theories), and/or because we watch others participating (social theories). A final internal or psychological factor that directly influences our sports participation decisions is attitudes. Attitudes are defined as learned thoughts, feelings, and behaviors towards some given object (in this case, sports participation). Our feelings (affective component of attitude) and beliefs (cognitive component) about sports participation certainly play a major role in determining our participation (behavioral component).

The external/sociological factors also influence the participant decision-making process. These factors include culture, social class, reference groups, and family. Culture is defined as the learned values, beliefs, language, traditions, and symbols shared by people and passed down from generation to generation. The values held by people within a society are a most important determinant of culture. Some of the core American values that influence participation in sports include achievement and success, activity, individualism, youthfulness, and fitness and health. Social class is another important determinant of participant decision making. Most people erro-

neously associate social class only with income. Our social class is also determined by occupation, education, and affiliations. Another important sociological factor is the influence of reference groups. Reference groups are individuals who influence the information, attitudes, and behaviors of other group members. For example, our friends may impact our decision to participate in a variety of recreational sports and activities. One reference group that has a great deal of influence over our attitudes and participation behavior is our family.

The final component of the model of participant behavior is situational factors. Every decision that we make to participate in a given activity has a situational component. In other words, we are always making a decision in the context of some unique situation. Five major situational influences that impact participant decision making include physical surroundings (physical environment), social surroundings (interaction with others), time (presence or absence of time), task definition (reason or occasion for participation) and antecedent states (physiological condition or mood prior to participation).

KEY TERMS & CONCEPTS

affective component	information search	reference groups
attitudes	learning	secondary reference groups
behavioral component	limited problem solving	selective attention
behavioral learning	Maslow's hierarchy of needs	selective interpretation
cognitive component	motivation	selective retention
cognitive learning	participant consumption behavior	simplified model of participant behavior
consumer socialization		
culture	perception	situational factors
decision-making process	personality	social class
evaluation of alternatives	post-participation evaluation	social learning
extensive problem solving	primary reference groups	socializing agents
family influence	problem recognition	sociological/external factors
habitual problem solving	psychological/internal factors	sports involvement

1. Define participant consumption behavior. What questions does this address with respect to consumers of sport? From a marketing strategy perspective, why is it critical to understand consumer behavior?

2. Outline the components of the simplified model of participant consumer behavior?

3. Outline the steps in the decision-making process for sports participation. What are the three types/levels of consumer decision making? How do the steps in the decision-making process differ for routine decisions versus extensive decisions?

4. Define personality. Why is it considered one of the internal factors of consumption behavior? Do you think personality is related to the decision to participate in sports? Do you think personality is linked to the specific sports we choose to play?

5. Describe Maslow's Hierarchy of Needs. How is Maslow's theory linked to sports marketing?

6. What is meant by the term *sports involvement* from the perspective of sports participants? How is sports involvement measured and used in the development of the strategic marketing process?

7. Define perception and provide three examples of how the perceptual processes apply to sports marketing.

8. Describe the three major learning theories. Which learning theory do you feel best explains the sports in which we choose to participate? Why is learning theory important to sports marketers?

9. Describe the three components of attitude. How do these components work together? Why must attitudes be measured to increase sports participation?

10. Define culture and explain the process of sports socialization. Describe the core American values.

11. Define social class and explain the characteristics of individuals at each level of the seven-tiered structure.

12. Explain how reference groups play a role in sports participation.

13. Discuss the traditional family structure and then the nontraditional family structures. How do today's nontraditional families influence sports participation? Is this for the better or worse?

14. Explain each of the five situational factors that influence the participant decision-making process.

1. Trace the simplified model of participant behavior for a consumer thinking about joining a health club. Briefly comment on each element of the model.

2. Ask three males and three females about the benefits they seek when participating in sports. What conclusions can you draw regarding motivation? Does there seem to be large gender differences in the benefits sought?

3. Interview five adult sports participants and ask them to describe the sports socialization process as it relates to their personal experience. Attempt to interview people with different sports interests to determine whether the socialization process differs according to the specific sports.

4. Watch three advertisements for any sporting goods on television. Briefly describe the advertisement and then suggest which core American value(s) are reflected in the theme of the advertisement.

5. Develop a survey instrument to measure attitudes towards jogging. Have ten people complete the survey and then report your findings. How could these findings be used by your local running club to increase membership (suggest specific strategies)? Are attitudes and behaviors related?

6. Interview five children (between the ages of 8 and 12) to determine what role the family and other reference group influences have had on their decision to participate in sports. Suggest promotions for children based on your findings.

7. Prepare a report that describes how time pressures are influencing sports participation in the United States. How are sports marketers responding to increasing time pressures?

INTERNET EXERCISES

1. Using the World Wide Web, prepare a report that examines sport participation in Australia. What are the similarities and differences in the sports culture of Australia versus the United States?

2. Find and describe two sports Web sites that specifically appeal to children. How does this information relate to the process of consumer socialization?

3. Find and describe a Web site for a health club. How does the information relate to the consumer decision-making process to join the club?

NOTES

1. Del Hawkings, Roger Best, and Kenneth Coney, *Consumer Behavior: Building Marketing Strategy*, 7th ed. (New York, NY: McGraw-Hill, 1998).

2. Ian P. Murphy, "Bowling Industry Rolls Out Unified Marketing Plan," *Marketing News*, January 20, 1997, 2.

3. Hawkings, Best, and Coney.

4. R.B. Cattell, H.W. Eber, and M.M. Tasuoka, *Handbook for the Sixteen Personality Factors Questionnaire* (Champaign, IL: Institute for Personality and Ability Testing, 1970).

5. Douglas M. Turco, "The X Factor: Marketing Sport to Generation X," *Sport Marketing Quarterly*, vol. 5, no. 1: 21–23.

6. Terry Lefton and Bernhard Warner, "Alt-Sportspeak: A Flatliner's Guide," *Brandweek*, January 27, 1997, 25–27.

7. H. Murray, *Exploration in Personality: A*

Clinical and Experimental Study of Fifty Men of College Age, (New York: Oxford University Press, 1938).

8. "You Can Buy a Thrill: Chasing the Ultimate Rush." <http://www.demographics.com/publications/ad/97_ad/9706_ad/ad970631.htm>.

9. Fred M. Beasley and Matthew D. Shank, "Fan or Fanatic: Refining a Measure of Sports Involvement," *Journal of Sport Behavior*, in press.

10. Ronald Paul Hill and Harold Robinson, "Fanatic Consumer Behavior: Athletics as a Consumption Experience," *Psychology & Marketing*, vol. 8, no. 2 (summer 1991): 79–99.

11. Beasley and Shank, in press.

12. Robert Sekular and Randolph Blake, *Perception*, 2nd ed., (New York, NY: McGraw-Hill, 1990).

13. John Kim, Jeen-Su Lim and Mukesh Bhargava, "The Role of Affect in Attitude Formation: A Classical Conditioning Approach," *Journal of the Accademy of Marketing Science*, vol. 26, no. 2 (1998): 143–152.

14. Harry Edwards. *The Sociology of Sport* (Dorsey Press: Homeword, IL, 1973).

15. Elizabeth Moore-Shay and Britts Berchmans, "The Role of the Family Environment in the Development of Shared Consumption Values: An Intergenerational Study" *Advances in Consumer Research*, vol. 2. Kim Corfman and John G. Lunch, Jr., eds. (Provo, VT: Association for Consumer Research, 1996) 484–490.

16. Howard Schlossberg. *Sports Marketing* (Cambridge, MA: Blackwell Publishers, 1996), 152.

17. "Something to Wish For: Time to Relax," *US News and World Report*, November 11, 1996, 17.

18. Diane Crispell. "Targeting Hunters." *American Demographics*. <http://www.demographics.com/publications/ad/94_ad/9401_ad/ad508.htm>.

19. Russel Belk, "Situational Variables and Consumer Behavior," *Journal of Consumer Research* (December 1975): 157–163.

Understanding Spectators As Consumers

After completing this chapter, you should be able to

- Understand the similarities and differences between spectator and participant markets

- Describe the eight basic fan motivation factors

- Explain how game attractiveness, economic factors and competitive factors relate to game attendance

- Describe the demographic profile of spectators and explain the changing role of women as spectators

- Understand the relationship between stadium factors and game attendance

- Discuss the components of the sportscape model

- Describe the multiple values of sport to the community

- Explain sport involvement from a spectator's perspective

- Discuss the model of fan identification

■ Some of the most enthusiastic spectators in the world are soccer fans.

In the previous chapter we examined participants as consumers. This chapter examines another group of consumers of great importance to sports marketers—spectators. Before we turn to our discussion of spectator consumption, two key points need to be addressed. First, the model of participant consumption behavior discussed in the previous chapter can also be applied to spectator consumption. Think for a moment about your decision to attend sporting events. Certainly, there are sociological factors that influence your decision. For instance, reference groups such as friends and family may have played a major role in influencing your decision to attend sporting events. Psychological factors, such as personality, perception, and attitudes, also impact your decision to attend sporting events. For example, the more ambitious and aspiring you are, the more likely you may be to attend sporting events. In addition, situational factors can affect your decision to attend sporting events. Maybe you were given tickets to the game as a birthday gift (e.g., task definition).

As you can see, the factors that influence participant decision making are also applicable to spectator decisions. However, the focus of this chapter is to understand why people attend sporting events and to examine what additional factors relate to game attendance. Rather than using the framework for participant consumption behavior, however, we will concentrate on the wants and needs of spectators. Understanding the consumer's needs and wants, in turn, is important when developing an effective marketing mix for spectators.

The second key point addresses the basis for considering spectators and participants as two separate markets. Many people who watch and attend sporting events also participate in sports, and vice versa. For example, you may watch March Madness and also play basketball on a recreational basis. Research has shown, however, that two different consumer segments exist.[1] In fact, marketing to "either participants or spectators would miss a large proportion of the other group." Let us look at Figure 6.1 to illustrate the differences between spectators and participants.

Each of the diagrams in Figure 6.1 depicts the potential relationship between spectator and consumer markets for golf, basketball, NASCAR, and running. Golf

figure 6.1

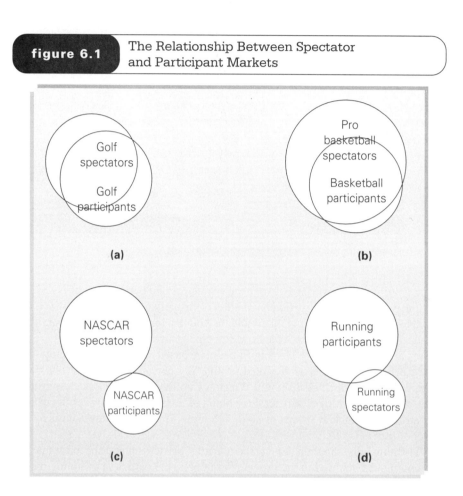

figure 6.1 The Relationship Between Spectator and Participant Markets

(a)

(b)

(c)

(d)

represents a sport where there is large crossover between participants and spectators. A study conducted by Milne, Sutton, and MacDonald supports this notion, finding that 84 percent of the golf participant market overlaps the golf spectator market.[2] In another study, it was found that 87.3 percent of the spectators in attendance at an LPGA event also participated in golf.[3]

A similar pattern is shown for basketball. The results of the study indicated an 81 percent overlap between basketball participation and watching pro basketball. Surprisingly, this same relationship did not exist for college basketball spectators. In that case, the overlap in the participation market and the college basketball spectator market was only 43 percent. The study also found that there was only a 36 percent overlap between spectators of professional basketball and spectators of college basketball—evidence that there are not only differences in spectators and participants, but among spectators at different levels of the same sport.[4]

The other two sports shown in Figure 6.1, NASCAR racing and running, demonstrate more extreme differences in the spectator and participant markets.

■ There is no overlap in the spectator and participant market for bull fighting.

There is virtually no overlap between the spectators and participants of NASCAR. Obviously, the NASCAR participant market is virtually nonexistent. However, new "fantasy camps" are springing up around the country for spectators who want to try racing. For example, at the Atlanta Motor Speedway, participants can enroll in classes at the Richard Petty Driving Experience based on their driving know-how. The "Rookie Experience" is designed for the "lay-person who has a strong desire to experience the thrill of driving a Winston Cup race car." For prices starting at $329.99, the rookie driver will get three hours of instruction, which results in eight laps around the track at speeds of up to 145 mph. The only requirement is a valid driver's license.[5]

The remaining diagram depicts the potential participant and spectator markets for running. As opposed to the previous examples, the participant running market is much larger than the spectator running market. In addition to the size of the markets, there are also differences in motivations for spectators and participants. Participants, for instance, may be motivated to run for reasons of personal improvement. On the other hand, spectators are likely to watch to provide support to a family member or friend.

In addition to looking at the overlap (or lack thereof) between participants and spectators on a sport-by-sport basis, other research has explored the differences between these two groups for sports in general. Table 6.1 summarizes the findings of a study conducted by Burnett, Menon, and Smart, which examined spectator and participant socioeconomic characteristics and media habits. Based on the results of this and other studies, it seems that sports participants and sports spectators represent two distinct markets that should be examined separately by sports marketers.

Before we explore spectators in greater detail, it is important to note that this market can be differentiated into two groups on the basis of consumer behavior. The first group consists of spectators who attend the sporting event. The second group of

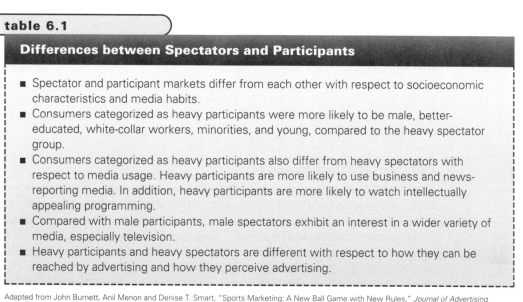

table 6.1

Differences between Spectators and Participants

- Spectator and participant markets differ from each other with respect to socioeconomic characteristics and media habits.
- Consumers categorized as heavy participants were more likely to be male, better-educated, white-collar workers, minorities, and young, compared to the heavy spectator group.
- Consumers categorized as heavy participants also differ from heavy spectators with respect to media usage. Heavy participants are more likely to use business and news-reporting media. In addition, heavy participants are more likely to watch intellectually appealing programming.
- Compared with male participants, male spectators exhibit an interest in a wider variety of media, especially television.
- Heavy participants and heavy spectators are different with respect to how they can be reached by advertising and how they perceive advertising.

Adapted from John Burnett, Anil Menon and Denise T. Smart, "Sports Marketing: A New Ball Game with New Rules," *Journal of Advertising Research* (September/October 1993): 21–33.

spectators consumes the sporting event through some medium (e.g., television, radio, Internet). This chapter is primarily concerned with understanding why consumers attend sporting events and what factors influence attendance. Let us begin by looking at some of the major factors that influence the decision to attend sporting events rather than watch them from the comfort of our homes.

Factors Influencing Attendance

It is opening day in Cleveland and the hometown Indians are set to take on the New York Yankees. Fred has gone to the traditional opening day parade and then attended the ball game for the past five years. The game promises to be a great one as the Indians are returning from last year's winning season and playing the rival Yankees. Fred will be joined at the game by his eight-year-old son and a potential business client.

As the hypothetical scenario illustrates, there are a variety of factors influencing Fred's decision to attend the season opener. He wants to experience the new stadium and watch the team that he has identified with since his childhood. As a businessman, Fred views the game as an opportunity to build a relationship with a potential client. As a father, Fred views the game as a way to bond with his son. In addition to these factors, Fred is prone to gambling and has placed a $50 bet on the home team. Finally, Fred thinks of opening day as an entertaining event that brings the whole community together and, as a lifelong resident, he wants to feel that sense of belonging.

Certainly, the interaction of the factors mentioned impacted Fred's decision to attend the game. Sports marketers must attempt to understand all of the influences on game attendance in order to market effectively to Fred and other fans like him. A variety of studies have examined some of the major issues related to game attendance, including fan motivation determinants, game attractiveness, economic factors, competitive factors, demographic factors, stadium factors, value of sport to the community, sports involvement, and fan identification. Let us explore each of these factors in greater detail.

Fan Motivation Factors

The foundation of any strategic sports marketing process is understanding why spectators attend sporting events. The basic motives for watching sports are categorized as self-esteem enhancement, diversion from everyday life, entertainment value, eustress, economic value, aesthetic value, need for affiliation, and family ties. It is important to note that these fundamental motives represent the most basic needs of fans. Because of this, the eight motives are often related to other factors that will be discussed later in the chapter such as sports involvement and fan identification. Let us now examine the eight underlying motives of fans identified in a study conducted by Wann.[6]

- **Self-Esteem Enhancement.** Fans are rewarded with feelings of accomplishment when their favorite players or teams are winning. More commonly called "fair weather fans," association with the team is likely to increase when the team is winning and decrease when the team is doing poorly.

    The phenomenon of enhancing or maintaining self-esteem through associating with winning teams has been called BIRGing, or basking in reflected glory.[7] When BIRGing, spectators are motivated by a desire to associate with a winner and thus present themselves in a positive light and enhance self-esteem. Likewise, spectators who dissociate themselves from losing teams because they negatively impact self-esteem accomplish this through CORFing, or cutting off reflected failure.

- **Diversion from Everyday Life.** Watching sports is seen as a means of getting away from it all. Most people think of sports as a novel diversion from the normal routines of everyday life.

- **Entertainment Value.** Closely related to the previous motive for attendance, sports serve as a form of entertainment to millions of people. As discussed in previous chapters, sports marketers are keenly aware of the heightened entertainment value of sports. In fact, one of the unique aspects of attending a sporting event is the uncertainty associated with the outcome. The drama associated with this uncertainty adds to the entertainment value of sports. Among spectators, the entertainment value of sports is thought to be the most highly motivating of all factors.

DAVID STERN

The Commissioner of the NBA since 1984, David Stern has earned his place in sports marketing history. Stern is currently called the best commissioner in sport, the best in NBA history, and perhaps the best of any sport, ever. Prior to Stern, the NBA had a shaky network reputation, plummeting attendance figures, and no television contract.

During his tenure as commissioner, Stern took a floundering NBA and turned it "into an entity that is the envy of professional sports—an innovative, multifaceted, billion-dollar global marketing and entertainment company whose future literally knows no bounds." Stern has redefined the NBA and focused his marketing efforts on licensing, special events, and home entertainment. The league has gone from the arena business to radio, television, concessions, licensing, real estate, and home video—all under Stern's leadership. When the NBA was experiencing a public relations nightmare because of the number of players believed to be on drugs, it was again Stern who cleaned up the mess.

The All-Star Weekend, the made-for-television NBA lottery, making basketball the most popular sport in America with kids, and marketing the NBA across the world are all part of the sports marketing legacy that is David Stern.

Adapted from E.M. Swift, "Corned Beef to Cavier," *Sports Illustrated*, June 3, 1991, 74–87.

A number of professional sports are attempting to find interesting and innovative ways to increase their entertainment value for the fans. John Madden, current Fox analyst and former Oakland Raider head coach, suggested that the NFL adopt his "fair-play game plan" which features the following: more protection for the quarterback; a quicker instant replay system; full-time and younger officials; more seasons before free agency; and more "event" promotion of games.[8] Baseball's new commissioner, Bud Selig, is trying to address the speed of play and has shaved an average of six minutes off each game in the 1998 season. In addition, Selig is considering more realignment of teams to increase fan interest and enthusiasm for the game.[9] Tennis, also suffering at the gate, has not seen any rule changes or major innovations since the addition of the break in the early 1970s. David Higedon, a tennis writer, has suggested that the entertainment value of tennis would be greatly improved by implementing some of the following ideas: allow only three second serves per game, stop quieting the crowds, eliminate five set matches, and shorten the season.[10] Even track and field marketers have considered shortening meets and changing the way the events are run (e.g., limit the shot put to one throw instead of six).[11]

■ **Eustress.** Sports provide fans with positive levels of arousal. In other words, sports are enjoyable because they stimulate fans and are exciting to the senses. For example, imagine the excitement felt by Indy fans when the announcer says,

■ Las Vegas: The capital of sports betting.

"Gentlemen, start your engines" or the anticipation surrounding the opening kick-off for fans at the Super Bowl.

■ **Economic Value.** A subset of sports fans are motivated by the potential economic gains associated with gambling on sporting events (see box). Their enjoyment stems from having a vested interest in the games as they watch. Because this motive is only present for a small group of spectators, the economic factor is the least motivating of all factors. However, the number of spectators that are gambling on sports continues to rise, especially among college students.

■ Sports betting on the rise at college campuses across the country.

The game was long over, but the action was just beginning. J.A. Davis, a 23-year-old Texas Tech senior, fought against the flow of departing fans as he weaved down the concrete aisles of Jones Stadium in Lubbock. He was in search of a better seat to catch the closing minutes of the Red Raiders' made-for-ESPN Thursday night football game against Nebraska. It didn't matter to Davis that Tech was already soundly beaten—the team trailed 35–16 with barely two minutes left to play—or that Nebraska had the ball. In his world, wins and losses are secondary to point spreads and over-unders, and on this day Davis had bet on the Cornhuskers, giving 25 points.

"Two hundred bucks I had riding on the game," recalls Davis. "Lots of people had Nebraska, giving 27, 28 points—you never bet on Texas Tech—but I got in with my bookie at 25." Nebraska, with third-and-one on the Tech 30, the clock running, Davis, dying the slow, hopeless death of a gambler longing for points from a team that doesn't need any. "I'm thinking, 'This can't be happening,'" says Davis. "I'm going to lose 200 bucks, 220 with the juice (i.e., the vigorish, the bookie's 10 percent commission on losing bets), and be down going into the weekend." Then a bettor's miracle occurred: The Huskers scored a trash touchdown, pushing the margin to 26, covering the spread and making Davis into a winner.

Meet the Juice Generation. For them, finance isn't a major, it's knowing how to spread $1,000 in wagers over 10 Saturday college football games and stay alive for Sunday's and Monday's NFL bets with a zero balance in their checkbook and their credit cards maxed out. Class participation is sitting in the back of a lecture hall with Vegas-style spreadsheets laid out, plotting a week's worth of plays on games from Seattle to Miami.

There is nothing in the collegiate rite of passage handbook about gambling. There are chapters on alcohol, drugs, and sex, but noth-ing about gambling. It's the dirty little secret of college life and is rampant and thriving in America. The outbreak may seem inconsequential, considering that legalized gambling is a growth industry in the United States. However, most of the gambling done on college campuses is illegal.

Studies done on campus gambling are scarce. In 1991, a study was conducted by Henry Lesieur, chair of the criminal justice department at Illinois State University, among college students at six universities in five states. His study concludes that 23 percent of college students gambled at least once a week.

The profile of the typical gambler is that there is no such thing as the typical gambler. Students from wealthy to modest backgrounds alike have thrown themselves into gambling. Some of the common characteristics include a degree of sports-obsessiveness (often an athletic past cut short by lack of talent); mostly male; a community in which to share betting tales (e.g., frat house); and usually higher levels of intelligence.

In addition, the sports betting behavior mirrors those of the adult public; NFL football is the most popular, followed by college football, college basketball, and the NBA. One exception is March Madness, the NCAA basketball tournament that rivals the NFL in wagering frequency.

Unfortunately for many college students, gambling is seen as a hobby rather than a problem. "We're working with the first generation that has been raised when gambling has been seen as a positive thing," says Roger Svendsen, director of the Minnesota Compulsive Gambling Hotline. "Instead of talking about gambling, we talk about gaming."

Says Lesieur, the gambling researcher, "What you have now, among college students, is a group of individuals who have no recollection of the time when gambling was outlawed. Gambling is simply around now. It's closer than ever before, and it's continuing to get closer."

- **Aesthetic Value.** Sports are seen by many as a pure art form. Basketball games have been compared to ballets, and many fans derive great pleasure from the beauty of athletic performances (e.g., gymnastics and figure skating).
- **Need for Affiliation.** The need for belonging is satisfied by being a fan. Research has shown that reference groups, such as friends, family, and the community, influence game attendance. The more an individual's reference group favors going to a game, the more likely they are to attend games in the future. In addition to influencing game attendance, one study found that reference groups can also impact other game-related experiences, such as perceived quality of the stadium, perceived quality of the food service, overall satisfaction with the stadium, and perceived ticket value. For instance, individuals who perceive their reference group as opposing going to games will also have less satisfaction with the stadium environment.
- **Family Ties.** Some sports spectators feel that attending sporting events is a means for fostering family togetherness. The entire family can spend time together and lines of communication may be opened through sports. Interestingly, women are more motivated than men to attend sporting events in order to promote family togetherness.[12]

Game Attractiveness

Another factor related to game attendance is the perceived attractiveness of each game. Game attractiveness is a situational factor that varies from game to game and week to week. The perceived quality of a single game or event is based on the skill level of the individuals participating in the contest (i.e., the presence of any star athletes), team records, and league standings. In addition to these game attraction variables, if the game is a special event (opening day, bowl game, all-star game), game attractiveness is heightened. The more attractive the game, the more likely attendance will increase.

Economic Factors

Both the controllable and uncontrollable economic factors can impact game attendance. The controllable economic factors include aspects of the sports marketing environment that can be altered by sports marketers, such as the price of tickets and the perceived value of the sports product. The uncontrollable economic factors are things such as the average income of the population and the economic health of the country.

Generally, the greater the perceived value of the game and the greater the income of the population, the greater the game attendance. Surprisingly, one study found that attendance has no relationship with increased ticket prices.[13] In other words, raising ticket prices does not negatively affect game attendance. Other researchers, however, have found just the opposite.[14]

Sports teams pay a high price in fan loyalty every time a player leaves to join another team, according to research by economics professors Steve Shmanske and Leo Kahane.[15] Their analysis of baseball rosters and financial data for major league teams in 1990–1992 shows that owners who trade players frequently to get a winning team may end up hurting their revenues instead.

Winning teams do attract fans. Each additional percentage point in a major league team's winning percentage attracts about 32,000 fans that season and 25,000 fans the next season. But exorbitant player contracts and frequent trades may hurt attendance. A $1 increase in the average price of a MLB ticket decreases attendance by about 180,000. And every time a regular player is traded to another team, attendance decreases. An average player's departure may cost 48,000 ticket sales. When a star leaves, as many as 84,000 tickets may not be sold. Given the average ticket price, the average player may be worth $420,000 to $540,000, and the star player may draw up to $730,000 in ticket sales. Trades are not necessarily bad for the baseball business, say the authors, but frequent trades are a sure way to alienate fans.

Competitive Factors

As discussed in chapter 3, competition for sporting event attendance can be thought of as either direct (other sports) or indirect (other forms of entertainment). Ordinarily, the lesser the competition for spectators' time and money, the more likely they will be to attend your sporting event.

One form of direct competition of interest to sports marketers is the televised game. Sports marketers need to understand spectators' media habits and motivations in order to appeal to this growing segment. In addition, sports marketers want to learn whether to treat the viewing audience as a separate segment or whether it overlaps with spectators who attend games.

Some of these issues were addressed in a series of studies conducted to understand consumers' motivations for watching televised sports. Overall, the excitement, enthusiasm, and entertainment value associated with the telecasts are the primary motivating factors.[16] Interestingly, the need for watching televised sports differed by gender. Women indicated that they were more motivated to watch sports for the social value and the fact that friends and family were already doing so. Men, on the other hand, were motivated to watch sports on television because they enjoy the telecasts and find them entertaining.

With respect to their viewing behavior, men are more interested in watching sports on television, want more sports coverage, watch more sports coverage, and follow it up by watching news reports of the action more frequently than their female counterparts. In short, men appear more highly involved in televised sports.

How does consuming the game via some alternative media like radio or television impact game attendance? One study examined the influence of television and radio broadcasting on the attendance of the NBA games. The results indicated that television broadcasts of home games would have a negative impact on attendance, with over 60 percent of the fans indicating that they would watch the game on television rather than attend. On the other hand, watching televised sports can also have a positive impact on home game attendance. For instance, the more one watches away games on television, the more one attends home games. In addition, the more one listens to the radio (for both home and away games), the greater the likelihood of attending home games.[17]

Demographic Factors

Demographic variables, such as population, age, gender, education, occupation, and ethnic background, are also found to be related to game attendance. Although the number of women attending sporting events is greater than ever before, males are still more likely to be in attendance. In addition, these men tend to be younger, more educated, and have higher incomes than that of the general population.

As you might imagine it is very difficult to come up with *the* profile of the typical sports fan because of the varying nature of sport. However, it is important not to generalize and run the risk of neglecting a potentially huge market (see Spotlight on Women's Sports Marketing).[18]

spotlight on women's sports marketing:

the woman as a spectator of men's sports

Women have been virtually ignored as spectators of men's sports until quite recently. Assuming that only men watch men's sport or only women watch women's sport is naive. Likewise, marketing to only half of the population for men's or women's sport is unjustifiable. Over half of the spectators who attend the Indianapolis 500 are women. The women's market for men's sport is waiting to be tapped. The NBA and NFL have already recognized this potential and have made commitments to develop this market.

Demise of Sexist Attitudes toward Women's Sports Participation

The recent recession and downward economic trends have been the real catalysts that are propelling companies to avidly pursue marketing to women who are active in sports and fitness. In difficult economic times, the sports interests of CEOs and their desire to rub elbows with celebrity male athletes are coming in second place to hard data on consumer interest and potential. Continuing to ignore the women's market—women as sports and fitness participants, spectators of men's sports, and male and female spectators of women's

sport—is bad business. Thus, simple economic necessity is forcing business to override its past prejudices, which have successfully limited and devalued the women's sports market.

We must also recognize that the parents of today are the first generation of mothers and fathers who expect that their daughters are guaranteed equal opportunity in everything from sport to business. These parents are supporting and encouraging their daughters' participation. As older generations disappear, grassroots support of girls and women playing sports will only increase the number of women who become involved in sport at earlier and earlier ages.

Spectators of Women's Sports

Both college- and professional-level men's sports have catered to males hooked on sports and willing to spend considerable money for good seats and parking. Corporations have paid many of these bills and written them off in the name of customer entertainment. However, ticket prices can only escalate so fast and arenas and stadia are only so large. Again, in the case of the male spectator, we have oversaturated the market. In big-time college sport and professional sport we have also priced families out of the picture. Athletes have often engaged in conduct unbecoming role models. This upward cost spiral coupled with the public perception of elite athletes as spoiled, selfish, and lawless has created a vacuum in its wake. Women's sports and, in many cases amateur and minor league men's professional sports, can be very inviting to families and men and women with more discriminating values who are ready to reassess their entertainment choices.

We must also recognize that women's sport is a new and different product. Men's basketball and women's basketball are two different products. The former is a contact sport and power game often played above the rim. The latter is more technically akin to baseball with regard to strategy and precision. These different games appeal to different spectators.

A look at the University of Texas, which has the first women's basketball program to demonstrate the presence of this new market for women's sport, illustrates the potential of this new market. Texas women's basketball was second in total basketball attendance in the Southwest Conference for many years—second only to the Arkansas men's team! The Lady Longhorns averaged 6,000 to 8,000 spectators a game and sold 5,000 to 6,000 season tickets at prices ranging from $60 to $70 each. Between sponsorships, advertising, and ticket sales, they bring in over $1 million a year.

Research on attendees of women's basketball games at the University of Texas showed that the most likely attendee who also watches men's athletic events is the baseball fan and not the men's football or basketball fan. In fact, there was less than a 5 percent overlap between those who purchased tickets and made contributions to men's sports and those who did the same for women's sports.

Research also showed that the majority of people who watched womens' sports were either young professionals with daughters or older, retired persons with high levels of disposable income. These spectators responded to a diversified value presentation that included quality sport, exemplary graduation rates, high standards of ethical conduct, and articulate young athletes who made contributions to their communities. These latter values were used to market the product and were extremely well received. If you asked Joe Q. Public about the Lady Longhorns, you would always get a response that included "great team, great kids, and they graduate too."

It is therefore reasonable to conclude that the possible recipient of this backlash against elite athlete greed and high prices for men's sports can be women's sports, if we have knowledgeable marketers who know how to position this new product to a different audience. Marketers need to recognize that the men's collegiate sport product has been sold with a narrow focus on winning potential. When a product lives or dies on the presence of one variable, it is a very dangerous way to do business. At the very least, men's and women's sport must structure their product presentation to appeal to a more diverse set of values: winning; 100 percent effort; fast, exciting, players who are serious students; articulate and talented young athletes; athletes who give back to their communities; and an honest athletic program.

Women's sports are in an ideal position to take advantage of this opportunity. These spectators appear to be different from men's sports spectators. Women's sports have not yet been tainted by the men's sport model value system. There should not be a problem positioning women's sports to demonstrate a commitment to diverse and positive values. There is a new and untapped women's sport market waiting to be exploited.

Source: Donna Lopiano. "Marketing Trends in Women's Sports and Fitness." Women's Sports Foundation. <http://www.lifetimetv.com/search/frameset.shtml/>. Courtesy of Women's Sports Foundation.

Stadium Factors

New stadiums are being built all around the country. Moreover, team owners who cannot justify or afford new stadiums are moving to cities that will build a new facility or attempt to renovate the existing stadium. Obviously, these stadium improvements are thought to impact the bottom line for team owners.

Stadium factors refer to variables such as the newness of the stadium, stadium access, aesthetics or beauty of the stadium, seat comfort, and cleanliness of the stadium. One study found that all of these factors are positively related to game attendance. That is, the more favorable the fans attitude towards the stadium, the higher the attendance.[19]

Similar results were found in study a conducted for *Money* magazine by IRC Survey Research Group.[20] This study looked at what 1,000 sports fans value when attending professional sporting events. The major findings, in order of importance, are

- Projected to be completed for Fall season 1999
- Will seat approximately 67,000
- Will have approximately 7,500 Parking Spaces
- Will have 140 Luxury Suites
- Will have 9,600 Club Seats with access to state-of-the-art club lounges on both sides of the stadium
- Situated on the east bank of the Cumberland River
- Open air stadium with natural grass field
- Includes finest amenities available in modern NFL stadium ranging from lockerrooms to upper concourse concession and novelty stands

- Financed in part through Permanent Seat Licenses, limited number of PSL's still available — call **1-888-PSL-SEAT.**
- Oilers will share the stadium with the Tennessee State University Tigers
- Stadium will host an annual college ball game "Music City Bowl", which will pit a Southeastern Conference team vs. an at-large opponent
- Gigantic state-of-the-art scoreboards in each end zone
- Stadium is designed to expand to as many as 75,000 seats for selected events

Tennessee's Future State-Of-The-Art Stadium

■ New sports facilities such as Tennessee Stadium influence attendance.

- Parking that costs less than $8 and tickets under $25 each
- Adequate parking or convenient public transportation
- A safe, comfortable seat that you can buy just a week before the game
- Reasonably priced snack foods, such as a hot dog for $2 or less
- Home team with a winning record
- A close score
- A hometown star who is generally regarded as being among the sport's ten best players
- Reasonably priced souvenirs
- A game that ends in less than three hours
- A wide variety of snack foods

Interestingly, the four most important things identified in the study were unrelated to the game itself. If you make people pay too much or work too hard, they would rather stay home. Apparently, only after you are seated in your comfortable chair with your inexpensive food do you begin to worry about rooting for the home team.

In addition, spectators were concerned about having a clean comfortable stadium with a good atmosphere. Part of the positive atmosphere is having strict controls placed on rowdy fans and having the option of sitting in a nonalcohol section of the stadium. An emerging area of some importance to new stadium design, as well as to stadium rehabilitation, is the need to provide more and larger restrooms. Because stadium atmosphere seems to be so important to fans, let us examine it in greater detail.

Sportscape

As you might have noticed, stadium atmosphere appears to be a critical issue in game attendance. Recently, studies have been conducted in the area of stadium environment or "sportscape."[21] **Sportscape** refers to the physical surroundings of the stadium that impact spectators' desire to stay at the stadium and ultimately return to the stadium. Figure 6.2 shows the relationship between these sportscape factors and spectator behavior.

As shown in Figure 6.2, sportscape factors include stadium access, facility aesthetics, scoreboard quality, seating comfort, and layout accessibility. Each of the sportscape factors serve as inputs to the spectator's affective response or judgment of pleasure or displeasure with the stadium. The affective response, as we learned in the previous chapter, is the "feeling" component of attitudes. Similarly, the affective response with the sportscape is the feeling of perceived pleasure or displeasure the spectator has with the stadium. The perceptions of the stadium sportscape are linked to behavioral responses or actions of the spectator. In this case, the two behavioral responses are the desire to stay in the stadium and repatronage, or returning to the stadium for future events. Let us further examine the sportscape factors and their impact on spectators' pleasure.

Stadium Accessibility   Many of us have left sporting events early to avoid traffic hassles or walked long distances to get to a game because of limited parking. For example, I recently attended a game at Wrigley Field in Chicago and, because of limited

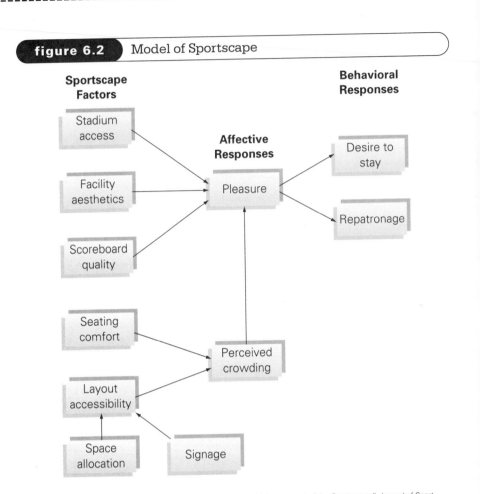

figure 6.2 Model of Sportscape

Sportscape Factors

Behavioral Responses

Stadium access

Facility aesthetics

Scoreboard quality

Seating comfort

Layout accessibility

Space allocation

Signage

Affective Responses

Pleasure

Perceived crowding

Desire to stay

Repatronage

Source: K.L. Wakefield, J.G. Bridgett, H.J. Sloan, "Measurement and Management of the Sportscape," *Journal of Sport Management*, vol. 10, no. 1 (1996): 16.

parking spaces, had to walk over three miles to get to the game. By the time I reached my seat, it was the third inning! This experience certainly resulted in displeasure with the entire game experience.

Stadium accessibility includes issues such as availability of parking, the ease of entering and exiting the parking areas, and the location of the parking relative to the stadium. From the spectator's perspective, anything that can make it easier to get in and out of the stadium quicker will positively impact a return for future games.

Facility Aesthetics Facility aesthetics refers to the interior and exterior appearance of the stadium. The exterior appearance includes stadium architecture and age of the stadium. New stadiums, with historic architectural designs, are springing up all over the country. Research has shown that newer stadia do increase game attendance.

The interior of the stadium includes factors such as color of the stadium walls, facades and seats, the presence of sponsors signage, and the presence of symbols from the team's past. For example, Cinergy Field in Cincinnati had no visible evidence of the team's history and legacy until recently, when three jerseys (Johnny Bench's, Fred Hutchinson's, and Joe Morgan's) were retired and displayed on the left field wall. It was, perhaps, the most sterile stadium in the country, and fans certainly expressed their displeasure. Compare this with Fenway Park in Boston, one of the oldest and most unique stadiums in the country. As former pitcher Bill Lee stated, "Fenway Park is a religious shrine. People go there to worship."

customers come first in latest stadium designs

As sightliness continues to improve and more amenities are added, it appears that stadium designers are focusing more attention than ever on customer satisfaction. In terms of facility design, the demand for club seats in stadiums continues to increase, following a path set by luxury suites a decade ago.

Clearly, the emphasis is on making stadiums more user-friendly. "There are more services for spectators and greater concentration on sightliness and intimacy now than in stadiums built in the 1960s and 1970s," said Don Dethlefs, a principal with Sink Combs Dethlefs of Denver.

In many ways, stadia of the present and future are being built with a clear eye on the past. The Ballpark at Arlington (Texas), Jacobs Field (Cleveland), and Oriole Park at Camden Yards (Baltimore) are all examples of modern-day stadia that offer services of today with the intimacy of an older facility. "A good example of that trend is a new minor league baseball park we're working on in Fargo, North Dakota," said Dethlefs. "To some extent, they want to model the park after Yankee Stadium. They're trying to recall a past closeness to the action."

Getting people close to the action is becoming more of a priority. "One way baseball parks accomplish this is with an uneven outfield, where they had been designed totally even and symmetrical," said Dethlefs. "A lot of

the sidelines at football stadiums are being reduced, as is the area around the foul line at baseball parks."

Helen Maib, an architect with HOK Sports Facilities Group in Kansas City, Missouri, sees a trend toward an increasing number of club seats in stadiums. "The market for luxury suites seems to have topped off somewhat; we don't think we'll see a higher number of luxury suites, percentage-wise," Maib said. "But there still seems to be a growing trend in the number of club seats."

Maib thinks the club seat factor may have economic roots. "A corporation may go in and buy four club seats, but it may be beyond their means to go in and buy a 12- to 14-seat luxury suite," she said. "Club seats offer the same amenities in terms of up-scale lounge space, and they're more flexible for the buyer to purchase the amount of seating they want."

An example of the club-seat trend is the new HOK-designed stadium for the Tampa Bay Buccaneers of the NFL, which will feature 10,000 club seats, far more than their current home at Tampa Stadium.

Dethlefs does not think the suite market has topped off, at least in what they offer. "We're seeing increased services, both in number and in how elaborate they are," he said. "The standard is going up all the time, both in suite size and amenities."

(continued)

Ray Ashe, an architect with Atlanta-based Rosser International, agrees. "Luxury boxes continue to be a hot item, both as a revenue producer and as prestige for the fan. ... A stadium club is always a plus, as is any type of priority seating, whether it is enclosed, covered, or anything else that would enhance the seat."

Spectators as a whole are demanding more amenities, Dethlefs noted. "We're seeing more concession points of sale, more choices on the menu, more portable carts and grills. ... There is a lot of money to be made from concessions if they are done well, and that aspect is becoming more of a focus in stadium design."

Permanent seat licenses, used in the financing of new NFL stadiums in Charlotte, North Carolina; Tampa, Florida; and St. Louis, Missouri are increasingly becoming a factor. "We're seeing PSLs everywhere from the NFL down to AAA minor league baseball parks being used with a lot of success," Maib said. "PSLs are being used to finance stadiums much as luxury suites and club seating has been used in the past."

Ashe is seeing more focus on creature comforts, particularly at the collegiate level. "A lot of college stadiums are up-grading their seating from benches to chairs. ... The traditional college stadium seating is wooden or aluminum benches, but that is changing." Another trend Ashe is seeing is the move from artificial turf back to natural grass at college football stadiums, both in new and existing facilities.

Source: Ray Waddell, "Customers Come First in Latest Stadium Designs," *Amusement Business*, July 24–30, 1995, 23.

Scoreboard Quality   One of the specific interior design considerations that represents a separate dimension of sportscape is scoreboard quality. In fact, the scoreboard in some stadiums is seen as the focal point of the interior. Throughout the game, fans continually monitor the stadium scoreboard for updates on scoring, player statistics, and other forms of entertainment, such as trivia contests, cartoon animation, and music videos. Examples of scoreboard quality range from the traditional Fenway Park with its manually operated scoreboard to the University of North Carolina with its recently installed videowalls.

The videowalls measure 16 by 14 feet and are hung at the four corners of the stadium, above the upper seating area. Steve Kirschner, from the UNC Office of Sports, states, "The fans' reaction to the newly installed videowalls was very positive. They loved the opportunity to see a great dunk from a different angle and a lot closer up than they normally would." Kirschner also points to the benefits the videowalls can have for the sports marketer, including the ability to broadcast live pre- and post-game interviews, generating fan excitement and promoting ticket and sponsor information.[22]

Perceived Crowding   As shown in Figure 6.2, seating comfort and layout accessibility are the two factors that were found to be determinants of spectators' perceptions of crowding. Perceived crowding, in turn, is thought to have a negative influence on spectator's pleasure. In other words, spectators' pleasure decreases as perceived crowding increases.

Perceived crowding not only has an impact on pleasure, but also spectator safety. For example, English football grounds are moving away from terraces (standing areas renown for hooliganism and violence) and towards a requirement of all-seater facilities. There has been a great deal of debate about reintroducing terracing. However, based on a report that identified all-seating as the factor that contributes the most to spectator safety, the British government has no plans to bring back terraces at English football grounds.[23]

Seating Comfort   Seating comfort refers to the perceived comfort of the seating and the spacing of seats relative to each other. Anyone who has been forced to sit among the more than 100,000 fans at a University of Michigan football game can understand the influence of seating on the game experience. Likewise, those who have been fortunate enough to view a game from a luxury box also know the impact of seating on enjoyment with the game.

Layout Accessibility   Layout accessibility refers to whether or not spectators can move freely about the stadium. More specifically, does the layout of the stadium make it easy for spectators to get in and out of their seats and reach the concession areas, restrooms, and so on. In order to facilitate access to these destinations, there must be proper signage to direct spectators and there must be adequate space allocated. Inadequate space and signage causes spectators to feel confused and crowded, therefore, leading to negative feelings about the game experience.

As stated previously, all of the sportscape factors impact spectators' feelings about the game experience. These positive or negative feelings experienced by spectators ultimately impact their desire to stay in the stadium and return for other games. Although all of the sportscape factors are important, research has shown that perceived crowding is the most significant predictor of spectators having a pleasurable game experience. In addition, the aesthetic quality of the stadium was found to have a major impact on spectators' pleasure with the game.[24]

The findings of the sportscape research presents several implications for sports marketers and stadium/facilities managers. First, stadium management should consider reallocating or redesigning space to improve perceived crowding. This might include enlarging the seating areas, walkways, and the space in and around concession waiting areas. Second, before spending the money to do major renovations or even building a new stadium to improve aesthetic quality, focus on more inexpensive alternatives. For instance, painting and cleaning alone might significantly improve the aesthetic value of an aging stadium.

The Crown in Cincinnati (formerly the Riverfront Coliseum) is an excellent example of how making renovations to an older facility can be an effective way to improve the sportscape. The $14 million spent on renovating the Crown included redesigning the building's entrance to improve traffic flow and increase the number of ticket windows. Additionally, the entrance will be repainted and retiled. On the interior, the walls were moved both to expand the size of the main concourse and concession areas and to double the number of restrooms. Moreover, all 15,000 seats were replaced. These changes have provided downtown Cincinnati with a first-class facility that spectators feel good about, at a cost much lower than new construction.[25]

Based on the studies conducted by Wakefield and his colleagues, there seems to be no doubt that the stadium atmosphere, or sportscape, plays a pivotal role in spectator satisfaction and attendance. Moreover, the pleasure derived from the sportscape causes people to stay in the stadium for longer periods of time. Certainly, having spectators stay in the stadium is a plus for the team who will profit from increased concession and merchandise sales. In describing the importance of the sportscape, Wakefield states "Effective facility management may enable team owners to effectively compete for consumers' entertainment dollars even when they may be unable to compete on the field."[26]

Value of Sport to the Community

Values, as you will recall, are widely held beliefs that affirm what is desirable. In this case, values refer to the beliefs about the impact of sport on the community. Based on the results of a recent study, spectators' perceptions of the impact of professional sport on a community can be grouped into eight distinct, value dimensions (see Table 6.2 for a brief description of values).

As you might expect, each of these values is related to spectators' game attendance and intentions to attend future games. For instance, spectators who believe sports enhances community solidarity are more likely to attend sporting events. Sports marketers should carefully consider these values and promote positive values when developing marketing strategy.

---

table 6.2

Eight Value Dimensions of Sport to the Community

- **Community Solidarity**—Sport enhances the image of the community, enhances community harmony, generates a sense of belonging, and helps make people feel proud
- **Public Behavior**—Sport encourages sportsmanship, reinforces positive citizenship, encourages obedience to authority, and nurtures positive morality
- **Pastime Ecstasy**—Sport provides entertainment and brings excitement
- **Excellence Pursuit**—Sport encourages achievement and success, encourages hard work, and encourages risk-taking
- **Social Equity**—Sport increases racial equality, promotes gender equity, and increases class equality
- **Health Awareness**—Sport eliminates drug abuse, encourages exercise, and urges an active lifestyle
- **Individual Quality**—Sport promotes character building and encourages competitive trait
- **Business Opportunity**—Sport increases community commercial activities, attracts tourists, and helps community economic development

Source: James J. Zhang, Dale G. Pease, and Sai C. Hui, "Value Dimensions of Professional Sport as Viewed by Spectators," *Sports and Social Issues*, February 21, 1996, 78–94. Reprinted by permission of Sage Publications, Inc.

Sports Involvement

In the previous chapter, involvement was examined in the context of sports participation. Measures of sports involvement have also been used to understand spectator behavior. From the spectators perspective, **sport involvement** is the perceived interest in and personal importance of sports to an individual attending sporting events or consuming sport through some other medium.

For instance, studies have looked at the involvement levels of golf spectators, baseball spectators, Division I women's basketball spectators and sports spectators in general.[27] In addition, a study has examined the cross-cultural differences in sport involvement (see Spotlight). Generally, these studies have shown that higher levels of spectator involvement are related to the number of games attended, the likelihood of attending games in the future, and the likelihood of consuming sport through media, such as newspapers, television, and magazines. Also of importance, high-involvement spectators were more likely to correctly identify the sponsors of sporting events.

spotlight on international sports marketing:

a comparative analysis of spectator involvement: United States vs. United Kingdom

As the field of sports marketing expands into international markets, the success of U.S. sports entities will be dependent on understanding the core consumer abroad—the international sports fan. Recently, a study was conducted to better understand the domestic and U.K. sports fan by measuring sports involvement and by exploring the relationship between sports involvement and sports-related behaviors.

The findings indicated that there are two dimensions of sports involvement that are consistent across the U.S. and U.K sample. The cognitive dimension refers to the way that consumers *think* about sports, and the affective dimension is the way that consumers *feel* about sports. Both the cognitive and affective factors were positively related to viewing sports on television, reading about sports in magazines and newspapers, attending sporting events, and participating in sports. That is, higher levels of involvement are related to

more viewing, reading about, and attending sporting events.

There were some differences in the responses of people from the United States and the United Kingdom. People from the United Kingdom spent less time each week watching sports on television; however, they were more likely to read the sports section of the newspaper on a daily basis. Compared to the U.S. sample, people from the United Kingdom were less interested in local sports teams as opposed to national teams. Finally, the British respondents were more likely than their American counterparts to perceive sports as necessary, relevant, and important.

There were no significant differences in the responses of people from the two countries concerning (1) the likelihood of planning your day around watching a sporting event (2) hours spent reading sports-related magazines, and (3) participation in sports-related activities.

Adapted from Matthew Shank and Fred Beasley, "A Comparative Analysis of Sports Involvement: U.S. vs U.K.," Advertising and Consumer Psychology Conference, Portland, Oregon, May 1998.

Fan Identification

Sports involvement was previously defined as the level of interest in and importance of sport to consumers. A concept that extends this idea to a sports organization is fan identification. Two contrasting examples of fan identification were seen recently with the movement of NFL franchises. When the Cleveland Browns moved to Baltimore, Browns fans became irate, holding protests and filing lawsuits trying to stop the team's move.[28] On the other hand, when the Houston Oilers moved to Nashville, relatively little fan resistance was observed, indicating low levels of fan identification.

Sports marketers are interested in building and maintaining high levels of fan identification for organizations and their players. If high levels of identification are developed, a number of benefits can be realized by the sports organization. Before examining the benefits of fan identification, let us take a closer at what it is. **Fan identification** is defined as the personal commitment and emotional involvement customers have with a sports organization.[29] Recently, a conceptual framework was developed by Sutton, McDonald, Milne, and Cimperman for understanding the antecedents and outcomes of fan identification.[30] The model is shown in Figure 6.3.

Managerial correlates are those things such as team characteristics, organizational characteristics, affiliation characteristics, and activity characteristics that directly contribute to the level of fan involvement. Team characteristics include, most notably, the success of the team. Typically, the more successful the team, the higher the level of fan identification—because people want to associate themselves with a winner (BIRGing). However, some fans see loyalty to the team to be more important than team success. For instance, the Boston Red Sox and the Chicago Cubs continue to have high levels of fan identification even though they have not won the World Series since the turn of the century.

Organizational characteristics also lead to varying levels of fan identification. In contrast with team characteristics, which pertain to athletic performance, organizational characteristics relate to "off-the-field" successes and failures. Is the team trying to

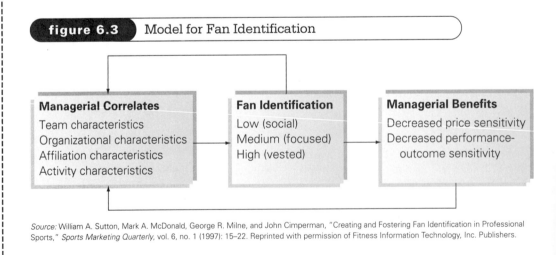

figure 6.3 Model for Fan Identification

Managerial Correlates	Fan Identification	Managerial Benefits
Team characteristics	Low (social)	Decreased price sensitivity
Organizational characteristics	Medium (focused)	Decreased performance-
Affiliation characteristics	High (vested)	outcome sensitivity
Activity characteristics		

Source: William A. Sutton, Mark A. McDonald, George R. Milne, and John Cimperman, "Creating and Fostering Fan Identification in Professional Sports," *Sports Marketing Quarterly*, vol. 6, no. 1 (1997): 15–22. Reprinted with permission of Fitness Information Technology, Inc. Publishers.

build a winning franchise or just reduce the payroll? Is the team involved in the community and community relations? Is the team owner threatening to move to another city if he or she does not have a new stadium built with taxpayers' monies? A recent example of the impact of team and organizational characteristics on fan identification was provided by the Florida Marlins. As soon as the team won the 1997 World Series (team characteristic that should foster high fan identification), the owner talked about selling the team, and the organization traded away several of its star players (organizational characteristic that will diminish fan identification).

Affiliation characteristics refer to the sense of community that a fan builds as a result of a team. According to Sutton et. al, "The community affiliation component . . . is defined as kinship, bond, or connection the fan has to a team. Community affiliation is derived from common symbols, shared goals, history, and a fan's need to belong."[31] As discussed in the study on the impact of sports on the community, the sports team provides fans with a way to feel connected to the community. Additionally, the more a fan's reference group (friends and family) favors going to games, the more the individual identifies with the team.[32]

Activity characteristics represent another antecedent to fan identification. In this case, activity refers to attending sporting events or being exposed to events via the media. As technology continues to advance, sports fans are afforded more and more opportunities to watch their favorite team via cable or pay-per-view, listen to games via radio, or link to broadcasts from anywhere via the Internet. With increased exposure, fan identification should be enhanced.

The interaction of the four preceding factors, will influence the level of fan identification. An individual's level of identification with a team or player can range from no identification to extremely high identification. However, for simplicity, Sutton et. al describe three distinct categories of fan identification.[33]

Low Identification

Fans who attend sporting events primarily for social interaction or entertainment benefit of the event characterize low-level identification. These "social fans" are attracted by the atmosphere of the game, promotions or events occurring during the competition, and the feelings of camaraderie that the game creates. Although this is the lowest level of fan identification, if fans are reinforced by the entertainment benefits of the game, then they may become more involved.

Medium Identification

The next higher classification of fan involvement is called medium identification, or focused fans. The major distinguishing characteristic of these fans is that they identify with the team or player, but only for the short term. In other words, they may associate with the team, or player, if it is having an especially good year. On the other hand, when the team starts to slump or the player is traded, "focused" identification will fade. As with low-level identification, a fan that experiences medium levels of identification may move to higher levels.

High Identification

The highest classification of fan involvement is based on a long-term commitment to the sport, team, or player. These vested fans often recruit other fans, follow the team loyally, and view the team as a vital part of the community. Fans classified as high involvement exhibit a number of concrete behavioral characteristics. Most importantly, high-identification fans are the most likely to return to sporting events. Moreover, high-involvment fans are more likely to attend home and away games, have been fans for a greater number of years, and invest more financially in being a fan.

Managerial Benefits

The final portion of the fan identification model put forth by Sutton et. al describes the outcomes of creating and fostering vested fans. One outcome is that high-identification fans have decreased price sensitivity. Price sensitivity refers to the notion that small increases in ticket prices may produce great fluctuations in demand for tickets. Fans that stick with the team for the long run are more likely to be season ticketholders or purchase personal seat licenses to get the right to purchase permanent seats. Fans that exhibit low levels of identification may decide not to purchase tickets, even for small increases in ticket prices.

Another outcome of high levels of fan identification is decreased performance-outcome sensitivity. Stated simply, fans that are vested will be more tolerant of poor seasons or in-season slumps. Fans will be more likely to stick with the team and not give up prime ticket locations that may have taken generations to acquire.

SUMMARY

In this chapter, we explored the spectator as a consumer of sport. Although there are many people who both participate and observe sports, research suggests that there are two distinct segments of consumers. For instance, participants tend to be male, better educated, and younger than spectators.

There are a variety of factors that influence our decision to attend sporting events. These factors include fan motivation, game attractiveness, economic factors, competitive factors, demographic factors, stadium factors, value of sport to the community, sports involvement, and fan identification. Fan motivation factors are those underlying reasons or needs that are being met by attending a sporting event. Researchers believe that some of the primary reasons that fans attend sporting events are to enhance self esteem, diversion from everyday life, entertainment value, eustress (feelings of excitement), economic value (gambling on events), aesthetic value, need for affiliation, and to be with family members.

Another factor that influences our decision to attend sporting events is game attractiveness. Game attractiveness refers to the perceived value and importance of the individual game based on what teams or athletes are playing (e.g., Is it the cross-town rival or is Ken Griffey Jr. in town?), the significance of the event to the league standings, whether or not the event is post-season versus regular season competition, or whether the event is perceived to be of championship caliber (e.g., the four majors in golf or the NCAA Final Four). In general, the greater the perceived attractiveness of the game, the more likely we will want to attend.

Economic factors also play a role in our decision to attend sporting events. As we discussed in chapter 3, the economic factors that may impact game attendance can be at the microeconomic level (e.g., personal income) or macroeconomic level (e.g., state of the nation's economy). Although these are uncontrollable factors, the sports organization can attempt to control the rising cost of ticket prices to make it easier for fans to attend sporting events.

Competition is another important factor that influences our decision to attend sporting events or observe them through another medium. Today, sports marketers must define the competition in broad terms—as other entertainment choices, such as movies, plays, and theater are competing with sporting events. Interestingly, sports organizations sometimes compete with themselves for fans. For example, one study found that televising home basketball games had a negative impact on game attendance.

Demographic factors such as age, ethnic background, and income are also related to spectator behavior. There is no such thing as a profile of the typical spectator. However, spectators are more likely to be male, young, more educated, and have higher incomes than that of the general population.

Perhaps the most important factor that influences attendance is the consumer's perception of the stadium. Stadium atmosphere appears to be a critical issue in attracting fans. The stadium atmosphere, or environment, has been referred to as the sportscape. Sportscape is the physical surroundings of the stadium that impact spectators' desire to stay at the stadium and ultimately return to the stadium. The multiple dimensions of sportscape include stadium access, facility aesthetics, scoreboard quality, seating comfort, and layout accessibility.

Another factor influencing game attendance and the likelihood of attending sporting events in the future is the perceived value of sport to the community. A recent study found that the more value attributed to sport, the more likely people were to attend. The value dimensions of sport to the community include community solidarity (bringing the community together), public behavior, pastime ecstasy (entertainment), pursuit of excellence, social equity, health awareness, individual quality (builds character), and business opportunities.

As discussed in the previous chapter, sports involvement referred to the consumer's perceived interest in and importance of participating in sport. Sports involvement has a related definition for those observing sporting events. High-involvement spectators are more likely to attend sporting events, read sports magazines, and plan their entire day around attending a sporting event.

A final factor that is related to spectator behavior is fan identification. Fan identification is the personal commitment and emotional involvement customers have with the sports organization. The characteristics of the team, the characteristics of the organization, the affiliation characteristics (sense of community), and the activity characteristics (exposures to the team) all interact to influence the level of fan identification. The higher the level of fan identification, the more likely fans are to attend events.

aesthetic value	family ties	self-esteem enhancement
demographic factors	fan identification	signage
diversion from everyday life	fan motivation factors	space allocation
economic factors	game attractiveness	sport involvement
economic value	layout accessibility	sportscape
entertainment value	need for affiliation	stadium access
eustress	scoreboard quality	stadium factors
facility aesthetics	seating comfort	

REVIEW QUESTIONS

1. Describe the differences and similarities between spectators and participants of sport.

2. Discuss the spectators' eight basic motives for attending sporting events. Which of these are similar to the motives for participating in sports?

3. Provide two examples of how game attractiveness influences attendance.

4. What are the economic factors that influence game attendance? Differentiate between the controllable and uncontrollable economic factors.

5. Describe the typical profile of spectators of women's sporting events. How would a sports marketer use this information in the strategic sports marketing process?

6. Discuss, in detail, the sportscape model and how the sportscape factors impact game attendance.

7. What are the value dimensions of professional sport to the community? How would sports marketers use these values in planing the strategic sports marketing process?

8. Define sports involvement from the spectator perspective. Why is it important to understand the levels of involvement among spectators?

9. Discuss, in detail, the model of fan identification and its implications for sports marketers.

10. Explain the relationship among the eight basic fan motivation factors and the other factors that influence game attendance (i.e., game attractiveness, economic factors, competitive factors, demographic factors, stadium factors, value to the community, sports involvement, and fan identification).

EXERCISES

1. Go to a high school sporting event, college sporting event, and professional sporting event. At each event, interview five spectators and ask them why they are attending events and what benefits they are looking for from the event. Compare

the different levels of competition. Do the motives for attending differ by level (i.e., high school, college, professional)? Are there gender differences or age differences among respondents?

2. Go to a sports bar and interview five people watching a televised sporting event. Determine their primary motivation for watching the sporting event. Describe other situations in which motives for watching sporting events vary.

3. Attend a women's sporting event and record the demographic profile of the spectators. What are your observations? Use these observations and suggest how you might segment, target, and position (market selection decisions) if you were to market the sport.

4. Attend a collegiate or professional sporting event. Record and describe all of the elements of sportscape. How do these impact your experience as a spectator?

5. Ask 10 consumers about the value that they feel a professional sports team would (or does) bring to the community. Then ask the same people about the value of college athletics to the community. Comment on how these values differ by level of competition.

6. How will marketing play a role in revitalizing the following sports: baseball, tennis, and cricket? How has marketing played a role in the increased popularity in the following sports: golf, basketball, and soccer?

INTERNET EXERCISES

1. Find examples via the Internet of how sports marketers have attempted to make it easier for fans to attend sporting events.

2. Locate two Web sites for the same sport—one for women and one for men (e.g., women's basketball and men's basketball). Comment on differences, if any, in how these sites market to spectators of the sport.

3. Locate two Web sites for the same sport—one American and one international (e.g., Major League Soccer and British Premier League). Comment on differences, if any, in how these sites market to spectators of the sport.

NOTES

1. John Burnett, Anil Menon, and Denise T. Smart, "Sports Marketing: A New Ball Game with New Rules," *Journal of Advertising Research*, (September/October 1993): 21–33.

2. George R. Milne, William A. Sutton, and Mark A. McDonald, "Niche Analysis: A Strategic Measurement Tool for Managers," *Sport Marketing Quarterly*, vol. 5, no. 3 (1996): 17–22.

3. Cited in Milne, Sutton, and McDonald, 17–22.

4. Milne, Sutton, and McDonald, 17–22.

5. *Richard Petty Driving Experience.* <http://www.racingschools.com/imecorp/petty.html>.

6. Daniel L. Wann, "Preliminary Validation of the Sport Fan Motivation Scale," *Journal of Sport & Social Issues*, (November 1995): 337–396. Reprinted by permission of Sage Publications, Inc.

7. See, for example, R.B. Cialdini, R.J. Borden, A. Thorne, M.R. Walker, S. Freeman, and L.R. Sloan, "Basking in Reflected Glory: Three (Football) Field Studies," *Journal of Personality and Social Psychology*, 34 (1976): 366–375.

8. Dave Anderson, "John Madden: Game Plan for a Better NFL" *Athlon Sports*, July 1998, 23–30.

9. Paul Falevi and Mark Mashe, "Baseball's Winning Streak for Fans" *The Washington Post National Weekly Edition*, August 1998, 18–19.

10. David Higdon, "13 Ways to Wake Up Pro Tennis" *Tennis*, May 1994, 43–46.

11. Jonathan Tesser, "S.O.S." *Sport Magazine*, August 1998, 88–89.

12. Wann, 337–396.

13. R.A. Baade and L.J. Tiechen, "An Analysis of Major League Baseball Attendance, 1969–1987," *Journal of Sport & Social Issues*, vol. 14 (1990): 14–32

14. Brad Edmondson. "When Athletes Turn Traitor." *American Demographics*. <http://www.demographics.com/publications/ad /97_ad/9709_ad/ad970916.htm> (September 1997).

15. Ibid.

16. Walter Gantz, "An Exploration of Viewing Motives and Behaviors Associated with Televised Sports," *Journal of Broadcasting*, vol. 25 (1981): 263–275.

17. James Zhang and Dennis Smith, "Impact of Broadcasting on the Attendance of Professional Basketball Games," *Sport Marketing Quarterly*, vol. 6, no. 1 (1997): 23–32.

18. Donna Lopiano. "Marketing Trends in Women's Sports and Fitness." *Women's Sports Foundation*. <http://www.lifetimetv.com/sports/index.html>.

19. Kirk L. Wakefield and Hugh J. Sloan, "The Effects of Team Loyalty and Selected Stadium Factors on Spectator Attendance," *Journal of Sport Management* (1995): 153–172.

20. Jillian Kasky, "The Best Ticket Buys for Sports Fans Today," *Money*, vol. 24, no. 10, October 1995, 146.

21. Kirk L. Wakefield, Jeffrey G. Blodgett, and Hugh J. Sloan, "Measurement and Management of the Sportscape," *Journal of Sport Management* (1996): 15–31.

22. *Electrosonic Project Briefing.* <http://www.electrosonic.com/briefing/arenas/ unc.html>.

23. "British Sports Minister says 'The Terraces are History'." <http://www.nando.net/newsroom/ spor.../feat/archive/102297/soc45127.html>. (October 1997).

24. Wakefield, Blodgett, and Sloan, 15–31.

25. Andy Hemmer, "Gardens Gets Skyboxes in Makeover," *Cincinnati Business Courier Inc.*, vol. 11, no. 48, April 10, 1995, 1.

26. Wakefield, Blodgett, and Sloan, 15–31.

27. Deborah L. Kerstetter and Georgia M. Kovich, "An Involvement Profile of Division I Women's Basketball Spectators," *Journal of Sport Management*, vol. 11, (1997): 234–249. Dana-Nicoleta Lascu, Thomas D. Giese, Cathy Toolan, Brian Guehring, and James Mercer, "Sport Involvement: A Relevant Individual Difference Factor in Spectator Sports," *Sport Marketing Quarterly*, vol. 4, no 4 (1995): 41–46.

28. Geoff Hobson, "Just Another Sunday," *The Cincinnati Enquirer*, December 7, 1996.

29. William A. Sutton, Mark A. McDonald, George R. Milne, and John Cimperman, "Creating and Fostering Fan Identification in Professional Sports," *Sport Marketing Quarterly*, vol. 6, no. 1 (1997): 15–22.

30. Ibid.

31. Ibid.

32. Kirk L. Wakefield, "The Pervasive Effects of Social Influence on Sporting Event Attendance," *Journal of Sport & Social Issues*, vol. 19, no. 4 (November 1995): 335–351.

33. Sutton, McDonald, Milne and Cimperman, 15–22.

Segmentation, Targeting, and Positioning

After completing this chapter, you should be able to

- Discuss the importance of market selection decisions

- Compare the various bases for marketing segmentation

- Understand target marketing and the requirements of successful target marketing

- Describe positioning and its importance in the market selection decisions

- Construct a perceptual map to depict any sports entity's position in the marketplace

Market selection decisions are the most critical elements of the strategic sports marketing process. In this portion of the planning phase, decisions are made that will dictate the direction of the marketing mix. These decisions include how to group consumers together based on common needs; who to direct your marketing efforts towards; and how you want your sports product to be perceived in the marketplace. These important market selection decisions are referred to as segmenting, targeting, and positioning (STP). In this chapter, we examine these concepts in the context of our strategic sports marketing process. Let us begin by exploring market segmentation, the first of the market selection decisions.

(S)egmentation

Not all sports fans are alike. You would not market the X-treme Games to members of the American Association of Retired People (AARP). Likewise, you would not market the PGA's Senior Tour to Generation Xers. The notion of mass marketing and treating all consumers the same has given way to understanding the unique needs of groups of consumers. This concept, which is the first market selection decision, is referred to as market segmentation. More specifically, **market segmentation** is defined as identifying groups of consumers based on their common needs.

Market segmentation is recognized as a more efficient and effective way to market than mass marketing, which treats all consumers the same. By carefully exploring and understanding different segments through marketing research, sports marketers determine which groups of consumers offer the greatest sales opportunities for the organization.

If the first market selection decision is segmentation, then how do sports marketers group consumers based on common needs? Traditionally, there are six common bases for market segmentation. These include demographics, socioeconomic group, psychographic profile, geographic region, behavioral style, and benefits. Let us take a closer look at how sports marketers use and choose from among these six bases for segmentation.

Bases for Segmentation

The bases for segmentation refer to the ways that consumers with common needs can be grouped together. Six bases for segmenting consumer markets are shown in Table 7.1.

Demographic Segmentation

One of the most widely used techniques for segmenting consumer markets is demographics. Demographics include such variables as age, gender, ethnic background, and family life cycle. Segmenting markets based on demographics is widespread for three reasons. First, these characteristics are easy for sports marketers to identify and measure. Second, information about the demographic characteristics of a market is readily available from a variety of sources, such as the government census data de-

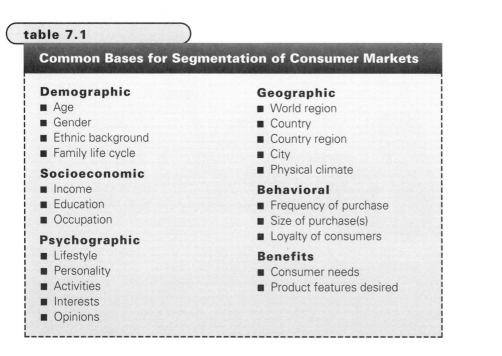

table 7.1

Common Bases for Segmentation of Consumer Markets

Demographic
- Age
- Gender
- Ethnic background
- Family life cycle

Socioeconomic
- Income
- Education
- Occupation

Psychographic
- Lifestyle
- Personality
- Activities
- Interests
- Opinions

Geographic
- World region
- Country
- Country region
- City
- Physical climate

Behavioral
- Frequency of purchase
- Size of purchase(s)
- Loyalty of consumers

Benefits
- Consumer needs
- Product features desired

scribed in chapter 4. Third, demographic variables are closely related to attitudes and sport behaviors, such as attending games, buying sports merchandise, or watching sports on television.

Age   Age is one of the most simplistic, yet effective demographic variables used to segment markets. Not only is age easy to measure, it is usually related to consumer needs. In addition, age of the consumer is commonly associated with other demographic characteristics, such as income, education, and stage of the family life cycle. A number of broad age segments exist such as the children's market, the teen market, and the mature market. Care must be taken, however, not to stereotype consumers when using age segmentation. How many 10-year-olds do you know who think they are 20, and how many 75-year-olds think they are 45?

Children. There has always been a natural association between children and sports. However, sports marketers are no longer taking the huge children's market for granted—and with good reason. Children have tremendous influence on purchase decisions within the family and are increasingly purchasing more and more on their own.[1]

Kids influence the sale of $165 billion of all products and services sold per year. In addition, children are believed to influence roughly 20 percent of all purchases in the United States. Approximately 8 percent of all sports equipment is purchased by children, and 10 percent of all sports equipment purchases are influenced by children.[2] Children are participating in sports and are identifying with teams, players, and brands at younger ages each year.

■ Professional sports are realizing the importance of the kid's market to their long-term success.

Thus, sports marketers have recognized the power of the kids' market. They realize that children will become fans and the season ticketholders of the future. As such, they have segmented markets accordingly. Here are some examples of how MLB teams have developed marketing mixes that will appeal to children.

- The Kansas City Royals gave kids 14 and under free admission with a paid adult admission during the second half of the 1995 season.
- On the day before the All-Star Game, the Chicago Cubs hosted an All-Star Kids Clinic, with attendance figures estimated at 5,000 kids.
- The Boston Red Sox held a "Kid's Opening Day" promotion where nine kids were chosen to run onto the field with the players before the game.[3]
- A new Playzone has been opened at Cinergy Field in Cincinnati that allows kids to play under the supervision of Red's employees during the game. Kids are given ID wristbands with their parents' seat location just in case they become lost.

In addition to these efforts, it has become commonplace in major league parks to let the kids run around the bases after selected games.

Major League Baseball is not the only sport to realize the importance of children to its success in the future. Tennis, for instance, is trying to increase its popularity by focusing on the children's market. The Tennis Industry Association (TIA) has teamed up with Turner Broadcasting's Cartoon Network in a series of promotions geared towards kids. The TIA's "Initiative To Grow the Game" seems to be working, because participation levels are increasing.[4]

The children's segment is also growing in importance for those organizations marketing to sports participants. For example, Ad-Teen, founded in 1996, is an exercise center that has specialized in children's fitness.

It is a rarity—a local fitness center exclusively for children that has adult-style equipment. Owner Don Lawson describes Ad-Teen, Inc. as a "Bally's for kids." Young clients get a complete supervised fitness program and access to scaled down cardiovascular and strength training equipment designed for smaller bodies.

There are few such clubs around the country, says Kathy McNeil, Director of Public Relations for the International Health Racquet and Sportsclub Association, a Boston-based trade association of 3,000 fitness centers. "Most of the fitness centers exclusively for young people do not place an emphasis on general fitness, but on specific sports training, such as gymnastics and karate." The ones that are not sports-specific usually target toddlers with chutes, slides, and ball pits.

Ad-Teen participants also find the center appealing. "At the fitness center I used to go to, I wasn't allowed to go near any of the machines—all I could do was take aerobics classes" says eight-year-old Emily Schreiber. "I especially like it here because I get to use the rower—my favorite way to exercise."

Mr. Lawson got the idea for Ad-Teen after watching a CBS report on *48 Hours* called "Generation X-tra Large" that focused on obesity and kids. Upon further investigation, Lawson learned that because of the popularity of computers, television, and cutbacks in physical education programs at schools, children weren't getting much exercise. Formal research also reinforced this notion. For instance, a 1989 University of Michigan National School Population survey says 68 percent of children fail to pass a minimum standard of fitness.

Sessions at Ad-Teen are tailored to meet the needs of each child, from weight loss maintenance to conditioning for a specific sport. The two-month program, consisting of 24 one-hour workout sessions and four nutritional classes, costs $500 and includes cardiovascular training with fitness machines, nutrition classes, and strength training.

Source: Reon Carter, "Club Get's Hip to Kid's Fitness," *Cincinnati Enquirer*, May 10, 1996, E1, E5. Courtesy of *Cincinnati Enquirer*.

Teens. The teen market is currently estimated at $95 billion and growing.[5] The number of teens is also expected to rise exponentially, because the U.S. Census Bureau projects that by 2010 there will be 30.81 million teens in the Unites States.[6] A global study conducted by DMB&B of 25,000 teens in 41 countries found that basketball is the most popular game on the planet. Over 70 percent of teens are involved in basketball, and 76 percent of the teens surveyed are familiar with the NBA logo.[7] Numbers like these are causing sports marketers to take a hard look at the teen market in all sports, as the following article illustrates.

younger crowd now driving golf

Once only a passion of an older generation, golf is now "chic" among the young. "They (teens) don't see the sport anymore as something their fathers play," says Brent Diamond, publisher of youth-targeted magazines, such as *Snowboard*, *Surfer*, and *Powder*. A quick

(continued)

look at the numbers substantiates this claim. Golf club sales for players from 14 to 17 years old more than doubled in 1995—from $18.4 million to $42.8 million. The number of junior golfers (between the ages of 12 and 17) grew nearly 17 percent.

Madison Avenue has played, and will continue to play, an important role in the image-building of golf. Nike and Tiger Woods will play a significant role in maintaining the positive momentum among teens. Woods' emergence has given the entire golf industry a huge boost in the teen market.

In addition to the advertising industry, the connection between golf and teens is being bolstered by cable television and Hollywood. In 1994, music video station VH1 launched its Fairway to Heaven golf tournament. "It was becoming apparent that golf was hip," said Joshua Katz, VH1 senior vice president of marketing. "Since we first aired the tournament, it has become a marquee franchise for our network. It's golf with a Rock n' Roll edge."

Hollywood is also helping the surge by producing golf-themed movies, such as *Happy Gilmore* and *Tin Cup*. Those two films alone grossed nearly $100 million combined in box office receipts, further evidence that golf is getting out of its stuffed shirts and into the hearts of teens.

Adapted from "Younger Crowd Now Driving Golf," *Cincinnati Enquirer*, October 31, 1996, D1, D4.

The Mature Market. Another market that is expected to increase at a staggering pace is the age 55 and older, mature market. The Bureau of Labor Statistics estimates that between 1987 and 2015 this segment will grow by 62 percent, compared to the 19 percent growth rate of the general U.S. population.[8] Stereotypically, the elderly are perceived to be inactive and thrifty. Nothing could be farther from the truth. The mature market is living longer and becoming more physically active. In addition, approximately 23 percent of Americans are 55 and older, controlling about 75 percent of the nation's wealth and about 50 percent of its discretionary income.[9] As a result, sports marketers are capitalizing on this growing market in a variety of ways.

Traditionally, senior citizen discounts have been promoted in Major League Baseball. For example, the Cincinnati Reds offer fans 65 and older the opportunity to purchase advance box and reserved seating at half price.

Other examples of sports markets being segmented by age can be seen in the growing number of "senior" sporting tours and events. The Senior Tour of the PGA has nearly the following of the regular tour events. Although not as successful as golf, other professional senior tours include tennis (both men's and women's) and bowling.

Seniors are also becoming more active as sports participants. The fastest growing participation sports for seniors, classified as age 55 and older, include exercising to music and running or walking on the treadmill. Table 7.2 shows some of the fastest growing activities for seniors.[10]

Gender More than 40 million women watch professional football on an average weekend.[11] More than 75,000 women are participating in organized ice or roller hockey

Three wars.
Three IRS audits.
Three kidney stones.

Anything but the cold.

Polartec® Series 300 fabric provides amazing warmth without weight. With over 160 other Climate Control Fabrics™, Polartec keeps you warm when it's cold, cool when it's hot, dry when you sweat. So you can perform at your peak. Look for the label.

POLARTEC
MALDEN MILLS

BELIEVE IN WHAT YOU WEAR.

■ Polartec is capitalizing on the growing mature market.

table 7.2

Fastest Growing Participation Sports for the Mature Market		
Sport/Activity	Number of Participants	Percent Change 1992–1996
Exercise to Music (*100+ days/year*)	884,000	257.9%
Treadmill (*100+ days/year*)	2,238,000	170.3
Resistance Machine (*100+ days/year*)	876,000	149.6
Golf (*25+ days/year*)	2,402,000	49.8
Fitness Walking (*100+ days/year*)	6,471,000	27.7

Source: Courtesy of Sporting Goods Manufacturers Association.

leagues in North America.[12] In fact, Manon Rheamue was signed as a goalie by the Tampa Bay Lighting in 1992 and was the first woman to ever play in a professional hockey game. The NBA now has two women referees. These examples, and many others, illustrate shifting gender roles in sport.

Historically, sports enthusiasts have been male. However, stereotypes are eroding quickly as women are becoming more involved in every facet of sport. More women are participating in sports, and more women are watching sports. Moreover, every attempt is being made to make women's sports equitable with their male counterparts. For example, in the 2000 Olympics in Sydney, women will compete in 24 of the 28 sporting events. In addition, the Sydney Olympics will feature 21 extra women's events across nine sports, such as the triathalon and tae kwon do.

All of this emphasis on women's sports translates into new opportunities for sports marketers. The women's segment is drawing much deserved attention as the Spotlight on Women in Sports Marketing illustrates.

spotlight on women in sports marketing:

as women take the field, firms deliver pitches

Almost everything about Rawlings's new softball helmet is unremarkable—until you check the back. Built into the hardplastic is an X-shaped opening. It's for a ponytail.

As girls and women discover sports, sports marketers such as Rawlings are discovering girls and women. Virtually ignored as participants, fans, and consumers just a few years ago, women now form a hot market for all things sports-related.

Reebok now makes a product that didn't exist a decade ago—$75 "elite" women's soccer shoes—endorsed by a player, Julie Foudy, who was obscure even in her sport until a few years ago. Louisville Hockey recently brought out a line of $99 women's hockey pants that feature a narrower waist, wider hips, and more pelvic and hip protection.

Thanks to the success of the new women's pro leagues, women are gaining their own group of marketable stars. Nike, lifting a page from its Michael Jordan playbook, brought out the first "signature" sneaker line for women in 1995 when it signed up basketball player Sheryl Swoopes. Rival player Nikki McCray signed a $1 million shoe deal with Fila. And coming soon: "The Lobo," Reebok's new basketball shoe, named for Rebecca Lobo.

The women's sports market has picked up such critical mass in recent years that two deep-pocketed publishers have begun to court it with glossy magazines. Condé Nast *Sports for Women*—from the publisher of *Vogue*, *Mademoiselle*, and *Vanity Fair*—launched its first issue last month. Time Warner, Inc. came out this fall with its second quarterly issue of *Sports Illustrated Women/Sports*, a spinoff from its weekly sports magazine. Time Warner says the magazine is a test and it hasn't committed to a full publication schedule yet. Condé Nast has committed $40 million to publishing monthly.

"We've had a whole generation [of girls] who've grown up playing sports, watching sports, who've now got their own [sports] role models," says Suzanne Grimes, Publisher of the Condé Nast magazine. "There's now a whole generation for which sports has become a natural part of their lives."

In fact, female participation rates in sports have been soaring for the past 20 years, helped along by Title IX of the Civil Rights Act, the 1972 law that required schools to equalize women's sports programs with men's. At the same time, the gold-medal performances of U.S. women's teams in softball, soccer, gymnastics, and basketball at the 1996 Olympics in Atlanta gave female athletes an unprecedented amount of exposure and glamour.

While 1 in 27 girls belonged to a school athletic team in 1970, 1 in 3 girls now plays some kind of school sport according to the National Federation of State High School Associations. The Women's Sports Foundation, which promotes participation, estimates that more than 40 million adult women now play some kind of sport.

The most high-profile changes in women's sports may be those involving women's professional leagues. Outside of tennis and golf, elite female athletes had virtually no options for playing after college only a few years ago. Recently, however, two women's professional basketball leagues and a women's professional softball league have sprung up. Professional women's soccer and ice hockey leagues may be next.

"It's just logic," said Donna Lopiano, Executive Director of the Women's Sports Foundation. "If you teach women how to play and they understand sports, they become passionately involved. They become participants and spectators." As women get more involved in sports, corporations are busy selling women's sports and athletes back to them.

Companies with an obvious sports tie-in—Nike and Reebok, for example—were the first to build ad campaigns around female athletes. But the list of women's sports sponsors now has grown well beyond those with something sports-related to sell.

General Motors, Kellogg's, Lee Jeans, and JC Penney, for instance, are all active sponsors of women's basketball. State Farm Insurance Co. will spend $5 million this year to underwrite women's professional skating, tennis, and golf and college volleyball. "We insure that girls will always get to play," says a magazine ad promoting the company's various tournaments and events.

State Farm ad director Richard Bugajski said that sponsoring a women's event generally costs far less than sponsoring a men's event and is less crowded with competing ads. "The ratings aren't all that great [for women's events on television], but that's okay … because we're reaching our audience at a low price relative to major league sports," he says. "It's a very efficient way to reach the audience we're after." Such promotions don't just plug a product, they generate goodwill among women, who appreciate that a company is taking a special interest in them, Bugajski said.

In women's sports sponsorship, "the medium is the message," says David Jacobson, Senior Editor of *IEG Sponsorship Report*, a Chicago newsletter. "Through sports, marketers communicate to women that they care about their concerns, certainly more so than the sponsor's competitor does." The newsletter estimates that companies will pay organizers more than $100 million this year to attach their names to women's sporting events of all kinds.

As a group of consumers, Jacobson adds, it doesn't hurt that "The Title IX generation"—generally speaking, women and girls under 40—is young, female, and relatively affluent—three of the most highly desirable attributes sought by any advertiser.

Ethnic Background   Segmenting markets by **ethnic background** is based on grouping consumers of a common race, religion, and nationality. Ethnic groups, such as African-Americans (13 percent of the U.S. population), Hispanic-Americans (11 percent of the U.S. population) and Asian-Americans (4 percent of the U.S. population) are increasingly important to sports marketers as their numbers continue to grow. When segmenting based on ethnic background, marketers must be careful not to think of stereotypical profiles, but to understand the unique consumption behaviors of each group through marketing research.

A recent example of how ethnic background can be an important consideration for sports marketers comes from Major League Soccer (MLS). Hispanic media in Dallas called for a boycott of the Burn's home opener due to the loss of three Hispanic players. The loss of these Hispanic players may have caused the Burn to lose over 10,000 fans in the first two home games. The majority of game-day ticket sales come from Hispanic fans who want to see Hispanic stars. The Burn estimates that its attendance is 45 percent Hispanic, although *Soccer America* editor Mark Woitalla says its much higher. Said Woitalla "It's more like 99 percent in the $9 (cheapest seats)."[13]

Another example of marketing to Hispanics is the introduction of "Deportes Hoy," the premier, Spanish-Languauge Sports Daily. The sports information product will be circulated in Los Angeles, Orange, and San Diego Counties and will be targeted to reach everyone from the occassional to the most highly involved sports enthusiasts.[14] Other examples of how athletes of color can influence market selection decisions are illustrated by the influx of Japanese pitchers to the major leagues (see spotlight).

Likewise, Fernado Valuenzala's career may have been revitalized by the San Diego Padres to appeal to the Hispanic market. Tiger Woods is unique because of his multiethnic background. He represents an opportunity to attract a variety of ethnic backgrounds to the sport of golf or to the products or services he endorses.

spotlight on international sports marketing:

japan's arms race

Hideo Nomo was the first of the Japanese exports to pitch in the Major Leagues. In 1995, he joined the Los Angeles Dodgers and immediately created a stir both on and off the field. In his first year, Nomo made the National League All-Star team and Asian-American fans flocked to Dodger Stadium to watch him pitch. These fans were armed with Japanese Flags and T-shirts emblazed with "Nomo the Tornado," the nickname for the first Japanese superstar to play in the majors.

One example of Nomo's tremendous appeal was when a 23-year-old Tokyo cook, flew to San Francisco during his week off to watch Mr. Nomo pitch, and then drove to Los Angeles to see him pitch again. Taking his seat at Dodger Stadium an hour and a half before the game, he shows off his $125 Dodger jersey and unrolls a placard with "NOMO" scrawled in the corners of a Japanese flag.

Nomo (since traded to the Mets) has seemingly paved the way for other Japanese pitchers to come to America and showcase their talents. In 1997, Shigeshi Hasegawa joined the Angels and Takashi Kashiwada signed with the New York Mets. Hideki Irabu signed with the New York Yankees for a whopping $12.8 million over four years before he ever threw a pitch on American soil![a] It is not surprising that these players were signed by teams in California and New York, both having large Asian-American populations.

Who else will follow Nomo? Most likely, there will be a steady stream of pitchers from Japan. Youngsters in Japan play baseball all the time, watch Major League Baseball on television, and dream of moving to America to make three times more money than they would receive in the Japanese major leagues.[b] Marketers would be the first to encourage these players to leave, as they represent an instant link to the growing Asian-American market.

[a] Emily Thorton and Joshua Kaufman, "Japan's Surge in Exported Arms," *Business Week*, June 23, 1997, 8.
[b] Steve Wulf, "Plenty More After Nomo; Thanks to Hideo Nomo, Major League Teams Now Look Upon Japan As the Land of the Rising Football," *Time*, March 24, 1997, 84–85.

Family Life Cycle   The **family life cycle** was a concept developed in the 1960s to describe how individuals progress through various "life-stages," or phases of their life. A traditional life cycle begins with an individual starting in the young, single "life stage." Next, an individual would progress through stages such as young, married with no children; young, married with children; to finally, older with no spouse. As you can see, the traditional stages of the family life cycle are based on demographic characteristics such as age, marital status, and the presence or absence of children.

Today, the traditional family life cycle is no longer relevant. In the 1990s, roughly half of all marriages end in divorce, and the number of single-parent households is on the rise. Changes in family structure such as these have led marketers to a more modern view of the family life cycle, shown in Figure 7.1.

Sports marketers segmenting on the basis of family life cycle have a number of options. Do they want to appeal to the young and single, the elderly couple with no kids living at home, or the family with young children? Sports that are growing in popularity, such as biking, segment markets based on a stage of the family life cycle. Just imagine the incompatible biking needs of a young, single person versus a young, married couple with children.

Professional sports has come under increased scrunity in the past decade for its lack of family values. Rising ticket prices, drunken fans, and late games have all been cited as examples of professional sports becoming "family unfriendly." Realizing this, sports marketers have tried to renew family interest in sports and make going to the game "fun for the entire family." As discussed in chapter 2, the Harlem Globetrotters have done this for years.

■ Kawasaki is segmenting on the basis of the family life cycle.

Along with the Globetrotters, there are many other examples of sports marketers trying to become more family friendly. For instance, the addition of Homer's Landing, an area where families can picnic before, during, and after the game, has become a "hit" for the St. Louis Cardinals. The Chicago Cubs and the other professional teams have initiated no-alcohol sections at their games to encourage a family environment. Moreover, many sports organizations have instituted family nights, which include tickets, parking, and food for a reduced price to encourage family attendance. For example, the Atlanta Braves offer "Grand Slam Family Specials," which include discounted bleacher tickets and free hot dogs, chips, and soft drinks for kids.[15]

Socioeconomic Segmentation

Thus far we have discussed demographic variables such as age, gender, ethnic background, and family life cycle as potential ways to segment sports markets. Another way of segmenting markets that has been found to be a good predictor of consumer behavior is through socioeconomic segmentation. As previously defined a consumer's **social class** is a division of members of a society into a hierarchy of distinct status classes, so that members of each class have relatively the same status and members of all other classes have either more or less status.

figure 7.1 Modern Family Life Cycle

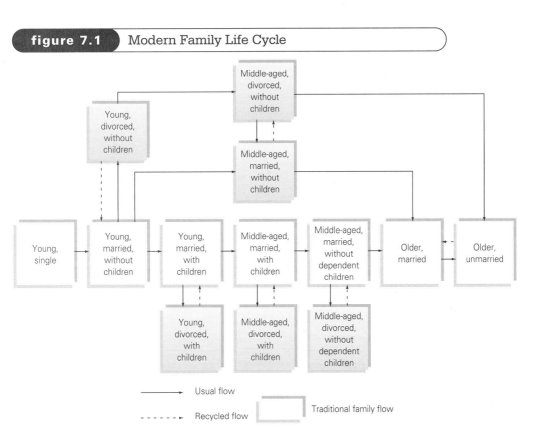

Young, single → Young, married, without children → Young, married, with children → Middle-aged, married, with children → Middle-aged, married, without dependent children → Older, married → Older, unmarried

Middle-aged, divorced, without children

Young, divorced, without children

Middle-aged, married, without children

Young, divorced, with children

Middle-aged, divorced, with children

Middle-aged, divorced, without dependent children

⟶ Usual flow

- - - - ▸ Recycled flow

☐ Traditional family flow

Source: Patrick Murphy and William Staples. "A Modernized Family Life Cycle," *Journal of Consumer Research* (June 1997):12–22. Reprinted with permission University of Chicago Press.

■ Polo is a sport that has typically appealed to the upper class.

Although most people immediately equate social class with income, income alone can be a poor predictor of social class. Other factors such as educational level and occupation also determine social standing. Usually, income, education, and occupation are highly interrelated. In other words, the higher the level of education, the higher the income and the more prestigious the occupation of an individual. Based on these factors (income, education, and occupation) members of a society are artificially said to belong to one of the social class categories. The traditional social class categories are upper, middle, and lower class Americans. Participation in certain sports has been associated with the various social strata. For instance, golf and tennis are called "country club" sports. Polo is a sport of the "rich and famous." Bowling is usually thought of as the "blue-collar" sport of the working class.

As with sex roles, the relationship between social class and sport is now shifting. Golf is now being enjoyed by people of all income levels. Attending a professional basketball or football game, once affordable for the whole family, can now only be enjoyed by wealthy corporate season ticketholders. In addition, NASCAR fans are stereotypically "good old boys" with "blue-collar" values. However, NASCAR has turned into a $2 billion-a-year industry and a marketing success story. During this tremendous growth, the sport is moving beyond its "good-ol'-boy" mentality and reaching a new market in yuppie America. Just consider the demographics of the NASCAR fan. Nearly a third of NASCAR fans have household incomes above $50,000 and more than a quarter hold professional or managerial jobs.[16]

Psychographic Segmentation

Psychographic segmentation is described as grouping consumers on the basis of a common lifestyle preference and personality. Psychographic segments are thought to be more comprehensive than other types of segmentation, such as demographics, behavioral, or geodemographic. As consumer behavior researcher Michael Solomon points out, "Demographics allow us to describe *who* buys, but psychographics allows us to understand *why* they do."[17] For this reason, many sports marketers have chosen to segment their markets on the basis of psychographics. In order to gain a better understanding of consumers' lifestyles, marketers assess consumer's **AIOs**, or statements describing activities, interests, and opinions. The three AIO dimensions are shown in Table 7.3.

Typically marketers quantify AIOs by asking consumers to agree or disagree with a series of statements reflecting their lifestyle. These statements can range from measures of general interest in sports to measures focusing on a specific sport. As seen in Table 7.3, many of these AIO dimensions relate indirectly or directly to sports. For example, sports, social events, recreation, and products may have a direct link to sports, while club memberships, fashion, community, and economics may be indirectly linked.

An example of psychographic segmentation in the golf market can be seen in Table 7.4. This figure illustrates a golfer's lifestyle based on research from *SRDS: The Lifestyle Market Analyst/National Demographic and Lifestyle 1996*. This type of

■ Volleyball and the beach lifestyle go hand in hand.

information examines activities and interests of golfers to determine what products and services might be successfully marketed to this group. For example, many professional golf tournaments are sponsored by large investment companies to capitalize on this popular activity of golfers.

Geographic Segmentation

Geographics is a simple, but powerful, segmentation basis. Certainly, this is critical for sports marketers and as long-standing as "rooting for the home team." All sports teams use geographic segmentation, however, it is not always as straightforward as it may initially seem. For instance, the Dallas Cowboys, Chicago Bulls, Atlanta Braves, and the Fighting Irish are all known as "America's Teams."[18]

table 7.3

AIO Dimensions

Activities	Interests	Opinions
Work	Family	Themselves
Hobbies	Home	Social issues
Social events	Job	Politics
Vacation	Community	Business
Entertainment	Recreation	Economics
Club membership	Fashion	Education
Community	Food	Products
Shopping	Media	Future
Sports	Achievements	Culture

Source: William Wells and Douglas J. Tigert, "Activities, Interests, and Opinions," *Journal of Advertising Research*, vol. 11 (August 1971): 27–35. Courtesy of the *Journal of Advertising Research*, The Advertising Research Foundation.

table 7.4

Golf Lifestyle Profiles Ranked by Index*

Top Ten Lifestyles		Bottom Ten Lifestyles	
Lifestyle	Index	Lifestyle	Index
Snow skiing frequently	187	Bible/Devotional reading	79
Tennis frequently	178	Sewing	83
Stock/Bond investments	158	Automotive work	87
Travel for business	157	Health/Natural foods	88
Frequent flyer	155	Needlework/Knitting	88
Wines	154	Science fiction	90
Real estate investing	151	Vegetable gardening	91
Watching sports on television	150	House plants	92
Own a vacation home	142	Own a cat	93
Boating/Sailing	142	Entering sweepstakes	93

Reprinted from the 1998 edition of *The Lifestyle Market Analyst*, published by SRDS with data supplied by Polk.
* (Index: U.S. Average = 100)

America's teams

The Boys, the Bulls, the Braves, and the Blue and Gold. "The reason these teams are followed so closely is plain and simple," says Fox TV's Vince Wladiaka, whose network contributes to the intense coverage. "If you win and have the ability to have something that makes you a consistent draw, you can be one of America's Teams."

Why are these America's teams? In part, it is the team's ability to win and the national exposure they receive. The Cowboys have three Super Bowls to their credit in the 1990s, along with extensive coverage by Fox and ABC, where Dallas dominates Sunday morning and Monday night ratings the way *Friends* dominates Thursdays. The Bulls have six NBA championships in the 1990s and coverage on NBC, TNT, and WGN, where the team is seen by between 2 and 18 million households about 100 times per year. Three World Series' appearances and one championship in the 1990s make up the credentials of the Braves. In addition, all 162 regular season games are telecast by ESPN, Fox, and TBS.

Finally, the Fighting Irish are the Associated Press' number-1-ranked team of all time and have been rated in the top six teams in five of the last eight seasons. Even more impressive is their one-of-a-kind deal with NBC Sports, the only network with an exclusive contract to televise a university's entire schedule.

So are the Cowboys the most popular of America's Teams? Based on television ratings, merchandising profits, and q-ratings (gauge of celebrity popularity), the answer is yes. The Boys are followed by the Bulls, the Irish, and the Braves, with all four well above their peers on these measures. Bulls' star Scottie Pippen says, "If you had to compare the Bulls and Cowboys, you'd have to go with the Cowboys because they have been popular longer."

"Worldwide, though, it might be different. Basketball is one of the top international sports. You go to a different country or different parts of Europe, the NFL is not as popular as the NBA." So would it be safe to say that the Bulls are the World's Team and the Cowboys are America's Team? Pippen says, "I would go with the Dream Team before I went with the Bulls. A lot of superstars on the Dream Team have fans in cities all over the world. The magnitude of being part of the Bulls is great, but worldwide, by no means is there any comparison to the Dream Team."

Adapted from Darryl Howerston, "America's Teams," *Sport*, November 1996, 33–38.

Geographic segmentation can be useful in making broad distinctions among local, regional, national, and international market segments. International or multinational marketing is a topic of growing interest for sports marketers. Witness, for example, Major League Baseball and the NBA both playing their first regular season games in Mexico, or the NFL discussing expansion into international markets. And let us not forget that minor international sporting event called the Olympic Games.

The physical climate also plays a role in segmenting markets geographically. Classic examples include greater demand for snow skiing equipment in Colorado and surfboards in Florida. However, Colorado ski resorts have the greatest number of sports tourists who come from Florida, hardly thought of as a snow ski mecca. Therefore, segments of sports consumers may exist in unlikely geographic markets. In this example, the psychographics of the sports consumer may be more important in predicting behavior than geographic location.

Although the climate plays an important role in sports, marketers have attempted to tame this uncontrollable factor. For instance, tons of sand were shipped to Atlanta, creating beachlike conditions, for the first ever Olympic beach volleyball competition. Domed stadiums, since the opening of the Astrodome in Houston, have also allowed sports marketers to tout the perfect conditions in which fans can watch football in the middle of a blizzard in Minnesota.

Behavioral Segmentation

For sports marketers engaged in the strategic sports marketing process, two common goals are attracting more fans and keeping them. Behavioral segmentation lies at the heart of these two objectives. **Behavioral segmentation** groups consumers based on how much they purchase, how often they purchase, and/or how loyal they are to a product or service.

Interestingly, in today's professional sports environment, loyalty is an increasingly important topic. Many professional sports teams have held their fans and cities hostage, and cities are doing everything they can to keep their beloved teams. For instance, in 1994, over half of the major professional sports franchises either moved into a new stadium or arena or had plans to build one.[19] Franchises and players within each team move so rapidly that fan loyalty becomes a difficult phenomena to capture. The day of the lifelong fan is over. Because of this, fans may identify more with individual players or even coaches (e.g., Cal Ripken Jr. and the Orioles, Tony Gwinn and the Padres, Joe Paterno and Penn State football) than they do with teams. This is true even in team-dominated sports, such as football. Prior to 1990, there was little movement of professional football teams. Since 1990, the Cardinals, Rams, Raiders, Browns, and Oilers have all moved.

Fans may be more concerned with the individual performance of Emmitt Smith, Dion Sanders, and Troy Aikman than they are with the Dallas Cowboys. Certainly, sports marketers have to monitor this trend of diminishing loyalty to a team. On the other hand, some sports fans show extreme loyalty by purchasing personal seat licenses. Personal seat licenses (PSLs) require fans to pay a leasing fee for their seats. This fee would guarantee the consumer his or her seat for several years. The PSL, of course, demonstrates the extreme devotion of a group of fans.

Along with behavioral segmentation based on loyalty to a team or sports product, consumers are frequently grouped on the basis of other attendance or purchase behaviors. For instance, lifelong season ticketholders represent one end of the usage contiuum, while those that have never attended sporting events represent the other end. A unique marketing mix must be designed to appeal to each of these two groups of consumers.

Benefits Segmentation

The focus of benefits segmentation is the appeal of a product or service to a group of consumers. Stated differently, **benefits segments** describe why consumers purchase a product or service or what problem the product solves for the consumer. In a sense, benefits segmentation is the underlying factor in all types of marketing segmentation in that every purchase is made to satisfy a need. Benefits segmentation is also consistent with the marketing concept (discussed in chapter 1) that states that organizations strive to meet customers' needs.

Major shoe manufacturers, such as Nike, focus on "benefits sought" to segment markets. Some consumers desire a high-performance cross-training shoe, while others want a shoe that is more of a fashion statement. In fact, one study asked consumers what is important to them when purchasing athletic footwear. The highest percentage of consumers indicated that "comfort, fit, and feel" was very important (83 percent), followed by "suits active lifestyle" (63 percent), "has performance advantages" (56 percent), and "has fashion advantages" (54 percent). As this research finding illustrates, different consumers desire different benefits from their athletic footwear.[20]

Golf ball manufacturers also try to design products that will appeal to the specific benefits sought by different groups of golfers. The Titleist HP2 Tour offers a soft feel, distance, and control all in one 2-piece ball, while the Titleist HP2 Distance gives remarkable distance and accuracy. Sports marketers really hit a home run when they design products like the HP2 Distance that satisfy multiple needs (i.e., distance and accuracy) of consumers.

Choosing More than One Segment

Although each of the previously mentioned bases for segmentation identify groups of consumers with similar needs, it is common practice to combine segmentation variables. An example of combining segmentation approaches is found in a study of the golf participant market.[21] A survey was conducted to determine playing ability, purchase behavior and the demographic characteristics of public and private course golfers. The resulting profile produced five disinct market segments that combine some of the various bases for segmentation discussed earlier in the chapter. These five segments are shown in Table 7.5.

Geodemographic Segmentation

One of the most widely used multiple segment approaches in sports is geodemographic segmentation. Although geographic segmentation and demographic segmentation are useful tools for sports marketers, combining geographic and demographic characteristics seems to be even more effective in certain situations. For instance, many direct marketing campaigns apply the principles of geodemographic segmentation.

The basis for **geodemographic segmentation** is that people living in close proximity are also likely to share the same lifestyle and demographic composition. Because lifestyle of the consumer is included in this type of segmentation, it is also known as geo-lifestyle. Geodemographics allows marketers to describe the characteristics of broad segments such as standard metropolitan statistical areas (SMSA) all the way down to census blocks (consisting of roughly 340 houses). The most common unit of segmentation for geodemography is the zip code. Claritias Inc., a marketing firm leading the charge in geodemographics, established the PRIZM system in 1970s. PRIZM is used to identify potential markets for products. Each unit of geography is classified as one of the 62 PRIZM clusters, which have been given names that best characterize those populations. Some examples of the PRIZM cluster categories are shown in Table 7.6.

Target Markets

After segmenting the market based on one or a combination of the variables discussed in the previous section, target markets are chosen. **Target marketing** is choosing the segment(s) that will allow an organization to most efficiently and effectively attain its marketing goals.

Sports marketers must make a systematic decision when choosing groups of consumers they wish to target. In order to make these decisions, each potential target market is evaluated on the basis of whether or not it is sizable, reachable, measurable, and exhibits behavioral variation. Let us look at how to judge the worth of potential target markets in greater detail.

table 7.5

Five Market Segments for Golf Participants

Competitiors (18.6 percent)
- Have a handicap of less than 10
- Indicate love of game
- Play for competitive edge
- Practice most often
- Most likely to play in league
- Own most golf clothing
- Are early adopters (e.g., third wedge)
- Buy most golf balls

Players (25.7 percent)
- Have handicap between 10 and 14
- Use custom club makers
- Practice a lot
- Like competition
- Exercise and companionship are important
- Most likely to take out-of-state golf vacation

Sociables (17.8 percent)
- Have handicap between 15 and 18
- Often play with family
- Purchase from off-price retailers
- Play for sociability
- Most likely to take winter vacation to warm destination

Aspirers (18.4 percent)
- Have handicap between 19 and 25
- Love to play; hate to practice
- Most inclined to use golf for business purposes
- Golf shows are important as source of information
- Competition and sociability are unimportant reason to play

Casual (19.5 percent)
- Have handicap of 26 or more
- Do not practice
- More women in this segment
- Play less frequently than other segments
- Own the least golf clothing
- Purchase the fewest golf balls
- Recreation is most important factor for play
- Exercise and companionship are moderately important
- Least likely to take a golf vacation
- Most likely to shop in course pro shop

Source: Sam Fullerton and H. Robert Dodge, "An Application of Market Segmentation in a Sports Marketing Arena: We All Can't Be Greg Norman," *Sport Marketing Quarterly*, vol. 4, no. 3 (1995): 43–47. Reprinted with permission of Fitness Information Technology, Inc. Publishers.

table 7.6

Sample PRIZM Cluster Categories and Descriptions

Kids and Cul-de-Sacs—Ranked number 1 of all 62 clusters in married couples with children and large (4 plus) families. As this characteristic governs every aspect of their lives and activities, one rightly pictures these neighborhoods as a noisy medley of bikes, dogs, rock music, and sports.

God's Country—Populated by educated, upscale professionals, married executives who choose to raise their children in the far exurbs of major metropolitan areas. Their affluence is often supported by dual incomes. Lifestyles are family and outdoor centered.

Towns and Gowns—Describes most of our nation's college towns and university campus neighborhoods. With a typical mix of half locals (towns) and half students (gowns), it is totally unique. Thousands of penniless 18- to 24-year-old kids, plus highly educated professionals with a taste for prestige products beyond their means.

Winners Circle—Second in American affluence and typified by new money, living in expensive new mansions in the suburbs of the nations major metros. These are well-educated, mobile executives and professionals with teen-aged families. Big producers, prolific spenders, and global travelers.

Source: How to Use PRIZM (Alexandria, VA: Claritas 1996). Courtesy of Claritas, Inc. of Arlington, VA.

Evaluation of Target Markets

Sizable

One of the first factors to consider when evaluating and choosing a potential target market is the size of the market. In addition to the current size of the market, sports marketers must also analyze the estimated growth of the market. The market growth would be predicted, in part, through environmental scanning, already discussed in chapter 3.

Sports marketers must be careful in choosing a target market that has neither too many nor too few consumers. If the target market becomes too large, then it essentially becomes a mass, or undifferentiated market. For example, we would not want to choose all basketball fans as a target market because of the huge variations in social class, lifestyles, and consumption behaviors.

On the other hand, sports marketers must guard against a target market that is too small and narrowly defined. We would not choose a target market that consisted of all left-handed, female basketball fans between the ages of 30 and 33 who live in San Antonio with income levels between $40,000 and $50,000. This market is too narrowly defined and would not prove to be a good return on our marketing investment.

One common trap that marketers fall into with respect to the size of the potential market is known as the majority fallacy. The **majority fallacy** assumes that the largest group of consumers should always be selected as the target market. Although, in some instances, the biggest market may be the best choice, usually the competition is the

table 7.7

Market Segments vs. Market Niches

Segment	Niche
Small mass market	Very small market
Less specialized	Very specific needs
Top down (go from large market into smaller pieces)	Bottom up (cater to the smaller pieces of the market)

most fierce for this group of consumers and, therefore, smaller more differentiated targets should be chosen.

These smaller, distinct groups of core customers that an organization focuses on is sometimes referred to as a market niche. **Niche marketing** is the process of carving out a relatively tiny part of a market that has a very special need not currently being filled. By definition, a niche is initially much smaller than a segment and consists of a very homogeneous group of consumers, as reflected by their unique need. The differences between market segments and niches are highlighted in Table 7.7.

One example of a niche market is individuals (as opposed to corporations) who have financially invested in the sports franchise through the purchase of season tickets for many seasons. In addition to their financial investment, these loyal fans have a high emotional investment in the team. In order to retain these valuable consumers, sports marketers must develop a specialized marketing mix to reinforce and reward the loyalty that these fans have shown to the organization.

Reachable

In addition to exploring the size of the potential target market, its ability to be reached should also be evaluated. Reach refers to the accessibility of the target market. Does the sports marketer have a means of communicating with the desired target market? If the answer to this question is no, then the potential target market should not be pursued.

Traditional means of reaching the sports fan include mass media, such as magazines, newspapers, and television. In today's marketing environment, it is possible to reach a very specific target market with technology such as the Internet. For instance, fans of women's soccer can interact on the "Women's Soccer Scene" at *www.requestltd.com/soccer/canadakicks/womenscene*. In addition to the Internet, satellite technology products, such as Primestar and DIRECTV are allowing sports fans all across the country access to their favorite teams. This, of course, opens new geographic segments for sports marketers to consider.

Measurable

The ability to measure the size, accessibility, and purchasing power of the potential target market(s) is another factor that needs to be considered. One of the reasons that demographic segmentation is so widespread is the ease with which characteristics such as age, gender, income level, and occupation can be assessed or measured. Psychographic segments are perhaps the most difficult to measure because of the complex nature of personality and lifestyle.

Behavioral Variation

Finally, if the target market is sizable, reachable, and measurable, sports marketers must examine behavioral variation. We want consumers within the target market to exhibit similar behaviors, attitudes, lifestyles, and so on. In addition, marketers want these characteristics to be unique within a target market. This component is the underlying factor in choosing any target market.

An example of behavioral variation among market segments is the corporate season ticketholder versus the individual season ticketholder. Although both corporate season ticketholders and individual season ticketholders may be fans at some level, their motivation for attending games and attitudes towards the team may be quite different. These variations would prompt different approaches to marketing to each segment.

How Many Target Markets?

Now that we have evaluated potential target markets, do we have to choose just one? The answer depends largely on the organization's marketing objectives and its resources. If the firm has the financial and other resources to pursue more than one target market, it does so by prioritizing the potential target markets.

The market distinguished as the most critical to attaining the firm's objectives is deemed the primary target market. Other, less critical markets of interest are called secondary, tertiary, and so on. Again, a unique marketing mix may need to be developed for each target market, so the costs associated with choosing multiple targets is sometimes prohibitive.

Positioning

Segmentation has been considered and specific target markets have been chosen. Next, sport marketers must decide on the positioning of their sporting events, athletes, teams, and so on. **Positioning** is defined as fixing your sports entity in the minds of consumers in the target market.

Before discussing positioning, three important points should be stressed. First, positioning is dependent on the target market(s) identified in the previous phase of the market selection decisions. In fact, the *same* sport may be positioned differently to distinct target markets. As the box on golf demonstrated earlier in the chapter, the positioning of golf is changing with the opening of a new target market—the young.

Second, positioning is based solely on the perceptions of the target market and how they think and feel about the sports entity. Sometimes positioning is mistakenly linked with where the product appears on the retailer's shelf or where the product is placed in an advertisement. Nothing could be further from the truth. Position is all about how the consumer perceives your sports product relative to competitive offerings.

■ Slazenger positioning its golf products as the "Standard of Excellence."

Third, the definition of positioning reflects its importance to all sports products. It should also be noted that sports leagues (ABA versus NBA), sports teams (e.g., Dallas Cowboys as America's Team), and individual athletes (e.g., Tiger Woods as the youthful, hip golfer or the NBA's eccentric bad boy, Dennis Rodman) all must be positioned by sports marketers.

How does the sports marketer attempt to fix the sports entity in the minds of consumers? The first step rests in understanding the target market's perception of the relevant attributes of the sports entity. The relevant attributes are those features and characteristics desired in the sports entity by the target market. These attributes may be intangible, such as a fun atmosphere at the stadium, or tangible, such as having cushioned seating. Golf club manufacturers such as Slazenger have positioned their equipment as the "standards of excellence" and having "impeccable quality."

In another example, consider the possible product attributes for in-line skates. Pricing, status of the name brand, durability, quality of the wheels, and weight of the skate, may all be considered product attributes. If serious, competitive skaters are chosen as the primary target market, then the in-line skates may be positioned on the basis of quality of the wheels and weight of the skate. However, if first-time, recreational skaters are considered the primary target market, then relevant product attributes may be price and durability. Marketers attempt to understand all of the potential attributes and then which ones are most important to their target markets through marketing research.

■ Dramatic differences in the positioning
of hockey and figure skating.

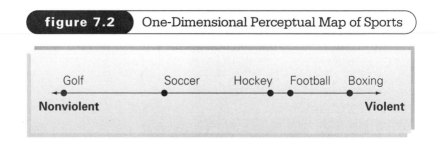

figure 7.2 One-Dimensional Perceptual Map of Sports

Golf   Soccer   Hockey   Football   Boxing

Nonviolent   **Violent**

Perceptual Maps

Through various advanced marketing research techniques, perceptual maps are created to examine positioning. **Perceptual maps** provide marketers with three types of information. First, perceptual maps indicate the dimensions or attributes that consumers use when thinking about a sports product or service. Second, perceptual maps tell sports marketers where different sports products or services are located on those dimensions. The third type of information provided by perceptual maps is how your product is perceived relative to the competition.

Perceptual maps can be constructed in any number of dimensions, based on the number of product attributes being considered. Figure 7.2 demonstrates a one-dimensional perceptual map, which explores the positioning of various spectator sports based on the level of perceived aggression/violence associated with the sports. This hypothetical example can be interpreted as follows: Boxing is seen as the most violent/aggressive sport, followed by football, hockey, and soccer. On the other hand, golf is the least aggressive sport. These results would vary, of course, based on who participated in the research, how aggression/violence is defined by the researchers, and what level of competition is being considered (i.e., professional, high school, youth leagues).

Although it is easy to conceptualize one-dimensional perceptual maps, the number of dimensions is contingent upon the number of relevant attributes to consumers. For example, LA Gear positions its shoes for multiple uses like aerobics, running, and casual wear. New Balance, however, positions its shoes solely on the basis of running.

table 7.8

Six Dimensions or Attributes of Sports	
Dimension 1	Strength, speed, and endurance vs. methodical and precise movements
Dimension 2	Athletes only as participants vs. athletes plus recreational participants
Dimension 3	Skill emphasis on impact with object vs. skill emphasis on body movement
Dimension 4	Skill development and practice primarily alone vs. primarily with others
Dimension 5	A younger participant in the sport vs. participant ages from young to older
Dimension 6	Less masculine vs. more masculine

Source: James H. Martin, "Using a Perceptual Map of the Consumer's Sport Schema to Help Make Sponsorship Decisions," *Sport Marketing Quarterly*, vol. 3, no. 3, (1994): 27–33.

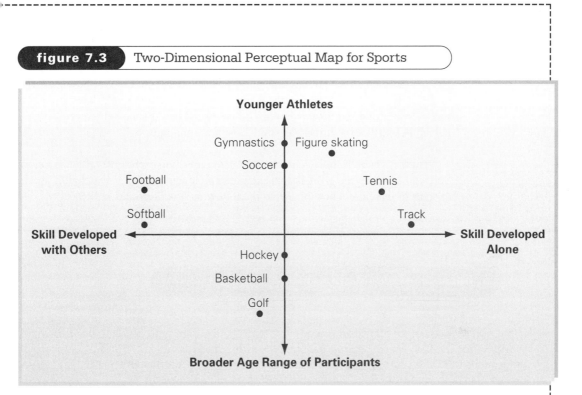

figure 7.3 Two-Dimensional Perceptual Map for Sports

A recent study using perceptual mapping techniques found that consumers identify six dimensions of sport (shown in Table 7.8). Although it is possible to create a six-dimensional perceptual map, it is nearly impossible to interpret. Therefore, two-dimensional perceptual maps were constructed that compared 10 sports on the six dimensions identified by consumers.

Figure 7.3 shows a two-dimensional perceptual map using Dimension 4 (skill developed primarily with others vs. skill developed alone) and Dimension 5 (younger athletes vs. broad age ranges of participants). Interpreting this perceptual map, football is considered a sport where the participants are younger athletes and skill is developed primarily with others. Compared with football, golf is seen as a sport for a broader range of participants with skills developed more on your own. Using these results, sports marketers can better understand the image of their sport from the perspective of various target markets and decide whether this image needs to be changed or maintained.

epositioning

As suggested, sport marketers may use the results of positioning studies to change the image of their sport. For instance, professional hockey is known for its aggressive play. Although this is appealing to some fans, it was not the image the NHL wanted to project. The NHL felt this aggressive play was overshadowing the essence of the game. Thus, NHL sought to **reposition** hockey and eliminate some of the undue violence of the sport. Repositioning is changing the image or perception of the sports entity in the minds of consumers in the target market.

One way that the NHL has repositioned professional hockey is to provide stiffer penalties for fighting. Morever, the NHL aired a series of humorous advertisements on ESPN that showed the players in a light-hearted way. Instead of featuring crushing body checks, the advertisemets show the nonaggressive, human side of the players.

Hockey is not the only sport attempting to reposition itself. Following the Latrell Sprewell incident, the NBA is also experiencing image problems. Baseball is another sport in search of a new image, as the following box illustrates.

baseball plays image game

In the split second before the Yankees won the World Series in 1996, Major League Baseball Enterprises CEO Greg Murphy flashed a concerned glance toward right field. Hundreds of New York City police officers were about to descend on the diamond if the Series ended.

"I asked the head of security to instruct them not to pull down their face shields and to smile at the crowd," said Murphy. "Those shields are so Darth Vader-like and so menacing. That's the last image that we want fans to take away from the celebration at the ballpark."

Murphy, who joined Major League Baseball in June 1996, knows that in sports marketing *image is everything*. The former Kraft and Pepsi-Cola executive says that over the next several months he hopes to reintroduce [reposition] America's once-favorite pastime to fans and corporations who have all but designated the game a sports dinosaur. He'll do it by targeting youth, women, and minorities; promoting a handful of star players; and aggressively wooing top companies in hopes of generating more than $500 million in corporate sponsorships before the end of 1996.

Top sports advertisers and marketers say baseball is ripe for a turnaround, but they worry the game is too caught up in its own traditions and history to "out-hip" aggressive competitors like the NFL, NHL, and NBA. Image experts say the World Series between New York and Atlanta added a much needed dash of panache to the sport. Yankee Stadium was filled with more Hollywood VIPs and corporate moguls than you usually see at a Los Anegeles Lakers game.

But getting fans to warm up to players might be tougher than baseball thinks. According to a study conducted by Market Evaluations, baseball stars often rank below those in other sports. The reason isn't clear, but marketers say baseball players might also be held to a higher standard than other athletes because of the game's traditional, wholesome, family orientation.

"Even when you have stand up guys like Cal Ripken or Frank Thomas, it's harder to sell an advertiser on a baseball player," says sports marketing consultant Nova Lanktree, who matches corporations with sports endorsers. She says the strike of 1994 has caused fans to view the players as greedy. One more reason to develop a new position for baseball.

Source: Dottie Enrico, "Baseball Plays Image Game," *USA Today,* October 28, 1996, B1, B2. Reprinted with permission.

C hapter 7 focuses on the critical market selection decisions, also referred to as segmentation, targeting, and positioning. Segmentation, the first market selection decision, is identifying consumers with common needs. Typically, the basis for segmentation of consumer markets include demographics, socioeconomics, psychographics, behavioral, and benefits. Marketers using demographic segmentation choose groups of consumers based on common ages, gender, ethnic background, and stage of the family life cycle. Geographic segmentation is grouping people who live in similar areas such as cities, states, regions of the country, or even countries (e.g., the United States versus international markets). Socioeconomic segmentation is based on grouping consumers of similar income levels, educational levels, and occupation. Psychographic segments are especially useful to sports marketers, as they are based on consumers' lifestyles, activities, interests, and opinions. Behavioral segments are groups of consumers that are similar on the basis of consumer actions, such as how often they purchase sports products or how loyal they are when purchasing a sports product. Finally, benefits segmentation are groups of consumers attempting to satisfy similar needs by consuming the sports product. Sports marketers may choose to segment their markets using one of the previously mentioned segmentation variables (e.g., demographics) or combine several of the bases for segmentation (e.g., geodemographic).

Once market segments have been chosen, the next market selection decision is picking a target market. Target marketing is choosing the segment or segments that will allow the organization to most effectively and efficiently acheive its marketing goals. When evaluating potential target markets, care should be taken to ensure that the markets are the right size (neither too large nor too small), reachable (accessible), measurable (i.e., size, purchasing power, and characteristics of the segments can be measured), and demonstrate behavioral variation (i.e., consumers share common characteristics within the target market).

The final market selection decision is positioning. After the target market has been chosen, sports marketers want to position their products or fix them in the minds of the target markets. Positioning is based on the perception or image that sports marketers want to develop or maintain for the sports product. For example, a minor league baseball team may wish to position itself as an inexpensive, family entertainment alternative. In order to understand how a sports product is positioned relative to its competition, perceptual maps are developed through marketing research techniques. By looking at perceptual maps, sports marketers can identify whether or not they have acheived their desired image or whether they need to reposition their sports product in the minds of the target market.

AIO dimensions

behavioral segmentation

benefits segmentation

demographic segmentation

family life cycle

geodemographic segmentation

geographic segmentation

market niche

market segmentation

market selection decisions

perceptual mapping

positioning

psychographic segmentation

repositoning

socioeconomic segmentation

target market

1. Describe the key components of market selection decisions and indicate how market selection decisions are incorporated into the larger strategic marketing process.

2. What is market segmentation? Provide some examples of how sports marketers segment the sports participant market (those who play) and the sports spectator market (those that watch).

3. Discuss the various ways to segment the sports market based on demographics. Which of the demographic bases are the most effective when segmenting the sports market and why?

4. Describe, in detail, the family life cycle and how it is used as a strategic tool when segmenting sports markets. What stage of the family life cycle are you currently in? How does this affect your sports participation and spectator behavior?

5. Provide examples of sports that you believe would appeal to each of the six social class categories (upper-upper through lower-lower). What sports appeal to all social class segments?

6. What are AIOs? Why is psychographic segmentation so difficult to practice?

7. Provide several examples of the growth of international sports marketing.

8. What is behavioral segmentation? What are some of the common behaviors that sports marketers would use for segmentation purposes?

9. Define benefits segmentation and discuss why benefits segmentation is considered to be at the core of all segmentation. What benefits do you look for when attending a sporting event? Does your answer vary from event to event?

10. Define a target market. What are the requirements for successful target markets (i.e., how should each target be evaluated)? Provide examples of sports products or services that target two or more distinct markets.

11. How many target markets should a sports marketer consider for a single product?

12. Describe positioning and discuss how perceptual mapping techniques are used by sports marketers. What is repositioning?

1. Find two advertisements for sports products that compete directly with one another. For example, you may wish to compare Nike running shoes with Reebok running shoes or King Cobra golf clubs with Taylormade golf clubs. How is each product segmented, targeted, and positioned? Are there more differences or similarities in these market selection decisions?

2. How is the health and fitness industry segmented, in general? Describe the segmentation, targets, and positioning of health and fitness clubs in your area.

3. You are hired as the director of sports marketing for a new minor league hockey franchise in Chicago, a city that already has an NHL team. Describe how you would segment, target, and position your new franchise.

4. Describe the primary target market for the following: NASCAR; the Kentucky Derby; "The Rhino" bowling ball; and the WNBA. Next, define a potential secondary target market for each of these sports products.

5. Interview five consumers who have recently attended a high school sporting event, five consumers who have recently attended a college sporting event, and five who have recently attended any professional sporting event. Ask them to identify why they attended this event and what benefits they were looking for? Were their needs met?

6. Develop a list of all the possible product attributes that may be considered when purchasing the following sports products: a tennis racquet, a basketball, a mountain bike. After you have developed the list of attributes, ask five people which attributes they consider to be the most important for each product. Do all consumers agree? Are there some attributes that you may have omitted? Why are these attributes important in positioning?

7. How do you think the following races are positioned: Boston Marathon, "Run Like Hell" 5K Halloween Race, and the Bowling Green 10K Classic? Draw a two-dimensional perceptual map to illustrate the positioning of each race.

8. Provide examples of individual athletes, teams, and sports (leagues) that have had to develop repositioning strategies.

 INTERNET EXERCISES

1. Using the Internet, find the demographic profile for fans attending LPGA (women's tour) versus PGA (men's tour). Are there differences? Use this information to comment on the market selection decisions for the LPGA.

2. Find two Internet sites that target children interested in sports and two Internet sites that target the mature market. Note any similarities and differences between the sites.

3. Find two Internet sites for soccer. One site should focus on U.S. soccer, while the other is international. Comment on the relative positioning of soccer in the United States versus abroad based on information found on the Internet.

1. "The Littlest Shoppers," *American Demographics,* February 1992, 48, 50.

2. "Young Consumers, Perils and Power," *The New York Times,* February 11, 1990.

3. John Erardi, "Indians Lead Way in Fan Relations," *Cincinnati Enquirer,* December 3, 1995, C10.

4. Claudia Deutsch, "Anyone for a Game of Tennis and 'Toons? Turner Promotes the Game to Children with its Cartoon Network," *The New York Times,* April 8, 1997, D8. Brian Clearly, "Cartoonizing Tennis," *Tennis,* November 1996, 14.

5. Michael Solomon, *Consumer Behavior,* 3rd ed. (Upper Saddle River, NJ: Prentice Hall, ed. 1996): 510.

6. Laura Zinn, "Teens: Here Comes the Biggest Wave Yet," *Business Week,* April 11, 1994, 76.

7. Cited in "New Consumer Product Offerings By NBA & WNBA." <http://www.newspage.com/cgi-bin/NA....y?story=v0120209.6is&date=19980121>.

8. W. Lazer and E. Shaw, "How Older Americans Spend Their Money," *American Demographics,* September 1987, 36–41.

9. C. Miller, "Misconception, Fear Stall Advance Into Mature Market," *Marketing News,* December 9, 1991, 11.

10. Sporting Goods Manufacturers Associations. "The Senior Sports Revolution." <http://www.sportlink.com>.

11. Margaret Littman, "Women Fans Have Gridiron Pros Grinning," *Marketing News,* February 2, 1998, 1, 14.

12. "Women's Hockey." *The Journal of Woman's Ice & Roller Hockey in North America.* <http://www.hockeyplayer.com/wh/information.htm>.

13. Welch Suggs, " Is Soccer Here to Stay?" *Dallas Business Journal.* (June 16, 1997) <http://www.amcity.com/dallas/stories/061697/story3.html>.

14. "Group Seven Communications, Inc. Launches 'Deportes Hoy', The Premier Spanish-Language Sports Daily," <http://guide-p.infoseek.com> (January 22, 1998).

15. John Erardi.

16. Adam Cohen, "Blowin' the Wheels Off Bubba," *Time,* February 26, 1996, 56.

17. Michael Solomon, *Consumer Behavior,* 3rd ed. (Englewood Cliffs, NJ: Prentice Hall, 1996).

18. "America's Teams," *Sport,* November 1996, 33–37.

19. "Touchdowns and Fumbles: Urban Investments in NFL Franchises." <http://www.cad.gu.edu.au/market/cy...rnal_of_sport_marketing/turco.html>.

20. "AFA National Consumer Survey." <http://www.sportlink.com/footwear/...market97/decisions_influences.html>.

21. Sam Fullerton and H. Robert Dodge, "An Application of Market Segmentation in a Sports Marketing Arena: We All Can't Be Greg Norman," *Sport Marketing Quarterly,* vol. 4, no. 3, (1995): 43–47.

CHAPTER

8

Sports Product Concepts

OBJECTIVES

After completing this chapter, you should be able to

- Define sports products and differentiate between goods and services

- Explain how sports products and services are categorized

- Define branding and discuss the guidelines for choosing an effective brand name

- Discuss the branding process in detail

- Examine the advantages and disadvantages of licensing from the perspective of the licensee and licensor

- Identify the dimensions of service quality and goods quality

- Define product design and explain how product design is related to product quality

■ This baseball, glove, and bat represent pure goods.

■ This competition represents a pure service.

Think about attending a Major League Baseball game at Wrigley Field in Chicago. Inside the stadium you find vendors selling game programs, scorecards, Major League Baseball licensed merchandise, and plenty of food and drink. An usher escorts you to your seat to enjoy the entertainment. During the game, you are exposed to more product choices.

Every game experience presents us with a number of opportunities to purchase and consume sports products. Some of the products, such as the scorecards, represent a pure good, while others, such as the game itself, represents a pure service. Each sports product represents a business challenge with incredible upward and downward potential. In this chapter, we will explore the multidimensional nature of sports products.

efining Sports Products

A **sports product** is a good, a service, or any combination of the two that is designed to provide benefits to a sports spectator, participant, or sponsor. Within this definition, the market concept discussed in chapter 1 is reintroduced. As you recall, the marketing concept states that sports organizations are in the business of satisfying consumers' needs. In order to do this, products must be developed that anticipate and satisfy consumers' needs. Sports marketers sell products based on the benefits that they offer consumers. These benefits are so critical to marketers that sometimes products are defined as "bundles of benefits." For example, the sport of snowshoeing has recently emerged as one of the nation's fastest growing winter sports. Ski Industry America, a trade association interested in marketing the sport of snowshoeing, suggests that the bundle of benefits this sports product offers include: great exercise, requires little athletic skill, and is much less expensive than skiing.[1]

In addition to sports and sporting goods, athletes can also be thought of as sports products that possess multiple benefits. For example, NBA teams are currently seeking players who can perform multiple roles on the court rather than having more specialized skills.[2] The player who can rebound, is great defensively, dribbles well, and can play the post is invaluable to the franchise. The classic example of the "hybrid" player with multiple skills was Magic Johnson who played center and guard in the 1980 NBA Finals. Today's NBA stars, such as Jordan, Pippen, and Hill, exemplify the versatile player who offers many benefits to the team. As the following article illustrates, Shaq is one big "bundle of benefits" both on and off the court.

shaq's a unique bundle of benefits

In music, marketing, movies, and basketball, Shaquille O'Neal has made his mark. Now that he's moved to the world's entertainment capital, Los Angeles, the 7-foot-1 center will grow even larger in the pop-culture world beyond sports. "Moving to the nation's number two media market (behind New York) automatically boosts his visibility tenfold," said Rob Kahane, whose Trauma Records is partnered with the O'Neal label. "I think Shaq's move to Los Angeles is huge."

Shaq's musical career as a rapper is going strong. His first two albums sold more than 500,000 copies each, and a third is on the way. O'Neal's movie career has not quite fared as well, however. His first movie—1994's *Blue Chips*—was not a major commercial success, and his second effort, *Kazaam*, was also dubbed a bust.

(continued)

Regardless of his successes and failures in the entertainment industry, O'Neal has proven himself as a marketing diesel. Shaq endorses consumer products from tacos to candy, and his move to Los Angeles will only help boost his marketing clout. And don't forget Reebok. The Los Angeles athletic shoe market has been dominated by Nike. Reebok believes, however, that Shaq's presence on the West Coast will boost shoe sales.

Sources: The Associated Press, "Shaq Attracts Cameras," *The Cincinnati Post*, July 20, 1996, p. 6D; Allison Samuels and Mark Starr, "Strutting His Stuff," *Newsweek*, November 4, 1996, 62.

Goods and Services as Sports Products

Our definition of products includes goods and services. It is important to understand the differences in these two types of products in order to plan and implement the strategic sports marketing process. Because services, such as watching a game, are being produced (by the players) and consumed (by the spectators) simultaneously, there is no formal channel of distribution. However, when you purchase a pure good, such as a pair of hockey skates, they must be produced by a manufacturer (e.g., Bauer), sent to a retailer (e.g., Sports Authority), and then sold to you. This formal channel of distribution requires careful planning and managing. Let us explore some of the other differences between goods and services.

Goods are defined as tangible, physical products that offer benefits to consumers. Obviously, sporting goods stores sell tangible products such as tennis balls and racquets, hockey equipment, exercise equipment, and so on. By contrast, **services** are usually described as intangible, nonphysical products. For instance, the competitive aspect of any sporting event (i.e., the game itself) or receiving an ice-skating lesson, reflect pure services.

It is easy to see why soccer balls and exercise equipment are classified as pure goods and why the intangible nature of the game constitutes a pure service, but what about other sports products? For example, sporting events typically offer a variety of pure goods (such as food, beverages, and merchandise). However, even these goods have customer service component. The responsiveness, courtesy, and friendliness of the service provider are intangible components of the service encounter.

Most sports products do not fall so neatly into two distinct categories, but possess characteristics of both goods and services. Figure 8.1 shows the goods-services continuum. On one end, we have sporting goods, and at the other end of the continuum we have almost exclusive, sports services. For example, a sports service

figure 8.1   The Goods-Services Continuum

Pure goods		Pure services
(tennis balls, hockey equipment)		(game itself)

that has received considerable attention in the past few years is the fantasy sports camp. Sports camps in a variety of team and individual sports have sprung up to appeal to the aging athlete. For instance, 30 people of age 30 or older pay $6,100 each to participate in a basketball camp run by former Lakers Magic Johnson and Jerry West. About the only tangible good that the participant leaves with are souvenirs of the camp, such as a uniform.

Thus far, the distinction between goods and services has been based on the tangible aspects of the sports product. In addition to the degree of tangibility, goods and services are differentiated on the basis of perishability, separability, and standardization. These distinctions are important because they form the foundation of product planning in the strategic sports marketing process. Because of their importance, let us take a look at each dimension.

Tangibility

Tangibility refers to the ability to see, feel, and touch the product. Interestingly, the strategy for pure goods often involves stressing the intangible benefits of the product. For example, advertisements for Nike's new F.I.T. performance apparel highlight not only the comfort of the product, but the way the clothing will make you feel like a champion. Similarly, Callaway's Great Big Bertha is paired with TAG Heuer watches in an advertisement that described how both are shaped by the spirit of Sports!

On the other hand, the strategy for an intangible service is to "tangibilize them."[3] For example, a major league team may wish to highlight the tangible comforts of its new facility rather than promote the game itself. Sportscape dimensions, or the tangible aspects of the stadium such as the stadium design, seating, and aesthetics should be stressed, especially when the team is performing poorly.

Standardization/Consistency

Another characteristic that distinguishes goods from services is the degree of **standardization**. This refers to receiving the same level of quality over repeat purchases. Because sporting goods are tangible, the physical design of golf balls are manufactured with very little variability. This is even more true today as many organizations focus on how to continuously improve their manufacturing processes and enhance their product quality.

Pure services, however, reflect the other end of the standardization/consistency continuum. For example, think about the consistency associated with different individual and team athletic performances. How many times have you heard an announcer state before a game, "Which team (or player) will show up today?" Meaning, will the team play well or poorly on that given day.

The Chicago Bulls may be one of the most consistent teams in the NBA because of their high winning percentage over the past few seasons. This, however, does not guarantee they will win the night you attend the game. Even the great Michael Jordan puts on a poor performance occasionally.

Consider another example of the lack of consistency within a sporting event. You may attend a doubleheader and see your favorite team lose the first game 14 to 5 and win the second game of the day by a score of 1 to 0. One of the risks associated with using individual athletes or teams to endorse products is the high degree of variability associated with their performance from day to day and year to year. Because sports marketers have no control over the consistency of the sports product, they must focus on those things that can be controlled, such as promotions, stadium atmosphere, and, to some extent, pricing.

Perishability

Perishability refers to the ability to store or inventory "pure goods," whereby services are lost if not consumed. Goods may be inventoried or stored if they are not purchased immediately, although there are many costs associated with handling this inventory. If a tennis professional is offering lessons, but no students enroll between the hours of 10:00 A.M. and noon, this time (and money) is lost. This "down time" in which the service provider is available but there is no demand is called **idle product capacity**. Idle product capacity results in decreased profitability. In the case of the tennis pro, there is a moderate inventory cost associated with the professional's salary.

Another example with much higher inventory costs is a professional basketball team that is not filling the stands. Consider the Dallas Mavericks, the NBA team with the poorest average attendance in the 1996–1997 season. The costs of producing one professional game include everything from the "astronomical" salaries of the players to the basic costs of lighting and heating the arena. If paying fans are not in the seats, the performance/service will perish, never to be recouped. As a general rule of thumb, the most perishable products in business are airline seats, hotel rooms, and athletic event tickets.

In an effort to reduce the problem of idle product capacity, sports marketers attempt to stimulate demand in off-peak periods by manipulating the other marketing mix variables. For example, if tennis lessons are not in demand from 10:00 A.M. to noon, the racquet club may offer reduced fees for enrolling during these times. Likewise, the Dallas Mavericks may offer a reduction in ticket prices or other promotions to stimulate fan interest.

Separability

Another factor that distinguishes goods from services is **separability**. If a consumer is purchasing a new pair of running shoes at a major shoe store chain, such as the Finishing Line, the quality of the good (the Reebok shoes) can be separated from the quality of the service (delivered by the Finishing Line sales associate). Although it is possible to separate the good from the person providing the service, these often overlap. What this suggests is that a manufacturer will selectively choose the retailers that will best represent their goods. In addition, manufacturers and retailers often provide detailed training to ensure that salespeople are knowledgeable about the numerous brands that are inventoried.

As we move along the goods-services continuum from pure goods toward pure services, there is less separability. In other words, it becomes more difficult to separate the service received from the service provider. In the case of an athletic event, there is no separation between the athlete, the entertainment, and the fan. The competition is being produced and consumed simultaneously. As such, sport marketers can capitalize on a team or athlete when they are performing well. When things are going poorly, they may have to rely on other aspects of the game (food, fun, promotions) to satisfy fans. The Colorado Rockies baseball club sold the exclusivity of their location at Coors Field to the fans. Virtually every game has been sold out since they entered the league in 1991 due to the marketing orientation of the Rockies.

Classifying Sports Products

In addition to categorizing products based on where they fall on the goods-services continuum, a number of other classification schemes exist. For sports organizations that have a variety of products, the concepts of product line and product mix become important strategic considerations. Let us look at these two concepts in the context of a goods-oriented sports organization and a services-oriented sports organization.

A **product line** is a group of products that are closely related because they satisfy a class of needs, are used together, are sold to the same customer groups, are distributed through the same type of outlets, or fall within a given price range. Wilson Sporting Goods sells many related product lines such as shoes, bats, gloves, softballs, golf clubs, and tennis racquets. The following spotlight provides an example of a new product line Huffy introduced to appeal to the female basketball participant.

spotlight on women in sports marketing:

huffy sports company introduces wnba product line

Huffy Sports Company, the world's leading manufacturer of basketball systems for home and institutional use, recently introduced a new product line of WNBA-licensed products. As the official backboard licensee of the WNBA, Huffy Sports is offering a WNBA/Rebecca Lobo portable basketball system (also available in a backboard and rim combination), as well as a WNBA team Mini-Jammer™ and Street Net™.

The explosive popularity of the WNBA, in combination with the rapid growth of women's basketball, has successfully helped launch Huffy Sports' WNBA branded products. "Today, females account for 38 percent of those playing basketball under the age of 18," Huffy Sports Marketing Manager Patrick

Ehren said. "The female market for basketball is rapidly expanding, and the WNBA is a great medium for Huffy Sports to reach that audience."

The flagship of Huffy Sports' WNBA product offering is the WNBA/Rebecca Lobo portable basketball system. Lobo, a forward/center with the WNBA's New York Liberty, has her image and autograph printed on the high-performance backboard.

For the true WNBA fanatics who take their game everywhere, Huffy Sports is offering a WNBA Mini-Jammer. The 24" mini-backboard highlights all eight WNBA team logos in full-color graphics. A white net, 10" diameter molded rim, 5" inflatable basketball, and mounting brackets are included with the unit.

(continued)

Rounding out Huffy Sports' WNBA product line is the company's WNBA Street Net. The answer for long lasting durability and safety, the Street Net is made from a "jersey-like" woven mesh that reduces the risk of entanglement and increases the net's life span. The Street Net also features the WNBA logo.

Huffy plans to continue developing its WNBA line, introducing new products at various price points in the months ahead. Lobo, who recently signed an exclusive product-endorsement contract with Huffy Sports, will support the licensed products through various retail appearances and promotions.

Source: "Huffy Company Introduces WNBA Product Line." <http://www.sportlink.com/new_products/huffy6.html>. Courtesy of Huffy Sports.

In Huffy's case, the WNBA product line is just one of many lines they offer consumers. The total assortment of product lines that a sports organization sells is the **product mix**. Table 8.1 illustrates the relationship between the product lines and product mix for Wilson Sporting Goods. The number of different product lines the organization offers is referred to as the breadth of the product mix. If these product lines are closely related in terms of the goods and services that are offered to consumers, then there is a high degree of product consistency.

Nike recently increased the breadth of its product mix by adding sports equipment. Product lines such as baseball bats and gloves, hockey sticks and skates, footballs, golf balls, and snowboards will also be sold under the new Nike equipment division.[4] The strategic advantage of this related diversification is the use of Nike's established marketing muscle. Synergy in distribution and promotion, as well as strong brand identification, should make Nike's launch into equipment a successful venture. Andrew Mooney, who heads the new equipment division certainly believes it will be profitable, "Within several years, we will be Nike's fastest growing division."[5]

table 8.1

Relationship Between Product Lines and Product Mix

Baseball	Basketball	Football	Hockey	Softball
Accessories	Accessories	Accessories	Hockey gloves	Accessories
Aluminum bats	Basketballs	Footballs	Pants	Bags
Bags	Uniforms	Football gloves	Shin guards	Balls
Baseballs		Protective	Shoulder pads	Aluminum bats
Batting gloves		equipment	Street hockey	Batting gloves
Gloves & mitts		Shoulder pads	equipment	Protective
Protective		Uniforms		equipment
equipment		Wristbands		Softball gloves
Uniforms				Uniforms
Wooden bats				

Source: "Wilson Sporting Goods Company." <http://www.wilsonsports.com>. Reprinted with permission of Wilson Sporting Goods Company.

Sports Marketing — hall of *fame*

PHIL KNIGHT

A former University of Oregon track-and-field athlete and Stanford MBA, Knight is the founder and current CEO of Nike, Inc. By all accounts, Nike and Knight are still changing the face of sports marketing. Knight started his multibillion dollar empire by selling his specialized running shoes out of the trunk of his car.

The ultimate driving force of Nike's success has been Knight's ability to attract top sports stars and build marketing campaigns around them. Nike's first celebrity athlete was the University of Oregon's track star, Steve Prefontaine. When Nike was surpassed by Reebok in the late 1980s, they landed their biggest success story ever—MJ, Michael Jordan. Quickly, Nike regained its position as market leader and has not relinquished it since.

Sources: Keith Elliot Greenberg, *Bill Bowerman and Phil Knight: Building the Nike Empire* (Woodbridge, CT: Blackbird Press, 1994); David R. Collins, *Philip H. Knight: Running with Nike* (Ada, OK: Garrett Educational Corp, 1992).

Today, Nike is focusing on increasing their talent pool of athletes and expanding their growing product lines into new sports such as hockey, golf, and soccer. For example, Tiger Woods recently joined the Knight stable for a $40 million, multiyear endorsement contract. In addition, Nike, under the leadership of Knight, is quickly moving into international markets. However their race with Reebok ends, Knight will always be remembered as the man who realized the true marketing power of sports celebrities.

1-800-749-2445

■ Nike extends their product lines.

The depth of the product lines describes the number of individual products that comprise that line. The greater the number of variations in the product line, the deeper the line. For example, the Wilson basketball product line currently features over a dozen different basketballs, seven of which are Grant Hill models (e.g., Synthetic Leather Grant Hill All-Star, Premium Rubber Grant Hill All-Star, Rubber Grant Hill Signature).

Now, think about how the product concepts might relate to a more service-oriented sports organization, like a professional sports franchise. All of these organizations have gone beyond selling the core product, the game itself, and moved into other profitable areas, such as the sale of licensed merchandise, memorabilia, and fantasy camps. In essence, sports organizations have expanded their product lines or broadened their product mix.

Understanding the depth, breadth, and consistency of the product offerings is important from a strategic perspective. Sports organizations might consider adding product lines, and therefore widen the product mix. For example, Nike is using this strategy and capitalizing on its strong brand name. Alternatively, the sports organization can eliminate weak product lines and focus on its established strengths. In addition, the product lines it adds may be related to existing lines (product line consistency) or may be unrelated to existing lines (product line diversification).

Another strategic decision may be to maintain the number of product lines, but add new versions to make the line deeper. For instance, the WNBA is deepening its product line from eight to ten teams for the 1998 season with the addition of Detroit and Washington, D.C.[6] Which of these product planning strategies requires examining the overarching marketing goals and the organizational objectives, as well as carefully considering consumers needs?

(P)roduct Characteristics

Products are sometimes described as "bundles of benefits" designed to satisfy consumers needs.[7] These "bundles" consist of numerous important attributes, or characteristics, that, when taken together, create the total product. These product characteristics, which include branding, quality, and design, are illustrated in Figure 8.2.

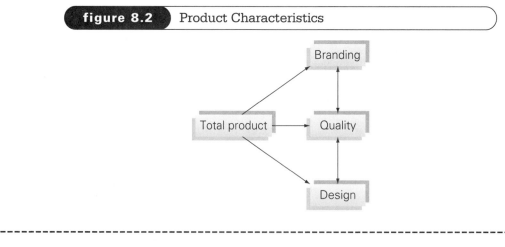

figure 8.2 Product Characteristics

It is important to note that each of the product characteristics interacts with the others to produce the total product. Branding is dependent on product quality, product quality is contingent on product design, and so on. Although these product features (i.e., branding, quality, and design) are interdependent, we will examine each independently in the following sections.

Branding

What first comes to mind when you hear University of Notre Dame, Green Bay, or adidas? It's likely that the Fighting Irish name, along with the Lucky Leprechaun ready to battle, comes to mind for Notre Dame. The Packers are synonymous with Green Bay, Wisconsin and the symbolic three stripes are synonymous with adidas. All of these characteristics are important elements of branding.

Branding is a name, design, symbol, or any combination that a sports organization uses to help differentiate its products from the competition. Three important branding concepts are brand name, brand marks, and trademarks. A **brand name** refers to the element of the brand that can be vocalized, such as the Nike Air Jordan, the Cincinnati Reds, and the University of Kentucky Wildcats. When selecting a brand name for sporting goods or a team name, considerable marketing effort is required to ensure that the name symbolizes strength and confidence. Because choosing a name is such a critical decision, sports marketers sometimes use the following guidelines for selecting brand names:

- The name should be positive, distinctive, generate positive feelings and associations, be easy to remember, and easy to pronounce. For team names, the positive associations include those linked with a city or geographic area.
- The name should be translatable into a dynamite attitude-oriented logo. As an example of a successful logo choice consider the San Jose Sharks of the NHL. Although the Sharks rank near the bottom of all sports franchises in wins, they rank in the top five in logo merchandise sales.[8]
- The name should imply the benefits the sports product delivers. For example, the name communicates the product attributes the target market desires.
- The name should be consistent with the image of the rest of the product lines, organization, and/or city. Again, this is especially important for cities naming their sports franchises. One example of this concept in action is MLS's Columbus Crew.[9] The Crew was chosen to represent the Columbus community in a positive manner. The name suggests the hard work, do-not-quit attitude that people in the Columbus community value.
- The name should be legally and ethically permissible. That is, the name cannot violate another organization's trademarks or be seen as offensive to any group of people. For example, a great many team names with reference to (and perceived negative connotations) Native Americans have been changed or are under scrutiny (e.g., Miami University of Ohio Redskins, Atlanta Braves, Washington Redskins).

As the article on the following page entitled "What's in a Name" illustrates, a good brand/team name means the difference between the success and failure of a franchise.

AquaSox, SeaWolves, Rampage, and Mud-dogs. These are minor league team names that were designed to be as unique and marketable as possible. Is this marketing creativity or a merchandising craze that has gone too far?

Just what is a Muddog? With a kid's fan club called the "Mud Puppies" and a ballpark known locally as the Dog Pound, it really doesn't matter. The Merrillville Muddogs have a name and logo that is tailormade for today's marketing and merchandising business.

"The name was developed by our owner, Dick Jacobson," notes Pat Krull, Assistant General Manager of the Muddogs. "He looked around the minor leagues and identified the trend of creature-oriented names—Sea Dogs, Mudcats, Crawdads, and RiverDogs. The northwest Indiana area is hardworking and blue-collar. The Muddog name and logo reflect that aspect of our community, from the spiked collar to the muscular arms."

When the Eastern League's New Britain Red Sox parted company with Boston and became the new Class AA affiliate of the Minnesota Twins, the time was right to capitalize on the current marketing craze. This led to the Hardware City Rock Cats.

This wild nickname emerged from a "name the team" contest, even though it wasn't one of the 400 different entries submitted. Many people suggested Hardware City because of the long-standing association with Stanley Tools and the hardware industry. Where the Rock Cats came from is not clear.

Though Christopher Whalen of the Rock Cats admits that the response from the older population was a bit cool at first, the name is catching on. "We are in Red Sox country, so the changing name and logo was dramatic. We now have full support of the community and we have gone national after we were adopted as the official minor league baseball team for the 200-station Sports Fan Radio Network, and in terms of merchandising, it's been a complete turnaround. We now ship merchandise from coast to coast and to Japan and Europe regularly."

In addition to the Rock Cats, here are just a few of the hottest minor league baseball merchandise sellers. Check out some of the names.

Augusta Greenjackets
Birmingham Barons
Bowie Baysox
Buffalo Bisons
Capital City Bombers
Carolina Mudcats
Charleston RiverDogs
Chattanooga Lookouts
Durham Bulls
Ft. Wayne Wizards
Greensboro Bats
Hickory Crawdads
Hudson Valley Renegades
Nashville Sounds
New Haven Ravens
Ottawa Lynx
Portland Sea Dogs
Rancho Cucamonga Quakes
Salt Lake City Buzz
Toledo Mud Hens
Trenton Thunder
Vermont Expos
West Michigan Whitecaps
Wilmington Blue Rocks

Source: Anthony Kalamut, "What's In a Name?" *Dugout*, August/September 1995, 27–29.

A **brand mark**, also known as the **logo** or **logotype**, is the element of a brand that cannot be spoken. One of the most recognizable logos in the world is the Nike Swoosh. Interestingly, Carolyn Davidson was paid just $35 in 1971 to create the logo that now adorns Nike products, as well as CEO Phil Knight's ankle in the form of a tattoo.

A **trademark** identifies that a sports organization has legally registered its brand name or brand mark and thus prevents others from using it. Unfortunately, product counterfeiting or the production of low-cost copies of trademarked popular brands is reaching new heights. Product counterfeiting and trademark infringement is especially problematic at major sporting events, such as the Super Bowl or Olympic Games. For example, Collegiate Licensing Co, which represents about 150 colleges, found some 3,000 counterfeit items at football bowl games and the NCAA basketball tournament.

The Branding Process

The broad purpose of branding a product is to allow an organization to distinguish and differentiate itself from all others in the marketplace. Building the brand will then ultimately impact consumer behaviors, such as increasing attendance, merchandising sales, or participation in sports. However, before these behaviors are realized, several things must happen in the branding process shown in Figure 8.3.

First, **brand awareness** must be established. Brand awareness refers to making consumers in the desired target market recognize and remember the brand name. Only after awareness levels reach their desired objectives can brand image be addressed. After all, consumers must be aware of the product before they can understand the image the sports marketer is trying to project.

After brand awareness has been established, marketing efforts turn to developing and managing a **brand image**. Brand image is described as the consumers' set of beliefs about a brand, which, in turn, shape attitudes. Brand image can also be thought of as the "personality" of the brand. Organizations that sponsor sporting events are especially interested in strengthening or maintaining the image of their products through association with a sports entity (athlete, team, league) that reflects the desired image. For instance, the marketers of the Cadillac STS have established sponsorships with tennis events to reinforce a brand image of power, grace, and control.

Sports marketers attempt to manage beliefs that we have about a particular brand through a number of "image drivers," or factors that influence the brand image. The image drivers controlled by sports marketing efforts include product features or characteristics, product performance or quality, price, brand name, customer service, packaging, advertising, promotion, and distribution channels. Each of these image drivers contribute to creating the overall brand image. After shaping a positive brand image, sports marketers can then hope ultimately to create high levels of brand equity.

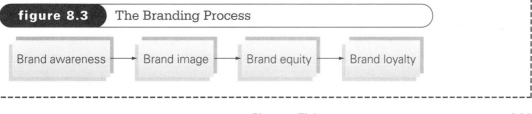

figure 8.3 The Branding Process

Brand awareness → Brand image → Brand equity → Brand loyalty

Another link in the branding process is developing high levels of brand equity. **Brand equity** is the value that the brand contributes to a product in the marketplace. In economic terms, it is the difference in value of having a branded product versus its generic equivalent. Consumers who believe a sport product has a high level of brand equity are more likely to be satisfied with the brand. The satisfied consumer will, in turn, become brand loyal or repeat purchasers.

How can marketers assess the equity of a brand such as the Yankees or Nike? One popular technique to measure brand equity evaluates a brand's performance across seven dimensions. Brand equity is then calculated by applying a multiple, determined by the brand's performance on the seven dimensions, to the net brand-related profits. These dimensions include: leadership or the ability of the brand to influence its market; stability or the ability of the brand to survive; market or the trading environment of the brand; internationality or the ability of the brand to cross geographic and cultural borders; trend or the ongoing direction of the brand's importance to the industry; support or the effectiveness of the brand's communication; and protection of the owners's legal title.[10]

Although there are a number of ways to measure brand equity in consumer goods, there have been very few attempts to look at the equity of sports teams. One exception was a study that measured the brand equity of MLB franchises.[11] To measure brand equity, the researchers first calculated team revenues for each franchise. These revenues are based on gate receipts, media, licensing and merchandise, and stadium-oriented issues, such as concession, advertising, and so on. The franchise value is then assigned a multiple based on growth projections for network television fees. Next, the total franchise value is subtracted from the value of a generic product to determine the brand equity. Because there is no such thing as a generic baseball team, the researchers used the $130 million fee paid by the two new expansion teams, Tampa Bay and Arizona. This $130 million fee represents the closest estimate to an unbranded team since they have yet to begin play.

Interestingly, only 7 of the 28 MLB teams show any brand equity. Based on the research, the following teams have positive brand equity (in rank order): New York Yankees, Toronto Blue Jays and New York Mets, Boston Red Sox, Los Angeles Dodgers, Chicago White Sox, and Texas Rangers. The teams with the lowest brand equity include the Montreal Expos, Pittsburgh Pirates, and Seattle Mariners. Given the fact that many of these "brands" have been around for decades, the brand equity for MLB franchises is surprisingly low.

While the previous study used an economic basis for determining brand equity, other research has employed less precise, qualitative approaches. For example, a panel of sporting goods industry experts were asked to name the most powerful brands in sport. In this study of equity, sports brands were defined as those who directly manufacture sporting apparel, equipment, and/or shoes. Nike is in a league of its own when it comes to branding. Ever since the introduction of the Air Jordan basketball shoe, Nike has grown geometrically since the days when Phil Knight (CEO) sold shoes out of the trunk of his car. Table 8.2 reports the 10 most powerful name brands in sports.

Brand loyalty is one of the most important concepts to sports marketers, because it refers to a consistent preference or repeat purchase of one brand over all others in a product category. Marketers want their products to satisfy consumers,

table 8.2

Top Ten Brand Names in Sports

1. Nike
2. Reebok
3. Spalding
4. Champion
5. Wilson
6. Russell
7. Rawlings
8. adidas
9. Titleist
10. Starter

Source: Frank Coffey, "The Top Brand Names in Sports," *Mark McCormack's Guide to Sports Marketing, International Sports Marketing Group,* 1996, 100–101. Courtesy of ISM GROUP, Inc., FL 33773.

so that decision making becomes a matter of habit rather than an extensive evaluation among competing brands. For example, Proctor & Gamble wants consumers to purchase Tide every time they need detergent, regardless of whether it is on sale or competitive products are being promoted.

To establish loyal consumers, Tide must address awareness and brand image. In 1987, brand managers of Tide decided that the awareness, image, and loyalty could be enhanced by establishing the Tide Racing NASCAR sponsorship. Today, Ricky Rudd drives the number 10 Tide car, and the NASCAR sponsorship has proven to be a tremendous success for P&G as loyal Rudd fans continue to be loyal to Tide products.

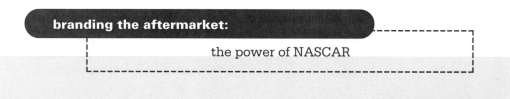

branding the aftermarket:

the power of NASCAR

During this century, as mass marketing has caught up with mass production, the one constant has been the significance of brands. In several notable cases, an entire product line has come to be known by the name of the pioneering brand. Some of our senior citizens still Hoover the carpet, then grab a cold one from the Frigidaire. And how many of us make Xerox copies on our Canon, blow our noses in a Kleenex, put a Band-Aid on a cut, Scotch tape a torn letter, eat Jell-O right out of the Tupperware container, and wear a Stetson in the Jacuzzi.

The ultimate goal of marketing is to have consumers subconsciously associate a brand name with a specific product. In sports marketing, brands such as Nike athletic shoes, Louisville Slugger baseball bats, Titleist golf balls, and Penn tennis balls are just a few names that have achieved this status.

(continued)

A growing trend in marketing sports products is to build official league endorsements. In other words, the brand is associated with the league rather than the specific sporting good. Consider the following: Wilson with the NFL, Rawlings with Major League Baseball, and Spalding with the NBA.

For over the last 10 years, NASCAR has been sitting on the tip of this iceberg, collecting money from a number of official product sponsors and merchandise licensees. For the first time, however, the NASCAR brand will appear on real automotive aftermarket (i.e., parts) products, not as an endorsement but as the actual brand or co-brand.

Research has indicated that NASCAR affiliation added value to packaging. We've been told countless times that more than 70 percent of NASCAR fans profess to be loyal to racing sponsors. That figure has been the big carrot-on-the-stick that's drawn so many sponsors into racing during the last decade. Now another figure is drawing the attention of the NASCAR licensing group.

Interbrand Schechter, a New York–based research company, has shown that 91 percent of the people said they would be more likely to purchase a product with the NASCAR name on it. Because of this research, NASCAR tested the aftermarket with an endorsement of Raybestos BruteStop brake pads by placing "Official Brakes of NASCAR" on the package. With decent sales and a couple of aftermarket retail chains outside regular distribution channels picking up the product, Raybestos was happy. So was the NASCAR marketing team.

Enter 76 NASCAR High Performance Motor Oil, an entirely new co-branded lubricant. "This isn't just re-branding an existing product," said Lany Higby, president of 76 Products Company. "We're introducing a new oil product, one that will be significantly superior to our own product today. We've been working on this particular product for the last couple of years," said Higby. "It was the happy coming-together of what we feel is a superior new product and NASCAR's branching out into the automotive aftermarket. From our standpoint, we felt it was very significant that NASCAR agreed to have its name on this product. The association with NASCAR frames this product in the consumer's mind."

So, what is a NASCAR product to be? Well, starting on familiar turf is usually safe. According to George Pyne, NASCAR Vice President of Licensing and Merchandising, "We'll be aligning ourselves with companies that have a long tradition of supporting NASCAR racing." Also, Pyne states that NASCAR automotive aftermarket products will fall into three basic categories: "There will be some racing lines. There will be lines that are geared to the professional mechanic, and some lines that are for the do it-yourselfer."

To support the new NASCAR-branded products, a host of multimedia advertising and promotions will surface. If you think your favorite driver is a huckster now, you ain't seen nothing yet. Here's a sample of what's in the pipeline: a line of high performance filters, a line of NASCAR ignition parts, and one of fuel system products. There will be NASCAR clutch components and NASCAR engine parts and gaskets. Also expect NASCAR engine additives and octane boosters. Down the road, look for NASCAR brake, power steering, and transmission fluids.

As far as adding new products, Pyne claims he's opting for the less-is-more approach. "When you put your name out everywhere," he offered, "it undermines the value of your brand, especially in the automotive aftermarket where we're really trying to capture a high-performance niche based on quality." So, don't expect NASCAR tongue depressors and hair spray just yet!

Source: Bill King, "Branding the Aftermarket," *Racer*, December 1996, 106. Courtesy of *Racer* Magazine.

In sports marketing, teams represent perhaps one of the most interesting examples of loyalty. It is common to hear us speak of people as being "loyal fans" or "fair-weather fans." The loyal fans endure all of the team's successes and hardships. As the definition implies, they continue to prefer their team over others. Alternatively, the fair-weather fan will jump to and from the teams that are successful at the time.

What are the determinants of fan loyalty to a team? Psychologist Robert Passikoff believes that the interaction of four factors create fan loyalty.[12] The first factor is the *entertainment value* of athletics. As we discussed in chapter 6, entertainment value is one of the underlying factors of fan motivation. In addition, entertainment was discussed as one of the perceived values of sports to the community. The second component of fan loyalty is *authenticity*. Passikoff defines authenticity as the "acceptance of the game as real and meaningful." *Fan bonding* is the third component of fan loyalty. *Bonding* refers to the degree to which fans identify with players and the team. The bonding component is similar to the concept of fan identification discussed in chapter 6. The fourth and final component of fan loyalty is the *history and tradition* of the team. For example, the Cincinnati Reds are baseball's oldest team and although they may be lacking in other dimensions of loyalty, they certainly have a long history and tradition with the fans in the greater Cincinnati area.

To measure fan loyalty, self-identified fans are asked to rate their hometown teams on each of the four dimensions. Interestingly, the fan loyalty measure does not specifically include a team performance component. Contrary to popular belief, Passikoff believes that winning and loyalty do not always go hand-in-hand. Table 8.3 provides the Fan Loyalty Index for Major League Baseball teams compiled in April 1997.

table 8.3

Fan Loyalty Index for Major League Baseball Teams (1997)*

Team	Index	Team	Index
Chicago White Sox	132	Pittsburgh Pirates	100
Kansas City Royals	129	Atlanta Braves	99
Detroit Tigers	127	Oakland Athletics	97
Cincinnati Reds	116	Seattle Mariners	97
Florida Marlins	116	Montreal Expos	96
St. Louis Cardinals	113	Los Angeles Dodgers	95
Cleveland Indians	111	Houston Astros	90
Toronto Blue Jays	111	San Francisco Giants	90
Baltimore Orioles	110	Chicago Cubs	86
Milwaukee Brewers	107	San Diego Padres	84
Philadelphia Phillies	105	Boston Red Sox	80
Arizona Diamondbacks	104	New York Mets	79
New York Yankees	104	Texas Rangers	74
Minnesota Twins	103	California Angels	73
Colorado Rockies	100		

* rating of 100 is the average team loyalty index

Source: Reprinted from *Forecast* newsletters with permission. © 1997, Cowles Business Media, Ithaca, New York.

In our society, loyalty to sports teams, at the high school, college, and professional levels, is perhaps higher than it is for any other goods and services that we consume. Unfortunately, team loyalty at the professional level is beginning to erode because of the constant threat of uprooting the franchise and moving to a new town. This is perhaps one reason for the increased popularity of amateur athletics. Colleges will not threaten to move for a better stadium deal, and athletes do not change teams for better contracts (although they do leave their universities early for professional contracts).

Licensing

The importance of having a strong brand is demonstrated when an organization considers product licensing. **Licensing** is a contractual agreement whereby a company may use another company's trademark in exchange for a royalty or fee. A branding strategy through licensing allows the organization to authorize the use of brand, brand name, brand mark, trademark, or trade name in conjunction with a good, service, or promotion in return for royalties. According to Sleight, "Licensing is a booming area of the sports business with players, teams, event names, and logos appearing on a vastly expanding range of products."[13] For example, the NFL has 150 licensees in apparel, sporting goods, basketball cards and collectibles, home furnishings, school supplies, home electronics, interactive games, home video, publishing, toys, games, gifts, and novelties.[14]

Because of the emergence of NFL Properties in 1963, licensing has become one of the most prevalent sports product strategies. From 1990 to 1994 the sale of licensed sports merchandise nearly doubled from $5.3 billion to $10.35 billion. However, over the past several years, licensing has maintained its growth or, in some cases, declined. *The Licensing Letter* reports that retail sales of licensed sports products reached $13.65 billion in 1997, a 1 percent decrease from 1996.

table 8.4	
1997 Retail Sales of Licensed Sports Products	
	(in billions)
NFL	$3.6
NBA	2.6
Colleges	2.0
NHL	1.2
MLB	1.9
Total	**$11.3**

Source: Sporting Goods Manufacturers Association.
Sports Licensed Products Report.
<http://www.sportlink.com
/research/...h/industry/98_licensed_report.html>.
Courtesy of Sporting Goods Manufacturers Association.

The 1997 retail sales of licensed sports products for the four major professional sports leagues and college/universities is shown in Table 8.4. This sales figure includes a variety of sports products such as sports memorabilia, novelty items, trading cards, and apparel. Clothing and apparel is estimated to account for nearly 60 percent of sales for all licensed sports products.

If done properly, licensing can be profitable to both parties in the exchange process. Licensing in sports marketing has tremendous implications for individual athletes, teams and leagues. The sale of licensed merchandise is not only skyrocketing in the United States, but also in Europe as the following Spotlight illustrates.

spotlight on international sports marketing:

europe gears up for rich pickens

Professional sports teams in the United States have long been aware that licensed products bring both recognition and revenues. In Europe, however, the most popular spectator sport, soccer, is only just beginning to grow its merchandise business, for which future potential is estimated at nearly the same volume as the major American sports.

Historically, the majority of the 700 or so top league teams in the 49 national member associations of the UEFA made little or no use of merchandising. On the other hand, a few clubs, especially in England and Germany, are making yearly profits running into the millions, thanks to merchandise sales.

German Budesliga club Bayern Munich, a team with a record number of national championship victories, recognized several years ago that one key to success on the soccer field is creative marketing and management off the pitch. In 1995, the club's turnover from sales of officially licensed products peaked at DEM40m ($60m), a figure expected to soar to almost DEM100m ($150m) by the turn of the century.

Over the years, Bayern Munich has built up its own commercial infrastructure, featuring a mail-order firm with a 20-person staff, sales promotions with direct mail, an annual 110-page, full-color catalogue containing 480 different items, and outlets at airports as well as merchandising shops at every authorized Opel retailer. The auto car manufacturer is the club's main sponsor.

"The likes of Bayern Munich or English Premier League side Manchester United, who run their own merchandising megastore, have clearly set role models for other clubs throughout Europe," according to Thomas Martens, Managing Director of Global Sportnet, based in Hamburg, Germany.

Global Sportnet specializes in different areas of football marketing in Europe, the main one being the acquisition and sales of worldwide television and advertising rights to European Cup games and qualifying games to the finals of the World Cup and European championships. At the same time, however, the company continues to expand its merchandising business throughout Europe.

Finding ways of generating new and reliable sources of income is not a new problem for many football managers. In the post-Bosman era, however, with players moving on free transfers, revenues from transfers can't be relied upon, and leave the

(continued)

clubs without one important means of balancing their budgets.

Although television is still the number one revenue producer for most soccer clubs in Europe, merchandising rivals soon will exceed ticket sales as an important revenue generator. "What a lot of smaller clubs realize now is that profits generated by sales of products bearing the team's logo and name are no longer restricted to a few big clubs, but can develop into a considerable economic factor for their own team," said Martens, whose company's global merchandising concept provides soccer clubs with a way of creating their own brands of merchandise. The centerpiece of the concept is a start-up package of a minimum 500 products, coupled with consultancy and management. Products are sourced from high-quality providers like American sportswear manufacturer Russell Corporation.

From this basis the clubs can build up their own merchandise. The scheme allows clubs to build at a healthy pace. Initially, the point of sale will be at the club's shop or the stadium. When certain quantities are reached, retail stores and mail order become part of the sales strategy. "The concept not only appeals to the traditional soccer nations in western and southern Europe but many of the small to medium-sized markets in eastern countries, where soccer is definitely the number one sport," explained Martens.

A further benefit for clubs becoming involved in the concept is that up to a solid 50 percent of sales profits remain with the club. "What we are offering is virtually the "Bayern Munich model," however on a smaller scale, more suitable to start with and tailored to each club's individual requirements. We do not intend to purchase a license but rather aim at a partnership, keeping the club totally involved in and allowing them tighter control of the brand name."

Since its launch in March, the Global Merchandising project has been well-received by teams from countries as different as Italy, Iceland, Austria, Poland, and the Republic of Ireland. In eastern Europe there is strong demand for a professional partner able to support product with consultancy. Among the pioneers are Polish First Division team, Lech Poznan, and the Slovakian side FC Dunajska Streda. Both clubs are beginning to control their merchandising programs and have created a strategic approach to this market segment.

With more purchasing power in the long run and changing consumption patterns in many developing countries, new relationships between fans and teams begin to build up. Surprisingly, many club officials still believe, mistakenly, that their fan base and overall attendances are too small to utilize their logo and name for merchandising. This misconception can prove expensive, when, in retrospect club managers realize they have lavishly wasted opportunities to generate additional income.

However, experience shows that once a club has decided to become involved, fellow league clubs soon follow. After the signing of Hungarian league side Debreceni Vastuas Sport Club in September, Global Sportnet has experienced "a number of other serious inquiries from other Hungarian teams."

In comparison to the American sports organizations, European soccer is much more fragmented, comprises nations with widely different economic situations and is, for these reasons alone, not as easy to market and manage as any of the major sports in the United States. No wonder that even in those leagues which are advanced in marketing terms, merchandising revenues trail far behind those of the American leagues.

The example set by Bayern Munich blazes a trail for many other European clubs. Bayern have been aggressive and kept full control of all activities because they saw the potential well in advance of other clubs. These clubs will soon follow with a new awareness that merchandising brings both recognition and revenues.

Source: "Europe Gears Up for Rich Pickens." *Sport Business International.* <http://www.sportbusiness.com>. Courtesy of Sport Business, Ltd.

Indeed, licensing is everywhere, but just what are the benefits of merchandise licensing? First, let us look at the advantages and disadvantages for the licensee.

Advantages to the Licensee
- The licensee benefits from the positive association with the sports entity. In other words, the positive attributes of the player, team, league, or event are transferred to the licensed product or service
- The licensee benefits from greater levels of brand awareness
- The licensee benefits by saving the time and money normally required to build high levels of brand equity
- The licensee may receive initial distribution with retailers and potentially receive expanded and improved shelf space for their products
- The licensee may be able to charge higher prices for the licensed product or service.

Disadvantages to the Licensee
- The athlete, team, league, or sport may fall into disfavor. For example, using an athlete such as Dennis Rodman is risky given his past behavior, off-the-court as well as on-the-court.
- In addition to the licensee, the licensor also experiences benefits and risks due to the nature of the licensing agreement.

Advantages to the Licensor
- The licensor is able to expand into new markets and penetrate existing markets more than ever before
- The licensor is able to generate heightened awareness of the sports entity and potentially increase its equity if paired with the appropriate products and services

merchandising mania:

down on the farm

Every minor league player dreams of making it to the "Big Show," and every minor league owner spends countless hours year-round attempting to put on a "Big Show." While the minor leagues provide a system for cultivating future stars, it is the big league clubs that supply the players in order for many of the smaller cities around the country to have live baseball. This relationship has turned towards the cultivation of cash, with revenues for minor leagues teams larger than anyone could ever imagine.

In 1995, 156 different teams played in one of the four classifications of the National Association of Professional Baseball Leagues—otherwise known as the minor leagues. Each of these franchises chases the same dream—success on the field, at the turnstile, and at the merchandise and concession stands.

(continued)

In 1990, the major leagues and the National Association negotiated a new Professional Baseball Agreement. In this agreement, guidelines were set for the division of broadcast monies, players' salaries, travel expenses, ballpark standards, and the like. With a new agreement, the face of minor league baseball changed dramatically.

One of the greatest benefits of the agreement has been the marketing arrangement between the National Association and Major League Baseball Properties (MLBP). This arrangement ensured that the merchandising of minor league baseball was placed at the hands of an experienced and successful group (MLBP).

Using the established relationships with MLBP and national manufacturers (e.g., New Era), the minor league clubs began receiving support in advertising, retail distribution, and point-of-purchase materials. This, in turn, meant higher product quality and better pricing, but most importantly it guaranteed access to national distribution.

In a few short years, the marketing of minor league baseball has grown from a few teams selling their merchandise aggressively to a free-for-all. Sales of minor league merchandise are showing staggering increases.

What started all of this? Money, of course. "Clubs get back what their logos generate," says Misann Ellmaker, the National Association' director of licensing. "Teams get paid through a royalty paid by the licensees, the money isn't shared. If the Hickory Crawdads sell a hat, they gain the revenue."

Source: Anthony Kalamut, "What's in a Name?" *Dugout*, August–September 1995, 27–29.

Disadvantages to the Licensor

■ The licensor may lose some control over the elements of the marketing mix. For instance, product quality may be inferior, or price reductions may be offered frequently. This may lessen the perceived image of the licensor.

Based on all of these considerations, care must be taken in choosing merchandising-licensing partnerships. Certainly, "the manufacturer of the licensed product should demonstrate an ability to meet and maintain quality control standards, possess financial stability, and offer an aggressive and well-planned marketing and promotional strategy."[15]

In addition to carefully choosing a partner, licensors and licensees must also be on the lookout for counterfeit merchandise. For instance, the NFL typically confiscates $1 million worth of fake goods during Super Bowl week. In 1996, the NBA snared $87 million worth of contraband, and one estimate has it that roughly $1 billion worth of counterfeit sports products hit the streets each year.

This problem has become so pervasive that the leagues now have their own logo cops who travel from city to city and event to event searching for violations. In addition to this form of enforcement, the Coalition to Advance the Protection of Sports Logos (CAPS) was formed in 1992 to investigate and control counterfeit products. CAPS has picked up $70 million worth of counterfeit products and production equipment since 1992. How can consumers guard against fakes? CAPS offers the following suggestions to consumers when purchasing sports products.[16]

- **Look for quality**. Poor lettering, colors that are slightly different from the true team colors, and background colors bleeding through the top color overlay are all signs of poor product quality.
- **Verification**. Counterfeiters may try to fake the official logo. Official items will typically have holograms on the product or stickers with moving figures, and embroidered logos should be tightly woven.
- **Check garment tags**. Poor quality merchandise is often designated by split garment tags. Rarely, if ever, will official licensed products use factory rejects or seconds.

Quality

Thus far we have looked at some of the branding issues related to sports products. Another important aspect of the product considered by sports marketers that will influence brand equity is quality. Let us look at two different types of quality: service quality and product quality.

Quality of Services

As sports organizations develop a marketing orientation, the need to deliver a high level of service quality to consumers is becoming increasingly important. For instance, at NFL Properties (NFLP), service quality is taken to the highest levels. NFLP is highly committed to understanding the individualized needs of each of its sponsors. Every sponsor of the NFL receives the name of a primary contact at NFLP who they can call at any time to discuss their marketing needs. They also recognize that each sponsor is in need of a unique sponsorship program, given their vastly different objectives and levels of financial commitment to the NFL.[17]

Although NFLP is an excellent example of an organization that values service quality, we have yet to define the concept. **Service quality** is a difficult concept to define, and as such, many definitions of service quality exist. Rather than define it, most researchers have resorted to explaining the dimensions or determinants of service quality. Unfortunately, there is also little agreement on what dimensions actually comprise service quality or how best to measure it.

Lehtinen and Lehtinen say that service quality consists of physical, interactive, and corporate dimensions.[18] The physical quality component looks at the tangible aspect of the service. More specifically, physical quality refers to the appearance of the personnel or the physical facilities where the service is actually performed. For example, the physical appearance of the ushers at the game may affect the consumer's perceived level of service quality.

Interactive quality refers to the two-way flow of information that disseminates from both the service provider and the service recipient at the time of the service encounter. The importance of the two-way flow of information is why many researchers choose to examine service quality from a dyadic perspective. This suggests gathering the perceptions of service quality from stadium employees, as well as fans.

The image attributed to the service provider by its current and potential users is referred to as corporate quality. As just discussed, product performance and quality is one of the drivers of brand image. Moreover, Lehtinen and Lehtinen also cited customer service as one of the image drivers. This suggests a strong relationship between corporate quality, or image of the team, and consumers' perceptions of service quality.

Groonos describes service quality dimensions in a different manner.[19] He believes service quality has both a technical and functional component. Technical quality is described as "what is delivered." Functional quality refers to "how the service is delivered." For instance, "what is delivered" might include the final outcome of the game, the hot dogs that were consumed, or the merchandise that was purchased. "How the service is delivered" might represent the effort put forth by the team and its players, the friendliness of the hot dog vendor, or the quick service provided by the merchandise vendor. This is especially important in sports marketing, as "the total game experience" is evaluated using both the "what" and "how" components of quality.

The most widely adopted description of service quality is based on a series of studies by Parasuraman, Zeithaml, and Berry.[20] They isolated five distinct dimensions of service quality. These **dimensions of service quality** comprise some of its fundamental areas and consist of reliability, assurance, empathy, responsiveness, and tangibles. Because of their importance in recent service quality literature, a brief description of each follows.

Reliability refers to the ability to perform promised service dependably and accurately. **Assurance** is the knowledge and courtesy of employees and their ability to convey trust and confidence. **Empathy** is defined as the caring, individualized attention the firm provides its customers. **Responsiveness** refers to the willingness to help customers and provide prompt service. **Tangibles** are the physical facilities, equipment, and the appearance of the service personnel.

In order to assess consumers' perceptions of service quality across each of the five dimensions, a 22-item survey instrument was developed by Parasuraman, Zeithaml, and Berry. The instrument, known as SERVQUAL, requires that the 22 items be administered twice. First, the respondents are asked to rate their expectations of service quality, and next, the respondents are asked to rate perceptions of service quality within the organization. For example, "Your dealings with XYZ are very pleasant" is a perception (performance) item, while the corresponding expectation item would be "Customers dealing with these firms should be very pleasant."

From a manager's perspective, measuring expectations and perceptions of performace allows action plans to be developed to improve service quality. Organizational resources should be allocated to improving those service quality areas where consumer expectations are high and perceptions of quality are low.

The original SERVQUAL instrument has been tested across a wide variety of industries, including banking, telecommunications, health care, consulting, education, and retailing. Most importantly, McDonald, Sutton, and Milne adapted SERVQUAL and used it to evaluate spectators' perceptions of service quality for a NBA team. The researchers fittingly called their adapted SERVQUAL instrument TEAMQUAL.[21]

In addition to finding that the NBA team exceeded service quality expectations on all five dimensions, the researchers looked at the relative importance of each of the five dimensions of service quality. More specifically, fans were asked to allocate 100 points among the five dimensions based on how important each factor is when evaluating the quality of service of a professional team sport franchise. As the results show in Table 8.5, tangibles and reliability are considered the most important dimensions of service quality. Tangibles, as you will recall from chapter 6, form the foundation of the sportscape, or stadium environment. This study provides additional evidence that the tangible factors, such as the seating comfort, stadium aesthetics, and scoreboard quality, play an important role in satisfying fans. Understanding fans' perceptions of TEAMQUAL is critical for sports marketers in establishing long-term relationships with existing fans and trying to attract new fans. As McDonald, Sutton, and Milne point out, "Consumers who are dissatisfied and feel that they are not receiving quality service will not renew their relationship with the professional sport franchise."

Quality of Goods

The quality of sporting goods that are manufactured and marketed have two distinct dimensions. The first dimension of quality is based on how well the product conforms to specifications that were designed in the manufacturing process. From

table 8.5

Importance Weights Allocated to the Five TEAMQUAL Dimensions

Dimensions	Allocation
Reliability—ability to perform promised services dependably and accurately	23%
Assurance—knowledge and courtesy of employees and their ability to convey trust and confidence	16
Empathy—the caring, individualized attention provided by the professional sports franchise for its customers	18
Responsiveness—willingness to help customers and provide prompt service	19
Tangibles—appearance of equipment, personnel materials, and venue	24

Source: Mark A. McDonald, William A. Sutton, and George R. Milne, "TEAMQUAL: Measuring Service Quality in Professional Team Sports," *Sport Marketing Quarterly*, vol. 4, no. 2 (1995): 9–15. Reprinted with permission of Fitness Information Technology, Inc. Publishers.

this standpoint, the quality of goods are driven by the organization and its management and employees. The other dimension of quality is measured subjectively from the perspective of consumers or end-users of the goods. In other words, whether or not the product performs its desired function. The degree to which the goods meet and exceed consumers' needs is a function of the organization's marketing orientation.

From the sports marketing perspective, the consumer's perception of quality is of primary importance. Garvin found eight separate quality dimensions, which include performance, features, reliability, conformance, durability, serviceability, aesthetics, and perceived quality (see Table 8.6).

Whether it is enhancing goods or service quality, most sports organizations are attempting to increase the quality of their product offerings. In doing so, they can

table 8.6

Quality Dimensions of Goods

Quality Dimensions of Goods	Description
Performance	How well does the good perform its core function? (Does the tennis racquet feel good when striking the ball?)
Features	Does the good offer additional benefits? (Are the golf clubheads constructed with titanium?)
Conformity to specifications	What is the incidence of defects? (Does the baseball have the proper number of stitches or is their some variation?)
Reliability	Does the product perform with consistency? (Do the gauges of the exercise bike work properly every time?)
Durability	What is the life of the product? (How long will the golf clubs last?)
Serviceability	Is the service system efficient, competent, and convenient? (If you experience problems with the grips or loft of the club, can the manufacturer quickly address your needs?)
Aesthetic design	Does the product's design look and feel like a high-quality product? (Does the look and feel of the running shoe inspire you to greater performance?)

Adapted from D.A. Garvin, "Competing on the Eight Dimensions of Quality," *Harvard Business Review,* November–December 1987, pp. 101–109. Copyright © 1987 by the President and Fellows of Harvard College; all rights reserved. Reprinted by permission of Harvard Business School Press.

better compete with other entertainment choices, more easily increase the prices of their products, influence the consumer's loyalty, and reach new market segments that are willing to pay more for a higher quality product.

Some sports franchises have been criticized for attempting to increase the quality of their overall products, while at the same time driving up the price of tickets. Unfortunately, it is becoming more costly for the "average fan" to purchase tickets to any professional sporting event. In this way, sports marketers have targeted a new segment (corporations) and overlooked the traditional segments.

Other criticisms have been directed at the NCAA and professional sports for making it too easy for athletes to leave school and turn professional. For example, in college basketball, there were 23 underclassmen who declared for early entry into the 1996 NBA draft. This may have detrimental effects on "product quality."

As a result of this exodus of stars, the college game is suffering. From a marketing standpoint, the fans are also suffering. Teams no longer stay together long enough to get and capture the imagination of fans. Atlantic 10 commissioner, Linda Bruno, stated "It seems as soon as college basketball hooks on to a star, he's suddenly a part of the NBA. Athletes leaving early have definitely hurt the college game." Rick Pitino, whose opinion is widely respected, adds, "Quite frankly, I think college basketball is in serious trouble." Interestingly, the early departures that are making the college game less appealing are doing nothing to strengthen the quality of the NBA. The NBA is saturated with players whose games never had a chance to grow or, as Stanford coach Mike Montgomery put it, "will have to be nurtured through [their] immaturity."[22]

A final product feature related to perceptions of product quality is warranties. **Warranties** are important to consumers when purchasing expensive sporting goods as they act to reduce the perceived risk and dissonance associated with cognitive dissonance. Traditional warranties are statements indicating the liability of the manufacturer for problems with the product. Interestingly, warranties are also being developed by sports organizations. The New Jersey Nets have offered their season ticketholders a money-back guarantee if they were dissatisfied with the Net's performance. With the price of tickets skyrocketing for professional sporting events, perhaps these service guarantees will be the wave of the future.

Product Design

Product design is one competitive advantage that is of special interest to sports marketers. It is heavily linked to product quality and the technological environment discussed in chapter 3. In some cases, product design may even have an impact on the sporting event. For example, the latest technology in golf clubs does allow the average player to improve his or her performance on the course. The same could be said for the new generation of big sweet spot, extra long tennis racquet. In another example, the official baseball used in the major league games was thought

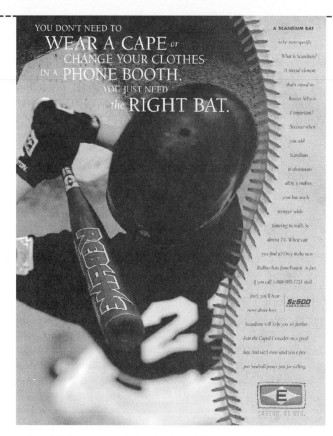

YOU DON'T NEED TO
WEAR A CAPE or
CHANGE YOUR CLOTHES
IN A PHONE BOOTH.
YOU JUST NEED
the RIGHT BAT.

A SCANDIUM BAT

EASTON. GO WIN.

■ Easton's high-tech product design is having an influence on baseball.

to be "juiced up." In other words, the ball was livelier because of the product design. As a result of this "juiced up" ball, home run production increased, much to the delight of the fans. From a sports marketing perspective, anything that adds excitement and conjecture to a game with public relation problems is welcomed. In the end, what matters is not whether the ball is livelier, but that the game is.[23]

Baseballs are not the only products that are having an impact on the outcome of sporting events. In 1997, players at the Australian Open complained about the product quality of the tennis balls being used. More specifically, many players complained about the balls being too soft and slow. As a result, Slazenger, the tennis ball supplier for the Australian Open, has ensured tournament officials and players that there will be "less fluffing of balls and as the game proceeds instead of the ball getting slower, it will get faster."[24]

Product design is important to sport marketers because ultimately it impacts consumers' perceptions of product quality. Moreover, organizations need to monitor the technological environment to keep up with the latest trends that may impact product design. Let us look at this relationship in Figure 8.4.

As you would imagine, the technological environment has a tremendous impact on product design decisions. In almost every sporting good category (e.g., exercise

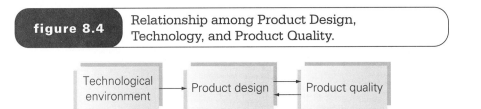

figure 8.4 Relationship among Product Design, Technology, and Product Quality.

Technological environment → Product design ↔ Product quality

equipment, golfing equipment, hunting equipment), sports marketers communicate how their brands are technologically superior to the competition.

The golf equipment industry thrives on the latest technological advances in ball and club design. Bicycle manufacturers stress the technological edge that comes with the latest and greatest construction materials. Tennis racquets are continually moving into the next generation of frame design and racquet length. NordicTrac exercise equipment positions itself as technologically superior to other competing brands. All of these examples illustrate the power of technology on product design.

The product design of sporting goods, in turn, influences consumer perceptions of product quality. By definition, **product design** includes the aesthetics, style, and function of the product. Two of the eight dimensions of the quality of goods are incorporated in this definition, providing one measure of the interdependency of these two concepts.

The way a good performs, the way it feels, and the beauty of the good are all important aspects of product design. Again, think of the numerous sporting goods that are purchased largely on the basis of these benefits. Consumers purchase golf clubs because of the way they look and feel. Tennis shoes are chosen because of the special functions they perform (cross-trainers, hiking, basketball) and the way they look (colors, style).

Color has historically been an important factor in the design of almost all licensed merchandise. Recent trends show that in hats, jerseys, and jackets, anything black is "gold." Although fans associate certain colors with their favorite teams (e.g., Dodger Blue or the Cincinnati Reds), MLB has started to experiment with licensed products that deviate from the traditional colors. Baby blues, electric oranges, and lime greens are replacing the traditional team colors and fans seem to be responding. For example, Cleveland (red and navy uniform colors) fans are purchasing jerseys in bright orange, the color of their arch-rival Baltimore Orioles.[25] Examples like these illustrate that color alone may be a motivating factor in the purchase of many sports products. As such, sports marketers must consider color to be critical in product design.

Figure 8.4 also shows that product quality may influence product design to some extent. Sports organizations are continually seeking to improve the levels of product quality. In fact, having high-quality goods and services may be the primary objective of many firms. As such, products will be designed in the highest quality manner with little concern about the costs that will be ultimately passed on to the consumers. Some major league sports organizations (e.g., New York Yankees, Dallas Cowboys) will design their teams to achieve the highest quality levels without cost consideration.

As new technologies continue to emerge, product design will become increasingly important. Organizations with a marketing orientation will incorporate consumer preferences to ensure that their needs are being met with respect to product design for new and existing products. What will the future bring with respect to product design, technology, and the need to satisfy consumers? One hint comes to us via the athletic shoe industry. With advances in technology, customized shoes are now being produced for professional athletes. Gone are the days when recreational athletes could wear the same shoes as their professional counterparts. Today's professional athletes are demanding custom fit, high-tech shoes, and weekend athletes will soon require the same. Shoe companies hope to sell customized shoes to the mass market within the next five years.[26]

Another perspective on the future of product design is that the design of products will stem from demand and changes in the marketing environment. One such change is the emergence of a viable market for women's sports products. Maria Stefan, executive director and vice president of the Sporting Goods Manufacturers Association (SGMA) believes that a number of changes are taking place in product design to accommodate women. "Instead of downsizing men's apparel, manufacturers...are producing garments for narrower backs, shorter arms, broader hips, narrower waists, and longer rises. Armholes are being recontoured. New fabric textures are being used to meet female standards for style and comfort."[27]

SUMMARY

Sport products are defined as goods, services, or any combination of the two that are designed to provide benefits to a sports spectator, participant, or sponsor. Within the field of sports marketing, products are sometimes thought of as bundles of benefits desired by consumers. As discussed in chapter 1, sports products might include sporting events and their participants, sporting goods, and/or sports information. The definition of sports products also makes an important distinction between goods and services.

Goods are defined as tangible, physical products that offer benefits to consumers. Conversely, services are intangible, nonphysical products. Most sports products possess the characteristics of both goods and services. For example, a sporting event sells goods (e.g., concessions) and services (e.g., the competition itself). The classification of a sports product as either a good or a service is dependent on four product dimensions: tangibility, standardization/consistency, perishability, and separability. Tangibility refers to the ability to see, feel, and touch the product. In other words, tangibility is the physical dimension of the sports product. Standardization refers to the consistency of the product or the ability of the producer to manufacture a product with little variation over time. One of the unique and complex issues for sports marketers is dealing with the inconsistency of the sports product (i.e., the inability to control the performance of the team or athlete). Perishability is the ability to store or inventory product. Pure services are totally perishable (i.e., you cannot sell a seat after the game has been played), while goods are not perishable and can be stored or warehoused. Separability, the final product dimension, refers to the ability to separate the good from the person providing the service. In the case of an athletic event, there is little separation between the provider and the consumer.

That is, the event is being produced and consumed simultaneously.

Along with classifying sports products by the four product dimensions, sports products are also categorized based on groupings within the sports organization. Product lines are groups of products that are closely related because they satisfy a class of needs, are used together, are sold to the same customer groups, are distributed through the same types of outlets, or fall within a given price range. The total assortment of product lines is called the product mix. This represents all of the firm's products. Strategic decisions within the sports organization consider both the product lines and the entire product mix. For instance, an organization may wish to add product lines, eliminate product lines, or develop new product lines that are unrelated to existing lines.

Products can also be described on the basis of three interrelated dimensions or characteristics: branding, quality, and design. Branding refers to the product's name, design, symbol, or any combination that is used by an organization to differentiate products from the competition. Brand names, or elements of the brand that can be spoken, are important considerations for sports products. When choosing a brand name, sports marketers should consider the following: The name should be positive and generate positive feelings; the name should be translatable into a exciting logo; the name should imply the benefits that the sports product delivers; the name should be consistent with the image of the sports product; and the name should be legally and ethically permissible.

The broad purpose of branding is to differentiate your product from the competition. Ultimately, the consumer will (hopefully) establish a pattern of repeat purchases for your brand (i.e., be loyal to your sports product). Before this can happen, sports marketers must guide consumers through a series of steps known as the branding process. The branding process begins by building brand awareness, in which consumers recognize and remember the brand name. Next, the

brand image, or the consumers' set of beliefs about a brand, must be established. After the proper brand image is developed, the objective of the branding process is to develop brand equity. Brand equity is the value that the brand contributes to a product in the marketplace. Finally, once the brand exhibits high levels of equity, consumers are prone to become brand loyal, or purchase only your brand. Certainly, sports marketers are interested in establishing high levels of awareness, enhancing brand image, building equity, and developing loyal fans or customers.

One of the important sports product strategies that is contingent upon building a strong brand is licensing. Licensing is defined as a contractual agreement whereby a company may use another company's trademark in exchange for a royalty or fee. The licensing of sports products is experiencing tremendous growth around the globe with the latest estimate (1997) reporting nearly $14 billion in the sale of licensed sports products. Advantages to the licensee (the organization purchasing the license or use of the name/trademark) include positive association with the sports entity, enhancing brand awareness, building brand equity, improving distribution and retail relationships, and having the ability to charge higher prices. Disadvantages to the licensee are the possibility of the sports entity experiencing problems (e.g., athlete arrested or team performing poorly or moving). On the other hand, the licensor (the sports entity granting the permission) benefits by expanding into new markets, which creates heightened awareness. However, the licensor may not have tight controls on the quality of the products being licensed under the name.

Quality is another of the important brand characteristics. The two different types of quality that impact brand image, brand equity, and, ultimately, loyalty are the quality of services and the quality of goods. The quality of services, or service quality, is generally described on the basis of its dimensions. Parasuraman, Berry, and Zeithaml describe service quality as having five distinct dimensions: reliability, assurance, empathy, responsiveness, and tangibles. Reliability refers to the ability to perform a promised service dependably and accurately. Assurance is the knowledge and courtesy of employees and their ability to convey trust and confidence. Empathy is defined as the caring, individualized attention the firm provides its customers. Responsiveness refers to the willingness to help customers and provide prompt service. Tangibles are the physical facilities, equipment, and the appearance of the service personnel. Using this framework, sports researchers have designed an instrument called TEAMQUAL to assess the service quality within sporting events.

The quality of goods is based on whether the good conforms to specifications determined during the manufacturing process and the degree to which the good meets or exceeds the consumer's needs. Garvin has conceptualized the quality of goods from the consumer's perspective. He found eight separate dimensions of goods quality, including performance, features, conformity to specifications, reliability, durability, serviceability, and aesthetic design.

Product design is the final characteristic of the "total product." Product design is defined as the aesthetics, style, and function of the product. It is important to sports marketers in that it ultimately impacts consumers' perceptions of product quality. For a sporting event, the product design might be thought of as the composition of the team. For sporting goods, product design has largely focused on the development of technologically superior products. In fact, the technological environment is thought to directly influence product design. Product design, in turn, enjoys a reciprocal relationship with product quality. In other words, product design impacts perceptions of product quality and may influence product design.

KEY TERMS & CONCEPTS

brand name	product lines	service quality dimensions
branding	product mix	services
branding process	product quality	sports product
goods	product warranties	standardization
licensing	quality dimensions of goods	tangibility
perishability	separability	TEAMQUAL
product design	service quality	trademark
product items		

REVIEW QUESTIONS

1. Define sports products. Why are sports products sometimes called "bundles of benefits?"

2. Contrast pure goods with pure services, using each of the dimensions of products.

3. Describe the nature of product mix, product lines, and product items. Illustrate these concepts for the following: Converse, Baltimore Orioles, and your local country club.

4. What are the characteristics of the "total product?"

5. Describe branding. What are the guidelines for developing an effective brand name? Why is brand loyalty such an important concept for sports marketers to understand?

6. Define licensing. What are the advantages and disadvantages to the licensee and licensor?

7. Describe service quality and discuss the five dimensions of service quality. Which dimension is most important to you as a spectator of a sporting event? Does this vary by the type of sporting event?

8. Describe product quality and discuss the seven dimensions of product quality. Which dimension is most important to you as a consumer of sporting goods? Does this vary by the type of sporting good?

9. How are product design, product quality, and technology interrelated?

EXERCISES

1. Think of some sports products to which consumers demonstrate high degrees of brand loyalty. What are these products, and why do you think loyalty is so high? Give your suggestions for measuring brand loyalty.

2. Interview the individual(s) responsible for licensing and licensing decisions on your campus. Ask them to describe the licensing process and what they feel the advantages are to your school.

3. Construct a survey to measure consumers' perceptions of service quality at a sporting event on-campus. Administer the survey to 10 people and summarize the findings. What recommendations might you make to the sports marketing department based on your findings?

4. Go to a sporting goods store and locate three sports products that you feel exhibit high levels of product quality. What are the commonalities among these three products? How do these products rate on the dimensions of product quality described in the chapter?

INTERNET EXERCISES

1. Search the Internet for a sports product that stresses product design issues on its Web site. Then locate the Web site of a competitor's sports product. How are these two products positioned relative to each other on their Web sites?

2. Search the Internet for three team nicknames (either college or professional) of which you were previously unaware. Do these team names seem to follow the suggested guidelines for effective brand names?

1. "Sports: Walk, Don't Schuss." <http://www.businessweek.com/1997/49/b3556153.htm>.

2. Hank Hersch, "Something Extra," *Sports Illustrated Presents Pro Basketball*, Fall 1996, 28–34.

3. Christopher Lovelock, *Services Marketing* (Englewood Cliffs, NJ: Prentice Hall, 1984).

4. Brian Metzler, "Just But It," *Skiing*, vol. 50, no. 4, December, 1997 p. 38. "Nike Profits up 12 Percent, Sees Growth Slowdown." <http://www.pathfinder.com/>. (September 18, 1997).

5. Jeff Jensen, "Nike Glides Into Hockey with Canstar Purchase" *Advertising Age*, vol. 65, no. 53, December 19, 1994, 34.

6. Tiesha Coleman. "NBA Announces WNBA Expansion Teams." *Huddlin with the Pros*. <http://www.huddlin.com/Dec/wnbat.htm>.

7. See for example, Coutland Bovee and John Thill, *Marketing* (New York, NY: McGraw-Hill, 1992), 252.

8. Calvin Sims, "It's Not Just How Well You Play the Game…," *The New York Times*, January 31, 1993. Mary Nemeth, James Deacon, and Rae Corelli, "The Selling of Sports," *Maclean's*, September 26, 1994, 33–35.

9. *The Columbus Crew*, <http:www.thecrew.com>.

10. Louis E. Boone, C.M. Kochunny, and Dianne Wilkins, "Applying the Brand Equity Concept to Major League Baseball," *Sport Marketing Quarterly*, vol. 4, no. 3 (1995): 33–42.

11. Ibid.

12. Brad Edmunson, "What Makes A Sports Fan?" *Forecast*. <http://www.demographics.com/publications/fc/97_fc/9709_fc/fc97093.htm> (September 1997).

13. S. Sleight, *Sponorship: What Is It and How to Use It?* (London: McGraw-Hill, 1989).

14. "New Consumer Product Offerings By NBA & WNBA." <http://www.newspage.com/cgi-bin/NA....y?story=v120209.6is&date=19980121>.

15. Eddie Baghdikian, "Building the Sports Organization's Merchandise Licensing Program: The Appropriateness, Significance, and Considerations," *Sport Marketing Quarterly*, vol. 5, no. 1 (1996): 35–41.

16. Robert Thurow, "Busting Bogus Merchandise Peddlers With Logo Cops," *The Wall Street Journal*, October 24, 1997, B1, B14.

17. Rick Burton, "A Case Study on Sports Property Servicing Excellence: National Football League Properties," *Sport Marketing Quarterly*, vol. v, no. 3 (1996): 23–30.

18. J.R. Lehtinen and U. Lehtinen, *Service Quality: A Study of Quality Dimensions* (Helsinki: Service Management Institute, 1982).

19. Christian Groonos, "A Service Quality Model and Its Marketing Implications," *European Journal of Marketing*, vol. 18 (1982): 36–44.

20. A. Parasuram, Valarie Ziethaml, and Len Berry, "A Conceptual Model of Service Quality and Its Implications for Future Research," *Journal of Marketing*, vol. 49 (1985): 41–50.

21. Mark A. McDonald, William A. Sutton, and George R. Milne, "TEAMQUAL: Measuring Service Quality in Professional Team Sports," *Sport Marketing Quarterly*, vol. 4, no. 2 (1995): 9–15.

22. Jack McCallum, "Going, Going, Gone," *Sports Illustrated*, vol. 84, no. 20 (May 20, 1996): 52.

23. Mark Starr with Todd Barrett, "Kiss That Baby Goodbye," *Newsweek*, May 10, 1993, 72.

24. Giles Smith, "Whingers Playing Different Ball Game to Amateur Types," *The Daily Telegraph*, February 22, 1997, 21.

25. Wendy Bounds and Stefan Fatsis, "Right Here! Get Yer Baseball Cap! Lime Green, Lavender, Baby Blue!" *The Wall Street Journal*, October, 13, 1997.

26. Joseph Pereira, "World-Class Athletes Now Rely on the Sole of a New Machine," *The Wall Street Journal*, September 23, 1997, A1, A10.

27. "Women's Sports Growth Sparks Manufacturing Innovation." <http://www.sportlink.com/industry/media/m97-15.html>.

Managing Sports Products

After completing this chapter, you should be able to

- Describe the characteristics of new products from an organizational and consumer perspective

- Explain the various stages of the new product development process

- Discuss the phases of the product life cycle and explain how the product life cycle influences marketing strategy

- Determine the factors that will lead to new product success

- Discuss the diffusion of innovations and the various types of adopters

■ The WNHL could be on the horizon.

spotlight on women in sports marketing:

introducing a new sports product

Following in the footsteps of women's basketball and softball, women's pro ice hockey could be on the horizon, starting with women's hockey having made its debut in the 1998 Olympic Winter Games in Nagano, Japan. To capitalize on the Olympic exposure and sign marquee players before they retire, there have been preliminary discussions about starting a women's pro ice hockey league next year.

"To know there is a possibility there would be somewhere for us to play after the Olympics, to maybe make a career out of it, it's everyone's dream," said Cammi Granato, a forward from Downers Grove, Illinois, whose brother, Tony, plays with the NHL's San Jose Sharks. Granato hopes the Winter Games generates the same interest for her sport that the 1996 Atlanta Summer Games helped create for several women's up-and-coming sports.

After the U.S. women's basketball team earned the gold medal, two women's pro basketball leagues were formed. Women's softball and soccer also were in the Olympic spotlight. The Women's Professional Fastpitch League opened its inaugural season in May, and the National Soccer Alliance is hoping to start a women's pro league next year.

Ed Saunders, a recent graduate of the University of New Hampshire, and Don Wilson, a construction contractor in West Islip, New York, said they have formed corporations with the intent of operating a women's pro ice hockey league. They are working on financial backing and logistics.

The National Hockey League has explored the possibilities, too. "We can say there are no immediate plans for that," said Bernadette Mansur, the NHL's vice president of corporate Communications. "We look at it as a possible future opportunity."

Saunders wants to start his league, with six, 20-player franchises located on the East Coast and Canada. He has consulted many of the top USA players, including Erin Whitten, a goaltender from Glens Falls, New York. "I've talked to most of the top U.S. players," Whitten said.

The Spotlight on professional women's ice hockey provides an interesting illustration of a new sports product that is on the verge of being introduced to the North American market. The growth of women's sports, the addition of women's ice hockey to the 1998 Winter Olympics, and the growing popularity of hockey as a spectator sport all suggest that the time is right for this new product. But you might be asking, "What's so new about hockey?"

There is obviously nothing new about hockey, and women have been playing organized hockey for years. However, very few sports fans, or even hockey fans, have been exposed to women's hockey. And none of us have watched women's *professional* hockey. The founders of the proposed league will have to keep this in mind when developing a marketing strategy for this "new" sports product.

ew Sports Products

Though it might seem that new products are easy to describe and think about, "new" is a relative term. Think about purchasing season tickets to your favorite college basketball team for the first time. You might consider this a new product even though the tickets have been available for many years. On the other hand, consider the WNBA. This sports product is new to all consumers and to the NBA, who is responsible for managing and marketing the league.

Regardless of how you define "new products," they are critical to the health of any sports organization for two reasons. First, new products are necessary to keep up with changing consumer trends, lifestyles, and tastes. Second, as unsuccessful sports products are dropped from the product mix, new products must be introduced continually to maintain business and long-term growth.

One of the key considerations for any sports organization is to continually improve the products it offers to consumers. New products seek to satisfy the needs of a new market, enhance the quality of an existing product, or extend the number of product choices for current consumers. Before discussing the process for developing new products, let us look at the different types of new sports products.

Types of New Products

As noted previously, there is no universally accepted definition of new products. Instead, new products are sometimes described from the viewpoint of the sports organization versus the consumer's perspective. The organization's definition of a new product is based on whether or not it has ever produced or marketed this particular product in the past. This can be important for organizations trying to understand how the new sports product "fits" with their existing products.

On the other hand, newness from the consumer's perspective is described as any innovation the consumer perceives as meaningful. In other words, the new product could be a minor alteration of an existing product or a product that has never been sold or marketed by any organization. Looking at new products from the consumer's viewpoint helps sports organizations understand the most effective way to market the product. Let us examine the types of new products from the organizational and consumer perspectives in greater detail.

Newness from the Organization's Perspective

New-to-the-World Products   Brand new sports innovations, such as the first inline skates, the first sailboard, or the advent of arena football, all represent new-to-the-world products. These products are new to the organization selling the product as well as to the consumers purchasing or using the product.[1]

Another interesting, new-to-the-world sports product is the corporate skybox for golf. Bill Rasmussmen (founder of ESPN in 1979) created Stadium Naples. This permanent, multideck grandstand looks like a ballpark, includes 50 condos priced from $750,000 to $1 million, and offers thousands of spectators views of closing holes. "Imagine Yankee Stadium with everything wiped between the foul poles and replaced by four golf holes," Rasmussen says.[2]

New Product Category Entries   Sports products that are new to the organization, but not to the world, are referred to as new product category entries. For example, Nike's recent venture into sports equipment is a new product category entry for the shoe and apparel market leader. Another example of new product category entries are the trend for media giants, such as Time-Warner (Atlanta Braves), Fox (LA Dodgers), Tribune Company (Chicago Cubs), and Walt Disney (Anaheim Angels and Mighty Ducks), to add professional sports franchises to their product mix.[3] These teams are not new to the fans, but new acquisitions for the organizations.

Sports Marketing  *fame*

BILL RASMUSSEN

Bill Rasmussen is hardly a household name, but all you have to do is mention four letters—ESPN—and his place in sports marketing history is secured. ESPN's founder developed the 24-hour sports programming channel in the fall of 1979. At that time, Rasmussen was simply looking for a way to broadcast the University of Connecticut basketball games when he happened upon satellite technology.

Today, ESPN reaches more than 70 million homes with its 8,760 hours of sports programming. A second channel, ESPN2, has been formed along with a host of new cable sports programming networks. All of these networks can thank Bill Rasmussen's desire to bring U Conn basketball to the people of Connecticut.

Source: Richard Hoffer, "Bill Rasmussen," *Sports Illustrated*, September 19, 1994, 121.

■ Easton's Redline glove represents a product line extension.

Product Line Extensions   Product line extensions refer to new products being added to an existing product line. For instance, the addition of interleague play in Major League Baseball or the new Nike tennis shoe called the Air Haze (Monica Seles's signature shoe named after her love of music from the 1960s) are product line extensions.

Product Improvements   Current products that have been modified and improved, such as the new and improved Air Jordan by Nike, are called product improvements. The latest version of the Air Jordan is one of 12 product improvements since the Air Jordan was launched in 1985. Another example of a product improvement is the Wilson Sledge Hammer 3.8 "Power Holes" racquet. This new and improved version of the Sledge Hammer features "elongated grommet holes on the inside of the racquet head, allowing the strings to move more freely upon ball impact, which helps players generate more power on off-center hits." If this new racquet offers a benefit that consumers are seeking (more power) and is believed to be improved, then it should be successful.

In another example of a product improvement, any sports team or individual that improves during the off-season can be considered a product improvement. Sometimes this improvement takes place because of trades or purchasing new players, and other times an enhanced product is the result of a new coach or players who are maturing and finally performing to their potential. In either case, product improvements represent an opportunity for sports marketers to promote the improvements (either real or perceived) in product quality.

Repositionings   As defined in chapter 7, repositioning is changing the image or perception of the sports entity in the minds of consumers in the target market. Sports products such as bowling and billiards are trying to reposition themselves as "yuppie sports activities" by creating tready and up-scale environments in sports facilities that are stereotypically grungy and old-fashioned.[4] Another repositioning example comes from the sport of cricket, which is trying to reposition itself as a sport for the young through a new advertising campaign.

The most common examples of new products are repositionings and product improvements because of the limited risk involved from the organization's perspective. The rearrangement of existing sports products also has its advantages. For example, this type of new product can be developed more quickly than new-to-the-world or new product category entrants, and it already has an established track record with consumers.

On the other hand, new-to-the-world products must undergo more careful research and development because they are new to the organization and to consumers. Moreover, more money must be invested because heavy levels of promotion are necessary to make potential consumers aware of the product. In addition, consumers must learn about the benefits of the new product and how it can help satisfy their needs.

Newness from the Consumer's Perspective

Another way to describe new products are from the perspective of consumers. New products are categorized as discontinuous innovations, dynamically continuous innovations, or continuous innovations.[5] The new products are categorized on the basis of the degree of behavioral change required by consumers. Behavioral changes refer to differences in the way we use a new product, think about a new product, or the degree of learning required to use a new product. For instance, a new extra-long tennis racquet does not require us to change the way we play tennis or to relearn the sport. On the other hand, extensive learning took place for many Americans exposed to soccer for the first time in the 1994 World Cup. Similarly, learning will have to occur for the many Americans who will watch the 1999 Cricket World Cup in Miami. Let us look at the three categories of new products from the consumer's perspective in greater detail.

Discontinuous innovations are somewhat similar to new-to-the-world products in that they represent the most innovative products. In fact, discontinuous innovations are so new and original that they require major learning from the consumer's viewpoint, and they require new consumption and usage patterns. Some of the "extreme sports," such as sky surfing, bungee jumping, and ice climbing, represent discontinuous innovations.

Many Southerners who have had limited access to ice hockey may view this sport as a discontinuous innovation. Interestingly, a recent study found that spectator knowledge of hockey was found to be a significant predictor of game attendance and intention to attend hockey games in the future. An equally important finding in the study was that knowledge of hockey may vary based on sociodemographic variables. In other words, the fan's age, gender, educational level, income, and marital status influence the degree of hockey knowledge.[6]

Dynamically continuous innovations are new products that represent changes and improvements but do not strikingly change buying and usage patterns. For instance, the titanium head and bubble shaft on a golf club or the aluminum bat are innovations that do not change our swing, but do represent significant improvements in equipment (and hopefully our game). When the shot-clock and three-point field goal were added to basketball, changes took place in how the game was played. Coaches, players, and fans were forced to understand and adopt new strategies for basketball. Most basketball enthusiasts think that these dynamically continuous innovations have improved the sport.

Another example of a dynamically continuous innovation is arena football. Arena football required spectators to relearn the rules of football and game strategy, although they essentially watch the game the same way. Based on the amount of television coverage, sponsorship dollars, and game attendance figures, it seems as though this dynamically continuous innovation has gained acceptance in most markets.[7]

■ Softspikes represents a dynamically continuous innovation that is gaining widespread consumer acceptance.

Continuous innovations represent an ongoing, commonplace change such as the minor alteration of a product or the introduction of an imitation product. A continuous innovation has the least disruptive influence on patterns of usage and consumer behavior. In other words, consumers use the product in the same manner that they have always used the product. Examples of continuous innovations include the addition of expansion teams for leagues such as MLB, the WNBA, or MLS. The NFL has also introduced a continuous innovation called Headliners. These toys, available at K-Mart, Wal-Mart, and Toys-R-Us, are three-inch miniature versions of 41 NFL players from 23 teams. Headliners are modeled after soccer players from the United Kindom's Premier League.[8]

We could debate which new product category best represents a team that has built a new arena and changed its venue or any new sports product. But, few new products fall neatly into the three categories. Rather, there is a continuum ranging from minor innovation to major innovation, based on how consumers perceive the new product. Knowing how consumers think and feel about a new product is critical information in developing the most effective marketing strategy. Before we talk more about the factors that make new products successful and spread through the marketplace, let us look at how new products are conceived.

(T)he New Product Development Process

Increased competition for sports and entertainment dollars, emergence of new technologies, and ever-changing consumer preferences are just a few of the reasons that sports marketers are constantly developing new sports products. As Higgins and Martin point out in their research on managing sport innovations, "Clearly, the list of innovations in sports is extensive and appears to be increasing at a rapid rate. This would suggest that spectators are seeking new and better entertainment and participants are seeking new and better challenges."[9]

Many new sports products are conceived without much planning, or happen as a result of chance. For instance, the sport of polo was created by British Cavalry officers in India who wanted to show off their horsemanship in a more creative way than the parade ground allowed them to. Although polo represents a sport that was developed by chance, this is more the exception than the rule. More often than not, sports organizations develop new products by using a systematic approach called the **new product development process**. The phases in the new product development process include idea generation, idea screening, analysis of the concept, developing the sports product, test marketing, and commercialization. Let us briefly explore each phase in the new product development process.

Idea Generation

The first phase of the new product development process is **idea generation**. At this initial phase, any and all ideas for new products are considered. Ideas for new products are generated from many different sources. Employees who work in product development teams, salespeople close to the consumers, consumers of sport, and competitive organizations are just a few of the potential sources of ideas for new sports products.

Naturally, a marketing-oriented sports organization will attempt to communicate with their consumers as much as possible to determine emerging needs. As we discussed in chapter 4, marketing research plays a valuable role in anticipating the needs of consumers. Moreover, environmental scanning helps sports organizations keep in touch with changes in the marketing environment that might present opportunities for new product development. For instance, in our opening scenario, the entrepreneurs who want to establish the women's professional hockey league understand that the environmental conditions are conducive to success.

Idea Screening

Once the ideas are generated, the next step of the product development process, idea screening, begins. During the **idea screening** phase, all of the new product ideas are evaluated, and the poor ones are weeded out. An important consideration in the ideas screening process is to examine the "fit" of the product with the organization's goals and consumer demand. The concept of new product fit is consistent with the contingency framework, which states that product decisions should consider the external contingencies, the internal contingencies, and the strategic sports marketing process. One formal idea screening tool for analyzing the "fit" of potential products is the new product screening checklist (see Table 9.1).

Sports marketers using some variant of this new product screening checklist would rate potential new product ideas on each item. As Table 9.1 indicates, a score of less than 30 would eliminate the new product from further consideration, whereas a score of 70 or more would be further developed. Obviously, each sports organization must design its own new product screening checklist to meet the demands of its unique marketing environment and organization.

Analysis of the Sports Product Concept or Potential

By the third phase of the new product development process, poor ideas have been eliminated. Now, the process continues as the firm begins to analyze potential new products in terms of how they fit with existing products and how consumers respond to these new products. As new product ideas begin to take shape, marketing research is necessary to understand consumers' perceptions of the new product concepts. One type of marketing research that is commonly conducted during the new product development process is referred to as concept testing.

During concept testing, consumers representative of the target market, evaluate written, verbal, and/or pictorial descriptions of potential products. The objectives of concept testing are to understand the target market's reaction to the proposed product, determine how interested the target market is in the product, and explore the strengths and weaknesses of the proposed product. In some cases, consumers are asked to evaluate slightly different versions of the product so that sports organizations can design the product to meet the needs of consumers.

table 9.1

New Product Screening Checklist

Rate the new-product concept using a 10 point scale. Score a "1" if the concept fails the question and a "10" if it meets the criterion perfectly.

Relative Advantage
Does the new product offer a cost advantage compared to substitutes?
Does the new product have a value-added feature?
Is your innovation directed at neglected segments of the marketplace?

Compatibility
Is the product compatible with corporate practices, culture and value systems (i.e., the internal contingencies)?
Is the new product compatible with the market's environment (i.e., the external contingencies)?
Is the new product compatible with current products and services being offered (i.e., product mix)?

Perceived Risk
Note on the following questions absence of risk should receive a higher score.
Does the consumer perceive an economic risk if he or she tries the new product?
Does the consumer perceive a physical risk in adopting the new product?
Does the consumer fear that the new technology will not perform properly?
Does the product offer a social risk to consumers?

A bottom line score of 100 (10 points for each question) suggests a new product winner. For most companies, a score of 70 or better signals a "go" decision on the new product concept. A risk-oriented company would probably consider anything that scores 50 or higher. A score of 30 or less signifies a concept that faces many consumer obstacles.

The most important reason for conducting a concept test is to estimate the sales potential of the new product. Often, this is done by measuring "intent to buy" responses from tested consumers. Using the results of concept testing, along with secondary data such as demographic trends, sports marketers can decide whether to proceed to the next step of the new product development process, drop the idea, or revise the product concept and reevaluate. Table 9.2 shows a hypothetical concept test for the Professional Beach Soccer Tour, a new sports product that has been on the market for roughly three years.

Developing the Sports Product

Based on the results of the concept test, design of the product begins in order to conduct further testing. Ideally, if the sports organization is employing a marketing-orientation, then the product design and development stem from the consumer's perspective. For instance, Nike began its product design efforts for a new baseball

■ Concept testing is used to understand consumer reactions to sports such as white water rafting.

<table>
table 9.2
</table>

Concept Test for the Professional Beach Soccer Tour

The sport of beach soccer is played on a 30-by-40-yard soft sand surface with five players on each team, including the goalie. There are three periods of 12 minutes each with unlimited player substitutions (as in hockey). In the event of a tie, the game goes into a 3-minute overtime period followed by sudden-death penalty kicks. The Professional Beach Soccer Tour would feature nation against nation (e.g., United States vs. Italy).

What is your general reaction to beach soccer?

How likely would you be to attend an event if the Tour stopped in your city?
Would definitely attend
Probably would attend
Might or might not attend
Probably would not attend
Would definitely not attend

What do you like the most about this concept of Professional Beach Soccer?
What could be done to improve the concept of Professional Beach Soccer?

glove by asking 200 college and minor league baseball players what they disliked about their current gloves. Eighteen months and $500,000 later, researchers have designed a prototype glove that is lightweight, held together with plastic clips and wire straps and resembles a white foam rubber clamshell. Nike is hoping that this space-age design is not perceived by baseball purists to be to far afield from traditional models.[10]

In the case of a sporting good, a prototype usually is developed so that consumers can get an even better idea of how the product will function and look. Today's superior engineering technology allows manufacturers to develop more realistic prototypes in a shorter period of time. It is common for prototypes to then be sent to select individuals for further testing and refinement. For instance, new golf, tennis, and ski products are routinely sent to club professionals for testing.

Another consideration in developing the sports product is making preliminary decisions with respect to the planning phase of the strategic sports marketing process. Potential market selection decisions (segmentation, target markets, and positioning) are considered. Furthermore, packaging, pricing, and distribution decisions are also deliberated. These basic marketing decisions are necessary to begin the next phase of new product development, test marketing.

Test Marketing

In the concept stage of new product development, consumers indicate that they would be likely to purchase the new product or service. Now that the product has been designed and developed, it can be offered to consumers on a limited basis to determine actual sales. Test marketing is the final gauge of the new product's success or failure.

Test marketing allows the sports organization to determine consumer response to the product and also provides information that may direct the entire marketing strategy. For instance, test markets can provide valuable information on the most effective packaging, pricing, and other forms of promotion.

The three types of test markets that may be conducted include standardized test markets, controlled test markets, and simulated test markets.[11] In standardized test markets, the product is sold through normal channels of distribution. A controlled test market, also known as a forced-distribution test market, utilizes an outside agency to secure distribution. As such, the manufacturer of a new product does not have to worry about the acceptance and level of market support from retailers or those carrying the product because the outside agency pays the retailer for the test. A simulated test market uses a tightly controlled simulated retailing environment or purchasing laboratory to determine consumer preferences for new sports products. This type of test market may be especially important in the future as more and more sporting goods and services are being marketed through the Internet.

Whatever type of test market is chosen, it is important to keep several things in mind. First, test marketing delays the introduction of a new sports product and may allow time for the competition to produce a "me-too" or imitation, product thereby negating the test marketer's investment in research and development. Second, costs of test marketing must be considered. It is common for the cost of test marketing to range from $30,000 to $300,000. Third, the results of test marketing may be misleading. Consumers may be anxious to try new sports products and/or competition may try to influence the sales figures of the tested product by offering heavy discounting and promotion of their own product. Finally, test marketing presents a special challenge for sports marketers because of the intangible nature of many sports services.

Commercialization

The final stage of new product development is **commercialization**, or introduction. The decision has been made at this point to launch full-scale production (for goods) and distribution. If care has been taken at the previous stages of new product development, the new product will successfully meet its objectives. However, even if a systematic approach to new product development is followed, more often than not sports products fail. Just what is it that makes a small portion of new sports products successful while the large majority fail? Let us look at some of the factors that increase the chances of new product success.

a successful new product?

NASCAR speedparks seem to have all the elements

Officials of St. Andrews Golf Corp. announced the signing of Jeff Gordon, a two-time NASCAR Winston Cup Champion, to serve as spokesperson for their new motorsports entertainment attraction called NASCAR SpeedPark.

Gordon said that he is thrilled to be associated with this new and innovative sports and entertainment project. "I got my start in racing on the Go-Kart tracks of California at the age of 9, and NASCAR SpeedParks will give hundreds of thousands of youth the chance to have a fun, safe, and professionally supervised experience with the fastest growing sport in America today, NASCAR racing," said Gordon.

There are currently two locations being considered for the first two NASCAR licensed SpeedParks, which will be the first in the company's aggressive roll-out schedule over the next four years. The first sites are to be developed in the Las Vegas and Southern California markets with additional sites planned for Florida and the Carolinas.

In order to capitalize on the power of the NASCAR brand identity, St. Andrews has been given the rights to identify each SpeedPark as the "Only Go-Kart Facility Officially Licensed by NASCAR." In addition, the SpeedParks will use the NASCAR trademarks, service marks, and other NASCAR registrations.

In another unprecedented move, St. Andrews will be teaming with Roush Racing to develop the Authentic Go-Karts. While at the parks, the drivers have the options of choosing from either a $\frac{5}{8}$ scale NASCAR Winston Cup Stock Car replica, a $\frac{5}{8}$ scale NASCAR Craftsman Truck Series replica, or a Jr. Stock Car replica.

Max Jones, general manager of Roush Racing adds, "The final product will be anything but a typical Go-Kart. We are testing all aspects of the Karts from the body materials, driver

(continued)

loading and unloading, engine performance and safety, tires, wheels, brakes, and other parts of the Kart; and then we will construct four prototype options of the most desirable configurations, at which point we will then configure the final Kart before we send it to the final manufacturing stage.

St. Andrews has also entered into a consulting agreement with Mach One Marketing Group to assist in the development and exe-cution of the sponsorship sales plan for the SpeedParks. "Our team's approach to sponsorship will leverage new opportunities for NASCAR sponsors at the grassroots level," said Hal Price, president of Mach One Marketing. "The NASCAR SpeedParks represent the testing grounds for sponsors to be creative and extend their forms of marketing into new athletic and entertainment activities."

Source: Jeff Gordon, "NASCAR/St. Andrews Golf Announce Expanded SpeedPark Program," *Business NewsBank,* May 29, 1996.

New Products Success Factors

The success of any new sports product, such as the NASCAR SpeedParks, depends on a variety of factors. First and foremost, successful products must be high quality, create and maintain a positive and distinct brand image, and be designed to consumer specifications. In addition to the characteristics of the product itself, the other marketing mix elements (pricing, distribution, and promotion) play a major role in the success of a new product. Finally, the marketing environment also contributes to the success of a new product. A brief description of these critical success factors are presented in Table 9.3. Let us evaluate how well the new NASCAR SpeedParks performs on each of the critical success factors.

Based on these critical success factors, would you predict that the NASCAR SpeedParks will be profitable? The NASCAR SpeedParks would seem to perform well on each of the product characteristics. Families can observe others enjoying the SpeedParks and try the sports product once with limited perceived risk. The NASCAR Go-Karts are safe and built for kids, so product complexity is low. With the NASCAR branding, the sophisticated engineering and the authenticity, the perceived advantage of these replica cars should be far greater than "just another Go-Kart." Finally, the SpeedParks are consistent with core values, such as safe and fun entertainment for the entire family.

In addition to the product considerations, other marketing mix considerations have also been well thought out for the NASCAR SpeedParks. Initially, the SpeedParks will be placed in parts of the country known for entertainment (e.g., Las Vegas) and/or the love of NASCAR racing (e.g., the Carolinas). Given the signing of Jeff Gordon and the agreement with the Mach One Marketing Group, promotion of the SpeedParks should be solid.

The marketing environment also appears to be ready for the introduction of the NASCAR SpeedParks. NASCAR is one of the fastest-growing spectator sports in the country and has a huge and loyal fan base. Moreover, there are other Go-Kart tracks, but none with the backing of NASCAR, so competition is limited. In summary, the NASCAR SpeedParks seem to perform well on all of the critical success factors, but only time will tell whether this new sports product will run the victory lap.

table 9.3

Critical Success Factors For New Products

Product Considerations

- **Trialability**—Can consumers try the product before he or she makes a purchase to reduce the risk?
- **Observability**—Can consumers see the benefits of the product or watch other use the product prior to the purchase?
- **Perceived complexity**—Does the new product appear to be difficult to understand or use?
- **Relative advantage**—Does the new product seem better than existing alternatives?
- **Compatibility**—Is the new product consistent with consumers' values and beliefs?

Other Marketing Mix Considerations

- **Pricing**—Do consumers perceive the price to be consistent with the quality of the new product?
- **Promotion**—Are consumers in the target market aware of the product and do they understand the benefits of the product?
- **Distribution**—Is the product being sold in the "right" places and in enough places?

Marketing Environment Considerations

- **Competition**—Are there a large number of competitors in the market?
- **Consumer tastes**—Does the new product reflect a trend in society?
- **Demographics**—Is the new product being marketed to a segment of the population that is growing?

Source: Courtland L. Bovée and John Thill, *Marketing* (New York: McGraw-Hill, 1992), 307–309.

Product Life Cycle

From the time a sports product begins the new product development process to the time it is taken off the market, it passes through a series of stages known as the product life cycle (PLC). The four distinct stages of the PLC are called introduction, growth, maturity, and decline. As shown in Figure 9.1, the traditional PLC was originally developed by marketers to illustrate how the sales and profits of goods vary over time. However, other sports products, like athletes, teams, leagues, and events, pass through four distinct phases over time. Regardless of the nature of the sports product, the PLC is a useful tool for developing marketing strategy and then revising this strategy as a product moves through its own unique life cycle.

The water-bike is an excellent example of a sports product whose life cycle mirrors the shape of the conventional PLC. The waterbike or personal watercraft, had tremendous growth in the early 1990s. Sales of waterbikes reached their peak in 1995 with 200,000 units sold.[12] However, unit sales have been decreasing since that year. Industry insiders would like to believe that the waterbike is in the maturity phase of

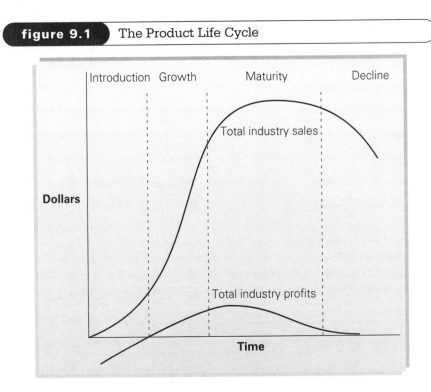

figure 9.1 The Product Life Cycle

Introduction Growth   Maturity   Decline

Total industry sales

Dollars

Total industry profits

Time

the PLC and that sales have merely reached their plateau. Others, however, contend that the industry has developed an image problem because of the safety and pollution issues associated with the activity. In this case, waterbike brands such as JetSki and SeaDoo, may need to find ways to extend the life of their products.

Before we explore the four phases of the PLC, keep several important factors in mind. First, the PLC originally was developed to describe product categories, such as waterbikes or baseball gloves, rather than specific brands, such as SeaDoo or Mizuno. Second, the product life cycle was designed to monitor the industry sales and profitability of goods rather than services. Third, the traditional shape and length of the product life cycle is generalized. In other words, it is assumed to look the same for all products. In reality, the length of the PLC varies for each sports product. Some products die quickly, some seem to last forever, and others die and are then reborn. Summarizing, sports marketers must carefully consider the unique PLC of each of their products on the market. Let us now explore how the PLC can be used for decision making in the strategic sports marketing process.

Introduction

When a new sports product first enters the marketplace, the introduction phase of the product life cycle (PLC) is initiated. The broad marketing goal of the first phase of the PLC is to generate awareness and stimulate trial among those consumers who are

■ Extending the product life cycle of the waterbike.

willing to try new products. Typically, profits are low because of the high start-up costs associated with getting the product ready to market.

During the introduction phase, pricing of the sports product is determined largely by the type of image that has been determined in the positioning strategy. Generally, one of two broad pricing alternatives is usually chosen during the introduction of the product. If the product strategy is to gain widespread consumer trial and market share, a lower price is set. This low pricing strategy is termed penetration pricing. On the other hand, a higher priced skimming strategy is sometimes preferred. The advantages of skimming include recouping the early marketing investment and production costs, as well as reinforcing the superior quality usually associated with higher prices.

Distribution of the new product is also highly dependent on the nature of the product. Usually, however, distribution is limited to fewer outlets. That is, there are a small number of places to purchase the product. Incentives are necessary to push the product from the manufacturer to the consumer. Promotion activity is high during the product's introduction in order to encourage consumers to try the new product. Additionally, promotion is designed to provide the consumers with information about the new product and to provide a purchase incentive.

Growth

Sales are usually slow as the new product is introduced. With the onset of the growth stage, sales of the product increase. In fact, a rapid increase in sales is the primary characteristic of the growth stage of the PLC. Because industry sales are growing, the broad marketing goal is to build consumer preference for your product and continue to extend the product line. Although competition is usually nonexistent or very weak at introduction, more competitors emerge during the growth phase. Promotion must stress the benefits of your brand over competitive brands.

For example, in 1990 Upper Deck introduced the first sports card using high resolution color photography. They literally could not print the cards fast enough, and demand skyrocketed with the subsequent product shortages. By the second year of production, Topps had introduced their competitive Stadium Club super premium line of cards. Demand for both cards was still good. However, Upper Deck would now forever be sharing a pie whose recipe they created.

During the growth stage, product differentiation occurs by making minor changes or modifications in the product or service. A premium is placed on gaining more widespread distribution of the product. Manufacturers must secure outlets/distributors at this early phase of the PLC so that the product is readily available. Finally, the prices during the growth phase are sometimes reduced in response to a growing number of competitors or held artificially high to enhance perceived quality. Let us look at some of the strategic decisions discussed thus far in the context of the Hawaiian Winter Baseball League.

Kurisu at the bat:
the growth of a league

When a group of minor league baseball owners pulled the plug on their Hawaiian winter league a few months before opening day in 1992, fanatical fans Duane Kurisu and his son were among the disappointed. Instead of just throwing his tickets in the trash, Kurisu decided to do something about it. The local real estate developer started his own league.

Since 1993, Kurisu's four Hawaii Winter Baseball League teams—the Honolulu Sharks, Maui Stingrays, Hilo Stars, and West Oahu Canefires—have played three 54-game seasons, becoming only the second U.S. off-season pro league after the Arizona Fall League.

Kurisu's market extends beyond Hawaii. His teams recruit players from North America, Japan, Taiwan, and Korea. Games are heavily attended by the East Asian tourists who throng to Hawaii. In addition, tickets are sold to tourists as well as to Hawaiian natives.

Kurisu admits that he got involved "because it was his passion for the game and desire to help rebuild Hawaiian tourism." Once committed, he poured over $5 million into the business. He began with gambling $1.5 million to hire staff, negotiate for players, develop team merchandise, and market tickets. In addition, he had to spend $500,000 to renovate several stadiums.

The new league spent $2.1 million in its first year, but took in only $600,000. "Starting a sports league is by far the most difficult thing that I have done," states Kurisu. The next year the league lost another $1.4 million and just when Kurisu thought it couldn't get worse, it did.

Major League Baseball announced that its teams would no longer pick up salaries for the talented young prospects they were trying out in the Hawaiian league. Rather than folding, Kurisu bit the bullet and paid full salaries for one season. Although attendance did increase, the league still lost $1.7 million in 1995.

Pleading desperation, Kurisu finally persuaded MLB to resume paying 40 percent of the players' salaries the next season. Kurisu also began refocusing his marketing efforts. Instead of trying to push a $5 ticket to Japanese tourists, he began putting together $75 packages including transportation from hotels, game tickets, an All-American hot dog dinner, and Japanese player autograph sessions.

Consistent with the growth phase of any product life cycle, Kurisu's aim in 1997 was to add two more teams and tap into the growing television market. Here, Kurisu may have his timing right. Satellite broadcasters are sprouting up all over Asia and looking for television programming. To aid in his efforts, Kurisu is opening a Tokyo office to drum up publicity and television contracts. It has been a tough haul, but it looks as if Casey Kurisu hasn't struck out—and there will yet be joy in Mudville (or Hawaii).

Source: Neil Weinberg, "Kurisu at the Bat," *Forbes*, September 23, 1996, 120.

Maturity

Eventually, industry sales begin to stabilize as fewer numbers of new consumers enter the saturated market. As such, the level of competition increases as a greater number of organizations compete for a limited or stable number of consumers. The primary marketing objective at maturity is to maintain whatever advantages were captured in growth and offer a greater number of promotions to encourage repeat purchases. Brand strategy shifts from "try me" to "buy one more than you used to." Unfortunately, profitability is also lessened because of the need to reduce prices and offer incentives.

If attempts to maintain sales and market share are unsuccessful in the maturity stage, an organization may try several alternative strategies to extend the PLC before the product begins to decline and eventually die. Let us look at how a once-invincible sports equipment manufacturer extended its PLC.

Schwinn back in the pack:

revving up the product life cycle for a declining brand

Having 101 years of experience manufacturing bicycles doesn't necessarily make you the leader of the pack. Schwinn Cycling and Fitness learned that painful lesson about three years ago after failing to ride on popular biking trends—including the mountain biking craze that boomed in the late 1980s—and was nearly bankrupt.

But the bicycle manufacturer, now headquartered in Boulder, has made a comeback. The charge now is to convince bicycle dealers and the casual biking public that the company has more to offer than the 1950s bikes equipped with white-wall tires, chrome fenders, and cantilever frames. While Schwinn still makes those bikes for nostalgia fans, its prize possessions these days are high–tech mountain bikes and flashy graphics that have moved Schwinn into the modern age.

"From a product standpoint, there's no question that we have caught up," said Chuck Ferries, chairman of the board. Shortly before its 100th birthday last year, the company became second only to Trek in unit volume sales

(continued)

at specialty bike shops. "They didn't take it seriously when it started in the 1980s so they missed a major trend," said Ferries, who was not with Schwinn at the time of near bankruptcy. "Sixty–five to 70 percent of all bike sales today are mountain bikes."

Schwinn's featured bikes for the next year are its BMX and freestyle bikes—an increasingly popular trend among people under age 30 that has led to the creation of new motocross tracks across the country. While those bikes have been good sellers partly because of Schwinn's exposure through professional racing teams and athletes, the challenge now is to capture the casual, weekend mountain biker—the type of person that Schwinn hopes will buy its middle-range bikes that cost $500 to $1000.

In the mountain-bike category, Schwinn is offering three levels of bikes: the entry-level Frontier, which ranges from $219 to $299; Mesa with upgraded components, $329 to $499; and Moab for experts, $599 to $899.

Dell Lee, who owns Littleton Cyclery & Fitness, was the most impressed with the long line of BMX and youth bikes—an indication that Schwinn is serious about attracting a larger share of those bikes in the market, he said. "I think a compliment to Schwinn is they're just like everybody else," he said. "They've survived. I think they're as viable as any other company."

Source: Emily Narvaes, "Schwinn Back in the Pack: Mountain Bike Boosts Company," *Denver Post*, May 15, 1996, C-01. Courtesy of the *Denver Post*.

Schwinn is an excellent illustration of a sports organization who realized it was rapidly moving toward extinction, decided to take corrective action, and developed and implemented new marketing strategies. Table 9.4 provides additional suggestions for sports marketers who wish to extend the PLC.

In another example, the United States Racquetball Association also realized that something needed to be done to rejuvenate the dying sport of racquetball. The Board of Directors agreed that a three-step plan to revitalize the sports.[13] The plan included (1) creating a vehicle to educate racquet club owners and managers about the economic benefits of the sport to their organization, (2) developing a system for club owners to implement the ideas described in the first step, and (3) designing a major

table 9.4

Extending the Product Life Cycle

- Develop new uses for products
- Develop new product features and refinements (line extensions)
- Increase the existing market
- Develop new markets
- Change marketing mix (e.g., new or more promotion; new or more distribution; increase or decrease price)
- Link product to a trend

Source: Joel Evans and Barry Berman, *Marketing*, 6th ed. (New York, NY: Macmillan, 1992), 439.

media event to generate more exposure and excitement in racquetball. Ultimately, an educational video was designed to address the issue of profitability and distributed to more than 2,000 clubs across the country. Most importantly, the Board of Directors agreed to support the idea of a U.S. Open event for racquetball to generate awareness and interest in the sport. The inaugural U.S. Open for racquetball was held in Memphis in 1996, which has helped spark interest in the declining sport.

Decline

The marketing goals for the decline stage of the PLC are difficult to pinpoint because decisions must be made regarding what to do with a failing product. These decisions are based largely upon the competition and how the sports organization chooses to react to the competition.

The distinctive characteristic of the decline phase of the PLC is that sales are steadily diminishing. Several alternative strategies might be considered during the decline phase. One alternative is referred to as deletion. As the name implies, the product is dropped from the organization's product mix. A second alternative, harvesting (or milking) is when the organization retains the sports product, but offers little or no marketing support. A final alternative is simply maintaining the product at its current level of marketing support in hopes that competitors will withdraw from the market that is already in decline.

Other Life Cycle Considerations

The PLC, although an excellent tool for strategic decision making, is not without limitations. These limitations include generalizing the length of the PLC, applying the PLC to broad product categories only, and using the PLC to analyze "pure" sporting goods only. Each of these potential weaknesses of the PLC model is discussed next.

Length and Shape of the PLC

Figure 9.1 depicted the traditional length and shape of the PLC. However, each product life cycle has its own unique shape and unique length depending on the product under consideration and the nature of the marketing environment. Several variants of the typical PLC length include the fad PLC, the classic PLC, and the seasonal PLC shown in Figures 9.2a–9.2c.

Fad The **fad** PLC (Figure 9.2a) is characterized by accelerated sales and accelerated appectance of the product followed by decline stages. Often sports marketers realize that their products will be novelty items that get into the market, make a profit, and then quickly exit. These one-time, short-term offerings would follow the volatile fad cycle. The ABA red, white, and blue basketball followed the fad cycle, as do many products in the golf equipment industry. For instance, in 1995, Callaway Golf introduced the revolutionary Big Bertha Iron, which outsold every other brand of iron. By 1996, just one year later, the Big Bertha Iron was obsolete.[14]

Another example of a fad cycle is the stadium seating and related memorabilia marketed and sold with the razing of the Cleveland Municipal Stadium in 1996. Pieces of the historic, former home of the Cleveland Browns were auctioned off with several

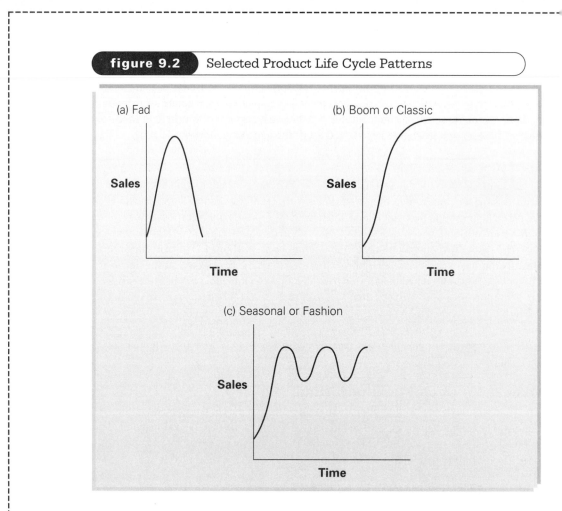

figure 9.2 Selected Product Life Cycle Patterns

(a) Fad

Sales

Time

(b) Boom or Classic

Sales

Time

(c) Seasonal or Fashion

Sales

Time

thousand fans in attendance. On the auction block were turnstiles, scoreboards, and a state flag that once flew over the stadium. Ticket-collector boxes, blueprints, and the toilet of former Browns owner Art Model were featured in a $23 auction catalog with 40 full-color pages. The locker belonging to former quarterback Bernie Kosar sold for around $2,000.

In a free auction preview, some 65,000 fans got one last chance to view the stadium, walk through a locker room, or stroll on the field. A few diehard-fans took away pieces of field sod or handfuls of gravel from the warning track. Prior to the auction, former Browns season ticketholders had the first option to purchase seats in the stadium, which held close to 80,000 fans. The seat prices range from $35 for a bench seat from the bleachers to $380 for a block of four wooden chairs.[15]

Classic Another variation of the PLC is characterized by a continuous stage of maturity (Figure 9.2b). Season tickets for the Green Bay Packers, Frisbees, baseball gloves and bats, tennis balls, and hockey sticks all represent other examples of the PLC known as the **classic**.

Seasonal   The **seasonal** life cycle is found in most sports where the sales of sports products rise and fall with the opening and closing day of the season. To combat the seasonal life cycle, some sports have adopted year-round scheduling. Most auto racing series are run on an 8- to 10-month schedule, giving sponsors almost year-round coverage. Professional tennis has also adopted a continual schedule, but as the following paragraph indicates, this may not be the best thing for thing for the sport.

When asked what he would do to cure the ills of tennis, former star and current TV analyst John McEnroe didn't hesitate before responding; "I would cut the amount of events. Now there are too many tournaments, so people don't have any idea about what's really important. I would make a schedule that would be like the baseball or basketball season, so we wouldn't go 12 months a year." Somewhat surprisingly, the NBA used the "less-is-more" strategy in 1984 when the league was plummeting in popularity. David Stern, then a rookie commissioner, significantly cut the number of televised games to increase long-term interest in the sport.[16]

The fad, classic, and seasonal life cycles are three common variants of the traditional PLC. Other products, however, seem to defy all life cycle shapes and lengths. Consider the old-fashioned roller skate. The roller skate was invented in 1863 and probably best followed the classic life cycle until the 1970s when disco fever swept the nation. During the *Saturday Night Fever* craze, skates quickly moved from a classic to a fad that eventually burned out. Recently, roller skating has experienced a resurgence, based, in part, on the late 1990s retro movement. Currently, inline skaters number about 27 million in the United States compared to 15 million roller skaters. However, skating continues to grow in popularity.[17]

The Level of Product

Another consideration for developing marketing strategy based on the PLC is the level of the product. Historically, the PLC was based on total industry sales for an entire product category, such as basketball shoes, bowling balls, mountain bikes, or golf clubs. Although examining the PLC by category is useful, it is also necessary to understand the PLC by product form and product brand.

Product form refers to product variations within the category. For example, titanium woods, metal woods, and "wood" woods represent three variations in product form in the golf club product category. The potential marketing strategies for each of these product forms differ by the stage of the PLC. The titanium woods are in the growth stage, metal woods are in maturity, and traditional woods are near extinction.

In addition to looking at the product category and form, it is also beneficial to examine various brands. Within the titanium wood form, there are a variety of individual brands, such as Taylor Made Burners, Callaway Big Berthas, and King Cobras. Each of these brands may be in different stages of the PLC. Therefore, sports marketing managers must give full consideration to variations in the PLC based on the level of the product (category, form, and brand).

Type of Product

The PLC originally was designed to guide strategies for goods. However, the notion of the PLC should be extended to other types of sports products. For instance, individual athletes can be thought of as sports products that move through a life cycle just as products do.

The phenomenal rise and success of Tiger Woods in the professional golf ranks has skyrocketed him out of introduction and into the growth phase of his PLC. The number of products that Woods endorses is rapidly increasing and more and more people are becoming aware of his "star" qualities. The Detroit Piston star, Grant Hill, also has emerged and continues in his growth stage. Recently, Hill signed an eight-year, $80 million shoe contract with Fila and is being touted as the next Michael Jordan for his skills both on and off the court. An aging star such as Steve Young of the San Francisco 49ers may be heading for retirement and decline in his individual PLC.

Interestingly, some individual athletes have a unique shape to their PLC. Think about the many professional boxers (who sometimes have had several PLCs) and baseball players (Daryl Strawberry, Eric Davis) who have come out of retirement to reintroduce themselves. Arnold Palmer, with his incredible staying power, will undoubtably stay in the maturity phase of his PLC and remain a classic even after playing in his last competitive golf tournament. Many aging golfers, such as Jim Colbert, who had almost no success on the regular PGA Tour are experiencing tremendous success on the Senior Tour. Unfortunately, many athletes experience a life cycle that is best represented by the fad PLC. For instance, Brian Bosworth (Seattle Seahawks linebacker), Mark "The Bird" Fiydrich (Detroit Tigers pitcher), and Buster Douglas (boxing) were all athletes who had short-term success only to quickly fall into decline for a number of reasons.

Sports teams also can pass through the various phases of the PLC. For instance, the Arizona Diamondbacks of Major League Baseball are in the introductory stage of their PLC. The Minnesota Twins, who may be moving to Charlotte, North Carolina, could be in the decline stage. These two product examples would each require completely different marketing strategies.

Professional and collegiate sports leagues also pass through the stages of the PLC. For example, professional tennis may be moving towards decline and is considering how to best extend its PLC. The ABL (women's professional basketball) and the CNBA (Chinese National Basketball League, discussed in the following spotlight) are currently in the introduction phase of their life cycles and, therefore, have directed their marketing efforts towards making fans aware of and generating interest in the leagues. On the collegiate side, Northwestern football, under coach Gary Barnett, has gone from decline to introduction to their current growth phase. Northwestern, the perennial football doormat of the Big Ten Conference, has recently enjoyed a number of successful seasons. As a result of their success, they are renovating and renaming their stadium and are enjoying a six percent increase in admissions applications.

high hoops for the east: introducing a professional league basketball in china

In basketball, nothing counts more than size, and China may be the ultimate proof of the axiom. The immensity of its population of 1.2 billion has prompted a very tall ambition among sports promoters, product sponsors, and the Communist government—that China could soon have the biggest collection of basketball fans on the globe. The clock has already started ticking on that dream: State television now broadcasts basketball at least five days a week, including both local games and those of America's National Basketball Association (NBA), and viewership is soaring. In the northwestern city of Jilin, cheerleaders in bikinis of purple and gold perform dance routines before games and during breaks. Two professional basketball leagues are already playing to packed school gymnasiums and university stadiums, with some players, coaches, and referees imported from the United States. The experience of sharing the court with former American professionals has already sharpened the Chinese hoopsters' game. "Some are even dunking the ball," says Joe Weakley, who left California in October to become coach of the two-month old Lions. "I never saw that before."

Basketball has been popular in China for years, particularly as a casual recreation at schools and in village squares. In 1994, the government decided that China's centrally controlled sports administration would have to loosen up, partly to improve the performance of Chinese athletes, but also to tap into professional sport's profit potential. A pro soccer league was quickly created, and a volleyball circuit was announced in December. All of the leagues are run by the State Physical Culture and Sports Commission, which shrewdly took the opportunity of investing in many of the newly formed teams. In 1994, the committee signed a deal with International Management Group (IMG), one of the world's largest sports marketing companies, to form the Chinese National Basketball League. The CNBL now has 12 competing clubs, television contracts, and big-name sponsors, such as Nike and Motorola. Last year, China made a slightly sweeter deal with a Hong Kong promotion company, Spectrum Group. That link produced the Chinese New Basketball Alliance, CNBA, which boasts eight teams and a large squad of foreign players, coaches, and refs. "The venture we're taking on is incredibly expensive," says Spectrum Chief Operating Officer Andy Jay, who notes that the league puts up its imported talent in five-star hotels. "But years down the road, if China keeps opening up, there will be more than one television station in each city, ticket sales will increase, and you'll have to make money."

Source: Anthony Spaeth, "High Hoops for the East," *Time*, January 20, 1997. Reprinted with permission of Time Life Syndication.

Each level of sports product must receive careful consideration by sports marketers because of the strategic implications. Sometimes the interaction of athlete, team, and league PLCs can make strategic decisions even more challenging. Take the case of Cliff Ronning of the Nashville Predators in the NHL. The expansion Predators might be seen in the introductory phase of the PLC, Cliff might be in growth, while the NHL is in maturity. As complex as this seems, sports marketers must remember not to neglect any of these products. Decisions will be made about the perceived relevance of each of these types of products.

(D)iffusion of Innovations

New sports/sports products, or **innovations**, are continually being introduced to consumers and pass through the various stages of the product life cycle as described in the previous section. Initially, the new sport/sports product is purchased or tried by a small number of individuals (roughly 2.5 percent of the marketplace). Then, more and more people begin to try the new product. Consider the "metal wood" in golf. When this innovation was first introduced in the late 1970s, only the boldest "pioneers" of golf were willing to adopt the new technology. Now, only a very small percentage of the golfing population do not carry metal woods in their bags.[18]

The rate at which new sports products spread throughout the marketplace is referred to as the "**diffusion of innovation**."[19] The rate of acceptance of a sport innovation is influenced by three factors, which are shown in Figure 9.3. The first factor impacting the rate of diffusion is the characteristics of the new product. These characteristics, such as trialability, observability, perceived complexity, relative advantage, and compatability, discussed earlier in the chapter in the context of new product factors. The interaction of these factors can accelerate or slow the rate of diffusion. Perceived newness, the second factor that influences rate of diffusion, refers to the type of new product from the consumer's perspective (continuous, dynamically continuous, and discontinuous innovations). Typically, continuous innovations have a faster rate of acceptance as they require no behavioral change and little disruption for the adopter. The third factor is the nature of the communication network. The rate and way in

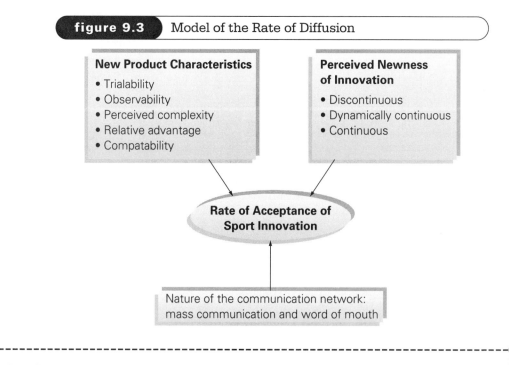

figure 9.3   Model of the Rate of Diffusion

New Product Characteristics

- Trialability
- Observability
- Perceived complexity
- Relative advantage
- Compatability

Perceived Newness of Innovation

- Discontinuous
- Dynamically continuous
- Continuous

Rate of Acceptance of Sport Innovation

Nature of the communication network: mass communication and word of mouth

which information is shared about a new sports product is critical to its success, as well as the speed of acceptance. Most marketers conceptualize the communications network for innovations as a two-step flow of information. In the first step, the initial consumers try a new product or opinion leaders are influenced by mass communication such as advertising, sales promotions, and the Internet. Then, in the second step, opinion leaders use word-of-mouth communication to provide information about the new product to the rest of the target market. Martin and Higgins believe that this two-step flow of information is especially important to sports innovations, because "unlike typical consumer purchase decisions, which involve only the individual, recent studies show that of the consumers who attend sporting events, less than two percent attend by themselves."[20]

The diffusion of innovations is an important concept for sports marketers to understand because of the its strategic implications. Stated simply, the marketer must know the stage of the life cycle and the characteristics of the consumers who are likely to try the product at any given stage. Let us examine the characteristics of each group as a product spreads throughout the marketplace.

Types of Adopters

Innovators represent those consumers who are the first to adopt a new sports product as it enters the marketplace. Because they are the first to adopt, these consumers carry the highest risk associated with the new product. These risks may either be social (what will others think of the product), economic (costs are high and drive up the price), and performance (will the product perform as it was intended). This younger and usually high-income group of consumers also is also known for the high degree of interaction and communication they have with other innovators.

The next group of consumers to adopt a new sports product is the **early adopters**. As with the innovators, this group is also characterized by high social status. It is perhaps the most important group to sports marketers, however, because they carry high degrees of opinion leadership and word-of-mouth influence. As just discussed, these individuals are the key players in communicating the value of new sports products to the majority of consumers.

Once the new sports product has spread past the early stages of the product life cycle, the **early majority** is ready for adoption. This group is above average in social status, but more deliberate in their willingness to try new products. In addition, this group is heavily influenced by information provided by the innovators and early adopters.

The **late majority** adopt innovations in the late stages of maturity of the product life cycle. As their name implies, over half (roughly 60 percent) of the market has now purchased/tried the new product before the late majority decide to do so. These individuals are skeptical and have less exposure to mass media.

The final group of adopters are known as **laggards**. These individuals are oriented toward the past and tend to be very traditional in the sports products that they choose. They begin to adopt products in the declining stage of the product life cycle. Clearly, prices must be reduced, and promotions encouraging trial and widespread distribution must all be in place in order for laggards to adopt new products.

(N)ew sports products are critical to the success of any organization. Newness, however, can be thought of in any number of ways. The organizational perspective on newness depends on whether or not the firm has marketed the product in the past. From the organizational perspective, new products are categorized as follows: new-to-the-world products, new product category entries, product line extensions, product improvements, and repositionings.

Conversely, newness from the consumer's perspective is based on the consumer's perception of whether the product represents an innovation. From the consumer's perspective, new products are classified as either discontinuous innovations, dynamically continuous innovations, or continuous innovations. Discontinuous innovations represent the most innovative new products, while continuous innovations are simply improvements or imitation products.

Regardless of how new products are classified, organizations are constantly searching for the next innovation that will help the firm achieve its financial objectives. Rather than leave this to chance, many organizations use a systematic approach called the new product development process. The new product development process consists of the following phases: idea generation; idea screening; analysis of the concept; developing the sports product; test marketing; and commercialization. Idea generation considers any and all ideas for new products from sources such as employees, competitors, and consumers. During the idea screening phase, these new product ideas are screened and the poorer ones are eliminated. To perform this task, organizations sometime use a new product screening checklist. In the third phase, analysis of the sports product concept, marketing research is used to assess consumer recreation to the proposed product. More specifically, concept tests are used to gauge the product's strengths and weaknesses, as well as the consumer's intent to use the new product. Next, a prototype of the new product is designed so that consumers can get an even better idea about the product. Additionally, preliminary decisions regarding marketing strategy are established. In the sixth stage, the new product is test marketed. Depending on the product and the market conditions, sports marketers may use either standardized, controlled, or simulated test markets. The final stage of the new product development process is commercialization in which the new product is formally introduced in the marketplace. Whether or not the product succeeds is a function of a number of factors, such as the product considerations (e.g., trialability, relative advantage), other marketing mix variable (e.g., pricing), and marketing environment considerations (e.g., competition).

As a new product reaches commercialization, it moves through a series of four stages known as the product life cycle, or PLC. The PLC is an important marketing concept in that the stage of the life cycle dictates marketing strategy. The four stages of the PLC include introduction, growth, maturity, and decline. At introduction, the marketing goal is to generate awareness of the new sports product. The broad goal of the growth phase is to build consumer preference for the sports product and begin to expand the product line. During maturity, the number of promotions are increased and marketers seek to maintain any competitive advantage they have obtained during growth. Finally, the product goes through decline, where decisions must be made regarding whether to delete the product or extend the life cycle.

Although each product has a life cycle, the length of that life and speed at which a product progresses through the four stages is unique for each product. Some sports products grow and decline at a rapid pace. These are known as fads. Other products, which seem to last in maturity forever, are called classics. The most common life cycle for sports products is known as seasonal. Other life cycle considerations are the level of product and the type of product. For example, sports marketers might analyze the life cycle of leagues, teams, and individual athletes, as well as other types of sports products.

The rate of diffusion is the speed at which new products spread throughout the marketplace. The rate of diffusion, or speed of acceptance, is based on three broad factors. These include the new product characteristics (e.g., trialability, observability), perceived newness (e.g., discontinuous innovation), and the nature of the communications network. It is critical that sports marketers monitor the rate of diffusion and understand the characteristics of consumers that try new products as they spread throughout the marketplace.

Innovators are the first group of consumers to try a new product. They are generally younger, have higher incomes, and have a strong tolerance for risk. The next group of consumers to try a sports product is the early adopters. This is a larger group than the innovators and, as such, they are key consumers to target. After the product has passed through the initial stages of the product life cycle, the early majority adopt the product. This group is above average in income, but more deliberate in trying new things. The late majority adopt the product during the late stages of maturity and finally the laggards may try new products. Strategically, sports marketers must adopt a different marketing mix when marketing to each of these new product adopter groups.

KEY TERMS & CONCEPTS

commercialization

continuous innovations

decline

developing the sports product

diffusion of innovations

discontinuous innovations

dynamically continuous innovations

early adopters

early majority

growth

idea generation

idea screening

innovation

innovators

introduction

laggards

late majority

maturity

new product category entries

new product development process

new product success factors

new sports product

new-to-the-world product

product life cycle

test marketing

types of adopters

REVIEW QUESTIONS

1. What is meant by a "new sports product?" Describe a "new sports product" from the organization's perspective and from the consumer's perspective.

2. What is the difference between discontinuous, dynamically continuous, and continuous innovations? Provide examples of each to support your answer.

3. Describe, in detail, the new product development process.

4. Why is test marketing so important to sports marketers in the new product development process? What are the three types of test markets? Comment on the advantages and disadvantages of each type of test market.

5. What are the critical success factors for new sports products?

6. Describe the product life cycle concept. Why is the product life cycle so critical to sports marketers? What is it used for? How can the product life cycle be extended?

7. What are some of the variations in the shape of the traditional product life cycle?

8. Define the diffusion of innovations. What are the different types of adopters for innovations? Describe the characteristics of each type of adopter.

EXERCISES

1. For each of the following sports products, indicate whether you believe they are discontinuous, dynamically continuous, or continuous innovations: WNBA, titanium golf clubs, and skysurfing.

2. Contact the marketing department of three sporting goods manufacturers or sports organizations and conduct a brief interview regarding the new product development process. Do each of the organizations follow the same procedures? Do each of the organizations follow the new product development process discussed in the chapter?

3. In what stage of the product life cycle is Major League Baseball? Support your answer with research.

4. Find an example of a "new sports product." Then, develop a survey using the critical success factors for new sports products and ask ten consumers to complete the instrument. Summarize your findings and indicate whether or not you think the new product will be successful based on your research.

5. Some people think that boxing may be in the decline phase of the product life cycle. Develop a strategy to extend the product life cycle of boxing.

INTERNET EXERCISES

1. Search the Internet and find examples of three "new sports products" that have recently been introduced in the marketplace.

2. Find three Internet sites of professional athletes in any sport. In what stage of the product life cycle are these athletes? Support with evidence found on the Internet.

3. Search the Internet for an example of a new sports product that could be classified as a fad. Describe the product and why you think the product is a fad.

1. William Zikmund and Michael d'Amico, *Marketing*, 4th ed. (St. Paul, MN: West, 1993).

2. Tim Rosaforte, "Building for the Future," *Sports Illustrated*, July 29, 1996, G15.

3. Ronald Grover, Amy Barrett, Richard Melcher, and Nicole Harris, "Playing for Keeps," *Business Week*, September 22, 1997, 32–33.

4. Mark Glover, "Taking the Cue—New Billiard Parlors Cater to Family Crowds and Aren't Shy About Giving Hustlers the Heave," *The Sacramento Bee*, January 15, 1996, p. E1. "Billiards Growing as a Participant Sport." <http://www.sportlink.com/individua...ng/96billpartstudy/96billpart.html> (May 1997).

5. See, for example, Del Hawkins, Roger Best, Kenneth Coney, *Consumer Behavior: Building Marketing Strategy*, 7th ed. (New York, NY: McGraw-Hill, 1998), 248–250.

6. James J. Zhang, Dennis W. Smith, Dale G. Pease, and Matthew T. Mahar, "Spectator Knowledge of Hockey as a Significant Predictor of Game Attendance," *Sport Marketing Quarterly*, vol. 5, no. 3 (1996): 41–48.

7. "League History." <http://www.iowabarnstormes.com/sidelines/history.html>. "Arena Football League History." <http://www.absorfw.com/JAWS/Arena/history.htm>.

8. Mark Curnutle, "Cheer for Favorite NFL Team with Action Figures, Phone Cards" *Cincinnati Enquirer*, September 2, 1996, C1.

9. Susan Higgins and James Martin, "Managing Sport Innovations: A Diffusion Theory Perspective," *Sport Marketing Quarterly*, vol. 5, no. 1, (1996):43–50.

10. Bill Richards, "Nike Plans to Swoosh into Sports Equipment But It's a Tough Game," *The Wall Street Journal*, January 6, 1998, A1.

11. Gilbert Churchill, *Basic Marketing Research*, 3rd ed. (Forth Worth, TX: Dryden Press, 1996).

12. Christopher J. Chipello, "Past the Crest: Backlash Beaches Water-Bike Craze," *The Wall Street Journal*, September 5, 1997, B1, B11.

13. Jim Hiser, "United States Open Racketball Championships...say What?" *Racquetball Magazine*, March–April 1996, 4–8.

14. James P. Sterba, "Your Golf Shots Fall Short? You Didn't Spend Enough," *The Wall Street Journal*, February 23, 1996, B7.

15. Patricia Davis, "A Stadium Is Going, Going, Gone; What Am I Bid for This Goal Post?" *The Wall Street Journal*, September 25, 1996.

16. David Hidgon, "Trim the Season to Grow the Game," *Tennis*, November 1996, 22.

17. Joseph Pereira, "Classic Roller Skates Return as Safety Fears Dull Blades," *The Wall Street Journal*, October 24, 1997, B1.

18. James P. Sterba, "Your Golf Shots Fall Short? You Didn't Spend Enough," *The Wall Street Journal*, February 23, 1996, B7.

19. Everett Rogers, *Diffusion of Innovations*, 3rd ed. (New York, NY: Free Press, 1983).

20. B.J. Mullin, S. Hardy, and William Sutton, *Sports Marketing* (Champaign, IL: Human Kinetics Publishers, 1993).

Promotion Concepts

After completing this chapter, you should be able to

- Identify the promotion mix tools
- Describe the elements of the communication process
- Understand the promotion planning model

- Compare the advantages and disadvantages of the various promotional mix tools
- Understand the importance of integrated marketing communication to sports marketers

Just ask anyone the first thing that comes to mind when they think of sports marketing, and they are likely to say, "Tiger Woods's Nike advertisements" or "Michael Jordan's Wheaties ads." As we have discussed, sports marketing is much more than advertisements using star athlete endorsers. It involves developing a sound product or service, pricing it correctly, and making sure that it is available to consumers when and where they ask for it. However, the necessary element that links the other marketing mix variables together is promotion.

Typically, promotion and advertising are used synonomously. **Promotion**, however, includes much more than traditional forms of advertising. It involves all forms of communication to consumers. For many organizations, sports are quickly becoming the most effective and efficient way to communicate with current and potential target markets. The combination of tools available to sports marketers to communicate with the public is known as the promotional mix and consists of the following **promotion mix elements**:

- *Advertising*—a form of one-way mass communication about a product, service, or idea, paid for by an identified sponsor.
- *Personal selling*—an interactive form of interpersonal communication designed to build customer relationships and produce sales or sports products, services, or ideas.
- *Sales promotion*—short term incentives usually designed to stimulate immediate demand for sports products or services.
- *Public or community relations*—evaluation of public attitudes, identification of areas within the organization that the sports population may be interested in, and building of a good "image" in the community.
- *Sponsorship*—investing in a sports entity (athlete, league, team, event, and so on) to support overall organizational objectives, marketing goals, and/or more specific promotional objectives.

Within each of the promotion mix elements are more specialized tools to aid in reaching promotional objectives. For example, sales promotions can take the form of sweepstakes, rebates, coupons, or free samples. Advertising can take place on television, in print, or as stadium signage. Sponsors might chose to communicate through an athlete, team, or league. Each of these promotional tools is a viable alternative when considering the most effective promotion mix for a sports organization. Regardless of which tool we choose, the common thread in each element of the promotion mix is communication. Because communication is such an integral part of promotion, let us take a more detailed look at the communications process.

Ⓒommunications Process

The communications process is an essential element for all aspects of sports marketing. **Communication** is the process of establishing a commonness of thought between the sender and the receiver. In order to establish this "oneness" between the

BILL VEECK

vn as the Promotion King of Baseball, Bill k single-handedly changed the course of ts marketing. Veeck pioneered promo- l events that today have become com- place. For instance, Veeck initiated Ladies t and Straight-A Night at the ballpark. One eck's most memorable promotions took e on August 19, 1951, when a pinch-hitter announced in the bottom half of the first ng in a game between the St. Louis ns and the Detroit Tigers. Over the furi- objections of the Detroit manager, Red e, the batter was declared a legitimate ber of the Browns. Bill Veeck, then owner e Browns, cautioned his pinch-hitter be- he left the dugout that "I've got a man in stands with a high-powered rifle, and if swing he'll fire."

What was the fuss? Veeck sent in a 3' 7" get named Eddie Gaedel to pinch-hit for Browns. Gaedel was promptly walked on straight pitches and removed from the game for a pinch-runner. Gaedel was quoted as saying "For a minute, I felt like Babe Ruth."

For all his successful promotions, Veeck is also remembered for one that turned sour in the mid-1970s. Called "Disco Demolition Night," the idea of the promotion was for fans to bring their disco albums to the ballpark to be burned in a bonfire. Unfortunately, fans stormed the field , a riot ensued, and the White Sox were forced to forfeit the second game of a doubleheader.

Veeck also instituted a promotion where fans were given signs with "yes" and "no" on them and asked to vote on strategy during a game. The "Grandstand Managers" led the Browns to a 5–3 victory. Promotions such as this led Veeck to be known as a true "fan's fan." He once stated that "every day was Mardi Gras and every fan was king." And "the most beautiful thing in the world is a ballpark filled with people." His marketing and fan orientation forged the way for later marketers of all sports.

d from: Bill Veeck, *Veeck as in Wreck: Autobiography of Bill Veeck* (New York, NY: Simon and Schuster, 1962).

sender and the receiver, the sports marketer's message must be transmitted via the complex communications process.

The interactive nature of the communications process allows messages to be transmitted from sports marketer (source) to consumer (receiver) and from consumer (source) to sports marketer (receiver). Traditionally, sports marketers' primary means of communication to consumers has been through the various promotion mix elements (e.g., advertisements, sponsorships, sales promotions, salespeople). Sports marketers also communicate with consumers via other elements of the marketing mix. For example, the high price of a NASCAR ticket communicates that it is a higher quality event than the more inexpensive Busch Grand National Series.

In addition to sports marketers communicating with consumers, consumers communicate back to sports marketers through their behavior. Most notably, consumers communicate whether or not they are satisfied with the sports product by their purchase behavior. In other words, they attend sporting events and purchase sporting goods.

The communications process begins with the source or the sender of the message. The source encodes the message and sends it through one of many potential

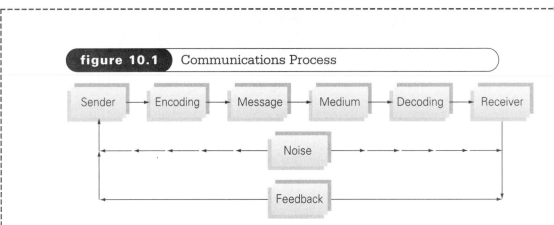

figure 10.1 Communications Process

Sender → Encoding → Message → Medium → Decoding → Receiver

Noise

Feedback

See, for example, Michael Solomon, *Consumer Behavior*, 3rd ed. (Englewood Cliffs, NJ: Prentice Hall, 1996).

communications media. Next, the message is decoded by the receiver of the message and finally feedback is given to the original source of the message. In the ideal world, messages are sent and interpreted exactly as intended. This, however, rarely occurs because of noise and interference.

Figure 10.1 shows a simplified diagram of the communications process. Each box in the figure represents one of the **elements in the communications process**. These elements include: the source, encoding, message, medium, decoding, receiver, feedback, and noise. In order to maximize communication effectiveness, it is necessary to have a better understanding of each of these elements in the communications process.

Source

The sender or **source** of the message is where the communication process always originates. In sports marketing, the source of messages is usually a star athlete. For example, you might think of Michael Jordan drinking Gatorade or Tiger Woods delivering a message of behalf of Rolex watches. Other popular athlete "sources," according to a 1996 survey conducted by Video Storyboard Tests,[1] that may not have come to mind include the following:

Shaquille O'Neal	Reebok, Pepsi, Taco Bell
Charles Barkley	McDonald's, Nike
Grant Hill	Fila, Sprite, Kellogg
Deion Sanders	Nike, Pepsi
Larry Bird	Converse, Miller Brewing
Arnold Palmer	Penzoil, Cadillac
Dennis Rodman	Nike, Pizza Hut
George Foreman	McDonald's (regional)
Wayne Gretsky	Campbell's Soup, L.A. Gear

■ Coaches, like Cincinnati's Bruce Coslet, are sources of marketing messages.

Although these sources are all individual athletes, there are many other sources of sports marketing messages. The source of a message might also be a group of athletes, a team, or even the league or sport. Additional sources of sports marketing messages are company spokespeople like Karsten Soldheim, the founder of Ping golf equipment, or coaches such as Bruce Coslet, seen in this advertisement trying to promote the sale of PSLs (personal seat licenses) for the Cincinnati Bengals.

Sources do not always have to be well-recognized and famous individuals to be effective. Sports marketers use actors playing the role of common, everyday sports participants to deliver their message from the perspective of the representative consumer of the sports product or service. Other effective sources are inanimate objects, such as Little Penny featured in the Nike advertisements. Additionally, sports marketers rely on sales personnel to convey the intended message to consumers. Informal sources, such as friends, family, and coworkers, are also sources of marketing information and messages. As we learned in chapters 5 and 6, reference groups play an important role in influencing purchase behavior and transmitting the marketing message.

Whatever the source, it is agreed upon by researchers that in order to be effective, the source must be credible. **Credibility** is the source's perceived expertise and trustworthiness. A very persuasive message can be created when a combination of these two factors (expertise and trustworthiness) is present in the source. For a source to be trustworthy, that person must be objective and unbiased. Certain athlete endorsers, such as Arnold Palmer, Mike Dikta, and Michael Jordan, are known for their perceived trustworthiness. We sometimes look to friends and family as information sources because of their objectivity. In fact, word-of-mouth communication is believed to be extremely persuasive because the source of the message has nothing to gain from delivering the message. Additional unbiased sources are those "man-on-the-street" testimonies by the common consumer. For example, many of us have seen infomercials that use "regular people" to describe how they lost weight or became physically fit by using the latest and greatest fitness equipment.

Source credibility is also enhanced when the sender of the message has perceived expertise. Naturally, athletes like Shaq, Penny Hardaway, Michael Jordan, and Grant Hill are believed to deliver expert messages when the product being promoted is related to athletics, or more specifically, basketball. At least this is what Nike and Fila are counting on. Nike pays Michael Jordan an estimated $20 million a year to be an "expert" endorser. Running second on the list of basketball endorsers is Grant Hill.

In September of 1997, Hill signed an $80 million deal over seven years with Fila.[2] Hill was picked for the NBA All-Star team his first three years in the league and was a member of the 1996 Olympic team. These basketball credentials should help Fila sell the shoe that bears Grant Hill's name. In fact, Fila is hoping that Hill will help build brand equity not just in the United States, but all over the world.

Other examples of athletes who endorse products related to their sport include race car drivers such as Jeff Gordon promoting Chevrolet and tennis players such as Michael Chang promoting Prince tennis equipment. The general rule of thumb is that the message is more effective if there is a match-up, or congruence, between the qualities of the endorser and the product that is being endorsed. In fact, the **match-up hypothesis** states the more congruent the image of the endorser with the image of the product being promoted, the more effective the message.[3]

Pennzoil® salutes Arnold Palmer, golfing legend, American hero, and, we're proud to say, our spokesman.

For every golfer in the world, we thank you Arnie.

■ Arnold Palmer: One of the most credible celebrity endorsers ever.

If the match-up hypothesis holds true, then why do companies pay millions of dollars to star athletes to promote their nonathletic products? For example, tennis star Pete Sampras endorses Pizza Hut, Movado watches, and RCA entertainment products. First, consumers have an easier time identifying brands that are associated with celebrity athletes. Second, athletes are used to differentiate competing products that are similar in nature. For instance, most consumers know and associate Shaquille O'Neal with Pepsi. Shaq's association helps to create and then maintain the desired image of Pepsi, which in turn differentiates it from Coke.

Encoding

After the source is chosen, encoding takes place. **Encoding** is translating the sender's thoughts or ideas into a message. In order to ensure effective encoding, the source of the message must make difficult decisions about the message content. Will the receiver understand and comprehend the message as intended? Will the receiver identify with the message?

Consider for a moment, the slogan "We Got Next" used to introduce the WNBA (see advertisement). The language of this message may be up-to-date and "cool," but it may also be misunderstood or misinterpreted by a large portion of the potential target audience. Likewise, even if the slogan is understood, it may be outdated quickly and seem "unhip" to the receivers of the message.

Sources have a variety of tools from which to encode messages. They can use pictures, logos, words, and other symbols. Symbols and pictures are often used in sports marketing to convey the emotional imagery that words cannot capture. The most effective encoding uses multiple media to get the message across (i.e., visually and verbally), presents information in a clear, organized fashion, and always keeps the receiver in mind.[4]

Message

The next element in the communications process is to develop the **message**, which refers to the exact content of the words and symbols to be transmitted to the receiver. Decisions regarding the characteristics of this message depend on the objective of the promotion, but sports marketers have a wide array of choices. These choices include one- versus two-sided messages, emotional versus rational messages, and comparative versus noncomparative messages.

The **sidedness** of a message is based on the nature of the information presented to the target audience. The messages can be constructed as either one-sided or two-sided. In a one-sided message, only the positive features of the sports product are described, whereas a two-sided message includes both the benefits and weaknesses of the product.

Another decision regarding the message in the promotion is whether to have an **emotional versus rational** appeal. A rational appeal provides the consumer with in-

WE GOT NEX

REBECCA LOBO . NEW YORK LIBERTY

www.wnba.com

■ How effective is the encoding in this message for the WNBA?

formation about the sports product so that he or she may arrive at a careful, analytical decision, and an emotional appeal attempts to make the consumer "feel" a certain way about the sports product. Emotional appeals might include fear, sex, humor, or feelings related to the hard work and competitive nature of sport.

A final message characteristic that may be considered by sports marketers is **comparative messages**. Comparative messages refer to either directly or indirectly comparing your sports product to one or more competitive products in a promotional message. For example, golf ball manufacturers often compare the advantages of their product to competitors' products.

Regardless of the message characteristics, the broad objective of promotion is to effectively communicate with consumers. What are some ways to make your sports marketing message more memorable and persuasive? Table 10.1 summarizes a few simple techniques to consider.

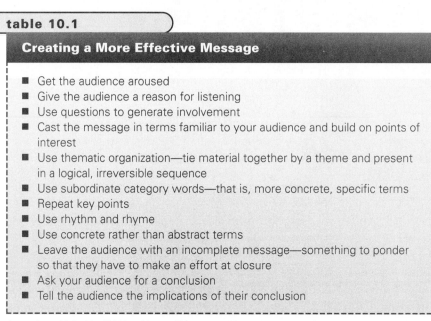

table 10.1

Creating a More Effective Message

- Get the audience aroused
- Give the audience a reason for listening
- Use questions to generate involvement
- Cast the message in terms familiar to your audience and build on points of interest
- Use thematic organization—tie material together by a theme and present in a logical, irreversible sequence
- Use subordinate category words—that is, more concrete, specific terms
- Repeat key points
- Use rhythm and rhyme
- Use concrete rather than abstract terms
- Leave the audience with an incomplete message—something to ponder so that they have to make an effort at closure
- Ask your audience for a conclusion
- Tell the audience the implications of their conclusion

Source: James MacLachlan, "Making a Message Memorable and Persuasive," *Journal of Advertising Research,* vol. 23, (December 1983–January 1984):51–59.

Medium

After the message has been formulated it must be transmitted to receivers through a channel, or communications **medium**. A voice in personal selling, television, radio, stadium signage, billboards, blimps, newspapers, magazines, and even athletes' uniforms all serve as media for sports marketing communication. In addition to these more traditional media, new communications channels such as the Internet and the multitude of sports specific cable programming (e.g., the Golf Channel) that are emerging and growing in popularity.

Decisions on which medium or media to choose depend largely on the overall promotional objectives. Also, the media decisions must consider the costs to reach the desired target audience, its flexibility, its ability to reach a highly defined audience, its lifespan, the sports product or service complexity, and the characteristics of the intended target market. These media considerations are summarized in Table 10.2. For example, sports marketers attempting to reach the mature market may choose television as a communications medium because the elderly watch 60 percent more television than average households. In addition, the mature market watches more baseball, golf, and bowling than the average household.[5] Other virtues of using television as a promotional medium are discussed in "The Power of Television".

table 10.2

Making Media Decisions

- Cost to reach target audience
- Flexibility of media
- Ability to reach highly specialized, defined audience
- Lifespan of the media
- Nature of the sports product being promoted (e.g., complexity of product)
- Characteristics of the intended target market

the power of television

No medium delivers like television, but with so many options, what's a company to do? Here are some ideas.

It's the perfect job for an armchair athlete. In Ann Arbor, Michigan, 10 cathode-frazzled researchers spend their work week watching hour after hour of sports broadcasts. Their employer, the research firm of Joyce Julius and Associates, analyzes around 15,000 hours of televised sports a year, monitoring the coverage sponsors get from their investment in televised competition. Sometimes it means going frame by frame, counting the number, position, and prominence of signs, endorsements, and logos. It takes an impressive eye for detail and plays havoc with keeping score, but the end result is a sponsorship valuation based on the rate of logo exposure and audible mentions of the sponsor compared to the cost of television advertising time.

This admirable devotion to duty—and the fact that Joyce Julius is retained by some of the top advertisers in the business—is testimony to the central role television plays in the sports sponsors' game plan. Used in the right way, it can be a marketer's dream, harnessing the thrill of top-level competition for a targeted mass audience of interested and involved consumers.

Clearly, there is no shortage of companies turning to television to peddle their products or burnish their image. Industry analysts expect them to spend roughly $3.5 billion on television advertising this year, paying out millions to run 30-second spots during everything from the Super Bowl to local college basketball games. They also will shell out an additional $3.5 billion on sports sponsorships, attaching their names and products to various events or leagues.

"The immediacy is a big part of the attraction (of sports for a sponsor)," says Barry Frank, head of IMG's television division, Trans World International. "The fact that it's live, it's exciting, and there's tension built into the game. And it's all on television."

John Mansell of Paul Kegan Associates, a California firm that follows the television business, breaks down the formula even further. "Sponsors want to be associated with something that is going to get exposure," he explains. "Sports are, on the whole exciting, and if it is exciting, then it is going to get exposure on television."

In a crowded and often unpredictable television marketplace, sports help focus the company's message to the people it wants to

(continued)

reach. And, hopefully, it also focuses the viewer's mind long enough to keep their channel-surfing fingers out of action and to let the marketer's message make an impact. Sports also deliver flexibility. From the blue-collar world of NASCAR racing (with sponsors like Winston, Tide, and Target Stores) to the high-brow realm of polo (Cartier, Mercedes, and Rolex), there is a sport to suit every product, image, and budget. If a company's pockets are deep, it can attach itself to an existing event, such as the Olympics or Super Bowl. Or, for considerably less, a firm can create its own event from the ground up. "It all depends on what a company is looking for," stresses TWI's Frank. "Is it looking to reach the most people? Is it looking to focus? Is it looking to use something that's got entertainment? Is it looking for a real high-quality rub-off? A company has to decide what its goals are and then find a way to use it."

TWI is the largest independent producer of sports programs in the world. Its weekly *Trans World Sports* show is seen in 76 countries by some 325 million households. Through IMG, it also puts sponsors, sports, and television together, often creating made-for-television events specifically for individual clients. "We start from scratch," Frank says. "Finding a venue, arranging dates, getting television exposure, booking competitors. There are existing events that can be used, but if they're any good, they're probably already taken. Either that, or someone wants too much money for them. Many times the best way to go is by having us start a special event for the company."

Consider how TWI helped Nutrasweet in figure skating. For just more than $1 million, the company backs two high-profile, prime-time competitions: the Nutrasweet World Professional Figure Skating Championships and the Nutrasweet Challenge of Champions. For that expenditure, the sweetener giant gets a package of benefits that Frank thinks makes more sense than existing events that are more costly and cluttered.

Their name is in each competition title," he says. "They have the only signage on the rink boards." They get seven or eight commercial spots in each telecast. They get an introduction to the program from the President or CEO, a little welcome on behalf of Nutrasweet. They entertain several hundred employees, customers, and business associates at the event. And they get choice seats and a party afterward that all the skaters attend. The events air on NBC and ABC, respectively, and get very high ratings. By and large, it is an excellent way to target spend a relatively small amount of money.

An integrated package like this, put together by an independent organizer like IMG, does, as Frank puts its, "cover all the bases." It delivers an audience likely to be interested in Nutrasweet products prime-time exposure and an upscale image "rub-off." But as anyone involved in the sports sponsorship business will tell you, "it all depends on your objectives." If a company's goal is public awareness of its name—not to define its image but simply to get its corporate name better known—a Nutrasweet-style deal might not be the best way to go. Sponsoring stadiums, teams, or even time clocks might make more sense. There's GM Place in Vancouver, British Columbia, and the MCI Arena in Washington, D.C., for example. The Bay Area's Candlestick Park is now 3Com Park after the computer manufacturer chose to pay an estimated $1 million to put its name on the historic stadium. At first glance it may not seem like such a great move, but the company gets regular exposure during national and local telecasts of NFL games, and last season millions of viewers heard the 3Com name for the first time. But there are drawbacks. Some Bay Area residents took offense when the venerable park changed its moniker. Adds Mansell: "You also keep hearing announcers on television having trouble with the name. They want to call it Candlestick Park or the Stick, and then its 'Oops, I mean 3Com.'"

Mansell puts together the *Media Sports Business* newsletter for Paul Kegan Associates, and he believes the driving force behind the ever-increasing corporate appetite for sponsoring sports is fueled simply by the public's ever-growing hunger for televised sports and the huge global growth of sports channels. There now are 33 such channels in the United States alone, almost triple the number of a decade ago. And the international numbers are increasing almost as fast. ESPN, for example, has launched six new networks internationally in the last year, giving it access to South America, India, Australia, and Asia."

Mansell thinks that the growing global presence of such television sports giants is one major reason NBC jumped in with its multibillion dollar bid for the rights to televise the next several Olympic Games. "It was partly because NBC feared that Rupert Murdoch was going to come in and bid for global rights," he says. "They wanted to at least preempt him domestically." Whatever the rationale, Mansell sees that sort of move as being just one more wave of the future. "More and more television entities will be bidding for worldwide rights," he says, "because more and more of them have an international presence."

Just as sports have changed television, television has changed sports. New technology has played its part. In golf, for instance, the comparatively new capability of covering every part of an 18-hole course opened up the idea of sponsoring individual holes. As a result, many par 3s in competitive golf now have special prizes attached for holes-in-one, and it's now common for sponsors to get their product on television by planting, say, a special prize automobile in the middle of a greenside lake. In motor racing, in-car cameras have opened up compelling ways of getting brand names in the picture. The over-the-shoulder shot allows for highly visible brand-name recognition on the driver's helmet and the windscreen, as well as on cars and clothing. And on beach volleyball's AVP tour, which has its own NBC television deal and

sponsors like Miller Brewing, an extremely tele-visual sport was made even moreso by designing everything from the arena to the dress code to work better on the small screen. Says IMG's Barry Frank, "As the media become more and more complex and there are more channels, it's harder to make an impact. Sports marketers are always looking for ways to make their broadcast and their sponsors stand out."

It's a far cry from advertising three decades ago. One Thursday in the early 1960s, for example, Ford bought every ad on all three networks for half an hour from 9:30 to 10:00 P.M. By the end of that evening, 60 percent of America had heard of Ford's newly-launched car, the Falcon. If Ford were to saturate all the networks in the same way today, it would be lucky to reach 40 percent of viewers.

The fragmenting of the network audience in general makes sports—especially the big-ticket events—one of the only television events that can pull in large ratings with consistency. And that's one of the main reasons why Peter McLoughlin, group director of corporate media for Anheuser-Busch, sees it as one of the few constants in an ever-changing media environment. "I always find it fascinating when you stop and think that *Monday Night Football* is the top-rated show among men 21 to 34 in the fall," he says. "Others come along and beat it every now and then. But the staying power of *Monday Night Football* is amazing. The audience is consistent year after year, and that shows the strength of sports.

"We could do more outside of television sports, but why would we?" asks McLoughlin. "Because of television, sports have been able to bring its excitement and competition to a vast audience over the years, and it's an audience that continues to grow. Whether it's through advertising or sponsorship programs, television sports works for us. And it works better than almost anything else."

Source: Martin Pearson, "The Power of Television," *Mark McCormack's Guide to Sports Marketing, International Sports Marketing Group,* 1996, 143–150. Courtesy of ISM Group, Inc., FL 33773.

Decoding

The medium carries the message to the receiver, which is where decoding takes place. **Decoding**, performed by the receiver, is the interpretation of the message sent by the source through the channel. Once again, the goal of communication is to establish a common link between sender and receiver. This can only happen if the message is received and interpreted correctly. Even if the message is received by the desired target audience, it may interpreted differently because of the receiver's personal characteristics and past experience. Additionally, the more complex the original message, the less likely it is to be successfully interpreted or decoded. As the following article illustrates, decoding a message is not always an easy task.

i got game

"I have a fantasy," I say. "I live in Three-Pointland. I live out beyond the arc. I launch from Three-Pointland. From Downtown, Way Downtown. From another area code. From another zip code. Nothing but net."

"Uh-oh," she says.

"I shoot the trey," I say. "I handle the rock. Protect it with my life, of course. I dish. I think of myself mostly as a number 1, but I could play the 2 in a pinch. The big thing is the trey. The trifecta. I lock and load, square to the basket. I get a good look. I launch!"

"College basketball, right?" she says. "I should have known. The leaves are gone. The days are getting colder. You're going into that hibernation thing again. You and the television. College basketball."

"It's not that I'm afraid to take the rock to the rack," I say. "I'll do that. I'll go into the paint, down the lane, set up on the blocks, clean the glass, rattle the tin, grab the orange, but my strength really isn't putbacks and slams. I'm a Three-Pointland sort of guy."

"I can never get it straight," she says. "Are those all separate games you watch from now until the end of March, or is it just one long, four-month production?"

"On defense, I'm in my man's face, in his shirt," I say, "I take the charge. I give the foul. I trap. I jump switch. I help out."

"I think it is just one long game," she says. "The uniforms change, and sometimes the lighting is different from different arenas and gyms, but the horn is always sounding— honk—and the same referees are blowing their whistles, and, for sure, the same two annoying voices are describing the action in their hyped-up, cliché-filled way. Is it a rule that college basketball broadcasters can never end a book about anything except college basketball, that they can have no knowledge except about college basketball? Or am I being a little harsh?"

"I know there will be potholes and strange twists and turns on the road to the Final Four, but I am ready for that," I say. "I'm not afraid to take control. I'll throw up the tough shot, the buzzer-beater, and it'll be good if it goes. Do you know what I mean?"

I will work the clock and hope to get the call. If need be, I'll launch a prayer.

"The thing that bothers me most about this college basketball is the overemphasis," she says. "Do any of these kids ever go to school? One night they're playing in Hawaii, and the next night they're in Alaska. Doesn't that make it a little hard to go to the library? Some of these teams are on television more than Oprah and Ricki Lake and Alex Trebek combined. I think Georgetown played Villanova a hundred times last year. At least it seemed that way. Bobby Knight and that red sweater could be part of the wallpaper. Is that the only sweater he owns?"

"I'm not afraid to go to the floor," I say. "I'm not afraid to set a pick. Give and go. Double-down. Shake and bake. Work without the ball. Run the break. Jump-start the offense. I'll get free with my drop step down low, my crossover dribble up high. I'll always be aware of the principle of verticality and will never put my hand in the cylinder except when I'm slamming the rock home to deliver a message."

"Is there one kid in all of college basketball who is pre-med?" she asks. "Is there one electrical engineer in the making? One English professor? I suppose there must be a couple, somewhere. The whole thing seems perverted to me. Kids from the West Coast go all the way to the East Coast to go to college. State universities fall all over each other to get tall kids from Nigeria and Serbia and Finland to go to their schools. Where's the sense in all this?"

"I'll box out. I'll put a body on people! I won't give up the baseline, but I'll hit the front end of the one-and-one, and I'll look for the cutters and the mismatches. I'll feed the hot hand, and i'll ice the shooter. I'll take off from the foul line. I'll alley and I'll oop."

"It just seems a little silly to me," she says. "The recruiting, the scandals, the money. All of this commotion…"

"Three-Pointland!" I say.

"It seems like so much…"

"Beyond the arc!"

"…gibberish."

(Pause for a program note: ESPN will televise 194 college basketball games this season. ESPN2 will televise 87. SportsChannel will televise 58. CBS will televise 50. ABC will televise 31. NBC will televise six. ESPN and ESPN2 will televise 22 women's games. These numbers do not count the telecasts of either the men's or women's NCAA tournaments.)

"All I know is that it's a new season," I say, "and I'm taking my game to the next level."

"Just make sure you close the door behind you," she says.

Receiver

The **receiver**, or the audience, is the object of the source's message. Usually, the receiver is the sports marketer's well-defined, target audience. However, and as previously mentioned, the receiver's personal characteristics play an important role in whether or not the message is correctly decoded. For example, the consumer's demographic profile (e.g., age, marital status, gender), psychographic profile (e.g., personality, lifestyle, and values) and even where they live (geographic region) may all impact the interpretation and comprehension of the sports marketing message.

Feedback

In order to determine whether or not the message has been received and comprehended, feedback is necessary. **Feedback** is defined as the response a target audience makes to a message. The importance of feedback as an element of the communication process cannot be overlooked. Without feedback, communication would be a one-way street, and the sender of the message would have no means of determining whether the original message should remain unchanged, be modified, or abandoned altogether.

There are several ways for the consumer or target audience to deliver feedback to the source of the message. The target market might provide feedback in the form of a purchase. In other words, if consumers are buying tickets, sporting goods, or other sports products, then the sports marketers message must be effective. Likewise, if consumers are not willing to purchase the sports product, then feedback is also being provided to the source. Unfortunately, the feedback in this case is that the message is either not being received or being incorrectly interpreted.

When using personal communication media, such as personal selling, feedback is received instantly by verbal and nonverbal means. Consumers will respond favorably by nodding their head in approval, acting interested, or asking intelligent questions. In the case of disinterest or inattention, the source of the message should make adjustments and change the message as it is being delivered to address any perceived problems.

Another common form of feedback comes through changes in attitude about the object of the message. In other words, the consumer's attitude shift towards a more favorable belief or feeling about the sports product, athlete, team, or sport itself. Generally, the more positive the attitude towards the message, the more positive the consumer's attitude towards the sports product. This should, in turn, lead to increases in future purchases. One of the many uses of marketing research is to gather feedback from consumers and use this feedback to create or redesign the strategic sports marketing process. The control phase of the strategic marketing process is dedicated to evaluating feedback from consumers and making adjustment to achieve marketing objectives.

Thus far, we have only examined feedback in one direction—from consumer of the product to the producer of the product. However, feedback is an interactive process. That is, consumers also receive feedback from the sports organization. Organizations let consumers know that they are listening to the "voice of the consumer" by reintroducing new and improved versions of sports products, changing the composition of teams and their coaches, adjusting prices, and even varying their promotional messages. For instance, the Montreal Expos lowered their ticket prices after receiving feedback from the fans that they would attend games offering promotions or special pricing.

Noise

The final element in the communication process is noise. Unfortunately, there is no such thing as perfect communication because of **noise**, or interference, in the communications process. This interference may occur at any point along the channel of communication. For example, the source may be ineffective, the message may be sent through the wrong medium, or there may be too many competing messages, each "fighting" for the limited information processing capacity of consumers.

When communicating through stadium signage, the obvious source of noise is the game itself. Noise can even be present in the form of ambush marketing techniques, where organizations attempt to confuse consumers and make them believe that they are officially affiliated with a sporting event when they are not. An excellent example of how noise can impact the communication process was the 1996 Olympic Games.

The 1996 Summer Olympic Games were, without question, the most commercial Olympics ever—with advertisements, logos, signage, and sponsorship tie-ins as far as the eye could see. Even some International Olympic Committee (IOC) members complained about the overcommercialization in Atlanta. Given this, it would be easy to make the argument that individual companies' Olympic marketing efforts probably got lost in the clutter and therefore to question whether they got their money's worth.

But perhaps the solution to the problem is not to cut down on the number of official sponsorship packages sold, but to do a much better job policing ambush marketers. After watching the Games on television more extensively than any other, what struck me the most was just how much of that clutter came from marketers who were not official Olympic sponsors—and just how invisible some of the actual sponsors appeared to be. Reebok may have paid $20 million for its official sponsor status, but competitor Nike's swoosh was everywhere—from its rock 'n' roll television commercials and its "@tlanta" Web site to athletes' jerseys and, of course, U.S.-track-star Michael Johnson's much-talked-about gold sneaks.

That's just one high-profile example, but marketers big and small tried to get in on the Atlanta Olympics for free. Even the Emporio Armani boutique in uptown Toronto displayed mannequins sporting gold medals in its window during the Games. Call it cheating, there's only one reason marketers do it: because they can. Expecting them to keep their hands out of the Olympic cookie jar when it's practically wide open to them is completely unrealistic. What marketers in their right mind would pass up the opportunity to associate their company—in any way possible—with the most-watched event in the world?

To be sure, the IOC did take some steps to try to limit what ambushers can do. They were on the lookout for those unlawfully using their trademarks (such as the rings or the word "Olympics"). And the Atlanta Committee for the Olympic Games (ACOG) planned a $10 million effort to stop ambush marketing, including hiring a firm to monitor advertising. ACOG even threatened to expose nonsponsors using Olympic symbols as "cheaters" in a print campaign.

But what good did this really do? If anything, the Atlanta Games were proof positive that companies don't have to dabble in trademark infringement (and risk heavy-duty legal bills) to ride the Olympic wave without paying multimillion dollar sponsorship fees to become "official." They can still sponsor teams or individual athletes who compete during the Games (like Helene Curtis and Donovan Bailey); they can still buy ample television airtime during Olympics broadcasts (take your pick); and they can still run promotional sweepstakes using trips to Olympic events as a prize.

Take Timex, for instance, whose competitor, Swatch, was the official Olympic timekeeper. The company, which sponsors athletes including diver Anne Montminy, rolled out a brilliant multimedia campaign through Ogilvy & Mather of Toronto that ran in Canada during the Olympics. One of the print ads had a turquoise Indiglo dot marking Atlanta on a map of North America. There was no use of trademarks or anything else "official," but Timex found a way in nonetheless.

"Ambush" marketers cannot be expected to trash their plans because their official sponsor competitors and the IOC do not like them. Clearly, something definitive must be done to stop this practice—and fast—or we may soon witness the erosion of an event that is not only the greatest demonstration of athletic wonder, but the most sought-after marketing opportunity on the planet.

Source: Lara Mills. "Ambush Marketing as an Olympic Event." <http://www.marketingmag.ca/Content/32.96/promo32_2.html>. Courtesy Lara Mills, *Marketing Magazine*, 1996.

Sports marketers must realize that noise will always be present in the communications process. By gaining a better understanding of the communications process, factors contributing to noise can be examined and eliminated to a large extent.

ⓟ romotion Planning

Armed with a working knowledge of the communications process, the sports marketer is now ready to design an effective promotion plan. Not unlike the strategic marketing process, promotional plans come in all shapes and sizes but all share several common elements. Our **promotional planning** document consists of four basic steps: (1) target market consideration (2) setting promotional objectives (3) determining the promotional budget and (4) developing the promotional mix.

Target Market Considerations

Promotional planning is not done in isolation. Instead, plans must rely heavily on the objectives formulated in the strategic sports marketing process. During the planning phase, target markets have been identified, and promotion planning should reflect these previous decisions. Promotional planning depends largely on who is identified as the primary target audience. One promotional strategy is based on reaching the ultimate consumer of the sports product and is known as a pull strategy. The other strategy identifies channel members as the most important target audience. This strategic direction is termed a push strategy. These two basic strategies are dependent upon the chosen target of the promotional efforts and guide subsequent planning. Let us explore the push and pull strategies in greater detail.

Push Strategy

A **push strategy** is so named because of the emphasis on having channel intermediaries "push" the sports product through the channel of distribution to the final consumer. If a push strategy is used, intermediaries such as a *manufacturer* might direct initial promotional efforts at a *wholesaler* who then promotes the sports product to the retailer. In turn, the *retailers* promote the sports product to the final user. When using a push strategy you are literally loading goods into the distribution pipeline. The objective is to get as much product as possible into the warehouse or store. Push strategies generally ignore the consumer. A variety of promotion mix elements are still utilized with a push strategy although personal selling is more prevalent when promoting to channel members closer to the manufacturer (i.e., wholesalers) than the end users.

Pull Strategy

The target audience for a **pull strategy** is not channel intermediaries but ultimate consumers. The broad objective of this type of promotional strategy is to stimulate demand for the sports product. So much demand, in fact, that the channel members, such as retailers, are forced to stock their shelves with the sports product. Since the end user, or ultimate consumer, is the desired target for a pull strategy, the promotion mix tends to emphasize advertising rather than personal selling. It is important to note that since sports marketing is based largely on promoting services rather than goods, pull strategies targeting the end user are more prevalent. In pull strategies, your objective is to get consumers to pull the merchandise off the shelf and out the door.

Although pull strategies are more common in sports marketing, the most effective promotion planning integrates both push and pull components. For example, marketing giant Procter and Gamble's (P&G) objective was to stimulate consumer demand for its Sunny Delight and Hawaiian Punch brands. To do so, P&G designed a promotion featuring UCLA basketball coach John Wooden and one of his star players, Bill Walton. The pull strategy offered consumers a Wooden and Walton autographed picture and coin set for $19.95 and proof-of-purchase. The push promotional strategy was directed at Sunny Delight and Hawaiian Punch distributors and retailers who carried the P&G brands. If the "trade" reached their performance goals during the promotion, they earned a framed picture of Walton and Wooden that was autographed and personalized for the distributor.

Promotional Objectives

After target markets have been identified, the next step in the promotion planning process is to define the **promotional objectives**. Broadly, the three goals of promotion are to inform, persuade, and/or remind target audiences. Consumers must first be made aware of the product and how it might satisfy their needs. The goal of providing information to consumers is usually desired when products are in the introductory phase of the PLC. Once consumers are aware of the sports product, promotional goals then turn to persuasion and convincing the consumer to purchase the product. After initial purchase and satisfaction with a given product, the broad promotional goal is then to remind the consumer of the sports product's availability and perceived benefits.

Informing, persuading, and reminding consumers are the broad objectives of promotion, but the ultimate promotional objective is to induce action. These consumer actions might include volunteering to help with a local 10k race, donating money to the U.S. Olympic Team, purchasing a new pair of in-line skates, or just attending a sporting event they have never seen. Marketers believe that promotions guide consumers through a series of steps in order to reach this ultimate objective—action. This series of steps is known as the hierarchy of effects (also sometimes called the hierarchy of communication effect).

The Hierarchy of Effects

The **hierarchy of effects** is a seven-step process by which consumers are ultimately led to action.[6] The seven steps include unawareness, awareness, knowledge, liking, preference, conviction, and action. As shown in Figure 10.2, consumers pass through each of these steps before taking action.

- *Unawareness*—During the first step, consumers are not even aware that the sports product exists. Obviously, the promotional objective at this stage is to move consumers towards awareness.

figure 10.2 Hierarchy of Effects

Action

Conviction

Preference

Liking

Knowledge

Awareness

Unawareness

- *Awareness*—The promotional objective at this early stage of the hierarchy is to make consumers in the desired target market aware of the new sports product. To reach this objective, a variety of promotional tools are used.

- *Knowledge*—Once consumers are aware of the sports product, they need to gather information about its tangible and intangible benefits. The primary promotional objective at this stage is to provide consumers with the necessary product information. An example of this was the 1994 World Cup Soccer Tournament hosted by the United States. The promotion campaign was designed to educate potential U.S. fans about the rules of the game and what to watch for during the course of a soccer match. Organizers hoped that once the fans became knowledgeable, they would then move to the next level of the hierarchy—liking.

- *Liking*—Having knowledge and information about a sports product doesn't necessarily mean that the consumer will like it. Generating positive feelings and interest regarding the sports product is the next promotional objective on the hierarchy. The promotion itself cannot cause the consumer to like the product, but research has shown the linkage between attitude towards the promotion (e.g., advertisement) and attitude towards the product.[7] The objective is to create a feeling of goodwill towards the product via the promotion.

- *Preference*—After consumers begin to like the sports product, the objective is to develop preferences. As such, the sports marketer must differentiate their product from the competition through promotion. The sports product's differential advantage may be found in an enhanced image and/or tangible product features.

- *Conviction*—Moving up the hierarchy of effects, consumers must develop a conviction or intention to take action. Behavioral intention, however, does not guarantee action. Factors such as the consumer's economic condition (that is, financial situation), changing needs, or availability of new alternatives may inhibit the action ever taking place. The objective of conviction step of the hierarchy of effects is to create a desire to act in the mind of the target audience.

■ Having greater knowledge of sports such as hockey, moves consumers through the hierarchy of effects.

■ *Action*—The final stage of the hierarchy and the ultimate objective of any promotion is to have consumers act. As stated previously, actions may come in a variety of forms, but usually include purchase or attendance.

Theoretically, the hierarchy of effects model states that consumers must pass through each of the stages in the hierarchy before a decision is made regarding purchase (or other behaviors). Some marketers have argued that this is not always the case. Consider, for instance, purchasing season tickets to a professional sport for business purposes. The purchaser does not have to like the sport or team in order to take action and buy the tickets. Regardless of what the hierarchy of effects proposes to do or not do, the fact remains that it is an excellent tool to use when developing promotional objectives. Knowing where the target audience is on the hierarchy is critical to formulating the proper objectives.

Establishing Promotional Budgets

The NHL experienced a 5,976 percent increase in annual spending on advertising from 1993 ($42,000) to 1996 ($2.51 million).[8] Although this exponential increase is uncommon, it is not unusual for sports organizations to allocate large amounts of their entire marketing budget to promotional efforts. In the case of the NHL, increases in advertising were needed to make potential fans more knowledgeable about and able to appreciate hockey. The NHL also wanted to reposition the league as the "Coolest Game on Earth," and keep up with the tremendous competitive threat of the NBA, MLB, and the NFL.

In theory, the promotional budget of the NHL would have been determined based on the many objectives set forth by the league's marketing strategy. In practice, **promotional budgeting** is an interactive and unscientific process by which the sports marketer determines the amount spent based on maximizing the monies available. Some of the ways promotional budgets may be established include arbitrary allocation, competitive parity, percentage of sales, and the objective and task method.

Arbitrary Allocation

The simplest, yet most unsystematic, approach to determining promotional budgets is called arbitrary allocation. Using this method, sports marketers set the budget in isolation of other critical factors. For example, the sports marketer disregards last year's promotional budget and its effectiveness, what competitors are doing, the economy, and current strategic objectives and budgets using some subjective method. The budget is usually determined by allocating all the money the organization can afford. In other words, promotional budgets are established after the organizations' other costs are considered. A sports organization that chooses this approach does not place much emphasis on promotional planning.

Competitive Parity

In the NHL, increases in promotional spending are largely based on keeping up with the other major league sports. Setting promotional budgets based on what competitors are spending is often used for certain product categories in sports marketing. For example, the athletic shoe industry closely monitors what the competition is doing in the way of promotional efforts. Reebok (annual budget of roughly $425 million), Fila, and Converse must keep pace with Nike's (annual budget of roughly $750 million) promotional spending if they intend to increase market share.[9]

One athletic shoe company that does not follow its competitors huge promotional spending is New Balance. The New Balance marketing budget will be increased to $13 million in 1998 (up from $4 million in 1997), and the company will venture into television advertising for the first time. Although this budget is just a fraction of its big name competitors, New Balance sales grew 16 percent in 1997 to $560 million. Instead of using glamous athlete endorsers, New Balance has paved its success by understanding its primary consumer—the 35–59-year-old baby boomer. To reach this growing market, New Balance has employed moderate prices, networks with podiatrists, and offers its running shoes in five widths (from AA to EEEE). With expected growth of 25 percent in 1998, New Balance represents a company that is expanding without excessive amounts of advertising.[10]

Percentage of Sales

The percentage of sales method of promotional budget allocation is based on determining some standard percentage of promotional spending and applying this proportion to either past or forecasted sales to arrive at the amount to be spent. It is common for the percentage to be used on promotional spending to be derived from some industry standard. For example, the athletic shoe industry typically allocates 5 percent of sales to promotional spending. Therefore, if a new athletic shoe company enters the market and projects sales of $1 million, then they would allocate $50,000 to the promotional budget. Likewise, if Converse totaled $7 million in sales in the previous year, then it might budget $350,000 to next year's promotional budget.

Although the percentage of sales method of budgeting is simple to use, it has a number of shortcomings. First, if percentage of forecast sales are used to arrive at a promotional budget figure, then the sales projections must be made with a certain degree of precision and confidence. If historical sales figures (e.g., last year's) are used, then promotional spending may be either too high or too low. For example, if Converse has a poor year in sales, then the absolute promotional spending would be decreased. This, in turn, could cause sales to slide even further. With sales declining, it may be more appropriate to increase (rather than decrease) promotional spending. A second major shortcoming of using this method is the notion that budget is very loosely, if at all, tied to the promotional objectives.

Objective and Task Method

If arbitrary allocation is the most illogical of the budgeting methods, then objective and task methods could be characterized as the most logical and systematic. The objective and task method identifies the promotional objectives, defines the communications tools and tasks needed to meet those objectives, and then adds up the costs of the planned activities.

Although the objective and task method seems the most reasonable, it also assumes that the objectives have been determined correctly and that the proper promotional mix has been formulated to reach those objectives. For instance, suppose the WNBA wanted to achieve an awareness level of 65 percent prior to opening night (June 21, 1997). To this end, sports marketers developed a promotional mix that included national advertising, related sales promotions, and public relations efforts in each of the eight WNBA cities. It is difficult to determine whether the money required to achieve this objective was spent in the most efficient and effective fashion.

Choosing an Integrated Promotional Mix

The final step in building an overall promotional plan is to determine the appropriate promotional mix. As stated earlier, the traditional promotional mix consists of advertising, personal selling, public relations, and sales promotions. The sports marketing manager must determine which aspects of the promotional mix will be best suited to achieve the promotional objectives at the given budget.

In choosing from among the traditional elements, the sports marketer may wish to broadly explore the advantages and disadvantages of each promotional tool. For example, personal selling may be the most effective way to promote the sale of personal seat licenses, but it is limited in reaching large audiences. Table 10.3 outlines some of the considerations when deciding on the correct mix of promotional tools.

Although the factors listed in Table 10.3 are important determinants of which promotional tools to use to achieve the desired objectives, there are other considerations. The stage of the life cycle for the sport product, the type of sports product, the characteristics of the target audience, and the current market environment must also be carefully studied. Whatever the promotion mix decision, it is critical that the various elements be integrated carefully.

table 10.3

Evaluating the Promotional Mix Elements

	Promotional Tools			
	Advertising	Personal Selling	Sales Promotion	Public Relations
Sender's control over the communication	Low	High	Moderate to low	Moderate to low
Amount of feedback	Little	Much	Little to moderate	Little
Speed of feedback	Delayed	Immediate	Varies	Delayed
Direction of message flow	One way	Two way	One way	One way
Speed in reaching large audiences	Fast	Slow	Fast	Typically fast
Message flexibility	None	Customized	None	Some
Mode of communication	Indirect & impersonal	Direct & face to face	Usually indirect & impersonal	Usually indirect & impersonal

Promotional planning for sports is becoming increasingly more complex. With the rapid changes in technology, new promotional tools are being used to convey the sports marketer's message. In addition, it is becoming harder and harder to capture the attention of target audiences and move them along the hierarchy of effects. Because of the growing difficulty in reaching diverse target audiences, the clarity and coordination of integrating all marketing communications into a single theme is more important than ever.

The concept under which a sports organization carefully integrates and coordinates its many promotional mix elements to deliver a unified message about the organization and its products is known as **integrated marketing communications**. Think for a moment about the promotional efforts of the WNBA. The promotional goals are to increase awareness and develop excitement about the league. To accomplish this, the WNBA will combine national advertisements, sponsorships, cable and network broadcast schedules, and tie-ins with the NBA. All of these communication medium must deliver a consistent message that produces a uniform image for the league to be successful. Not only must the WNBA deliver an integrated promotional mix, the league's sponsors and the eight new teams must also transmit a unified message.

The primary advantage of integrating the promotional plan includes more effective and efficient marketing communications. Unfortunately, determining the return on investment (ROI) for an integrated promotion plan is still difficult, if not impossible. Northwestern University Professor Don Schultz has identified four types of information that must be available in order to begin to measure ROI for integrated communications.[11] These factors include

- *Identification of specific customers*—identification of specific households, including information on the composition of that household in order to make inferences.
- *Customer valuation*—placing a value on each household based on either annual purchases or lifetime purchases. Without this information on the purchase behavior of the household or individual, the calculation of ROI is of limited value to the marketer.
- *Track message delivery*—understanding what media consumers or households use to make their purchase decisions, and how a household receives information and messages over time. In addition, this involves measuring "brand contacts" or when and where consumers come into contact with the brand.
- *Consumer response*—in order to establish the best ROI, behavioral responses are captured. In other words, consumer responses such as attitudes, feels and memory are deemed unimportant and purchases, inquiries, and related behaviors (e.g., coupon redemption) are evaluated.

SUMMARY

(P) romotional planning is one of the most important elements of the sports marketing mix. Promotion involves communicating to all types of sports consumers via one or more of the promotion mix elements. The promotion mix elements include advertising, personal selling, sales promotions, public relations, and sponsorship. Within each of these promotion mix elements are more specialized tools to communicate with consumers of sport. For example, advertising may be developed for print media (e.g., newspapers, magazines) or broadcasts, (e.g., radio, television). However, regardless of the promotion mix element that is used by sports marketers, the fundamental process at work is communication.

Communication is an interactive process that is established between the sender and the receiver of the marketing message via some medium. The process of communication begins with the source or sender of the message. In sports marketing, the source of the message might be an athlete endorser, team members, a sports organization, or even a coach. Sometimes the source of a marketing message can be friends or family. The effectiveness of the source in influencing consumers is based largely on the concept of source credibility. Credibility is typically defined as the expertise and trustworthiness of the source. Other characteristics of the source, such as gender, attractiveness, familiarity, and likability may also play important roles in determining the source effectiveness.

After the source of the message is chosen, message encoding occurs. Encoding is defined as translating the sender's thoughts or ideas into a message. The most effective encoding uses multiple ways of getting the message across and always keeps the receiver of the message in mind. Once encoding takes place, the message is more completely developed. Although there are any number of ways of constructing a message, sports marketers commonly choose between emotion (e.g., humor, sex, or fear) and rational (information-based) appeals.

The message, once constructed, must be transmitted to the target audience through any number of media. The traditional media include television, radio, newspapers, magazines, and outdoor (billboards, stadium signage). Nontraditional media, such as the Internet, are also emerging as powerful tools for sports marketers. When making decisions about what medium to use, marketers must consider the promotional objectives, cost, ability to reach the targeted audience, and the nature of the message being communicated.

The medium relays the message to the target audience, which is where decoding occurs. Decoding is the interpretation of the message sent by the source through the medium. It is important to understand the characteristics of the target audience to ensure that successful translation of the message will occur. Rarely, if ever, will perfect decoding take place, because of the presence of noise.

The final elements in the communications model are the receiver and feedback. The message is directed to the receiver, or target audience. Again, depending on the purpose of the communication, the target audience may be spectators, participants, or corporate sponsors. Regardless of the nature of the audience, the sports marketer must understand as much as possible about the characteristics of the group to ensure an effective message is produced. Sports marketers determine the effectiveness of the message through feedback from the target audience.

Understanding the communications process provides us with the basis for developing a sound promotional plan. The promotional planning process includes target market considerations, setting promotional objectives, determining the promotional budget, and developing the promotional mix.

The first step in the promotional planning process is to consider the target market identified in the previous planning phase of the strategic sports marketing process. The two broad target market considerations are the final consumers of the sports product (either spectator or participants) or intermediaries, such as sponsors or distributors of sports products. When communicating to final consumers, a pull strategy is used. Conversely, push strategies are used to promote through intermediaries. After target markets are considered, promotional objectives are defined. Broadly, objectives may include informing, persuading, or reminding the target market. One model that provides a basis for establishing promotional objectives is known as the hierarchy of effects, which states that consumers must pass through a series of stages before ultimately taking action (usually defined as making a purchase decision). The steps of the hierarchy of effects include unawareness, awareness, knowledge, liking, preference, conviction, and action. Once objectives have been formulated, budgets are considered. In the ideal scenario, budgets are linked with the objectives that have been set in the previous phase of the promotion planning process. However, other common approaches to promotional budgeting include arbitrary allocation, competitive parity, and percentage of sales. Most sports organizations use some combination of these methods to arrive at budgets. The final phase in the promotion planning process is to arrive at the optimal promotion mix. The promotion mix includes advertising, personal selling, public relations, sales promotion, and sponsorship. Decisions about the most effective promotion mix must carefully consider the current marketing environment, the sports product being promoted, and the characteristics of the target audience. Ideally, the sports marketer designs an integrated promotion mix that delivers a consistent message about the organization and its products.

arbitrary allocation

communication

comparative message

competitive parity

credibility

decoding

elements in the
communications process

emotional versus rational
appeal

encoding

feedback

hierarchy of effects

integrated marketing
communication

medium

message

message characteristics

noise

objective and task method

percentage of sales

promotion

promotion mix elements

promotional budgets

promotional objectives

promotional planning

pull strategy

push strategy

receiver

sidedness

source

target market considerations

1. Define promotion and then discuss each of the promotion mix elements.

2. Describe the elements of the communication process. Why is communication so important for sports marketers? What is the relationship between communication and promotion?

3. Define the source of a sports marketing message and provide some examples of effective sources. What is source credibility? What are the two components of source credibility?

4. What is meant by encoding? Who is responsible for encoding sports marketing messages?

5. Discuss the various message characteristics. What are the simple techniques used to create more effective messages?

6. Why is television considered to be the most powerful medium for sports marketing messages?

7. Define feedback. How is feedback delivered to the source of the message?

8. Outline the basic steps in promotion planning.

9. What is the fundamental difference between a push strategy and a pull strategy?

10. Describe the three broad objectives of any type of promotion. What is the hierarchy of effect, and how is this concept related to promotional objectives?

11. What are the various ways of setting promotional budgets? Comment on the strengths and weaknesses of each.

12. Comment on how you would choose among the various promotion mix tools. Define integrated marketing communication.

1. Evaluate the promotion mix used for the marketing of any intercollegiate women's sport at your university. Do you feel the proper blend of promotional tools are being used? What could be done to make the promotional plan more effective for this sport?

2. Find any advertisement for a sports product. Then describe and explain each of the elements in the communications process for that ad. Do the same (i.e., explain the communications process) for the following scenario: A salesperson is trying to sell stadium signage to the marketing director of a local hospital.

3. Conduct an interview with the Marketing Department of a local sports organization and discuss the role of each of the promotional tools in the organization's promotion mix. In addition, ask about their promotional budgeting process.

4. Describe three television advertisements for sports products that are designed to inform, persuade, and remind consumers. Do you feel the advertisements are effective in reaching their promotional objectives?

5. Locate advertisements for three different sports products. Comment on which response on the hierarchy of effects you believe each advertisement is trying to elicit from its target audience.

6. Find an example of a comparative advertisement. What do you feel are the advantages and disadvantages to this type of message?

INTERNET EXERCISES

1. Using the Internet, find an example of an advertisement for a sports product and a sports-related sales promotion. For each, discuss the targeted audience, the promotional objectives, and the message characteristics.

2. How do organizations get feedback regarding their promotions via the Internet? Find several examples of ways of providing sports marketers with feedback about their promotions.

3. Consider any sports product and find evidence of advertising and sales promotion *not* on the Internet. Then locate the product's promotion on the Internet. Comment on whether or not this organization practices integrated marketing communications.

NOTES

1. Melanie Wells, "All's Not Well in Celebrity Pitchdom," *USA Today*, November 4, 1996, B1.

2. Joseph Pereira, "Fila Scores on an Assist From Grant Hill," *The Wall Street Journal*, November 5, 1996. Stefan Fatsis, "Grant Hill Signs New Fila Deal For $80 Million," *The Wall Street Journal*, September 23, 1997.

3. Michael Kamins, "An Investigation into the Match-Up Hypothesis in Celebrity Advertising: When Beauty May Be Only Skin Deep," *Journal of Advertising*, vol. 19, no. 1 (1990):4–13.

4. Charles Lamb, Joesph Hair and Carl McDaniel, *Principles of Marketing*, 2nd ed. (Cincinnati, OH: South-Western Publishing, 1994) 487.

5. Solomon, 527–528.

6. Robert Lavidge and Gary Steiner, "A Model for Predictive Measurements of Advertising Effectiveness," *Journal of Marketing*, vol. 24 (1961):59–62.

7. Rajeev Batra and Michael Ray, "Affective Responses Mediating Acceptance of Advertising," *Journal of Consumer Research*, vol. 13 (September 1986):236–239. Leon Shiffman and Leslie Kanuk, *Consumer Behavior*, 4th ed. (Englewood Cliffs, NJ: Prentice Hall, 1996), 237–239.

8. "Sports Advertising Expenditures-1996," Competitive Media Reporting, New York.

9. Joseph Pereira, "Sneaker Company Tags Out-of-Breath Baby Boomers," *The Wall Street Journal*, January, 16, 1998, B1–B2.

10. Ibid.

11. Don Schultz, Stanley Tannenbaum, and Robert Lauterborn, *Integrated Marketing Communications: Putting it Together and Making it Work* (Lincolnwood, IL: NTC Publishing Group, 1992). Don Schultz, "Rethinking Marketing and Communications' ROI," *Marketing News*, December 2, 1996, 10. Don Schultz and Paul Wang, "Real World Results," *Marketing Tools*, April/May 1994.

CHAPTER 11

Promotion Mix Elements

After completing this chapter, you should be able to

- Describe each element of the promotion mix, in detail

- Understand the basic process for designing a successful advertising campaign

- Discuss emerging forms of promotion

- Outline the strategic selling process and explain why sports marketing should use this process

- Identify the various forms of promotion

- Specify the importance of public/community relations to sports marketers

■ Stadium signage was one of the earliest forms of promotion.

In 1996, the Optimum Group, one of America's leading sales promotion agencies, designed a unique sales promotion for Hiram Walker. The promotion was designed to increase short-term sales of Canadian Club Classic (a 12-year-old whiskey). In this case, the promotion (called a premium) was a baseball card signed by one of four Hall of Fame players, including Willie Stargell, Billy Williams, Ernie Banks, and Brooks Robinson. With each purchase of a 750 ml bottle of Canadian Club Classic, consumers were able to collect one card from the series of cards.

In addition to the end users, Hiram Walker distributors were also involved in the sales promotion. Distributors could win a customized shelf unit to display the set of baseball cards and autographed baseballs. They could win these items for participating in the promotion and selling the idea to their retailers. The prizes motivated distributors to push cases into their retail accounts. According to Tom Wessling, senior vice president of sales and marketing for the Optimum Group, the promotion was a huge success. In fact, it was so well received that a second series of cards was issued. In order to make the sales promotion work, personal selling was needed to secure the baseball legends. Other forms of communication were also necessary to inform the Hiram Walker distributors and consumers about the promotion.

As demonstrated in the Hiram Walker promotion, sports marketers must carefully integrate the promotion mix elements to establish successful promotions to consumers and trade. In the previous chapter we explored the importance of communication and the basic concepts of promotional planning. The purpose of this chapter is to examine each of the **promotional mix elements** in greater detail. By doing so, sports marketers will be in a better position to choose the most effective promotional elements for the construction of the promotional plan. Let us begin by looking at one of the most widely used forms of promotion—advertising.

Advertising

Advertising remains one of the most visible and important marketing tools available to sports marketers. Although significant changes are taking place in the way sports products and services are advertised, the reasons for advertising remain the same. Advertising creates and maintains brand awareness and brand loyalty. In addition, advertising builds brand image and creates a distinct identity for sports products and services. Most importantly, advertising directly impacts consumer behavior. In other words, it causes us to attend sporting events, buy that new pair of running shoes, or watch the NCAA Women's Basketball tournament on television.

Most of us associate the development of an advertisement with the creative process. As you might imagine, advertising is more than a catchy jingle. In order to develop an effective advertisement, a systematic process is employed. Some of the steps in this process are very similar to the promotional planning process discussed in chapter 10. This is not unexpected, as advertising is just another form of communication, or promotional tool, used by sports marketers.

The advertising process is commonly referred to as designing an advertising campaign. An advertising campaign is a series of related advertisements that communicate a common message to the target audience (see Figure 11.1). The advertising campaign (similar to the promotional planning process) is initiated with decisions about the objectives and budget. Next, creative decisions, such as the ad appeal and execution, are developed. Following this, the media strategy is planned and finally, the advertising campaign is evaluated. Let us explore each of the steps in designing an advertising campaign in greater detail.

Advertising Objectives

The first step in any advertising campaign is to examine the broader promotional objectives and marketing goals. The overall objectives of the advertising campaign should, of course, be consistent with the strategic direction of the sports organization. The specific objectives and budgeting techniques for advertising are much the same as those discussed in chapter 10. Namely advertising is designed to inform, persuade, remind, and cause consumers in the target market to take action.[1] In addition to these broad objectives, advertising objectives are sometimes categorized as either direct or indirect.

The purpose of **direct objectives** in advertising is to elicit a behavioral response from the target audience. In sports marketing, this behavioral response may be in the form of purchasing tickets to a game, buying sporting goods that were advertised on the Internet, or even volunteering at a local event. Sometimes, an advertisement asks consumers to make multiple behavioral responses—for instance, watch the draft on

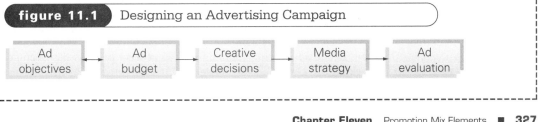

figure 11.1 Designing an Advertising Campaign

Ad objectives → Ad budget → Creative decisions → Media strategy → Ad evaluation

TNT, head to the Sports Authority, and check out the NBA Web site (www.nba.com) are all directives of an advertisement for the NBA draft show.

Direct advertising objectives can be further categorized into two distinct types: advertising to end users and sales promotion advertising. Both of the direct response objectives, however, are designed to induce action.

Advertising by sports organizations to end users   In this case, the objectives of advertising are not to enhance the perceived image of the event, the team, or the league, but rather to generate immediate response. With this type of objective, the sports marketer is attempting to build immediate sales. As such, the specific objective of advertising to end users is usually stated in terms of increasing sales volume.

Sales promotion advertising   It is common for contests, sweepstakes, coupons, and other forms of sales promotions to be advertised via any number of medium. As such, the objectives of direct response advertisement are to have consumers participate in the contests/sweepstakes or redeem coupons. Objectives, therefore, are measured in terms of the level of participation in the sales promotion.

Indirect objectives are based on establishing prebehavioral (i.e., prior to action) responses to advertising. That is, accomplishing goals, such as increasing awareness, enhancing image, improving attitudes, or educating consumers. These indirect objectives should, in turn, lead to more direct behavioral responses. Consider the advertisement for the Goodwill Games featuring Dan O'Brian which states simply "The Worlds' Best Athletes On The World's Biggest Stage." The objective of this advertisement is to generate awareness of the Games, inform potential consumers about the dates of the Games, and to enhance the image of the Games. Ultimately, the advertisements sponsors (most notably TBS and the Goodwill Games) hope that these indirect objectives will lead to the behavior response of viewing.

Indirect objectives, such as image enhancement, are always present to some extent in advertising. Sports leagues, such as the WNBA, use indirect advertising ("We Got Next") to generate awareness and interest in the league, while individual teams in the league are more concerned with direct, behavioral objectives ("Come Watch Us").

Advertising Budgeting

As with advertising objectives, budgeting methods for an ad campaign are largely the same as those for other forms of promotion. For example, techniques such as competitive parity, objective and task, and percentage of sales are again relevant to advertising. Whatever the methods used, it is important to remember that advertising budgets should ideally stem from the objectives that the advertising is attempting to achieve. However, other factors, such as monies available, competitive activity, and how the sports organization views the effectiveness of advertising, should be kept in mind.

Creative Decisions

After the objectives and the budget have been established, the creative process becomes the focus of the advertising campaign. The **creative process** has been defined as generating the ideas and the concept of the advertisement. Advertising

1-800-305-2420

■ Nike advertisement using a direct objective.

and sports marketing agencies hire individuals who possess a great deal of creativity, but even the most innovative people use a systematic process to harness their creativity.

To begin the creative process, most advertising agencies prepare a creative brief. The purpose of any creative brief is to understand clients' communication objectives so that the creative process will be maximized. The **creative brief** is a tool used to guide the creative process towards a solution that will serve the interests of the client and their customers. When used properly, the creative brief can be thought of as a marketing-oriented approach to the design of an advertising campaign. Table 11.1 shows a sample of the creative brief used by The Optimum Group (mentioned at the beginning of the chapter).

The three outcomes of the creative process are (1) identifying benefits of the sports product, (2) designing the advertising appeal—what to say, and (3) developing the advertising execution—how to say it. Each of these three elements in the creative decision process are discussed.

Identifying Benefits

Designing a distinctive advertising campaign involves identifying the key benefits of the sports product. We have briefly discussed the importance of understanding benefits in the context of segmenting consumer markets. As defined in chapter 7, benefits describe why consumers purchase a product/service or what problem the product solves for the consumer. For advertising purposes, describing the benefits or reasons why consumers should buy the sports product is a must. Marketing research is used to understand the benefits desired or perceived by consumers who might use or purchase the sports product.

table 11.1

The Creative Brief

"Thinking about the situation is much better than hoping."

Strategic thinking leads to insight which leads to high-quality execution.
Question: Why do a creative brief?
Answer: Our objective is to help our clients build their business. To do that, we must learn as much as we can so we can best deploy our creative resources to help the client meet their business objectives.

Creative brief elements

1. Project description
2. Target audience description (demographics, psychological data, etc.)
3. Long-term strategy
4. Competitive distinctiveness
5. Desired customer response (1-2 "desires" maximum) e.g., trial, change perception
6. Mandatory executional elements (1-2 maximum)
7. Known key customer insights

What does the creative brief do?

1. Raises key issues about the business
2. Organizes learning already known about the consumer or business
3. It suggests areas for needed additional learning
4. It can help uncover new insights important to helping the customer
5. It contributes to the creative process

Questions to ask when developing a creative brief

1. Are there proven insights from other products or categories that we could use?
2. Is there a negative perception in category or product that our client's product could refute? Is there a tradeoff or compromise that the client's product could eliminate?
3. Are there specific usage habits that could be leveraged into strong executions? How can we breathe creative life into research reports?
4. Is there a potential consumer negative in your principal competitor's strength?
5. Is there a perceived standard of excellence in your category? How does your brand compare to it? Can you create a standard of excellence for your brand?
6. What are the realities of how the client's brand fits their customer's needs? How does this affect the consumer's mindset when considering the alternatives available in the product category?
7. Is there a positive piece of consumer psychology your product can latch onto? Is there an emotional side to the client's brand? How does it interrelate with the practical side?
8. How does the client's consumer perceive their "brand"—not the product—"the brand"?

©1996 Optimum Group

Advertising Appeals

Understanding benefits and developing **advertising appeals** go hand in hand. Once the desired benefits are uncovered, the advertising appeal is developed around these benefits. In short, the advertising appeal recounts *why* the consumer wishes to purchase the sports product. The major advertising appeals used in sports marketing include health, emotion, fear, sex, and pleasure.

Health appeals are becoming prevalent in advertising, as the value placed on health continues to increase in the United States. Obviously, advertisements for the fitness industry and fitness centers capitalize on this growing concern of Americans. One important consideration when using health appeals in advertisements is the demographic profile of the target audience. According to the Health and Fitness Expo, the strongest growth in health-club membership is in the 35–54-year-old age range. Additional research has shown that the largest segment of the fitness club industry is middle-income working women who are not looking for "glamour and cache" in a gym. Moreover, the number of health-club members age 55 and older more than doubled between 1988 and 1995. Those age 45–54 posted the second largest gain in health club membership at 61 percent. The demographic of the audience and the health benefits desired from fitness centers should be carefully studied in the advertising process.[2]

A number of **emotional appeals**, such as fear, humor, sex, pleasure, and the drama associated with athletic competition, are also used in sports marketing promotions. One of the unique aspects of sports marketing is the emotional attachment that consumers develop for the sports product. As discussed in chapter 6, many fans have high levels of involvement and identification with their favorite athletes and teams.[3] Some fans may even view themselves as part of the team. Recognizing this strong emotional component, many advertisers of sport use emotional appeals. The infamous "Thrill of victory and agony of defeat" message used for decades for ABC's *Wide World of Sports* opening captures the essence of an emotional appeal. Emotional appeals that allow fans to relive the team's greatest moments and performances of past years are often used to encourage future attendance.

One specific type of an emotional appeal is a fear appeal. **Fear appeals** are messages designed to communicate what negative consequences may occur if the sports product or service is not used or is used improperly. Scare tactics are usually inappropriate for sports products and services, but in some product categories moderate amounts of fear in a message can be effective. Consider, for example, messages concerning exercise equipment or health-club membership. Many promotional campaigns are built around consumers' fears of being physically unfit and aging. Even athletic promoters use moderate fear appeals by telling consumers that tickets will be sold out quickly and that they should not wait to purchase their seats. Effective sports marketers identify their sports products as solutions to the common "fears" of consumers. For example, manufacturers of bike and skateboard helmets are quick to cite the plethora of head injuries that result without the use of proper headgear.

Another emotional appeal is sex. **Sex appeals** rely on the old adage that "sex sells." Typically, marketers who use sex appeals in their messages are selling products that are sexually related, such as perfumes and clothing. This is true also in sports marketing, as demonstrated by Polo Sport fragrance by Ralph Lauren or the Michael Jordan cologne, which made $60 million in sales during its first six months on the market. Even more recently, Nike has developed an advertising campaign for Nike FIT, featuring star athletes such as Scotty Pippen, Gabrielle Reece, and Michael Johnson baring it all.

In sports marketing, sex appeals are sometimes used, but this is always a delicate subject. ProBeach Volleyball has been criticized for relying too much on the sex appeal of its players (both male and female) to attract fans. Most notably, top player Gabrielle Reece has been used as a model in *Sports Illustrated's* swimsuit edition and in other advertisements. Additionally, Major League Soccer has come out with a series of advertisements promoting the sex appeal of its players.

Pleasure or fun appeals are designed for those target audiences that participate in sports or watch sports for fun, social interaction, or enjoyment. These advertising appeals would stress the positive relationships that can be developed among family members, friends, or business associates by attending games and/or participating in sports. A recent advertisement by a major credit card company captured the pleasure of a father taking his son to a baseball game. The essence of the appeal was that although you might not be able to afford it at the time, you will never be able to replace the priceless moment of taking your child to his or her first ball game.

Advertising Execution

The **advertising execution** should answer the appeal that the advertiser is trying to target. In other words, it is not what to say, but how to say it. Let us look at some of the more common executional formats, such as message sidedness, comparative advertisements, slice of life, scientific, and testimonials.

One executional format is whether to construct the message as **one-sided** or **two-sided**. A one-sided message conveys only the positive benefits of a sports product or service. Most sports organizations don't want to communicate the negative features of their products or services, but this can have its advantages. Describing the negatives along with the positive can enhance the credibility of the source by making it more trustworthy. In addition, discussing the negative aspects of the sports product can ultimately lower consumers' expectations and lead to more satisfaction. For instance, you rarely hear a coach at any level talk about how unbeatable a team or player is. Rather, the focus is on the weaknesses of the team, which reduces fan (and owner) expectations.

Comparative advertisements, another executional format, contrasts one sports product with another. When doing comparative advertisements, sports advertisers stress the advantages of their sports product relative to the competition. For new sports products that possess a significant differential advantage, comparative advertisements can be especially effective. The risk involved with comparative advertisements is that consumers are exposed to your product as well as the competitor's product.

Because of the unique nature of sport, many advertisements are inherently comparative. For example, boxing advertisements touted the "Fight of the Century" between Muhammed Ali and Joe Frazier. In fact, there have been many "Fights of the Century" advertisements that are strikingly similar, comparing two boxers' strengths

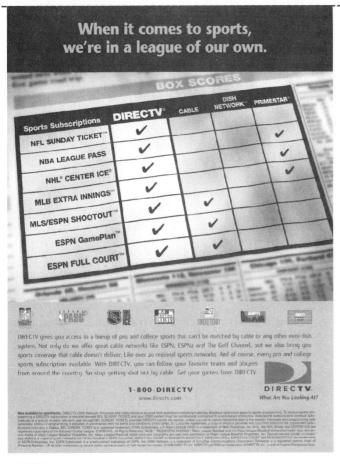

■ DIRECTV uses comparative advertising.

and weaknesses. Other sporting events, such as the made-for-television Skin's Game, use a similar comparative format for promoting the events. Many home teams skillfully use comparative advertisements to attract moderately involved fans interested in the success of the local team. These fans are attracted by the allure of the visiting team or one of its star athletes. For instance, many basketball advertisements promote the big-name athletes of the opposing team, rather than highlight their own stars.

Slice-of-life executional styles show a "common" athlete or consumer in a common, everyday situation where the consumer might be using the advertised sports product. A slight variation of this style is the **lifestyle** execution, wherein the advertisement is intended to portray the lifestyle of the desired target audience. For example, the 'Just Do It' campaign uses a slice-of-life format that appeals to the participant in each of us. More recently, the "I Can" campaign has expanded and updated Nike's once-popular and currently old-fashioned slogan. Bob Wood, Nike's vice president of USA Marketing, states that the new slogan "reflects the deep emotional connection that people have with sports in feeling good about participating and setting personal goals."[4]

In another slice-of-life example, Zest soap ran a very effective campaign for their product using football star Ironhead Hayward as their "showering" spokesperson.

Another executional style that is also readily used in sports advertising is called **scientific**. Advertisers using this style feature the technological superiority of their sports product or use research/scientific studies to support their claims. For instance, many golf ball manufacturers use scientific claims to sell their product. Wilson's Staff Titanium was touted as "Golf's First Titanium Core Ball." Maxfli markets the Maxfli MD Tungsten with its heavier tungsten core, which makes the ball fly farther, and the Titleist Professional ball, which has a core of corn syrup, water, and salts, surrounded by a rubber and plasticlike covering. As Bill Morgan, Titleist's vice president of golf ball research admits, "A lot of times, chemical words or technical words are talked about in marketing and nobody really knows what they are talking about. But it sounds high tech. There is a little deception there, really."

One of the most prevalent executional styles for sports advertising is the use of **testimonials**. Testimonials are statements about the sports product given by endorsers. These endorsers may be the "common" athlete, professional athletes, teams, coaches and managers, owners, or even inanimate objects. For example, in advertising designed to increase tennis participation among children, kids are seen playing with cartoon characters. Michael Jordan and his "Space Jam" friends represents another example of inanimate objects used as endorsers.

Why are athlete testimonials so popular among sports advertisers? The answer to this question is the ability of sports celebrities to persuade the target audience and move them towards purchase. Athletes' persuasive power stems from their credibility and, in some cases, attractiveness. **Credibility** refers to the expertise and the trustworthiness of the source of the message. **Expertise** is the knowledge, skill, or special experience possessed by the source about the sports product. Of course, successful athletes who promote products needed to participate in their sport have demonstrable expertise. Examples of the athlete-athletic product match-up include Michael Jordan, Grant Hill, Cheryl Swoopes—basketball shoe contracts; Tiger Woods, Greg Norman, Jack Nicklaus—golf equipment; Jeff Gordon, Dale Jarrett—automotive industry; Ken Griffey, Jr., Barry Larkin—baseball gloves; Pete Sampras, Michael Chang, Monica Seles—tennis racquets; and Brett Hull—hockey equipment.

The other dimension of source credibility is **trustworthiness**. This refers to the honesty and believability of the athlete(s) endorser(s). Trustworthiness is an intangible characteristic that is becoming harder and harder for professional athletes to establish. Today's consumers realize that athletes with already large salaries are being paid huge sums of money for endorsements. Because of this, the athlete's believability is often suspect. Nevertheless, even some of the highest paid athlete endorsers, such as Michael Jordan, Arnold Palmer, and Tiger Woods, seem to have established themselves as trustworthy sources of information.

In addition to credibility, another factor that makes athletes successful endorsers is **attractiveness**. Although attractiveness is usually associated with physical beauty, it appears to have another, nonphysical dimension based on personality, lifestyle, and intellect. Attractiveness operates using the process of identification, which means that the target audience identifies with the source (athlete) in some fashion. Gatorade's

■ These successful professional golfers create a powerful image for Ralph Lauren's Polo Golf.

classic "I wanna be like Mike" campaign, featuring Michael Jordan, is a good example of the identification process.

Who are the most successful and appealing athlete endorsers? In 1997, a study was conducted by Burns Sports Celebrity Service, Inc. to answer this question.[5] The survey asked 300 creative directors at national advertising agencies and corporate marketing executives who hire athletes to rate the most appealing athlete endorsers. Not surprisingly, the results indicated that the appeal of Tiger Woods, the recent Masters Champion, is growing at an extremely rapid pace. Woods has firmly established himself as one of the top sports celebrity endorsers today (see Table 11.2). Burns Sports' President, Bob Williams, believes that, "If Tiger Woods takes an aggressive approach accepting endorsements, he could become the first athlete to earn a billion dollars in endorsements. Woods' golf career could last thirty years or more, unlike athletes from other sports whose average career is in the single digits. Hence, the real opportunity to earn a billion dollars from endorsements is within reason for a megastar like Tiger Woods."

table 11.2

Top Athlete Endorsers

Burns' Most Appealing Athlete Endorser	Highest Paid Athlete Endorser*
1) Tiger Woods	1) Michael Jordan: $40,000,000
2) Michael Jordan	2) Shaquille O'Neal: $17,000,000
3) Grant Hill	3) Arnold Palmer: $15,000,000
4) Dennis Rodman	4) Andre Agassi: $13,000,000
5) Ken Griffey, Jr.	5) Dennis Rodman: $ 9,000,000

Source: Courtesy of Burns Sports Celebrity Services, Inc.

Although athlete endorsers, such as those listed in Table 11.2, can be extremely effective, there are risks involved. Athletes are costly, may have career threatening injuries, or just do foolish things. Here are just a few examples of the many athlete endorsers gone bad.

In an unprecedented move, the Golden State Warriors terminated Latrell Sprewell's four-year, $32 million contract after he threatened to kill his coach, P.J. Carlesimo, during a scrimmage. After exchanging words, Sprewell grabbed Carlesimo and choked him for 10 to 15 seconds before the other players could stop him. The NBA suspended him for one year without pay, and Converse terminated Sprewell's endorsement deal, which was estimated to pay between $300,000 and $600,000 annually. Amazingly, Sprewell's supension was reduced, and he was reinstated with his team after winning an abritration decision filed by Sprewell and the NBA players union.

Dennis Rodman, a notorious bad boy, was fined $50,000 for making derogatory comments about Mormons during the 1997 NBA Championship Series against the Utah Jazz. The fine was Rodman's third of the season. His previous two incidents involved kicking a courtside photographer ($25,000) and striking Joe Wolf of the Bucks ($7,500). In response to Rodman's insensitive comments, his television advertisements for Carl's Jr. (fast food restaurant) were yanked permanently. Robert W. Wisely, senior vice president of marketing for Carl Karcher Enterprises, commented that "Derogatory comments made about any religious or racial group are inexcusable."

O.J. Simpson was enjoying a successful run with Hertz when he was charged with the murder of his former wife, Nicole Brown Simpson. In another football example, Brett Favre, the 1995 NFL MVP quarterback, estimates that his 46 days in a drug rehabilitation clinic cost him the opportunity to take part in a number of high-paying endorsements.[6]

In still other examples, Steffi Graf and her father were charged with tax evasion. Magic Johnson's public announcement that he was HIV positive caused a stir with his sponsors. John Daly (problems with alcohol) and Fuzzy Zoeller (racist remarks after the 1997 Masters) represent two examples of problematic endorsers in golf. And the list goes on and on.

table 11.3

Guidelines for Using Sports Celebrities as Endorsers

- Sports celebrities are more effective for endorsing sports-related products. Match-up hypothesis again holds true—does not matter if consumers recognize the it athlete if they cannot remember the product that is being endorsed
- Long-term relationships or associations between the product and the endorser are key—cannot be short-term or one-shot deals to be effective. Examples include Arnold Palmer with Penzoil and Michael Jordon with Nike
- Advertisements using athlete endorsers who appear during contests or events in which the athlete is participating are less effective
- Athletes who are overexposed may lose their credibility and power to influence consumers. Tiger Woods's manager Hughes Norton of IMG says that he is planning to limit the golfing phenom to an association with just five global brands to avoid overexposure

Adapted from: Amy Dyson and Douglas Turco, "The State of Celebrity Endorsement in Sport," *Cyber-Journal of Sport Marketing*, <http://www.cad.gu.edu.au/cjsm/dyson.htm>.

For these reasons, many sports advertisers are shying away from individual athletes and using teams or events as their advertising platform. Nonetheless, many sports celebrities are still being used as endorsers. Table 11.3 presents some general guidelines for using sports celebrities in your organization's advertising campaign. One promising alternative that reduces the risk of potential problems is to use athletes who are no longer alive.

One promising alternative that reduces the risk of potential problems, is to use athletes that are no longer alive. Recently, Nike ran a series of 10 commercials using former Green Bay Packer coach Vince Lombardi. Other corporations have featured departed stars in their ad compaigns including Citibank (Babe Ruth), Microsoft (Lou Gehrig and Jesse Owens), McDonald's, Coca-Cola, Apple Computer, General Mills (Jackie Robinson), and Miller Brewing (Satchel Paige). Dead athletes are more cost effective, scandalproof, and are icons in the world of sports. Ruth was chosen to represent Citibank in an upcoming campaign—49 years after his death and 62 since his last homer—for similar reasons. "Babe's an American sports icon, instantly recognizable," says Ken Gordon, a Citibank vice president, explaining why Ruth got the nod over contemporary ballplayers.[7]

Media Strategy

As presented in the previous chapter, a medium or channel is the element in the communications process by which the message is transmitted. Traditional mass media, such as newspapers, television, radio, or magazines, are usually thought of as effective ways of carrying advertising messages to the target audience. However, new technologies are creating alternative media. The Internet, for example, represents an emerging medium that must be considered by sports advertisers. Deciding what medium or media to use is just one aspect in developing a comprehensive media strategy.

Media strategy addresses two basic questions about the channel of communication. First, what medium or media mix (combination of medium) will be most effective in reaching the desired target audience? Second, how should this media be scheduled to meet advertising objectives?

Media Decisions or Media Selection

The far-ranging (and growing) number of media choices make selecting the right media a difficult task. Choosing the proper media requires the sports advertiser to be mindful of the creative decisions made earlier in the advertising process. For instance, an emotional appeal—best suited to television—would be difficult to convey using print media (see article "Power of Print"). It is also critical that the media planner keep the target market in mind. Understanding the profile of the target market and their media habits is essential to developing an effective advertising campaign.

power of print

Marketers will spend billions of dollars sponsoring sports events and advertising goods and services around those events. The stakes are especially high in an Olympic year, and dozens of companies have raised their marketing budgets to link their products and logos to events, promotions, and athletes. They will pour much of that money into television, but a sizable amount will go to another vital, sometimes underutilized and often forgotten medium: the printed word.

"Effective use of the print media can have several advantages over other outlets," says Bob Dorfman, a San Francisco advertising copy writer for Foote, Cone & Belding and the producer of the *Marketer's Professional Scouting Report*, a publication that tracks the endorsement value of athletes. "For one, you're no longer limited to the business pages; now your company name is in the sports section as well," he explains. "Also, there will be some rub-off on your company or product, resulting in residual allegiance. And you get instant personality for whatever it is you're selling."

However, maximizing dollars spent doesn't mean merely throwing money at an event or an advertisement. Sports marketing through print requires savvy, patience, and a keen sense of the medium's pluses and pitfalls. If a title sponsorship is done poorly, for example, discerning editors and journalists will leave out the corporate affiliation, lessening the likelihood that the public will see its sponsorship—and name—in newspapers and magazines. Or even worse, they could end up resenting it. When 3Com bought the rights to call San Francisco's storied Candlestick Park "3Com Park," the media did not embrace the name immediately. "You have to understand the environment in which you are doing something," cautions one sports marketer. Even so, the name change garnered volumes of national media attention, prompting another marketer to concede that "Any name recognition is better than none." In short, there's a certain artfulness in approaching the print media for optimum corporate exposure.

Unappreciated as it may be sometimes, the print medium has special qualities that differentiate it from radio and television. To be sure, marketers are more or less restricted to black and white words on paper and accompanying photos that are locked in still, two-dimensional space and cannot move or talk. And for those reasons alone, television may be more powerful. But more cost-effective? That depends. More information can be communicated on a newspaper page than in a 30-second television spot. And if the advertisement is compelling, readers are apt to spend more time—undivided time since they won't be straying from their sets to get something from the refrigerator—with the promotion.

Another advantage of print over broadcasting is timing. Companies can turn promotions around lickety-split, thereby cashing in on events or other newsworthy happenings that tout their products or sponsorship. For example, marketers frequently produce congratulatory print advertisements for a sponsoring figure who has just won an MVP award, easily within a day's time. Television commercials, needless to say, require extensive lead time, which can result in costly errors. A few years ago, Reebok botched its "Dan vs. Dave" campaign in preparation for the decathlon competition at the 1992 Olympics in Barcelona between two American athletes. However, one of them, Dan O'Brien, failed to qualify for the U.S. team. Simply put, print provides more latitude to be creative and to respond in a timely way to the vicissitudes of the sporting world, where events can shift overnight.

How can a company tilt the odds in its favor of seeing its name or logo in the paper? Consider what Nissan did last year. A longtime sponsor of what had been known as the Nissan Los Angeles Open, the automobile company felt that even when it took over title sponsorship several years ago, it still was not getting the print publicity it deserved. "After about eight years of modest results, you need some return," says Nissan's John Gill, who handles events for both the Nissan and Infiniti lines. So the company decided to alter the name of the event, and the Nissan L.A. Open became simply the Nissan Open. The outcome was dramatic; newspaper references to Nissan jumped from under 1 million to 3.5 million. "Instead of giving us only opening line mention, we got many more subsequent mentions" in coverage, a proud Gill says. "That verified what we suspected. It gave the press fewer opportunities to exclude our name."

Another firm that has enjoyed tremendous exposure by marketing through print is Chicago-based Cotter & Co., which owns True Value hardware stores and sponsors the NFL's True Value Man of the Year award. The company combines print advertising with local promotion to capitalize on its backing of the award, which honors players who make significant contributions on and off the field, a philosophy that fits well with the hardware store's image.

Thirty players are selected each season, one from each NFL team, along with a national winner. True Value has added sponsorship of Major League Baseball's Roberto Clemente Award, which also recognizes off-the-field contributions. The two awards give True Value a synergy that the company plans on marketing aggressively in print advertising and other local events.

Marketers need more than the printed word to get the most from a sponsorship event. Visuals, too, are a vital component in getting the word out there. In most cases, capturing logos and products on the pages of newspapers and magazines is a matter of stacking the odds in a company's favor. That is because serendipity often plays the biggest role in what images find their way into print. The key is: signage, signage, signage.

Mundane as it may sound, plastering logos is a time-tested method of increasing coverage. Most companies do this, hanging banners and emblazoning T-shirts, towels, and interview rooms with corporate insignias. True Value, for one, plans to advertise its sponsorship of the Roberto Clemente Award with rotating signs in ballparks across the land.

Some companies are taking these strategies to the next level. Last year, Canada's

(continued)

Corel Corp., one of the world's largest computer software manufacturers, signed a three-year pact with the Women's Tennis Association (WTA) for tour sponsorship. Already one of the biggest print advertisers around, the company will likely exceed the $40 million it spent last year on promoting itself through the press. Corel has been working with the WTA to create additional categories of player rankings, such as the "Top Ten Rookies" and the "Top Ten Movers and Shakers" to display at tournaments sites to augment media interest in a wider range of players. The software company also is looking at publishing these same categories-cum-photos in *Tennis* magazine as a way of associating their backdrops and logos with the players. What's more, Corel will be floating a hot air balloon (its version of the Goodyear blimp) at various events, like it did at the WTA Championships last November. And later this year, Corel will provide computer terminals at tour events so journalists can download photographs and information on players to accompany stories. "We understand very well how print media is used for exposure," says Pat Reid, the company's director of sponsorship and promotion. "If you're not organized and not thinking about the print media, you won't get anywhere."

Getting somewhere also demands maintaining cordial and professional relations with the media, a fact not lost on companies with ambitious plans like Corel. "We plan to service them like never before," Reid says, displaying a realistic understanding about the power of a friendly relationship.

An outgrowth of this evolving relationship finds many companies now partnering with national magazines in producing special advertising "features," most of which run opposite traditional advertisements touting products. For example, Nissan runs a special advertisement called "Hometown Heroes," profiling local athletes who make contributions to home communities. Procter and Gamble's Old Spice profiles amateur athletes with its Athlete of the Month. American Honda Motor Company sponsors the "Honda Scholar Athlete of the Year," and the list goes on. These quasi-advertisements serve a clear purpose: They link sports to a feel-good charity or cause while at the same time providing advertising mileage.

In the end, it is hard to say whether the print medium is a more effective means of reaching the public per dollar than other media. But one thing is for certain: Print is important, and it pays to recognize that. With print, companies can increase brand loyalty, build name recognition, and ultimately sell more goods and services. Which is why understanding its power can make a big difference to the bottom line.

Adapted from Douglas O. Robson, "The Power of Print," *Mark McCormack's Guide to Sports Marketing*, International Sports Marketing Group, 1996, 136–141.

Every type of media has strengths and weaknesses that must be considered when making advertising placement decisions. As the previous article illustrates, print may be the most cost effective medium for sports marketers. Table 11.4 demonstrates selected advantages and disadvantages when choosing advertising media.

Alternative Forms of Advertising

Because of the advertising clutter present in traditional advertising media, sports marketers are continually evaluating new ways of delivering their message to consumers. Alternative forms of advertising range from the more conventional stadium signage to the most creative media. Consider the following innovative illustrations of alternative forms of advertising: The International Cricket Council has allowed players to sell the top 23 cen-

table 11.4

Profiles of Major Media Types

Medium	Advantages	Limitations
Internet	Allows messages to be customized, reaches specific market interactive capabilities	Clutter, audience characteristics, hard to measure effectiveness
Newspapers	Flexibility; timeliness; good local market coverage; broad acceptability; high believability	Short life; poor reproduction quality; small pass-along audience
Television	Good mass market coverage; low cost per exposure; combines sight, sound, and motion; appealing to the senses	High absolute costs; high clutter; fleeting exposure; less audience selectivity
Direct mail	High audience selectivity; flexibility; no ad competition within the same medium; allows personalization	Relatively high cost per exposure; "junk mail" image
Radio	Good local acceptance, high geographic and demographic selectivity; low cost	Audio only, fleeting exposure; low attention ("the half-heard" medium) fragmented audiences
Magazines	High geographic and demographic selectivity; credibility and prestige; high-quality reproduction; long life and good pass-along readership	Long advertisement purchase lead time; high cost; no guarantee of position
Outdoor	Flexibility; high repeat exposure; low cost; low message competition; good positional selectivity	Little audience selectivity; creative limitations

Adapted from Philip Kotler and Gary Armstrong, *Marketing: An Introduction*, 4th ed. (Upper Saddle River, NJ: Prentice Hall), 471.

timeters of their bats for advertising; and thirty-five public golf courses in Connecticut have signed up for a program that will put advertisements in the bottom of their holes. Who knows where advertisements will appear next, perhaps Dennis Rodman's head?

Stadium Signage

Stadium signage, or on-site advertising, is back.[8] For some time, nary a sign was found on the outfield wall of a MLB team or on the boards at an NHL game. Now, stadium signage prevails on every inch of available space. Not unlike other forms of advertising, stadium signage is designed to increase brand or corporate awareness, create a favorable image through associations with the team and sport, change attitudes or maintain favorable attitudes, and ultimately increase the sale of product.

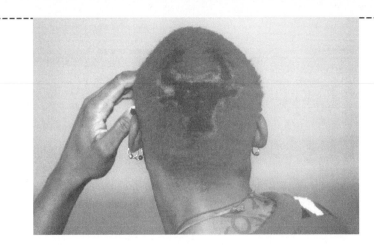

■ Can Dennis Rodman's head be an alternative advertising medium?

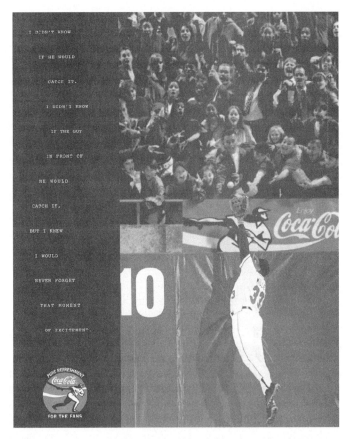

■ Coca Cola creates a positive association with baseball by using stadium signage.

One current estimate is that $15 billion is spent each year on stadium signage, but this is expected to increase, given the advent of new technologies where stadium billboards can be changed and customized to local markets.[9] As the following article illustrates, there is sometimes more to a stadium sign than meets the eye.

virtual advertising

First used by a minor league baseball team in 1995, the latest technological advancement in sports stadium signage is called the "virtual advertisement" or "virtual sign". Virtual advertisements or signs are ads that aren't really there. The ads can appear on the field, ice, tennis court, or just about anywhere, but can only be seen by the television viewing audience rather than those in attendance. The technology called L-VIS was developed by Princeton Video Image of Princeton, New Jersey. The system can distribute different video images simultaneously to different audiences around the globe, and as such is geared primarily for large global advertisers. As PVI vice president Sam McCleary points out, "The L-VIS system allows advertisers to modify the message to fit the market. Customized signage by market is an increasingly more valuable component to marketing."[a]

Other benefits of virtual signs include state-of-the-art graphics, a way to hold viewers attention, and cost effectiveness. For instance, a half-inning of virtual advertising costs $20,000, roughly the same as a 30-second conventional commercial. In addition, virtual signage will help keep the stadium and playing surfaces free of unwanted signage. This may even help the players as signage on the ice or right behind home plate or a tennis end-line may be disturbing.[b] McCleary says that viewers "don't seem to make the distinction" between real signage and virtual signage.[c] Most importantly, virtual signage will give teams the opportunity to be flexible and creative with potential sponsors. Virtual signs have appeared in overseas broadcasts of rugby, cricket, and soccer and could be appearing soon in boxing, basketball, baseball, football, and tennis coverage.[d]

[a] Chad Rubel, "What You See on TV Is Not What You Get at Stadium," *Marketing News*, May 6, 1996, 2.
[b] Brian Fenton, "Truth in Advertising," *Popular Mechanics*, January, 1997, 34.
[c] William Power "The Virtual Ad: On TV You See It, at Games You Don't" *The Wall Street Journal*, July 30, 1998, B1, B10.
[d] Michael Bürg "Signs of the Times," *MediaWeek* , March 4, 1994, 14.

Although stadium signage can be an effective means of advertising, it can also be costly. For instance, the rotating scorer's and press table stadium signage can cost between $50,000 and $100,000 for NBA games, given the current demand for the space. How is expensive stadium signage sold and justified by sports marketers? First, research has shown that locations considered to be part of the game (e.g., scorer's table or on the ice) are more effective than those locations removed from the action (e.g., scoreboards). One researcher found that spectators had improved recognition of and attitudes towards eight courtside advertisers for a NCAA Division I men's basketball team. This finding is, of course, extremely important to sponsors considering the cost and effectiveness of this type of stadium signage.[10]

Other Outdoor

A new form of outdoor advertising is also becoming popular at national sporting events. This type of outdoor promotion uses live product demonstrations or characters to attract fans' attention. For example, the U.S. Army staged a live combat reenactment prior to the start of the Charlotte 500 NASCAR race. In another example, Juan Valdez, the very recognizable brand character for Columbia Coffee, showed up in the stands of the U.S. Open tennis tournament. Similarly, Ronald McDonald attended the Kentucky Derby and a Chicago Bulls game to promote the Arch Deluxe sandwich from McDonald's.

In a related fashion, sports marketers sometimes use variations of product placement techniques. Product placement occurs when manufacturers pay to have their products used in television shows, movies, and other entertainment media. For instance, General Motors featured their GM pickup in the opening ceremonies of the 1996 Olympic Games in Atlanta as part of the theme, "a typical Friday night in America." Reebok was prominently featured in the movie *Wayne's World*, and perhaps the earliest sports product placement was when James Bond, 007, used Slazenger golf balls on the links in the classic *Goldfinger*. In the ultimate product tie-in, the Anaheim Mighty Ducks of the NHL were named after the series of movies created by their parent company, Disney.

Are these product placements effective? Generally, product placements and live product demonstrations seem to work. After all, it is hard to miss a man dressed up like Juan Valdez in the midst of a crowd of tennis fans or Garth from Wayne's World fully attired in Reebok apparel. The advantages that have been cited for these alternative forms of advertising include[11]

- **Exposure**—a large number of people go to the movies, rent movies, or could be exposed to a live-product demonstration if they are attending a sporting event or watching television.
- **Attention**—Moviegoers are generally an attentive audience. Sports spectators are also a captive audience when they are waiting for the action to begin.
- **Recall**—research has shown that audiences have higher levels of next-day recall for products that are placed in movies than for traditional forms of promotion.
- **Source association**—for product placements, the audience may see familiar and likable stars using the sports product. As such, the product's image may be enhanced through association with the celebrity.

Another alternative form of advertising is using the athlete as a "human billboard."[12] The history of athletes wearing an advertisement can be traced back to the 1960s, when organizations began establishing relationships with stock car drivers. Soon, the practice of drivers wearing patches on their clothing spread to other sports, such as tennis and golf. The use of athletes as advertisers is much more common in individual sports because these individuals have the ability to negotiate and wear whatever they want, as opposed to the tight controls imposed on athletes in team sports by their respective leagues.

Today, the use of athletes as "human billboards" is part of the integrated marketing communications plan rather than a stand-alone promotion. Steve Elkington of

■ These runners all exemplify the human billboard.

the PGA Tour wears Buick visors, sweaters, and shirts, in addition to the other advertisements and promotions he performs for Buick. The major appeal of this form of advertising is the natural association (classical conditioning) that is formed in consumers' minds between the athlete and the organization or product.

How much does it cost sponsors to rent advertising space on an athlete's body? An IndyCar driver's helmet might cost between $50,000 and $250,000, depending on the driver. The precious space on a professional golfer's visor would cost between $250,000 and $500,000. Although these prices may seem outrageous, organizations are willing to pay the price for the exposure and enhanced brand equity.

Internet

Another major player in the world of advertising media is the Internet. As discussed in chapter 3, the Internet has already become a valuable source of sports information for participants and fans. In addition, the Internet is fast becoming the favorite promotional medium for sports marketers. A total user base of 30 million people, along with an expected growth rate of 10 percent per month, are among several of the benefits to sports marketers.[13] Let us take a look at some of the other advantages to promotion via the Internet.

Perhaps the most substantial advantage to using the Internet as a promotional tool is the good fit between the profile of the sports fan and the Internet user. The typical Internet user is described as an entertainment-minded, educated male between 18 and 34 years old. For instance, the demographic profile of ESPNET SportsZone is 96 percent male, with 80 percent between the ages of 18 and 34.[14] Sound familiar? These characteristics closely match the traditional sports fan. In addition, the Internet is the ideal medium to target college sports fans due to greater access and usage rates among students. Generally, the Internet allows the sports advertiser to reach an extremely focused targeted market.

www.nhl.com

The official NHL Website wires together players and fans. And the assist goes to IBM.

■ The Internet has become a popular advertising medium.

Another distinct advantage of promotion via the Internet is the interactive nature of the medium. Promotions attract the attention of the target audience and then create involvement by having consumers point and click on the information that they find of interest. For instance, TaylorMade Golf has an interactive advertisement found on the golf.com Web site (www.golf.com). A point and click of the mouse will take consumers to the TaylorMade homepage, which features a media center, retail locator, golf talk, pro shop, staff players, information about TaylorMade, and international information. As the Web page suggests "Welcome to TaylorMade Golf. Find Your Game with our new and innovative golf products. Enjoy your stay and putter around for awhile."

Other advantages of the Internet versus more traditional media include the Internet's ability to be flexible. Web promotions can be updated, and changes can be made almost instantly. This flexibility is a tremendous advantage for sports marketers, who are constantly responding to a changing environment. In fact, the Internet seems to the perfect tool for sports marketers using the contingency framework for strategic planning.

A final benefit of promotion via the Internet is its cost effectiveness. The Internet provides organizations with a means of promoting sports to consumers all over the globe at a low cost. The ability to reach a geographically diverse audience at a low cost is one of the primary advantages of Internet promotion.

Although there are many advantages, promotion via the Internet can also pose potential problems. As with other forms of advertising, it is difficult to measure the effectiveness of sports promotion over the Internet. Often, marketers use the "number of hits" as a proxy for effectiveness, but this cannot be used to determine the interest level of the consumer or purchase intent.

Promotional clutter is another difficulty with Internet promotions. As the Internet becomes a more popular advertising medium, more organizations will compete for the audience and its attention. In order to break through the clutter, sports marketers must design new Internet promotions. Differentiating among Web promotions will become increasingly important in gaining the attention of consumers and developing a unique position for organizations.

A final disadvantage of promotion on the Internet is its inability to reach certain groups of consumers. Although the Internet is a great medium to reach younger, college-educated, computer-literate consumers, it may be extremely inefficient in trying to promote to the mature market or, perhaps, consumers of lower socioeconomic standing.[15]

Although we have looked at some of the pros and cons of promotion via the Internet, the fact remains that the Internet is here to stay. The low costs, ability to target sports fans and participants, and high flexibility far outweigh the disadvantages of this medium. Certainly, sports marketers should consider the Internet as another important tool in his or her integrated communications efforts.

Choosing a Specific Medium

Once the medium or media mix is chosen by the sports organization along with the advertising agency, the specific medium must be addressed. In other words, if the advertisement will appear in a magazine, then the choice of magazine will be most effective. Do we want our advertisement to promote the 1998 gold-medal U.S. Women's Hockey Team to appear in *Sports Illustrated*, *Sport Magazine*, *The Hockey News*, or some combination of these specific media? To answer this question, we must consider our reach and frequency objectives.

Reach refers to the number of people exposed to an advertisement in a given medium. For the advertiser who wishes to generate awareness and reach the largest number of people in the target audience, perhaps *Sports Illustrated*, with a circulation of 3.2 million, would be the most effective media.[16] However, if the target audience is women, then *Sports Illustrated* might be reaching people who are not potential users.

The reach of an advertisement is determined by a number of factors. First, the nature of the media mix influences reach. The general rule is that the greater the number of media used, the greater the reach. For example, if the advertising campaign for U.S. Women's Hockey was broadcast on television, printed in magazines, and also appeared on the Internet, reach would be increased. Second, if only one medium is to be used, increasing the number and diversity within this medium will increase the reach. For instance, if cable television was chosen as the sole medium for the U.S. Women's Hockey campaign, reach would be increased if the commercial was aired on ESPN, Lifetime, and Fox Sports versus ESPN alone. Finally, reach can be enhanced by airing the advertisements during different times of the day or day parts. The advertisement might be shown at night after 9:00 P.M. and also in the morning to reach a greater percentage of the target audience.

Along with reach, another consideration in making specific media decisions is frequency. **Frequency** refers to the number of times the individual or household is exposed to the media vehicle. An important point is that frequency is measured by the number of exposures to the media vehicle rather than the advertisement itself. Just because an advertisement is shown on television during the Super Bowl does not mean that the target audience has seen it. Consumers might change channels, leave the room, or simply become involved in conversation. A recent study examined this issue using Super Bowl viewers in a bar setting.[17] It found that visual attention levels for the game are similar to attention levels for the advertisements, attention to commercials vary by their location in the cluster of advertisements and time of game, and that Super Bowl commercials may receive more attention than commercials on other programs.

Media Scheduling

Four basic media scheduling alternatives are considered once the medium (e.g., magazines) and specific publications (e.g., *Sports Illustrated*) are chosen. These schedules are called continuous, flighting, pulsing, and seasonal. A **continuous schedule** recognizes that there are no breaks in the demand for the sports product. This is also called steady, or "drip," scheduling. During the advertising period, advertisements are continually run. Most sporting goods and events are seasonal and therefore do not require a continuous schedule. Some sporting goods, such as running shoes, have roughly equivalent demand and advertising spending throughout the year.

A **flighting schedule** is another alternative, where advertising expenditures are varied in some months and zero is spent in other months. Consider the case of the Houston Astros. Heavy advertising expenditures are spent in March, April, and May leading up to the season. Reminder-oriented advertising is placed over the course of the rest of the season, and no advertising dollars are spent in the winter months. This type of scheduling is most prevalent in sports marketing due to the seasonal nature of most sports.

A **pulsing schedule** is a variant of the flighting schedule. Ad expenditures may vary greatly, but some level of advertising is always taking place. Although it sounds similar to a flighting schedule, remember that a flighting schedule has some months where zero is being spent on advertising.

Personal Selling

Now that we have looked at the advertising process in detail, let us turn to another important element in the promotion mix—personal selling. Personal selling is used in a variety of ways in sports marketing, such as securing corporate sponsorships, selling luxury suites or boxes in stadiums, and hawking corporate and/or group ticket sales. In the marketing of sporting goods, the primary applications of personal selling are to get retailers to carry products (push strategy) and consumers to purchase products (pull strategy).

Personal selling represents a unique element in the promotion mix because it involves personal interaction with the target audience rather than mass communication to thousands or millions of consumers. The definition of personal selling reflects this important distinction between personal selling and the other promotion tools. **Personal selling** is a form of person-to-person communication in which a salesperson works with prospective buyers and attempts to influence their purchase needs in the direction of his or her company's products or services.

All of the advantages of personal selling described in Table 11.5 make it an attractive promotional tool, so the ability to use personal selling to develop long-term relationships with consumers is becoming more and more important to sports marketers. In fact, building long-term relationships with consumers has become one of the critical issues for marketers in the 1990s.[18] Formally, **relationship marketing** is the process of creating, maintaining, and enhancing strong, value-laden relationships with customers and other stakeholders.[19]

As Kotler and Armstrong point out, the key premise of relationship marketing is that building strong economic and social ties with valued customers, distributors, dealers, and suppliers leads to long-term profitable transactions. Many sports organizations are realizing that it is cheaper to foster and maintain strong relationships with existing customers rather than find new customers or fight the competition for a stagnant consumer base.

Two examples of building relationships with consumers of sport were described in a recent article entitled "Pursuing Relationships in Professional Sport."[20] In the first example, a promotion was developed by the Pittsburgh Pirates and Giant Eagle Supermarkets. The basic premise of the promotion was that fans could earn discounts and

table 11.5

Benefits of Personal Selling

- Personal selling allows the salesperson immediately to adapt the message he or she is presenting based on feedback received from the target audience
- Personal selling allows the salesperson to communicate more information to the target audience than does other forms of promotion. Moreover, complex information can be explained by the salesperson
- Personal selling greatly increases the likelihood of the target audience paying attention to the message. It is difficult for the target audience to escape the message because communication is person-to-person
- Personal selling greatly increases the chances of developing a long-term relationship with consumers, due to the frequent person-to-person communication

special offers at Pirates' games by participating in the Giant Eagle preferred shoppers program. For example, fans with an Advantage Card (given to program participants) were offered discounted ballpark meals for a month, half-price tickets to five games throughout the season, and discounts on Pirates' merchandise. The relationship-building program was deemed successful by the Pirates, Giant Eagle, and the fans.

Another relationship-building effort was designed for the fans of the San Diego Padres. The program, initiated in the 1996 season and called the Compadres Club, rewarded fans for attending predetermined numbers of games. In addition, the fans could receive frequency points based on player performance. Ultimately, fans could redeem their frequency points for Padres merchandise, posters, and dinners. For example, the top earners receive an authentic baseball bat autographed by a Padres player and presented on the field at a special pregame ceremony. More than 50,000 fans enrolled in the program's initial year, and the Padres gathered a wealth of information on its fans.

Although both the Pirates and the Padres have developed marketing programs to build relationships with fans, the importance of personal selling should not be overlooked. Personal selling was necessary for the Pirates to communicate the benefits of the partnership to Giant Eagle. As a result of selling a successful program to Giant Eagle, the company increased its Pirates-related marketing budget by roughly 25 percent. The Padres, armed with a database of the demographic and buying habits of its most loyal fans, will use personal selling to secure additional sponsorship and advertising dollars.

The Strategic Selling Process

Now that we have defined personal selling and discussed some of its major advantages, let us examine how the selling process operates in sports marketing. As previously discussed, sports marketers are generally concerned with selling an intangible service versus a tangible good. Most salespeople view the selling of services as a much more difficult process, because the benefits of the sports product aren't readily observable or easily communicated to the target audience. It is much easier to sell the new and improved Champagne Ti Bubble 2 Metalwood when the consumer can see the design, feel the weight of the club, and swing the club. In essence, the product sells itself. Contrast this with the sale of a luxury box to a corporation in a stadium that is yet to be built. Selling this sports product is dependent on communicating both the tangible and intangible benefits of the box to the prospective buyer. In addition to the problems associated with selling a service versus a good, the sale of many sports products require several people to give their approval before the sale is complete. This factor also makes the selling process more complex.

In the everchanging world of sports marketing, the "good ol' boy" approach to selling is no longer valid. To be more effective and efficient in today's competitive environment, a number of personal selling strategies have been developed. One process, developed by Robert Miller and Stephen Heiman, is called **strategic selling**.[21]

Miller and Heiman suggest that the first step in any strategic selling process is performing an analysis of your current position. In this instance, position is described as understanding your personal strengths and weaknesses as well as the opportunities and threats that are present in the selling situation. In essence, the salesperson is constructing a mini-SWOT analysis. Questions regarding how prospective clients feel about you as a salesperson, how they feel about your products and services, who the competition is, and how they are positioned must all be addressed at the initial stages of the strategic selling process.

Good salespeople realize that they must adapt their current position for every account before they can be successful. In order to change this position, six elements in the strategic selling process must be considered in a systematic and interactive fashion. These elements, which must be understood for successful sales, include buying influences, red flags, response modes, win-results, the sales funnel, and the ideal customer profile. Let us take a brief look at how these elements work together in the strategic selling process.

Buying Influences

A complex sale was earlier defined as one where multiple individuals are involved in the buying process. This is true with large organizations considering a sponsorship proposal or families considering the purchase of exercise equipment for a new workout facility in their home. One of the first steps in the strategic sales process is to identify all of the individuals involved in the sale and to determine their buying roles.

Roles are patterns of behavior expected by people in a given position. Miller and Heiman believe that there are generally four critical buying roles that must be understood in a complex sale (no matter how many people play these roles). The **economic buying role** is a position that governs final approval to buy and that can say yes to a sale when everyone else says no, and visa versa. The **user buying role** makes judgments about the potential impact of your product/service on their job performance. These individuals will also supervise and/or use the product, so they want to know "what the product/service will do for them." The **technical buying role** screens out possible suppliers on the basis of meeting a variety of technical specifications that have been determined in advance by the organization. The technical buyers also serve as gatekeepers, who screen out potential suppliers on the basis of failing to meet the stated specifications. Finally, the **coach's role** is to act as a guide for the salesperson making the sale. The coach is a valuable source of information about the organization and can lead you to the other buying influences. As Miller and Heiman point out, identifying the individuals playing the various roles is the foundation of the strategic selling process.

Red Flags

Once the individuals have been identified, the next step in the strategic selling process is to look for red flags, or things that can threaten a complex sale. Red flags symbolize those strategic areas that can require further attention in order to avoid mistakes in positioning. In addition, red flags can be used to capitalize on an area of strength. Some of the red flags that can threaten a complex sale include either missing or uncertain information, uncontacted buying influences, or reorganization. For example, any uncontacted buying influences is considered a threat to the sale. These uncontacted buying influences are analogous to uncovered bases in baseball. Teams cannot be fielded or successful when there is no shortstop or catcher. Likewise, a sale cannot be successful until all the relevant players have been contacted.

Response Modes

After the buyer(s) have been targeted and you have correctly positioned your products/services by identifying red flags, the next step in the strategic selling process is to determine the buyer's reaction to the given sales situation. These varying reactions are categorized in four response modes. These modes include the growth mode, trouble mode, even keel mode, and overconfident mode.

The **growth mode** is characterized by organizations who perceive a discrepancy between their current state and their ideal state in terms of some goal (e.g., sales or profits). In other words, the organization needs to produce a higher quality sports product or put more people in the seats in order to grow. In this situation, the probability of a sale is high.

The second response mode is known as the **trouble mode**. When an organization is falling short of expectations, it is in the trouble mode. Here again, there is a discrepancy between the current and ideal states. In the growth mode the organization is going to improve upon an already good situation. However, the trouble mode indicates that the buyer is experiencing difficulties. In either case, the potential for a sale is high.

The **even keel mode** presents a more difficult case for the salesperson. As the name implies, there is no discrepancy between the ideal and current results and therefore, the likelihood of a sale is low. The probability of a sale can be enhanced if the salesperson can demonstrate that a discrepancy actually exists, the buyer sees growth or trouble coming or there is pressure from another buying influence.

The final response mode is termed **overconfident**. Overconfidence is generally the toughest mode to overcome from the salesperson's perspective in that the buyers believe things are too good to be true. Just think about individual athletes or teams who are overconfident. Invariably they lose because of their false sense of superiority. Organizations that are overconfident are resistant to change because they are exceeding their goals (or at least they think so), so sales are difficult. Major League Baseball did nothing to bring back fans after the disasterous strike of 1994 and 1995. After all, attendance and licensing revenue had been running at peak levels before the strike. As a result of their overconfidence and failure to act, MLB is still trying to figure out how to recapture their lost fan base.

In this stage of the strategic sales process, the response mode of the organization should be analyzed. In addition, each of the buying influences should be examined to determine their perception of the current situation. By analyzing the buying influences and their perceptions, the salesperson is in a position to successfully adapt his or her approach to meet the needs of each buying influence and each customer.

Win-Results

Much of sports marketing today is based on the premise of strategic partnerships. The same is true for the strategic sales process. In strategic partnerships, the sales process produces satisfied customers, long-term relationships, repeat business, and good referrals. To achieve these outcomes, the salesperson must look at clients as partners rather than competition that must be beaten.

Miller and Heiman define the **win-results** concept in the strategic selling process as an objective result that gives one or more of the buying influences a personal win. The key to this definition is understanding the importance of both wins and results. A result is the impact of the salesperson's product or service on one or more of the client's business objectives. Results are usually tangible, quantifiable, and affect the entire organization. Wins, on the other hand, are the fulfillment of a promise made to oneself. Examples of personal wins for the potential client include gaining recognition within the organization, increasing responsibility and authority, and/or enhancing self-esteem. It is important to realize that wins are subjective, intangible, and do not benefit all the people in the organization the same way.

The Sales Funnel

The sales funnel is another key element in the strategic sales process. This is a tool that is used to organize all potential clients, as opposed to developing a means for understanding an individual client. Basically, the sales funnel is a model that is used to organize clients so that salespeople might organize their efforts in the most efficient and effective manner. After all, allocating time and setting priorities are two of the most challenging tasks in personal selling.

The sales funnel divides clients into three basic levels—above the funnel, in the funnel, and the best few. Potential clients exist above the funnel if data (e.g., a call from the prospective client wanting information or acquiring information from personal sources) suggests that there may be a possible fit between the salesperson's products or services and the needs of the potential client. The salesperson's emphasis at this level is to gather information and then develop and qualify prospects.

Potential clients are then filtered to the next level of the sales funnel. If clients are placed in the funnel (rather than above it), then the possibility of a sale has been verified. Verification occurs once a buying influence has been contacted and indicates that the organization is in either a growth or trouble response mode. Remember that these two response modes represent ideal conditions for a sale to occur.

When all the buying influences have been identified, red flags have been eliminated, and win-results have been addressed, sales prospects can be moved from in the funnel to the "best few." At this final level of the sales funnel, the sale is expected to happen roughly 90 percent of the time.

Ideal Customers

The ideal customer concept in strategic selling extends the notion of the sales funnel. In this case, all potential customers outside the funnel are evaluated against the hypothetical "ideal customer." The strategic sales process is based on the belief that every sale is not a good sale. The ideal customer profile is constructed to cut down on the unrealistic prospects that shouldn't be in the sales funnel in the first place.

When constructing the ideal customer profile, the salesperson must judge each prospect with respect to organizational demographics, psychographics, and corporate culture. Current prospects can then be evaluated against the ideal customer profile to determine whether or not additional time and energy should be invested.

Sales Promotions

Another promotion mix element that communicates to large audiences is sales promotions. **Sales promotions** are a variety of short-term, promotional activities that are designed to stimulate immediate product demand. A recent Pizza Hut sales promotion illustrates how a simple game promotion can impact short-term sales. The promotional idea was that every quarterback sack tallied by the Baltimore Raven's defense would result in $1 off a pizza. What sounded like a great idea turned into a relative nightmare, as the Ravens recorded nine sacks on that day, turning the cost of a large pizza to a paltry $1.69. Pizza Hut stores in the Baltimore area were swamped with some consumers waiting as long as three hours to cash in on the deal.[22]

The sales promotions used in sports marketing come in all shapes and sizes. Think about some of the sales promotions that you may be familiar with. Examples might include the Bud Bowl; Straight-A Night at the ballpark; a lifesize, cutout figure of Shaquille O'Neal placed inside Taco Bell restaurants; coupons for reduced green fees at public golf courses; a sweepstakes to win a free trip to the SuperBowl; a mail-in for Campbell's Soup "Stars on Ice" soup bowl; and many others.

As stated in the definition, all forms of sales promotions are designed to increase short-term sales. Additional objectives may include increasing brand awareness, broadening distribution channels, reminding consumers about the offering, or inducing trial to win new customers. To accomplish these objectives, sports marketers use a variety of sales promotion tools.

Premiums

Premiums are probably the sales promotion technique most associated with traditional sports marketing. **Premiums** are items given away with the sponsors product as part of the sales promotion. Baseball cards, NASCAR model car replicas, water bottles, hats, refrigerator magnets, posters, and almost anything else imaginable have been given away at sporting events. While premiums are often given away to spectators at events, they can also be associated with other sporting promotions. For example, *Sports Illustrated* magazines gives away hats, T-shirts, and videos to induce potential consumers to subscribe. In another example, NHL Mastercard is giving away a hat with the logo of the fan's favorite team for opening a line of credit.

Although premiums can bring people to games who would not otherwise attend, they can also have negative consequences and must be carefully planned. In the now defunct World Hockey Association (WHA), the Philadelphia Blazers handed out souvenir pucks at the first home game. Unfortunately, the game had to be postponed because the ice was deemed unfit for skating. When the Blazer's Derek Sanderson announced the game cancellation to the crowd at center ice, he was pelted with the pucks.[23] In a similar scenario, the LA Dodgers had to forfeit a game because fans began throwing baseballs (that they had been given) onto the field, endangering players and other fans. The Dodgers can also be used to illustrate the height of premium marketing. In 1984, the Los Angeles Olympic Games created a regionwide craze for pin collecting. Sensing the "legs" of this mania, the Dodgers created six pin-give-away nights at their stadium, Chavez Ravine. They picked games that would typically have low attendance. The result was that all six of these games sold out on the strength of a $.60 per unit collector's pin!

Contests and Sweepstakes

Sweepstakes and contests are another sales promotional tool used by sports marketers to generate awareness and interest among consumers. Contests are competitions that award prizes on the basis of contestants' skills and ability, whereas sweepstakes are games of chance or luck. As with any sales promotion, the sports marketing manager must attempt to integrate the contest or sweepstakes with the other promotion mix elements and keep the target market in mind.

One of the classic contests sponsored by the NFL was the punt, pass, and kick competition. In this competition, young athletes competed for a chance to appear on the finals of nationally televised NFL games, making the NFL the winner for promoting youth sports. Other contests have capitalized on the growing popularity of rotisserie sports. Dugout Derby, Pigskin Playoff, and Fairway Golf are all examples of "rotisserie" contests conducted via toll free numbers where fans could earn prizes for choosing the best fantasy team or athletes. In return, marketers capture a rich database of potential consumers.[24]

Diet Coke is promoting a chance to win a golfing trip for four to the Hawaiian Islands. Other sweepstakes are taking advantage of the Internet and its growing audience. For example, Speedstick is offering sports fans a chance to win two NHL season tickets for their favorite team. The sweepstakes is being promoted through the ESPN Web site, and the only information required to win this prize is a name and e-mail address. Again, the brand managers for Speedstick are collecting a database of potential consumers of their product by running this sales promotion. The typical by-product of this database would be a bounceback trial offer or a high-value coupon mailed to respondents.

Sampling

One of the most effective ways of inducing customers to try new products that are being introduced is **sampling**. Unfortunately, it is very difficult to give away a small portion of a sporting event. However, sports have been known to put on exhibitions to give consumers a "taste" for the game. Squash demonstration matches have been held in the middle of New York's Grand Central Station, attracting thousands of fans who would have never otherwise been exposed to the sport. The Olympics, of course, uses demonstration sports such as roller hockey and Tae Kwon Do to provide a "sample" of the action to spectators. If fan interest is high enough (i.e., attendance), the sport can then become a medal sport in the next Olympiad.

Point-of-Purchase Displays

Point-of-Purchase, or **P-O-P displays** have long been used by marketers to attract consumers' attention to a particular product or retail display area. These displays or materials, such as brochures, cut-outs, and banners, are most commonly used to communicate price reductions or other special offers to consumers. For instance, tennis racquet manufacturers, such as Prince, design huge tennis racquets, which are then displayed in the storefronts of many tennis retail shops to catch the attention of consumers.

Coupons

Another common sales promotion tool is the coupon. **Coupons** are certificates that generally offer reductions in price for sports products. Coupons may appear in print advertisements, as part of the product's package, inserted within the product packaging, or be mailed to consumers. Although coupons have been found to induce short-term sales, there are disadvantages. For instance, some marketers feel that continual coupon use can detract from the image of the product in the mind of consumers. In addition, most coupon redemption is done by consumers who already use the product, therefore limiting the use of coupons to attract new customers.

Public Relations

The final element in the promotional mix that we will discuss is public relations. Quite often, public relations gets confused with other promotional mix elements. Public relations is often mistaken for publicity. This is an easy mistake to make because the goals of public relations and publicity are to provide communication that will enhance the image of the sports entity (athlete, team, or league). Before we make a distinction between public relations and publicity, let us define public relations. **Public relations** is the element of the promotional mix that identifies, establishes, and maintains mutually beneficial relationships between the sports organizations and the various publics on which its success or failure depends.

Within the definition of public relations, reference is made to the "various publics" with which the sports organization interacts. Brooks divides these publics into the external publics, which are outside of the immediate control of sports marketers, and the internal publics, which are more directly controlled by sports marketers. The external publics include the community (city and state officials, community members, corporations, and so on), sanctioning bodies (e.g., NCAA), intermediary publics (sports marketing agencies), and competition (other sports or entertainment choices). The internal publics, such as volunteers, employees, suppliers, athletes, and spectators are associated with manufacturing, distributing, and consuming the sport itself.[25]

Sports marketers have a variety of public relations tools with which they can communicate with the internal and external publics. The choice of tools depends on the public relations objective, the targeted audience, and how public relations is being integrated into the overall promotional plan. These tools and techniques include generating publicity (news releases, press conferences) participating in community events, producing written materials (annual report, press guides), and even lobbying (e.g., personal selling necessary for stadium location decisions).[26]

One of the most important and widely used public relations tools is publicity. Publicity is the generation of news in the broadcast or print media about a sports product. The news about a sports product is most commonly disseminated to the various sports publics through news releases and/or press conferences. Although public relations efforts are managed by the sports organization, publicity can sometimes come from external sources. As such, publicity might not always enhance the image of the sports product. Because publicity is often outside the control of the sports organization, it is seen as a highly credible source of communication. Information that is coming from "unbiased" sources, such as magazines, newspaper articles, or the televised news, is perceived to be more trustworthy.

In addition to publicity, another powerful public relations tool used to enhance the sports organization's image is **community involvement**. Recently, a study was conducted to determine what, if anything, professional sports organizations are doing in the area of community relations. The survey specifically examined the NBA, NHL, NFL, and MLB to determine how they are involved in community relations and how important community relations is to their overall marketing program. All of the responding teams indicated that they were involved in some sort of community programs, with the most common form of community involvement being (1) sponsoring public programs (e.g., food and toy drives, medical programs and services, auctions and other fundraisers) (2) requiring time commitment from all of the sports organizations employees (3) partially funding programs and (4) providing personnel at no charge. Interestingly, the study found no differences among the importance of community relations by type of league. In other words, the NBA, NHL, NFL, and MLB are all equally involved in community relations.[27]

There are a variety of public relations techniques that can help achieve public relations and promotion objectives. When developing an integrated marketing communications strategy, sports marketers need to know how to coordinate public relations efforts with the other promotional mix tools. Additionally, sports marketers must understand how to best synthesize each of the public relations tools. The follow example illustrates how Quaker State planned, implemented, and evaluated an integrated public relations and sponsorship plan. As you read, pay special attention to how the public relations tools were carefully blended to achieve Quaker State's objective of establishing a mutually beneficial relationship within the Dallas–Fort Worth community.

quaker state long drive competition

In March 1996, Quaker State (QS) moved its headquarters to Irving, Texas, a suburb between the cities of Dallas–Fort Worth. To quickly establish the company in its new community, Ketchum Associates, the PR firm for Quaker State, suggested that QS participate in the Byron Nelson Golf Classic because it is a major national event in Dallas–Fort Worth and also a huge charity event. Because they were so late to the game, all of the prime sponsorships were purchased months before. And even the minor ones that were still available were far too expensive for QS.

QS needed a quick, low-budget, and high-impact alternative. With this in mind, Ketchum convinced the Salesmanship Club (the charity

(continued)

sponsor of the Byron Nelson) to admit an entirely new category for corporate sponsorships—a longest drive competition, or rather, the "Quaker State Long Drive" (QSLD). This would be a first-of-its-kind event during a PGA Tour tournament. The QSLD, which linked a QS product benefit with the obvious golf interpretation, generated extensive local and national media coverage for QS.

Public Relations Objective

To quickly establish QS as a good corporate citizen within its new community, a low-budget, high-profile community effort was devised. Target audiences included the Dallas–Fort Worth business community, event audience, QS employees, and potential buyers of QS products. The more specific objectives included:

- Participating in a high-profile, cost-effective local event to increase community awareness about QS's presence in Dallas–Fort Worth
- Creating a QS-owned "event within an event" that would generate coverage about the company
- Increasing newsworthiness of QS's participation by including a donation to charities identified by players winning the QSLD competition

Research identified the annual Byron Nelson Golf Classic because of its high profile as a Dallas–Fort Worth (DFW) community event (it is the largest charity tournament on the PGA tour) and because it could reach the target audiences quickly and efficiently. Research also determined that a long-drive contest had never been held during the PGA Tournament. This led to the creation of the QSLD, an event-within-an-event that QS could own, one that would separate the company from other tournament sponsors.

The QSLD concept combined QS, famous for motor oil and other auto products, with a long-drive competition, which helped the company drive a subtle product message. The QSLD concept was simple for all parties to understand, and the novelty of a long-drive competition in a PGA Tour event generated strong interest from the players and media.

Implementing the Public Relations Plan

Ketchum developed a three-phase program that would generate coverage about the QSLD before, during, and after the tournament. This included a press conference with tournament namesake Byron Nelson, on-site interviews with the distance measuring crew, and daily updates about the winner of the QSLD competition. The activities were executed as follows:

Pre-Event Publicity:

- Ketchum contacted DFW print and broadcast media and began working with media on-site to create excitement about the first-ever long-drive competition in a PGA Tour event
- Coordinated inclusion of QSLD in *Dallas Morning News* pre-event special section about the Byron Nelson
- Scheduled media interviews for local television crews with the distance measuring crew on the 16th hole as they prepared for the tournament
- Distributed media alert regarding press conference to announce QS's sponsorship of the Nelson and the QSLD competition

Event Publicity:

- Coordinated a press conference at the tournament site with golfing legend Byron Nelson and QS Chairman Herb Baum, who announced the company's sponsorship and presented a $10,000 check to Nelson
- Distributed alerts about the QSLD and an advisory regarding the $10,000 check presentation to key DFW and on-site media
- During the tournament, monitored the progress at the QSLD hole and provided media with periodic updates of players' performances

- At the end of each day, developed a release announcing the winner of that day's QSLD, and their chosen charity for the $2,500 daily donation

Post-Event Publicity:

- To wrap-up the success of the QSLD competition, Ketchum issued a final news release summarizing the daily winners and their charities, as well as the CEO's reaction to the program
- Distributed copies of the release to national sports media to generate additional coverage
- Followed-up with all of the involved media and created a videotape incorporating all of the television coverage for QS to use internally as an example of how to leverage a corporate sponsorship successfully.

Evaluation

Overall results By sponsoring the sixteenth hole as the QSLD hole during the 1996 Byron Nelson Golf Classic, the company achieved and surpassed its objective of increasing regional awareness of the company's new presence in Irving, Texas. In addition to media coverage on every local television station and five mentions in the *Dallas Morning News*, the QSLD was mentioned on *ABC Sports* and USA Network coverage of the Byron Nelson.

Media results The QSLD winner was announced in every day's Byron Nelson section of the *Dallas Morning News*. Each local network affiliate covered the QSLD (either at the press conference, in features about the distance measuring crew, or interviews with players about their performance). Also, the competition was used in portions of two national network sports shows—on *ABC Sports* and USA Network Sports, according to producers. Coverage of the QSLD competition (not including the USA Network story) totaled over 8.5 million impressions nationwide, and more than 6.5 million locally.

In addition, the event was received well by the golfers—as evidenced by the humor of Corey Pavin, Justin Leonard, and the other pros who joked about their performances at the QSLD hole. The final results were so positive that Ketchum suggested that QS trademark the long-drive competition for future PGA Tour events.

Source: "Quaker State Long Drive Competition," PR Central<http://www.prcentral.com/c97longdrive.htm>.

SUMMARY

(C) hapter 11 focuses on gaining a better understanding of the various promotional mix elements. Advertising is one of the most visible and critical promotional mix elements. Although most of us associate advertising with developing creative slogans and jingles, there is a systematic process for designing effective advertisements. Developing an advertising campaign consists of a series of five interrelated steps, which include formulating ad objectives, designing an ad budget, making creative decisions, choosing a media strategy, and evaluating the advertisement.

Advertising objectives and budgeting techniques are similar to those discussed in chapter 10 for the broader promotion planning process. Advertising objectives are sometimes categorized as either direct or indirect. Direct advertising objectives, such as advertising by sports organizations to end user and sales promotion advertising, are designed to stimulate action among consumers of sport. Alternatively, the goal of indirect objectives is to make consumers aware, enhance the image of the sport, or provide information to consumers. After objectives have been determined, budgets for the advertising campaign are considered. Budget techniques, such as competitive parity, objective and task, arbitrary allocation, and percentage of sales, are commonly used by advertisers.

Once the objectives and budget have been established, the creative process is considered. The creative process identifies the ideas and the concept of the advertisement. In order to develop the concept for the advertisement, benefits of the sports product must be identified, ad appeals (e.g., health, emotional, fear, sex, pleasure) are designed, and advertising execution decisions (e.g., comparative advertisements, slice of life, scientific) are made. After creative decisions are crafted, the next phase of the advertising campaign is to design media strategy. Media strategy includes decisions about the what medium (e.g., radio, television, Internet) will be most effective and how to best schedule the chosen media.

Another communications tool that is part of the promotional mix is personal selling. Personal selling is unique in that person-to-person communication is required rather than mass communication. In other words, a salesperson must deliver the message face-to-face to the intended target audience rather than through some nonpersonal medium (e.g., a magazine). Although there are many advantages to personal selling, perhaps none is greater than the ability to use personal selling to develop long-term relationships with customers.

In today's competitive sports marketing environment, a number of strategies have been developed to maximize personal selling effectiveness. One process, designed by Miller and Heiman, is called the strategic selling process and consists of six elements. The elements that must be considered for successful selling include buying influences, red flags, response modes, win-results, the sales funnel, and the ideal customer profile.

Sales promotions are another element in the promotional mix that are designed primarily to stimulate consumer demand for products One of the most widely used forms of sales promotion in sports marketing includes premiums, or items that are given away with the core product being purchased. In addition, contest and sweepstakes, free samples, point-of-purchase displays, and coupons are forms of sales promotion that often are integrated into the broader promotional mix.

A final promotional mix element considered in chapter 11 is public, or community relations. Public relations is the element of the promotional mix that identifies, establishes, and maintains mutually beneficial relationships between the sports organization and the various publics on which its success or failure depends. These publics include the community, sanctioning bodies, intermediary publics, and competition. Other publics include volunteers, employees, suppliers, participants, and spectators. The tools with which messages are communicated to the various publics include generating publicity, participating in community events, producing written materials such as annual reports and press releases, and lobbying.

KEY TERMS & CONCEPTS

advertising	advertising objectives	creative decisions
advertising appeal	buying influences	direct objectives
advertising budgeting	comparative advertisements	emotional appeals
advertising execution	coupons	fear appeals

health appeals	premiums	sex appeals
ideal customer	profit appeals	slice-of-life advertisements
indirect objectives	promotional mix elements	stadium signage
media scheduling	public relations	strategic selling process
media strategy	response modes	sweepstakes and contests
one-sided versus two-sided	sales funnel	testimonials
personal selling	sales promotion	win-results
pleasure appeals	sampling	
P-O-P displays	scientific advertisements	

REVIEW QUESTIONS

1. What are the major steps in developing an advertising campaign?
2. Explain direct advertising objectives versus indirect advertising objectives.
3. Describe the creative decision process. What are the three outcomes of the creative process?
4. Discuss, in detail, the major advertising appeals used by sports marketers. Provide at least one example of each type of advertising appeal.
5. What are the executional formats commonly used in sports marketing advertising?
6. Comment on the advantages and disadvantages of using athlete endorsers in advertising.
7. What two decisions do advertisers make in developing a media strategy? What are the four basic media scheduling alternatives? Provide an example of each type of media scheduling.
8. Discuss the strengths and weaknesses of the alternative forms of advertising available to sports marketers.
9. When is personal selling used by sports marketers? Describe, in detail, the steps in the strategic selling process.
10. Describe the various forms of sales promotion available to sports marketers.

EXERCISES

1. Design a creative advertising strategy to increase participation in Little League Baseball.
2. Design a survey instrument to assess the source credibility of 10 professional athletes (of your choice) and administer the survey to 10 individuals. Which athletes have the highest levels of credibility, and why?

3. Attend a professional or collegiate sporting event and describe all of the forms of advertising you observe. Which forms of advertising do you feel are particularly effective, and why?

4. Visit a sporting goods retailer and describe all of the sales promotion tools that you observe. Which forms of sales promotion do you feel are particularly effective, and why?

5. Interview the director/manager of ticket sales for a professional organization or collegiate sports program to determine their sales process. How closely does their sales process follow the strategic selling process outlined in the chapter?

6. Interview the marketing department (or director of community/public relations) from a professional organization or collegiate sports program to determine the extent of their community or public relations efforts. How do sports organizations decide which community events/activities to participate in?

INTERNET EXERCISES

1. Using the Internet, find two examples of advertisements for sports products that use indirect objectives and two examples of advertisements that use direct objectives.

2. Find 10 advertisements on the Internet for sports products and describe the executional format for each advertisement. Which type of execution format is most commonly used for Internet advertising?

NOTES

1. See, for example, Joel Evans and Barry Berman, *Marketing*, 6th ed. (New York: Macmillan, 1994), 610.

2. Hilary Stout, "Shedding Glitz, Lucille Roberts Gains Health-Club Niche," *The Wall Street Journal*, October 6, 1997, B1.

3. William A. Sutton, Mark A. McDonald, George R. Milne, and John Cimperman, "Creating and Fostering Fan Identification in Professional Sports," *Sport Marketing Quarterly*, vol. 6, no. 1 (1997):15–22.

4. "Nike Just Does New Slogan: 'I Can,'" ESPN SportsZone. <http://espnet.sportszone.com/other/news/971230/00514522.html>.

5. "Tiger Woods Tops Michael Jordan in Survey of Most Appealing Product Endorser." *Burns Sports Celebrity Service, Inc.* <http://www.burnssports.com/experts.htm>.

6. "Favre Estimates Drug Rehab Cost $2 Million in Endorsements." <http://www4.nando.net/newsroom/ap/.../feat/archive/082996/gbp50152.html>. (August 29, 1996).

7. Mark Hyman, "Dead Men Don't Screw Up Ad Campaigns," *Business Week*, March 10, 1997, 115.

8. Douglas M. Turco, "The Effects of Courtside Advertising on Product Recognition and Attitude Change," *Sport Marketing Quarterly*, vol. 5, no. 4 (1996): 11–15.

9. Jay Gladden, "The Ever Expanding Impact of Technology on Sport Marketing, Part II," *Sport Marketing Quarterly*, vol. 5, no. 4 (1996): 9–10.

10. Turco, 11–15.

11. George Belch and Michael Belch, *Advertising and Promotion: An Integrated Marketing Communications Perspective*, 4th ed. (New York: Irwin, McGraw-Hill, 1998), 431–434.

12. Joe Layden, "Human Billboards," *Mark McCormack's Guide to Sports Marketing*, International Sports Marketing Group, 1996, 129–136.

13. Chad Rubel, "It's Okay to Think Cheap in Starting a Net Plan," *Marketing News*, January 29, 1996, 12.

14. Jay Gladden, "Sports Market Bytes: The Ever Expanding Impact of Technology on Sport Marketing, Part I," *Sport Marketing Quarterly*, vol. 5, no. 3 (1996): 13–14.

15. Rachel Johns, "Sports Promotion & The Internet," *Cyber-Journal of Sport Marketing*. <http://www.cad.gu.edu.au/market/cv...urnal _of_sport_marketing/johns.htm>.

16. "Top Magazines by Paid Circulation: Six Month Averages Ended June 30, 1997." <http://adage.com/ns-search /datapla...3/aaaa004Chf33977&NS-doc-offset=0&>.

17. Fred Beasley, Matthew Shank, and Rebecca Ball, "Do Super Bowl Viewers Watch the Commercials," *Sport Marketing Quarterly*, forthcoming.

18. Philip Kotler and Gary Armstrong, *Marketing: An Introduction*, 4th ed., (Upper Saddle River, NJ: Prentice Hall, 1997).

19. Ibid.

20. Sean Brenner, "Pursuing Relationships in Professional Sport," *Sport Marketing Quarterly*, vol. 6, no. 2 (1997): 33–34.

21. Robert Miller and Stephen Heiman, *Strategic Selling* (New York: Warner Books, 1985).

22. "Ravens Fans Fill Up on Pizza After Great Snacks." <http://espnet.sportszone.com/nfl/news/971117/ 00457511.html>.

23. Ed Willes, "A Legacy of Slapstick and Slap Shots," *New York Times*, November 30, 1997, 33.

24. Howard Schlossberg, *Sport Marketing* (Cambridge, MA: Blackwell, 1996).

25. Christine Brooks, *Sports Marketing: Competitive Business Strategies for Sports* (Upper Saddle River, NJ: Prentice Hall, 1994).

26. William Zikmund and Michael d'Amico, *Marketing*, 4th ed., (St. Paul, MN: West, 1993).

27. Denise O'Connell, "Community Relations in Professional Sports Organizations," Unpublished Masters Thesis, The Ohio State University.

CHAPTER 12

Sponsorship Programs

After completing this chapter, you should be able to

- Comment on the growing importance of sports sponsorships as a promotion mix element

- Design a sponsorship program

- Understand the major sponsorship objectives

- Provide examples of the various costs of sponsorship

- Identify the levels of the sports event pyramid

- Evaluate the effectiveness of sponsorship programs

When Swatch signed on as official timekeeper of the 1996 Centennial Olympic Games, they knew everyone would find it hard to believe. In fact, early research showed that most consumers assumed that a competitor was the official timekeeper. Consumers remembered Swatch as an inexpensive, plastic watch with crazy designs that everyone used to wear in the mid-1980s. Swatch saw the Olympic Games as an opportunity to re-introduce the company to the public as a brand that is not only affordable and fun, but is also committed to cutting-edge technology and the utmost quality and precision.

Sponsorship Objectives

- In a sea of Olympic sponsorships, make Swatch stand out from the crowd
- Use the Olympics to remind consumers of Swatch's sense of fun, surprise, and *joie de vivre*
- Show off the technological innovations in timing Swatch brought to the Games and get consumers thinking, "If Swatch is qualified to time the Olympic Games, it must be a high-quality watch"

Strategies

Position Swatch as a Clearinghouse for Olympic Stories. Months before the Olympics began, a public relations agency retained by Swatch developed relationships with the media assigned to cover the Olympic Games. Swatch was positioned as "the place to go" to get your Olympic stories—human interest, celebrity, or technology-driven.

Execution: When the media arrived in frenzied Atlanta, the agency made their jobs easier by virtually producing stories for them (including Swatch, of course).

For newspapers and television stations from around the world, the public relations agency coordinated human interest stories on the Swatch Pavilion and the Olympic collectible craze, highlighting Swatch Olympic watches and pins.

A special opportunity was created for E! Entertainment in which Olympic gold medalist Janet Evans tried on Olympic Swatch watches and talked about what a quality watch it was to wear while she was swimming.

Months before the Olympics began, the agency positioned Swatch timing engineers as expert resources, available to thoroughly explain and demonstrate to the media how Swatch timing was improving the accuracy of the Olympic Games. During the games, the efforts paid off with feature stories in the *New York Times* and *USA Today*. When another company's scoring and results system failed, the agency made sure the media knew Swatch was still doing its job flawlessly, as reported by *NBC Nightly News* and the *Chicago Tribune*.

Utilize Swatch Olympic Legends to Communicate Key Messages. In March 1996, the agency launched the Swatch Olympic Legends Collection, 10 watches designed in collaboration with famous Olympians, including Mark Spitz, Nadia Comaneci, Dan Jansen, and Katarina Witt. Swatch had the opportunity to work with these "legends" as spokespeople, who could communicate Swatch's messages and impart the excitement, glory, and emotion of the Olympic Games.

Execution: Presenting these athletes as a media draw became another successful way to make consumers aware of Swatch's role in the games.

To introduce the Swatch Olympic Legends Collection to the media, the agency invented the "Swatch Olympic Legend Awards," a ceremony held at New York's All-Star Cafe to honor the 10 Olympians recognized with Swatch watches. Local crews, E! Entertainment, and *Extra* attended, along with the editors of almost every major fashion magazine.

On *The Oprah Winfrey Show*, a program recognized as a proven "product seller," Mark Spitz presented Oprah with his signature Swatch watch.

An exclusive opportunity was coordinated by the agency for nationally syndicated *Extra*, in which Olympic legend Nadia Comaneci surprised opening ceremonies singer and superstar Celine Dion (on-air) with a "Nadia" Swatch watch, moving Dion to tears.

Think on Your Feet; Make the Most of Every Situation. The chaotic, fast-paced, high-intensity Olympic environment is unlike anything that exists in the real world. Once the games began, it was important that the agency's two-person, on-site team keep its eye out for potential public relations opportunities and make the most of every situation that arose.

Execution: Some of Swatch's most important Olympic public relations hits can be credited to the agency's ability to turn on a dime.

Virtually overnight, the agency turned a party at the Hard Rock Cafe for Swatch guests into a media event by arranging for kids from the Swatch Olympic Youth Camp to share a special night-on-the-town with Dream Teamer Hakeem Olajuwon. Media were invited to follow the kids as they presented Hakeem with a giant Swatch watch. In addition to Hakeem, other famous Olympians and the mayor of Atlanta were captured by *Entertainment Tonight*, CNN, and 15 additional camera crews from around the world.

When Centennial Olympic Park re-opened after the tragic bombing, the agency made last-minute arrangements for Olympian Dan Jansen to hand out free ice cream to the crowds in front of the Swatch Pavilion in the park. Equally important, the agency got the media there, with *USA Today* running a photo and caption.

Sponsorship Evaluation

Media and consumers alike saw Swatch as a star performer of the Olympic Games—the *Chicago Tribune* gave Swatch a "gold medal" and called them the "surprise of these games."

The media portrayed Swatch as fun, energetic, and full of life—partying at the Hard Rock Cafe, hanging out with Celine Dion, having a ball in the Swatch Pavilion, trading Swatch pins, collecting Olympic Swatch watches, and so on. Swatch was perceived as hip and new.

Swatch timing was taken seriously by the media and lauded for the new innovations it brought to the 1996 Centennial Olympic Games.

Swatch garnered over 300 million print and electronic media impressions, including *NBC Nightly News*, E! Entertainment, *Entertainment Tonight*, *Extra*, MSNBC, Fox National Newsfeed, NBC National Newsfeed, MTV, *Good Day New York*, *Good Day Atlanta*, National Public Radio, *Seventeen*, *Men's Health*, *Self*, *USA Today*, the *Chicago Tribune*, the *Los Angeles Times*, and the *New York Times*.

Source: "Swatch: The Official Timekeeper of the Centennial Olympic Games." PR Central. <http://www.prcentral.com/c97olympic.htm>.

rowth of Sponsorship

The opening scenario is just one example of a company using sponsorship to help achieve its marketing objectives. A wide variety of organizations are realizing that sports sponsorships are a valuable way to reach new markets and retain an existing customer base. Sponsorships can increase sales, change attitudes, heighten awareness, and build and maintain relationships with consumers. It is no wonder that sponsorships became the promotional tool of choice for marketers in the 1990s. Before we turn to the growth of sponsorship as a promotional tool, let us define sponsorship.

In chapter 10, sponsorships were described as one of the elements in the promotional mix. More specifically, **sponsorship** was defined as investing in a sports entity (athlete, league, team, or event) to support overall organizational objectives, marketing goals, and/or promotional strategies.

The sponsorship investment may come in the form of monetary support and/or trade. For example, Kellogg's has agreed to a three-year deal to sponsor the British Olympic Teams. Kellogg's will supply the team with breakfast cereals, in addition to providing monetary support. In this case, Kellogg's is sponsoring the entire British Olympic team rather than individual athletes or individual sports. They do this to support their marketing objective of increasing sales of Kellogg's brand cereals in Great Britain.[1] Understanding how sponsorship can help achieve marketing goals and organizational objectives will be discussed when we look at the construction of a sponsorship plan or program. For now, let us turn our attention to the dramatic growth of sponsorship as a promotional tool.

In our brief discussion of sponsorship, we have alluded to the "dramatic growth" of sponsorship, but just how quickly is sponsorship growing? Take a look at the following facts and figures regarding sponsorship activities:

- IEG (International Events Group) estimates that $6.8 billion have been spent by companies sponsoring special events in 1998. Of this $6.8 billion, $4.56 billion (or roughly 67 percent) have been spent to sponsor sporting events.[2]
- Motor sports sponsorships totaled $998 million in 1997, making this sport first in sponsorship dollars spent. Golf, with $614 million in sponsorship, is the second highest sport for sponsorship spending.[3]
- Sponsorship growth has exceeded traditional forms of promotion. For example, in 1997, advertising expenditures grew six percent while sponsorship sales steadily grew nine percent.[4]
- In 1997, companies spent $307 million in sports sponsorships of Olympic teams and competitions according to IEG.[5] This number is projected at $396 million for 1998.
- In one of the largest single sponsorship programs, Coke spent $40 million to become the official sponsor for the 1996 Olympic Games. It is also believed that Coke spent another $500 million to carry out the activities related to being an official sponsor (e.g., advertisements, building an Olympic pavilion in Atlanta, sales promotions) in an integrated marketing communications effort.[6]
- Estimates from the Institute of Sports Sponsorship (ISS) suggest that the British sponsorship industry has been seriously undervalued in the past and may be worth up to £1 billion in 1997.[7]

Not unlike other forms of promotion, sponsorship marketing is also reaching its saturation point in the marketplace. Consumers are paying less attention to sports sponsorships as they become more the rule than the exception. Sponsorship clutter is causing businesses, such as Swatch, to design more systematic sponsorship programs that stand out in the sea of sponsorships. In addition, businesses are fighting the clutter of sponsoring mainstream sports by exploring new sponsorship opportunities (e.g.,

X-Games, women's sports, Paralympics) and by becoming more creative with existing sponsorship opportunities.

One example of a creative sponsorship approach in a traditional sports medium comes from the world of professional soccer. The pre-game event at a New York/New Jersey Metrostars MLS game was called "Rhett Harty Haircut Day" and sponsored by Conair hair care products. The event was named after the key defensive player for the team who is famous for sporting a clean-shaven head. Conair offered a free "zip" haircut to the first 200 fans, a T-shirt featuring Harty's picture on the front and a Conair logo on the back, a $2 rebate coupon for a Conair haircut kit, and a free ticket to the game. Harty also appeared at the event to sign autographs and demonstrate the product. Although the event focused on Conair's HotHead Clippers, the larger goal was to get Conair's name out to soccer fans. In addition to generating tremendous exposure for Conair, the Metrostars win by increasing attendance and fan support.[8]

The Conair/Metrostars example illustrates the nature of sponsorship. In essence, a sports sponsorship program is just another promotion mix element to be considered along with advertising, personal selling, sales promotions, and public relations. One difference, however, between sponsorship and the other promotion mix elements is that sports marketing relies heavily on developing successful sponsorship programs. In fact, sponsorship programs are so prevalent in sports marketing that the field is sometimes defined in these terms. The rest of this chapter is devoted to understanding how to develop the most effective sponsorship program.

Designing a Sports Sponsorship Program

Sports sponsorship programs come in all shapes and sizes. Following are just a few examples:

- Adam and Eve, the nation's largest mail-order marketer of adult novelties, is sponsoring NASCAR driver Richard Bailey's Late Model Stock Division Car.[9]
- AND 1 sportswear company has signed multiyear sponsorship deals with Temple University, Grambling University, George Washington University, and Rutgers University to provide uniforms, practice gear, and warm-up suits for the men's and women's basketball programs.[10]
- Albert Belle has signed a deal with Taco Bell to promote the "Belle Card," which offers Taco Bell customer discounts.[11]
- Reebok and the WNBA and the ABL have signed multiyear deals making Reebok the official footwear supplier of both women's professional basketball leagues.[12]
- Alltel, a telecommunications and information services company, signed a 10-year, $6.2 million deal to rename Jacksonville Municipal Stadium, Alltel Stadium.[13]
- Honda signed a three-year exclusive automotive sponsorship with Little League Baseball.[14]

What do each of these sponsorship examples have in common? First, they were developed as part of an integrated marketing communications approach in which sponsorship is but one element of the promotion mix. In addition, each of the sponsors has carefully chosen the best sponsorship opportunity (with individual athletes, teams, and leagues) to meet their organizational objectives and marketing goals.

In order to carefully plan sponsorship programs, a systematic process is being used by an increasing number of organizations. The process for designing a sports sponsorship program is presented in Figure 12.1. Before explaining the process, it is important to remember that sponsorship involves a marketing exchange. The sponsor benefits by receiving the right to associate with the sports entity (e.g., team or event), and the sports entity benefits from either monetary support or product being supplied by the sponsor. Because the marketing exchange involves two parties, the sponsorship process can be explored from the perspective of the sponsor (for example, Nokia) or the sports entity (for example, Sugar Bowl). We will look at the process from the viewpoint of the sponsor rather than the entity sponsored.

As shown in the model, decisions regarding the sponsorship program are not made in isolation. Rather, the sponsorship program is just one element of the broader promotional strategy. It was suggested earlier that all the elements in the promotional mix must be integrated to have the greatest and most effective promotional impact. However, sponsorship decisions influence much more than just promotion. Sponsorship decisions can impact the entire marketing mix. For example, Nike recently signed a 10-year, $200 million contract to sponsor Brazil's World Championship soccer club. This will certainly present an opportunity for Nike to design and market a number of product tie-ins (shoes and apparel) to the sponsorship.[15] There are two important things to consider before signing a sponsorship agreement: (1) all your organization is getting is the right to be called a sponsor, not a completed sponsorship plan and (2) you should spend two to three times your sponsorship fee to leverage your relationship as a sponsor—if you do not have the funds to promote, do not buy the sponsorship.

When designing the sponsorship program, the initial decisions are based on sponsorship objectives and budgets. These two elements go hand in hand. Without the

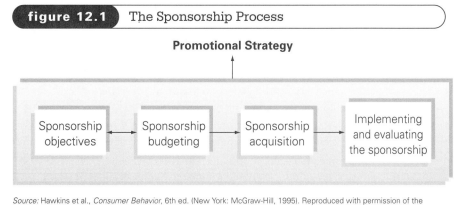

figure 12.1 The Sponsorship Process

Promotional Strategy

Sponsorship objectives → Sponsorship budgeting → Sponsorship acquisition → Implementing and evaluating the sponsorship

Source: Hawkins et al., *Consumer Behavior*, 6th ed. (New York: McGraw-Hill, 1995). Reproduced with permission of the McGraw-Hill Companies.

money, the most meaningful objectives will never be reached. Alternatively, appropriate objectives must be considered without total regard to cost. If the objectives are sound, senior-level managers will find a way to allocate the necessary monies to sponsorship.

After the objectives and budget have been agreed upon, the specific sports sponsorship opportunity is chosen from the hundreds available. For example, Pepsi receives approximately 500 sponsorship proposals each year, and Penzoil reports that they receive 200 proposals annually. Others estimate that several corporations receive over 100 sponsorship proposals each week! Regardless of the exact number, there are a wealth of sponsorship opportunities available to potential sponsors. Here's an illustration of how Aspen's Spirit of Skiing event is presenting information to potential sponsors.[16]

table 12.1

Sponsorship Opportunity

Aspen—The Spirit of Skiing: A Benefit for Gilda's Club and Aspen School of Music

Sponsorship Level	Description of Benefits
Gold Sponsor $50,000	Gold Sponsors receive VIP credentials for 10 guests, 5 Obermeyer fashion ski jackets, 5 gift bags, 10 tickets to the benefit concert, and 5 deluxe Ritz Carlton hotel rooms. Sponsor's name and logo appear on the event banners, racer bibs, publicity, and materials.
Silver Sponsor $30,000	Silver Sponsors Club receive VIP credentials for 6 guests, 3 Obermeyer fashion ski jackets, 3 gift bags, 6 tickets to the benefit concert, and 3 deluxe Ritz Carlton hotel rooms. Sponsor's name and logo appear on the event banners, racer bibs, publicity, and materials.
Bronze Sponsor $20,000	Bronze Sponsors Club receive VIP credentials for 4 guests, 2 Obermeyer fashion ski jackets, 2 gift bags, 4 tickets to the benefit concert, and 2 deluxe Ritz Carlton hotel rooms. Sponsor's name and logo appear on the event banners, racer bibs, publicity, and materials.
Official Sponsor $10,000	Official Sponsors receive VIP credentials for 2 guests, 1 Obermeyer fashion ski jacket, 1 gift bag, 2 tickets to the benefit concert, and 1 deluxe Ritz Carlton hotel room. Official Suppliers receive banners on the race course.
Individual Participant $600.00	Individuals can participate in the event in one of the following ways: 3-day lift ticket, concert ticket, or entry in Pro-Am race.
$300.00	3-day lift ticket or entry in Pro-Am race.

Source: "Aspen—The Spirit of Skiing." <http://www.aspen.com/aspenonline/d...spiritofskiing>. Courtesy of Kiki Cutter.

When choosing from among many sponsorship opportunities, three decisions must be addressed. The first decision is whether to sponsor a local, regional, national, or global event. Second, the organization must choose an athletic platform. For instance, will the organization sponsor an individual athlete, team, league, or stadium. Third, once the broad athletic platform is chosen, the organization must decide on a specific sports entity. For example, if a league is selected as the athletic platform, will the organization sponsor the WNBA, the MLS, or the NFL?

The final stage of the sports sponsorship process involves implementation and evaluation. Typically, the organization wishes to determine whether their desired sponsorship objectives have been achieved. Measuring the impact of sponsorship on awareness levels within a targeted audience is a relatively easy marketing research task. However, as the costs of sponsorships continue to increase, there is a heightened sense of accountability. In other words, organizations wish to assess the impact of sponsorship on the bottom line—sales. As Glenn Wilson, professor at Griffith University, points out, "The task of assessing the financial benefit [of sponsorship] remains a difficult one."[17]

Now that we have a rough idea of how the sponsorship process works, let us explore each stage of the sports sponsorship model in greater detail.

Sponsorship Objectives

The first stage in designing a sponsorship program is to carefully consider the sponsorship objectives. Because sponsorship is just one form of promotion, the sponsorship objectives should be linked to the broader promotional planning process and its objectives. The promotional objectives will, in turn, help achieve the marketing goals, which should stem from the objectives of the organization. These important linkages were stated in our definition of sponsorship.

Not unlike advertising objectives, sponsorship objectives can be categorized as either direct or indirect. **Direct sponsorship objectives** have a short-term impact on consumption behavior and focus on increasing sales. **Indirect objectives** are those that ultimately lead to the desired goal of enhancing sales. In other words, the sponsor has to generate awareness and create the desired image of the product before consumers purchase the product. The indirect sponsorship objectives include generating awareness, meeting and beating competition, reaching new target markets, building relationships, and improving image.[18]

One of the reasons that sponsoring sporting events has risen in popularity is that sponsorship provides so many benefits to those involved in the partnership. In other words, both the sponsor and the sports entity (event, athlete, league) gain from this win–win partnership. Let us look at some of the primary objectives of sponsorship, from the sponsor's perspective.

Awareness

One of the most basic objectives of any sponsor is to generate awareness or raise levels of awareness of its products and services, product lines, or corporate name. Sponsors must understand which level to target (i.e., individual product versus company name) based on the broader promotional or marketing strategy. For a new company or product, sponsorship is an important way to generate widespread awareness in a short period of time.

From the event or sports entity's perspective, having a large corporate sponsor will certainly heighten the awareness of the event. The corporate sponsor will design a promotional program around the event to make consumers aware of the sponsor's relationship with the event. The corporate sponsor will also want to ensure that their promotional mix elements are integrated. In other words, advertising, sponsorship of the event, and sales promotion will all work in concert to achieve the desired promotional objectives. However, a recent study conducted by Hoek, Gendall, Jeffcoat, and Orsman[19] found that sponsorship generated higher levels of awareness than advertising. In addition, sponsorship led to the association of a wider range of attributes with the brand being promoted than did advertising.

Competition

Another primary objective of sponsorship is to stamp out or meet any competitive threats. Many corporate sponsors claim that they are not that interested in sponsorship opportunities, but that they cannot afford not to do so. In other words, if they do not make the sponsorship investment, their competitors will do so. Sponsorship is thought of as a preemptive tactic that will reduce competitive threat. Reebok's increased sponsorship of the 1996 Olympic Games was based on its sagging performance behind its competitor Nike.[20] Coke sponsors virtually every national governing body of U.S. Olympic sports. They promote only a handful of these sports, but their sponsorship of the others effectively keeps archenemy Pepsi out of any chance of ambushing their Olympic efforts.

Unfortunately, the sponsoring company can still be harmed by competitors who use ambush marketing tactics. **Ambush marketing** is a planned effort (campaign by an organization) to associate themselves indirectly with an event in order to gain at least some of the recognition and benefits that are associated with being an official sponsor.[21] One of the earliest examples of ambush marketing at its finest was Nike's 1984 "I Love LA" marketing campaign. Although not an official Olympic sponsor, this campaign inextricably tied Nike to the city and event. Most sports marketers consider this ambush campaign the catalyst for the steady rise in ambush marketing practices.[22]

Today, many examples of ambush marketing exist. However, the Olympic Games seems to be the "sporting event of choice" for ambush marketers. Consider these 1996 Olympic ambush moments:[23]

- The U.S. Postal Service wanted to establish full-service post offices within the Olympic areas, but was denied since UPS was the official overnight postal carrier of the games. In another ambush attempt on UPS, Federal Express ran advertisements promoting its official sponsorship of the U.S. Men's Basketball Dream Team.

- Nike (which, incidentally, has its own director of ambush marketing) advertised its new shoes during a telecast of the Olympic Games by purchasing spots on NBC affiliates rather than the network. Nike also produced a commercial rather than informational Web site (Nike@Lanta) that went uncontested by ACOG. Finally,

Nike's name and logo were erected on a building overlooking Atlanta's Olympic Park. What is amazing is that the building was constructed specifically for the purpose of ambush marketing.

Do ambush marketing tactics work for organizations that do not want to pay the cost for official Olympic sponsorship? The answer to this question seems to be an overwhelming yes. Studies have shown that most consumers cannot correctly identify the true Olympic sponsors. Let us look at some of the evidence that supports the success of ambush marketing techniques.[24]

- 64 of 138 total respondents believed AT&T was the official long-distance supplier to the 1994 Summer Olympic Games, while 70 indicated that ambushers Sprint and MCI were the official suppliers

- 59 respondents believed Jeep was the official auto of the 1994 Summer Olympic Games, while 41 indicated that ambusher Chevrolet was the official automobile

- 68 percent of respondents incorrectly judged Wendy's to be the official sponsor versus 55 percent of consumers who correctly identified McDonald's

- Although 72 percent of respondents correctly identified Visa as the official sponsor, 52 percent incorrectly thought the sponsor was American Express.

Because ambush marketing tactics are effective and consumers do not really care (only 20 percent of consumers said that they were angered by corporations engaging in ambush marketing), it appears that there is no end in sight for this highly competitive tactic. However, some preventative measures are taking place to protect the investments of the actual sponsors of the Olympic Games.

ACOG contracted with an advertising intelligence firm to monitor all television and radio advertisements for ambush attempts. In addition, ACOG sent 900 letters to corporate executives informing them of their intent to identify and remove ambush attempts. If a company was found to have engaged in ambush attempts, ACOG threatened to take out full-page advertisements in national newspapers to embarrass the offending organization.[25]

New legislation is continuing to emerge to prevent ambush marketing. In Australia, new anti-ambush legislation was recently announced by the Federal Minister for Sport, Territories, and Local Government to protect sponsors and organizers of the 2000 Summer Games in Sydney. Moreover, the Sydney Olympic Games Organizing Committee (SOGOC) launched a $2 million dollar advertising campaign against ambushers. The advertisements will feature six Olympians and highlight the contributions made to the games by the official sponsors.[26] Hopefully, the advertising campaign will create awareness and recognition of the real sponsors.

Reaching Target Markets

Reaching new target markets is another primary objective of sponsorship programs. One of the unique features and benefits of sponsorship as a promotional medium is its ability to reach people who are attracted to sports entities because they share a common interest. Therefore, sporting events represent a natural forum for psychographic segmentation of consumers. That is, reaching consumers with similar activities, interests, and opinions (AIOs). Steve Goldstein, vice president of public relations and event marketing for IDV/Hublein, sums it up nicely by saying, "Sports marketing [sponsorships] allows us to reach our consumers where they live and play. Used effectively, it can reach more efficiently than traditional advertising."

Consider the following examples of how sponsors have attempted to reach new and sometimes difficult to capture audiences: The X-Games represent a perfect opportunity to reach Generation Xers, a target market that is "difficult to reach through traditional media." Another target market that has been neglected includes the millions of disabled Americans.

disabled athletes go for sponsorship gold

Scot Hollonbeck remembers the days when, as a young wheelchair racer, his primary sponsor was a funeral home. "I'd wear his patch in the race," Mr. Hollonbeck says of the funeral-home director. "He'd pay gas money" for travel. Today, marketing opportunities for elite disabled athletes like Mr. Hollonbeck are beginning, however slowly, to move beyond the local businesses. Corporate endorsements, speaking fees, prize money, and more are making their way into disabled sports. Perhaps most important, television is giving the movement some much-needed exposure.

If any single event, however, could catapult Mr. Hollonbeck and his colleagues into the mainstream, it might be this 10-day extravaganza—the 1996 Paralympic Games, an Olympics for disabled athletes.

Highlights of the event, to be held largely in Atlanta's Olympics venues, will be carried on CBS and cable television outlets. Attendance, fueled by a flashy opening ceremony hosted by Christopher Reeve, was estimated to hit 1.5 million, which made it the world's best attended spectator sporting event in 1996 after the Olympics.

Begun in 1960 as an event "parallel" to the Olympics, the Paralympics have blossomed into a major competition, drawing some 3,500 participants—including blind cyclists, para-

plegic power lifters, and amputee runners—from about 100 nations competing in 17 sports. For these games, organizers have tried to carry things one step further, converting them from a mostly charity event to a full-fledged marketing opportunity. Twenty-seven companies, including Coca-Cola, IBM, Motorola, and Turner Broadcasting, have signed up for sponsorships and supplier arrangements for between $2 million and $6 million.

"The way we're presenting the movement is entirely new," says Andy Fleming, chief executive of the Atlanta Paralympic Organizing Committee. Sponsors say their decision to include the event in their marketing program is no longer solely a matter of altruism. "It is a serious marketing opportunity," says Paul Harman, who heads BellSouth Corp.'s Olympics and Paralympics sponsorship programs. The latter event, he acknowledges, is not "nearly as mature as the Olympic marketing opportunity; they're on the up-and-coming track." But with millions of Americans considered to be disabled, he adds, "That is a big market to look at. It certainly gets our attention."

BellSouth—which paid an estimated $4 million for its sponsorship and is providing goods for the event—is marketing its participation in television advertisements and signs in the Olympic stadium. The company is also spon-

(continued)

soring the Paralympics' medal ceremonies.

"Without a doubt, we see this as a tremendous marketing opportunity," Mr. Harman concludes. Says Peter de Tagyos, sponsorships director for AT&T Corp., "Clearly it is a marketing opportunity in the classic sponsorship sense. It is also a labor of love."

This infusion of capital, however, has not leveled the playing field for either disabled athletes or for organizers of their sporting events. Mr. Hollonbeck may earn $4,000 for winning a big race, but that compares with tens of thousands of dollars for able-bodied runners in major events. For organizers of the Paralympics, meanwhile, slow sponsorship sales meant a planned $100 million budget was whittled to $89 million, causing cuts in spending on advertising, sports officials' uniforms, the so-called look of the event (banners and signs), publications, and more.

But only a few years ago, it would have been difficult to envision any major corporate sponsorship for a disabled-sports event—or for its athletes. "I'm here to say you can race wheelchairs for a living," says the affable Mr. Hollonbeck, a 26-year-old with a stunning physique. In addition to his winnings on the race circuit and his temporary marketing job with Coca Cola, Mr. Hollonbeck makes his living through speeches and endorsements. Support of various kinds comes from big-name companies, including Quickie, a maker of wheelchairs.

Clearly, much of the earning power of disabled athletes comes from the power of their stories. Mr. Hollonbeck, a talented athlete, played several sports growing up. At age 14 he was a determined runner and swimmer. Then, at 5:20 A.M. in his hometown of Rochelle, Illinois, the young Mr. Hollonbeck set off for swim practice on his bicycle. He was hit by a drunken driver and hospitalized with a severed spinal cord.

Mr. Hollonbeck was paralyzed from the waist down. Recovery was arduous, as he was strapped to a hospital bed that rotated (to prevent pressure sores), periodically leaving him staring at the floor. It was during a session of "floor time," as he calls it, that Mr. Hollonbeck heard an announcement that would change his life. It was 1984, and the Los Angeles Olympics were playing on the hospital television. The 300-meter wheelchair race would be coming up next, a broadcaster said. "I looked across the room and said to my mother, I want to do that," Mr. Hollonbeck remembers.

Like most elite athletes, he has experienced the ups and downs of competition, finishing a disappointing tenth in the World Championships in 1990, yet winning two golds and one silver two years later in the Paralympic Games in Barcelona, Spain. The next year, a crash in a race broke both his arms, leaving him immobilized again. His second-place finish last week in a 1,500-meter exhibition race during the Olympic Games here attests to the fact that he is back.

Mr. Hollonbeck has yet to strike real sponsorship and endorsement gold. But his profile is rising. Georgia Power Company ran photos of Mr. Hollonbeck's face and arm muscles in a two-page magazine advertising spread touting "power" and "efficiency in motion." The advertisement ran in *Newsweek*, *Sports Illustrated*, and other publications.

Still Mr. Hollonbeck is far from satisfied. Recently, a sense of duty and a $700 stipend persuaded him to pose for photos for two billboards. The advertisements would promote the Atlanta Paralympics and also contain the company's name. But when the company presented him with what it considered good news—the campaign would expand to 95 billboards—Mr. Hollonbeck was livid. He called off the agreement. "If I don't give [my service] a value," he says, "I do a disservice to the movement.

"They want it all for free," he says of Paralympics sponsors. "They'll say, 'We're promoting the Paralympics. We're doing it for you. It's charity.' I say bull—. They're doing it because it's good for business."

Source: Thomas Emory, Jr., "Disabled Athletes Go for Sponsorship Gold," *The Wall Street Journal*, August 9, 1996, B6.
Reprinted by permission of *The Wall Street Journal*, ©1996 Dow Jones & Company, Inc. All Rights Reserved Worldwide.

■ Disabled athletes now compete in the Paralympic Games.

With the growth of the Paralympic Games and programs like Sporting Chance, which provides opportunities for people with disabilities to participate in sports, marketers are now addressing this market. Furthermore, women represent a growing target market for many marketers interested in sports sponsorship opportunities.

 spotlight on women in sports marketing

factors affecting corporate sponsorship of women's sport

There is little doubt that women's sport and the consumers that follow it are becoming the greatest growth sector for sports marketers as we near the next millennium. The growth of women's sports is taking place at all levels. More and more women are participating in sports and watching sports, which has created opportunities for equipment and apparel manufacturers as well as for broadcast media. In addition, marketing to women through the athletic medium has become an interesting and valuable tool for corporate America. In

(continued)

short, women are becoming the target market of choice for sports marketers.

Although women are growing in importance to sports marketers, relatively little is known about the sponsorship decisions relative to women's sport. A recent study by Nancy Lough of Kent State University was designed to better understand corporate sponsorship of women's sport. The following are summarized results of the research.

What are the benefits realized by corporations that have sponsored women's sports?

Benefits	Rank (1 is the greatest perceived benefit)
Extended audience profile	1
Demographic fit	
Size	
Extended media coverage	2
Local	
National	
Public relations factors	3
Customer presence	
Hospitality provided	
Community leader presence	

What factors are influential in the development of corporate involvement in sponsorship?

Category	Rank (1 is the greatest perceived benefit)
Budget considerations	1
Cost effectiveness	
Affordability	
Access to potential buyers	
Targeting of market	2
Demographic fit	
Access to users of product	
Immediate audience	
Size	
Proposal considerations	3
Competent staff running event	
Evaluation procedures described	
and/or employed	

What factors are utilized by corporations in sponsorship selection decisions?

Category	Rank (1 is the greatest perceived benefit)
Meeting sponsorship goals	1
Achievement of objectives	
Cooperation of organizers w/sponsors	
Value/ROI	
Performance of event organizers	
Corporate direction/strategy	
Positioning/Image	2
Product-Sport image fit	
Image-Target market fit	

Category	Rank (1 is the greatest perceived benefit)
Targeting Women	3

- Visible connection of sponsor and women's event
- Women as potential consumers of company's products
- Ability to promote sales to women
- Unique opportunity vs. other options
- Research supporting involvement with women's sport

In addition to these findings of women's sport sponsorship, Lough offers the following observations:

- Gender-appropriate sports are still the most attractive to sponsors of women's sport
- Sponsors are interested in creating ties to the sport or event image via media coverage and/or advertising
- Corporate interest in sponsoring women's sports will continue to grow
- Establishing the Women's Sport Cable Channel will give sponsors the perfect vehicle to reach this emerging market
- As competition for ownership of women's events increases, so too will the value of sponsorships
- Women's sports sponsorship appears to represent a better value than a comparably priced sports package.

Source: Nancy L. Lough, "Factors Affecting Corporate Sponsorship of Women's Sport," *Sport Marketing Quarterly*, vol. 5, no. 2 (1996):11–19. Reprinted with permission of Fitness Information Technology, Inc. Publishers.

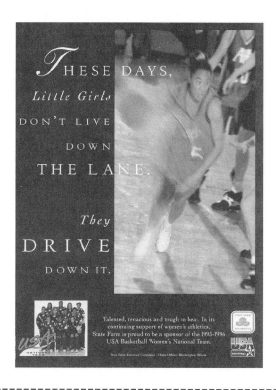

■ Corporate sponsorship targeting women's sport.

Relationship Marketing

As discussed in the previous chapter, building long-term relationships with customers is one of the most important issues for sports marketers in today's competitive marketing environment. Building relationships with clients or putting the principles of relationship marketing to work is another sponsorship objective. Corporate hospitality managers see to it that sponsors are given ample space to "wine and dine" current or perspective clients. The prevalence of luxury boxes at stadiums or arenas is just one small piece of evidence that corporate sponsors will go to great lengths and spend great amounts of money to build and maintain working relationships with their clients.

One example of an organization using sponsorship to build relationships with its clients is United Distillers, who produce Johnny Walker whiskeys.[27] Johnny Walker was the titled sponsor of the 1997 Ryder Cup, pitting the United States against Europe. The 1997 Ryder Cup by Johnny Walker presented an exceptional opportunity to build relationships with corporate clients. Maxine Longmuir of Johnny Walker said, "The sponsorship is not just about television figures and exposure. We entertained over 1,000 clients with a variety of two-, three-, and four-day packages." The whiskey company was entertaining an estimated 380 people a day from around the globe, while 650 guests were enjoying the hospitality from the fourth hole. These guests included distributors and clients who purchase Johnny Walker products. Certainly, an enjoyable way to achieve a sponsorship objective.

The community is another public with which sponsors want to build relationships. As you will recall from the previous chapter, one of Quaker State's primary objectives in sponsoring the Byron Nelson Classic was to establish a link with the Dallas–Fort Worth community. Many corporate sponsors believe that returning something to the community is an important part of sponsoring a sporting event. Haruo Murase, president and CEO of Canon USA, Inc., who is the title sponsor of the Canon Greater Hartford Open PGA TOUR event, explains why he believes supporting the community is critical:

We at Canon are proud of the part we play in sponsoring the Canon Greater Hartford Open, one of the top fund raisers on the PGA TOUR. The Canon GHO helps us fulfill our goal of being a good corporate citizen. The tournament raises more than $1 million a year that is being used for service programs that help the young, elderly, and disadvantaged in the greater Hartford community. We feel quite privileged to be able to make such a contribution each year.[28]

Image Building

Perhaps the most important reason for sponsorship of a sports entity at any level is to maintain or build an image. Image building is a two-way street for both the sponsoring organization as well as the sports entity. The sponsoring organization associates itself and/or its brands with the positive images generated by the unique personality of the sporting event. Ferrand and Pages describe the process of finding a congruence between event and sponsor as "looking for the perfect wedding."[29] The researchers also point out that "any action toward sponsoring an event should begin with an analysis of the common and unique attributes of the event and the brand or product."

figure 12.2) Sponsorship Match-Up

Consider an event like the Summer Extreme Games (X-Games), which possess a well-defined image that includes characteristics such as aggressiveness, hip, cool, no fear, and no rules. The image of extreme sports such as skysurfing, street luge, or the adventure race will certainly "rub off" or become associated with the sponsoring organization. Taco Bell, Nike, and Mountain Dew will take on the characteristics of the extreme sports, and the image of their products will be maintained or enhanced.

In chapter 10, the **match-up hypothesis** was described as the more congruent the image of the endorser with the image of the product being promoted, the more effective the message. This simple principle also holds true for sponsorship. However, the image of the sports entity (remember this may be an event, individual athlete, group of athletes, or team) should be congruent with the actual or desired image of the sponsor's organization or the product being sponsored. In Figure 12.2, we can see how the image of Taco Bell has shifted toward the X-Games and how the image of the X-Games also shifts towards the sponsor.

Sometimes the "match up" between sponsor and sports entity is not seen as appropriate. For example, Anheuser Busch's $50 million sponsorship of the 2002 Winter Olympics in Salt Lake City, Utah, may be scrutinized because of the religious beliefs of Mormons. Anheuser Busch may be forced to call their products malt beverages. The following spotlight illustrates another problematic, alcohol-related match-

spotlight on international sports marketing

brewers' soccer sponsorship draws fire

When angry fans from Britain's Chelsea soccer club stormed the field after losing to the Millwall team, alcohol was widely blamed as the catalyst. The so-called lager louts didn't have to look far for suggestions on what to imbibe. Chelsea players sport the logo of Aldoph Coors Company, while Millwall's sponsor is Seagram Company's Captain Morgan rum. Chelsea is a member of England's Premier League, which is sponsored by big British brewer Bass PIC's Carling Black Label brand.

"It's quite obvious the role that alcohol plays in acting as a fuel for disorder," says Mark Bennett, a spokesman for the Alcohol Concern, a pressure group in the United Kingdom that wants brewers voluntarily to drop their name from team shirts.

(continued)

Certainly, the rash of violence in European football is enough to make any image-conscious corporate sponsor nervous. The brewers deny their marketing efforts contribute to any violent behavior. "Football fans drink beer, and there's no denying that," says Jonathan Nye, Bass's sponsorship manager. Bass says its soccer-sponsorship activities do not encourage fans to drink more alcohol, only to switch to the Carling brand. "There's no correlation that shows beer sponsorship encourages anything to do with the violence or soccer troubles at all," adds Mr. Nye.

Even so, the troubled alliance of beer sponsors, soccer clubs, and the rowdy fans who love them both has prompted widespread criticism and even spurred some countries to ban alcohol-related advertising on team jerseys and in stadiums.

"We don't consider beer and liquor and cigarettes to go along with football and sports in general," says Jim Hansen, general secretary of the Danish Football Association. "I think the general feeling here is that there is a problem."

In France, no football team is sponsored by an alcohol brand, and alcohol advertising is not permitted in the stadiums. In England, the Football Association Cup, which has never had an alcohol sponsor, a few years ago turned down an offer by Foster's Brewing Company to sponsor the event.

Efforts to curb football violence throughout Europe in the past several years have focused on the role of alcohol. Four years ago, during a European Cup competition in Rotterdam, officials banned drinking at a match and closed city bars to curb violence. And although alcohol is not universally banned at football matches, various countries have imposed strict regulations about when and where alcohol can be consumed.

Nonetheless, alcohol companies have clamored to sponsor football clubs, a move that gives them regular access to their target market of beer-drinking sports fans—with the added hope that fans will become as loyal to the sponsor as they are to the football club itself. Analysts say a team's reputation for violence is unlikely to tarnish the brand's image among loyal football fans.

Source: Tara Parker-Pope, "Brewers' Soccer Sponsorship Draws Fire," *The Wall Street Journal*, February 27, 1995, B1, B8. Reprinted by permission of *The Wall Street Journal* © 1995 Dow Jones & Company, Inc. All Rights Reserved Worldwide.

Sales Increases

The eventual objective for nearly all organizations involved in sponsorship programs is to increase sales. Although sometimes there is an indirect route to sales (i.e., the hierarchy of effects model of promotional objectives, which states that awareness must come before action or sales), the major objective of sponsorship is to increase the bottom line. Organizations certainly would not spend millions of dollars to lend their names to stadiums or events if they did not feel comfortable about the return on investment. Likewise, the events are developed, in some cases (e.g., the Skins Game, the World's Fastest Human Race between Michael Johnson and Donovan Bailey), for the sole purpose of making a profit. Without sponsorship, the event would lose the ability to do so.

It is clear that when organizations are considering a sponsorship program, the first step is to determine the organizational objectives and marketing goals that might be achieved most effectively through sponsorship. However, the primary motivation for organizations participating in sports sponsorships is still unclear. Historically, organizations entered into sponsorships to create awareness and enhance the image of their brands, product lines, or corporations. Three recent studies examining the primary reasons for engaging in sponsorship found increasing awareness and enhancing com-

table 12.2

Importance of Sponsorship Objectives

Objectives	Mean Importance Rating
Increase sales/market share	6.14
Increase target market awareness	6.07
Enhance general public awareness	5.88
Enhance general company image	5.47
Enhance trade relations	4.60
Enhance trade goodwill	4.55
Involve community	4.48
Alter public perception	4.15
Enhance employee relations	3.84
Block competition	3.68
Develop social responsibility	3.13
Develop corporate philanthropy	3.12

Source: Doug Morris and Richard L. Irwin, "The Data-Driven Approach to Sponsorship Acquisition," *Sport Marketing Quarterly*, vol. 5, no. 2 (1996):7, 9. Reprinted with permission of Fitness Information Technology Inc. Publishers.

pany image to be the most important objectives. More recently, studies have shown that increasing sales and market share are the primary motives of sponsorship (see Table 12.2).

Regardless of the relative importance of the various sponsorship objectives, organizations must carefully evaluate how the sponsorship will help them achieve their own unique marketing objectives. Along with examining the sponsorship objectives, the organization must find a sponsorship opportunity that fits within the existing promotion budget. Let us look briefly at the basic budgeting considerations, the next step in the sponsorship model.

Sponsorship Budgeting

As with the promotional budget, the methods of determining the sponsorship budget include competitive parity, arbitrary allocation, percentage of sales, and the objective and task method. Because the fundamentals of these budgeting methods have already been discussed, let us examine the sponsorship budgeting process at several organizations.

The only generality to be made about the budgeting process is that decision-making varies widely based on the size of the company and its history and commitment to the practice of sponsorship.[30] Larger organizations that have used sponsorship as a form of communication for many years tend to have highly complex structures and those new to sponsorship tend to keep it simpler.

Consider, for example, the budgeting process at Anheuser Busch. Anheuser Busch's budgeting process begins with determining the corporatewide marketing budget. This is usually anywhere from three to five percent of the previous year's sales (percentage of sales method discussed in chapter 11). The total budget is then divided among the company's 32 brands, with Budweiser, the flagship brand, receiving the largest share of the budget. The final decision on budget allocation is made by two high-level management teams who receive and review potential sponsorships. The first team looks at how the managers plan on supporting their sponsorships with additional promotional mix elements such as point-of-sale merchandising. The second team hears the brand managers present their case and defend their budget.

Although Anheuser Busch's budgeting process represents a more complex and structured approach, Marriott uses a simpler technique. Marriott, a relative newcomer to sports sponsorship, leaves the whole business to its corporation's hotel and time-share properties. The same practice holds true for Philip Morris, where managers of individual brands like Virginia Slims decide which sponsorship opportunities to pursue and how much money to allocate. The brand managers of Yukon Jack and Jose Cuervo, two alcoholic beverage brands of IDV/Hublein, also make their budgeting decisions independently. Yukon Jack and Jose Cuervo spend 60 percent and 30 percent, respectively, of their marketing budget on sponsorship.[31]

Once specific budgets are allocated, the organization must look for sponsorship opportunities that will meet objectives and still be affordable. To accommodate budgetary constraints, most sports entities offer different levels of sponsorship over a range of sponsorship fees. One example of the cost of sponsorship and the tangible benefits received by the sponsor is the Giant Eagle LPGA Classic (see Table 12.3).[32] The professional golf tournament in Warren, Ohio, attracts an almost equal number of men (48 percent) and women (52 percent) who have attended or graduated college and have an average household income of $65,000. Sponsorship packages are presented in the following areas: skyboxes, souvenir program/pairings guide, course promotions, and corporate hospitality. The preceding example demonstrates the potential costs of sponsoring a sporting event. Table 12.4 shows several other miscellaneous sponsorship fees. It is important to note that the sponsorship fee is not the only expense that should be considered by organizations. As Brant Wansley of BrandMarketing Services, Ltd., points out, "Buying the rights [to the sponsorship] is one thing, capitalizing on them to get a good return on investment is another. . . . Purchasing a sponsorship is like buying an expensive sports car. In addition to the initial cost, you must invest in the maintenance of the car to ensure its performance."[33] Sponsorship must be integrated with other forms of promotion to maximize its effectiveness. Rod Taylor, senior vice president of the Optimum Group, adds, "The only thing that you get as a sponsor is a piece of paper saying you've paid to belong. It is up to you as the marketer to convince consumers that you do, in fact, belong!"

An excellent example of an organization leveraging its sponsorship is Anheuser Busch in the 1996 Summer Olympics. In addition to print and broadcast advertisements, Anheuser Busch produced commemorative Olympic cans and accompanying P-O-P displays to stimulate sales at the retail level. Bob Lachky, group vice president of Budweiser brands at Anheuser Busch, says, "When you can drill [sponsorship] all the way through every element of the marketing mix—from advertising all the way through point-of-sale . . . and if you can get something that looks seamless from top to bottom, you're going to have a successful promotion."[34]

table 12.3

Sponsorship Opportunities: Giant Eagle LPGA Classic

Community Club

Entertain your guests among tournament sponsors and enjoy complimentary food and beverage service in the exclusive Community Club pavilion.

- Individual Community Club pass: $550
- 6 Community Club passes: $3,150
- 10 Community Club passes: $5,000
- 15 Community Club passes: $7,125

Packages of six or more include 2 VIP Parking passes and identification on the sponsor board and Web site

Corporate Hospitality Tents

Separate yourself from the competition by entertaining your guests in the exclusivity and privacy of a Corporate Hospitality Tent. Each package includes:

- 25 weekly Corporate badges
- Four VIP Parking passes
- 2' × 2' sign featuring your company logo
- Private rest room facilities
- 20 percent discount off Souvenir Program advertising
- Right to purchase additional tickets, up to 20% of your daily allotment, at a discounted rate
- Identification on the tournament sponsor board and Web site

Package A: $7,900

- 16' × 16' tent with 16' × 16' fenced patio
- 300 tickets, 60 each day Wednesday–Sunday

Package B: $10,750

- 20' × 20' tent with 20' × 16' fenced patio
- 625 tickets, 125 each day Wednesday–Sunday

Package C: $13,900

- 20' × 30' tent with 30' × 16' fenced patio
- 1,000 tickets, 200 each day Wednesday–Sunday

Skyboxes

Skyboxes combine the benefits of premium seating and corporate hospitality to create a distinctive entertainment venue.

Executive Skybox: $4,500

- 20 reserved seats in your private section
- 100 tickets, 20 each day Wednesday–Sunday
- 100 transferable Executive Skybox passes, 20 each day Wednesday–Sunday
- Cash bar access and wait staff service
- 2 VIP Parking passes

(continued)

table 12.3 *(continued)*

Sponsorship Opportunities: Giant Eagle LPGA Classic

18th Green VIP Skybox: $250
- One reserved seat in the 18th Green VIP Skybox
- Five tickets, one each day Wednesday–Sunday
- Five transferable VIP Skybox passes, one each day Wednesday–Sunday
- Cash bar access and wait staff service
- Identification on the sponsor board and Web site (four-seat minimum)

9th Green VIP Skybox: $200
- One reserved seat in the 9th Green VIP Skybox
- Five tickets, one each day Wednesday–Sunday
- Five transferable VIP Skybox passes, one each day Wednesday–Sunday
- Cash bar access and wait staff service
- Identification on the sponsor board and Web site (four-seat minimum)

Souvenir Program

An annual collector's item, the Giant Eagle LPGA Classic Souvenir Program is complimentary to all tournament spectators.

Type	Tickets	Price
Back Outside Cover, Four-Color	Two Season Clubhouse badges, Four Good-Any-One-Day passes	$3,500
Full-Page, Four-color	Two Season Clubhouse badges, Two Good-Any-One-Day passes	$2,000
Full-Page, Black and White	Two Season Clubhouse badges, Two Good-Any-One-Day passes	$1,500
Half-Page, Black and White	Eight Good-Any-One-Day passes	$1,000
Quarter-Page, Black and White	Four Good-Any-One-Day passes	$ 550

Pairing Guide

A daily guide to all the tournament action from Wednesday–Sunday, your advertisement appears adjacent to each day's pairings.

- Inside Panel—Sunday only: $3,450
- Outside Panel: $4,750
- Inside Panel: $5,250
- Inside Panel under Course Map: $6,000

Each panel includes one full-page, four-color ad in the Souvenir Program and one Classic Ticket Package.

- Promotional Tents: $3,100
- Daily interaction with tournament spectators awaits organizations that utilize a Promotional Tent.
- 10′ × 10′ Promotional Tent
- Two 8′ tables and four chairs
- One Classic Ticket Package

table 12.3 *(continued)*

Sponsorship Opportunities: Giant Eagle LPGA Classic

Staff tickets

Tee Sponsorship: $3,500

Uniting prominent signage on the tee and a two-page spread in the Souvenir Program provides Tee Sponsors with integrated exposure to tournament spectators.

- Logo identification on the hole, par, yardage sign
- One full-page, four-color ad in the Souvenir Program facing the hole layout

Leaderboard Advertising: $2,950

Courtesy of Giant Eagle LPGA Classic.

table 12.4

The Cost of Sponsorship

Corporate box at the United Center, home of the NBA Chicago Bulls	$220,000/year
Corporate name and logo on the white part of the fuselage of the *James Cook, Around-the-World*, prop airplane adventure	$8,000
Right to become the title sponsor or rename the Tot Trot in Boston (5k run/walk for stroller pushers)	$7,500
Corporate logo worn by professional rodeo contestant on the back of the shirt and 9 square inches on the left front pocket of shirt	$5,000
Sponsorship for English soccer's Premier League	$14.8 million/year
Official supplier for MLB (gives the company exclusive rights to MLB trademarks and collective use of team designations in advertising, packaging, merchandising, and promotions)	$10 million/year

Choosing the Sponsorship Opportunity

Once sponsorship objectives have been carefully studied and financial resources have been allocated, organizations must make decisions regarding the appropriate sponsorship opportunity. Whatever the choices, thoughtful consideration must be given regarding the potential opportunities.

Choosing the most effective sponsorship opportunity for your organization necessitates a detailed decision-making process. Several researchers have examined the organizational decision-making process in attempts to understand the evaluation and selection of sponsorship opportunities. A conceptual model of the corporate decision-making process of **sport sponsorship acquisition** developed by Arthur, Scott, and Woods is shown in Figure 12.3.

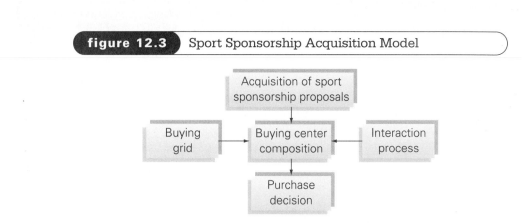

figure 12.3 Sport Sponsorship Acquisition Model

Acquisition of sport
sponsorship proposals

Buying
grid

Buying center
composition

Interaction
process

Purchase
decision

Reprinted by permission from D. Arthur, D. Scott, and T. Woods, "A Conceptual Model of the Corporate Decision-Making Process of Sport Sponsorship Acquisition," *Journal of Sport Management*, vol. 11, no. 3 (1997): 229.

The process begins with the acquisition of sponsorship proposals. Generally, this is a reactive process in which organizations receive the multitude of sponsorship possibilities from sports entities wishing to secure sponsors. Within the sponsorship proposal, potential sponsors commonly look for the following information to assist in decision making:

- Fan attendance/demographic profile of fans at the event
- Cost/cost per number of people reached
- Length of contract
- Media coverage
- Value-added promotions
- Sponsorship benefits

After the proposals have been acquired, the next step is to form the buying center. The buying center is the group of individuals within the organization who is responsible for evaluating and choosing the sponsorship. The buying center usually consists of four to five individuals who each play a unique role in the purchase. Typically, these roles are described as gatekeepers, influencers, decision makers, and purchasers. These roles were previously discussed in the context of personal selling. You will recall that one of the sales activities was to identify the individuals within the organization who performed these roles. Similarly, the sponsorship requester must learn who these individuals are before submitting the proposal. Hopefully, the proposal can then be tailored to meet the unique needs of the individuals who comprise the buying center.

Gatekeepers control the flow of information to the other members of the buying center. They are able to pass on the relevant proposals to other group members and act as an initial filtering device. The **influencers** are individuals who can impact the decision-making process. These individuals often have information regarding the sports entity that is requesting the sponsorship. The influencers have acquired this information through contacts that they have in the community or industry. The **decision maker** is the individual within the buying center that has the ultimate responsibility to accept or reject proposals. In our earlier examples, describing the budgeting process for Jose Cuervo and Yukon Jack, the brand managers were the ultimate decision makers in the sponsorship acquisition process. Finally, the **purchasers** are responsible for negotiating contracts and formally carrying out the terms of the sponsorship.

The composition of the buying center, in terms of the number of individuals and the interaction between these individuals, is a function of the type of sponsorship decision. The buying grid refers to the organization's previous experience and involvement in sponsorship purchases. If this is the first time the organization has engaged in sport sponsorship, then more information will be needed from the sponsorship requester. In addition, the buying center will have additional members with greater interaction. On the other hand, if the sponsorship is simply being renewed (also known as a straight sponsorship rebuy), the buying center will play a less significant role in the decision-making process.

The next step in the sponsorship acquisition model is to make the purchase decision. Typically, it takes an organization three to six weeks to make a final sponsorship decision. While this may seem slow, purchasing a sponsorship is a complex decision that requires the coordination and interaction of all the members in the buying center.

The purchase decision consists of three interrelated steps. In the first step, the organization must consider the desired scope of the sponsorship (e.g., international versus local). To do this a simple scheme for categorizing sponsorship opportunities has been developed, called the Sport Event Pyramid. The second interrelated step requires the organization to select the appropriate athletic platform for the sponsorship. Does the organization want to sponsor an event, a team, a league, or an individual athlete? Finally, after the organization has chosen the scope of sponsorship and the athletic platform, it specifies the particular sports entity. After the final decision is made, a quick audit can be conducted to determine whether or not the organization has made the appropriate choice of sponsorship. Let us examine the three steps in the purchase decision-making process in greater detail.

Determining the Scope of the Sponsorship

The first step in the purchase decision phase of sponsorship acquisition is to determine the desired scope of the sponsorship. David Shani and Dennis Sandler have developed a way to categorize various sponsorship opportunities called the **Sports Event Pyramid**.[35] The Sports Event Pyramid is an excellent first step in reducing the number of sponsorship proposals to a smaller subset.

The Sports Event Pyramid consists of five levels: global events, international events, national events, regional events, and local events. Each level of the Sports Event Pyramid classifies events on the basis of the width and depth of interest in the event. Shani and Sandler describe the width as the geographic reach of the event via the various communications media, and the depth of the event refers to the level of interest among consumers.

Global events are at the apex of the pyramid. As the name implies, global events have the broadest coverage and are covered extensively all over the world. In addition to their wide coverage, global events generate a great deal of interest among consumers. Shani and Sandler suggest that the World Cup and the Olympic Games are the only examples of truly global events. Corporations that wish to position themselves in the global market should be prepared to pay top dollar for sponsorship of these events due to the tremendous reach and interest in the events.

International events are the next level in the hierarchy. For any event to be considered international in scope, it might (1) have a high level of interest in a broad, but not global, geographic region, or (2) be truly global in scope but have a lower level of interest in some of the countries reached. Examples of international events include Wimbledon, European Cup Soccer, America's Cup (yachting), the Rugby Union World Cup, and the Pan-American Games. Sponsoring these types of events is useful for corporations that have more narrowly targeted global markets.

Extremely high interest levels among consumers in a single country or two countries is categorized in the Sports Event Pyramid as a **national event.** National events, such as the World Series, the NCAA Final Four, and the Super Bowl, attract huge audiences in the United States.

Regional events have a narrow geographic focus and are also characterized by high interest levels within the region. The Big East conference tournament in basketball and the Boston Marathon are considered good examples of regional events.

In the lowest level of the pyramid are **local events**. Local events have the most narrow geographic focus, such as a city or community, and attract a small segment of consumers that have a high level of interest in the event. High school sports, local races, and golf scrambles are examples of local events.

The primary purpose of the pyramid is to have marketers first develop an understanding of what level of sponsorship is consistent with corporate sponsorship objectives and budgets. Next, the corporation can decide upon which specific sporting events at the correct level present the best match. The organization may start small and choose to sponsor local events at the beginning. The larger the organization gets, the more likely it will be involved in sponsorship at each of the five levels of the pyramid. For example, Coca Cola is deeply involved in sponsorships at all five levels.

Although the Sports Event Pyramid is a great tool for marketers developing a sponsorship program, it does have some potential flaws. First, the local events are shown at the base of the pyramid. To some, this may imply the broadest geographic focus while, in fact, the local events have the most narrow focus. Second, it may be extremely difficult to categorize certain events. For example, the Super Bowl is cited as a national event that, by definition, has a one- or two-country focus with a high level of interest. The Super Bowl, of course, is broadcast in hundreds of countries, but may have limited interest levels in most. Therefore, it is uncertain as to whether the event should be categorized as a national event, an international event, or both.

Determining the Athletic Platform

After the general level of sponsorship reach is considered via the sponsorship pyramid, a more specific sponsorship issue must be considered. Namely, choosing the appropriate athletic platform. University of Michigan Professor Christine Brooks defines the **athletic platform** for sponsorship as being either the team, the sport, the event, or the athlete.[36] Additionally, choice of athletic platform could be further subdivided on the basis of level of competition. For instance, common levels of competition include professional, collegiate, high school, and recreational.

The choice of athletic platform (or, in some instances, platforms) is based on sponsorship objectives, budget, and geographic scope. More specifically, when selecting the athletic platform, several factors should be considered.

- What is the sponsorship budget? What type of athletic platform is feasible given the budget?
- What is the desired geographic scope? How does the athletic platform complement the choice made in the sports sponsorship pyramid?
- How does the athletic platform complement the sponsorship objectives?

Let us take a closer look at each of the broad choices of athletic platform for sponsorship. These include athletes, teams, sports/leagues, and events.

Athletes   We have previously examined the opportunities and risks of athletes as endorsers in chapters 10 and 11. To summarize, athletes can have tremendous credibility with the target audience and can create an immediate association with a product in the consumer's mind. For example, NASCAR fans talk about Ricky Rudd driving the "Tide Car" or Sterling Martin driving the "Coors Light" car. The problem, however, is that athletes can perform poorly or be seen as troublemakers. Moreover, professional athletes are also frequently labeled as "spoiled brats."

One athlete that has not yet made it big with sponsors because of her perceived negative image is Venus Williams. This 17-year-old tennis star seems to be in a position to make it big in the sport and with sponsors, but currently only has a five-year, $3 million deal with Reebok. Problems with Venus include a father who has complained about racism in the sport of tennis and fellow professionals criticizing her for "standoffish behavior."[37]

In addition to these negative issues, Venus's age may be seen as a problem. Most sponsors, having been burned in the past by teenage sensations that go sour, will want to wait until the athlete has proven him or her self before spending huge sums of money for sponsorship. On the other hand, sponsors trying to promote a young, cool image for their products may see Venus's age as a huge benefit. Whichever is the case, this example does illustrate the complexities of using an individual athlete as the athletic platform for sponsorship.

TIGER WOODS

Although sports marketing takes on many different meanings to different people, its essence is captured in the 21-year-old, multimillion dollar phenom named Eldrick "Tiger" Woods. Tiger seems to have it all. He's handsome, charming, young, multiethnic, and, most important, is oozing talent. Tiger's sponsors certainly think that he is worth the money. Nike, Titleist, and the All-Star Cafe have all purchased a piece of Tiger for a total of $67 million in sponsorship fees.

PGA Tour Commissioner Tim Finchem has stated that "It's conceivable that in terms of overall impact on the sport—when you figure in media, dollars on the table for him, his ability to be a role model—that if he succeeds he might be the most important player ever. He has the potential to have a profound impact on our sport as an entertainment sport. He could have a real impact on the overall growth of the game, which would be a much more

lasting impact than the week-to-week sort of Tigermania which has been referred to."

The sport of golf has already seen short-term benefits of the new Tiger era. For example, the final round of the 1996 Masters drew a rating of 14.1 and a 31 share. Translated, this means that roughly 14 million viewers watched the tournament. In a related example, attendance at the Motorola Western Open is expected to increase from 170,00 to 250,000 because of Tiger.

Nike is also reaping the benefits of its $40-million contract with Tiger. The company estimates that its golf revenues will total $180 million by the end of fiscal 1998. That figure represents a 60 percent increase from the previous year. Tiger is also expected to help the entire golf equipment industry grow at a significant pace. Thomas Crow, Cobra golf founder and vice chairman, states that "All the manufacturers have an opportunity to feed off Tiger."

Source: "Tiger, Inc.," *Business Week*, April 28, 1997, 32–36; John Feinstein, "Tiger By the Tail," *Newsweek*, September 9, 1996, 58–61.

Teams   Teams at any level of competition (little league, high school, college, and professional) can serve as the athletic platform. Although sponsorship is typically associated with professional teams, college athletic departments also rely heavily on sponsorship partnerships.

The marketing of collegiate sports has skyrocketed in recent years. Anywhere from 10 percent to 20 percent of college basketball tournaments have title sponsors. One estimate states that corporations spend nearly $70 million annually on college sports sponsorships. Bill Battle, owner and CEO of the Collegiate Licensing Company, which handles licensing for about 150 schools, estimates the college market to be roughly $2.5 billion per year. Add to that the multimillion-dollar television contract and deals that most university coaches have with Nike, Reebok, and adidas, and college athletics is a huge business.[38]

Becoming the official outfitter for a university's athletic teams has become especially lucrative for colleges and has given sponsors great exposure. For instance, Ohio State University signed a $9.25-million contract with Nike to fuel the growth of the university's athletic program. Nike will provide OSU's athletic department with an annual allocation of $1.85 million, to be distributed in four ways: (1) $1 million in footwear, apparel, and equipment for more than 800 athletes and coaches in 34 sports,

■ Sponsorship of teams can occur at any level of competition.

(2) $725,000 cash to augment the salaries of head coaches, purchase needed equipment, and improve substandard facilities and technology, (3) $100,000 cash for marketing and advertising, to fund two internships in the athletic program's marketing department and to fund 20 scholarships for youths to attend OSU's summer sports camps, and (4) $25,000 cash for new computer equipment in the student-athlete counseling center.[39]

foot fight goes to adidas

If anyone notices what brand of shoes the Notre Dame football team has on this fall, adidas American, Inc. will be happy. Adidas beat out Nike and the team's footwear supplier of the last several years, Reebok, for the right to shoe not only the Fighting Irish football team, but most of the university's other varsity teams as well.

Under a five-year agreement announced by adidas earlier this year, the company will give Notre Dame all the shoes its varsity athletes need, plus it will pay an undisclosed amount. Shoe companies are willing to pay for the privilege of outfitting Notre Dame athletes because it is good advertising.

Not only will "Irish" players be wearing shoes with adidas's trademark three stripes, but the agreement calls for Coach Bob Davie to dress for games in adidas sportswear. It is the same sort of arrangement that kept Lou Holtz storming the sidelines in recent years clad in clothing bearing small Reebok logos.

This is the first time Notre Dame has signed a multisport deal with a single shoe supplier. In the past, head coaches have been free to negotiate, and profit from, shoe deals for their particular teams. Strictly speaking, Notre Dame coaches are not obligated to switch to adidas, but most are expected to.

(continued)

The athletic department considered offers from Reebok, Nike, and adidas. It gave adidas the nod because of the company's commitment to service. Adidas has stationed a representative in South Bend to handle the Notre Dame account exclusively.

Not that it had any bearing on its winning the account, but adidas has been lucky for Notre Dame in the past. "We've had them on for our last four national championships," said Bubba Cunningham, 1984, 1988 MBA, associate director of athletics. He was referring to the titles won in women's soccer in 1995, men's and women's fencing in 1994, women's fencing in 1987, and football in 1988.

Source: Ed Cohen, "Foot Fight Goes to adidas," *Notre Dame Magazine,* Summer 1997, 12. Courtesy of *Notre Dame* magazine and Ed Cohen.

Sport/League   In addition to sponsoring teams, some companies choose to sponsor sports or leagues. One example of this is General Motors and the WNBA. Dean Rotondo of General Motors states that "The WNBA sponsorship ensures a commitment GM has made to women's sports." One advantage to sponsoring women's sports and the WNBA is that there is less sponsorship clutter. Fewer companies are sponsoring women's sports/leagues and those that do are creating a unique position and differentiating themselves.[40]

MCI is a corporation that has chosen an integrated approach in sponsoring a number of sports/leagues. MCI's athletic platform at the sport/league level includes being the official communications company of Major League Baseball, Historic Sportscar Racing, CART, and is also the official telecommunications company of NASCAR.

Nike is also well known for their sponsorship of sports and leagues. In 1990, the "Nike Tour" was established as a breeding ground for golf professionals who have not cracked the PGA. Although the Nike Tour was initially thought of as the "minor league" of professional golf, it has become a viable tour in and of itself. Since 1990, Nike Tour purses have doubled from $3 million to $6.25 million. Also, the top 15 players on the Nike Tour money list automatically become eligible for the PGA Tour.[41]

Nike has also thrown itself into the sponsorship of soccer. By agreeing to pay the U.S. Soccer Federation $120 million over eight years, Nike has boosted U.S. soccer into the big leagues. Nike aspires to dominate the world's most popular sport and capture the largest share of the billions being spent on soccer shoes and apparel. In addition to their deal with the U.S. Soccer Federation, Nike currently spends about $3 million sponsoring MLS, the premier professional league in the United States.[42]

Lately, leagues have been trying to organize themselves to become more attractive to sponsors. MLS is structured as a single entity, which means that each team owner has a financial stake in the league. This is different from the other professional sports leagues, which consist of individual franchise owners (i.e., every person for him- or herself). This structure decreases the opportunity for ambush marketing and offers organizations an integrated sponsorship and licensing program.[43]

The MLS was not the first league to think about how best to serve the interests of sponsors. NFL Properties was designed in 1963 primarily to meet and beat the competition posed by Major League Baseball. The league, in attempting to offer a competitive advantage to sponsors, built a system whereby potential sponsors receive collective and individual team rights. That is, sponsors can create opportunities or promotions that feature all NFL teams and/or local teams in a local market.[44]

Sponsors choose to use the power of the league and its recognizable league logo and therefore support all the teams. From the sponsors' perspective, this represents easy and less expensive one-stop shopping. As Burton points out, "If an NFL corporate partner had to design individual local contracts to secure key markets, the collective local team fees would quickly surpass the single sponsorship fee." By allowing sponsors the opportunity to receive collective team rights, the league gains enhanced exposure. An example of this national exposure through marketing collective team rights include Coke's "Monsters of the Gridiron."

Events   An athletic platform that is most commonly associated with sports marketing is the event. Examples of sporting events sponsorship are plentiful, as are the opportunities to sponsor sporting events. In fact, sometimes the number of events far outweighs the number of potential corporate sponsors. For example, the city of Winnipeg is about to stage two national and international sporting events over the space of 16 months. In a city that ranks the eighth largest in Canada and has a population of only 680,000, the challenge will be to find enough corporate sponsors. In response to this challenge, event organizers will be forced to be more creative in designing sponsorship packages that appeal to organizations of all size.[45]

The advantages to using an event as an athletic platform are similar to those benefits gained by using other athletic platforms. For instance, the event will hopefully increase awareness and enhance the image of the sponsor. In addition, the event often allows the consumer a forum to purchase the sponsor's products. For example, Penn might sponsor the U.S. Open and sell its product at the event to a captive audience with a lifestyle and consumption behaviors that are highly desirable to this tennis equipment manufacturer. In another example, Guinness Brewing has signed on as the first global sponsor of the 1999 Rugby Union World Cup and will also be the competition's official beer supplier. You can bet the Guinness will be flowing at the event.

As with the other athletic platforms, one of the primary disadvantages of using events as the athletic platform is sponsorship clutter. In other words, sponsors are competing with other sponsors for the attention of the target audience. One popular way to combat this clutter is to become the title sponsor of an event. Every college football bowl game now has a title sponsor, with the exception of the Rose Bowl—and this too will change. Recently, the Rose Bowl announced that in 1999 it will add a sponsor's tag line. More formally, this is called a presenting sponsor (i.e., the Rose Bowl presented by AT&T).

Choosing the Specific Athletic Platform
The choice of a particular athletic platform follows the selection of the general platform. At this stage of the sponsorship process, the organization makes a decision

regarding the exact athlete(s), team, event, or sports entity. For instance, if the organization decides to sponsor a professional women's tennis player, who will be chosen—Steffi Graf, Venus Williams, Monica Seles, or Anna Kournikova? As with the previous decisions regarding sponsorship, the choice of a specific sponsor is based largely on finding the right "fit" for the organization and its products.

A recent trend is for sports marketers to ensure and control the "fit" by manufacturing their own sporting events. For example, Nike has created a new division to create and acquire global sporting events. By creating their own events, Nike will be able to control every aspect of how the event is marketed. Moreover, Nike will be able to develop events that are the perfect fit for their multiple target markets.[46] Other organizations, such as Honda, are also pursuing a similar strategy. They have put pressure on their advertising agency to develop sporting events that will be the ideal match for the Honda target market.

Once the decision regarding the general level of sponsorship and the specific athletic platform have been addressed, it may be useful to review carefully the choice(s) of sponsorship before taking the final step. To do so, Brant Wansley of BrandMarketing Service, Ltd. offers the following suggestions for choosing a sponsorship:[47]

- Does the sponsorship offer the right positioning?
- Does the sponsorship provide a link to brand image?
- Is the sponsorship hard for competitors to copy?
- Does the sponsorship target the right audience?
- Does the sponsorship appeal to the target audiences' lifestyle, personality, and values?
- How does the sponsorship dovetail into current corporate goals and strategies?
- Can the sponsorship be used for hospitality to court important potential and current customers?
- Is there a way to involve employees in the sponsorship?
- How will you measure the impact of the sponsorship?
- Can you afford the sponsorship?
- How easy will it be to plan the sponsorship year after year?
- Does the sponsorship complement your current promotion mix?

Sponsorship Implementation and Evaluation

Once the sponsorship decisions are finalized, plans are put into action and then evaluated to determine their effectiveness. Do sponsorships really work? The findings to this million-dollar question are somewhat mixed. In chapter 16 we will discuss the techniques organizations use to determine whether or not the sponsorship has met their objectives. For now, let us look at the results of several studies that have been conducted to determine consumer response to sponsorship. In a poll conducted by Performance Research, more than half of the respondents indicated that they would be "not very likely" or "not at all likely" to purchase a company's products because it was an Olympic sponsor.[48]

Most studies report that sponsorship is having a positive impact on their organizations. For example, Visa reported that its affiliation with the Olympic Games has steadily increased brand awareness from 52 percent (after the 1988 Winter Games) to 66 percent (after the 1994 Winter Games) to roughly 75 percent (after the 1996 Summer Games). Delta Air Lines also increased awareness levels from 38 percent to 70 percent due to its Olympic sponsorship. The ESPN Chilton Poll reports that 51 percent of consumers are at least a little more likely to purchase a product or service of a company that sponsors the Olympics.[49] In another study, roughly 60 percent of consumers indicated that they "try to buy a company's product if they support the Olympic Games."[50]

On the other hand, some researchers have found that the majority of consumers say sponsorship makes no difference to them and their purchase behavior. One potential reason for these less than encouraging findings is the amount of sponsorship clutter. For example, some 250 marketers were sponsors, suppliers, or licensees for the 1996 Olympic Games in Atlanta. David F. D'Allessandro, senior vice president of the John Hancock Company, said, "The clutter will be so enormous that I'm not sure the public walks away with any distinctive view of you."[51]

The effectiveness of sponsorships has also been examined in other countries. Recently, a study was conducted by Ishikawa, Stotlar, and Walker to determine whether Japanese consumers had a positive image of the sponsors of the Lillehammer Winter Olympic Games held in 1996.[52] In addition, the study explored whether purchase behaviors would be altered because of Olympic sponsorship.

Based on a survey of 212 consumers, the researchers found that Japanese consumers had neither a positive nor a negative image of the sponsors of the Olympic Games, with only 30 percent indicating that they had a favorable image of the sponsors. Even more importantly, about 80 percent of the survey respondents stated that the sponsors' affiliation with the Olympics would have no impact on their purchase behaviors.

These results illustrate important cross-cultural differences in perceptions of Olympic sponsorship. Some research has shown that American consumers were affected in their purchase behaviors based on Olympic sponsorship. Also, Americans had favorable images of those organizations affiliated with the Olympics. Based on these findings, potential sponsors must realize that cultural differences do exist among consumers with respect to sponsoring the Olympic Games. Strategies suggested by the authors to enhance sponsorship ROI include developing long-term involvement in the sponsorship, use of collateral advertisements to reinforce Olympic sponsorship, and advertising more heavily during the Olympic season to more strongly associate their products with the Olympic Games.

The element of the promotional mix that is linked with sports marketing to the greatest degree is sponsorship. A sponsorship is an investment in a sports entity (athlete, league, team, event) to support overall organizational goals, marketing objectives, and/or promotional objectives. Sports sponsorships are growing in popularity as a promotional tool for sports and nonsports products (and organizations). For example, an estimated $4.56 billion was spent on sports sponsorships in 1998. Because so much emphasis is placed on sponsorship, organization must understand how to develop the most effective sponsorship program.

The systematic process for designing a sponsorship program consists of four sequential steps, which include setting sponsorship objectives; determining the sponsorship budgeting, acquiring a sponsorship, and implementing and evaluating the sponsorship. Because sponsorship is one of the promotional mix elements, it is important to remember the relationship it has with the broader promotional strategy. As suggested in chapters 10 and 11, all of the elements of the promotional mix must be integrated to achieve maximum effectiveness.

The sponsorship process begins by setting objectives. These objectives, not unlike advertising objectives, can be categorized as either direct or indirect. Direct sponsorship objectives focus on stimulating consumer demand for the sponsoring organization and its products. The sponsoring company benefits by attaching their product to the sports entity. The sports entity also benefits by increased exposure given by the sponsor. As such, both parties in the sponsorship agreement benefit through the association. Indirect objectives may also be set for the sponsorship program. These objectives include generating awareness, meeting and beating the competition, reaching new target markets (e.g., disabled) or specialized target markets (e.g., mature market), building relationships with customers, and enhancing the company's image.

After objectives have been formulated, the sponsorship budget is considered. The techniques for setting sponsorship budgets are also in accord with the promotional budgeting methods discussed in the previous chapter. Generally, sponsorship of sporting events is not an inexpensive proposition—especially given the threat of ambush marketing. Ambush marketing is the planned effort by an organization to associate themselves indirectly with an event in order to gain at least some of the recognition and benefits that are associated with being an official sponsor. In past years, the Olympics have been a playground for ambush marketing techniques. For example, Nike, not an official sponsor of the 1996 Summer Olympics, constructed a building overlooking the Olympic Park to associate themselves with the festivities of the Olympic Games. Today, more stringent policing and regulation of ambush marketing is occurring by the sporting event organizers to protect the heavy financial outlay of official sponsors.

The third step of the sponsorship process is to choose the sponsorship opportunity, or acquire the sponsorship. This means making decisions about the scope of the sponsorship, choosing the general athletic platform, and then choosing the specific athletic platform. The scope of the sponsorship refers to the geographic reach of the sports entity, as well as the interest in the entity. Shani and Sandler describe the scope of athletic events using a tool called the Sports Event Pyramid. The Sports Event Pyramid is a hierarchy of events based on geographic scope and level of interest among spectators. The five-tiered hierarchy ranges from international events, such as the Olympic Games, to local events, such as a Little League tournament in your community. Once the scope of the sponsorship has been chosen, the athletic platform must be determined. The athletic platform for a sponsorship is generally a team, sport, event, or athlete. Additionally, the athletic platform could be further categorized on the basis of level of competition (i.e., professional, collegiate, high school, or recreational).

Decisions regarding the choice of athletic platform should be linked to the objectives set in the previous stages of sponsorship planning. After choosing the general athletic platform, the potential sponsor must select the specific platform. For example, if a collegiate sporting event is to be the general platform, then the specific athletic platform may be the Rose Bowl, the Championship Game of the Final Four, or a regular season baseball game against an in-state rival.

The final phase of the sponsorship process is to implement and evaluate the sponsorship plans. Organizing a sponsorship and integrating a sponsorship program with the other promotional mix elements requires careful coordination. Once the sponsorship plan is put into action, the most critical question for decision makers is "Did the program deliver or have we met our sponsorship objectives?" The implementation and evaluation of the strategic sports marketing process and, more specifically, sponsorships is considered in chapter 16.

KEY TERMS & CONCEPTS

ambush marketing tactics

athletic platform

awareness

competition

image building

reaching target markets

relationship marketing

sales increases

sponsorship

sponsorship budgeting

sponsorship evaluation

sponsorship objectives

sponsorship program

sports event pyramid

REVIEW QUESTIONS

1. Define sponsorship and discuss how sponsorship is used as a promotional mix tool by sports marketers? Provide evidence to support the growth of sports sponsorships worldwide.

2. Outline the steps for designing a sports sponsorship program.

3. Discuss, in detail, the major objectives of sports sponsorship from the perspective of the sponsoring organization.

4. What is ambush marketing, and why is it such a threat to legitimate sponsors? What defense would you take against ambush marketing tactics as a sports marketer?

5. In your opinion, why are sports sponsorships so successful in reaching a specific target market?

6. How are sponsorship budgets established within an organization?

7. Describe the various levels of the sponsorship pyramid. What is the sponsorship pyramid used for, and what are some potential problems with the pyramid?

8. Define an athletic platform. In determining what athletic platform to use for a sponsorship, what factors should be considered?

9. What questions or issues might an organization raise when choosing among sponsorship opportunities?

10. Describe the different ways that sports sponsorships might be evaluated. Which evaluation tool is the most effective?

EXERCISES

1. Design a proposed sponsorship plan for a local youth athletic association.

2. Provide five examples of extremely good or effective match-ups between sporting events and their sponsors. In addition, suggest five examples of extremely poor or ineffective match-ups between sporting events and their sponsors.

3. Find at least one example of sponsorship for each of the following athletic platforms: individual athlete, team, and league.

4. Contact an organization that sponsors any sport or sporting event and discuss how sponsorship decisions are made and by whom. Also, ask about how the organization evaluates sponsorship.

5. Design a survey to determine the influence of NASCAR sponsorships on consumers' purchase behaviors. Ask 10 consumers to complete the survey and summarize the findings. Suggest how NASCAR might use these findings.

INTERNET EXERCISES

1. Search the Internet and find an example of a sponsorship opportunity at each level of the Sponsorship Pyramid.

2. Locate at least three sports marketing companies on the Internet that specialize in the marketing of sponsorship opportunities. What products or services are these organizations offering potential clients?

NOTES

1. "Sport in Brief: Olympic Games" *The Guardian*, January 13, 1998, 22.

2. "IEG Network." <http://www.sponsorship.com/forum/FAQ.htm>.

3. "IEG Sponsorship Report, Annual Sponsorship Spending Within the Top Five Sports Areas" (Chicago: IEG, 1998).

4. "IEG Sponsorship Network, FAQ." <http://www.sponsorship.com/forum>.

5. "IEG Sponsorship Report, Annual Sponsorship Spending Within the Top Five Sports Areas" (Chicago: IEG, 1998).

6. David Shani and Dennis Sandler, "Climbing the Sports Event Pyramid," *Marketing News*, August 26, 1996, 6.

7. "The Institute of Sports Sponsorship." <http://www.internetsolutions.co.uk.../pages/iss_newsletter.html#billion>.

8. Gail Gaboda, "Conair Creates a Buzz at N.Y. Soccer Game," *Marketing News*, vol. 31, no. 18, September 1, 1997, 8.

9. "The Business of Sport." <http://www.bizsports.com>.

10. Ibid.

11. Ibid.

12. Ibid.

13. Ibid.

14. Ibid.

15. Linda Himelstein, "The Game's The Thing At Nike Now," *Business Week*, January 27, 1997, 88. Oscar Waters, "Nike Hopes for Big Kicks From Brazilian Soccer," *St. Louis Post-Dispatch*, December 16, 1996, B19.

16. "Aspen—The Spirit of Skiing." <http://www.aspen.com/aspenonline/d...spiritofskiing>.

17. Glenn Wilson, "Does Sport Sponsorship Have a Direct Effect on Product Sales?" *Cyber-Journal of Sports Marketing*. <http://www.cad.gu.edu.au/market/cy...rnal_of_sport_marketing/wilson/htm>.

18. See, for example, Nigel Pope. "Overview Of Current Sponsorship Thought." <http://www.cad.gu.edu.au/cjsm/pope21.htm>. R. Abratt, B. Clayton, and L. Pitt, "Corporate Objectives in Sports Sponsorship," *International Journal of Advertising*, vol. 6 (1987):299–311; Christine Brooks, *Sports Marketing:Competitive Business Strategies for Sports* (Englewood Cliffs, NJ: Prentice Hall, 1994).

19. Janet Hoek, Philip Gendall, Michelle Jeffcoat, and David Orsman, "Sponsorship and Advertising: A Comparison of Their Effects," *Journal of Marketing Communications* (1997):21–32.

20. Dawn Chmielewski, "Reebok Banking on Olympics," *Business NewsBank*, March 6, 1996.

21. D.M. Sandler and D. Shani, "Ambush Marketing: Who Gets the Gold?" *Journal of Advertising Research*, vol. 29 (1989):9–14.

22. *Atlanta Constitution Journal*. <http://www.atlantagames.com/WEB/oly/getcoke2.html>. (December 29, 1995).

23. Peter J. Graham, "Ambush Marketing," *Sport Marketing Quarterly*, vol. 4, no. 1 (1997):10–12.

24. Howard Schlossberg, *Sports Marketing* (Cambridge, MA: Blackwell Publishers, 1996).

25. Graham, 10–12.

26. Chris Pritchard, "Aussie Olympic Committee Takes on Ambush Marketing." <http://marketingmag.ca/Content/32.97/int1.html>.

27. "Ryder Cup Provides Perfect Stage," *Sport Business International*. <http://sportbusiness.com/NewArchitecture>.

28. "Good Golf, Good Deeds," Special Advertising Section of *Sports Illustrated*, August 19, 1996.

29. Alain Ferrand and Monique Pagés, "Image Sponsoring: A Methodology to Match Event and Sponsor" *Journal of Sport Management*, vol. 10, no. 3 (July 1996):278–291.

30. Roger Williams, "Making the Decision and Paying for It," *Mark McCormack's Guide to Sports Marketing, International Sports Marketing Group*, 1996, 166–168.

31. Roger Williams, "Making the Decision and Paying for It," *Mark McCormack's Guide to Sports Marketing, International Sports Marketing Group*, 1996, 166–168; Paula Hendrickson, "Sports Marketing: Gaining the Competitive Advantage," *Sales and Marketing: Strategies & News*, (May/June 1997), vol. 7, no. 4.

32. "Giant Eagle LPGA Classic." <http://www.lpgaclassic.com/spon_opps.htm>.

33. Brant Wamsley, "Best Practices Will Help Sponsorships Succeed," *Marketing News*, September 1, 1997, 8.

34. "Scoring With Sports Fans," *BEVERAGE Industry*, November 1996, 46, 48, 49.

35. David Shani and Dennis Sandler, "Climbing the Sports Event Pyramid," *Marketing News*, August 26, 1996, 6.

36. Brooks, 1994.

37. Brad Wolverton, "So Far, She's Not The Venus De Moola," *Business Week*, September 29, 1997, 140.

38. Dianna P. Gray, "Sponsorship on Campus," *Sport Marketing Quarterly*, vol. v, no. 2 (1996): 29–34; Sporting Goods Manufacturers Association, "Sports Licensed Products Report." <http://www.sportlink.com/research/...h/industry/98_licensed_report.html>.

39. Bob Baptist, "Nike Deal Means A Lot to OSU," *Columbus Dispatch*, December 29, 1995, 2F.

40. Margaret Littman, "Sponsors Take to the Court with the New Women's NBA," *Marketing News*, March 3, 1997, 1, 6.

41. Leonard Shapiro, "Under the PGA's Wing, Nike Tour Starting to Fly" *Washington Post*, March 5, 1998, 32. T.R. Reinman, "Nike Tour is Long on Desire, Short on Tents and Skyboxes," *The San Diego Union Tribune*, March 10, 1998, D4.

42. Stefan Fatsis, "Nike Kicks in Millions to Sponsor Soccer in U.S.," *The Wall Street Journal*, October 22, 1997, B1, B8.

43. "A Look Back at the First Two Years of MLS." <http://www.mlsnet.com/about/#The Structure>.

44. Rick Burton, "A Case Study on Sports Property Servicing Excellence: National Football League Properties," *Sport Marketing Quarterly*, vol. 5, no. 3 (1996): 23–30.

45. Nancy Boomer. "Winnipeg's Next Flood." <http://www.marketingmag.ca/Content/1.98/special1.html>.

46. Jeff Jenson, "Nike Creates New Division to Stage Global Events," *Advertising Age*, September 30, 1996, 2.

47. Wamsley, 1997

48. Howard Schlossberg, *Sports Martketing* (Cambridge, MA: Blackwell Publishers, 1996).

49. "ESPN Chilton Sports Poll Olympic Report." <http://research.chilton.net/sr0696sp.htm>.

50. Stuart Elliott, "After $5 Billion is Bet, Marketers Are Racing to Be Noticed Amid the Clutter of the Summer Games," *New York Times*, July 16, 1996, D6.

51. James Crimmins and Martha Horn, "Sponsorship From Management Ego to Marketing Success," *Journal of Advertising Research*, vol. 36, no. 4 (July 1996).

52. Senji Ishikawa, David K. Stotlar, and Marcia L. Walker, "Olympic Games Marketing in Japan," *Sport Marketing Quarterly*, vol. 5, no. 4 (1996): 17–25.

Distribution Concepts

After completing this chapter, you should be able to

- Describe the core distribution concepts in sports marketing

- Discuss the various types of channels of distribution

- Explain the nature of sports retailing and discuss the current state of the sports retailing industry

- Explore the major issues in facilities and stadium management and marketing

- Understand the role of sports media in the distribution process

In October 1996, a new division of the NFL was developed to launch the sport around the globe. As vice president for television distribution for the NFL, Ann Murray is responsible for ensuring that the world has an opportunity to view NFL action. Having held a similar job at the NBA, she certainly knows the ropes and can quickly put her finger on the difference between the two roles. "One of the big challenges facing the NFL is that the sport isn't widely played," she said.

In the Super Bowl, she has an ideal shop window for the NFL television product. The global audience for Super Bowl XXXI was around 800 million, watching in 150 countries, including Thailand where an enthusiastic local commentary helps bring the game to the local audience.

In many ways, television has assumed a dual role. On one hand, the pictures are the perfect ambassador for the sport, introducing new audiences to the spectacle. On the other hand, television distribution is an important revenue stream. Asked whether the NFL was prepared to deal pictures for guaranteed exposure in order to spread the gospel, Murray seems willing to keep her options open.

"I believe that if people see something as valuable, they will pay for it. If they spend money, they will make sure it succeeds," she said. "Our objective is to get the best possible exposure. That could mean being open to barter arrangements, which may not involve money but could take other things into consideration. "We want to bring more value to our package, to make sure people are satisfied and get real value for their investment."

The NFL sees television as a key building block, and innovative broadcasters like the United Kingdom's Channel 4 have won praise for the way they have approached an unfamiliar subject and delivered it to their domestic audience in a style that makes football familiar and accessible.

The increasing number of overseas players in the league is also helping broadcasters tailor output to particular markets. But for the time being at least, football remains a mystery to many. "People outside the U.S. do not always know how huge and powerful this product is," said Murray. And while she may not be convinced that there will ever come a time when the sport is played as widely as, say, soccer, she is certain that international television deals will, over time, let millions around the world "feel the power" and allow the NFL to develop a strong overseas business.

Adapted from "Delivering the NFL to the World," Sport Business International. <http://www.sportbusiness.com>.

Historically, distribution has been one of the most important marketing functions. The ability of consumers to purchase or gain access to sports products in a timely fashion at a convenient location is the essence of the distribution function. Without distribution, every consumer interested in purchasing a new pair of Nike running shoes would need to travel to one of their manufacturing facilities around the world. Without the sports media, another form of distribution, we would have to travel with our favorite major league team to away games to watch the action. As illustrated in the opening scenario, without distribution, football fans from around the world would have to come to the United States to see the Super Bowl.

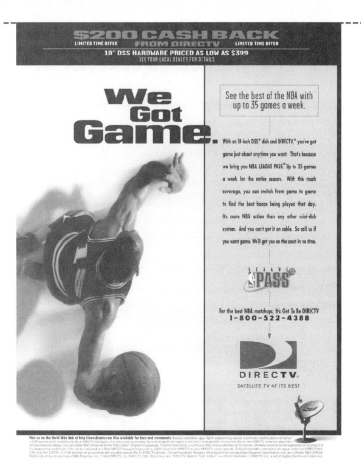

■ DIRECTV distributes customized sports programming to consumers.

Fortunately, we are able to purchase our Nike shoes from department stores, sporting goods outlets, catalogs, shoe stores, and a variety of other convenient sources. We can tune in and watch every one of our team's games because of specialized, cable television programming, such as DIRECTV.

Just what length will sports marketers go to to bring their products to consumers? Consider the following examples:

■ The Buffalo Bills chartered an Amtrak train that ran 290 miles from Albany to Buffalo, bringing fans to games. With minimal publicity, 980 people purchased tickets to the first tailgate party on rail. Another 1,500 people put their name on the waiting list. The response has local and state officials debating whether to spend millions on rail improvements that would bring the fans practically to the stadium's front gate. A few other NFL teams offer commuter rail packages to their stadiums, but none has brought in fans from so far. Bill Munson, the Bills' assistant general manager, says, "We feel this train is an important part of what we want to try to do to become as regional as we can."[1]

- A recent survey shows that Greg Norman is the professional golfer from whom most golfers would like to take a lesson. Unfortunately, there is one small problem—Norman's busy schedule will not allow it. However, the solution is much simpler. If you cannot take the people to Norman, maybe you can take Norman to the people. That is what Earl Takefman, CEO of Visual Edge Systems, is trying to do with the interactive video called "One-on-One with Greg Norman." Specially equipped trucks will carry software video gear and other equipment necessary to analyze the golfer's swing and then compare it with Norman's swing sequence. The trucks will travel to PGA tour stops, golf outings, and charity events. The cost will be about $40 for a lesson, or event organizers can buy the use of the truck for member-guest events, pro-ams, or corporate affairs.[2]

- In September 1995, a baseball game was broadcast live over the Internet for the first time. The game, featuring the Seattle Mariners against the New York Yankees, was carried by ESPN Sportzone. Regardless of what part of the world you were in, the sport of baseball could be brought to you.[3]

Distribution planning, as shown in the foregoing examples, is a complex process to understand because of the many shapes it takes in sports marketing. For sporting goods, **distribution** involves moving the product from producer to end users. This task is accomplished through a **channel of distribution**, or a coordinated group of individuals or organizations that route the sports product to the final consumer. Those individuals or organizations that take part in the distribution process are referred to as **channel members**. Channel members are responsible for facilitating the exchange between manufacturers or service providers and consumers.

For sporting events, there is a direct channel of distribution. The fans attending the event are consuming it as quickly as the sports product (entertainment) is being produced. Consumers that are not attending a sporting event may also want access to the event. In this case, the sports marketer must seek alternative ways to deliver the sporting event to a widespread audience. Television, radio, or the Internet can be considered a distribution medium for fans who wish to consume the game via one of the many broadcast media.

Distribution is also important to sports marketers who are seeking new markets in which to sell existing sports products. Sports marketers are developing new **sports delivery systems** to bring their sports to new markets. In addition to televising games worldwide, the NFL may play several regular season games in Mexico to promote the sport of football south of the border. NASCAR has also distributed its product internationally, holding several events in Japan each year.[4] Likewise, in October 1997, the NHL broke the ice in Japan by holding its first-ever official league game outside of North America.[5] As discussed in the following article, the NBA will not be left behind in the race to gain international distribution and increase the fan base.

Cedric Didier was cheering. The 24-year-old basketball nut from Grenoble had traveled four hours to see the McDonald's Championship in Paris, but hardly to root for the home team. "Michael, Michael," yelled Didier, decked out in a Chicago Bulls jersey, as Michael Jordan swished another two-pointer. Said Didier, "Jordan is the best player in the world, and the Bulls are the best team in the world."

On October 16–18, 1997, at Paris's 13,000-seat Berry arena, the Bulls—sans Scottie Pippen and Dennis Rodman—proved that again. As they eased by two European teams to win the tournament, the sold-out games underlined how the soaring worldwide appeal of the NBA has seduced even the supposedly anti-American French. The Bulls also made another point: Namely, that when it comes to marketing U.S. products abroad, Jordan and the NBA are a pretty unbeatable team. In fact, a lot of marketers would do well to follow the bouncing ball.

Since the Dream Team captured the 1992 Olympic gold medal, sales outside the United States of NBA-licensed basketballs, backboards, T-shirts, and caps have soared from $10 million to $500 million. "We saw this, and we jumped," says NBA Commissioner David Stern. A decade ago, the NBA had no international staff or foreign offices. Today, it has 80 workers in 11 offices abroad and plans to double both numbers this year. "We're spending a lot, but we're already profitable," says Paul Zilk, the NBA's international director. Compare that with the National Football League's World League: It has lost an estimated $100 million since its 1990 launch. Even nonsports ventures such as Disneyland Paris are still struggling.

Admittedly, the NBA enjoys several built-in advantages over baseball or American football. Hardly any baseball fields exist in Europe. And imagine trying to explain a squeeze play to a Frenchman. By contrast, Yvan Mainini, the French Basketball Federation's president, says basketball was first played in Paris in 1873, only two years after the game was invented in Massachusetts. "We have 450,000 players in France," Mainini says. Pro leagues exist throughout the continent but are particularly strong in southern Europe.

The NBA has shrewdly transformed these European hoop dreams into a marketing lay-up. When Europe's state broadcasting monopolies were broken up in the 1980s, the league rushed in with attractive offers to newly formed commercial and cable channels. "Michael Jordan came along at the same time that global television was experiencing outstanding growth," Stern says. Some 191 countries now televise NBA games—in 40 languages. Many get broadcasts free of charge or for a minimal fee. "The point isn't to get revenues as much as exposure," Stern explains.

But perhaps the NBA's biggest feat—and its most important lesson for other U.S. companies going global—is restraint. It refuses to start its own European league. "We don't have a Manifest Destiny," says Stern. Even though Disney's theme park outside Paris is recovering, the Mouse blundered by barging into France with an attitude. It has been forced to write off much of its huge investment in oversized hotels and parking lots. Unlike Americans, Europeans prefer to visit the park just for the day and often come by train.

A European NBA could provoke a similar culture clash. Many big European cities do not have American-style indoor arenas, and a new league would be a declaration of war against local basketball groups.

Transatlantic basketball tensions were already surfacing at the championships. After the Bulls beat his team 89–82, Bozidar Maljkovic, coach of PSG Racing, derided the

(continued)

constant television time-outs and the NBA's showbiz approach—the mascots, vast video screens, and cheerleaders. The French Federation's Mainini says, "The NBA thinks about selling shirts. We think about basketball." And the NBA's global glow could fade after Jordan hangs up his sneakers. "When he retires, there is going to be a void no one can fill," concedes Stern.

But the McDonald's Championship was nothing but net for Jordan and the NBA. When European teams played each other, the arena was almost empty. When the Bulls took center stage, the fans—and more than 1,000 journalists—piled in. The crowd, especially teens who, polls show, prefer basketball to soccer, went wild over Jordan's acrobatics. "No French player comes close," said 16-year-old Solien Mekki.

Even for superstar Jordan, the adulation this far from home seemed surprising. "When I first came into the league, I could sit outside [at the cafes] and not be bothered," he recalled. This trip, he could not leave his hotel without being mobbed. Michael may long for those peaceful days, but David Stern is not complaining.

Source: William Erickson, "Michael, the NBA, and the Slam Dunking of Paris," *Business Week,* November 3, 1997, 82. Reprinted from November 3, 1997 issue of *Business Week* by special permission, copyright © 1997 by The McGraw-Hill Companies, Inc.

In this chapter, distribution will be examined from three distinct perspectives. First, we will explore basic distribution concepts for the delivery of sports products. Second, the distribution function will be investigated from the sporting event standpoint. Ticket distribution and the stadium as "place" will be examined as a portion of this distribution function. Finally, distribution will be discussed from the viewpoint of sports media, or those organizations interested in bringing sporting events to widespread audiences.

(B)asic Distribution Concepts

As stated earlier, distribution involves getting sports products to consumers. This is accomplished through a channel of distribution that is defined as organizations or individuals who direct the flow of sports products from producer to consumer. The organizations or individuals who make up the channel of distribution are commonly referred to as **channel members**. Channel members include producers, intermediaries, and consumers. Producers of sports products may range from two teams competing products a manufacturer of sporting goods, such as Starter. As we discussed in earlier chapters, the ultimate consumers of the sports products are either spectators or sports participants.

Intermediaries are organizations or individuals that are in the middle (thus, the term *middlemen*) of producers and consumers. The two most common types of intermediaries for sporting goods are wholesalers and retailers. Wholesalers sell to other intermediaries, such as retailers and/or other wholesalers. Retailers, such as The Sports Authority or Oshman's, sell to ultimate consumers, or end users. Although these are traditional intermediaries for sporting goods, intermediaries are also present in the channel of distribution for attending sporting events or watching sports. For instance, the ticket distribution agency (or the scalper) can be considered an intermediary in getting you to the sports product. In addition, the televised sporting event is distributed to you via a cable or a national network. In this case, the media can be thought of as an intermediary.

One job of the sports marketer is to ensure that products flow smoothly through this "pipeline" of intermediaries to you, the ultimate consumer. Through the proper management of channels of distribution, products arrive to consumers in the most timely and cost-effective manner. Intermediaries, in fact, make this possible. In the next section, we will look at why intermediaries advance the distribution process.

Intermediary Functions

Intermediaries perform a number of broad functions in the distribution process. Each of these broad functions is essential to the distribution process. The structure of the distribution channel and the type of sports product dictate the functions of the intermediary. It is important to realize that, in most cases, the functions are necessary and cannot be eliminated, although responsibilities can be shifted among channel members.

The first channel function is referred to as the **information function**. Because intermediaries such as sporting goods retailers are closer to the end users of the product, they are in a position to provide insight into consumer needs and the benefits desired by consumers. Aside from marketing research, channel intermediaries may also help producers monitor the marketing environment. For example, a retailer monitors trends in consumer demand for products and informs the manufacturer of the sporting good. The information can also flow in the other direction. That is, retailers provide consumers with information to assist in purchase decisions. Intermediaries such as the sports media also need to provide information to consumers regarding the nature of the broadcast.

Another of the core intermediary functions of channel members is **marketing communications**. As we learned in chapters 10 and 11, the communications function involves a number of activities, such as advertising and promotion, personal selling, and public relations. Typically, many of the marketing communications functions are performed by retailers to stimulate demand of end users. For example, Lady Foot Locker promotes Avia shoes using a collegiate woman athlete. The objective of this promotion is to increase demand for Avia and for Lady Foot Locker.

The **physical distribution** function is perhaps most synonymous with distribution activities. Without physical distribution, products would not be moved from producer to consumer. Imagine having to drive to Louisville every time you wanted to purchase a baseball bat or to Beaverton, Oregon (or some foreign country) to buy Nike shoes. One of the critical issues facing distribution is that deliveries are made in a timely fashion. New technologies are emerging, such as a computerized order processing system that reduces the time between placing an order and receiving goods.

Inventory management is yet another of the important functions performed by channel intermediaries. Inventory management tasks include ordering the correct assortment of merchandise (i.e., popular product lines and items), maintaining appropriate levels of merchandise, and storing the merchandise that has been ordered. Today, just-in-time (JIT) management systems are being used to minimize the amount of inventory that needs to be stored. In essence, goods arrive when needed to reduce inventory costs.

■ *Golf Day* illustrates direct marketing in action.

Although each of these functions is necessary, the channel member who performs each is largely dictated by the type of channel. In other words, various routes can be navigated from producer to consumer. In the next section, we will examine several of the more common marketing channels for sports products.

Types of Channels

Channels of distribution can vary in length, depending on the total number of channel members. Broadly speaking, channels can be described as either direct or indirect. **Direct channels** are the shortest in length because producer and end user are the only two channel members (see Figure 13.1).

With the increasing number of direct mail catalogues for sports and the use of the Internet for shopping, direct distribution is becoming a popular channel for sports marketers. Virtually all types of sporting goods can be purchased using direct mail. For example, discounted golf equipment can be purchased from GolfSmith or GolfWorks catalogues, running shoes and gear can be purchased from California Best or Roadrunner catalogues, volleyball equipment is sold in the magazine *Volleyball*, and tennis equipment is sold in the magazine *Tennis*. The following article looks at the plusses and minuses of buying equipment via direct mail.

figure 13.1 Direct Channel of Distribution

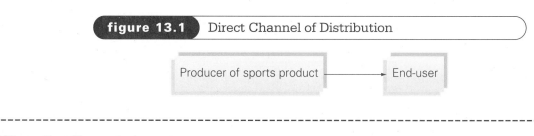

What is the deal with all these mail-order racquet ads in the back of this magazine? Answer: It could be a pretty good deal, especially if your top shopping priority is price or if you are looking for a discontinued model.

Buying racquets, shoes, and tennis accessories by mail is an option chosen by 18 percent of players, according to a survey in *Tennis Buyer's Guide*, *Tennis* magazine's affiliated trade publication. The biggest advantage to letting your fingers do the shopping through the back of the book could be saving money—25 percent and up, according to Tracy Leonard, *Tennis's* equipment advisor.

To put that to the test, we asked five mail-order companies to give us their best price on the Head Big Bang, which was advertised in our September issue. Quotes ranged from $149 to $189 strung, compared to the average store price of $199 unstrung, according to Head.

But while the mail-order route generally is cheaper, one trade-off is the customization of the new racquet. "A good pro or tennis shop is going to weigh and balance and string your new racquet to your exact specifications and customize the grip for you," says one manufacturer who, like most brands, distributes his products to both retails shops and mail-order companies. "If you're a serious player, you may save some money on the racquet if you buy it by mail, but you could end up spending more by the time you bring it in for the special grip or strings."

But the notion that the mail-order option is a price-only consideration is wrong, according to David Hirschfeld, a partner in Holabird Sports, one of the largest mail-order companies. "We like to think of ourselves as the L.L. Bean of tennis—our emphasis is on total value, not just price," he says. "We carry the entire line of most of the manufacturers and give customers a fair price and good service before and after the sale." He points out that Holabird has a full-time staff of eight certified stringers and knowledgeable tele-salespeople, and his mail-order division is as service-oriented as his retail shop in Baltimore. "The other thing we offer is that we don't try to persuade buyers into any particular brand the way a lot of club pros do who are paid by the manufacturers to push their brands. We don't care what you buy … just that you buy." One mail-order advantage is that the companies usually have a wider range of grip sizes and carry more models—including discontinued models—than stores.

But the biggest drawback to the mail-order option is that you cannot try out the racquet, which is not important if all you want is to replace your existing stick with the same model. There is, of course, the option of trying out the racquet at your local club or tennis specialty store and then ordering it by mail, if you do not mind getting the evil eye from the shop when you come in to get it restrung or regripped.

Another disadvantage to mail-order racquet shopping is that, often, manufacturers give the retail outlets a head start on new products before they distribute them to the mail-order companies. It is a system that works like movie releases—the theaters get them before the video stores.

If you decide to exercise the mail-order option, shop around.

Adapted from Bill Gray, "The Pros and Cons of Buying Mail-Order Racquets," *Tennis*, November 1995, 79–80.

The other type of channel structure is called an **indirect channel** because intermediaries are present. Two common indirect channels of distribution look like the following:

Producer ⟶ Wholesaler ⟶ Retailer ⟶ Consumer
Producer ⟶ Retailer ⟶ Consumer

As you can see, wholesalers and retailers are all added to the distribution process when indirect channels are being utilized. In addition, agents or brokers, who have the legal authority to act on behalf of the producer, can become important members of an indirect channel. Sports agents, in fact, are intermediaries who act on the behalf of athletes who are being purchased by the consumer (in this case the sports organization).

Single versus Multiple Channels

The previous section provided a brief discussion of traditional channel structure. Another decision that must be made by sporting goods manufacturers is whether to use a single-channel versus a multiple-channel strategy. A **single-channel strategy** is described as using only one channel of distribution to reach potential consumers. For example, Sea Ray boats are sold through authorized Sea Ray dealerships around the world. This channel structure allows the manufacturer greater control over the entire distribution process.

The other more common alternative for channel design is to distribute sports products via **multiple channels**. In this case, more than one channel structure is utilized. For example, Calloway golf clubs can be purchased in golf specialty stores, through direct mail-order catalogs, and at pro shops. Professional and college athletic programs also offer multiple channels of distribution. Games and events can be attended, watched on television, listened to on the radio, or even broadcast via the Internet. For many sports organizations, multiple channels are considered advantageous because they allow multiple opportunities or places to purchase the sports product, and they reach different market segments.

Degrees of Market Coverage

One of the coverages related to the idea of single versus multiple retailing channels is determining the desired level of market coverage. **Market coverage** refers to the number of outlets used in the distribution of the sports product. The extent of market coverage is defined in terms of exclusive, selective, or intensive distribution.

Exclusive distribution occurs when only one outlet is used to market products per geographic market. For instance, the phrase "exclusive coverage" of sporting events illustrates the concept of exclusive distribution. NBC has the exclusive rights to televise the Summer Olympic Games in 2000, 2004, and 2008.[6] Moreover, NBC has exclusive coverage of the 2002 and 2006 Winter Olympics. Other examples of exclusive distribution include the long-standing coverage of the Masters and the NCAA Basketball Tournament by CBS.

Selective distribution, as the name implies, refers to making products available in several, but selectively chosen, outlets. For instance, the NFL selectively distributes its regular season contests on Fox, CBS, ESPN, and ABC. **Intensive distribution** involves selling sports products in a large number of available outlets. Nike athletic shoes, for example, are sold in Niketown retail stores, Nike outlet shops, a number of retail athletic shoe stores (e.g., Foot Locker, Just For Feet), department stores, discount stores, and catalogues. As such, Nike has chosen an intensive distribution strategy. However, specific models of Nike shoes are selectively or exclusively distributed.

Sports Retailing

A critical member of most channels of distribution for sporting goods is the sports retailer. Sports retailers, such as The Sports Authority, Foot Locker, and Dick's Sporting Goods, are linked with sports marketing in that they provide products to the final consumer so that he or she may participate in sports. By definition, **sports retailers** are channel members who are involved in all the activities of selling products and services to end users, or final consumers.

In this definition of sports retailing, a few important points must be considered. First, retailers are channel members who differentiate themselves from other channel members in that they sell to end users, or consumers, who use the products or service. If more than 50 percent of an organization's sales are to end users, they may be called retailers. However, if less than 50 percent are sold to final consumers, the organization is considered a wholesaler. By contrast, a wholesaler purchases products that are sold to other businesses for resale.

Second, retailers are involved in a variety of activities, such as promotion, creating a desirable store image in which to shop, and providing wide assortments of sporting goods to consumers. Each of these retailing activities will be explored in the next section of this chapter.

Third, the definition of sports retailing points to the notion of selling not only goods, but providing needed services. Most sports retailers provide both goods and services to consumers. For example, a tennis retailer will sell equipment and apparel and also provide racquet repair and stringing services. Some tennis retailers may offer lessons, as well. Other sports retailers may provide ticket distribution services for sporting events.

Some sports retailers, such as health and fitness clubs, are known as service retailers because they primarily offer services rather than goods to end users. Other examples of service sports retailers would be golf club repair shops and tourist attractions, such as the Baseball Hall of Fame and the Louisville Slugger Museum. In addition, the rapidly expanding field of sports medicine, which not only rehabilitates you when you are injured but also helps to make you a better athlete, is a sports retailer.

The Number and Types of Sports Retailers

The continued reduction in the total number of sporting goods outlets and the consolidation of key players continues. According to a 1997 study by Sportstyle, the top 10 sporting goods retailers accounted for 5,103 outlets in 1996 versus 4,804 in 1995—an increase of 6 percent, countering the overall trend toward fewer retail locations.[7] The small, independent retailer and regional chains continue to be under pressure and fall victim to the industry's consolidation. One of the great names in sporting goods retailing, Herman's, closed its doors in 1996 after a 60-year run.

The large retailers continue to transform the marketplace. Woolworth's has put together an empire of brands, including Foot Locker, Lady Foot Locker, Kid's Foot Locker, and Champs, while an investment group owns MC Sports, Big 5, and Gart Sports. There is The Sports Authority, with sales over a billion dollars and 199 stores, continuing to build "big-box" stores in the United States and expanding internationally.

Jack Smith, 60, is a good customer for his own wares. He runs 15 miles a week, plays tennis twice a week, and golfs at least once a week. A big wheel in sporting goods retailing, the trim 6-footer is chairman of The Sports Authority, Inc. (revenues of $1 billion), the world's largest chain concentrating solely in sporting goods.

He runs 138 superstores, with an average of 42,000 square feet of selling space, situated in 26 states from Massachusetts to California and in Canada. Fort Lauderdale–based Sports Authority is at the forefront of the consolidation movement. Its closest rivals, Sports & Recreation and Sportmart, each have only about half of Sports Authority's revenues.

Smith's stores are for—well, for Jack Smiths. The emporiums are stacked floor to ceiling with basketballs, bats, irons, hockey pucks, fishing rods, sneakers, and skis in just about every conceivable shape, size, and quality.

Retailing has been in a well-documented slump, and sporting goods stores have not avoided it. The Sports Authority has. "My numbers make me want to tap dance on Wall Street," says the Philadelphia native. In 1995, his net income rose 32 percent, to $22.3 million, outpacing sales, which were up 25 percent. His same-store sales rose 1.1 percent, despite store openings in existing markets. Both of his rivals reported net income that was down more than 50 percent.

What is Smith's secret? The same as that of any category killer, from Home Depot to Toys "R" Us. His stores are so densely stocked that it is practically impossible to walk out without whatever you were looking for.

Carrying heavy inventories without tight controls is, of course, a recipe for bankruptcy. Smith wisely invested in computer systems early on to monitor inventory at each store on a daily basis. Orders are automatically transmitted to suppliers, who ship to stores directly. That allows Smith to turn inventory faster than competitors, avoid overstocking, and keep costs down by eliminating the need for a distribution center.

Smith aims to press home his advantage over his rivals. He plans to increase his market share both with new stores and by buying existing stores. In July, for instance, he bought leases on seven stores from bankrupt Sportstown.

Smith did not invent the idea of a category killer in sporting goods. In the early 1980s, he was an executive at Herman's Sporting Goods, Inc., and tried to emulate them. He could not pull it off. In 1981, Smith quit Herman's, by then owned by a British company, and interested venture capitalists in picking up Grace's idea of a sporting goods category killer. By 1990, he was running eight stores, mainly in Florida, and was convinced he could make the idea work. Smith's minichain caught the eye of Joseph Antonini, then chairman of Kmart Corporation, who acquired it for $75 million. Backed by Kmart capital, Smith now had the wherewithal to go all out for expansion. By fall 1994, The Sport's Authority hit 100 stores.

Then Kmart fell on hard times—which turned out to be a break for Smith. First, Kmart sold 71 percent of The Sports Authority to the public for around $270 million—14.1 million shares at $19 each. And this past fall it sold the remaining 29 percent for another $160 million. The Sports Authority is now an independent company with nearly 21 million shares; Smith owns 216,000 shares and options worth over $5 million.

For now, at least, it looks like clear sailing. The Sports Authority has no long-term debt and can use its entire cash flow for expansion. This year, Smith plans to open 30 new stores. Duff & Phelps retailing analyst Richard Nelson predicts that the company will earn $28 million, or $1.35 a share, on sales of almost $1.3 billion this year.

Ask Jack Smith to name his business heroes. Not missing a beat, he names Charles

Several of the large retail chains are experimenting with a format featuring even more square footage. However, the expansion rate of the "big-box" outlets will slacken as the U.S. market becomes saturated, even for these megastores. The "big-boxes" and the power center concept (huge shopping centers with four or five "superstores"), which have risen in number to over 400 in the United States, have victimized the strip malls and mall shopping centers. It is clear that the very large retailers have successfully built up the capital necessary to invest in establishing a network of stores in key locations in major marketplaces. They are now competing head-on for market share. The smaller, independent retailer can still compete by offering superb personal service to the customer. These niche retailers will find success by adopting a "boutique" approach—less merchandise but more selective—combined with superior merchandising and personalized post-purchase customer contact.[8]

Sports Retailing Mix

Like all marketers and retailers, sports retailers must also design an effective marketing mix for their retail environment. With the nature of sports retailing constantly changing, sports retailers must be able to quickly adapt their marketing mix to meet the changing needs of consumers.

The first step in designing an effective retail marketing mix is to understand just who your customers are or who you want them to be. Sports retailers segment and target groups of consumer in a number of ways. Some sports retailers, such as Lady Foot Locker, use demographic segmentation and target women. Other retailers, such as the many tennis and ski shops, segment on the basis of psychographics and lifestyle, knowing that a large proportion of consumers who ski also participate in tennis.

Just as in the broader strategic sports marketing process, after target markets have been chosen the next step in retailing is to develop a unique position in the marketplace. If you recall, positioning was defined in chapter 7 as fixing the sports product in the mind of consumers. In retailing, positioning is fixing the retail outlet in the minds of consumers. This is accomplished by developing a marketing mix that will be the most appealing to the chosen target market and that will create the desired image. Let us examine retailing mix decisions and retail image in greater detail.

Sports Retailing Products

One of the biggest challenges facing sports retailers is choosing the right product mix to satisfy their target market(s). Remember, the product mix describes all of the different product lines that are carried by the organization, as well as the depth and breadth of that assortment. In sports retailing, this translates into decisions about what sports products to carry and what variety and depth of product lines to carry in each sport. For example, some sporting goods retailers may not choose to sell hunting and fishing equipment, while others may specialize in only these two sporting activities. Obviously, these two sports retailers would be positioned very differently from each other.

An excellent example of a sports retailer that has chosen to differentiate itself based on the type of merchandise carried is Play It Again Sports. These retailers specialize in selling preowned (used) sporting goods at a fraction of the cost of new products. Consumers bring in their old merchandise and may either sell it or trade it for other merchandise. By selling used sporting goods, Play It Again Sports targets price-sensitive consumers who, for whatever reason, do not want to pay a lot for their sporting goods.

Planning the assortment of goods and services to offer consumers is often referred to as merchandising. In fact, merchandising is at the heart of sports retailing. If sports retailers did not provide some assortment of products, stores would have to be highly specialized. For example, you would have to go to a soccer store for shin guards, a baseball store for a glove, a hockey store for a stick, and so on.

Merchandisers are also concerned with the issue of presenting the products in the retail environment. The type of merchandise sold by a sports retailer and the way that it is presented to consumers have a tremendous impact on the image of the retailer. Store layout and the way the products are stocked will be critical to the atmosphere of the retail outlet. Nike Town outlets could sell their actual products on a fraction of the retail space they actually use. If they reduced their space, however, they would not convey the sports experience message that they are trying to transmit to consumers.

A recent trend in sports merchandising is to carry products in the retail environment that are not necessarily focused on sports. This practice of selling "unrelated merchandise" is referred to as scrambled merchandising. Sports retailers are beginning to scramble merchandise by offering consumers a much wider variety of active wear and clothing than they have ever done in the past. In addition, some stores are beginning to offer consumers a wide array of sports services, such as batting cages, a bowling center, basketball courts, and workout facilities.

Sports Retailing Pricing

Pricing decisions also allow sports retailers to differentiate themselves from competitors. Many independent and smaller sporting goods retailers charge higher than normal prices and position themselves as excellent customer service providers. Sports retailers, such as the nearly 450 "team stores" across the country that specialize in college and professional licensed merchandise, may also charge higher prices for their deep but narrow product lines. In contrast, sports discounters, such as Hibbett Sporting Goods, offer lower prices and a wider assortment of products.

Again, the decision of what price strategy to follow at the retail level is based on the target market that has been chosen, the desired positioning, and the competition. It is important to understand that not all consumers are necessarily looking for the lowest price. The various categories of price orientation among consumers are presented in Table 13.1.

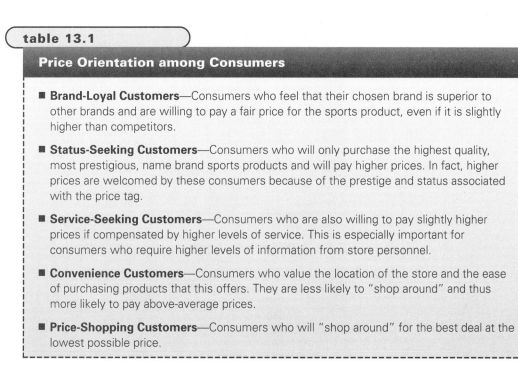

table 13.1

Price Orientation among Consumers

- **Brand-Loyal Customers**—Consumers who feel that their chosen brand is superior to other brands and are willing to pay a fair price for the sports product, even if it is slightly higher than competitors.

- **Status-Seeking Customers**—Consumers who will only purchase the highest quality, most prestigious, name brand sports products and will pay higher prices. In fact, higher prices are welcomed by these consumers because of the prestige and status associated with the price tag.

- **Service-Seeking Customers**—Consumers who are also willing to pay slightly higher prices if compensated by higher levels of service. This is especially important for consumers who require higher levels of information from store personnel.

- **Convenience Customers**—Consumers who value the location of the store and the ease of purchasing products that this offers. They are less likely to "shop around" and thus more likely to pay above-average prices.

- **Price-Shopping Customers**—Consumers who will "shop around" for the best deal at the lowest possible price.

Source: Joel Evans and Barry Berman, *Marketing*, 6th ed. (New York, NY: Macmillan, 1994), 680.

Again, the sports retailer must identify the price orientation of its target market and plan the rest of the retail mix accordingly. For instance, the independent sports retailer may charge more but offer higher levels of customer service, convenience, and, hopefully, establish "store-loyal" consumers. On the other hand, sports superstores may offer limited service but the lowest prices in town.

Sports Retailing Distribution

The most critical retail distribution decision is the location of the store. As the old saying goes, the three most important factors in the success of a retail outlet are location, location, location. Although this is generally true, certain types of shoppers, as we have learned, are more price sensitive than others and will be willing to travel to more remote locations to get the best deals. Alternatively, the prestige shopper may have to go out of his (or her) way to purchase that one-of-a-kind product.

Because location is so critical, how do retailers choose the ideal location? As with all retail mix decisions, store location is largely a function of the target market and positioning. Table 13.2 presents general guidelines for choosing a store location.

Sports Retail Promotions

Retail promotions refer to decisions sports retailers make with respect to the proper mix of personal selling, advertising, sales promotions, and public relations. Promotional

■ Retailers like Kmart appeal to price shopping customers.

decisions also play a key role in retail positioning, or establishing the store in the mind of the target market.

Typically, advertising at the local retail level has short-term, direct objectives for stimulating sales. Sports retail advertising tends to emphasize price discounts and is usually run in conjunction with other sales promotions. Ultimately, retailers' advertising wants to draw consumers to a specific store with the hope that once they arrive, they will make multiple purchases.

At the national level, retail advertising tends to be more institutional, stressing the image of a chain of stores. These national advertisements promote the atmosphere of the store, product selection/brand names carried, and often feature a well-known athlete endorser. For example, a FOOTACTION advertisement uses Denver Broncos quarterback John Elway and also features the Reebok brand logo. FOOTACTION hopes to enhance its image through association with a name brand shoe and the high-profile Super Bowl champion of 1997.

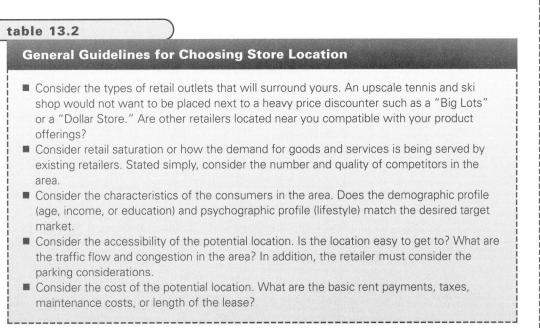

table 13.2

General Guidelines for Choosing Store Location

- Consider the types of retail outlets that will surround yours. An upscale tennis and ski shop would not want to be placed next to a heavy price discounter such as a "Big Lots" or a "Dollar Store." Are other retailers located near you compatible with your product offerings?
- Consider retail saturation or how the demand for goods and services is being served by existing retailers. Stated simply, consider the number and quality of competitors in the area.
- Consider the characteristics of the consumers in the area. Does the demographic profile (age, income, or education) and psychographic profile (lifestyle) match the desired target market.
- Consider the accessibility of the potential location. Is the location easy to get to? What are the traffic flow and congestion in the area? In addition, the retailer must consider the parking considerations.
- Consider the cost of the potential location. What are the basic rent payments, taxes, maintenance costs, or length of the lease?

Source: Patrick Dunne, Robert Lusch, Myron Gable, and Randall Gebhardt, *Retailing* (Cincinnati, OH: South-Western, 1992).

Personal selling at sports retailers is also an essential part of the retail promotional mix. The amount of personal selling is often a key positioning factor for sports retailers. Sales personnel are an important part of a consumer's perception of a retailer. The level of knowledge and the customer service the sales personnel possess can shape the image of the retailer. In essence, sales personnel are a retailer's foot soldier in the constant war for consumers' discretionary income.

Retail Image

As previously stated, the retailer's positioning strategy is thoughtfully carried out by choosing the appropriate marketing mix and by creating the desired store image. In fact, nothing may be as important to a sports retailer than the image of the store. Most retailers have realized that they need to create an image that consumers find entertaining and fun. Simply putting quality products on the shelves is no longer acceptable. As such, sporting goods retailers are undergoing a "Disneylike" transformation. According to Reebok's Meers, "If the retailers look around and see a sterile environment that just shows product, they should understand that they will have to change their presentation."[9]

Just what makes up store image? This concept is as difficult to describe as someone's personality. In fact, a good way to conceptualize store image is to think of it as "store personality" made up of many tangible and intangible traits. Retail store image is made up of a number of interrelated factors that together produce the overall store experience (see Table 13.3). These factors include atmospherics, location, store sales personnel, clientele, types of merchandise carried, and types of

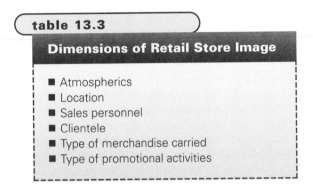

table 13.3

Dimensions of Retail Store Image

- Atmospherics
- Location
- Sales personnel
- Clientele
- Type of merchandise carried
- Type of promotional activities

promotional activities. As we discussed, the dimensions of retail store image in greater detail, pay special attention to the relationship between each factor and the marketing mix.

Atmospherics

The term that best encompasses the many facets of in-store image is atmospherics. **Atmospherics** is a retail store's visual, auditory, and olfactory environments, designed to attract and keep consumers in the store. Of all the factors that comprise retail store image, atmospherics is perhaps the most important in creating and reinforcing the store image. In addition, store atmosphere plays a role in encouraging people to visit a store, stay in a store for longer periods of time, and make more impulse purchases. In fact, some research suggests that atmosphere becomes even more important as the number of competing stores increases and as these stores begin to carry similar products at similar prices.

As seen in this definition, the three dimensions of atmospherics are the visual, auditory, and olfactory. Each of these dimensions relates to the consumer's senses and has an impact on the overall "feel" of the sports retail outlet. The visual dimension refers to those things that we can see in the store environment, such as the way the merchandise is displayed, the store layout, the color of the walls and carpeting, the in-store promotional displays, lighting, and even the appearance of employees. The auditory dimension of atmosphere refers to the sounds that are present in the retail environment. Most notably, music is an integral part of any sports retailing environment. The sports marketer must carefully choose the music/sounds that are consistent with the desired store image and target market. For example, you might want to play up-tempo, high-energy music in a store selling aerobics and exercise equipment and soft, relaxing music in a store specializing in golf equipment.

NikeTown is well-known for its visual and auditory effects within the store. For example, just look at this description of NikeTown in San Francisco:

Customers ascend from the ground floor to the third floor of this 49,840 square-foot sports showcase store on an escalator flanked by the multimedia collage wall featuring graphics video and archival displays. The three-story Town Square central space contains a full height concept pavilion, surrounded by product pavilions. The Town Square area features four banks of video monitors with inspirational videos designed by Nike Film and Video. On the screens customers will see footage of Nike athletes on the field, on the course, on the court, and on the lanes. Above, shoppers circulate through the upper floor on translucent glass bridges (etched with the Nike Waffle outsole pattern).[10]

The olfactory dimension is based on the sense of smell. Studies have shown that smell influences the amount of time consumers spend in a retail setting, purchase intentions, and spending behavior. Although smell has the greatest impact on our emotions, memory, and purchase behavior, it is seldom considered by retailers. In the future, sports retailers might manipulate the olfactory environment of their stores by producing scents that replicate the "smell of the ballpark" that consumers remember from their childhood.

Location

Location of the store was previously discussed in the context of the retail mix. First, the location of the store in relation to the community is a determinant of image. For instance, is the store in a downtown metropolitan area, in a suburban neighborhood, or in a rural community? Secondly, important to the store's image is the location of the store with respect to the store cluster. In other words, is the store located in a shopping center, in a strip mall, or perhaps in an outlet mall? Finally, the location of the store relative to surrounding stores is an important element in establishing and maintaining the retail image.

All of these location factors interact to create part of the image. A golf specialty store located in an upscale part of the community that is surrounded by other high-end retailers creates an extremely positive image for that store. In fact, this is an especially important part of image because even those consumers who never enter the store will still form an image of the store because of the location factors.

Sales Personnel

Store sales personnel are also an important ingredient in the image of the retail outlet, for a number of reasons. First, the physical appearance of the sales staff may enhance or detract from the store image. For example, the sales personnel at The Finish Line are required to wear striped referee shirts to create a "sports authority image." Second, the level of customer service provided by the sales personnel adds to the "service image" of the store.

Customer service refers to the activities that take place before, during, and after the transaction. It is the knowledge and caring that sales personnel provide customers. Studies that examine the traits of successful sales personnel have shown the importance of the role of empathy, or the ability to feel as the customer does and put oneself in the other's position to appreciate his or her situation. Most researchers have found that empathy is a highly desirable characteristic in personal selling. However, a recent study found that sales performance and empathy are not related in a linear fashion. In other words, the sales performance does not directly increase as empathy increases.[11]

In addition, and of special importance to those sports retailers that target consumers with a service orientation, customer service means the extent to which extra services are provided to consumers. For example, golf pro shops will often let you play a few rounds with a set of clubs before making a purchase decision or bicycle shops will offer test rides and maintenance discounts for consumers.

Clientele

Other consumers who shop at the same retailer comprise the clientele. The demographic and psychographic characteristics of the target market can influence the overall image of the store. For example, if trendy, high-income consumers are seen shopping at a tennis and ski shop, then the store will take on some of the characteristics of the consumers. In turn, consumers who desire to be seen as more trendy may visit this store to enhance their self image. This is another demonstration of the "match-up" hypothesis, or image congruence hypothesis, discussed in chapter 11. Rather than the match-up between celebrity endorser and product being featured in the ad or the match-up between sponsor and event, we have the congruence between consumer and retail outlet.

Merchandise Assortment

Another essential, if not the most important, determinant of store image is the type of merchandise carried. If the merchandise is considered to be high quality and high priced, the image of the store will follow. In the Kentucky Store, all of the merchandise carried is licensed by the University of Kentucky and the NCAA. The image of the store is directly related to the image of the University of Kentucky and its prominent and successful basketball program.

Promotional Activities

The nature and number of promotional activities a sports retailer implements is another factor that may impact store image. It is important to remember that promotional activities do not just include the advertising done by the sports retailer. It also includes the personal selling that impacts customer service, sales promotions, sponsorships, and public relations.

The greater the number of promotional activities, the greater the communication the sports retailer has with its target audience. As such, the retailer increases their chance to develop or maintain its image with every promotional opportunity. However, this is not to say that all promotional activities are viewed positively. For example, some consumers may equate continual price discounting of merchandise with a lower quality of product.[12] This could have a detrimental effect on overall store image.

As you have seen, store image is a function of many different factors. Perhaps one way to think about these factors is that each one is somehow related to the retailing mix. The critical principle to be gathered from the previous discussion of retailing image is that image is a powerful tool sports retailers use to differentiate themselves from their competition.

Nonstore Retailing

Another form of retailing that is growing in popularity is nonstore retailing. As the name implies, nonstore retailing are purchases made outside of the traditional retail outlet and usually in the home. Interactive shopping via the Internet, television home shopping networks, and mail-order retailing are all types of nonstore retailing. It is predicted that as many as 40 percent of all shoppers will try some form of home shopping within the next several years. Generally, consumers are shopping at home for convenience, time savings, potentially lower prices, and no pressure from salespeople.[13]

Somewhat surprisingly, consumer safety may also be a reason that consumers are shopping at home.[14] One study reports that consumers no longer feel safe in heavily crowded malls or downtown shopping areas. This finding has tremendous implications for sporting goods retailers and for professional sports franchises. Strategies need to be developed and implemented to promote a safe environment for shopping or attending events. This also has implications for the location of new sports facilities. A number of new stadiums are being built in impoverished areas to spur economic development. If this finding can be generalized, then sports organizations may need to rethink where they are "relocating" and rebuilding.

Internet Shopping

One of the fastest growing home shopping media is the Internet. About 44 million adults (23 percent of the population) use the Internet regularly according to Mediaweek Research.[15] The Yankee Group estimates 5.7 million households shopped online in 1997. This number is projected to grow to 35 million by the year 2000.[16] However, that percentage of on-line shoppers is predicted to grow with further advances in technology and consumer acceptance. Other factors that will help increase the amount of Internet shopping include addressing concerns with security of payment and being assured companies on the Web are reputable.

One of the primary advantages of Web shopping is the ability of sports marketers to reach a highly uniform target market. In other words, the target market on the Internet is highly homogeneous and has very similar interests and behaviors. This target marketing approach, driven by the rapid growth in computer technology, has facilitated the use of database marketing techniques.

Database marketing measures customers' buying behavior so the sports marketer is able to distinguish loyal fans from first-time purchasers. Once these loyal customers are captured on the Internet, they can be reached when they go on-line next time or via more traditional direct marketing approaches, such as being mailed postcards inviting them to attend a pre-game team function or social event for fans after the game. Sports marketers have recently started to successfully use these traditional database marketing techniques.

Stadium as "Place"

As we discussed earlier in the chapter, the distribution channel for services, such as attending a sporting event, varies dramatically from the distribution of a sporting good. The primary distinction is that the game is produced and consumed simultaneously at the "place" of distribution. As such, the service "factory," or place where the service is consumed, becomes an integral part of the service experience for consumers. The following article provides an elegant description of the stadium experience and its importance to sport.

Walt Disney said at the opening of Disneyland in 1955, "It will be a place for people to find happiness and knowledge." In an ideal world, the same aspirations should be expressed at the opening ceremony of a modern stadium—unfortunately, this is not the case.

These special places—these cathedrals of sport we call stadia—have not lived up to their potential since they evolved out of the codification of sport last century. That is unfortunate, because stadia are very special buildings: They are designed to bring communities together, to react with each other and as one with the event. We gather inside them to celebrate a unique experience—whether it is a sporting event or music event. But these buildings, which have taken on the responsibility of providing us with this special experience, are often dull and uninteresting places. Sometimes they lack the most basic amenities and are bleak and unfriendly; their owners are obsessed with head counts at the turnstiles rather than the heartbeats of experience.

The good news is that these inhospitable concrete bowls are dying.

A New Generation

Great performances are difficult to achieve in a hostile environment, any more than spectator commitment can be expected from people who have to queue, are jostled and uncomfortable, have restricted views, and are herded out at the end of the event.

A new generation of stadia are in the making and will live up to their potential of being very special places. But mediocrity in design, management, catering, safety, or comfort has no place in the new sporting cathedrals. At long last we have woken up to the fact that the long-term health of any stadium is directly dependent on two things: the quality of the event and the quality of the spectator experience. The people creating these buildings are learning to protect those qualities, creating venues that can command the respect and admiration of the athletes and the spectators.

There is no doubt that the average living room provides a higher level of comfort than most stadia, and television coverage generally provides a better view of the game, with the added benefit of close-ups, replays, commentary, and interviews. But the critical ingredient that sets the live experience apart from its televised replica is this—the crowd: this gathering of people focusing on a show of human endeavor.

The Experience

This physical and emotional experience is the product the stadium sells, and it is unique in modern life. The opportunity to be part of the crowd, to cheer and applaud at the same time as 100,000 other people just like us, to join in the wave, the national songs or the club chant, provides a deep bonding reassurance that we are part of a whole.

The spirit, the camaraderie, the emotion, and the atmosphere of a great sporting occasion are improved by a great stadium. The venue is not a passive backdrop, but is a set that can enhance the experience through its design and its management. It is this experience that is the core business of the stadium, and it must be nurtured and encouraged if it is to survive and prosper.

Source: "The Death of the Stadium." *Sport Business International.* <http://www.sportbusiness.com>. Courtesy of Sport Business, Ltd.

The Emergence of New Venues

For the last 15 years, almost every city and their professional sports franchise has talked about building a new facility or renovating an existing facility. In some areas, such as Greater Cincinnati, there are even proposals to build three new stadia—one for the Bengals (football), one for the Reds (baseball), and one for NASCAR racing. Moreover, an estimated $7 billion will be spent on new stadia in the United States as nearly 50 professional sports teams either will be playing or expect to play in a venue within the next few years.[17]

Rather than build a new facility, some sports complexes are choosing less costly renovations. For example, Wembley Stadium in London will soon be receiving a face-lift. In an effort to attract events such as soccer's World Cup in 2006 and the World Athletic Championships in 2003, Wembley Stadium will be shutting its doors for re-modeling in mid-1999.[18]

The English Sports Council has agreed to release the first part of $194.6 million to begin the improvements of the new "English National Stadium." Chairman for the English Sports Council, Sir Rodney Walker, stated that with a "world class, state-of-the-art stadium [England] can confidently put forward strong bids for world class events."

Who will be asked to pay for these major stadium renovations or sparkling new arenas? Although the logical answer to this question would be the millionaire owners or huge corporations who own the teams, 80 percent of all monies come from the tax-payers. Ironically, the average citizen may not be able to afford the price of admission to the new stadium or arena that he or she just helped fund. The stadium that the tax-payers just funded may be obsolete in less than 10 years. For example, the Miami Heat of the NBA built a brand new facility for the expansion team in 1988, but it already is being replaced by a new and improved $200 million arena. As business consultant Marc Ganis pointed out, "It was obsolete before the concrete dried."[19]

The primary reason the stadium was quickly outdated was the absence of luxury seating and other amenities that are standard in today's new arenas. Modern sports complexes with luxury boxes, restaurants, and other entertainment facilities seem to be guaranteed revenues for owners. For instance, Seattle Mariners' owner Ken Behring says he can add $15 million a year to the team's revenues from luxury boxes alone in a new site. Andrew Zimbalist, an economist at Smith College, agrees. He believes that a new stadium or arena can add between $10 million and $40 million to a team's annual income.

What are new stadiums doing to enhance the entertainment value of attending games? Built for the 1996 Summer Olympics, the Atlanta Braves' Turner Field provides an excellent example of the latest in stadium design. The field has been described as an entertainment park complete with interactive batting cages, picnic areas, restaurants, and sports museums. In addition, fans can announce the game and purchase a tape of their broadcast. The primary goal of these modern theme parks is to create value for the price of admission and attract more families to the games. The reality is that the majority of fans want these new sports venues—even if the funding comes out of their own pockets.[20]

Along with an entertaining stadium atmosphere, the location of new stadiums can play a major role in attendance. A recent trend in stadium design is to construct "old-style" ballparks. Having a "retro" park is based not only on the stadium's appearance, but also the feeling of how the ballpark fits in with the surrounding neighborhood. For instance, Camden Yards in Baltimore is highlighted by a warehouse that sits outside the stadium and provides part of the old feel that is attractive to fans. This old feel at Camden Yards is maintained down to the most minute details, such as the typeface and lettering used on signage.

table 13.4

Five Newer Ballparks and Percentage of Capacity Based on Average Attendance Since Opening

Camden Yards, Baltimore	97% of capacity
Coors Field, Denver	94% of capacity
Jacobs Field, Cleveland	94% of capacity
The Ballpark at Arlington, Texas	69% of capacity
Comiskey Park, Chicago	66% of capacity

Adapted from Cliff Peale, "Adding Spice to the Ballpark," *Cincinnati Post*, October 2, 1996, 5B.

Table 13.4 provides an objective look at how the newer ballparks are faring in terms of attendance. Note that Camden Yards, Coors Field, and Jacobs Field are "retro parks" that are situated in neighborhood settings, while The BallPark at Arlington and Comiskey Park are more modern facilities with respect to location.

Ticket Distribution

Revenues generated through media continue to rise in the revenue mix of professional sports teams. Even with this trend in broadcast revenues, ticket revenues remain critical to the financial health of sports organizations. As such, ticket distribution practices are one of the most important considerations of sports marketing managers.

A common misperception is that ticket distributors simply provide fans with tickets at a convenient location. However, ticket distributors, not unlike the channel members for other sports products, provide a variety of necessary functions. Modern ticket distribution tasks include marketing the game, advertising, sales force management, sales force operations, technical support, and customer service. As such, these tasks have an impact on the fan's overall satisfaction with the sporting experience. In addition, if these functions are performed effectively and efficiently, fans may also benefit from lower prices.

As Miller and Fielding point out in their recent study of 113 professional sports franchises, ticket distribution practices of professional sports franchises have evolved over the years.[21] In 1968, Ticketron became the first organization to offer computerized distribution services. Today, 67 percent of the responding professional sports franchises use outside ticket distribution services. Somewhat surprisingly, 81 percent of the franchises stated that the ticket agencies sell less than 33 percent of their tickets. This can be explained by the large percentage of season ticket sales for professional sports. In fact, some of the franchises that do not employ ticket agencies sell all of their tickets on a seasonal basis.

Although ticket distribution agencies generally provide a much-needed service for fans and professional sports franchises, they have also received a great deal of criticism from consumers. The primary complaint is that ticket distribution agencies add

table 13.5

Advice for Sports Marketing Managers Involved with Ticket Distribution Agencies

- No one agency operates as a monopoly, so negotiate for the best deal
- Require that the ticket agency's staff has proper training in customer service
- Require that the ticket agency's staff know your facility inside and out
- Inquire about the bonus provisions paid to you in exchange for long-term agreements
- Consider limiting the number of service fees that the ticket agency charges fans
- Negotiate the hours that the box office is open for consumers
- Retain the right to audit the ticket distribution agency
- Carefully consider the location and number of ticket distribution sites with the agency
- Decide on who will incur costs, such as ticket production on information systems
- Determine the agency's position on refunds or cancellations
- Agree on the appropriate number of phone lines to be used
- Require the ticket agency to communicate all service fees prior to the transaction
- Specify the amount of liquidation damages in case a breach of contract occurs
- Determine whether controls are in place to safeguard against employees involved in the scalping market
- Require that the ticket agency use print technology to guard against counterfeiting
- Understand the state laws regarding ticket distribution practices
- Determine whether your contract with the ticket agency conflicts with existing contracts
- Clarify whether the ticket distribution agency can subcontract to other distributors
- Agree that your franchise may provide ticket distribution for charitable events
- Agree that your franchise may provide ticket distribution for season tickets and other promotional packages

Source: Lori K. Miller and Lawrence W. Fielding, "Ticket Distribution Agencies and Professional Sport Franchises: The Successful Partnership," *Sport Marketing Quarterly*, vol. 6, no. 1 (1997): 47–55.

an "excessive" service fee to the face value of the ticket. The agencies feel the service fee is reasonable to cover the costs of providing the basic distribution tasks (e.g., handling charge, mailing charge), but fans feel like they are being "ripped off." Not only does this cause problems for the distribution agent, but the negative feelings also spill over onto the professional sports franchise. Twenty-seven percent of those professional sports franchises responding to the survey indicated that they receive more than 50 complaints each year from dissatisfied consumers regarding service fees. Table 13.5 provides sports marketers with suggestions for dealing with ticket distribution agencies.

Sports Media as Distribution

Another form of distribution that is continuing to grow in importance to sports is the sports media. Network and cable television, radio, and the Internet can all be considered channel intermediaries that deliver the sports product to the final consumer. Sports media, most notably television, has been considered the driving force of sports marketing in the 1990s. Let us look at what Dick Ebersol, president of NBC Sports and voted the most powerful person in sports in 1996, had to say about the significant role of the media in sports:

Look at the impact of television on the growth of sports. Because advertiser interest is so strong, the broadcast and cable networks are in a position to pay much more money for rights than anyone would have imagined 15 to 20 years ago. That means more money has gone to the leagues and teams. The results? Expansion, newer stadiums, and the ability of many of these teams to attract free agents.

As long as sports—particularly on television—is a worthwhile business enterprise, the people at the top of The Sporting News' *list [of the most powerful people in sports] will keep the tent poles firmly in place. If interest falls, the poles will crack and the tent will come down. And the interest is from the fan. Your living room is the voting booth, and your remote control is the voting device. Though you did not elect us, your "votes" send us a clear message about what you want to see.[22]*

Another way to examine the growing importance of the media as a distribution tool is to look at the trend in revenues among sports franchises. Twenty-five years ago, the majority of revenues generated by professional sports franchises were based on gate receipts. For example, in 1974, 55 percent of the operating income of NFL franchises was generated from ticket sales and 34.5 percent from media revenues. Table 13.6 shows the average gate and media receipts for major league sports in 1996.

There has been a tremendous shift in all of the sports, with the exception of hockey, towards a reliance on media revenues. In fact, the NFL media revenues more than double the gate receipts. Media revenues will only increase with the recent television rights agreements reached between the NFL and the major networks for $17.6 billion.

table 13.6

Average Gate and Media Revenues for Major League Sports in 1996*

Sport	Average Gate Receipt	Average Media Receipt
MLB	25.7	25.2
NFL	22.6	43.0
NHL	25.6	6.3
NBA	23.3	21.2

* all values in millions

Source: Financial World Magazine. <http://www.financialworld.com/archives>.

The NFL's new pacts with ABC, ESPN, CBS, and Fox show once again just how much the television networks, their ratings battered by cable, video, satellite television, and the Internet, simply must have national sports to stay relevant in a splintering media market. "We anticipated we would get a big boost, but nothing like this," said Rich McKay, general manager of the Tampa Bay Buccaneers. "This is unbelievable." Here are the fees paid by each network for the television rights to the NFL:[23]

Network	Rights Fees (in billions)
ABC	4.4 for Monday Night
CBS	4.0 for AFC
FOX	4.4 for NFC
ESPN	4.8 for Sunday Night

Why are networks willing to pay these astronomical prices to televise football? Is this a reasonable price for networks to pay? Consider the benefits:[24]

- Professional football and other professional sports are the last bastion of a guaranteed mass audience. In particular, big-time sports programming delivers the young, male target market that advertisers want to reach.

- Television ratings for football are declining, but at a slower rate than the ratings for other network programming. For instance, *Monday Night Football*'s (which incidentally gets $360,000 per 30-second advertising spot) ratings have dropped about 16 percent, while the ratings of ABC have declined about 35 percent.

- On cable television, professional football remains the most watched programming.

- The networks use the NFL telecasts to create and enhance their image. In addition, they are saving money that they would have had to spend on developing other programming. And compared to the 10 percent success rate for new programs, broadcasters know sports leagues (usually) finish their seasons.

- Despite inroads by the NBA, professional football remains the United States's favorite spectator sport, says the Chilton/ESPN Sports poll, with about one-fourth of all Americans picking it as their favorite.

Aside from the traditional media, other distribution systems that allow the fans to customize their own sports products are becoming popular. Direct broadcast satellite services that use a DSS system allow fans to subscribe to all the major league sports, collegiate sports, and the more than 25 specialty sports networks (e.g., the Golf Channel, SpeedVision). For instance, DIRECTV's NBA League Pass allows fans to watch more than 40 games a week outside of their local area. Even more importantly, the fans are able to choose which games they want to watch. As more distributors, such as DIRECTV and Primestar, compete for subscribers, the number of games to choose from should increase.

Q. Briefly describe the sports products offered by DIRECTV.

A. With more than 175 available channels, DIRECTV is able to offer special subscription packages to every major professional sport, including NFL Sunday Ticket (National Football League), NBA League Pass (National Basketball Association), NHL Center Ice (National Hockey League), MLB Extra Innings (Major League Baseball), and MLS/ESPN Shootout (Major League Soccer). DIRECTV also carries special packages for college football and basketball. Each sports subscription offers subscribers an extensive choice of out-of-market games to select from.

Q. Which sports subscriptions are the most popular?

A. The most popular professional package on DIRECTV is NFL Sunday Ticket, followed by MLB Extra Innings, NBA League Pass, and NHL Center Ice.

Q. What plans do you have to extend the product mix?

A. DIRECTV is currently evaluating the addition of international sports coverage—both on a subscription and pay-per-view basis.

Q. Describe your typical DIRECTV sports consumer.

A. The typical DIRECTV sports subscriber is male, married, 34–45 years old, with a household income of over $45,000 per year. Most DIRECTV subscribers live in urban/suburban areas and reside in single-family households.

Q. How many homes are equipped with a DSS system (the technology necessary to receive DIRECTV)?

A. To date (January 1998), DIRECTV has more than 3.3 million subscribers in the United States.

Q. What is the consumer's perception of the price for DIRECTV?

A. The consumer perception of the price for DIRECTV has dramatically changed over the past year. Consumers are now aware that hardware cost is below $200. However, most consumers are unaware of the monthly fees or sports subscription prices (primarily because we have not focused our marketing on monthly programming costs).

Q. What types of advertising are most effective in reaching your target market?

A. To reach the sports enthusiast, we use a combination of television (national and cable) and print (magazine and newspaper) advertising. For television, we focus on highly rated or high-profile sports programming—Super Bowl pre-game shows, NBA playoffs and finals, College Basketball (March Madness), MLB All Star Game, World Series, NFL pre-season, game, and NFL playoffs. These media vehicles provide broad reach coverage of our targeted sports audience.

In cable, we maintain continuity schedules on ESPN SportCenter and Fox Sports News. This strategy balances our broad reach broadcast strategy with high frequency, plus year-round coverage to avid sports fans. In print, we use highly targeted sports publications for highly specific sports packages. Not surprisingly, we have received the best results when we placed ads in *Sports Illustrated, The Sporting News, Baseball Weekly*, and *USA Today*.

Q. Who do you see as competition for DIRECTV?

A. Our biggest competitor is cable television. Currently, there are 99 million television households in the United States. Cable claims roughly 65 million of those homes. As DIRECTV grows, we continue to draw subscribers from formerly cabled homes, as well as homes that are not currently passed by cable. Among the direct broadcast satellite (DBS) providers, our primary competitors are Primestar and Echostar/DISH Network service. DIRECTV is the leader among all DBS providers with about 55 percent market share.

Along with television, radio and Internet broadcasts are other sports media for distributing games. The power of the radio is usually underestimated, as some fans live and die by their ability to listen to their favorite team from other states. For example, fans as far away as Tulsa, Oklahoma or Cincinnati, Ohio are able to receive all of the St. Louis Cardinals baseball broadcasts transmitted from KMOX-AM, aptly dubbed the "Sports Voice of St. Louis." The broadcast of games via the Internet even takes this one step further. Fans from all over the world are able to listen to NHL and NBA games on their computers. In the near future, these games will also be video broadcast via the Internet. MLB recently demonstrated the first live video relay of a game. Although the technology is not quite ready, consumers will soon be able to enjoy their favorite teams from anywhere on the planet.[25]

Sports Marketing hall of fame

ROONE ARLEDGE

[te]levision has done more for sports and [spo]rts marketing than anything, then Roone [Arle]dge is the man who has done the most to [gui]de the course of sports television. He is re[spo]nsible for, among other things, creating [th]e *World of Sports, The American Sports[man]*, and *Monday Night Football*. In addition, [mo]dern television coverage of the Winter and

Summer Olympics was defined by Arledge's production of the 1964 Mexico City games.

Arledge, later to become the president of ABC News, pioneered sports broadcasts by using instant replay, handheld cameras, isolation cameras, graphics, and field microphones. All of these things have brought the fans closer to the game.

[Sourc]e: Steve Rushin, "Roone Arledge," *Sports Illustrated,* September 19, 1994, 55.

(T) he focus of chapter 13 is the distribution element of the sports marketing mix. Distribution refers to the ability of consumers to receive sports products in a timely fashion at a convenient location. The complex process of distribution has many meanings in sports marketing. In this chapter, we explored distribution from three distinct perspectives: distribution concepts for the delivery of sporting goods; distribution to consumers who attend sporting events; and distribution to consumers who experience the event via one of several sports broadcast media.

One of the most important concepts in the distribution of sporting goods is the channel of distribution. A channel of distribution is an organization or individual who directs the flow of sports products from producer to consumer. The individuals or organizations who comprise the channel include producers or manufacturers, intermediaries, and consumers. As discussed in chapter 1, all of these channel members play an important role in the sports industry.

Producers are those sports entities that manufacture the sports product. This may be two competing athletes or the manufacturer of sporting goods needed to participate in sports events. Intermediaries are organizations that are in the middle of the channel of distribution, and thus they perform a number of functions (e.g., providing information, promotion, physical distribution, inventory management) that help sports products flow smoothly from producer to consumer. Two common intermediaries for sporting goods are wholesalers and retailers.

The strategies used to select channels of distribution depend on a number of factors, such as the type of product, the phase of the product life cycle, the characteristics of the target market, and the organizational objectives and marketing goals of the producer. These factors are all considered when deciding which type of channel structure to pursue and the distribution intensity. The types of channels that may be used range from direct channels of distribution with no intermediaries to more complex and lengthy structures. The distribution intensity, or degree of market coverage, refers to the number of outlets being used to sell the sports products. The extent of market coverage ranges from intensive distribution, which seeks to sell the sports product in as many places as possible, to exclusive distribution, in which the sports product is available only at one location.

Sports retailers are an important member of most channels of distribution. By definition, retailers are involved in all the activities of selling products and services to end users or final consumers. Critical to the success of sports retailers is the designing of an effective and coordinated retail mix. Similar to the marketing mix, the retailing mix consists of sports products, pricing, place, and promotion. To support the retailing mix, sports retailers seek to create a unique image for their retail outlets. The store image of the retailer is influenced by factors such as atmospherics, location, sales personnel, clientele, types of merchandise carried, and types of promotional activities. Finally, nonstore retailing is growing in importance to sports marketers, as more and more products are being sold via home shopping media such as the Internet, television, and direct mail.

The second broad sports distribution issue discussed in this chapter is distributing the sport product to spectators who are attending events. Two primary issues in distribution to spectators at the event are the stadium as retailer and ticket distribution. New stadiums are being constructed at an alarming pace, as owners of professional sports franchises realize the potential for increased revenues through personal seat licenses and luxury boxes. Interestingly, the taxpayers are choosing to subsidize the cost of these "entertainment" venues as the owners threaten to move the team if new facilities are not built. Ticket distribution is another important component of the complex distribution process in sports marketing. Ticket distribution tasks involve more than just handling transactions at the ticket booth. Other functions such as marketing the game, advertising, sales force management and operations, technical support, and customer service, are also ticket distribution responsibilities. The nature of the tasks performed by the ticketing agency has an impact on fans' overall satisfaction with the sporting experience.

The third issue in the distribution of sports products is to provide the game experience to spectators not at the event, but through a mediated source such as television or the Internet. One example of the importance of media to the sports industry is to consider the astronomical $17.6 billion television rights agreement between the NFL and the four major networks. In professional sports like football, the media revenues more than double the teams' take at the box office. In addition to the traditional broadcast media, new companies such as DIRECTV and Primestar are offering satellite services that allow consumers more sports programming than ever before.

KEY TERMS & CONCEPTS

channel intermediaries

channel members

channel of distribution

direct channels

distribution

exclusive distribution

indirect channels

information function

intensive distribution

intermediary functions

inventory management function

market coverage

marketing communications
   function

multiple channels

physical distribution function

selective distribution

single channels

sports delivery system

sports retailing

REVIEW QUESTIONS

1. Define distribution planning for sports marketers. What is meant by the terms *channel of distribution* and *channel members*?

2. What are some of the emerging ways of delivering sports products to widespread audiences?

3. Describe, in detail, the significant functions of channel intermediaries.

4. What are the major types of channels of distribution? Provide an example of each type of channel of distribution. What are the pros and cons of purchasing sports products through direct channels of distribution?

5. Differentiate between single versus multiple channels of distribution. Do professional sports franchises use single or multiple channels of distribution for ticket sales? For merchandise?

6. What is meant by degree of market coverage? Compare exclusive distribution, selective distribution, and intensive distribution. How would you determine which degree of market coverage to use for any given sports product?

7. Discuss the current state of sports retailing? What are the dimensions of the retail store image?

8. Describe what is meant by non-store retailing. What is the quickest growing form of non-store retailing?

9. Why are sports media considered a form of distribution?

EXERCISES

1. Choose any sports product and describe the channel of distribution(s) used for that product.

2. Decide on the appropriate market coverage—intensive, selective, or exclusive— for the following sports products: New York Rangers hockey; Reebok golf shoes; Speedo swimwear.

3. Comment on some of the consequences (positive and negative) of "selling out" any professional sporting event.

4. Conduct a brief environmental analysis (opportunities and threats portion of the SWOT analysis) to determine what type of sports retail outlet you feel will be successful in the coming years.

5. Discuss the trends in sports retailing with the store manager of a local sporting goods outlet. What products are performing well, and which ones are phasing out? How does the store manager develop his or her strategic plan?

6. Design a survey to assess the impact of using celebrity athletes to endorse sporting goods retailers (e.g., Terry Bradshaw for Dicks Sporting Goods chain). Have 10 consumers complete your survey and report the findings. What are the implications of your results to strategic market planning?

7. Visit a local sporting goods retailer and comment on how the outlet targets its marketing efforts towards women. Is the emphasis placed on women more or less than you expected? Discuss the retailer's store image.

8. Perform a search for information regarding the television rights for the NBA, NHL, and PGA. How do these compare with the NFL? Comment on why these other sports organizations cannot demand the fees paid to the NFL.

INTERNET EXERCISES

1. Find a virtual sporting goods retailer via the Internet. Comment on the advantages and disadvantages of Internet shopping.

2. Find an Internet site for a stadium that has been recently been built. Comment on the atmospherics of the stadium as described on the Web site.

3. Perform a search for three sites that provides sports news. Which do you feel is the best site and why?

1. The Associated Press, "Bills Begin Running Football Fans in on a Rail," *Cincinnati Enquirer*, November 23, 1996, 5.

2. Adam Barr, "Can't Go to Norman? Bring Him to You," *Golfweek*, October 12, 1996, 26.

3. Tom Farrey, "Internet Broadcast in Wave of Future," *The Seattle Times*, August 31, 1995, D1.

4. Corinne Economaki, "Out of the Box," *Brandweek*, November 17, 1997, 23–25.

5. Peter Lardner, "NHL Stars Break the Ice in Tokyo," *Reuters Ltd.*, October 1, 1997.

6. Michael Hiestand, "NBC, Olympics Cut Marketing Deal," *USA Today*, March 16, 1997, 2c; "TV Sports: The $3.5 Billion Ticket," *Broadcast and Cable*, May 13, 1996, 34–39.

7. Sporting Goods Manufacturers Association. "1998 State of the Industry Report." <http://www.sportlink.com/research/1998_research/industry/98soti.html>.

8. Sporting Goods Manufacturers Association. "1998 State of the Industry Report." <http://www.sportlink.com/research/1998_research/industry/98soti.html>.

9. Jerry Schwartz, "Longtime Makers of Sporting Goods Consider the Possibility that their Game Has Passed Them By," *New York Times*, February 25, 1997, C9.

10. "Nike Town San Francisco, Retail San Francisco Info." <http://info.nike.com/retail/info_sanfran.html>.

11. "New Survey Indicates How to Increase Consumer Confidence In Shopping Online," <http://biz.yahoo.com/prnews/980127/va_better_1.html>.

12. Ibid.

13. "Why We Might Shop at Home." <http://www.duke.edu/~bjones/lit/iiiwhy.html>.

14. Ibid.

15. "Web Usage Grows," *Editor and Publisher*, vol. 131, June 13, 1998, 40.

16. Patricia Riedman, "Junglee Helps Shoppers Do Online Comparisons," *Advertising Age*, April 13, 1998, 28.

17. Edward Robinson, "It's Where You Play that Counts," *Fortune*, July 21, 1997, 54–56; "Taxpayers Take a Beating on New Stadiums," *USA Today Magazine*, April 1996, 14.

18. "Wembley Gets Go-Ahead to Rebuild Stadium." *The PointCast Network*. <http://www.pointcast.com> October 8, 1997.

19. "The Death of the Stadium," Sport Business International. <http://www.sportbusiness.com>.

20. Cliff Peale, "Adding Spice to the Ballpark," *Cincinnati Post*, October 2, 1996, 5B.

21. Lori K. Miller and Lawrence W. Fielding, "Ticket Distribution Agencies and Professional Sport Franchises: The Successful Partnership," *Sport Marketing Quarterly*, vol. 6, no. 1 (1997): 47–55.

22. Dick Ebersol. "The Box and 1." *The Sporting News*. <http://www.sportingnews.com/features/powerful/ebersol.html>.

23. "ABC, ESPN 'Ready for some Football'; NBC, TNT Left Out by NFL." <http://www.espnet.sportzone.com/nfl/news/980113/00533127.html>.

24. Stephan Fatsis and Kyle Pope, "Why TV Networks Splurge on NFL Deals," *The Wall Street Journal*, December 12, 1997, B1, B8.

25. Mark Hyman, "Do You Love The Orioles and Live in L.A.?" *Business Week*, May 12, 1997, 108.

14

Pricing Concepts

OBJECTIVES

After completing this chapter, you should be able to

- Explain the relationship among price, value, and benefits

- Understand the relationship between price and the other marketing mix elements

- Describe how costs and organizational objectives impact pricing decisions

- Explain how the competitive environment influences pricing decisions

Five weeks after moving into one of the most modern and striking arenas in the world, with stars such as Adam Oates and Peter Bondra leading the team to a solid first half of the 1997–1998 season, the Washington Capitals should be riding high at the box office.

They are not.

Instead, the Capitals (22–17–8) often have been playing before a quiet, half-empty MCI Center while their sister team, the NBA Wizards, thrives before an average attendance of 19,329 in the 19,740-seat venue. The Capitals had fallen to 20th among 26 NHL teams in ticket sales as of last week, averaging 14,676 tickets sold per game, a 7 percent decline from last year, according to NHL ticket reports.

The Capitals averaged 13,668 in their first 10 home games this season at U.S. Airways Arena in Landover. In the 12 games they've played downtown at MCI Center, where they moved December 5, the average has increased to 15,643.

Still, "this is so disappointing," said Francis Rose, who sold hockey memorabilia for five years at Capitals games at U.S. Airways Arena. Rose, 32, closed his booth January 12 because he didn't do enough business during games to pay the increased rents at MCI Center. "We were told the days of 7,500, 8,500 nights were over."

Susan O'Malley, who runs both teams as president of Washington Sports, said better days are ahead, and attendance will build as the season progresses. "We're getting the Caps going," said O'Malley, who works for Abe Pollin, owner of the two teams. "Next year we are going to see an explosion."

The Capitals left behind a chunk of their family-oriented and individual fan base in the Maryland suburbs when they moved to MCI Center. They said they are in the midst of a multiyear move from that family base to an audience drawn from downtown business establishments and the Virginia suburbs.

The Northern Virginia effort—and the convenience of the Metro subway system—has yet to yield consistently large crowds. The team's 6,668 season ticket holders (including approximately 2,000 club seat holders that see both teams) are well below last year's NHL season ticket average of 11,159 per team. The increase in ticket prices this year (ranging from $19 to $60, compared with last year's $12 to $45) is also a factor.

The most dramatic drop has been among fans who purchase tickets one game at a time. They include Lee Chisenhall, 36, of Solomons in southern Calvert County. Chisenhall said he probably will see one Caps game this year compared with five or six last season, mostly because the team raised ticket prices and moved farther away.

"It's a lot more expensive and it's longer for me to get to," said the Baltimore Gas & Electric employee, who has attended one game this year because he had a free ticket. "If they were one of the top teams or in contention, I'd go, but because they're mediocre, I'd just as soon" go see the Chesapeake Icebreakers, an East Coast Hockey League team that plays in Show Place Arena in Prince George's County.

O'Malley said she thinks the occasional fan will return by the end of the season. "It's hard to tell whether we lost them or whether they are holding off until the second half of the year," O'Malley said. "Did the guy that buys three or four games say, `I'm not coming to Landover' or `I will wait until the new arena opens in February' or `I'm not coming [the entire season]?' We won't know until April."

Even the Capitals' game-day ticket buyers, known as "walk-ups" in the industry, dwindled to almost zero in the first half of the season after numbering 400 a game last year in Landover.

There have been signs that interest is stirring. After hitting low spots against the New York Islanders (11,217 on December 16) and Florida Panthers (10,414 on December 18), the impulse buyers arrived with a vengeance to see the ever-popular Mighty Ducks of Anaheim (19,011 on New Year's Day) and the New York Rangers (19,740 on January 3). (The announced attendance is the number of tickets sold, not the number of people in the seats, which can be thousands less). Individual tickets jumped to 6,000 for the Pittsburgh Penguins game on December 26, and walk-ups were a healthy 1,700. But that was the day after Christmas, and the Penguins usually draw a big crowd wherever they play. The real test will be whether the Capitals can increase their season ticket base.

That could take years. It took 10 years for O'Malley to raise the Wizards' season ticket base from 2,500 when she took over in 1988 to 10,000 now.

She is committed to success. "We're going to do the same thing with the Capitals that we did with the Wizards," she said. The plan calls for 3,000 new fans to sample each game through discount ticket promotions with sponsors such as Chex Cereal or on special nights such as "College Night," "Student Achievement Night" and "Adam Oates Weekend." The Capitals follow up the fans' visit through direct mail and phone calls that invite them to join a 10-game ticket plan. Then they try to move the ticket holder to a 20-game plan and eventually to season tickets.

The question is: Will it work for hockey the same way it did for basketball?

Some observers think it's going to be difficult. They say that Washington is not a hockey town the way it is a football and basketball town. The Redskins, for example, are a regular sellout, except for 3,000 club seats at the new Jack Kent Cooke Stadium. Also, most of the ice rinks and youth hockey teams are in the suburbs, far from the downtown arena.

Several marketers said the team needs to develop more passion among fans through image advertising, even among the suit-and-tie crowd, or risk permanently losing its fan base, as the NFL Oakland Raiders did for more than a decade after moving to Los Angeles, then returning to half-empty crowds at Oakland–Alameda County Coliseum.

"I just don't see advertising for them anywhere," said Bruce Zalbe, president of Bethesda-based Hot Events, a sports and entertainment marketing firm. "You don't see Adam Oates on the side of a bus. You don't hear much about the team. They need to advertise more to market themselves to people who are not regular or hard-core fans. You have to create excitement about your team."

Source: Thomas Heath, "Caps Downtown: A Tough Ticket to Sell," *Washington Post*, January 15, 1998, E1. © 1994, *The Washington Post*. Reprinted with permission.

If you were an executive for an NHL franchise such as the Washington Capitals, what price would you charge your fans? What factors would you consider when making your pricing decision in a continually changing marketing environment? How would you estimate the demand for tickets? Will the financial benefit of increasing prices offset the negative fan relations?

In this chapter, we will explore the subjective nature of pricing sports products. More specifically, we will consider how factors such as consumer demand, organizational objectives, competition, and technology impact pricing. Also, we will examine how pricing interacts with the other elements of the marketing mix. Let us begin by developing a basic understanding of pricing.

■ To some, golf lessons may be priceless.

What Is Price?

Price is a statement of value for a sports product.[1] For example, the money that we pay for being entertained by the Boston Celtics is price. The money that we pay for shorts featuring the Notre Dame logo, is price. The money we pay for a personal seat license, which gives us the right to purchase a season ticket, is price. The money we pay on tuition to the Dave Pelz Golf Academy is price. In all these examples, the price paid is a function of the value placed on the sports product by consumers.

the value of a seat:

seat licenses hated, but they work

Personal Seat Licenses, or PSLs, are one of the new sports marketing "buzzwords" of the 1990s. This increasingly common phenomenon is a sports-stadium financing strategy in which fans pay thousands of dollars for rights to future tickets. With stadium costs soaring to $200 million-plus in a time of scarce public resources, PSLs—like million dollar salaries for .220 hitting infielders and $50 pay-per-view fights that last 90 seconds—have become a permanent fixture in the economics of professional sports. In fact, PSLs are also familiar at the collegiate level, with many seat locations being tied into required annual donations to the booster clubs.

"Basically you were giving people legacy rights for their tickets," says Max Muhleman, sports marketing executive who developed the idea of the PSL for the then expansion, Charlotte Hornets in 1987.

With the Hornets leading the league in attendance during three of their first four years, however, tickets became a scarce—and valuable—commodity in Charlotte. Against that backdrop, Muhleman came across a classified ad in a Charlotte newspaper asking for $5,000 for the rights to two seats.

"I called early in the morning and asked the guy, 'Is this a joke?' " Muhleman recalled. "And he said, 'No, I sold them to the first caller and you're about the tenth caller. I should have asked $10,000.'" For Muhleman, the realization that fans were willing to spend thousands of dollars simply for the right to buy future tickets caused the proverbial light to go on over his head. Today, licenses for prime midcourt seats cost as much as $25,000.

The Pros

To those who support—however grudgingly— the seat license concept, the idea is a way of minimizing the public money needed to build major facilities. In return, the fan also receives something of value: the right to control the destiny of his seats, even after he stops buying them. Until now, in most professional sports, when a season ticket holder stopped renew-

ing his order, his seats usually reverted back to the team for sale—though in a limited number of cases immediate family members could sometimes acquire them. Under the new plan, charter season ticket holders could pass on their seats to friends or even sell them, though no one saw much value in that possibility.

The Cons

Detractors feel that PSLs are simply a slick marketing gimmick that dramatically escalates major ticket costs, shifting more fan dollars to wealthy team owners and players. One man, in a Charlotte newspaper, stated that "Football is a working person's game" and that PSL prices had made Ericsson Stadium (home of the Carolina Panthers) the preserve of "wine and cheesers." "I thought I could send a kid to college, house him, feed him, and buy him a car for what these seats cost," said Charlotte real estate broker Walker Wells, who three years ago paid $42,000 for 14 seat licenses.

Adapted from Barry Horstman, "Seat Licenses Hated, but They Work," *Cincinnati Enquirer*, September 23, 1996, 1A, 3A.

The essence of pricing is the exchanging process discussed in chapter 1. Price is simply a way to quantify the value of the objects being exchanged. Typically, money is exchanged for the sports product. We pay $26 in exchange for admission to the sporting event. However, the object of value that is being exchanged does not always have to be money. For instance, Play It Again Sports, a new and used sporting goods retailer, allows consumers to trade their previously owned sports equipment for the store's used or new equipment. This form of pricing is more commonly referred to as barter or trade. It is common for kids who exchange baseball cards to use this form of trade. Many golf courses hire retirees and pay them very low wages in exchange for free rounds of golf.

Regardless of how pricing is defined, value is the central tenet of pricing. The value placed on a ticket to a Bulls game is based on the relationship of the perceived benefits to the price paid.[2] Stated simply,

$$\text{Value} = \frac{\text{Perceived Benefits of Sports Product}}{\text{Price of Sports Product}}$$

The perceived benefits of the sports product, or what the product does for the user, are based on its tangible and intangible features. The tangible benefits are important in determining price because these are the features of the product that a consumer can actually see, touch, or feel. For example, the comfort of the seats, the quality of the concessions, and the appearance of the stadium are all tangible aspects of a sporting event. The intangible benefits of going to a sporting event may include spending time with friends and family, feelings of association with the team when they win (e.g., BIRGing) or 'being seen' at the game.[3]

The perceived benefit of attending a Chicago Bulls game is a subjective experience based on each individual's perception of the event, the sport, and/or the team. One consumer may pay a huge amount to see the game because of the perceived benefits of the product (mostly intangible), while another consumer may attend the game only if given a ticket. In either case, the perceived benefits either meet or exceed the price, resulting in "perceived value."

For the high-involvement sports fan, the Bulls ticket represents a chance to be able to tell his grandchildren that he saw the greatest player of all time, Michael Jordan. To the no- or low-involvement individual, the same game may appear to be a complete waste of time. Again, it is important to recognize that the value placed on attending the sporting event is unique to each individual, even though they are consuming the same product (in this case, the Bulls game). As researcher Valerie Zeithaml points out, "What constitutes value—even in a single product category—appears to be highly personal and idiosyncratic."[4]

Using a different example, a Reggie Jackson rookie baseball card in mint condition may be priced at $600. A collector or baseball enthusiast may see this as a value because the perceived benefits outweigh the price. On the other hand, the noncollector (or to the mom or dad who threw our cards away) may perceive the card as having barely more value than the cost of the paper on which it is printed.

In yet another example, professional sports franchises are assigned monetary values based on tangibles such as gate receipts, media revenues, venue revenues (e.g., concessions, stadium advertising, and naming), players costs, and operating expenses. Further consideration in the value of a professional sports franchise is brand equity, a highly intangible characteristic. Since 1995, NBA franchises have increased the most in value (an average of 30 percent), followed by NFL (28 percent), NHL (27 percent), and MLB (21 percent).[5] Table 14.1 provides a list of the franchises having the highest values in each sport and the respective percentage change in franchise value since 1995.

Two important points emerge from the previous examples of value. First, value varies greatly from consumer to consumer because the perceived benefits of any sports product will depend on personal experience. Second, pricing is based on perceived value and perceived benefits. As such, consumers' subjective perceptions of the sports product's benefits and image are fundamental to setting the right price. In this case, image really is everything.

All too often, price is equated incorrectly with the objective costs of producing the sports product. Because many sports products are intangible services, setting prices based on the costs of producing the product alone becomes problematic. For instance, how do you quantify the cost of spending time with your friends at a sporting event or having the television rights to broadcast NFL games?

table 14.1

Top Franchise Values

	1997 Value	Two Year Change
NFL		
Dallas Cowboys	$320 million	34%
St. Louis Rams	243 million	59
Miami Dolphins	242 million	30
MLB		
New York Yankees	241 million	30
Baltimore Orioles	207 million	26
Atlanta Braves	199 million	66
NBA		
New York Knicks	250 million	44
Phoenix Suns	220 million	41
Chicago Bulls	214 million	29
NHL		
Chicago Black Hawks	151 million	48
New York Rangers	147 million	36
Detroit Red Wings	146 million	18

Source: "Sports Values." *Financial World Magazine.* <http://www.financialworld.com/archives/1997/June /AllValuations.html>.

Sports Marketing hall of *fame*

PETE ROZELLE

Rozelle led the National Football League for y three decades, helping it survive bidding with three rival leagues and three players s, before retiring unexpectedly in 1989. Rozelle's pioneering sports marketing ac- lishments include *Monday Night Football* the Super Bowl, which blossomed into rica's most-watched sporting event. The er of the Super Bowl" put the NFL on tele- n just about everywhere and transformed vay Americans spend Sunday afternoons. Rozelle arrived at about the same time e rival American Football League, a de-

velopment that created competition for play- ers and television ratings. In 1962, Rozelle negotiated a $9.3 million television contract with CBS, a deal that earned him re-election as commissioner and a $10,000 bonus that pushed his salary to $60,000. By 1966, the two warring leagues, weary of the battle for player talent, merged, creating a single pro- fessional football league, with Rozelle as commissioner. The merger also produced a world championship game, which would eventually come to be known as the Super Bowl.

(continued)

It was Rozelle who brought sports into 10 figures when he negotiated a landmark five-year, $2.1 billion contract with television's three major networks in 1982. Then he expanded to cable, selling a Sunday night series to ESPN in 1986. The current television contract, for which Rozelle set the groundwork, gets $1.58 billion for four years from Fox alone, more than 2,000 times what Rozelle got in his first contract with CBS in 1962.

Along with these accomplishments, Rozelle's biggest contribution may have been introducing revenue-sharing in pro football 30 years before it created havoc in other sports. Doing so allowed teams in minor markets like Green Bay to equally share TV revenues—the biggest part of the NFL pie—with teams in New York, Chicago, and Los Angeles.

Rozelle is also credited, along with Roone Arledge, for creating *Monday Night Football*, now the nation's longest-running sports series. Because the NFL had an agreement not to televise on Friday night or Saturday in competition with high-school and college football, he decided Monday night would be the obvious time to showcase a single game nationally. Overall, Rozelle's impact was as much social as it was financial. He changed the nation's leisure habits and lifestyle by making Sunday afternoons and Monday nights sacred during football seasons.

Source: "Innovator Rozelle dies at 70," *Cincinnati Enquirer,* December 7, 1996, C1, C5.

(T)he Determinants of Pricing

Now that we have discussed the core concept of price, let us look at some of the factors that impact the pricing decisions of sporting marketers. Pricing decisions can be influenced by internal and external factors, much in the same way that the contingency framework for sports marketing contains both internal and external considerations. **Internal factors**, which are controlled by the organization, include the other marketing mix elements, costs, and organizational objectives. **External (or environmental) factors** that influence pricing are beyond the control of the organization. These include consumer demand, competition, legal issues, the economy, and technology. Figure 14.1 illustrates the influence of the internal and external forces on pricing decisions. Let us look at each of these forces in greater detail.

| figure 14.1 | Internal and External Influences on Pricing |

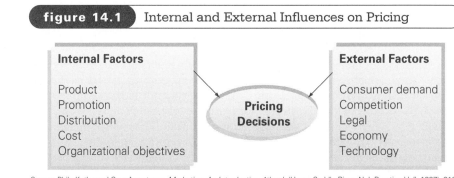

Internal Factors

- Product
- Promotion
- Distribution
- Cost
- Organizational objectives

Pricing Decisions

External Factors

- Consumer demand
- Competition
- Legal
- Economy
- Technology

Source: Philp Kotler and Gary Armstrong, *Marketing: An Introduction,* 4th ed. (Upper Saddle River, N.J: Prentice Hall, 1997), 312.

Internal Factors

Other Marketing Mix Variables

Price is the element of the marketing mix that has been called a "pressure point" for consumers. That is, price can make or break a consumer's decision to purchase a sports product. Although price is critical, the other **marketing mix variables** must be carefully considered when determining the price of a sports product. Pricing must be consistent with product, distribution, and promotional planning. For marketing goals to be reached, all of the marketing mix elements must work in concert with one another.

How is price connected to other marketing mix variables? Let us begin by examining the relationship between price and promotional planning. Each of the promotional mix elements discussed in chapter 10 (advertising, public relations, personal selling, sales promotions, sponsorships) is related to price. Broadly, the promotion function communicates the price of the sports product to consumers. For example, advertisements often inform consumers about the price of a sports product. In comparative advertisements, the price of a sports product versus its competition may be the central focus of the message.

Many forms of sales promotion are directly related to price. For example, price reductions are price discounts designed to encourage immediate purchase of the sports product. Coupons and rebates are simply another way for consumers to get money back from the original purchase price. Moreover, premiums are sometimes offered for reduced prices (or for free) to build long-term relationships with consumers. For instance, members of the St. Louis Blues' Junior BlueNote Club receive coupons for discounted Blues merchandise at BlueNote Sports Shops.

The relationship between pricing and promotion also extends to personal selling. Depending on the sports product, sales personnel sometimes negotiate prices. Although not the case for most sports products, some prices are negotiable. The sale of boats, golf clubs, squash lessons, scalped tickets, and luxury boxes each represents an example of a sports product that has the potential for flexible pricing.

The public relations component of the promotional mix is also related to pricing in several ways. First, publicity and public relations personnel often stress the value of their ticket prices to potential consumers. For example, the Cincinnati Reds public relations department includes information about how little a family of four will have to spend to attend a game. Additionally, the Reds may emphasize that they have the lowest average prices in baseball at $8.37 per ticket, compared to other major league sports and teams.[6]

Second, public relations is important in the launch of a new sports product. Media releases that alert the public to the features of the new product, as well as the pricing, are an important aspect of creating awareness. In addition, sources not only inside but also outside of the sports organization play roles in providing information about changes to the product. For instance, when a professional sports team raises its ticket price, you can bet that the story will generate "negative public relations."

A final link between price and promotion is the cost of the promotion itself. The price of running a promotion may influence potential consumers. The price of a

Super Bowl advertisement (roughly $1.3 million for a 30-second spot in 1998),[7] upon becoming public knowledge, may shape consumers' expectations and perceptions of not only the advertisement, but the product and the company as well. Consumers' expectations for advertisements featured during the Super Bowl are generally higher because of the hype and the advertisement's high price tag. At the same time, the high levels of free publicity generated by Super Bowl advertisements, both prior to and after the event itself, can offset the exorbitant expense and render the advertisements cost effective.

The distribution element of the marketing mix is also related to pricing. The price of a sports product is certainly dictated (in part) by the choice of distribution channel(s). In a traditional channel (manufacturer of the sporting good to wholesaler to retailer to consumer), the costs of covering the various functions of the channel members are reflected in the ultimate price charged to consumers. In a more nontraditional channel, such as purchasing a product over the Internet, prices are generally reduced. For example, the Great Big Bertha driver may cost $500 in a golf specialty store but is sold for hundreds of dollars less via the Internet.

The retailer is also a common member of the distribution channel that shapes pricing decisions. More specifically, the type of retailer selling the sporting good or facility where the sporting event takes place will impact price perceptions. For instance, consumers expect to pay more for golf equipment in a country club pro-shop than they do at a local golf discount outlet. Likewise, consumers who attend a baseball game at Coors Field in Denver expect to pay higher ticket prices for the state-of-the-art facility than do consumers at an aging facility like Pittsburgh's Three Rivers Stadium. A concern facing professional sports is that the new sports palaces being built around the country may drive the common fan out of professional sports markets.[8]

A final element of the marketing mix related to price is the sports product itself. The price of attending a sporting event is related to expectations of service quality. The higher the ticket price being purchased, the higher fan expectations of customer service. Likewise, the higher the price of the sporting good, the higher the consumer expectations of product quality. In this way, price is used to signal quality to consumers, especially to those who have little or no previous experience using the sports product.[9]

Pricing is also used to differentiate product lines within the sports organization. An organization will offer product lines with different price ranges to attract different target markets. For example, Converse still offers a canvas basketball shoe at a low price for traditionalists who prefer canvas over the more popular—and more expensive—leather style.

The product life cycle also suggests the strength of the price-product relationship. As illustrated in chapter 9, pricing strategies vary throughout the stages of the product life cycle. For example, during the introductory phase, products are typically priced either low to gain widespread acceptance or high to appeal to a specific target market and signal quality. Product prices are slashed during the decline phase of the life cycle to eliminate inventory and related overhead costs.

The design of sports products is the final factor that demonstrates the close relationship between product and price. Product design and pricing are interdependent. Sometimes, product design is altered during the manufacturing process to achieve a target price. For instance, Wayne Huizenga's dismantling of the Florida Marlins following their 1997 World Series triumph was a dramatic move to reduce the payroll. In this case, the product design refers to the quality of the team; the manufacturing process is the team's performance on the field. Unfortunately, the team and its fans may suffer from this move to achieve target price. Other times, prices must be adjusted (usually upward) to achieve the desired product design. New York Yankee owner George Steinbrenner has historically spent large sums of money to build a winning team, with mixed results.

Clearly, price is closely associated with the rest of the marketing mix. Usually, there are two ways of coordinating the element of price with the rest of the marketing mix variables: nonprice competition and price competition. Let us look at these two distinctly different pricing strategies in greater detail.

Price versus Nonprice Competition

Nonprice competition is defined as creating a unique sports product through the packaging, product design, promotion, distribution, or any marketing variable other than price.[10] This approach permits a firm to charge higher prices than its competitors because its product has achieved a competitive advantage. In turn, consumers are often willing to pay more for these products because the perceived benefits derived from the product are believed to be greater. Nevertheless, an element of risk is attached to using this nonprice competition approach.

Consider a commodity like a golf ball. Bridgestone may adopt a nonprice competition strategy for its brand of golf balls (Precept) by featuring the packaging, the product design, or something other than price. This can be a risky strategy for Bridgestone. What if consumers fail to recognize the superiority of the Precept golf ball? They may instead purchase a competitor's lower priced golf ball that offers the same benefits.

When adopting the distinctly different **price competition** strategy, sellers primarily stimulate consumer demand by offering consumers lower prices. For example, minor league franchises successfully use price competition to attract dissatisfied fans unable or unwilling to spend large sums of money to attend major league sporting events. In response to a price competition strategy, and to offset its own higher ticket costs, a major league franchise is likely to stress the greater intangible benefits associated with attending its more prestigious events. These benefits include the higher quality of competition, the more exciting atmosphere, and the greater athletic abilities of the stars.

Costs

Costs are those factors associated with producing, promoting, and distributing the sports product. Consider the cost of owning a minor league hockey franchise. To produce the competition or event, players are necessary. These players require salaries and equipment in order to perform. In addition, these players require support personnel such as coaches, trainers, and equipment managers, and so on. Also, these players need a place to play, which includes the costs of rent, utilities, cleaning, and maintenance. These represent some of the basic costs for producing a hockey game. However, they do not tell the entire story.

In addition to these core costs, other costs can include advertising, game promotions, and the salaries of front-office personnel (secretaries, general managers, and scouts). Team transportation is another cost. All of these costs, or the total cost of owning a minor league hockey franchise, can be expressed as the sum of the variable costs and fixed costs, as shown

$$TC = FC + VC$$

where TC = total cost
FC = fixed cost
VC = variable costs

Fixed costs are the sum of the producer's expenses that are stable and do not change with the quantity of the product consumed. Almost all costs associated with the minor league hockey team in the preceding example would be considered fixed. For example, rent on the arena, salaries, and transportation are all fixed costs. They do not vary at all with the amount of the product consumed (or in this case the team's attendance). The bulk of the game promotions are determined prior to the season and, as a result, are considered fixed costs, too.

Variable costs are the sum of the producer's expenses that vary and change as a result of the quantity of the product being consumed. Advertising may represent a variable cost for the minor league hockey franchise. If advertising expenditures increase from one month to the next because the team is doing poorly at the box office, then the dollar amount spent varies. Similarly, advertising could represent a variable cost if additional advertising or promotions are used because attendance is higher than expected.

Although an athletic team experiences very few variable costs in the total cost equation, a manufacturer of pure sporting goods would encounter a significantly greater number of variable costs. Usually, variable costs for manufacturing a sporting good range between 60 percent and 90 percent of the total costs. For example, the cost of the packaging and materials for producing the good varies by the number of units sold.

Costs are considered an internal factor that influences the pricing decision because they are largely under the control of the sports organization. The minor league hockey team management makes decisions on player salaries, how much money to spend on advertising and promoting the team, and how the team travels. These costs loom large in the sport franchise because they impact the prices charged to the fans.

It's a great day to take in a ball game, don't you think? With our hustling, bustling jaunt through the economy, we probably deserve a relaxing afternoon of hot dogs and peanuts with my favorite baseball team—the Shady Valley Primadonnas. Of course the hot dogs and peanuts are overpriced, and you might need a second mortgage on your house to buy the ticket, but the expense is worth watching the finest athletes in the world display their world-class athletic abilities. We might even coax an autograph from the Primadonnas' all-star centerfielder—Harold "Hair Doo" Dueterman.

Are These Guys Worth It?

While we thoroughly enjoy the game—the Primadonnas come from behind to win in the bottom of the ninth—our favorite player, Hair Doo, strikes out four times and commits an error in centerfield. This raises a really, really important question in the grand scheme of the universe: Is Hair Doo worth his $10 gadzillion salary? Should Hair Doo get 100 times the salary of an average, overworked, underappreciated member of the third estate?

Hair Doo's salary really raises another more general question: Why does anyone get paid what they get paid? Any questions we ask about Hair Doo Dueterman's salary could also be asked about the wage of any average, overworked, underappreciated member of the third estate—Hair Doo's numbers just happen to be bigger. Because wages and salaries are nothing more than prices, the best place to look for answers is the market.

The Market Says Yes!

Let's first ponder the supply side of the market. Hair Doo performs his athletic prowess before thousands of adoring fans—supplies his labor—because he's willing and able to take on his designated duties for a mere $10 gadzillion. If Hair Doo wasn't willing and able to play baseball for $10 gadzillion, then he would do something else.

Hair Doo's willingness and ability to play our nation's pastime depends on his opportunity cost of other activities, such as deep sea diving, coal mining, ballet dancing, or game show hosting. By selecting baseball, Hair Doo has given up a paycheck plus any other job-related satisfaction that could have been had from those pursuits. He's decided that his $10 gadzillion salary and the nonmonetary enjoyment of playing baseball outweigh his next best alternative. We should have little problem with this decision by Hair Doo, because we all make a similar choice. We pursue a job or career that gives us the most benefits.

But … (this is a good place for a dramatic pause)…someone also must be willing to pay Hair Doo Dueterman $10 gadzillion to do what he does so well. This is the demand-side of the process, which we affectionately call the market. It deserves a little more thought.

The someone who's willing to pay Hair Doo's enormous salary, the guy who signs Hair Doo's paycheck, is the owner of Shady Valley Primadonnas—D. J. Goodluck. You might remember D. J.'s grandfather from Fact 3, "Our Unfair Lives," a wheat farmer on the Kansas Plains who had the good fortune of homesteading 160 acres with a BIG pool of crude oil beneath. (The Goodlucks still visit the toilet each morning in a new Cadillac. They did, however, sell their ownership in Houston, Texas, and bought South Carolina.)

Why on earth would D. J. and his Shady Valley Primadonnas baseball organization pay Hair Doo this astronomical $10 gadzillion salary? D. J. must have a pretty good reason. Let's consider D. J.'s position.

Hair Doo's statistics are pretty impressive. In the past five years he's led the league in umpire arguments, souvenir foul balls for adoring fans, product endorsements for nonbaseball-related items, and instigation of bench-clearing fights. All of these have made Hair Doo an all-star, number-one fan attraction.

(continued)

While Hair Doo may or may not help the Shady Valley Primadonnas win the championship, he does pack fans into the stands. And he's packed fans into the stands for the past five years.

Fans in the stands translates into tickets for the Shady Valley Primadonnas, national television broadcasts, and revenue for D. J. Goodluck. D. J. is willing to pay Hair Doo $10 gadzillion to perform his daring do, because Hair Doo generates at least $10 gadzillion in revenue for the team. If Hair Doo failed to generate revenue equal to or greater than his $10 gadzillion salary, then D. J. would trade him to the Oak Town Sludge Puppies (the perennial last-place cellar-dwellers in the league), send him to the minor leagues, or just release him from the team.

The bottom line on Hair Doo's salary is the same for any average, overworked, underappreciated member of the third estate—an employer is willing and able to pay a wage up to the employee's contribution to production. If your job is making $20 worth of Hot Mamma Fudge Bananarama Sundae's each day, then your boss—Hot Mamma Fudge—would be willing to pay you $20 a day.

Many Are Worth Even More

As entertainers, athletes are paid for fan satisfaction. The more fans who want to see an athlete perform, the more an athlete is paid. In fact, most athletes—even those who make gadzillions of dollars for each flubbed fly ball, dropped pass, and missed free throw—probably deserve even higher salaries. The reason is competition. The degree of competition on each side of the market can make the price too high or too low. If suppliers have little or no competition, then the price tends to be too high. If buyers have little or no competition, then the price tends to be too low.

In the market for athletes, competition is usually less on the demand side than on the supply side. The supply of athletes tends to be pretty darn competitive. Of course, Hair Doo is an all-star player, but he faces competition from hundreds of others who can argue with umpires and hit foul balls into the stands.

The demand side, however, is less competitive. In most cases, a particular team, like the Shady Valley Primadonnas, has exclusive rights to a player. They can trade those rights to another team, like the Oak Town Sludge Puppies, but the two teams usually don't compete with each other for a player's services. There are a few circumstances—one example is "free agency"—where two or more teams try to hire the same player, but that's the exception rather than the rule.

With little competition among buyers, the price tends to be on the low side. This means that Hair Doo Dueterman's $10 gadzillion salary could be even higher. It means that the Shady Valley Primadonnas probably get more, much more, than $10 gadzillion from ticket sales and television revenue. It means that D. J. Goodluck would probably be willing and able to pay more, much more, than $10 gadzillion for Hair Doo Dueterman's athletic services. The only way to find out how much Hair Doo is worth to the Shady Valley Primadonnas is to force them to compete for Hair Doo's services with other teams.

This is a good place to insert a little note on the three estates. Most owners of professional sports teams, almost by definition if not by heritage, tend to be full-fledged members of the second estate. The players, in contrast, usually spring from the ranks of the third. The idea that one team owns the "rights" of a player stems from the perverse, although changing notion, that the third estate exists for little reason other than to provide second-class servants for the first two estates.

Colleges Are Worse

If professional athletes who get gadzillions of dollars to play are underpaid, how do college athletes, who get almost nothing, compare? It depends on the sport.

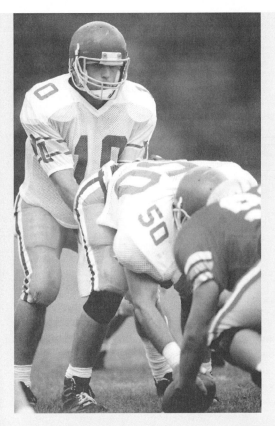

■ Should college athletes be paid?

Big-time college sports, especially football and basketball, are highly profitable entertainment industries. Millions of spectators spend tons of money each year for entertainment provided by their favorite college teams. Star college athletes can pack the fans into the stands as well as star professional athletes. With packed stands come overflowing bank accounts for the colleges.

What do the athletes get out of this? What are their "salaries?" Being amateurs, college athletes aren't paid an "official" salary. They are, however, compensated for their efforts with a college education, including tuition, books, living accommodations, and a small monthly stipend. While a college education isn't small potatoes—$100,000-plus at many places—this compensation tends to fall far short of the revenue generated for the school. The bottom line is that big-time college athletes, like the pros, are usually underpaid.

The reason is very similar to that of the professional athletes. College athletics have limited competition among the "employers" but a great deal of competition among the "employees." Many more high-school athletes hope to play big-time college ball than ever realize that dream. And while different colleges may try to hire—oops, I mean recruit—the same athlete, the collegiate governing bodies, most notably the National Collegiate Athletic Association, limit the degree of competition and fix the "wage" athletes can receive. You often hear about the NCAA penalizing a college because it went "too far" in its recruiting efforts. This translates into the charge that college paid an athlete

(continued)

"too much" to play, such as new cars, bogus summer jobs with high wages, and cash payments from alumni.

Underpayment is most often a problem for big-time football and basketball revenue-generating sports. Athletes in sports with less spectator interest, such as tennis, gymnastics, or lacrosse, actually may be overpaid based on their contribution to their colleges' entertainment revenue.

Here's a tip to keep in mind in the high-priced world of athletics:

Athletes are paid based on their contribution to fan satisfaction. If you think athletes are paid too much, then don't contribute to their salaries by attending games or watching them on television. If, however, you enjoy their performance and are willing to pay the price of admission, then worry not about their pay.

Source: Orley Amos, "Those Astronomical Athlete Salaries," *A Pedestrian Guide*. <http://amos.bus.okstate.edu/guide/IS02.html>. Courtesy of Orley M. Amos, Jr.

American athletes are not the only ones enjoying big paydays. British sports stars are also reaping the benefits of endorsement deals, sponorship fees, and all of the money coming into sports through television rights (see Table 14.2). However, these earnings pale in comparison to their American counterparts.

The increasing cost of player salaries has been passed on, in part, to the fans. Table 14.3 shows an example of the Fan Cost Index (FCI) for the NBA. The FCI represents the total dollar amount that a family of four would have to pay to attend a home game. This total cost includes the price of four tickets, two small beers, four sodas, four hot dogs, parking, two game programs, and two twill caps. The other costs indicate the pricing of one unit. In other words, the cost of one beer at the Knicks game is $5.25.

table 14.2

British Sports Top Money Earners in 1997

Athlete	Sport	Earnings
Lennox Lewis	Boxing	$10.6 million
Naseem Hamed	Boxing	$ 9.6 million
Damon Hill	Formula One	$ 8.7 million
Alan Shearer	Soccer	$ 5.8 million
Johnny Herbert	Formula One	$ 4.1 million
David Coulthard	Formula One	$ 3.3 million
Ryan Giggs	Soccer	$ 2.7 million
Paul Ince	Soccer	$ 2.7 million

Source: Agence France Presse, "British Footballers Profit From Cash Boom," November 17, 1997, <http://www.afnews.org/newsroom/spo.../feat/archive/111797/soc27044.html>.

table 14.3

Team Marketing Report's NBA Fan Cost Index (1996-97 season)

Team	Beer	Soda	Hot Dog	Park	Program	Cap	Ticket Average	FCI
1. New York	$5.25	$2.35	$3.25	$17.00	$5.00	$20.00	$42.14	$268.45
2. Portland	$4.00	$2.00	$1.75	$10.00	$4.00	$12.00	$47.49	$254.98
3. Chicago	$4.50	$2.50	$2.75	$10.00	$5.00	$15.00	$42.97	$251.88
4. L.A. Lakers	$4.00	$2.25	$2.25	$ 7.00	$5.00	$18.00	$38.39	$232.58
5. Seattle	$4.00	$2.00	$2.50	$10.00	$5.00	$12.00	$39.76	$229.03
6. Boston	$3.50	$2.25	$2.50	$15.00	$5.00	$10.00	$39.25	$228.00
7. Houston	$3.50	$1.75	$2.00	$ 0.00	$4.00	$15.00	$41.92	$227.68
8. Orlando	$3.75	$1.75	$2.50	$ 5.00	$5.00	$13.00	$40.07	$223.78
9. New Jersey	$4.50	$2.25	$3.00	$ 6.00	$5.00	$18.00	$34.09	$218.37
10. Washington	$4.50	$2.50	$2.00	$ 7.00	$4.00	$15.00	$36.39	$217.56
11. Philadelphia	$4.00	$2.00	$2.25	$ 8.00	$4.00	$18.00	$34.86	$216.46
12. Phoenix	$3.75	$2.00	$2.50	$ 6.00	$4.00	$10.00	$38.80	$214.70
13. Utah	$3.50	$2.00	$2.00	$ 7.00	$3.00	$15.00	$35.81	$209.22
14. Golden State	$5.00	$2.75	$2.50	$ 8.00	$4.00	$15.00	$31.77	$204.07
15. Miami	$3.50	$2.00	$2.75	$10.00	$4.00	$10.00	$34.66	$202.63
16. Indiana	$3.50	$2.00	$2.00	$ 5.00	$4.00	$10.00	$36.29	$201.15
17. Detroit	$4.25	$2.00	$2.25	$ 6.00	$4.00	$12.00	$34.05	$199.71
18. Sacramento	$3.25	$2.25	$2.50	$ 6.00	$3.00	$16.00	$32.01	$197.55
19. Cleveland	$3.50	$1.50	$2.00	$ 8.00	$4.00	$16.00	$31.59	$195.36
20. Denver	$3.25	$2.50	$2.75	$ 5.00	$5.00	$15.00	$28.56	$186.73
21. San Antonio	$3.50	$2.00	$2.00	$ 6.00	$5.00	$12.00	$30.89	$186.56
22. Minnesota	$3.50	$2.25	$2.50	$ 5.00	$5.00	$15.00	$27.38	$180.51
23. Atlanta	$3.00	$1.75	$2.50	$ 7.00	$5.00	$13.00	$27.61	$176.44
24. Toronto	$2.75	$1.41	$0.79	$ 7.00	$4.00	$ 7.00	$33.00	$175.93
25. Dallas	$3.00	$1.50	$1.75	$ 6.00	$4.00	$12.00	$28.78	$172.14
26. Vancouver	$3.53	$1.48	$2.22	$ 7.00	$4.00	$ 7.00	$30.09	$171.82
27. L.A. Clippers	$4.75	$2.25	$2.75	$ 7.00	$3.00	$13.00	$24.81	$167.72
28. Milwaukee	$3.50	$2.00	$2.00	$ 6.00	$4.00	$10.00	$26.67	$163.69
29. Charlotte	$3.00	$1.50	$1.50	$ 4.00	$4.00	$10.00	$25.57	$152.28

Source: Team Marketing Report's NBA Fan Cost Index 1996-1997, Team Marketing Report, Inc. Chicago, Illinois. Reprinted with permission.

There are many recent examples of professional teams that attempt to control their costs. They may decide to reduce payrolls by trading players with top salaries and not actively pursue players in the high-priced free agent market. Teams may elect not to travel first class. Cincinnati Reds owner Marge Schott wanted to eliminate the organ player so she would not have to pay him. These types of cost-cutting or controlling decisions may impact employee satisfaction, fan support, and, consequently, long-term profits.

Although cost is usually considered to be an internal, controllable factor for organizations, it can have an uncontrollable component. For instance, the league imposes a minimum salary level for a player that is beyond the control of the individual team or owner. The costs of raw materials for producing sporting goods may rise, representing a cost increase that is beyond the control of the manufacturer. Players' unions for professional teams may set minimum standards for travel that are not under the individual team's control. All of these examples describe the uncontrollable side of costs that must be continually monitored by the sports marketer.

Organizational Objectives

The costs associated with producing a good or service are just one factor in determining the final price. Cost considerations may determine the "price floor" for the sport product. In other words, what will be the minimum price that an organization might charge to cover the cost of producing the sports product? Covering costs, however, may be insufficient from the organization's perspective. This depends largely on the organization's objectives. As we have stressed throughout this text, marketing mix decisions—including pricing—must consider the broader marketing goals. Effective marketing goals should be consistent with the organizational objectives.

There are four categories of **organizational objectives** that influence pricing decisions. These include income, sales, competition, and social concerns. **Income objectives** include achieving maximum profits or simply organizational survival. In the long term, all professional sports organizations are concerned with maximizing their profits and having good returns on investment. Alternatively, amateur athletic events and associations are in sports not necessarily to maximize profits but to "stay afloat." Their organizational objectives center around providing athletes with a place to compete and covering costs.

Sales objectives are concerned with maintaining or enhancing market share and/or encouraging sales growth. If increasing sales is the basic organizational objective, then a sporting goods manufacturer or team may wish to set lower prices to encourage more purchases by existing consumers. In addition, setting lower prices or offering price discounts may encourage new groups of consumers to try the sports product. By doing so, the team may increase fan identification and, ultimately, fan loyalty. This will, in turn, lead to repeat purchases.

Another broad organizational objective may be to compete in a given sports market. An organization may wish to meet competition, avoid competition, or even undercut competitive pricing. These **competitive objectives** are directly linked to final pricing decisions. Traditionally, professional sports franchises are the "only game in town," so competitive threats are less likely to dictate pricing as they would in other industries.

A final organizational objective that influences pricing is referred to as a **social concern**. Many sports organizations, particularly amateur athletic associations, determine the pricing of their sporting events based on social concerns. For example, consider a local road race through downtown St. Louis on St. Patrick's Day. The organizational objective of this race is to encourage as many people as possible to participate in the community and festivities of the day. As such, the cost to enter the race is minimal and designed only to offset the expense of having the event.

Regardless of which organizational objective is established, each has a large role in setting prices for sports products. In practice, more than one objective is typically set by the sports organization. However, prices can be determined more efficiently and effectively if the organization clearly understands its objectives. Let us look at an example of how the MLS mission statement provides a direction for pricing.

Major League Soccer's mission statement is

*To create a **profitable** Division I professional outdoor soccer league with players and teams that are competitive on an international level, and to provide **affordable** family entertainment. MLS brings the spirit and intensity of the world's most popular sport to the United States. Featuring **competitive ticket prices** and family-oriented promotions such as "Soccer Celebration" at the stadium, MLS appeals to the children who play and the families who support soccer. MLS players are also involved with a variety of community events.*[11]

As indicated in the mission statement, MLS is concerned with profitability for its league and teams. Moreover, the pricing of MLS games should be affordable so that families who support soccer will be financially able to purchase tickets, reflecting a social concern. Finally, the mission statement reflects the competitive nature of pricing. The interaction of the organizational objectives of the MLS should exert a great influence on the price that fans pay to see U.S. professional soccer.

External Factors

Thus far, we have described the internal, or controllable, determinants of pricing and factors that are believed to be under the control of the sports marketer. The uncontrollable, or external, factors also play an important role in pricing decisions. The uncontrollable factors that influence pricing include consumer demand, competition, legal issues, the economy, and technology. Let us turn our discussion to each of these major, external factors.

Consumer Demand

One of the most critical factors in determining the price of a sports product is **consumer demand**. Demand is the quantity of a sports product that consumers are willing to purchase at a given price. Generally, consumers are more likely to purchase products at a lower price than a higher price. More formally, economists refer to this principle as the **law of demand**.[12] To better understand the nature of the law of demand and its impact on any given sports product, let us examine the price elasticity of demand.

Price elasticity explains consumer reactions to changes in price. **Price elasticity** measures the extent to which consumer purchasing patterns are sensitive to fluctuations in price. For example, if the St. Louis Cardinals raise their general admission prices from $5.00 to $7.50, will the demand for general admission seats decline? Similarly, if the ticket prices are reduced by a given amount, will the demand increase?

Mathematically, price elasticity is stated as

$$e = \frac{DQ/Q}{DP/P}$$

where e = price elasticity
DQ/Q = percentage change in the quantity demanded
DP/P = percentage change in the price

Consumer price elasticity may be described in one of three ways: elastic demand, inelastic demand, or unitary demand. **Inelastic demand** states that changes in price have little or no impact on sales. In the previous example, demand would have probably been inelastic, because even relatively large increases in the ticket prices would have had little impact on the number of fans attending each game. If demand is inelastic, then e is less than or equal to 1 (see Figure 14.2a). Because of the great demand for tickets, the Chicago Bulls or Green Bay Packers could probably raise their minimum ticket price to $150 and still sell out all of their games.

Elastic demand refers to small changes in price producing large changes in quantity demanded. For example, if the average price of a ticket to a Toronto Raptors game is reduced from $33.00 to $25.00, and if the number of units sold increases dramatically, then demand is considered elastic, because e is greater than 1 (see Figure 14.2b).

Finally, **unitary demand** is defined as a situation where price changes are offset exactly by changes in demand. In other words, price and demand are perfectly related. A small change in price produces an equally small change in the number of units sold. Similarly, a large change in price causes an equally large change in the number of units sold. In a situation where demand is unitary, e is equal to 1 (see Figure 14.2c).

figure 14.2   Price Elasticity of Demand

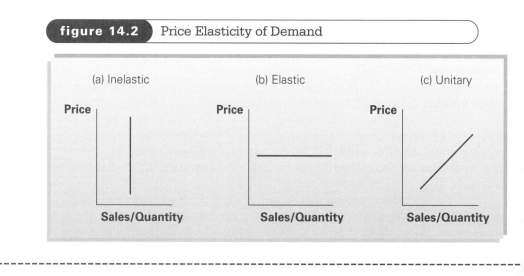

(a) Inelastic   (b) Elastic   (c) Unitary

Price   Price   Price

Sales/Quantity   Sales/Quantity   Sales/Quantity

■ Soccer is one of the fastest growing participant sports in the United States.

Estimating Demand

The basic notion of demand allows sports marketers to explore the relationship between price and the amount of sports product that is sold. In practice, a sports marketer cannot continually change the price of a product and then determine the impact of this price change. Rather, the sports marketer must develop estimates of demand. The three basic factors that are used to estimate demand are consumer trends and tastes, availability of substitute sports products, and the consumer's income. Let us briefly explore the three demand factors.

Consumer Tastes   **Consumer tastes** play an influential role in estimating demand. Consumer demand for football is at an all-time high,[13] which influences ticket prices (and the price of rights to televise football). Similarly, soccer and golf are the hottest participant sports according to the Sporting Goods Manufacturers Association (see Table 14.4). The increased demand for soccer and golf equipment will also impact pricing to consumers.

---

table 14.4

Ranking the Hottest Activities			
	1996	1997	1998
Soccer	3	2	1
Golf	5	4	2
Basketball	4	3	3
In-Line Skating	1	1	4
Roller Hockey	2	4	5
Softball	—	13	6

Source: Sporting Goods Manufacturers Association. 1998 State of the Industry Report.
<http://www.sportlink.com/research/1998_research/industry/98soti.html>.

With sophisticated statistical techniques, sports marketers can understand what, when, and how factors are influencing consumer tastes and the likelihood of purchasing products. For example, demand for a new design of in-line skates in any given market may be expressed as a function of a number of factors other than price. These factors can include the number of consumers currently participating in this recreational activity, the desire of recreational skaters to have more technologically advanced skates, the amount that the new skates have been advertised or promoted, or the availability of the skates.

Marketing research (as discussed in chapter 4) allows us to estimate demand for new and existing sports products. Firms conduct research to determine consumers' past purchase behavior and the likelihood of their buying a new product. In addition, businesses rely on environmental scanning to monitor changes in the demographic profile of a market, changes in technology, shifts in popular culture, and other issues that may impact the size or tastes of the consumer market.

Environmental scanning and marketing research assist sports marketers in understanding what consumers expect and are willing to pay for sports products. Let us look at how consumers evaluate price (see Figure 14.3).

In the **consumer pricing evaluation process**, acceptable price ranges are determined by consumers' expectations. These expectations are influenced by communicating with other consumers (i.e., word of mouth), promotions or advertising, and, to some extent, past experience in purchasing the products. If the gap between expectations and the actual price is too large, a problem arises for the sports organization. If prices are much higher than expected, the consumer will be much less likely to purchase. On the other hand, if prices are much lower, then the quality of the sports product may be called into question.

The sport of professional boxing provides an excellent example of the role past experience plays in determining an acceptable price range for consumers. Recently, fan satisfaction with professional boxing has reached an all-time low because of the short length of heavyweight fights and the heavyweight prices paid by pay-per-view

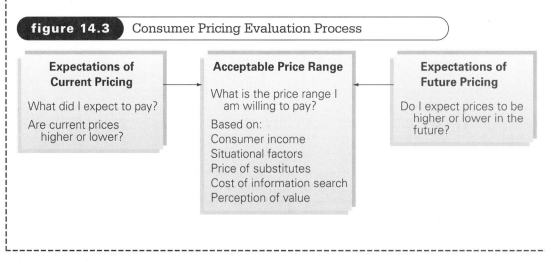

| figure 14.3 | Consumer Pricing Evaluation Process |

Expectations of Current Pricing

What did I expect to pay?

Are current prices higher or lower?

Acceptable Price Range

What is the price range I am willing to pay?

Based on:
Consumer income
Situational factors
Price of substitutes
Cost of information search
Perception of value

Expectations of Future Pricing

Do I expect prices to be higher or lower in the future?

(PPV) customers to watch these fights. To combat this problem of short telecasts, Cablevision, which broadcast the November 1996 title fight between Evander Holyfield and Mike Tyson, introduced a controversial pricing strategy. Consumers who wished to view the fight paid a $10-a-round price with a $50 cap.[14]

This innovative strategy apparently sparked a 200 percent jump in sales in Cablevision's 1.9 million PPV homes (a PPV record). Equally important, the product quality was not called into question. Cablevision paid a flat fee (roughly $4 million) for the rights to the fight, and the boxers did not receive any additional money based on the fight's length.

Along with a consumer's previous experience with pricing, expectations of future pricing also influence the acceptable range of prices a consumer is willing to pay. For example, when a technically superior form of the sports product, such as Upper Deck's Super Premium Baseball Cards, is in the introductory phase of the product life cycle, little competition exists and start-up costs are high. Most consumers would expect the price of this product to drop over time, and some may be willing to wait for this to occur. On the other hand, sports fans may expect ticket prices to continually rise in the future and purchase season tickets immediately rather than waiting for the inevitable higher prices.

Along with expectations of current and future prices, a number of other individual consumer judgments will also play a role in determining the acceptable price range for any given sports product. As shown in Figure 14.3, these variables include consumer income, situational factors, price of substitutes, cost of information search, and perceptions of value.

Consumer income, one of the three demand factors, refers to the consumer's ability to pay the price. Generally, the higher the consumer's income, the wider the range of acceptable prices. For example, a sports fan who has an annual income of $100,000 might perceive a $7 increase in ticket prices as still within his or her price range. However, the same $7 increase in price may be unaffordable to the fan earning $30,000 per year. Significantly, both fans may find the increase in ticket prices unacceptable, but only the latter finds it unaffordable.

The **situational factors** that may impact a consumer's acceptable range of prices include the presence or absence of time, the usage situation, and social factors. Consider the following situations and how each might impact the price you would be willing to pay. First, you are getting ready for a much-anticipated round of golf when you discover that you only have one ball left in your bag. Typically, you purchase golf balls at your local discount store for roughly $4 a sleeve (package of three). Given the situation, (absence of time) you are forced to "cough up" $8 at the pro shop for the three balls needed to get you through the round. This absence of time to shop for less-expensive golf balls caused the acceptable price range to double in this situation.

The next scenario illustrates how your usage situation influences the range of acceptable prices. Imagine that you are purchasing a new set of golf clubs that will be used only once or twice a month at the local public course. In this situation, the acceptable price range for this set of clubs might be from $200 to $300. It is likely that you may even purchase less expensive, previously owned clubs. On the other hand, if you are planning to use the clubs once or twice a week and are more concerned about their quality and your image, the acceptable range of prices would increase.

The final situation places you in the position of purchasing tickets for the Charlotte 500 NASCAR race. The cost of purchasing one ticket in the grandstand is approximately $80. You are not a huge NASCAR fan and the thought of spending $80 for a ticket seems disagreeable. However, a group of your best friends are attending the event and encourage you to "go along for the ride." You agree and purchase the ticket because of the social situational influence.

Another interesting social situational influence is referred to as the "**mob effect**." The mob effect (or the crowd effect) describes a situation in which consumers feel it is socially desirable to attend "special" sporting events, such as the NBA Finals, Bowl Games, or World Series. Because these events constitute unique situations that can never be duplicated, consumers are willing to pay more than usual for the "right" to be a part of the mob (or crowd).

An additional consumer determinant of acceptable prices is the expected **price range of substitute products**. The prices of competitive products will have a major influence on what you deem acceptable. If a sports organization's pricing becomes out-of-line (higher) versus competition, then consumers will no longer pay the price.

The **cost of information search** also determines what a consumer considers acceptable. A consumer wishing to purchase a series of tennis lessons has a relatively low cost of information search because information is easily obtained from friends or by calling various tennis professionals. In this case, the cost of the search is less than the benefit of finding the best value. Interestingly, in purchasing a sports product, the cost of information search may be negligible because fans may find the search itself to be intriguing.

Finally, as discussed previously, **perception of value** will dictate acceptable price ranges for sports products. Remember, perceptions of value will vary from individual to individual and are based on the perceived benefits. The greater the perceived benefits of the sports product, the higher the range of acceptable prices. Most people would consider $200 an outrageous price to attend a single pro football game. However, that cost might look like the bargain of a lifetime if that single game were the Super Bowl.

Availability of Substitute Products   Another demand factor, other than price alone, that may impact demand is the **availability of substitute products**. Generally, as the number of substitute products for any given sports product increases, demand for the product will decrease. Consider the case of almost any professional sports franchise and substitute products. Typically, there is no substitute product for the professional sports team. Therefore, demand remains relatively unchanged, even when ticket prices are increased (in other words, demand is highly inelastic). For example, there is no substitute product for the St. Louis Cardinals, although baseball is played in St. Louis at the collegiate, high school, and amateur levels. However, consumers may choose to spend their sports dollars on purchasing televised broadcasts of the Cardinals, rather than pay the price increase.

Consumer's Income   The final demand factor that influences the consumer's ability to purchase the sports product is the **consumer's income**. Simply stated, the more income a consumer realizes, the higher the demand for various sports products. This "income-related" demand factor is related to the cost of the sports product under consideration. That is, the higher the cost of the sports product, the more "consumer income" matters.

The potential consumer's personal income and ability to purchase products is also highly related to the state of the economy, in general. The economy is one of the "other external factors" that influences pricing, which will be discussed in the next section.

Economy

The current economic cycle also influences pricing decisions. A recessionary period, for instance, is characterized by reduced economic activity. During these times, there is a reduced demand for goods and services. In addition, unemployment rates are typically higher. Although this sounds grim for consumers and sports fans, imaginative sports marketers might be able to take advantage of these slowdowns in the economy by holding or slightly reducing prices while stressing the continued value of the sports product.

Periods of inflation also require a pricing review. During inflationary periods, the cost of inputs (e.g., supplies, raw materials) necessary to produce the sports product will rise and ultimately increase prices to consumers. Rather than increase prices, sports marketers may adopt a cost reduction strategy during inflation. Such a strategy necessitates reducing or stabilizing costs of producing the product so consumer prices need not be increased.

Whatever the phase of the economic cycle, it is important to understand the direct relationship between pricing and the economy. In the preceding discussion, prices were adjusted due to changes in the economy. The prices set by manufacturers and sports organizations equally have a tremendous impact on the demand for these products and services and, in turn, affect the economy.

Competition

As stated earlier, **competition** is one of the most critical factors in determining prices. Every sports organization must closely monitor the pricing structure of competing firms in order to successfully implement prices for its own products. One key to understanding the relationship between price and competition is exploring the sports organization's competitive environment. These four competitive environments include pure monopolies, oligopoly, monopolistic competition, and pure competition.

Most professional sports organizations operate in a pure monopoly, which means that they are the only seller who sets the price for a unique product. With the exception of New York, Chicago, and California, there are few areas large enough to support two professional sports franchises in the same sport (e.g., the Cubs and White Sox). As such, most professional sports are free to manipulate prices as they wish. The same would hold true for many college athletic programs, where college sports may be "the only show in town."

An oligopoly is where a small number of firms control a market. Conditions for an oligopoly exist when no one seller controls the market, but each of the few sellers has an impact on the market. In the sports industry, an example of an oligopoly is the sports news networks where ESPN, CNN, and Fox have dominant control over the market.

In the case of many sporting goods, monopolistic competition is the norm. There are dozens of brands with identical products to sell. This competitive environment requires both price competition and nonprice competition. For example, all tennis balls are designed the same, but the many different brands compete based on lower prices and/or other marketing mix elements (promotions, product image, sponsorships). The same holds true for golf balls, basketballs, and so on.

Pure competition is a market structure that has so many competitors that none can singularly influence the market price. The market conditions that must exist for pure competition include homogeneous products and ease of entry into the market. Although pure competition exists in industries selling uniform commodities such as agricultural products, it does not exist in the sports industry.

Legal Issues

In addition to the other external factors, sports marketers must consider legal constraints imposed on pricing. Several key laws that affect sports marketers were presented in chapter 3. Table 14.5 presents U.S. legislation that specifically impacts the pricing of sports products.

Technology

Without a doubt, all sports products are becoming more and more technologically advanced. The trend towards technology can have an indirect or direct influence on pricing decisions. Experience tells us that greater technology costs money. The high cost of research and development, as well as the higher costs for production and materials, drive up the price of the sports product. For example, if our stadiums are equipped with mini-screen monitors at every seat, the consumer would be expected to pay the

---

table 14.5

Laws Influencing the Pricing of Sports Products

- **Sherman Act, 1890:** Establishes illegality of restraint of trade and price fixing. It also restricts the practice of predatory pricing to drive competition from the marketplace through pricing.
- **Clayton Act, 1914:** Restricts price discrimination.
- **Robinson-Patman Act, 1936:** Limits the ability of firms to sell the same product at different prices to different customers.
- **Wheeler-Lea Act, 1938:** Ensures that pricing practices are not deceiving to consumers.
- **Consumer Goods Pricing Act, 1975:** Eliminates some control over retail pricing by wholesalers and manufacturers. It allows retailers to establish final retail prices in most instances.

price for this technology in the form of higher ticket prices. In this case, an advance in technology has a direct impact on the pricing.

Although technology and higher prices are typically thought to go hand in hand, technology doesn't always have to increase pricing. For example, a consumer may be able to buy a King Cobra titanium driver for $250 using electronic commerce (in other words, purchasing it through the Internet). The same driver may cost $50 to $100 more if purchased in a traditional retail outlet. In this case, technology is having an indirect influence on pricing, happily reducing the price of goods to consumers.

SUMMARY

The pricing of sports products is becoming an increasingly important element of the sports marketing mix. Price is a statement of value for a sports product, and understanding consumers' perceptions of value is a critical determinant of pricing. Value is defined as the sum of the perceived benefits of the sports product minus the sum of the perceived costs. The perceived benefits of the sports product, or what the product does for the user, are based on its tangible and intangible features. Each consumer's perception of value is based on his or her own unique set of experiences with the sports product.

A variety of factors influence the pricing decisions for any sports product. Similar to the internal and external contingencies that impact the strategic sports marketing process, pricing influences can be categorized as internal or external factors. Internal factors are those under the control of the sports organization, such as the other marketing mix elements, cost, and organizational objectives. External factors are those factors beyond the control of the sports organization that influence pricing. These include consumer demand, competition, legal issues, the economy, and technology.

Marketing mix elements other than price must be carefully considered when determining the price of the sports product. Promotional mix elements (for example, advertising, sales promotions) often communicate the price (or price

reductions) of the sports product to consumers. The channel of distribution that is selected influences the price of sports products. For instance, consumers expect to pay higher prices (and are charged higher prices) when purchasing tennis equipment from a pro shop versus directly from the manufacturer. Product decisions are also highly related to pricing. Simply, price is used to signal product quality. Generally, the higher the price that is charged, the greater the perceived quality of the product.

Two distinct pricing strategies that emerge based on the emphasis of marketing mix elements are price and nonprice competition. As the name suggests, nonprice competition tries to establish demand for the sports product using the marketing mix elements other than price. Price competition, on the other hand, attempts to stimulate demand by offering lower prices.

In addition to other marketing mix variables, costs play a major role in pricing decisions. Costs are those factors that are associated with producing, promoting, and distributing the sports product. The total cost of producing and marketing a sports product is equal to the sum of the total fixed costs and the total variable costs. The fixed costs, such as players' salaries, do not change with the quantity of the product consumed, whereas variable costs change as a result of the quantity of the product being consumed. Today, the costs of running a professional sports franchise are skyrocketing because of players' salaries.

A final internal factor that influences pricing is organizational objectives. The four types of pricing objectives include income objectives, sales objectives, competitive objectives, and social objectives. Typically, a combination of these four objectives is used to guide pricing decisions.

External factors, which are beyond the control of the organization, include consumer demand, competition, legal issues, the economy, and technology. Demand is the quantity of a sports product that consumers are willing to purchase at a given price. Price elasticity measures the extent to which consumer purchasing patterns are sensitive to fluctuations in price. For some sports products, such as a ticket to the Super Bowl, demand is relatively inelastic, which means that changes in price have little impact on game attendance. However, when demand is elastic, small changes in price may produce large changes in quantity demanded. Sports marketers try to estimate the demand for products by examining consumer trends and tastes, determining the number of substitute products, and looking at the income of the target market.

One of the most critical factors in determining pricing for sports products is to examine the prices charged for similar products by competing firms. Most professional sports franchises operate in a monopolistic environment in which no direct competitors exist. Because of this market condition, the price of attending professional sporting events is continually increasing. In fact, many "average" fans believe that they are being priced out of the market and can no longer afford the cost of admission. In addition to competition, laws influence the pricing structure for sports products. For example, the Sherman Act was designed to protect freedom of competition, thereby freeing prices to fluctuation subject to market forces. The phase of the economic cycle is another important consideration in pricing. During periods of inflation, prices may rise to cover the higher costs, and during periods of recession, prices may be lowered. Finally, advances in technology are related to pricing decisions. Typically, consumers are willing to, and expect to, pay more for "high-tech" sports products. However, this is not always the case, as sometimes technological change can reduce pricing by facilitating marketing of the sports product.

KEY TERMS & CONCEPTS

competition

competitive objectives

consumer demand

consumer income

costs

economy

estimating demand

expected price

external factors influencing
  pricing

fixed cost

income objectives

internal factors influencing
  pricing

law of demand

legal issues

marketing mix variables

nonprice competition

organizational objectives

personal seat licensing

price

price competition

price elasticity

price inelasticity

sales objectives

situational factors

social concerns

technology

total cost

unitary demand

value

variable cost

1. Define price, perceived value, and perceived benefits. What is the relationship among price, value, and benefits?

2. Discuss the advantages and disadvantages of personal seat licenses from the consumer's perspective and the sports organization's perspective.

3. Outline the internal and external factors that impact pricing decisions. What is the primary difference between the internal and external factors?

4. Provide examples of how the marketing mix variables (other than price) influence pricing decisions.

5. Define fixed costs and variable costs and then provide several examples of each type of cost in operating a sports franchise. Do you believe costs should be considered controllable or uncontrollable factors with respect to pricing?

6. What are the four organizational objectives, and how does each influence pricing? Which organizational objective has the greatest impact on pricing?

7. What is meant by the law of consumer demand? Explain the difference between elastic and inelastic demand.

8. Describe, in detail, how sports marketers estimate the demand for new and existing sports products. What are the three demand factors, and which do you believe is the most critical in estimating demand?

9. What laws have a direct impact on pricing? Briefly describe each law.

10. How do advances in technology influence pricing? How does the economy influence pricing decisions?

11. Describe the different types of competitive environments. Why is competition considered one of the most critical factors influencing pricing?

1. Interview five consumers and ask them, "If a new athletic complex was built for your college or university basketball team, would you be willing to pay higher seat prices?" Summarize your results and discuss the findings in terms of perceived value and perceived benefits.

2. Interview five consumers and ask them to describe a sports product that they consider to be of extremely high value and one they consider to be of extremely poor value. Why do they feel this way?

3. Find two examples of sports products that you consider to compete solely on the basis of price. Provide support for your answer.

4. For any professional sports franchise, provide examples of how the rest of its marketing mix is consistent with its pricing.

5. Provide two examples of sports organizations that have (either in whole or in part) a social concern pricing objective.

6. Interview five people to determine whether demand could be characterized as elastic or inelastic for the following sports products: season tickets to your favorite basketball team's games, golf lessons from Greg Norman, and Nike Air Jordans.

7. Provide examples of how technology has increased the ticket prices of professional sporting events. Support your examples from a cost perspective.

INTERNET EXERCISES

1. Using the Internet, find three examples of promotions for sport products that provide consumers with pricing information.

2. Find an example of a sports product that is being sold via the Internet for a lower price than offered via other outlets. How much cheaper is the sports product? What does the consumer have to give up to purchase the product at a lower price over the Internet?

NOTES

1. See, for example, William Zikmund and Michael d'Amico, *Marketing*, 4th ed., (St. Paul, MN: West, 1993).

2. Christopher Lovelock, *Services Marketing*, 3rd ed. (Upper Saddle River, NJ: Prentice Hall, 1996).

3. See, for example, R.B. Cialdini, R.J. Borden, A. Thorne, M.R. Walker, S. Freeman, and L.R. Sloan, "Basking in Reflected Glory: Three (Football) Field Studies," *Journal of Personality and Social Psychology*, no. 34 (1976): 366–375.

4. Valerie Zeithaml, "Consumer Perceptions of Price, Quality, and Value: A Means-End Chain Model and Synthesis of Evidence," *Journal of Marketing*, vol. 52 (July 1988): 2–21.

5. "Sports Values." *Financial World Magazine*. <http://www.financialworld.com/archives/1997/June/AllValuations.html>.

6. Chuck Johnson, "Baseball Ticket Prices Rise, Remain Bargain," *USA Today*, January 22, 1998, 1C.

7. Ellen Neuborne, with Roger Crockett, *Business Week*, February 2, 1998, 70. *Adweek*, vol. 39, no. 3, January 19, 1998, 5.

8. Rick Morrissey, "Sold Out While Owners Chase Higher Revenues, Average Fan Pays the Price," *Rocky Mountain News*, February 18, 1996, 16B.

9. See, for example, A.R. Rao and K.B. Monroe, "The Effect of Price Brand Name and Store Name on Buyers' Perceptions of Product Quality," *Journal of Marketing Research* (August 1989): 351–357; J. Gotlieb and D. Sarel, "The Influence of Type of Advertisement, Price, and Source Credibility on Perceived Quality," *Journal of the Academy of Marketing Science* (Summer 1992): 253–260.

10. See, for example, Zikmund and d'Amico, 1993.

11. "Major League Soccer, The Objectives." <http://www.mlsnet.com/about>.

12. See for example, Joel Evans and Barry Berman, *Marketing*, 6th ed. (New York: Macmillan, 1994), 677.

13. Richard Turner, "Send in the Refs," *Newsweek*, November 25, 1996, 91–93. Stephan Fatsis and Kyle Pope, "Why Networks Will Splurge on NFL Deals," *The Wall Street Journal*, December 12, 1997, B1, B8.

14. Rudy Martzke, "SET Expects Pay-Per-View Recordbreaker," *USA Today*, November 8, 1996, 2C.

CHAPTER **15**

Pricing Strategies

O B J E C T I V E S

After completing this chapter, you should be able to

- Understand the components for designing a successful pricing strategy

- Explain and apply the different ways to arrive at an approximate price level (differential pricing, new sports product pricing, psychological pricing, product mix pricing and cost-based pricing)

- Describe how and when price adjustments should be made in the final stage of pricing

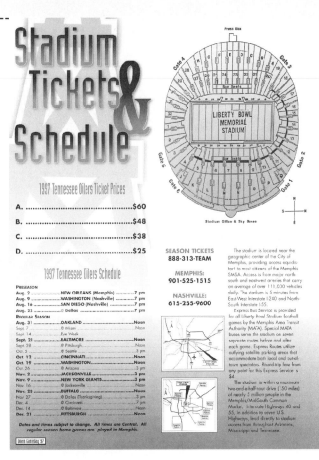

■ Ticket prices for the Tennessee Oilers.

In the previous chapter, we discussed the internal (controllable) and external (uncontrollable) influences on pricing decisions made by a sports organization. The focus of this chapter is to describe a strategic process for determining price within the context of these internal and external factors. Setting approximate prices to achieve the sports organization's objectives is largely based on choosing from among several pricing strategies. The various pricing strategies that we will discuss include differential pricing, new sports product pricing, psychological pricing, product mix pricing, and cost-based pricing.

Differential Pricing Strategy

One of the most common pricing strategies for sports marketers is known as differential pricing. **Differential pricing** is selling the same product or service to different buyers at different prices. Because the market is heterogeneous and unique target markets exist, differential pricing strategies are common practice.

Theoretically, differential pricing may constitute the illegal practice of price discrimination—the practice of charging different prices to different buyers for goods of like grade and quality. However, differential pricing in sports marketing is considered legal if the product in question is a service rather than a good and if the price discrimination does not substantially lessen competition.[1]

Second-market discounting is the most common differential pricing strategy used for pricing sporting events. **Second-market discounting** occurs when different prices are charged to different segments of consumers. For example, students are given a $4 discount off the regular price of admission to the Cincinnati Cyclones hockey games. Similarly, faculty and student discounts are common when attending collegiate sporting events.

Second-market discounting is also prevalent in sports participation. Golf courses commonly offer different pricing for weekend versus weekday tee times. In fact, courses also offer discounts for greens fees during nonpeak times, such as after 6:00 P.M. Similarly, ice rinks offer reduced pricing in the summer to estimate demand.

New Sports Product Pricing Strategy

As the name implies, new sports pricing strategies are used when the sports organization sets approximate price levels for products being introduced for the first time in the marketplace. Regardless of which of these pricing strategies are utilized, competition is a major consideration in setting prices at the introductory stage of the product life cycle.

The two pricing strategies that are commonly employed for new products include penetration pricing and price skimming. **Penetration pricing** is when the new sports product is being introduced at a low initial price relative to the competition. This low price will encourage consumers to try the product or service, especially when consumers are price sensitive. In addition, penetration pricing is useful when demand is relatively price elastic, that is, when small decreases in price produce high levels of increased demand for the product. Generally, penetration pricing is useful for gaining a large market share and generating high sales volume as a sport product is being introduced.

One example of penetration pricing strategy being used to stimulate demand for a new product is the WNBA. Most of the teams in the league offer tickets for as low as $6 and as high as $25. The Cleveland Rockets offer tickets for $6, $8, $10, and $15. This, of course, is a far cry from the NBA and its average ticket price of nearly $35. The WNBA's decision to use penetration pricing is an attempt to expose as many fans as possible to women's games, so they can see the high quality and entertaining brand of basketball being played by women. Similarly, the MLS, also in the introductory phase of its product life cycle, has adopted penetration pricing. Another example of penetration pricing would be when the San Diego Clippers moved their NBA franchise to Los Angeles. This move brought them head-to-head with the more successful LA Lakers franchise. The "new" LA Clippers discounted their tickets in an effort to build fan attendance during their first few seasons.

Price skimming is an entirely different pricing strategy, in which a sports organization initially sets high prices or charges prices higher than the competition. Price skimming refers to the practice of skimming the "cream of the top" of the market. In other words, targeting those consumers who are price insensitive. The price must not be too high, but high enough to induce certain target markets to adopt the new product. In order to successfully adopt a price skimming strategy, the sports organization must be certain that the rest of the marketing mix is consistent with the pricing. In other words, if the price is high, perception of product quality and image must be high, distribution must be more selective, and the promotional strategy must be image enhancing.

The risk of using a price skimming approach is that competitors or "knockoff/imitation" products may quickly enter the market and attempt to grab sales and market share by offering a comparable product at a substantially lower price. An added danger of price skimming is that fewer consumers are likely to pay the higher prices for the products. Given this, it is important for the sports organization to monitor sales and charge a high enough price to be profitable. Golf and tennis tournaments use price skimming techniques effectively to sell their best seats to a select few customers.

Other issues that may lead to decisions of penetration versus skimming pricing include:[2]

- *Production capacity*—Limited production capacity tends to favor a skimming strategy because the marketer may be more assured that you can sell all you can produce. A good example of this is limited stadium seating, where the sports organization can only accomodate a relatively small number of fans and, therefore, charges higher prices because it is relatively assured of sell-outs. This happens for many teams in the United States and abroad, as the following article suggests.

spotlight on international sports marketing

fans forced to meet cost of loving football

Arsenal may be supplanting Chelsea as the favored home of foreign players, but Chelsea's position as the most expensive ground to watch football in the FA Carling Premiership is safe. The top ticket price for the coming season at Stamford Bridge will be $75, which represents a 25 percent increase on last season, itself a 14 percent hike on 1995–1996, and makes the best Chelsea tickets around 15 percent more expensive than the good seats at their big London rivals. Tony Banks, Labour's Chelsea-supporting sports minister, has been rather quiet on the subject of the club's ticket prices, but it can hardly fit in with his principle of bringing sport to the people.

Alas, Chelsea's rapid ticket inflation is far from unique in the top flight. Research published recently by Case Associates, the think-tank run by Simon Bishop and Cento Veljanovaski and backed by Ashurst Morris Crisp, the city lawyers, showed that the price of tickets for top teams rose by 222 percent between 1985 and 1995. This compares with a 52 percent increase in the Retail Price Index, a 51 percent jump in average cinema ticket prices and—to stretch the leisure choice comparison to its logical conclusion—a 99 percent jump in the price of lager.

There is an argument that you are getting a better class of football for your money. If you compare the old first division with the Premiership today, there has been the influx of leading foreign players, such as Eric Cantona, Dennis Bergkamp, and Gianfranco Zola.

How, though, does football explain the inflation in the lower divisions? The first division prices have risen by 169 percent over 10 years when compared with the old second division; and new second division prices show a 151 percent jump. Even the lowest division of the Football League has seen a 145 percent hike in the cost of admission.

There are various reasons for this. Most clubs would argue, with some justification, that the amounts that they have had to spend upgrading their grounds to all-seat stadiums after the Taylor report into the Hillsborough disaster have justified putting up prices. Yet, by the same token, many top clubs are now gaining so much from merchandise and food and drink sales at their bright new grounds that this pays for the cost of upgrading. Selling off their old grounds for redevelopment has also been a lucrative trade.

The report, though, poses the question of whether top-flight football may be pricing it-self too highly, supporting the proposition put forward by Doug Ellis, the chairman of Aston Villa, that pay-per-view television might hit attendance hard at the leading clubs. Case estimates that the live televising of Premiership matches by BSkyB, in which News International, publisher of the *Times*, has a 40 percent stake, cuts attendance at the games by up to 10 percent. However, the Premier League's figures show an increase in the average attendance at matches of more than 30 percent since the BSkyB contract started. Last year, BSkyB showed 230 live matches, with the average gate in the Premiership 28,434.

Yet it looks like the high price of tickets may increase the appeal of pay-per-view. It has been generally assumed that pay-per-view will be priced at about $15 a game, but Case points out that, at $30 a game, it would still seem cheap when compared with the cost of a parent and two children paying upwards of $95 to attend a live match. At $30 a game, the report predicts that, by 2004, the value of pay-per-view to Premier League could be as much as $2.3 billion a year. It is on its way. There is a debate in football about when it will happen, but what it may do is hold back the rampant ticket inflation that is threatening to price many real supporters out of the game.

Source: Jason Nisse, "Fans Forced to Meet Cost of Loving Football," *London Times*, July 21, 1997, 39. ©Times Newspapers Limited, 1997.

- *Rate of technological change*—In the sporting goods industry, where there are rapid changes in product design based on technology (e.g., skiing, tennis, golf), skimming strategies may be more appropriate.
- *Barriers to entry*—If there is some barrier (e.g., patent or high start-up costs) that will reduce the threat of competition, a skimming pricing strategy may be more appropriate.
- *Economic conditions*—In periods of high inflation, a price skimming strategy is recommended. The sports organization would want to charge "all that the market could bear" because the additional revenues will be worth much less in the future.

- *Desired image*—If the desired position of the sports product is higher quality and prestige, then a price skimming strategy would be consistent. However, price penetration may be useful for a sports organization stressing good value for the price. Realistically, the NFL could charge $1,000 per seat for a Super Bowl ticket and still sell every seat due to the tremendous prestige of this event.

Psychological Pricing Strategies

Why would anyone purchase a pair of Air Jordans for $140, "the Biggest Big Bertha" driver for $500, or a courtside ticket to the New York Knicks basketball game for $1,000? One possible answer is that price says something about the quality of the product or service. Perhaps, even more importantly, the price that consumers are willing to pay says something about the person and their self-concept. This notion of pricing being based on the consumer's emotion and image, rather than economics alone, is known as **psychological pricing**.

Several different types of psychological pricing are commonplace in sports marketing. In the examples just listed, prestige pricing is being used for setting approximate price levels for sports products. **Prestige pricing** is setting an artificially high price to provide a distinct image in the marketplace. Examples of prestige pricing include professional basketball teams charging extremely high ticket prices for courtside seats. For example, the Philadelphia 76ers recently raised the ticket prices of front-row seats from $165 to $200 per seat.

Another example of prestige pricing comes from the world of professional golf. As part of a special spectator package called GolfWatch, 1,000 fans are provided access to the action from inside the traditional gallery ropes. The fans will be provided with this exclusive viewing area, an on-course concierge, hospitality oases, and other extras not given to the average paying customer. However, the price tag for the prestigous spectator accommodations will be roughly $1,500 per head.[3]

Sports marketers also utilize a psychological pricing strategy known as reference pricing. In **reference pricing**, consumers carry a frame of reference in which they evaluate products. Typically, these referenced prices are based on past experience with the product or service or by gathering high levels of information when evaluating alternative products. Knowing this, sports marketers might provide consumers with comparative information on various brands so that consumers "feel" like they are getting a deal. Often, lesser-known brands might be featured next to name brands in sporting goods retailers to reflect the value.

A variant of reference pricing is known as the "**lure of the middle pricing**." A new product is introduced into the product line at a price higher than the current highest priced product. In essence, consumers are now attracted to the midpriced product (formerly the highest priced product). Its selling price has not been altered, but its reference price has changed.

Odd–even pricing is another form of psychological pricing that may be used in conjunction with other strategies. Consumer perceptions are altered by using an odd-number price ($9.95) versus an even-number price ($10). Interestingly, consumers might perceive the odd-number pricing as a greater value than the $10 even with a meaningless $.05-cent difference in price. Likewise, consumers associate even pricing with higher quality products or services. Ticket pricing for most sporting events follows an even pricing strategy, while many sporting goods are sold using odd-pricing.

A final psychological pricing strategy is called **customary** or **traditional pricing**. Consumers' expectations of price and beliefs about what prices are historically charged for sports products form the basis of traditional pricing. For instance, many Major League Baseball franchises try to keep bleacher seating at or below $7, to uphold the tradition of the "cheap seat." Any attempt to dramatically increase these customary prices usually elicits a highly negative reaction among consumers. Unfortunately, other related products (e.g., concessions, merchandise) may be increased to offset the inexpensive ticket prices for bleachers or general admission seating.

Product-Mix Pricing Strategies

One of the pricing objectives discussed in the previous chapter was profit oriented. This pricing objective suggests that firms can set prices to achieve maximum profitability. In this case, pricing strategy may be guided by exploring the profitability of an entire product mix or product line, rather than setting prices for individual products independently. As such, pricing decisions made around the entire mix of products become more complex due to the various factors that influence demand for each product. Let us take a look at the more commonly used product mix pricing strategies.

In chapter 8, we learned that a product line is a group of products that are closely related because they satisfy a class of needs, are used together, are sold to the same customer groups, are distributed through the same type of outlets, or fall within a given price range. Product line pricing establishes a range of selling prices and price points within that range.[4] Some of the items are priced lower and designed to appeal to a more price-sensitive group of consumers; other items within the product line are higher priced and targeted to a more affluent or price-insensitive group of consumers. Product-line pricing strategies are used for selling tickets to most sporting events. For example, the Washington Capitals offer tickets to all regular season home games at the MCI Center for $19, $30, $40, $50, $60, and $95. Sports card manufacturers also use product-line pricing strategies when they offer special, limited edition card sets at grossly inflated prices. The only thing "limited" in these sets is often the value to the consumer.

When using product-line pricing strategies, sports marketers must be careful in choosing the approximate prices to set for the various products within the line. The image of the higher-priced products might suffer if consumers apply the limited quality and features of the lower-priced items to the upper-end items. On the other hand, the higher-priced items within the line may enhance the image of the lower-priced sports products.

Frequently, marketers are exposed to the perceptual law that states "the whole is greater than the sum of its parts." This is the basic premise of bundle pricing. A **bundle**

pricing strategy refers to the grouping of individual sports products and services into a "single package" price. Golf and tennis balls are each sold using bundle pricing, with multiple balls being lumped together in one sleeve or canister and sold at a single price. Another example of a bundling strategy is when sweatpants and jacket are sold together as a single unit for a single price.

Often, we hear of golf vacation packages that incorporate greens fees, breakfast, lodging, and sometimes travel costs into one low price. This is usually more attractive to the potential consumer, because prices are generally lower for the package than they would be for the individual items and greater convenience is offered. Another example of bundle pricing in sports marketing is the bundling of individual game tickets into a "mini" season ticket package. For example, the Miami Dolphins offer their fans the "Special Teams Package." This ticket bundling package offers fans the opportunity to purchase seats for one preseason and two regular season games at a discount of $2 per ticket off the single game price. In yet another example, the Goodwill Games in New York offer discounts of 20 percent on tickets for groups of 20 or more.

Finally, price bundling occurs when selling season tickets for nearly all sports. For instance, the Tampa Bay Mutiny of Major League Soccer offer a season ticket package for $396, which includes much more than just the ticket. Fans receive discounts on team merchandise, free merchandise, pre-game "M" Club party with complimentary appetizers, pre-game chalk talk by the Tampa Bay Head Coach John Kowalski, an invitation to a Mutiny pre-season practice, free Mutiny T-shirt, a free Mutiny newsletter and media guide, a ticket exchange program, $25 gift certificate at one of four area soccer stores, $3 savings off game day tickets, and a free photo of Carlos Valderramma.[5]

The converse of bundle pricing strategy is **captive product pricing** where multiple sports products are separated and sold at a single price. In captive product pricing, sports manufacturers or organizations sell products and services that are used in conjunction with or in addition to the primary product. Typically, the primary product is sold at a low price and profits are made on the purchase of additional product(s). For businesses providing services, this type of pricing strategy is referred to as **two-part pricing**, where the service charge has a fixed fee and a variable component based on usage.

Consider purchasing a ticket to a sporting event. The ticket price represents a fixed fee, and the additional products and services consumed while watching the event vary based on the individual consumer. Most people at the event will have something to eat or drink and possibly purchase other souvenir items. Using a captive pricing strategy involves charging a moderate price for the ticket to enter the event and then setting higher markups on the related items. Anyone who has attended a major sporting event and has paid $2.50 for a soft drink and $4 for a hot dog has experienced captive pricing techniques at work (although fans often sneak in their own food and drink).

Another familiar example of a two-part pricing strategy is country club membership. Typically, fixed fees are charged for membership and monthly dues and then additional fees are assessed for using other facilities, such as the golf course, tennis courts, or dining. In fact, many golf courses (to the dismay of people who enjoy walking) require golfers to use carts to speed up play and course throughput increase or the number of golfers that participate each day.

■ Racquet club membership often uses two-part pricing strategies.

Cost-Based Pricing Strategies

Perhaps the most straightforward of all pricing strategies are **cost based**. As the term implies, the sports organization examines all of the costs associated with producing the sporting good or event before determining the price. Traditionally, organizations that utilize cost-based methods will set costs to achieve the desired levels of profitability. The lowest possible selling price a firm can charge and still attain its profit objectives is known as the price floor. A sports organization will be reluctant to price its products below the price floor, since doing so will result in the organization eventually running itself into the ground. To avoid this problem, sports marketers put a great deal of emphasis on understanding the costs associated with producing any given product.

Cost-plus pricing represents the simplest type of cost-based pricing strategy. In this strategy, the price is derived by computing the total cost (fixed + variable costs) of producing the individual product and then adding an additional cost to achieve the desired profitability. This extra charge, which is added to the cost of the product, is referred to as a standard markup. Let us look at an example of cost-plus pricing for a souvenir baseball autographed by Cal Ripken, Jr. of the Baltimore Orioles and trace how a $6.50 baseball is sold for $79.95. The initial cost of the baseball is $6.50, but Cal Ripken is paid $20.00 for signing each ball (incidentally, Ripken will sign roughly 10,000 balls each year). The next cost to add is a licensing fee of $2.50, paid to Major League Baseball for each ball and $2.00 for a nameplate, holder, and certificate of authenticity. The marketing company, Score Board, Inc. adds in a $14.00 markup, selling each ball for about $45.00 wholesale. Finally, retailers like Hammacher Schlemmer markup each ball $34.95 to cover their costs and make a profit. The cost to you, the collector, is $79.95.[6]

How do sports marketers decide upon the size of the markup on products and services? As stated before, profit objectives and consumer demand typically drive the percentage markup. In addition, the markup is based on the effort required to sell products and services (the more effort and time, the greater the markup), the quantity of products and services sold (the greater quantity sold, the less the markup), and also industry standards (use markup similar to that of the competition).

Target profit pricing is another variation of the cost-based methods. Here, sports marketers set approximate prices based on the target profit they have determined when setting objectives. In order to decide on price levels, a break-even analysis is typically conducted.

The basic premise of this **break-even pricing strategy** is for the firm to determine the number of units it will have to sell at a given price to break even (or recoup costs). Simply stated, if it costs the Ohio State University approximately $375,000 to operate their women's basketball program each year and they generate $375,000 in total revenues each year, then the program has "broken even."

spotlight on women in sports marketing:

the cost side of breaking even

Women have more opportunity to play major college sports than ever before, but the recent gains still fall short of achieving gender equity. That was the major finding of a survey of 107 Division 1A schools conducted by Gannett News Service during 1995–96. More specifically, the study found the following:

- The average spending on overall operations of a women's athletic program increased 167 percent over the last five years, but was still minimal compared to the amount spent on men's programs.
- The operating expenditures for men's programs averaged almost $2.4 million versus an average of $687,789 for women's programs.

- Overall, schools spent an average of $6.27 million per year on men's programs, when all costs including operations, coaches salaries, tuition, and recruiting expenses are included. The comparable average for women was $2.3 million.
- In men's basketball, the average operating cost more than doubled during the five-year span of 1991–1996 to $541,728. During the same period, women's costs nearly tripled, but only to $209,734 (still less than half of the men's operating cost).
- **Money In and Money Out**: Revenue from football programs account for 45 percent of NCAA Division 1A athletic funds. Football was also the chief expense, at 23 percent.

Revenues		Expenses	
Football	45%	Administration	45%
Other	34	Football	23
Men's Basketball	17	Nonrevenue Women	12
Nonrevenue Men	2	Nonrevenue Men	9
Women's Basketball	1	Men's Basketball	7
Nonrevenue Women	1	Women's Basketball	4

■ Non-revenue-generating sports such as wrestling have been eliminated from many college athletic programs.

■ **Comparing Expenses:** Men's basketball operating expenses are more than twice those of women's basketball. Here's a comparison of the top 10 sports, by expense, for men's and women's programs in 1996.

Men	Expenses	Women	Expenses
Football	$150,764,234	Basketball	$22,344,635
Basketball	57,964,941	Volleyball	9,715,380
Baseball	13,752,929	Track	8,263,927
Track	9,311,899	Softball	5,861,526
Tennis	5,073,124	Soccer	5,411,365
Golf	4,892,028	Tennis	5,266,277
Swimming	4,064,110	Swimming	4,791,837
Wrestling	3,209,280	Gymnastics	3,885,721
Soccer	2,847,675	Golf	3,578,917
Ice Hockey	1,936,732	Rowing	1,831,792

Source: Tom Witosky, "Separate, Still Not Equal," *The Cincinnati Enquirer,* March 2, 1997, C9. Courtesy of Tom Witosky.

In order to look at the number of units needed to break even at any given price, the following formula is applied:

$$\text{Break-Even Point} = \frac{\text{Fixed Cost}}{\text{Price} - \text{Variable Costs Per Unit}}$$

To illustrate, suppose we wanted to calculate the break-even point for a new fiberglass hockey stick. If the fixed costs for the stick are estimated to be $1.5 million, the variable costs per unit are $5, and the suggested selling price is $25, then the company would need to sell 75,000 hockey sticks to break even.

$$\text{Break-Even Point} = \frac{\$1.5 \text{ million}}{\$25 - \$5.00/\text{unit}}$$

$$\text{Break-Even Point} = 75,000 \text{ sticks}$$

If the price of the hockey stick is decreased by $5 to a selling price of $20, then the new break-even point would be 100,000 hockey sticks. The problem, however, is that the marketing manager cannot necessarily predict the impact the price change will have on the demand for the product. Dropping the price may not lead to an increase in demand large enough to still break even.

It is important to remember that when using a target profit pricing objective, the firm is not content to merely break-even but seeks to earn a profit. That is, revenues must be greater than costs. Clearly, price plays a critical role in assuring profit objectives are met.

ⓟrice Adjustments

As with most things in sports marketing, prices are dynamic. Initial prices are determined by a variety of internal and external issues that are continually changing with new market conditions. For instance, more or less competition may provide the impetus for price changes. Also, prices may be adjusted to stimulate demand for sporting products when sales expectations are not currently being met. Finally, prices might be adjusted to help meet the objectives that have been developed. The next section explores some of the ways in which price adjustments are implemented by sports marketers.

Price Reductions and Increases

In 1996, the Detroit Tigers were having such a terrible season on the field and at the gate that they decided to reduce ticket prices midseason to boost attendance. The same strategy was used by the Oakland Athletics. The A's reduced parking charges from $7 to $5, decreased upper-reserved seating from $7 to $5, and dropped bleacher seat prices from $4.50 to $4.00. In addition, the A's were planning on reducing food and concession prices in an all-out effort to increase attendance.

The A's and Tigers' examples notwithstanding, sports organizations rarely reduce or increase the price charged to consumers during the course of the season to stimulate demand. It is much more common, however, for marketers of sporting goods to reduce and increase prices. Typically, **price reductions** are efforts to enhance sales and achieve greater market share by directly lowering the original price. In addition to the direct reductions in price, rebates or bundling products are other types of price breaks commonly employed. Simply said, the Los Angeles Dodgers will never have an end-of-the-season sale of tickets. You will, however, be able to find any number of sales of baseball equipment at the end of the summer.

Whatever the form of price reductions, they are frequently risky for sports manufacturers for a number of reasons. First, consumers may associate multiple price reductions with inferior product quality. Second, consumers may associate price reductions with price gouging (always selling products at a discount so the initial price must be unreasonably high). Third, price reductions may wake a sleeping dog and cause competition to counter with its own price decreases. Finally, frequent price changes make it more difficult for the consumer to establish a frame of reference for the true price of sports products. If tennis balls regularly sell for $4.99 for a package of three, and I conduct three sales over the season that offer the balls for $2.99, then what is the perceived "real" price?

Price increases represent another important adjustment made to established prices. In recent years, many sports organizations have had to increase prices for a variety of reasons, even though consumers, retailers, and employees discourage such actions. One of the primary reasons for increasing prices is to keep up with cost inflation. In other words, as the cost of materials or running a sports organization increases, prices must be increased to achieve the same profit objectives. Another reason for implementing a price increase is because there is excess demand for the sports product. For example, if the Boston Celtics have season tickets sold out for the next 10 years, then slight increases to these ticket prices may be acceptable.

Because of the negative consequences of raising prices, sports organizations may consider potential alternatives to straight price increases. These alternatives include eliminating any planned price reductions, lessening the number of product features, or unbundling items formerly "bundled" into a low price.

If there are no viable alternatives to increasing prices, it is important to communicate these changes to fans and consumers in a straightforward fashion to avoid potential negative consequences. Remember, much of pricing is based on consumer psychology. If fans or consumers of sporting goods are told why prices are being increased, they may feel that price increases are justified.

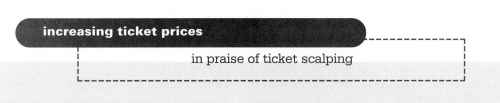

increasing ticket prices

in praise of ticket scalping

Suppose you and your buddy had two tickets to the Super Bowl. Because you were at the front of the ticket line, you had good seats. Unexpectedly, your boss, in spite of your apoplectic protests, sends you both on an emergency business trip.

So what do you do with the tickets? Give them away? Not likely. You paid full freight for them. Let them go unused and eat the $250 per ticket? You have got to be kidding. Sell them to your neighbor for what you paid for them? Maybe, but the odds on the game have narrowed, and the tickets seem worth a lot more.

What about scalping them for maybe $1,500 each, the market price on the street? What's wrong with that? Whose tickets are they, anyway?

Any normal NFL fan (and any market economist) would say nothing at all because that is the market price. And besides, they're your tickets, right?

Well, no, say the owners of the teams. By scalping the tickets, you are making a profit that belongs to us. Or in the words of Jerry Colangelo, president of the Phoenix Suns, in a 1995 exchange with Arizona State University students, scalpers "made money off of him without his permission and that was not right." Further, he noted that he paid taxes on the money he earned on the original sale, and the scalpers paid no taxes on the resale. Peter Luukko, CEO of the Core States Center in Philadelphia, puts it differently: By selling your tickets on the scalping market, you are stealing from the teams.

Of course, scalping is against the law in about half the states and in most of the cities where major sporting and concert events are

(continued)

held. There are several reasons for the laws. First, most of them were passed when markets were not in favor and government regulation was. Second, there is a fairness issue: All the tickets to a popular event should not go to the wealthiest people; some should be rationed to lower, income buyers and "true fans" on a first-come, first-served basis.

Third, the owners of the teams and the promoters of the events want a sellout, both for public relations purposes and to maximize revenues from parking, popcorn, and pizza sales at the game. They dread a bust, a lousy game at which the parking lot ticket price before the game falls, signaling empty seats, less revenue, and general embarrassment.

Finally, owners, officials, and fans alike are rightly concerned with two aspects of scalping: the hassling of fans at the stadium and the possibility of sales of counterfeit or misrepresented tickets.

Fallout from scalping, good and bad. Dennis McGlynn, the president and CEO of Dover Downs (Delaware) Entertainment, where NASCAR auto racing draws thousands of fans, notes that his track can be the fall guy. "When a scalper sells tickets for $290, promising they are on the straightaway right near the finish, when in fact they are bleacher seats on the far turn that any fan could have bought for $32, Dover Downs gets the flak for misrepresentation." And the scalper has moved to the next event.

These pressures have resulted in all sorts of antiscalping statutes. Sometimes, to be sure, the law of unintended consequences strikes. A few years back the city of Cleveland began enforcing a 50-year-old statute that prohibits the reselling of two or more tickets "at a price varying from the regularly advertised box-office price."

In 1995, more than two dozen fans were busted by the Cleveland police for trying to sell something like $24 worth of Indians tickets for $20 just to get rid of them. Even the mayor recognized the folly of such a policy and stopped enforcing the law. So some teams have established "Scalp-Free Zones" at the stadium where fans can sell tickets at face value or lower—but not at more than face value.

But there is a better idea. Stephen K. Happell and Marianne Jennings, professors at Arizona State University, proposed letting the market work. Scalping, they note, is inevitable and a fact of life at every stadium at every event. So why not set aside an area at the stadium where scalpers have the right to operate and trade tickets at will? Scalpers would buy a license, bringing some revenue to the owners, and the designated areas would keep scalpers from harassing uninterested fans. Tickets would be available to fans who want them—and without the fear of being nabbed as a criminal if they buy them.

Happell and Jennings persuaded the city of Phoenix to adopt such a plan in 1995, and it has been working well. They correctly predicted that if all the scalpers were aggregated in one place, the market would clear and the price of scalped tickets would fall. Tickets to Phoenix Suns' games dropped to face value, and even at the 1996 Super Bowl in Phoenix, fans could buy tickets at face value, almost unheard of at America's premier sporting event.

In other words, let the market work and everyone wins—the owners reinforce their ticket-pricing structure, fans get tickets, crime is reduced, and nobody is hassled. Only you and your buddy are at risk, for your $1,250-per-ticket profit may evaporate. But, hey, you win some and lose some, right?

Source: Pete du Pont. "In Praise of Ticket Scalping." <http://www.intellectualcapital.com/issues/97/1204/iced.asp> (December 4, 1997). With permission of Intellectual Capital.com (www.intellectualcapital.com).

An important concept when making price adjustments (either up or down) is known as the **just noticeable difference**, or **JND**.[7] The just noticeable difference is the point at which consumers detect a difference between two stimuli. In pricing, the two stimuli are the original price and the adjusted price. In other words, do consumers perceive (notice) a difference when prices are increased or decreased from their previous price? The following examples illustrate the importance of the just noticeable difference.

Dick's Sporting Goods may sell Wilson softball gloves at a regular price of $39.99 (note the psychological price strategy of odd pricing being used). With softball season right around the corner, Dick's decides to reduce prices and sell the gloves for $34.99. Does this $5 reduction surpass the difference threshold? In other words, does the consumer feel that there is a noticeable difference between the regular price and sale price? If not, then the price reduction will not be successful at stimulating demand.

Let us continue the example of the Wilson softball glove. Suppose, now, that because of the increasing cost of raw materials needed to produce the gloves, the price has to be increased from $39.99 to $44.99. Again, the sports marketer has to determine whether or not consumers will notice this increase in price. If not, then the price increase may not have negative consequences for the sale of Wilson softball gloves.

Price Discounts

Combined with straight price decreases, **price discounts** are other incentives offered to buyers to stimulate demand or reward behaviors that are favorable to the seller. The two major types of price discounts that are common in sports marketing are quantity discounts and seasonal discounts.

Quantity discounts reward buyers for purchasing large quantities of a sports product. This type of discounting may occur at all different levels of the channel of distribution. Using the previous softball glove example, Wilson may offer a quantity discount to Dick's Sporting Goods for sending in a large purchase order. Consumers hope that Dick's Sporting Goods will pass the savings on to them in the form of price reductions. The purchase of group ticket sales is another common example of quantity discounts in sports marketing.

Seasonal discounts are also prevalent in sports marketing because of the nature of sports. Most sports have defined seasons that are observed by both participants and spectators. Seasonal discounts are intended to stimulate demand in off-peak periods. For example, ski equipment may be discounted in the summer months to encourage consumer demand and increase traffic in skiing specialty stores. Manufacturers might also offer seasonal discounts to retailers in off-seasons to help level out production schedules.

In addition to sporting goods, seasonal discounts are often offered for ticket prices to sporting events. The Thiftway ATP (tennis) and Kroger Senior Classic (golf) events provide discounts for customers purchasing tickets in advance during the winter months for these summer events.

■ Ski resorts may use seasonal discounting.

SUMMARY

(T)his chapter discusses several pricing strategies that are used to determine the price of sports products. The pricing strategies examined in chapter 15 include differential pricing, new sports product pricing, psychological pricing, product mix pricing, and cost-based pricing.

Differential pricing is selling the same sports product to different buyers at different prices. When using differential pricing, care must be taken not to discriminate against consumers. As you will recall from the previous chapter, the Robinson–Patman Act of 1936 limits the ability of firms to sell the same product at different prices to different customers. The most common form of differential pricing is second-market discounting, where different prices are charged to different segments of consumers.

New sports product pricing strategies are used to determine the selling price for sports products that are about to be introduced to the marketplace. The two new sports product pricing strategies that are commonly employed are penetration pricing and price skimming. Penetration pricing strategies attempt to stimulate demand and product trial

by offering the new sports product at a low price. Alternatively, price-skimming strategies set prices at or above the competition to enhance perceived product quality.

Psychological pricing strategies are based on the image that the organization wants to project for its sports product. Prestige pricing, reference pricing, odd–even pricing, and traditional pricing are all different types of psychological pricing. Prestige pricing uses high prices to convey a distinct and exclusive image for the sports product. Reference pricing uses the consumers' frame of reference that is established through either previous purchasing experience or high levels of information search. Odd–even pricing is setting prices at odd numbers (e.g., $9.95) to denote a lower price or a "good deal" or setting prices at even numbers (e.g., $10.00) to imply higher quality. Finally, traditional pricing uses historical or long-standing prices for a sports product to determine the pricing.

Product mix strategies consider all of the organization's products at set prices to maximize the profitability of each individual product. Product line pricing, a type of product mix strategy, sets price steps (also known as price points) between products in the line to appeal to different groups of consumers. Another product mix strategy, called price bundling, clusters two or more sports products into a single packaged price. Conversely, captive product pricing unbundles two or more sports products and sells each at a separate price. This type of product mix strategy is also referred to as two-part pricing.

Cost-based pricing strategies calculate all of the costs associated with producing and marketing a sports product and then determine the price based on the total cost. The simplest type of cost-based strategy is known as cost-plus pricing, where total costs are determined and an additional cost is added to achieve the desired profitability. Another cost-based method is target profit pricing, which sets approximate prices based on the target profit that the organization determined when setting objectives. In order to decide on price levels using any of the cost-based methods, a break-even analysis is typically conducted.

Once the price of the sports product has been determined, adjustments are constantly necessary as market conditions, such as consumer demand and change. Price reductions or increases are used to reach pricing objectives that have been determined. Generally, price reductions are used to help achieve sales and market share objectives, whereas increases are used to keep up with rising costs. Regardless of whether adjustments are made to raise prices or lower prices, an important consideration in pricing is the concept known as the JND, or just noticeable difference. The JND is the point at which consumers can detect a "noticeable" difference between two stimuli—the initial price and the adjusted price. Depending on the rationale for price adjustments, sports marketers sometimes want the change to be above the difference threshold (i.e., consumers will notice the difference) and sometimes it will be below the difference threshold (i.e., consumers will not notice the difference).

KEY TERMS & CONCEPTS

break-even pricing

bundle pricing

captive product pricing

cost-based pricing strategies

cost-plus pricing

customary pricing

differential pricing

just noticeable difference (JND)

new sports product pricing

odd–even pricing

penetration pricing

prestige pricing

price adjustments

price discounts

price skimming

pricing strategy model

product line pricing

product mix pricing strategies

psychological pricing strategies

quantity discounts

reference pricing

seasonal discounts

second-market discounting

target profit pricing

two-part pricing

REVIEW QUESTIONS

1. Outline the steps for developing a pricing strategy. How do the internal and external factors affect this process?

2. Discuss differential pricing strategies. What is second-market discounting?

3. Describe the major differences between penetration pricing and price skimming. What conditions lead sports marketers to use penetration pricing versus price-skimming strategies?

4. What is psychological pricing? Provide several examples of reference pricing for sports products. Do you feel odd–even pricing is an effective psychological pricing strategy? Why?

5. Discuss the various product mix pricing strategies. Keeping the overall strategic marketing process in mind, why are product mix strategies so important?

6. Define cost-based pricing. Why are cost-based pricing strategies considered to be the simplest way of establishing prices? Explain the logic of break-even analysis.

7. What are the risks associated with reducing the price of sports products? Describe two common types of price discounting.

EXERCISES

1. Design a study that will establish a consumer's just noticeable difference for two sports products: (1) a season ticket package initially priced at $250 and (2) a soccer ball initially priced at $23.95. What are your findings? Does the initial price (the starting point) matter?

2. Calculate the break-even point for a manufacturer of golf balls, given the following: the fixed costs for the balls are estimated to be $1.3 million, the variable costs per unit are $2, and the suggested selling price is $10.

3. Name two sports products that use price-skimming strategies and two sports products that use a penetration pricing strategy. Comment on how the rest of the marketing mix follows the pricing strategy. Do you agree with the sports marketers' pricing decision?

4. Conduct a simple study of odd–even pricing by producing a rough (mock-up) advertisement for a sports product. Produce two versions of the advertisement—one using odd pricing for the sports product and an identical version using even pricing for the sports product. Then measure demand for the product (potential sales) by assessing purchase intent and consumer perceptions of quality. Which product will sell the best (odd priced or even priced)? Which product is perceived to be of higher quality (odd priced or even priced)?

5. Interview the organizer of a local/neighborhood road race (e.g., 5K or 10K) and determine the costs of staging such an event. Categorize the costs as either fixed or variable. Assess the role of cost in the price of the entry fee for participants.

1. Using the Internet, find an example of price bundling sports products.

2. Using the Internet, find an example of product line pricing for the pricing of a sponsorship package (i.e., sponsorship levels at different prices).

3. Searching the Internet, find an example of a sports product that uses prestige pricing. Comment on the construction of the Web site itself. Is it consistent with the prestige pricing?

NOTES

1. See, for example, William Zikmund and Michael d'Amico, *Marketing*, 4th ed. (St. Paul, MN: West, 1993).

2. Eric Berkowitz, Roger Kerin, Steven Hartley, and William Reidelius, *Marketing*, 3d ed. (Homewood, IL: Irwin, 1992) 339–340.

3. "Diamond Vision," *Sports Illustrated*, July 29, 1996, G22.

4. Joel Evans and Barry Berman, *Marketing*, 6th ed. (New York, NY: Macmillan, 1994) 720.

5. "Tampa Bay Mutiny." <http://www.tampabaymutiny.com/main2.htm>.

6. Sabra Chartrand, "When the Pen Is Truly Mighty," *The New York Times*, July 14, 1995, D1.

7. See, for example, John Mowen and Michael Minor, *Consumer Behavior*, 5th ed. (Upper Saddle River, NJ: Prentice Hall, 1998) 70.

CHAPTER **16**

Implementing and Controlling the Strategic Sports Marketing Process

OBJECTIVES

After completing this chapter, you should be able to

- Describe how the implementation phase of the strategic sports marketing process 'fits' with the planning phase

- Explain the organizational design elements that impact the implementation phase

- Identify the general competencies and the most important skills that effective sports marketing managers possess

- Describe the basic characteristics of TQM programs and how TQM might be implemented in sports organizations

- Identify some of the guidelines for designing reward systems

- Define strategic control and how the control phase of the strategic sports marketing process 'fits' with the implementation phase

- Explain the differences among planning assumption control, process control, and contingency control

Dressed in baggy khakis and a rumpled blazer, 25-year-old James "Jake" Weinstock might be mistaken for a struggling actor. When he stabs at his unruly locks and gushes about hitchhiking in Zimbabwe, he projects the boyish charm of Tom Hanks in *Big*. In the Wild East, however, where the high-octane capitalism of the post-Soviet era has turned convention on its head, appearances can be deceiving.

Though he looks like a slacker, the history major from the University of Pennsylvania could teach a Harvard MBA a thing or two. Straight out of college and with little experience in business, Weinstock and two other partners raised $2.5 million to realize a dream of starting a business in Russia, a country Weinstock fell in love with while roaming the world during a year's leave of absence from Penn. In the year and a half of teeth-grinding frustration since the enterprise was conceived in a Moscow bar, he has hopped across continents in search of start-up capital, boned up on accounting and contract law, and staved off the Russian mafia.

Rattled Rivals

The result: a soccer-field-size, state-of-the-art Gold's Gym in Moscow's center—the name licensed from California's renowned Gold's Gym, which has 500 franchises around the world. The facility has shaken up the city's sluggish health-club industry and rattled its once-complacent Russian rivals. With Astro-turfed tennis courts, a Nike-built basketball court, high-tech Cybex workout machines, tanning salons, a Western-style emphasis on service, a day-care center, and in-house medical staff, Gold's has fired up the city's fitness-starved business community. In the run-up to February's grand opening, the gym has been taking members at reduced rates, which include hefty corporate discounts. Weinstock has fielded hundreds of calls from affluent Muscovites and expatriate residents, signing up more than 400.

"I'm biting my nails. We're just this close to the end," says Weinstock in the gym's bare-bones office, his words almost drowned out by the rattle of jackhammers and the roar of blowtorches as workers race around the clock to meet the opening deadline.

Dreams

Weinstock was merely upholding his family's independent streak when, after only six months of employment, he chucked his comfortable marketing job at Moscow's Ernst & Young for "plain pasta dinners" and heady dreams. Both Weinstock's parents are also boss-dodgers: His mother, a freelance editor, worked for *The New Yorker*, while his father runs his own small consulting firm. Weinstock's brothers are writers. "I wanted to do my own thing," he says. "And the fact that it's so difficult here makes success that much more rewarding."

An avid sports fan who claims he would join a pickup basketball game anywhere, Weinstock got the idea for a gym venture on his second day in Moscow. An expatriate fraternity brother introduced him to 31-year-old Paul Kuebler, at that time financial director at Andersen Consulting. "The project was a perfect fit for both of us: making money while having fun," says Weinstock. Kuebler had been at Andersen for almost eight years and was itching for something more adventurous. In May 1995, he brought on board a Russian friend of two years, Vladimir Grumlik. Then things really began to roll.

Weinstock is not unique in the New Russia. Other brash, adrenaline-charged Generation Xers, both Russians and Westerners, have braved the chaos and rampant criminality of post-Soviet Russia to follow their stars—opening diners, movie theaters, casinos, and even banks, and transforming the city's landscape in the process.

Weinstock and his partners are among the few entrepreneurs, however, who braved quitting their jobs without the security of prior backing, simply hoping venture capital might emerge in time to save them.

Their gamble paid off. But raising capital was much tougher than just passing the hat. Despite a licensing agreement with Gold's and an upbeat business plan that promised a 60–70 percent return, few investors in either Russia or the United States took the bait. "Our proposal was a bit offbeat: too small for the big funds and too big for the small ones," says Kuebler, who admits that he naively expected things to fall into place within three months of leaving Andersen last October.

The venture seemed doomed when the Communists swept to victory in December's parliamentary elections, just when Weinstock was in New York seeking investors. Potential financiers, already wary of both Russia and Weinstock's youth, lost interest when the specter of communism reappeared.

Character

The partners did not despair, however. Smashing open their combined nest eggs of about $150,000—Weinstock claims that even his high school ball-boy savings went into the project—and with a little help from friends and relatives, they persisted. When a Boston real-estate developer, Commonwealth Property Investors (CPI), decided to pump in a cool million last June after a presentation by the two Americans, things began to click. "Jake and Paul's character was crucial in our decision. They're mature, levelheaded, dedicated, and complement each other well. I was impressed that they staked their nest eggs on this project," says CPI's Moscow rep, Greg Getshow. He added that although Gold's was not in CPI's line of business, it was excited by the idea.

With CPI's $1 million paving the way, 10 other private investors jumped on board, a Russian among them. The savvy partners say they made sure, however, to keep a control-ling interest in the business, which is registered as an offshore company in Cyprus with a local Russian subsidiary.

Keen to upstage Reebok International, Ltd. and increase its visibility in Moscow, Nike, Inc., while wary of sponsoring an exclusive gym, agreed to build a basketball court, on the condition that it be made available on demand for company-sponsored sports clinics for the young. It is also providing staff outfits.

Investors agree that the Americans' fluency in Russian helped. More important, their extensive contacts with Moscow officialdom through a trustworthy local partner helped seal their backing. Vladimir Grumlik, an intense, no-nonsense former athlete who once sold Nikes in Russia's caviar capital, Astrakhan, got to know Moscow officials through his earlier business ventures. He has been crucial.

Grumlik scoured Moscow for potential gym sites, helping to find a crumbling but spacious soccer arena belonging to the Stadium of Young Pioneers, a now-privatized wing of the Soviet-era youth organization. They got the building under a 25-year renewable lease. "I love working with Paul and Jake. They're more responsible and farsighted than the Russians I've dealt with," says Grumlik. And with his sports mentor, Alexei Spirin, a World Cup Russian soccer referee, he helped them strike the kind of deal that in Moscow keeps the mafia at arm's length. A power broker back in Soviet times, Spirin is cozy with Moscow's elite and knows well how to make things happen in Russia.

"On Spirin's recommendation, we hired a security firm tied to the former KGB," says Kuebler. "We pay them above-market rates plus a 'consulting' fee, and they make sure no one messes with us." The cost is no more than 5 percent of revenue.

No Pool

While the security issue may be resolved for now, the partners still have plenty to worry about. Competitors have their knives out for the brash American upstarts. "They're just a

(continued)

bunch of kids with no experience," sniffs Olga Antonova, manager of their biggest rival, World Class Fitness, which has more than 3,000 members. Spurred by Gold's debut, World Class has spruced up service, extended hours, and is rushing to open a new gym.

And while Gold's equipment might be a notch above its competitors', Gold's lacks the clincher—a swimming pool. Then there's the cost: A year's membership, while $500 cheaper than many rival gyms, still runs $2,500. Says Greek businessman Konstantinos Tsakonas: "[Membership in] the Gold's franchise in Cyprus costs $600. Why are they charging me four times more?" Many of the city's wealthy, including expats, prefer working out in cheaper Soviet-style sports clubs. And while the partners are chummy now, Russians have been known to fall out, often violently.

Some outsiders, however, are cautiously optimistic. "This city could absorb scores more world-class gyms. If Gold's doesn't alienate Russians by being too American, it could take off," says Andrei Kulikov, a correspondent for the Russian sports daily, *Sport Ekspress*.

Even before liftoff, Weinstock is amazed by what's happened. "I never imagined we'd come this far," he says. "When I can have a cafe latte and watch people enjoying themselves, then I'll finally be able to relax."

Maybe. But if members sign up in droves and if branches appear in St. Petersburg and Ukraine as planned, Weinstock should not count on relaxing for long.

Source: Vajai Maheshwari "All Set to Muscle in on Moscow," *Business Week*, December 16, 1996. Reprinted from *Business Week* by special permission. Copyright © 1996 by the McGraw-Hill Companies, Inc.

The opening scenario presents an excellent example of how sports organizations operate in uncertain and changing conditions. Moreover, sports organizations must consider the internal and external environments and formulate a plan that achieves a "fit" with these environments. The strategic sports marketing process is ultimately directed towards the achievement of the organization's mission, goals, and objectives. The contingency theory of sports marketing suggests that there are a variety of marketing plans that can achieve these goals. However, not all of these plans are equally effective. Likewise, organizations have a variety of ways to implement and control the strategic sports marketing plan they have developed, all of which are not equally useful for putting the plan into action. Thus, sports marketers should allocate the time and effort necessary to develop a program that will lead to the desired outcomes and most effectively implement and control the planning process.

The remainder of this chapter looks at the last two phases of the strategic marketing process—implementation and control. We will begin by examining a model of implementation process and the organizational design elements that facilitate or impede the execution of the marketing plan. Then we will shift our focus to the control phase and look at some of the common forms of strategic control.

Ⓘmplementation

Implementation can be described as putting strategy into action or executing the plan. As illustrated in the opening scenario, Jake Weinstock's dream of opening the first Gold's Gym in Moscow was realized after overcoming considerable obstacles. Although most sports marketers need not worry about the Russian mafia, they do need to continually monitor the implementation process to make sure that plans are being carried out in the correct manner.

To successfully manage the implementation process, the sports marketer must consider a number of organizational design elements. These organizational design elements include communication, staffing, skills, coordination, rewards, information, creativity, and budgeting. Implementation must begin with **communication**. Effective communication requires a leadership style that allows and encourages an understanding of the marketing plan by all members of the sports marketing team. A second critical element involves **staffing** and developing the **skills** in those people who are responsible for carrying out the plan. These people must also be placed within the organization so that they can work together to implement the plan, thus a third critical design element is **coordination**. **Rewards** that are congruent to the plan can provide the motivation and incentives necessary for people to work effectively toward the achievement of the goals and objectives outlined within the plan. **Information** must be available to those people who will carry out the plans so that effective decisions can be made throughout the implementation phase. Effective work environments also allow for and encourage **creativity** from individuals who are expected to find ways to carry out the strategic marketing plan. Finally, a supportive **budgeting** system is critical to the successful achievement of strategic goals and objectives. These seven organizational design elements of implementation and their relationship to the strategic sports marketing process are outlined in Figure 16.1.

Each of these seven elements must be carefully considered within the strategic marketing process by the sports marketing manager. The implementation design must be appropriate for the plan. In other words, a "fit" between the planning phase and the implementation phase is required. Thus, a change in the strategic marketing plan of a sports organization could lead to the need to make changes in one or more of these design elements. Let us look at each of the seven design elements in greater detail.

Communication

Effective communication is critical to the successful implementation of the strategic sports marketing plan. Before we discuss the issues involved in effective communication, it is important to understand the importance of having a leader who is committed to the strategic sports marketing plan. Without such commitment, the best communication efforts will be ineffective. The values of the marketing leader not only affect the strategic sports marketing process, but also the way the plan will be implemented. Strategy leadership requires a "champion," someone who believes so strongly in the strategic marketing plan that he or she can share the "what," "why," and "how" with those who will be responsible for its implementation.

The commitment of the leader to the plan usually dictates the level of commitment among those who will carry it out. In addition, different strategies require different skills, even among leaders. Therefore, when strategy changes, a change in leadership often follows. That relationship may also be reversed. A change in leadership will often lead to a change, or at least an adjustment, to the strategy. In fact, because of the close relationship between strategy and leadership, it is sometimes

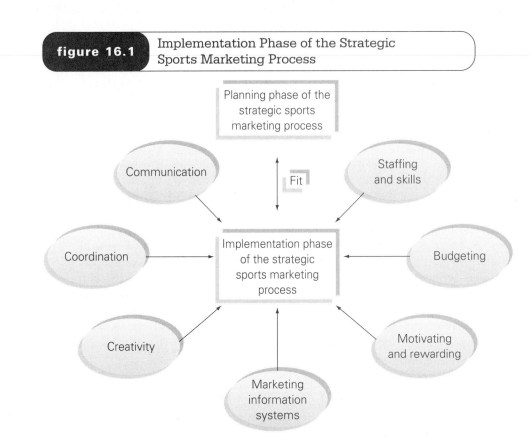

figure 16.1 Implementation Phase of the Strategic Sports Marketing Process

Planning phase of the strategic sports marketing process

Communication

Staffing and skills

Fit

Coordination

Implementation phase of the strategic sports marketing process

Budgeting

Creativity

Motivating and rewarding

Marketing information systems

necessary to bring in outside sports marketers to implement a changed or new strategy. Organizations will also often bring in someone new when they believe a new marketing strategy is needed to enhance performance.

For example, Jim Ritts, commissioner of the Ladies Professional Golf Association was hired to broaden the reach of the league and bolster its marketing efforts. Having a marketing and media background, Ritts was thought to have the skills required to grow the tour. Although this is challenging, Ritts has had the support of players, sponsors, and golf industry executives. In addition, Ritts has the popularity of golf and women's sports on his side. For instance, in 1995 some 5.4 million women hit the links—a number that has grown exponentially over the last decade.

Ritts claims that the real key to his success is luring sponsors with a "national agenda." Companies such as State Farm Mutual, which has held the State Farm Rail Classic in Springfield, Illinois, for three years, have renewed agreements, and new sponsors have signed on. Most notable is a five-year commitment from ITT Company for a November tour-ending championship in Las Vegas to be aired on ABC.[1]

Organizational leadership sets the tone for communication within the sports organization. Communication may be formal or informal and may utilize a number of different channels. For example, some organizations may require all communications

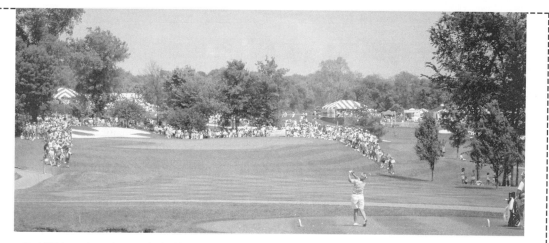

■ The LPGA is growing under strong leadership.

be written and meetings be scheduled and documented. Other organizational leaders may have an informal, open-door policy and allow for more "spur of the moment" meetings and "hallway" discussions. Either policy can be effective when it comes to implementing strategy within the sports organization, as long the necessary information is clearly and accurately communicated.

Strategy was once considered a "top-down" only process where those who had a "big-picture" view of the organization were considered the best candidates for formulating strategy. This often led to huge communication requirements as organizational leaders attempted to inform those who had to carry out the strategy about not only the strategy, but the rationale for strategic choices made by the top management. Experience has shown that the communication process is easier when those who are expected to implement the plan are involved throughout the process. Thus, involving the entire sports marketing team throughout the strategic sports marketing process can usually be more effective than attempting to communicate the plan after it has been developed.

Even when everyone responsible for implementing the plan is involved in its development, strategic sports marketing plans should be communicated often. Due to the contingent nature of the strategic sports marketing process, plans and circumstances can change, and people can forget the original plan and the basic premise upon which the plan was formulated. Employees can learn about or be reminded about the content and purpose of the plans in a variety of ways. This information can be communicated in regularly scheduled meetings or at gatherings where the strategic plan is the primary agenda item. Printed material can also be useful. Some sports organizations may give employees desk items, such as calendars or paperweights, with keywords that remind them of the strategy. They may even program screen savers on computers with words that will remind employees of the strategic thrust of the marketing plan. Promotional literature that can be displayed around the office or sent to employees through e-mail is also useful. In essence, sports marketing organizations that can provide daily reminders of the strategy are more likely to keep everyone involved on the same strategic path. Many forms of internal promotion can be used to achieve this goal.

Communication with groups and individuals outside of the marketing department is also important. Many such individuals and groups, both within the organization and outside of the organization, have a stake in the marketing strategy and can have an impact on the implementation of the plan. For example, it is important to inform other departments within the sports organization who affect or are affected by the strategy or the strategic marketing direction. For example, many teams are in the process of trying to develop long-term relationships with their fans. One of the ways to build these relationships is to allow fans more access and contact with the players. At the collegiate level, Xavier Women's Basketball Team has implemented a Kid's Club where young Musketeer fans are sent a handwritten note by a member of the team inviting them to a pregame pizza party. This creative plan can only be executed by communicating its importance to coaches and members of the XU team.

As with internal promotion, external promotion and communication of the strategic sports marketing plan can take many forms. Some channels for these communications include Web sites, annual reports, mailers, marketing specialties such as calendars, or meetings. Again, the key to effectively communicating to outside or inside groups is committed and competent leadership. It is with this leadership and effective communication efforts that the foundation for successful implementation of the strategic sports marketing plan is provided.

Sports Marketing Hall of fame

GARY DAVIDSON

Gary Davidson was once called the man who has had the greatest impact on professional sports in America. A former lawyer, Davidson founded and served as president of the American Basketball Association (ABA), the World Hockey Association (WHL), and the World Football League (WFL) in the late 1960s and early 1970s.

These leagues, of course, offered alternatives for professional athletes that would have never otherwise existed. By breaking the virtual monopoly held on talent by the existing NBA, NHL, and NFL franchises, Davidson attracted stars such as Wayne Gretzky, Bobby Hull, "Dr. J." Julius Erving, and Rick Barry to play in his rebel leagues. Davidson and his leagues are also credited with some major rule changes that subsequently were adopted by the existing professional leagues. For instance, the three-point shot was created to add excitement to the ABA and has changed the entire course of modern basketball.

In addition to his ambush marketing tactics, Gary Davidson broadened the scope of professional sports. He placed professional franchises in cities that were previously considered too small to support major league sports. For example, San Antonio and Indianapolis were two of his original ABA teams that are now successful NBA franchises. Davidson's leagues have benefited the fans, the players, and major league sports.

Source: Steve Rushin, "Gary Davidson," Sports Illustrated, September 19, 1994, 145.

Staffing and Skills

As we just discussed, it is critical to the success of the strategic sports marketing plan to have a leader who can "champion" and communicate the strategy. As important as the leader is to effective implementation, it is equally important to have a staff who cares about and is capable of implementing the strategy. A group of individuals must be assembled who have the appropriate mix of backgrounds, experiences, know-how, beliefs, values, work and managerial styles, and personalities.

It is important to consider strategy prior to hiring and training new employees and in retraining those who are already with the marketing team. This is especially vital in managerial or other key positions. However, staffing for the implementation of strategic sports marketing plans must go much deeper into the organizational ranks. In fact, putting together an effective marketing team is one of the cornerstones of the implementation process.

A few studies have examined the relationship between types of strategy and staff characteristics. One study of corporate executives and their perceptions regarding the relationship between managerial characteristics and strategy offered two interesting findings.[2] First, experience and exposure to a particular type of strategy has been viewed by corporate executives as being essential for managers. Previous experience and exposure to a strategy can provide an opportunity for these experienced individuals to provide important input into the implementation of the plan. However, the second finding suggests that a "perfect match" between managerial characteristics and strategy is likely to result in an overcommitment to a particular strategy. In other words, managers may not be able to change strategic direction when contingencies change if they are perfectly matched in education, training, experience, and personality to one particular strategy. These findings may be particularly relevant for sports organizations. Because sports organizations operate in changing, uncertain, and unpredictable environments where the internal and external contingencies can change frequently, staffing must consider the capacity for change among employees.

To develop a staff capable of implementing the strategy, three categories of characteristics must be considered: education, training, and ability; experience and previous track record; and personality and temperament. With any team-building activity, it is important to consider the compatibility of the individuals who will work together to implement the strategic sports plan.

Just what skills are necessary to land and keep your dream job in sports marketing? The answer to this question is best addressed in two parts. First, what knowledge is required for an individual to be successful in all sports management positions? In other words, what are the foundation skills for a successful career. Second, what are the marketing-specific core competencies of the sports marketing manager?

In addressing the first question, the general competencies necessary for all sports marketing management careers include the following:[3]

- to direct the work effort of people or groups of people
- to interrelate with the community
- to negotiate in order to arrive at a solution to a problem

- to function within a specified budget
- to use supervision techniques
- to evaluate the results of your decisions in light of work objectives
- to self-evaluate employee's job performance
- to use problem-solving techniques
- to interpret basic statistical data
- to speak before large audiences
- to apply the knowledge of the history and evolution of sport into the structure of today's society
- to appreciate the psychological factors that pertain to an athlete's performance and attitude on the playing field

These general skills are required of all sports marketing managers to some extent, but what about more specific marketing skills? Recently, this question was posed to sports marketing professionals employed in sports marketing firms, amateur sports organizations, professional sports organization, and college athletics. The results of this study are presented in Table 16.1.

Remember, changes in strategy may lead to modification of the staff and skill base. Thus, employee training and retraining is often an important part of the implementation process. As strategy is developed and the implementation plan formulated, sports marketers must consider not only new staffing needs, but also new skill needs. Training and retraining programs should be designed and included in the implementation plans so that the staff is prepared to implement the new or modified strategy. Until all of the staff and skills are in place, it is unlikely that the sports organization can proceed with the successful implementation of the marketing plan.

Coordination

Successful implementation of the marketing plan depends not only on capable and committed leadership who can effectively communicate internally and externally and a staff with the necessary skills, but also on the effective organization of those people and their tasks. Structure helps to define the key activities and the manner in which they will be coordinated to achieve the strategy. A fit between strategy and structure has been shown to be critical to the successful achievement of strategy and the performance of organizations. According to one important study of organizations, when a new strategy is chosen, a decline in performance was observed and administrative problems occurred until a new method of organizing people and activities was put into place. Once the new method was implemented, organizational performance began to improve, and the strategy was more likely to be achieved.[4] Thus, the strategic marketing plan must dictate how people and tasks are organized.

One way of coordinating people and tasks in a sports organization is by practicing Total Quality Management (TQM). Quality improvement programs have become an important and powerful tool for organizations of the 1990s, including sports

table 16.1

Most Important Skills for Sport Marketing Managers

Presented in Rank Order Where 1 Is the Most Important Skill and 20 Is the Least Important Skill

1. Establish a positive image for your sporting organization
2. Achieve sponsors' promotional goals
3. Stimulate ticket sales
4. Maximize media exposure for events, athletes, sponsors
5. Acquire sponsors through personal contacts
6. Maintain good relations with community, authorities, partners
7. Acquire sponsors by formal presentations
8. Develop special promotions
9. Improve budget construction
10. Negotiate promotion contracts
11. Evaluate sports marketing opportunities and performance
12. Design and coordinate content of events
13. Coordinate press coverage of events
14. Create contracts
15. Provide corporate hospitality of events
16. Build public image and awareness of athletes
17. Schedule events and facilities
18. Establish event safety factors
19. Build rapport with editors, reporters, and other media reps
20. Buy and resell media rights

Source: Peter Smolianov and David Shilbury, "An Investigation of Sport Marketing Competencies," *Sport Marketing Quarterly*, vol. 5, no. 4 (1996): 27–36. Reprinted with permission of Fitness Information Technology, Inc. Publishers.

organizations.[5] Nearly all major corporations and industries in the United States have adopted some type of quality initiative to meet competitive challenges. Traditionally, TQM programs have been focused on manufacturing quality. To manufacturers of sporting goods, quality is likely to mean an excellent consistency of goods and deliveries made by their suppliers. In a manufacturing environment, TQM has been primarily concerned with both the counting and reduction of defects and reducing the cycle time taken to complete any given process.

Even though TQM philosophies originally were used in manufacturing companies, a large number (69 percent) of service organizations are also using the principles of TQM. Although the nature of services is vastly different from those of manufactured products (see chapter 8), Roberts and Sergesketter argue that the fundamental quality issues are similar.[6] A service organization, as with a manufacturing organization, must concentrate on the reduction of defects and cycle times for important processes. As such, the philosophies of TQM are just as applicable for sports services as they are for manufacturing.

Although TQM represents a quality philosophy, there is little agreement as to what TQM (or quality) actually is and how best to manage the TQM process in an organization.[7] Evans and Lindsay define TQM as an integrative management concept for continuously improving the quality of goods and services delivered through the participation of all levels and functions of the organization.[8] In addition, TQM is described as incorporating design, control, and quality improvement, with the customer as the driving force behind the process.

Although the definitions of TQM may vary on the basis of wording and relative emphasis, all quality improvement programs share a common set of features or characteristics.[9] These characteristics, include, but are not limited to, the following:

1. **Customer-driven quality**—quality is defined by customers, and all TQM practices are implemented to please the customer;
2. **Visible leadership**—top management is responsible for leading the quality charge and places quality above all else;
3. **Data-driven processes**—all TQM processes are driven by data collection, use of measurement, and the scientific method; and
4. **Continuous improvement philosophy**—it is always possible to do a better job, and continual, small changes in improvement are just as critical as an occasional major breakthrough.

Rewards

As we have just discussed, the execution of strategy ultimately depends upon individual members of the organization. Effective communication, staffing, skill development and enhancement, and coordination are vital to implementation efforts and should be planned for and considered throughout the strategic sports marketing process. Another critical component in the design of an implementation plan is to provide for motivating and rewarding behavior that is strategy supportive. Thus a reward system is a key ingredient in effective strategy implementation.

There is no one "correct" reward system. From a strategic perspective, rewards must be aligned with the strategy; therefore, the best reward system is "contingent" upon the strategic circumstances. These rewards and incentives represent another choice for management. Thus, reward systems will reflect the beliefs and values of the individuals who design them. However, in order to successfully motivate desired behavior, reward systems must consider the needs, values, and beliefs of those who will be "motivated" by and receiving the rewards.

Management can choose from several types of motivators, which can be classified on the basis of three types of criteria. Motivators can be positive or negative; monetary or nonmonetary; and long run or short run. Some examples include compensation (salary and/or commission), bonuses, raises, stock options, benefits, promotions, demotions, recognition, praise, criticism, more (or less) responsibility, performance appraisals, and fear or tension.

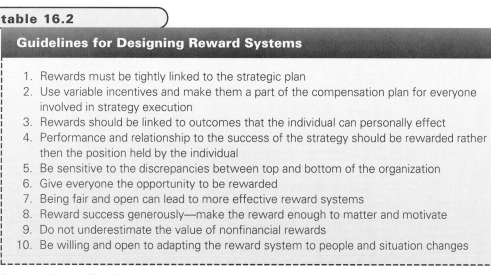

table 16.2

Guidelines for Designing Reward Systems

1. Rewards must be tightly linked to the strategic plan
2. Use variable incentives and make them a part of the compensation plan for everyone involved in strategy execution
3. Rewards should be linked to outcomes that the individual can personally effect
4. Performance and relationship to the success of the strategy should be rewarded rather then the position held by the individual
5. Be sensitive to the discrepancies between top and bottom of the organization
6. Give everyone the opportunity to be rewarded
7. Being fair and open can lead to more effective reward systems
8. Reward success generously—make the reward enough to matter and motivate
9. Do not underestimate the value of nonfinancial rewards
10. Be willing and open to adapting the reward system to people and situation changes

Source: John Pearce and Richard Robinson, *Formulation, Implementation, and Control of Competitive Strategy*, 5th ed. (Boston: Irwin, 1994).

Experience has shown that positive rewards tend to motivate best in most circumstances; however, negative motivators are also frequently used by organizations. Many organizations assume that only financial motivators will lead to desired behaviors. However, many organizations have obtained great success with nonfinancial rewards. Typically, a combination of both provides optimal results. Timing is also an important consideration in motivating performance with reward systems. Rewards systems should be based on both short-term and long-term achievements so that employees can receive both immediate feedback and yet be motivated to strive for the longer term strategic goals.

Although reward systems are contingent upon the internal and external contingencies and the specific circumstances around which a sports marketing group must operate, there are some important general guidelines for developing effective reward systems (see Table 16.2).

In summary, reward systems are critical to the successful achievement of the strategic sports marketing plan. In order to be effective, these systems must motivate behavior that "fits" with and ensures adequate attention to the strategic plan.

Information

Accurate information is an essential guide for decision making and action and necessary for all phases of the strategic sports marketing process. Execution of the sports marketing plan depends on effective information systems. These systems should provide the necessary information, but should not offer more than is needed to give a reliable picture of issues critical to the implementation of the strategy.

Reports of information must be timely. The flow of information should be simple, including all the critical data being reported only to the people who need it. In other words, reports do not necessarily need "wide distribution."

In order to aid strategy implementation, information reports should be designed so as to make it easy to flag variances from the strategic plan. In designing these reports, the critical questions to ask are

1. Who is going to need this information?
2. For what purpose will they need it?
3. When do they need it?

The NHL provides an example of a sports organization who enhanced their ability to implement marketing strategy through an information system.[10] One of the organizational objectives of the NHL was to make better use of emerging technologies. Towards this end, the NHL formed a strategic alliance with IBM called NHL-ICE (Interactive Cyber Enterprises). NHL-ICE will implement information programs for the media, fans, coaches, and players. The NHL-ICE programs include redesigning the NHL Web site, implementing a real-time scoring system that captures statistics for every hockey game, and integrating network computing solutions into the marketing of the league's products and services. Gary Bettman of the NHL Commission states that "NHL-ICE is an integrated approach where technology will provide tangible benefit to everyone who cares about hockey."

Creativity

The design of the strategic sports marketing plan's implementation phase is concerned with putting in place an effective system for executing marketing programs that will lead to the achievement of goals and objectives developed by the organization. The premise of this book is that the changing and uncertain environments in which sports organizations operate often require the need to adjust or change plans based on changing internal and external contingencies. Innovative plans and processes are vital to finding a fit with those contingencies. Thus, innovation, in the context of the strategic sports marketing process, is concerned with converting ideas and opportunities into a more effective or efficient system.

The creative process is the source of those ideas and therefore becomes an important component in the successful formulation and implementation of strategic sports marketing plans. Without creative endeavors, innovation is unlikely, if not impossible. An increase in creative efforts should likewise lead to an increase in innovative plans and processes.

When we talk about creativity it is important to consider both the creative process and the people who engage in that process. The creative process can be learned and used by virtually anyone. However, some people have more experience with and confidence in their ability to be creative than others.

Many organizations can encourage creativity within their employees. This process of creating and innovating within an organization has been referred to as intrapreneurship, or corporate entrepreneurship. Intrepreneurial efforts have become popular in recent years as organizations have acknowledged the value of innovation in changing and uncertain environments. The watchword of today's businesses, sports organizations included, is change. As we discussed, innovation is vital to an organization's ability to change and adapt to internal and external contingencies. There are two general steps that can lead to an increase in the number of creative efforts and the resulting innovations: education and training regarding the creative process and establishing an organizational culture and internal environment that encourages creativity.

The Creative Process

Although creativity is usually associated with promotion, it is important for all elements of the marketing mix. To be competitive, sports organizations must be creative in their pricing, in developing new products and services, and in getting new sports products to the consumer. The first step in increasing creative efforts within a sports organization is educating employees about the creative process. Creativity is a capability that can be learned and practiced. It is a distinctive way of looking at the world and involves seeking relationships between things that others have not seen.

Although they are referred to by different names, there are four commonly agreed-upon steps in the creative process. They are knowledge accumulation, incubation, idea generation, and evaluation and implementation.

The *knowledge accumulation phase* is an often overlooked, but absolutely vital, stage in the process of creating. Extensive exploration and investigation must precede successful creations. Because creations are simply putting together two existing ideas or tangibles in a new way, it is necessary to have an understanding of a variety of related and unrelated topics. This information gathering provides the creator with many different perspectives on the subject under consideration. Information can be gathered through reading, communication with other people, travel, and journal keeping. Simply devoting time to natural curiosities can be useful in this stage. The key is that the more the creator can learn about a broad range of topics, the more he or she will have to choose from as the new creation is being developed.

In phase two, *the incubation period*, the creative individual allows his or her subconscious to mull over the information gathered in the previous stage by engaging in other activities. The creative effort is dropped for other pursuits. Routine activities, play, rest, and relaxation can often induce the incubation process. "Getting away" from the creative endeavor allows the subconscious mind to consider all the information gathered.

Often, when the creator least expects it, solutions will come. The next stage, *idea generation*, is the stage that is often portrayed as the "lightbulb" coming on in one's mind. The opportunity for this has been set, however, in the first two phases. As the body rests from the research and exploration, the subconscious mind sees the creative opportunity or the "light."

The last stage, *evaluation and implementation*, is often the most difficult. It requires a great deal of self-discipline and perseverance to evaluate the idea and determine whether or not it will lead to a useful innovation. Following through with that implementation is often even more challenging. This is especially true because those individuals who are able to generate creative ideas are often not the ones who can turn those ideas into innovations. Often creators will fail numerous times as they attempt to implement creative efforts.

Encouraging Intrapreneurship

Creative efforts and the innovations within organizations are a function of both individual and organizational factors. Entrepreneurial employees add value to the organization and enhance implementation by finding creative ways to achieve the strategic plan. However, these efforts can flourish only if organizational features foster creativity. In order to encourage an intrepreneurial environment, staff members must be rewarded for entrepreneurial thinking and must be allowed and even encouraged to take risks. Failure and mistakes must be allowed and even valued as a means to creative and innovative expression.

The key to successfully creating a climate that encourages creativity and innovation is to understand the components of such an atmosphere. Those components include management support, worker autonomy, rewards, time availability, and flexible organizational boundaries. To understand these components, consider the following guidelines used at 3M Company.[11]

- **Don't kill a project**—If an idea does not seem to find a home in one of 3Ms divisions at first, 3M staff member can devote 15 percent of his or her time to prove it is workable. In addition, grant money is often provided for these pursuits.
- **Tolerate failure and encourage risk**—Divisions at 3M have goals of 25–30 percent of sales from products introduced within the last five years.
- **Keep divisions small**—This will encourage teamwork and close relationships.
- **Motivate champions**—Financial and nonfinancial rewards are tied to creative output.
- **Stay close to the customer**—Frequent contact with the customer can offer opportunities to brainstorm new ideas with them.
- **Share the wealth**—Innovations, when developed, belong to everyone.

The Federation Internationale de Football Association (FIFA), the governing body of soccer, is an example of an organization that attempted to introduce a number of creative ideas and innovations to the 1998 World Cup in France. Innovations ranged from increasing the number of teams that were allowed to compete in the World Cup to playing rock music after every goal. The most controversial innovation was on the field as referees were instructed to strictly reinforce an old rule permitting no tackling from behind. Finally, FIFA also sanctioned the use of ballboys along the field to speed up play when a ball went out of bounds.[12]

Sports television programmers are continually looking for innovation and creativity to attract viewers. Not long ago there were no flashing hockey pucks, no net cams, and no microphones clipped to managers or coaches. One innovation in sports programming that has received positive feedback is the camera analysis of a baseball bat in motion. ESPN presents information on bat speed and the length of time that the bat is level through the strike zone. This innovation allows viewers to see that the classic advice of "swing level" holds true.[13]

Budgeting

Budgets are often used as a means of controlling organizational plans. However, the budgeting process can be an important part of the implementation plan if budget development is closely linked to the sports marketing strategy. In fact, the allocation of financial resources can either promote or impede the strategic implementation process.

Marketers within the sports organization must typically deal with two types of budgetary tasks. First, they must obtain the resources necessary for the marketing group to achieve the marketing plan goals. Second, they must make allocation decisions among the marketing activities and functions. These two types of activities require working with individuals and groups internal and external to the sports marketing function.

In order to develop strategy-supportive budgets, those individuals responsible should have a clear understanding of how to use the financial resources of the organization most effectively to encourage the implementation of the sports marketing strategy. In general, strategy-supportive activities should receive priority budgeting. Depriving strategy-supportive areas of the funds necessary to operate effectively can undermine the implementation process. However, overallocation of funds wastes resources and decreases organizational performance.

In addition, just like the rest of the strategic sports marketing process, the budgeting process is subject to changing and often unpredictable contingencies that may necessitate changes in the marketing budget. A change in strategy nearly always calls for budget reallocation. Thus, those individuals who are responsible for developing budgets must be willing to shift resources when strategy changes.

Control

In the uncertain and changing environments in which sports organizations operate, it is critical to consider four questions throughout the strategic sports marketing process.

1. Are the assumptions on which the strategic marketing plan was developed still true?
2. Are there any unexpected changes in the internal or external environment that will affect our plan?
3. Is the marketing strategy being implemented as planned?
4. Are the results produced by the strategy the ones that were intended?

These questions are considered the basis of strategic control and the fundamental issues to be considered in the control phase of the strategic sports planning process model. **Strategic control** is defined as the critical evaluation of plans, activities, and results—thereby providing information for future action. As illustrated in Figure 16.2, the control phase of the model is the third step to be considered. However, it is important to note that the arrows allow for "feedforward." In other words, even though we consider control as the third phase of the model, it is considered as earlier phases of the process are developed. Once the initial plan is developed, the assumptions on which the plan was developed and the internal and external contingencies must be examined and monitored. As the implementation process is set in place and as the plan is executed, strategic control reviews the process as well as the outcomes. Variances from the original assumptions, plans, and processes are noted and changes are made as needed.

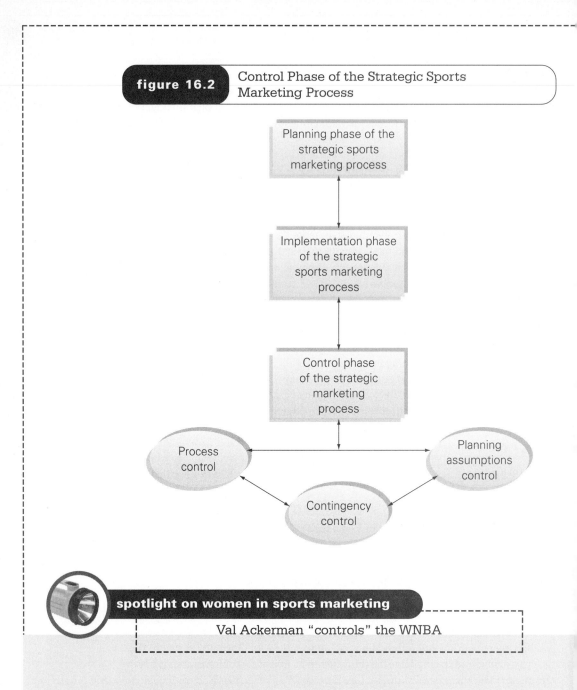

figure 16.2 Control Phase of the Strategic Sports Marketing Process

Planning phase of the strategic sports marketing process

Implementation phase of the strategic sports marketing process

Control phase of the strategic marketing process

Process control

Planning assumptions control

Contingency control

spotlight on women in sports marketing

Val Ackerman "controls" the WNBA

In its second season, the WNBA is continually examining the organizational objectives that were set for the league and determining whether the league is on course. Leading the effort to understand how the WNBA is faring against its goals is league president, Val Ackerman.

In her "Mid-Point State of the League" address, Ackerman stated, "Business is good and getting better. But work remains to be done."[a] The work that Ackerman is referring to is trying to build repeat business among fans coming to WNBA games and trying to bolster television ratings. With per game attendance averaging 10,001 and season ticket sales running 72 percent above last year's, the league attendance goals seem to be being met. Although the television ratings have slipped slightly from last year, Ackerman is still confident. Televised league games are reaching about 2.5 million homes each week, and coverage has been expanded to include 100 of the 160 league games.[b]

[a] W.H. Stickney, Jr. "Ackerman Pleased with Steady Growth," *The Houston Chronicle*, July 25, 1998, 4.
[b] Antonya English, "WNBA is Catching On," *St. Petersburg Times*, August 8, 1998, 2C.

The three types of strategic control that sports marketers must consider are planning-assumptions control, process control, and contingency control. The following sections outline each of these three types of control.

Planning-Assumptions Control

As we have discussed throughout this text, it is vital to understand internal and external contingencies and formulate strategic sports marketing plans that establish a fit with those contingencies. During the planning phase, it is often necessary to make assumptions about future events or contingencies about which we do not have complete information. In addition, individual planners may perceive and interpret data differently. In other words, the strategic sports marketing plan is based on a number of situation-specific premises and assumptions. This level of control attempts to monitor the continuing validity of these assumptions. Thus, in this first type of control, the sports marketer asks the question: "Are the premises or assumptions used to develop the marketing plan still valid?" In order to fully evaluate the responses to this question, the assumptions used during the development of the marketing plan must be listed. This step is vital to the success of this control mechanism so that those individuals who are responsible can monitor them throughout the process.

Because of the complexity of the decision-making process, it may be impossible to monitor all of the assumptions or premises used to formulate the strategic sports marketing plan. Therefore, it is often practical not only to list the premises, but also to prioritize them based on those that may most likely effect a change in the marketing plan.

Although all assumptions should be considered in this form of control, there are two categories of premises that are most likely to be of concern to the sports marketer: external environmental factors and sports industry factors. As we discussed earlier, strategic sports marketing plans are usually based on key premises about many of these variables. Some examples of external environmental factors include technology, inflation, interest rates, regulation, and demographic and social changes. The relevant sports industry in which a sports organization operates is also usually a key premise aspect in designing a marketing plan. Competitors, suppliers, league regulations, and leadership are among the industry-specific issues that need to be considered when identifying the critical assumptions used to develop the strategic plan.

Although monitoring the premises or assumptions used to develop the strategic sports marketing plan is vital to the control phase of the strategic sports marketing process, it is not sufficient. In other words, this form of control does not measure how well the actual plan is progressing nor is it able to take into account the aspects of the internal and external environment that could not be detected during the planning phase when the premises were developed. Thus, effective control must consider two additional forms of evaluation: process control and contingency control.

Process Control

Process control monitors the process to determine whether it is unfolding as expected and as desired. This type of control measures and evaluates the effects of actions that have already been taken in an effort to execute the plan.

Because of changes in premises and contingencies, the realized strategic marketing plan is often not the intended strategic marketing plan. Changes and modifications to the plan usually occur as a result of the process control activities carried out by marketers. In other words, during this stage of control, sports marketers attempt to review the plan and the implementation process to determine whether both remain appropriate to the contingencies. Either the marketing plan or the implementation process put in place to execute the plan may not proceed as intended. These variances may lead to a need to change the plan or the process or both. Thus, the key question asked by this form of control is: "Should either the strategic plan or the implementation process be changed in light of events and actions that have occurred during the implementation of the plan?" It is important to note that to change or modify the marketing plan or implementation process is not necessarily a decision to avoid. The benefit of this form of control is that sports marketers can minimize the allocation of resources into a strategic plan or implementation process that is not leading to achievement of the objectives and goals deemed important by the sports organization.

In order to answer the preceding question, two measures are typically used: *monitoring strategic thrusts* and *reviewing milestones*. As we discussed earlier, the strategic sports marketing plan is a means of achieving strategic and financial organizational goals and marketing objectives. An important part of evaluating the plan and process is to review the achievement of these objectives and goals during the execution of the plan. Because objectives are not time specific or time bound (as discussed in an earlier chapter), strategic thrusts can be examined to evaluate progress in the direction of strategic and financial objectives. On the other hand, reviewing milestones typically examines achievement of marketing objectives. Let us look at each of these two forms of process control more closely.

Monitoring Strategic Thrusts

Monitoring strategic thrusts attempts to evaluate or monitor the strategic direction of the plan. As a part of the overall strategic plan, smaller projects are usually planned that will lead to the achievement of the planned strategy. Successful pursuit of these smaller projects can provide evidence that the strategic thrust is the intended one. On

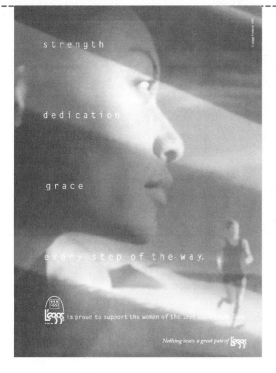

■ Sponsorship represents a strategic thrust that must be monitored.

the other hand, if these projects are getting lost to other "nonstrategic" projects, it could mean that the overall strategy is not progressing as planned.

One strategic thrust of special interest to sports organizations and organizations marketing their products through sports is, of course, sponsorship. Determining the effectiveness of a sponsorship program is becoming more and more important as the costs of sponsorship continue to rise. Just how, then, do we measure or determine whether we are seeing a return on our marketing investment. Lesa Ukman, president of IEG Chicago, which publishes the IEG sponsorship report, believes sponsorship return can be measured. Ukman stresses the following regarding sponsorship measures:[14]

Sponsorship return can be measured. The key lies in defining objectives, establishing a presponsorship benchmark against which to measure, and maintaining consistent levels of advertising and promotion so that it is possible to isolate the effect of sponsorship.

The lack of a universal yardstick for measuring sponsorship is a problem, but it is also an opportunity. The problem is that sponsorships often are dropped, not because they don't have measurement value, but because no one has actually measured the value.

The lack of a single, standardized measurement is also an opportunity because it means sponsors can tailor their measurement systems to gauge their specific objectives.

Although there are no universal measures, here are a few of the more popular ways of measuring sponsorship effectiveness against the objectives of awareness and exposure, sales, attitude change, and enhancing channel-of-distribution relationships:

■ Sponsors such as Jaguar and Castrol must design controls to evaluate sponsoship effectiveness.

■ Number of stories and mentions in popular media, such as newspapers, televised shows, and magazines, serve as a measure of exposure. For example, John Hancock Financial Services measures the impact of its football bowl sponsorship using this method. In one year, approximately 21 binders of newspaper clippings were collected at an estimated advertising equivalency of $1 million.[15]

Awareness is also assessed through "media equivalencies." That is, determining how much "free" time the sponsor has accumulated through television coverage. For example, Julius Joyce and Associates has estimated that at the Masters golf tournament, Nike's logo was on-screen during Sunday's CBS coverage for 16 minutes and 31 seconds, translating to $1,685,000 in on-air Nike exposure.[16]

■ Sales figures for products and services can be examined both prior to (pre) and after (post) the event to estimate the potential impact of the sponsorship. Other methods of tracking sales include looking at sales for the sponsorship period versus the same time period in prior years or measuring sales in the immediate area versus national sales. In addition, sales might be tied directly to the sponsored event. For example, discounts for products might be offered with proof of attending the event (show ticket stub), therefore the number of redemptions might be tracked. Of course, many other factors, such as competitive reaction and additional sales promotions, will influence the sales figures.

One final variation of measuring the impact of sales is to involve the sales force in tracking the value of leads and contacts generated through sponsorship.

■ In order to assess consumer attitudes towards various products and services, as well as the sponsored event, research is conducted in the form of surveys or in-depth interviews. This primary market research is used to gauge the image of the event and its sponsors, attitudes that consumers have toward the event and its sponsors, and awareness of events and sponsors' products and services. Let us look at the following example taken from the Western Open golf tournament, which is featured on CBS over the Fourth of July holiday.[17]

In early 1994, Motorola decided to become a title sponsor of the Western Open golf tournament. Motorola's objectives where to enhance awareness levels and change attitudes towards Motorola's products and services among their target market. In this case, the target audience was defined as adults in the United States with annual household income levels of $25,000 or more and who indicated that they regularly or sometimes follow professional golf.

Their research approach consisted of a two-phased, before and after design that would help understand whether or not promotional objectives were being met. Phase one consisted of a telephone survey of a representative sample of 500 eligible adult respondents two months prior to the tournament. The purpose of this survey was to determine general awareness levels and attitudes of Motorola's products and services. Phase two was a follow-up telephone survey of a second representative sample two weeks after the tournament to assess whether awareness and attitudes had changed.

The research found that over one-third of the golf enthusiasts interviewed had watched the Motorola Western Open on CBS. Using aided recall, one of four respondents was able to identify Motorola's title sponsorship of the tournament. Large groups of respondents reported that Motorola's title sponsorship of the tournament directly influenced their attitudes toward the company. Nearly half of the respondents agreed Motorola's image as a quality company improved because of the sponsorship. In addition, nearly 40 percent of the respondents in the follow-up study claimed that they now had even higher regard for Motorola than before the event. Almost 33 percent stated that they were now more likely to purchase Motorola's products, and 26 percent reported that their awareness of the company's products and services had increased.

When determining the impact of sponsorship on channels of distribution, it is common practice to track the number of outlets carrying the given product before and after the sponsored event. Additionally, sponsors may wish to assess the number of retailers or dealers participating in a program versus previous promotions. Finally, companies may measure incremental display at the point-of-purchase in retail outlets.

For example, Kraft General Food, Inc.'s primary objective for sponsorship of a NASCAR team for Country Time Drink Mix was to enhance distribution in the Southeast and in-store merchandising nationally. To this end, Kraft created a promotion in which consumers could get to ride in a race car simulator with proof of purchase. The simulator increased sales 66 percent in the Southeast and generated more than 40 incremental case displays at each retail stop nationwide.[18]

Milestone Review

The second form of process control focuses on reviewing milestones. Marketing managers at sports organizations usually establish milestones that will be reached during the execution of the marketing plan. These milestones may be critical events, major allocations, achievements, or even the passage of a certain amount of time. As these milestones are reviewed on a continuous basis, an evaluation of the advisability of continuing with the plan and the process is afforded.

Financial Analysis

Financial information can be used to understand and control the process of strategic marketing plan implementation. It is important for any sports organization to have a good accounting system. In terms of process control, the accounting system can provide

- A ready comparison of present financial performance with past performance, industry standards, and budgeted goals
- Reports and financial statements that can be used to make appropriate strategic decisions
- A way of collecting and processing information that can be used in the strategic sports marketing process

Two important components of a good accounting system are the *income statement* and *balance sheet*. Income statements provide a summary of operating performance. These documents summarize both money coming into and going out of the sports organization and/or the marketing department or division. Because income statements are a good measure of customer satisfaction and operating efficiency, they should be prepared frequently—at least every three months, if not monthly. Balance sheets, on the other hand, provide a summary of the financial health of the sports organization at a distinct point in time. The balance sheet provides the sports marketer with a summary of what the organization is worth, what has been invested in assets, such as inventories, land, and equipment, how the assets were financed, and who has claims against the assets. Tables 16.3a and 16.3b provide simple examples of the information typically found on income statements and balance sheets.

table 16.3a

Rich Creek Rockers

Income Statement for the Year Ended December 31, 1998

Revenues:		
Single game admissions	$140,000	
Season ticket holders	275,000	
Concessions	250,000	
Advertising revenue	95,000	760,000
Expenses:		
Cost of concessions sold	100,000	
Salary expense—players	235,000	
Salary/wages—staff	130,000	
Rent	150,000	615,000
Profits before taxes		145,000
Income tax		33,000
Income after taxes		$112,000

table 16.3b

Rich Creek Rockers

Balance Sheet at December 31, 1998

Assets		Liabilities and Owner's Equity	
Cash	$10,000	Accounts payable	$20,000
Accounts receivables	82,000	Capital stock	50,000
Equipment	40,000	Retained earnings	62,000
Total assets	$132,000	Total liabilities and owners equity	$132,000

One of the more useful methods of financial analysis for control purposes is known as *ratio analysis*. Financial ratios are computed from income statements and balance sheets. These ratios can tell the sports marketing manager much about the progress and success of the strategic sports marketing plan. In other words, using financial ratios can help a sports marketing manager assess whether the marketing strategy continues to provide an appropriate fit with internal and external contingencies. There are several types of financial ratios that can be categorized as

- **Profitability ratios**—Provide an indication of how profitable the organization or division is during a period of time
- **Liquidity ratios**—Indicates the ability of the organization to pay off short-term obligations without selling off assets
- **Leverage ratios**—Measure the extent to which creditors finance the organization
- **Activity ratios**—Measures the sales productivity and utilization of assets
- **Other ratios**—Determine such things as return to owners in dividends, the percentage of profits paid out in dividends, and discretionary funds

Table 16.4 lists some of the more commonly used ratios, how each is calculated, and what each can tell the sports marketing manager. Examples of how these ratios are applied and interpreted are shown in Table 16.5.

Contingency Control

The third form of control, **contingency control**, is based on the assumption that sports marketers operate in an uncertain and unpredictable environment and that the changing nature of the internal and external environments may lead to the need to reassess strategic choices. Although it is included as a part of the control phase, this form of control should be of concern throughout the strategic sports marketing process.

The goal of contingency control is to constantly scan the relevant environments for internal and external contingencies that could affect the marketing planning process. Unlike planning assumptions control, the goal here is to remain unfocused so that any

table 16.4

Summary of Selected Key Financial Ratios

Ratio	Calculation	Question(s) answered
Gross profit margin	$\dfrac{\text{Sales-Cost of goods sold}}{\text{Sales}}$	What is the total margin available to cover operating expenses and provide profit?
Net profit margin	$\dfrac{\text{Profits after taxes}}{\text{Sales}}$	Are profits high enough given the level of sales? Are we operating efficiently?
Return on total assets	$\dfrac{\text{Profit after taxes}}{\text{Total assets}}$	How wisely has management employed assets?
Asset turnover	$\dfrac{\text{Sales}}{\text{Average total assets}}$	How well are assets being used to generate sales revenue?
Current ratio	$\dfrac{\text{Current assets}}{\text{Current liabilities}}$	Does our organization have enough cash or other liquid assets to cover short-term obligations?
Debt-to-assets load	$\dfrac{\text{Total debt}}{\text{Total assets}}$	Is the organization's debt excessive?
Inventory turnover	$\dfrac{\text{Cost of goods sold}}{\text{Average inventory}}$	Is too much cash tied up in inventories?
Accounts receivables turnover	$\dfrac{\text{Annual credit sales}}{\text{Accounts receivables}}$	What is the average length of time it takes our firm to collect for sales made on credit?

unanticipated events will not be missed. In other words, the "big picture" is of most concern in this phase of control. The primary question to be addressed here is: "How can we protect our marketing strategy from unexpected events or crises that could affect our ability to pursue the chosen strategic direction?"

Attempts to control without a prestructured list of variables of concern may not seem to make sense at first. However, it is easier to understand this form of control if one thinks in terms of how a crisis usually occurs. The daily events leading up to an unpredicted event lead to a focus in the form of a crisis. Previously unimportant or unnoticed events become more problematic until an actual crisis requires some action. Learning to notice and interpret signals thus becomes an important way to circumvent crises. Thus, the goal of contingency control is to learn to notice these signals and to have a plan of action in place to cope with a crisis if it occurs.

table 16.5

Examples of Financial Ratios

Net profit margin $\dfrac{112{,}000}{760{,}000} = 14.7\%$

Interpretation Approximately 15 percent of sales is yielding profits. This percentage should be compared to industry (similar sports organizations) averages and examined over a period of several years. Declining or subpar percentages could mean expenses are too high, prices are too low, or both.

Return on assets $\dfrac{112{,}000}{132{,}000} = 84.8\%$

Interpretation This is a measure of the productivity of the assets in the sports organization. Once again, this number should be compared to similar sports organizations and examined over several years. If this number is declining, it may indicate that assets are not being used as effectively and/or efficiently as they were in previous years.

Inventory turnover $\dfrac{2{,}500{,}000}{100{,}000} = 25 \text{ times}$

Interpretation Inventory turnover is a measure of the number of times inventory is sold during a period of time. Assuming an average inventory of $100,000 (beginning inventory + ending inventory/2) the inventory (in this example—concessions) was sold 25 times. If this number is higher than the average for this type of sports organization, then ordering costs may be too high and stockouts may be occurring. If the number is lower, it may mean too much inventory is being stored, tying up money unnecessarily, and the products (in this case—food) may lack freshness.

Sports scandals and crises are not infrequent. Anyone who reads a newspaper sports section has observed situations that could lead to a public relations nightmare for a sports organization. Consider the gambling scandal at Boston College where a large number of players were involved in large bets made with bookies. The front page headline in *USA Today* read "Gambling Scandal Rocks Boston College." With a history of gambling and game fixing, and the school's image as a Catholic Jesuit institution and the timing (before the biggest game of the year—Notre Dame) the scandal had the potential to provide a public relations disaster. However, Boston College was actually able to use this "crisis" to boost its own credibility through swift actions to inititate its own investigation and calling in the District Attorney's office.[19]

Although a crisis is typically unpredictable, it is useful to plan so that the chosen response can be not only faster, but also more effective. A crisis plan should include the following:[20]

- Well-defined organizational response strategies
- Specific procedures that will lead to more efficient and effective response
- Steps that will deal effectively with potential media impact and will enhance image
- Efficient ways to deal with a variety of problems that could occur

Moreover sports organizations may benefit from an informal and a formal crisis response plan. The key is that any crisis plan should offer priorities for proactive and reactive response under a variety of circumstances. It should have the capacity to both alert and calm people during an unexpected event that could have potential for major consequences.

SUMMARY

Implementing and controlling the strategic sports marketing process is the emphasis of chapter 16. After the planning phase of the strategic marketing process is completed, the implementation and control phases are considered. Implementation is described as an action step where strategic marketing plans are executed. Without the proper execution, the best plans in the world would be useless. To facilitate the implementation process, seven organizational design elements must be addressed. The organizational design elements include communication, staffing and skills, coordination, rewards, information, creativity, and budgeting. To begin, the organization must effectively communicate the plan and its rationale to all of the members of the sports marketing team who will play a role in executing the plan. In terms of staffing and skills, there must be enough people and they must have the necessary skills and expertise to successfully implement the strategic marketing plan. Research has shown that the skills deemed most important for sports marketing managers include establishing a positive image for your sports organization, achieving sponsors' promotional goals, stimulating ticket sales, maximizing media exposure for events, athletes, and sponsors, and acquiring sponsors through personal contacts.

Coordination is another of the organizational design elements that influences implementation. Coordination involves determining the best structure for the organization to achieve the desired strategy. Research has shown the importance of good fit between structure and successful implementation. One way of coordinating people and tasks that has received considerable attention over the last decade is through total quality managements (TQM). TQM philosophies are based on aligning the organizational structure to best meet the needs of the customers.

Another important organizational design element that impacts implementation is the rewards structure of the sports organization. With proper pay and incentives, employees may be motivated to carry out the strategic plan. Some guidelines for designing effective rewards systems include linking rewards to the strategic plan, using a variety of incentives; link performance with rewards, give everyone the opportunity to be rewarded, and be willing to adapt the rewards system.

Information is one of the most essential elements of effective implementation. To aid in the gathering and dissemination of information for strategic decision making, organizations must design information systems. Before gathering information, consideration must be given to who is going to need this information, for what purpose the information is needed, and when do they need it?

Fostering creativity, another organizational design element, is yet another important aspect of implementation. Creativity and innovation within the organization is called intrapreneurship or corporate entrepreneurship and is developed through education and training. In order to enhance employee creativity the creative process, consisting of four steps, is used by organizations. These steps include: knowledge accumulation, idea generation, evaluation, and implementation. Efforts to encourage intrapreneurship are also enhanced by creating an organizational environment that cultivates such thinking.

The final organizational design element that has a direct impact on implementation is budgeting. Without proper monies, the strategic sports marketing plan cannot be properly implemented or carried out. Budgets must be secured for all marketing efforts within the larger organization. Once these monies are obtained, they must then be allocated within marketing to achieve specific marketing goals that have been prioritized.

After plans have been implemented, the control phase of the strategic sports marketing process is considered. Strategic control is defined as the critical evaluation of plans, activities, and results, thereby providing information for future action. In other words, the control phase explores how well the plan is meeting objectives and makes suggestions for adapting the plan to achieve the desired results. Three types of strategic control considered by sports marketers include planning-assumptions control, process control, and contingency control.

Planning-assumptions control asks whether the premises or assumptions used to develop the marketing plan are still valid. Two categories of assumptions that should receive special consideration from sports marketers are those concerned with the external contingencies and the sports industry. Because plans are typically developed by carefully considering the external environment and the sports industry, assumptions with respect to these two issues are critical.

Process control considers whether the plan and processes used to carry out the plan are being executed as desired. The key issue addressed by process control is whether the planning or implementation processes should be altered in light of events and actions that have occurred during the implementation of the plan. In order to make decisions about whether plans or the implementation process should be changed, sports organizations review milestones that have been set or monitor strategic thrusts. Milestones such as financial performance, are more specific objectives that can be examined, while strategic thrust evaluates whether the organization is moving towards its intended goals.

KEY TERMS & CONCEPTS

activity ratios	financial analyses	process control
budgeting	implementation	profitability ratios
communication	information	ratio analyses
contingency control	leverage ratios	rewards
control	liquidity ratios	staffing and skills
creative process	milestone review	total quality management
creativity	monitoring strategic thrusts	
crisis plan	planning-assumptions control	

1. What are the organizational design elements that must be managed for effective implementation?

2. Why must there be a fit between planning and implementation phases of the strategic sports marketing process?

3. What are some of the common ways of communicating with groups both inside and outside the sports organization?

4. What are the marketing-specific core competencies of the sports marketing manager?

5. Define TQM. What are the common characteristics of any TQM program? Why is it important for sports organizations to practice a TQM philosophy?

6. What are the guidelines for designing rewards systems?

7. What is intrapreneurship? What are the four steps in the creative process? How can sports organizations encourage intrapreneurship?

8. Define strategic control. What are the three types of strategic control that sports marketers must consider?

9. What two measures are typically used during process control?

10. How can we evaluate sponsorship effectiveness?

11. Describe the different financial ratios that can be calculated to assess whether a sports organization's financial objectives are being met.

12. What are the fundamental components of a crisis plan?

1. Describe three sports organizations that have a strong leader who communicates well outside the sports organization. What are the common characteristics of these leaders and why do these leaders communicate effectively?

2. How does the training that you are receiving compliment the marketing-specific skills required of sports marketing managers?

3. Locate the organizational charts for the marketing department of two professional sports organizations. How will this structure facilitate or impede the implementation of their strategic marketing effort?

4. Design a rewards system to encourage intrapreneurship.

5. Discuss the last three major "crises" in sport (at any level). How did the organizations or individuals handle these crises?

6. Discuss how being the quarterback of a football team is similar to being a marketer responsible for implementing and controlling the strategic sports marketing process.

7. Interview three marketing managers who are responsible for sponsorship decisions in their organization. Determine how each evaluates the effectiveness of their sponsorship.

1. Browse the Web site of the National Sporting Goods Association (www.sportlink. com) and discuss how the information found on this site might be useful for developing a strategic marketing plan for the new International Basketball League (IBL).

2. Find two Web sites that would provide sports marketing managers with information about whether their planning assumptions regarding demographics of the U.S. population remained valid.

3. Find examples of three nonsports organizations that advertise on ESPN's Web site (www.espnet.sportzone.com). How might these companies evaluate the effectiveness of their Web-based advertising?

NOTES

1. Gail De George, "LPGA Comes Blasting Down the Fairway," *Business Week*, July 15, 1996.

2. A. K. Gupta and V. Govindarajan, "Build, Hold or Harvest: Converting strategic intentions into reality," *Journal of Business Strategy* (Winter 1984):41.

3. Peter Smolianov and Dr. David Shilbury, "An Investigation of Sport Marketing Competencies," *Sport Marketing Quarterly*, vol. 5, no. 4 (1996):27–36.

4. A. D. Chandler, *Strategy and Structure* (Cambridge, MA: MIT Press, 1963).

5. L. Marlene Mawson, "Total Quality Management: Perspectives for Sport Managers," *Journal of Sport Management*, vol. 7 (1993):101–106.

6. Harry Roberts and Bernard Sergesketter, *Quality Is Personal* (New York: Free Press, 1993).

7. George Easton and Sherry Jarrel, "The Effects of Total Quality Management on Corporate Performance: An Empirical Investigation," *Journal of Business,* vol. 71, no. 2:253–261.

8. James Evans and William Lindsay, *The Management and Control of Quality*, 2nd ed., (St. Paul, MN: West, 1993).

9. Ibid.

10. "NHL teams with IBM to promote and enhance hockey through new alliance, NHL-ICE." <http://issc2.boulder.ibm.com/telmedia/prnhl996. htm>; "NHL-ICE: A Virtual Power Play." <http://domino.www.ibm.com/ebusine...s/ 35E438D34E58CD4A852651E00639D54>.

11. Russell Mitchell, "Masters of Innovation," *Business Week*, April 10, 1989, 58–63.

12. Patrick Halverson, "From Ball Boys to Golden Goals—Did the Changes Work? Tournament Innovations—The Seniors and the Frivolous," *Financial Times*, July 7, 1998, 19.

13. Wayne Scanlon, "TV Shows the Swing is Still the Thing," *The Ottawa Citizen*, July 3, 1998, F1.

14. Lesa Ulkman, "Evaluating ROI of a Sponsorship Program," *Marketing News*, August 26, 1996, 5.

15. "And Now a Word From Our Sponsors." *Marketing Tools*, June 1995. <http://www.demographics.com/publications/ mt/95_mt/9506_mt/mt169.htm>; John Burnett, Anil Menon, and Denise Scott, "Sports Marketing: A New Ball Game with Old Rules," *Journal of Advertising Research*. (September/October, 1993): 21-38.

16. "The Business of Sports." <http://www.bizsports.com/newsarchive/430new. htm>.

17. "Measuring Effectiveness for Motorola." <http://www.prcentral.com>.

18. Lesa Ulkman, "Evaluating ROI of a Sponsorship Program," *Marketing News*, August 26, 1996, 5.

19. Rudy Martzke, "Scandal Turns Notre Dame–BC Game Into Bonus for CBS," *USA Today*, November 8, 1996, 2C; "Crisis in Sports: Boston College Today but Who's Next?" <http://mediachallenge.com/hotcorner/boston.html>.

20. "Defining Crisis and Crisis Planning." <www.sports.mediachallenge.com\crisis\index. html#feature>.

Career Opportunities in Sports Marketing

Many of us have dreamed of becoming a professional athlete. Unfortunately, reality sets in rather quickly. We discover that we cannot throw a 90 mile-per-hour fastball or even touch the rim—much less slam dunk. However, there are many other opportunities for careers in sports. In fact, there are a wide variety of sports careers in sports marketing. In this appendix, we will explore some of the career options in sports marketing and present some interview and resumé writing tips for landing that dream job. Finally, we will examine some additional sources of information on careers in sports marketing.

Before we look at some of the career alternatives in sports marketing, it is useful to think about how the concepts discussed in this text can be useful in your job search. As you know, the strategic marketing process begins by conducting a SWOT analysis. You should build a SWOT into your career planning. First, ask questions about your own strengths and weaknesses. You can be sure that the organizations that you interview with will be asking similar questions. Next, try to identify the opportunities that exist in the marketplace. What sports are hot? Where are the growth areas in sports marketing?

The next step of your strategic career search should be to gather information and conduct research on prospective employers. Research might be conducted by talking to people within the organization to gain a better understanding of the culture. In addition, observation might take place both before and certainly during the interview.

Next, you need to consider your target market. Do not apply for all of the sports marketing jobs in the world. Target the job opportunities based on location, type of position, and how the position or organization fits with your current and potential strengths. You also need to position yourself. Remember, careers in sports marketing are in demand and you need to find a way to market yourself and stand out from the competition.

The marketing mix variables also should be considered in your job search. The product, in this case, is you. You are the bundle of benefits that is being offered to the prospective organization. You should also enter into the strategic career search with some understanding of price. What is the value you attach to the service and expertise that you will provide? Are the salary and benefits package being offered a satisfactory exchange?

Your resumé, cover letter, interviewing skills, and ability to sell yourself are the elements of the promotion mix. Each of these elements communicates something about you to prospective employers. Finally, the place element of the marketing mix is the   location in which you are willing to work.

From this brief discussion, you can begin to understand that finding the right job for yourself in sports marketing can be done in a systematic, organized fashion. By using the basic principles of the strategic marketing process, you will be in a better position to land your dream job. Let us turn our attention to some of the job opportunities that exist in the field of sports marketing.

Job Opportunities in Sports Marketing

There a wide variety of jobs in sports marketing that may be of interest to you. Here are just a few of the opportunities that exist. As you look through this section, pay attention to the sample advertisements and the qualifications that are stressed for each position. In addition, remember not to suffer from marketing myopia when you look for your first job. Have a broad perspective and think of your first job as an entrée into the sports industry.

Internships

Nearly 70 percent of sports marketing executives began their careers interning for a sports organization, and 90 percent of sports organizations offer some type of internship. Many sports marketing students believe that they will secure high-paying, glamorous, executive-level positions upon completion of their degree. The truth is that jobs in sports marketing are so competitive that internships are usually the only route to gaining the experience needed for a permanent position. By working as an intern, you become familiar with the organization and learn about the sports industry. In turn, the organization learns about you and reduces its risk in hiring you for a permanent position.

Sample Advertisements

- **Sales and Marketing Manager**—Interns will assist the marketing department in the following areas: sponsorship fulfillment, lead qualification, sampling/couponing programs, health and fitness expo at the Los Angeles Convention Center and race day festival. Must be hardworking, detail-oriented, friendly, energetic, and computer-literate, and have good communication skills. Hours would be flexible to fit interns' schedule.
- **Marketing Intern**—We have an opening for a sports marketing intern to assist in marketing programs designed to facilitate the growth of our products and services. Ideal person should have a sports marketing or sports management background. Computer, organization, and strong communication skills are essential. Internet experience preferred.

Facilities Management

Whatever the sport, there must be a place to play. From brand new multimillion-dollar sports complexes such as the Bank One Ballpark in Arizona to community centers used for recreational sports, facilities management is an important function. Although facilities management positions are more managerial in nature, they do include a strong marketing emphasis. For example, facilities managers are expected to perform public and community relations tasks, as well as have a strong promotion management background.

Sample Advertisements

- **Advertising and Public Relations Manager**—Opportunity for a creative, energetic, hands-on individual to develop and implement advertising and PR program for an established golf course facility. Minimum of five years experience in advertising, design, broadcast production, and media planning. Desktop experience a must. Internet experience a plus. Must be able to maximize pre-established budgets.

- **Facility Manager**—The Special Events Center is seeking candidates for the position of Facility Manager. Candidates should be sales and marketing driven with experience in event planning, marketing and promotions, and facility management. Bachelor's degree with three years related experience required. Primary liaison between users and facility staff. Provide leadership in event planning, on-site event management, and customer service.

Professional Services

As the sports industry grows, the need for more and more business professionals in all areas is increasing. Today, sports careers are automatically associated with being a sports agent because of the Jerry McGuire "show me the money" phenomenon. However, professional services are also needed in sports law, advertising, accounting, information systems, marketing research, finance, and sports medicine. Having the appropriate educational background before attempting to secure sport industry experience is a must. Salaries for professional services positions vary greatly depending on the job type and responsibilities.

Sample Advertisements

- **Director of Special Olympics**—Seeking persons with excellent communication, fundraising, and management skills. Special Olympics is a year-round program of sports training and competition for children and adults with mental retardation. Responsibilities include planning and organizing competitive events, training programs, public awareness campaigns, and fundraising activities. Candidates for position must possess excellent communication and fund-raising skills as well as administrative, organizational, and volunteer management experience. Previous Special Olympics experience not required, but helpful.

- **Global Advertising/Merchandising Manager**—Multinational manufacturer of cycling components. Responsible for leading the creation and execution of global advertising; athlete and event sponsorship; media planning and communication; global product merchandising; global cost center management. This position requires an analytical thinker with excellent leadership and execution skills. A successful candidate is an MBA who has in-depth knowledge of ad strategy, planning, and production.

Health and Fitness Services

As the sports-participant market continues to grow, so will jobs in the health and fitness segment of the sports industry. Numerous jobs are available in management and sales for health clubs. Additionally, health and fitness counseling or instruction (e.g., personal trainer, aerobics instruction) represents another viable job market in health and fitness. Careers in sports training and sports medicine are also growing in number. In addition to working for sports organizations as a trainer or physical therapist, a number of sports medicine clinics (usually affiliated with hospitals) are targeting the recreational participant and creating a host of new jobs in the prevention or rehabilitation of sports injuries.

Sample Advertisements

- **Director of Campus Recreation**—Major responsibilities: provide opportunities to enhance participant fitness, personal skills, and enjoyment for a variety of student recreational activities; supervise, coordinate, and evaluate the activities of the department; prepare operating and capital expenditure budgets; develop goals, objectives, policies, and procedures; and perform personnel administration within the department. Qualifications: Master's degree and three years experience in recreation or a similar field, two years experience in administrative position, and current CPR and first aid certification required.

- **Fitness Club Operations Director**—Oversee all pool and tennis associates. Duties include hiring, training, supervising, and reviewing the performance of staff; administering weekly payroll; designing employees work schedules; and overseeing maintenance/cleanliness of facilities and inventory. Bachelor's degree; minimum two years experience in athletic club/resort and one year in club management; basic knowledge of tennis, fitness and aquatics; and excellent communication skills. Sales and marketing experience, with a strong member services background and experience developing/implementing member retention programs preferred.

Sports Associations

Nearly every sport has a governing body or association that is responsible for maintaining the integrity and furthering the efforts of the sport and its constituents. Examples of sports associations include Federation International Football Association (FIFA), National Sporting Goods Association (NSGA), United States Tennis Association (USTA), and the Thoroughbred Racing Association (TRA). Each sport association has executive directors, membership coordinators, and other jobs to help satisfy members' needs.

Sample Advertisements

- **U.S. Tennis Association**—Assist Director of Marketing in sponsorship, donations, and ad sales. Professional tournament operations for one tournament and booth promotions at all Northern California tournaments.

- **Research Associate**—A non-profit golf association. Duties include survey research, statistical analysis, report writing, and database management. Knowledge of SAS and related Bachelor's degree a must. Proficiency required in mapping, spreadsheet, and word processing software. Position requires demonstrated experience in technical writing and good verbal communication skills. Knowledge of the golf industry a plus. Entry level position.

Professional Teams and Leagues

Along with being a sports agent, the types of jobs most commonly associated with sports marketing are in the professional sports industry segment. Working as the director of marketing for one of the "big four" sports leagues (NBA, MLB, NHL, or NFL), or one of the major league teams, almost always requires extensive experience with a minor league franchise or college athletic program and a minimum of a Master's degree. Job responsibilities include sales, designing advertising campaigns to generate interest in the team, and supervision of game promotions and public relations.

Sample Advertisements

- **Assistant Marketing Director**—Develops season ticket campaign strategies, negotiates advertising and media tradeouts, directs promotion coordinator, sales representative. Master's degree preferred; bachelors degree required, preferably in marketing. Excellent communication skills a must. Should have extensive experience in working with corporate sponsors and developing a client base to support athletic sales.
- **Advertising Sales**—Major sports league seeks account executive to sell print advertising for event publications. The ideal candidate will possess two to four years consumer or trade publication sales experience; excellent written and verbal communication skills; a proven track record of increasing sales volume; and the ability to work in a fast-paced environment and the flexibility to travel.

College Athletic Programs

If your ultimate career objective is to secure a position with a professional team or league, college athletic departments are a great place to start. Nearly all Division I and Division II athletic programs have marketing, sales, and public relations functions. In fact, most of the larger Division I programs have an entire marketing department that is larger than most minor league franchises.

Sample Advertisements

- **Coordinator of the Goal Club**—Responsibilities include identifying, cultivating, soliciting, and stewarding donors together with managing special events and direct mail programs. Candidates must possess a bachelor's degree and two or three years of fundraising experience.
- **Athletic Recruiting Coordinator**—Responsibilities include developing and organizing a vigorous recruiting program for eight sports within the guidelines of NCAA III, represent the athletics department at college fairs, and coordinate all recruiting activities with the admissions department.

Sporting Goods Industry

Sporting goods is a $62 million dollar industry that is growing and presents career choices in all of the more traditional marketing or retailing functions. Opportunities include working for a sporting goods manufacturers (e.g., Nike, adidas, Callaway, or Wilson) or retailers such as Dick's, Sports Authority, or Footlocker.

Sample Advertisements

- **Associate Buyer**—Lady Foot Locker is looking for a professional. To qualify you will need chain store buying experience. Sporting goods exposure a plus.
- **General Manager/Catalog Division**—An outdoor recreation equipment retailer in the burgeoning backpacking/mountaineering/climbing industry is looking for a hands-on GM with full responsibility for its fast growing catalog division. Responsibilities include bottom-line profitability, strategic planning/execution, financial planning, marketing, prospecting, circulation and database management, catalog development and production, purchasing and inventory control, and systems coordination. Qualifications include five-plus years management in a mail order operation.

Event Planning and Marketing

Rather than work for a specific team or league, some sports marketers pursue a career in events marketing. Major sporting events such as the World Series, All-Star games, or the Olympics do not happen without the careful planning of an events management organization. The largest and most well-known events management company is the International Management Group (IMG) headed by Mark McCormack with offices worldwide. Event marketers are responsible for promoting the event and selling and marketing sponsorships for the event.

Sample Advertisements

- **Event Management Leader**—A service management association serving the bowling industry. Candidates will have a Bachelor's degree in business or hotel management along with a proven track record of professional event production.
- **Event Planner**—National sports marketing firm organizing sports leagues and special events for young professionals, is seeking an entry-level candidate to assist with operations and promotions of sports leagues, parties, and special events. Should be sports minded, extremely outgoing, and organized for this very hands-on position.

Researching Companies

The previous section should have given you a good idea of the types of job opportunities in sports marketing. Having considered your options, it is now time to get serious about finding that first job that will launch an exciting career. You will soon send out cover letters and resumé. Realize that they must be tailored to each position and organization. If they are not, the prospective employer will sense you have not done your homework. Your research efforts should include the following types of information: age of the organization, services or product lines, competitors within the industry, growth patterns of the organization and of the industry, reputation and corporate culture, number of employees, and financial situation.

Today, most of the organizational information can be obtained quickly and easily via the Internet. Other popular sources of industry and company information include the following: *Team Marketing Report's Inside the Ownership of Professional Sports Teams*, *Million Dollar Directory* (Dun & Bradstreet)*, Standard and Poor's Register*, and *Ward's Business Directory of U.S. Private and Public Companies.*

Cover Letters and Resumes

Once you have researched prospective employers, you are ready to communicate with the organizations that you wish to pursue. Let us look at how to construct simple, yet persuasive, cover letters and resumés. Remember, these documents are within your complete control (think of this as an internal contingency); use this to your advantage and present yourself in the best possible light. Let us begin with the fundamentals of cover letter preparation.

Cover Letters

The major objective of any cover letter is to pique the interest of the prospective employer. First impressions are everything and the cover letter is the employer's first glimpse of you. There are a few basic guidelines that you can follow to make your cover letters more effective.

In the first paragraph, state the letter's purpose and how you found out about the position. Follow this with an overview of your most impressive job-related attributes such as skills, knowledge, and expertise. Obviously, the attributes you choose should relate to the position in mind. The third part of the cover letter should stem from all the research previously gathered on the organization. Show off your knowledge of the company and their current needs. Finally, let the organization know how you can help solve their current needs. Stress the fit between your background and values and the organization's culture.

Resumés

Now that your cover letter has been constructed, you are ready to begin work on an effective resumé. Here are seven tips for writing a resumé that are guaranteed to tell your story.

1. **Be Thorough**—A good resume should give the employer an indication of your potential based on your previous accomplishments. Include things such as job-related skills, previous work experience, educational background, volunteer experiences, special achievements, and personal data.

   Activities that you might deem to be unimportant could provide a great deal of insight into your ability to succeed on the job. For example, how about the student that has coached a little league team throughout his or her collegiate career? Some candidates might view this as totally unrelated to the job. However, the wise candidate will see how this activity could be used to demonstrate unique aspects of their personality such as patience, leadership, and good organizational skills.

2. **Be Creative**—Most students are under the false impression that there is a right way and a wrong way to organize their resume. In fact, most career development

centers use a boilerplate format making every student's resumé standard and neglecting the job and the industry.

All resumés should include topical areas such as job objectives, skills, knowledge, accomplishments, personal data, education, employment history, observations of superiors, and awards. The way you organize and write these sections is limited only by your imagination. The most important thing to remember is that the format should reflect both you and the job you are seeking.

3. **Use Quotations**—A powerful tool that is not widely used in resumé preparation is the use of quotations. These quotes can be found in old performance evaluations or letters of recommendation. Here is an example of a quote that was used to reinforce the strength of an application.

> *"Ms. Beasley has contributed in a positive manner to the success of the athletic department at WPU by organizing and implementing an effective game day promotional plan."*
>
> Tim White, promotions manager, athletic department, WPU.

Quotes like this can provide further evidence of your abilities while relieving you of having to toot your own horn.

4. **Make the Resumé Visually Appealing**—Looks are everything. In one study, 60 percent of employers indicated that they formed an opinion about the candidate on the basis of their resumé's appearance. The resumé that looks good will be given more consideration than one that does not. The resumé that is badly written and produced will be tossed, regardless of the applicant's qualification. A few things to think about when designing your resumé include length (keep it to one page), paper (high-quality stock in white or off-white), spelling, grammar, and neatness (any error is unacceptable).

5. **Include a Career Objective**—Most employers consider the career objective to be the most important part of the resumé. Why? A specific career objective indicates that you know what you want in a job. This type of goal-directed behavior is what employers want to see in a candidate.

On the other hand, some resumé preparation experts strongly disagree with this line of reasoning. They argue that by placing an objective on your resumé, you are limiting the potential position. In other words, if you leave your options open, the employer will direct your resumé to the job that best suits your qualifications.

The best advice is to have multiple resumés prepared and ready to go with multiple career objectives. Most people have multiple career interests and do not have to settle for just one job. If you are truly practicing target marketing, you should have several different resumés ready. You should try to make the career objective sound like the description of the job you are targeting. Here is a sample career objective for a student who wishes to pursue a public/community relations position at a major university or professional sports franchise:

> *Public Relations Assistant—Interested in copy writing, editing, writing speeches and news releases, photography, graphics, etc. Desire experience on organization's internal*

and external publications. Good writing and speaking skills with communications background should assist in advancement to a management position within the athletic department of a major university or professional sports organization.

6. **Honesty Is the Best Policy**—Employers are checking prospective candidates' qualifications more than ever before, due to a wave of people falsifying their credentials. Obviously, deceiving the employer about what you have done, or what you are able to do, is no way to start a positive relationship.

7. **Spread the Word**—You should seek feedback and constructive criticism about your resumé by showing it to everyone you know. Ask for comments from other students, your professors, and career development specialists at school. In addition, you should circulate it among people in the sports industry. Resumé writing is a dynamic process that requires constant changes and improvement.

(I)nterviewing

Most jobs in sports marketing require a high degree of interpersonal communication; therefore, the interview becomes a place to showcase your talents. Each person should have his or her own interview style, but here are some tips that should assist all job candidates with their interviewing skills.

1. **Be Mentally Prepared**—As with athletes, mental preparation is the name of the game for job seekers. Most job candidates do not come to the interview fully prepared. To get ready, you should have thoroughly researched the sports organization. Next, you need to learn as much as possible about the person or people who will be conducting the interview. Being mentally prepared means being able to ask intelligent questions. Naturally, the types of questions you ask will vary by the position of the interviewer. Here are just a few of the potential questions that you might ask of the personnel manager or human resource representative:

   - What do employees like best about the company? What do employees like least about the company?
   - How large is the department in which the opening exists? How is it organized?
   - Why is this position open?
   - How much travel would normally be expected?
   - What type of training program does a new employee receive? What type of professional development programs are offered? Who conducts them?
   - How often are performance reviews given and how are they conducted?
   - How are raises and promotions determined? What is the salary range of the position?
   - What are the employee benefits offered by the company?

   Possible questions for your potential supervisor include:

   - What are the major responsibilities of the department?
   - What are the major responsibilities of the job?

- What would the new employee be expected to accomplish in the first six months or year of the job?
- What are the special projects now ongoing in the department? What are some that are coming in the future?
- How much contact with management is there? How much exposure?
- What is the path to management in this department? How long does it typically take to get there, and how long do people typically stay there?

Here are some questions that might be asked of would-be colleagues:

- What do you like most or least about working in this company? What do you like most or least about working in this department?
- Describe a typical workday.
- Do you feel free to express your ideas and concerns? Does everyone in this department?
- What are the possibilities here for professional growth and promotion?
- How much interaction is there with supervisors, colleagues, external customers? How much independent work is there?
- How long have you been with the company? How does it compare with other companies where you have worked?

2. **Be Physically Prepared**—Image is important to all organizations, and a large part of the image that you project is largely a function of your physical appearance. In other words, if you look the part, the chances of getting the job increase exponentially. The key to dressing for an interview is not only to be professionally dressed, but to convey an image that is consistent with the company and the position. An interview is not the time to redefine the meaning of professional dress. Make sure you feel comfortable in the clothes that you choose to wear to the interview. If you look good and feel good, you will undoubtedly convey these positive feelings throughout the interview.

3. **Practice Makes Perfect**—Many marketing experts have discussed the similarities between finding a job and personal selling. When you are job hunting, you are, in essence, marketing or selling yourself. If you were selling a product, you would strive to become as familiar as possible with that product. You would not only learn the positive features and benefits of the product, but understand the limitations of the product. In this case, you have to know everything the interviewer could conceivably ask about you. This should not be difficult, but you have to be prepared. The best way to prepare is through practice and repetition, so that you feel confident answering questions about yourself.

   The following is a list of questions regarding school, work, and personal experiences that are often asked during the interview. The more you have thought about these questions prior to the interview, the better your responses. Questions pertaining to school experiences might include:

- Which courses did you like most? Why?
- Which courses did you like least? Why?
- Why did you choose your particular major?

- Why did you choose to go to the school you attended? What did you like most or least about this school?
- If you could start college again, what would you do differently?

Questions pertaining to work experiences might include:

- What did you like most or least about the job?
- What did you like most or least about your immediate supervisor?
- Why did you leave the job?
- What were your major accomplishments during this job?
- Of all the jobs you have had, which did you like the most and why? Of all the supervisors you have had, which did you like the most and why?

Questions pertaining to personal experiences might include:

- Of all the things that you have done, what would you consider to be your greatest accomplishment and why?
- What do you consider to be your major strengths? What do you consider to be your major weaknesses?
- What kind of person do you have the most difficulty dealing with? Assuming that you had to work with such a person, how would you do it?
- What do you think are the most valuable skills you would bring to the position for which you are applying?
- What are your shorts-term goals (within the next five years), and what are your long-term goals?

4. **Maintaining a Proper Balance**—A good interviewee will know when to talk and when to listen. Your job is to present a complete picture of yourself without dominating the conversation. The best strategy for success is adapting to the interviewer and following his or her lead. When you are answering questions, do not let your mouth get ahead of your mind. Take a moment to think and construct your answers before rushing into a vague and senseless reply.

5. **The Interview Process Does not End with the Interview**—After the interview be sure to write a letter expressing your thanks and desire for future consideration. It is a good idea to mention something in the body of the letter that will trigger the memory of the interviewers. Look for unique things that happened or were said during the interview and write about these. Too often, students neglect writing this simple letter and lose the opportunity to present their professionalism one more time.

Where to Look for Additional Information

Beatty, Richard. 1996. *The Perfect Cover Letter*, 2nd ed. New York: John Wiley and Sons.

Carter, David. 1994. *You Can't Play the Game If You Don't Know the Rules: Career Opportunities in Sports Management*. San Luis Obispo, CA: Impact.

Fischer, David. 1997. *The 50 Coolest Jobs in Sports: Who Got Them, What They Do, and How Can You Get One!* New York: Arco.

Grappo, Gary Joesph, and Adele Beatrice Lewis. 1998. *How to Write Better Resumes*, 5th ed. Barrons Educational Series.

Karlin, Leonard. 1997. *Careers in Sports.* E.M. Guild Publishers.

Taylor, John. 1992. *How To Get a Job in Sports*. New York: Macmillan.

Tepper, Ron. 1998. *Power Resumes*. New York: John Wiley and Sons.

Yate, Martin John. 1997. *Cover Letters That Knock 'Em Dead*, 3rd ed. Adams.

www.onlinesports.com/pages/jobs.html

www.sportline.com/u/sportscareers

www.sportlink.com/employment/jobs/

www.sportscareers.com

www.sportsjobs.com

www.teammarketing.com/jobopps.htm

Sports Marketing Sites of Interest on the Internet

Category	URL	Annotation
Professional sports	www.nba.com	Official site of the NBA (basketball)
	www.nhl.com	Official site of the NHL (hockey)
	www.nfl.com	Official site of the NFL (football)
	www.majorleaguebaseball.com	Official site of MLB (baseball)
	www.mls.com	Official site of MLS (soccer)
	www.wnba.com	Official site of WNBA (women's basketball)
	www.ableague.com	Official site of ABL (women's basketball)
	www.pga.com	Official site of PGA (golf)
	www.lpga.com	Official site of LPGA (women's golf)
	www.nascar.com	Official site of NASCAR racing
	www.pba.org	Official site of PBA (bowling)
	atptour.com	Official site of ATP (tennis)
	www.minorleaguebaseball.com	Official site of Minor Leagues (baseball)
International sports	www.sportcal.co.uk	Database of international sporting events
	www.isma.org	International Sports Marketing Association
	www.ausport.gov.au	Australian Sports Directory
	www.asma.asn.au	Australian Sports Marketing Association
	www.e-sports.com/select/Olympics	Olympics information
	www.olympics.nbc.com	Olympics information
	www.olympics.nbc.com/usoc/ paralympics	Paralympic information
	www.worldleague.com	Official site of World Football League (WFL)
	www.cfl.ca	Official site of Canadian Football League (CFL)
Sports media	espnet.sportszone.com	ESPN Sports
	www.cnnsi.com	CNN and *Sports Illustrated*
	www.sportingnews.com	The *Sporting News*
	www.sportsline.com	CBS Sports
	www.nbc.com/sports	NBC Sports
	www.sportsnetwork.com	Sportsnetwork
	www.cardmall.com/sportsmap	Sports News
	www.businesswire.com/sportlink	Daily Sports Press Releases
	www.sportstrend.com	Magazine serving the sporting goods industry
Women in sports	www.fiat.gslis.utexas.edu/ ~lewisa/womsprt.html	Links to women in sports
	www.lifetimetv.com/WoSport	Women's sports
Careers and educational opportunities in sports	www.sportsjobs.com	Job openings in the sports and recreation industry

Category	URL	Annotation
	www.sportlink.com/employment/ jobs/	Job openings in the sports and sporting goods
	www.sportscareers.com	Job openings in the sports and recreation industry
	www.sportline.com/u/sportscareers	Job openings in the sports and recreation industry
	www.onlinesports.com/pages/ jobs.html	Job openings in the sports and recreation industry
	www.sirc.ca/peprgs.html	Recreation and sports science programs in the United States and abroad
	www.teammarketing.com/ jobopps.htm	Job openings in the sports and recreation industry
Sporting goods industry information	www.sportlink.com	SGMA's site for sporting goods information
	www.nsga.org	National Sporting Goods Association site
College sports	www.ncaa.com	Official site of the NCAA
Sports marketing industry information and research	www.teammarketing.com	General sports marketing information
	www.bizsport.com	General sports marketing information
	www.cad.gu.edu.au/ market/cyber-journal_of_sport_ marketing/cjsm.htm	*Cyber-Journal of Sports Marketing*
	www.playlab.uconn.edu/frl.htm	Sports marketing literature review
Other sports	www.autononomy.com/soccer.htm	Soccer links
	www.speedsouth.com	Motor racing links
	www.flakezine.com	Snowboarding
	www.usagymnastics.org/usag	Gymnastics
	www.churchilldowns.com	Horse racing
	www.thoroughbredtimes.com	Horse racing
	www.baseball-links.com	Baseball links
	www.debbiwilkes.com	Inside the figure skating community
	www.rollerhockey.com	Roller Hockey International League links
	www.tennis.com	Tennis links
	www.uhu.com/boxing	Boxing links
	www.foxnet.net/users/bowling/ sites.html	Bowling links
	www.skicentral.com	Skiing links
Indexes	www.tns.les.mit.edu/cgi-bin/sports	Index of internet sports pages
	sports.yahoo.com	Index for general sports information
	www.swv.ie/sport/index.htm	Index for general sports links
	members.tripod.com/~hoovsworld/ index.html	Index for general sports links
	ww.total.net/~fletch/idx.html	Index for general sports links
	www.hsv.tis.net/~thompson/ sachome.html	Index of sports franchise addresses
	www.oldsport.com	Index of general sports and sporting goods links

advertising

A form of one-way mass communication about a product, service, or idea paid for by an identified sponsor.

advertising appeals

The reason that the consumer wishes to purchase a sports product.

agent

Intermediaries whose primary responsibility is leveraging athletes' worth or determining their bargaining power.

amateur sports participants

Participants who do not receive compensation for playing a sport.

ambush marketing

A planned effort or campaign, by an organization to associate itself indirectly with an event in order to gain some of the recognition and benefits associated with being an official sponsor.

assurance

The knowledge and courtesy of employees and their ability to convey trust and confidence.

athletes

Participants who engage in organized training in order to develop skills in particular sports.

athletic platform

The type of sports entity (team, sport, event, or athlete) chosen to produce the best return on sports sponsorship objectives.

atmospherics

A retail store's visual, auditory, and olfactory environments that are designed to attract and keep consumers in the store.

attitude

Learned thoughts, feelings, and behaviors toward a given object.

behavioral segmentation

The process of grouping consumers based on how much they purchase, how often they purchase, or how loyal they are to a product or service.

benefits segmentation

The process of grouping consumers based on why they purchase a product or service or what problem the product solves for the consumer.

brand equity

The value that a brand contributes to a product in the marketplace.

brand image

The consumers' set of beliefs about a brand, which shapes their attitudes.

brand loyalty

A consistent preference for, or repeat purchase of, one brand over all others in a product category.

brand mark

The element of a brand that cannot be spoken (also known as the *logo* or *logotype*)

brand name

The element of the brand that can be vocalized, such as the Nike Air Jordan, the Cincinnati Reds, or the University of Kentucky Wildcats.

branding

Any combination of name, design, and symbol that a sports organization uses to help differentiate its products from the competition.

bundle pricing

The grouping of individual sports products and services into a single-package price.

channel of distribution

A coordinated group of individuals or organizations that route a sports product to the final consumer.

cognitive dissonance

Feelings of doubt or anxiety that may occur after consumers have made an important participation decision.

communication

The process of establishing a commonness of thought between the sender and the receiver.

competition

A contest among sellers trying to reach their market objectives by filling the same customer need.

contingency framework for strategic sports marketing

A system for understanding and managing the complexities of the sports marketing environment.

consumer demand

The quantity of a sports product that consumers are willing to purchase at a given price.

control

The process of measuring results, comparing the results to the marketing objectives, communicating the results to the entire organization, and modifying plans to achieve the desired results.

convenience sampling techniques

Sample elements are chosen based on being readily available to the researcher.

cost-based pricing

The pricing schemes in which the sports organization examines all of the costs associated with producing the sports product and then determines the price.

coupons

Certificates that offer reductions in price for sports products.

creative brief

A tool used to guide the creative process toward a solution that will serve the interests of the client and their customers.

credibility

The expertise and the trustworthiness of the source of a message.

culture

The shared values, beliefs, language, symbols, and tradition that are passed on from generation to generation by members of a society.

cultural values

Widely held beliefs that affirm what is desirable by members of a society.

demographic environment

Observing and monitoring trends and shifts in the population.

differential pricing

Selling the same product or service to different buyers at different prices.

diffusion of innovation

The rate at which new sports products spread throughout the marketplace and are accepted by consumers.

distribution

The movement of a sports product from producers to consumers.

economic activity

The flow of goods and services between producers and consumers.

empathy

The caring, individualized attention a firm provides its customers.

environmental scanning

A firm's attempt to continually acquire information on events occurring outside the organization.

eustress

Positive levels of arousal that are provided to spectators of sports.

evaluative criteria

Features and characteristics that potential consumers look for when choosing a sport in which to participate.

exchange

A marketing transaction in which the buyer gives something of value to the seller in return for goods and services.

experimentation

Research in which one or more variables are manipulated while others are held constant in order for results to be measured.

external contingencies

All influences outside of the organization that can impact the organization's strategic marketing process.

facility aesthetics

The interior and exterior appearance of a stadium.

fad

A product life cycle characterized by accelerated sales and accelerated acceptance of the product followed by a rapid decline.

family life cycle

A progression of individuals through various life stages (e.g., young and single, married with children.)

fan identification

The personal commitment and emotional involvement customers have with a sports organization.

fixed costs

The sum of the producer's expenses that are stable and do not change with the quantity of the product consumed.

focus group

A structured discussion with 6–10 people led by a moderator.

frequency

The number of times an individual, or a household, is exposed to a media vehicle.

geodemographic segmentation

The process of grouping consumers who live in close proximity and are also likely to share the same lifestyle and demographic composition.

goal

A short-term purpose that is measurable, challenging, attainable, and time specific.

goods

Tangible physical products that offer benefits to consumers.

idle product capacity

"Down time" in which the service provider is available, but there is no demand for the sports product.

implementation

Decisions in the strategic sports marketing process such as who will carry out the plans, when the plans will be executed, and how the plans will be executed.

inelastic demand

A situation in which changes in price have little or no impact on demand.

information search

When a participant seeks relevant information that will help them resolve the problem.

innovations

New sports products that are continually being introduced to consumers.

integrated marketing communications

The concept by which a sports organization carefully integrates and coordinates its many promotional mix elements to deliver a unified message about the organization and its products.

intermediaries

Organizations or individuals that are in the middle of producers and consumers; also called middlemen.

internal contingencies

All influences within the organization that can impact the organization's strategic marketing process.

inventory management

Ordering the correct assortment of merchandise, maintaining appropriate levels of merchandise, and storing the merchandise that has been ordered.

judgment sample

Sample elements chosen subjectively and based on the judgment of the researcher that they best serve the purpose of the study.

learning

Relatively permanent changes in response tendencies due to the effects of experience.

licensing

A contractual agreement whereby a company may use another company's trademark in exchange for a royalty or fee.

majority fallacy

The false assumption that the largest group of consumers should always be selected as the target market.

market segmentation

Grouping consumers together based on common needs.

market selection decisions

Choosing market segments, target markets, and positioning in the planning phase of the strategic sports marketing process.

marketing orientation

Concentration on understanding the consumer and providing a sports product that meets consumers' needs, while achieving the organization's objectives.

marketing research

The systematic process of collecting, analyzing, and reporting information to enhance decision making throughout the strategic sports marketing process.

match-up hypothesis

The belief that the more congruent the image of the endorser with the image of the product being promoted, the more effective the message.

media

The element in the communications process by which the message is transmitted.

mob effect

A situation in which consumers feel it is socially desirable to attend "special" sporting events.

motivation

An internal force that directs behavior toward the fulfillment of needs.

multiple channels

Using more than one channel of distribution to reach potential consumers.

new product category entries

Sports products that are new to the organization, but not to consumers.

new-to-the-world products

Brand new sports innovations such as the first in-line skates, the first sailboard, or the advent of arena football.

niche marketing

The process of carving out a relatively tiny part of a market that has a very special need not currently being filled.

nonprice competition

The creation of a unique sports product through the packaging, product design, promotion, distribution, or any marketing variable other than price.

organizational culture

The shared values and assumptions of organizational members that shape an identity and establish preferred behaviors in an organization.

organizational objectives

Signposts that help an organization focus on its purpose as stated in its mission statement.

organized sporting events

Sporting competitions that are sanctioned and regulated by a controlling authority such as a league, association, or sanctioning body.

participant-consumption behavior

Actions performed when searching for, participating in, and evaluating the sports activities that consumers feel will satisfy their needs.

perception

The complex process of selecting, organizing, and interpreting sports-related stimuli.

penetration pricing

Selling a new sports product at a low initial price relative to the competition in order to gain market share.

perceived risk

The uncertainty associated with decision making and the concern for the potential threats of making the wrong decision.

personal seat licenses (PSLs)

A sports stadium financing strategy in which fans pay for rights to purchase future tickets.

personal selling

A form of person-to-person communication which a salesperson works with prospective buyers and attempts to influence their purchase needs in the direction of his or her company's products or services.

personal training

Products designed to benefit participants in sports at all levels of competition (e.g., fitness centers and health services, sports camps and instruction).

personality

A set of consistent responses an individual makes to the environment.

point-of-purchase (P-O-P) displays

A promotional display designed to attract consumers' attention to a particular product or retail display area.

positioning

Fixing the sports product in the minds of the target market by manipulating the marketing mix.

premiums

Items given away with the sponsors product as part of the sales promotion.

prestige pricing

Setting an artificially high price to provide a distinct image in the marketplace.

price

A statement of value for a sports product.

price competition

Stimulating consumer demand primarily by offering consumers lower prices.

price discounts

Incentives offered to buyers to stimulate demand or reward behaviors that are favorable to the seller.

price elasticity

The extent to which consumer purchasing patterns are sensitive to fluctuations in price.

price reductions

Efforts to enhance sales and achieve greater market share by directly lowering the original price.

price skimming

Selling a new sports product at a high initial price relative to the competition to enhance perceived quality.

primary data

Data gathered for the specific research question at hand.

problem definition

Specifying what information is needed to assist in solving problems or identifying opportunities.

problem recognition

Discrepancy between a consumer's desired state and an actual state large enough and important enough to activate the entire decision-making process.

product design

The aesthetics, style, and function of the sports product.

product life cycle

A useful tool for developing a marketing strategy and then revising this strategy as a product moves through the stages of introduction, growth, maturity, and decline.

product line

A group of products that are closely related because they satisfy a class of needs, are used together, are sold to the same customer groups, are distributed through the same type of outlets, or fall within a given price range.

product mix

The total assortment of product lines that a sports organization sells.

projective techniques

Any variety of methods that allow respondents to project their feelings, beliefs, or motivations onto a relatively neutral stimulus.

product line extensions

New products being added to an existing product line.

promotional mix elements

The combination of elements—including advertising, personal selling, sponsorship, public relations, and sales promotion—designed to communicate with sports consumers.

psychological pricing

Pricing based on the consumer's emotion and image, rather than economics alone.

public relations

The element of the promotion mix that identifies, establishes, and maintains a mutually beneficial relationship between the sports organizations and its publics.

quantity discounts

Rewarding buyers for purchasing large quantities of a sports product by lowering prices.

quota sampling

Sample elements chosen on the basis of some control characteristic or characteristics of interest to the researcher.

reach

The number of people exposed to an advertisement in a given medium.

reference groups

Individuals who influence the information, attitudes, and behaviors of other group members.

reliability

The ability to perform a promised service dependably and accurately.

repositioning

Changing the image or perception of the sports entity in the minds of consumers in the target market.

research design

The framework or plan for a study that guides the collection and analysis of data.

research proposal

A document that describes all the information necessary to conduct and control a study.

responsiveness

The willingness to help customers and provide prompt service.

sales promotions

A variety of short-term promotional activities designed to stimulate immediate product demand.

sample

A subset of the population from which data is gathered to estimate some characteristic of the population.

sanctioning bodies

Organizations that not only market sports products, but delineate and enforce rules and regulations, determine the time and place of sporting events, and provide athletes with the structure necessary to compete.

seasonal discounts

Reduction in prices to stimulate demand during off-peak periods.

secondary data

Data that has been collected previously but is still relevant to the research question.

services

Intangible, nonphysical products.

simplified model of the consumer-supplier relationship

A framework for describing the various products, suppliers and consumers in the sports industry.

single channel strategy

Using only one channel of distribution to reach potential consumers.

situational factors

Temporary factors within a particular time or place that influence the participation decision-making process.

spectators

Consumers who derive their benefit from the observation of the event.

sport

A source of diversion, or a physical activity, engaged in for pleasure.

sporting goods

Tangible products that are manufactured, distributed, and marketed within the sports industry.

sportscape

The physical surroundings of a stadium that impact spectators' desire to stay at and ultimately return to the stadium.

sport sponsorship acquisition

A reactive process whereby organizations receive sponsorship possibilities from sports entities wishing to secure sponsors.

sports camps and instruction

Organized training sessions usually designed to provide instruction in a specific sport.

sports equipment manufacturers

Organizations responsible for producing and sometimes marketing sports equipment used by consumers who are participating in sports at all different levels of competition.

sports information

Products that provide consumers with news, statistics, schedules, and stories about sports.

sports involvement

The perceived interest in and personal importance of sports to an individual sport consumer.

sports marketing

The specific application of marketing principles and processes to sports products and to the marketing of nonsports products associated with sport.

sports product

A good, a service, or a combination of the two that is designed to provide benefits to a sports spectator, participant, or sponsor.

sports retailers

Channel members who are involved in all the activities of selling products and services to end users or final consumers.

sports sponsorship

Exchanging money or product for the right to associate a name or a product with a sports entity.

social class

The homogeneous division of people in a society sharing similar values, lifestyles, and behaviors that can be hierarchically categorized.

sociological factors

Influences outside of the individual participant that influence the decision-making process.

strategic control

The critical evaluation of plans, activities, and results, providing information for future strategic action.

strategic sports marketing process

The process of planning, implementing, and controlling marketing efforts to meet organizational objectives and satisfy consumers' needs.

strategic windows

A period of time during which the characteristics of a market and the distinctive competencies of a firm fit together well.

tangibles

The physical facilities, equipment, and appearance of the service personnel.

target marketing

Choosing the segment(s) that will allow an organization to attain its marketing goals most efficiently and effectively.

test marketing

Introducing a new product or service in one or more geographic areas on a limited basis.

trademark

An identifier that indicates a sports organization has legally registered its brand name or brand mark, thus preventing others from using it.

value

The perceived benefits of a sports product, or what the product does for the user, based on its tangible and intangible features.

variable costs

The sum of the producer's expenses that vary as a result of the quantity of the product being consumed.

vision

A long-term roadmap to guide where the organization is headed.

warranties

Statements indicating the liability of the manufacturer for problems with the sports product.

Chapter 1

3 The Coca Cola Company; **11** Ken Karp/Simon & Schuster-PH College; **14** PhotoDisc, Inc.; **14** Easton, Inc.; **15** Ricoh Corporation; **20** National Baseball Hall of Fame & Museum, Inc.; **22** U.S. Tennis Association

Chapter 2

40 Harlem Globetrotters; **46** PhotoDisc, Inc.; **48** NBA Properties, Inc.; **50** Cleveland Golf Company; **55** Monica Almeida/New York Times Pictures; **56** David Geoffrey & Associates d.b.a. Slazenger Golf

Chapter 3

68 IBM Corporation; **70** Wilson Sporting Goods Company; **71** Canon U.S.A., Inc.; **73** PhotoDisc, Inc.; **90** Nike Advertising

Chapter 4

110 PhotoDisc, Inc.; **113** Alliance Research, Inc.

Chapter 5

134/137/143/146/150/158/162 PhotoDisc, Inc.

Chapter 6

170 Elise Amendola/AP/World Wide Photos; **172/176** PhotoDisc, Inc.; **176** Northern Kentucky University; **182** Tennessee Oilers

Chapter 7

200 Ken Karp/Simon & Schuster-PH College; **203** Polartec/Malden Mills Industries; **208** Kawasaki Motors Corp., U.S.A.; **210/211** PhotoDisc, Inc.; **220** David Geoffrey & Associates d.b.a. Slazenger Golf; **220** G. Paul Burnett/AP/World Wide Photos; **221** Larry Salzman/AP/Wide World Photos

Chapter 8

230 (2) PhotoDisc, Inc.; **237** Nike Advertising; **256** Easton, Inc.

Chapter 9

264 Seattle Ice Breakers; **267** Easton, Inc.; **269** Softspikes, Inc.; **273/279** PhotoDisc, Inc.

Chapter 10

299 Cincinnati Bengals; **300** Pennzoil Products Company; **303** WNBA; **315** PhotoDisc, Inc.

Chapter 11

326 Ron Frehm/AP/Wide World Photos; **329** Nike Advertising; **333** DIRECTV, Inc.; **335** Polo Ralph Lauren Corporation; **342** The Coca Cola Company; **342** Beth A. Keiser/AP/Wide World Photos; **345** Jim Sulley/AP/Wide World Photos; **346** IBM Corporation

Chapter 12

377 Nadeau/AP Wide World Photos; **379** State Farm Insurance Companies; **393** Larry Fleming/Simon & Schuster-PH College

Chapter 13

405 DIRECTV, Inc.; **410** Trend Lines, Inc.; **418** Kmart Corporation

Chapter 14

440/451/457 PhotoDisc, Inc.

Chapter 15

468 Tennessee Oilers; **475/477/482** PhotoDisc, Inc.

Chapter 16

493 Jack Stohlman/LPGA Ladies Professional Golf Association; **507** Sara Lee Corporation; **508** Jose Goitia/AP/Wide World Photos